D0279815

JAMES II

JAMES, DUKE OF YORK
(from the picture by Lely at St. James's Palace)

JAMES II

BY

F. C. TURNER
M.A. (Oxon)

EYRE & SPOTTISWOODE
LONDON

First published 1948
Reprinted 1950

This book is printed in Great Britain for Eyre & Spottiswoode (Publishers) Ltd., 15 *Bedford Street, London, W.C.*2, *by Richard Clay and Company, Ltd., Bungay, Suffolk*

PREFACE

In writing this book I have been very much indebted to Mr. Esmond de Beer, who has throughout my work on both parts of the subject given me invaluable advice in my search for authorities; he has also, at great cost of time, read through the whole of the first part and annotated it with great minuteness, enabling me to remove a host of minor errors and causing me to re-examine many of my conclusions. I am also very grateful to Mr. Alan Fremantle, who read my book at an early stage and made many suggestions which I have adopted; he has also given me valuable help in correcting proofs. On particular points I have had the expert assistance of Mr. E. D. Cuming and Mr. Francis Colmer.

My thanks are due also to the secretary and staff of the London Library, without whose assistance I could have done very little, in particular to the late Mr. G. E. Manwaring, who placed his great knowledge of historical literature at my disposal and was an unfailing and patient guide.

I have based my work entirely on original authorities. I have, however, derived great assistance both in sources and in interpretation of them from a number of modern works. I have also occasionally taken from them quotations from documents not accessible to me. Chief among these are:—

- Osmond Airy, *Charles II.*
- Bagwell, *Ireland under the Stuarts.*
- Miss Barbour, *Arlington.*
- Arthur Bryant, *Charles II*; *Pepys, the Saviour of the Navy.*
- Julia Cartwright, *Sacharissa.*
- Ruth Clark, *Sir William Trumbull in Paris.*
- Keith Feiling, *English Foreign Policy, 1660–1667*; *History of the Tory Party, 1660–1702.*
- Miss H. C. Foxcroft, *Halifax.*
- M. and S. Grew, *The English Court in Exile.*
- F. M. G. Higham, *King James II.*
- Lodge, *History of England from the Restoration to the Death of William III.*
- W. L. Mathieson, *Politics and Religion in Scotland.*
- Ogg, *The Reign of Charles II.*
- R. S. Rait, *The Parliaments of Scotland.*
- Leopold von Ranke, *History of England, principally in the XVIIth century.*
- Eva Scott, *The King in Exile* ; *The Travels of the King.*
- Tedder, *The Navy of the Restoration.*

In the few cases in which I have used particular references which I have found in modern books I have made due acknowledgement. If I have anywhere omitted to do so it is by inadvertence, for which I apologise. All writers on this period must acknowledge their debt to Macaulay, "robust rather than subtle" (in Miss Foxcroft's phrase), complacent in his Victorianism and with all the prejudices of his period, especially those of the Whig party, completely unjudicial in his treatment of individuals, but amazingly accurate in the realm of fact and suceeding, in spite of his faults, in giving a balanced and very readable account of the events which led up to the Revolution of 1688.

F. C. TURNER.

Newick, Sussex.

AUTHOR'S NOTE ON THE SECOND IMPRESSION

I TAKE the opportunity afforded by reprinting to make certain corrections in detail to the necessity for which my attention has very kindly been drawn by correspondents and reviewers. In this connection I wish to convey my very grateful thanks to: Mr. Andrew Sparkes of Corpus Christi College, Oxford (various errors in the text); Mr. Trevor Roper, tutor of Christchurch, Oxford, and reviewer in the *New Statesman and Nation* (for the substitution throughout of "Christ Church" for "Christchurch"); Mr. L. Pettit of Hove (p. 169, note); Mr. J. J. Dwyer, reviewer in the *Tablet* (pp. 116 and 280); Mr. R. W. Lee of Oxford (p. 428, note); Mr. J. B. Whitmore, F.S.A. (p. 429, note 2); and Mr. J. A. Chapman of Glasgow (p. 474).

F. C. TURNER.

Henfield, Sussex, February 1950.

CONTENTS

PART I

JAMES, DUKE OF YORK, 1633–1685

PART II

KING JAMES II, 1685–1701

PART I

JAMES, DUKE OF YORK

1633–1685

His brother, though oppressed with vulgar spite,
Yet dauntless and secure of native right,
Of every royal virtue stands possessed,
Still dear to all the bravest and the best.
His courage foes, his friends his truth proclaim,
His loyalty the King, the world his fame.
His mercy even the offending crowd will find,
For sure he comes of a forgiving kind.

Dryden: "Absalom and Achitophel".

CHAPTER I

THE CIVIL WAR

JAMES, Duke of York and Albany, was born at St. James's Palace on October 14, 1633, the third of the six children of the King and Queen. At the time of his birth his father, King Charles I, was thirty-three, and his mother, Henrietta Maria, twenty-four; his brother Charles was his senior by three years, and his sister Mary, who was to marry William II of Orange and to become the mother of William III, by two years; Elizabeth, who died in 1650 a prisoner of the Parliament, was born in 1635; Henry, Duke of Gloucester, in 1639, and Henrietta, who married Philip, Duke of Orleans, and negotiated the Treaty of Dover, in 1644. Of his near relatives by far the most important was his maternal uncle, the French King, Louis XIII. Louis died in 1642, and James never saw him; his son, who succeeded him as Louis XIV, was born in 1638, and was thus James's first cousin, and his junior by five years; another maternal uncle was the older Louis's brother, Gaston, Duke of Orleans, and two maternal aunts were married to Philip IV of Spain and to the Duke of Savoy. On his father's side the relatives were fewer and less distinguished, but the brother of James's grandmother, Anne of Denmark, was King of that country, and James's widowed aunt, Elizabeth, who had been Queen of Bohemia, was the mother of Charles Lewis, the Elector Palatine.

James's ancestry was on his father's side mainly Scotch, and on his mother's side French and Italian. His nearest English relations came to him through Margaret Tudor, who five generations before him had married James IV of Scotland; and Margaret herself was not of pure English blood—of her four grandparents, three were English and one Welsh. But at no time of his life did James admit that he was anything but an Englishman, and in this he resembled George III, who also boasted English nationality, though for nine generations no ancestor of his had been born on English soil. James spent little more than eighteen months of his life in Scotland, and there is no sign in any of his numerous letters from that country of any pride in, or affection for it. At two periods of his life he vaguely dreamed of mastering England by Scottish arms, but he never, like his brother, signed the Covenant, or, like his grandson, donned the kilt, in furtherance of such an enterprise.

In one of their despatches the French ambassadors report a conversation they had had with James:

> He replied that we could not change his mind, though we were always trying to do so; that he was English and consequently very stubborn. "But," we rejoined, "you are French on one side, you ought to make allowance for that." He replied, "The English are stubborn when they are in the right, and when they are not, then the French can be obstinate too." And on that he left the room and went to his prayers.

As a young man he conceived a considerable affection for his mother's country, and it seems probable that, had the course of events taken a different turn, he would have settled down quite happily as a naturalised Frenchman, he would have found congenial occupation in the French Army, and he would have been more at home in the political atmosphere of France than he ever was in that of England. But even in such circumstances it is difficult to imagine James commanding troops in a war against the country of his birth; in later life, when, from his own point of view, he had much to complain of in the behaviour of the English, he did not in his heart want them to be beaten even when they were fighting against him. One of the chief elements in the tragedy of his life was the lack of mutual understanding between him and the people he loved so well.

James was christened on November 24, and his sponsors were Frederick Henry, Prince of Orange, his aunt, the unfortunate Elizabeth, Queen of Bohemia, and her son, Charles Lewis, the Prince Palatine. The immediate attendants, whom he shared with his older brother and sister, were of three grades: nurses, the cofferess (an occupation which the *Oxford English Dictionary* has overlooked) and rockers, on behalf of whom payment was made in April 1635 by the Exchequer of £610, for what period it is not stated; and it is also recorded that one Mary Godbolt, a rocker, received on retirement from service a gift of £150. The Countess of Dorset was governess to the two boys, and she disbursed about £1500 a year to tradesmen for wares delivered for their use. The purchasing power of money was immensely greater than it is at the present day—perhaps five times as great—and we may conclude that the young Princes were very well done and that their little Court was well paid. James was destined for the post of Lord High Admiral of England before he was three, when he was four and a half he was formally appointed to that office. At the age of ten he was also a colonel in the Royal Army. In January 1644 he received a writ of summons to the House of Lords, sitting at Oxford.

In January 1642 Charles found the London mob an impossible neighbour, and took his wife and family to Hampton Court and then to Windsor. From Windsor the King made a journey to Dover, avoiding London, to see the Queen and Princess Mary embark for Holland. James and his younger brother and sister were meanwhile sent to St. James's. When in March Charles went north and made York his headquarters, James was for a time at Richmond, but the King very soon sent the Marquess of Hertford to fetch him, a service which was performed against the express prohibition of Parliament.

Not long after James's arrival at York his father very injudiciously employed him in what is generally recognised as the first incident of the Civil War. Hull at that time was a great magazine of arms and ammunition, the Governor, Sir John Hotham, had been appointed by the King, and no one at that time doubted his loyalty. The Parliament had already directed their attention to the magazine and had ordered its removal to the Tower, in case Charles should attempt to seize it. It is probable that had the King ridden straight into the town with a body of attendants he would have met with no resistance. He chose, however, to send James with his tutors and equerries as for a party of pleasure, conveying at the same time to the Governor his own intention of dining with Sir John next day. Sir John had time to consider where he stood, and when next day the King appeared at the gates he found them shut and the garrison standing to arms. Charles was compelled to swallow this rebuff, and it was only with difficulty that he persuaded Hotham to release James and his attendants.

Both James and his brother Charles were at the Battle of Edgehill, which was fought a few days after James's ninth birthday. The two royal children had an exciting time. The King started with the boys beside him in the rear-guard; but early in the action he found it necessary to take charge of the leading troops, and looked round for someone to conduct the Princes to a place of safety. The Duke of Richmond refused, and the Earl of Dorset when he was given the order "answered with an oath, that he would not be thought a coward for the sake of any king's son in Christendom and therefore humbly desired His Majesty to commit that charge to some other man", a remark that made such an impression on James that he quoted it forty years later. Finally Sir William Howard yielded to the royal command, collected an escort and conducted the boys to some sort of shelter in farm buildings near the field. Here they were discovered by a part of the enemy's horse, but fortunately the number of the Princes' escort appeared greater than it actually was, and they escaped capture.

From Edgehill Charles and James accompanied their father to Banbury and then to Oxford, which they reached on October 29. From this date until the capture of the city by Fairfax on June 24, 1646, Oxford was the Royalist headquarters, and except for a few weeks in the late summer of 1643, when he accompanied his father to Bristol and to the abortive siege of Gloucester, James lived continuously there. His father was with him in the intervals of his campaigns and his mother paid a visit of nine months, July 1643 to April 1644. James was thus deprived of the continuous influence of both his parents at the formative age of nine to twelve, and he was to be still less in their company in the succeeding years. There is nothing that is known of the character of Henrietta Maria which suggests that she was a good mother to her sons, but Charles I was steady and upright in his private life and was devoted to his children; at the same time, unfortunately, he was completely dominated by his wife, and he would not have been allowed much control over them. Neither Charles nor Henrietta was a competent instructor in statecraft (Charles II's shrewdness derived in part from his grandfather); but possibly his father's example might have kept James, at any rate, steadier in his resistance to carnal temptation and preserved him in later life from many hours of bitter remorse. A pleasant story of King Charles's way with his sons has survived: "The old King was always very severe in the education of his present majesty: insomuch that at St. Mary's in Oxford he did once hit him on the head with his staff when he did observe him to laugh (at sermon time) upon the ladies that sat against him."

Of James's education in the narrow sense of the word we know practically nothing directly. He had as tutors when he was at Oxford, Broughton, Brian Duppa and Croucher, who were all three Fellows of colleges; one Massonett taught him writing, and the same man was his sub-tutor in the spring of 1646 and his "sub-lector" at The Hague in 1648; he also taught both Princes French. During the exile Massonett showed an intriguing spirit: he allowed himself to be made a tool by Hyde's enemies and concocted evidence against that counsellor; he also worked as a spy for Thurloe; in this last capacity he evidently escaped detection, for in 1664 we find Massonett physician to James's household on a salary of £40 a year—clearly a man of many accomplishments but no great virtue. No doubt, like most royal children, James had plenty of tutors and obeyed none. An injunction conveyed from his father early in 1647, that he should "ply his book more and his gun less", tells us nothing; such advice is common form among fathers. But he was probably from early boyhood fond of the open air. At the time of the Restoration a little panegyric on James appeared which shows in its muddled style evidence of hurried composition; from this work we learn that:

> his ingenious towardliness was not ignorant how much learning adds to nature, which made him eager after that accomplishment, though I cannot say he ever minded to make study his business, being so averse from prying upon his book, that he cared not to plod upon his games; for his active soul was more delighted with quick and nimble recreations, as running, leaping, riding.

Certainly James in later life showed few signs of a liberal or exact education: he had, as far as we know, no interest in literature, and he was not a patron of the arts; nor does it appear that, in spite of the appearance of his name as a vice-president of the Royal Society, he had even Charles's superficial curiosity about science; he did, however, pay the expenses of Thomas Smith ("Rabbi" or "Tograi" Smith, who figured prominently in the affair of Magdalen College in 1687) in his journey to the Levant "for the advance of learning", and this may not have been an isolated act. In Brussels, at the age of seventeen, he was taken to Masses "in order to hear good music", but it was suspected that this was a mere pretext, and that the real object was his conversion. At the same time it is quite possible that James had a real interest in music. As a young man he took some pains to learn the guitar (he used his talent on one occasion as an excuse for obtaining access to a lady's boudoir), and he is said to have played accompaniments on that instrument to his brother's vocal duets with the celebrated bass singer John Gostling; he was probably a considerable patron of Henry Purcell: in 1685 he paid up his arrears of salary as organist of the Chapel Royal and composer of the King's Music,[1] and commissioned him in 1688 to write an anthem in celebration of the Queen's pregnancy; Purcell composed several of his most famous works for other special occasions in James's reign.

The English of James's letters is undistinguished and pedestrian, and it is often difficult to catch his meaning at a first reading; and good letter-writing was then one of the ordinary accomplishments of a gentleman. Such parts of his memoirs as have survived furnish evidence of confusion of mind in the frequent repetitions in similar words of accounts of the same incidents. In the whole of his writings, of which a tremendous bulk has survived, there are very few of those turns of

[1] So says Purcell's biographer (A. K. Holland, *Henry Purcell*, 1932), but he furnishes no references and there is no record of such payments in the Calendar of Treasury Books: an entry in this Calendar for April 14, 1685, gives the name of thirty-six musicians who were to perform at the coronation with Dr. Staggins as Master of the King's Music, and Henry Purcell is mentioned last but one.

expression which indicate that a writer is interested in writing as an art; "like so many young spaniels that run and bark at every lark that springs" (a description of the Exclusionists) is almost a unique flight of fancy. Part of these defects was no doubt personal and ineradicable by education. James had no humour—if we except a very occasional sardonic grimness in his description of the misfortunes of someone he disliked—and no gift of intimacy; and this last deficiency is closely associated with a quality of which all his letters give evidence—a narrow egotism which makes no pretence whatever at being interested in the concerns of his correspondent. But over and above all this there remains an irreducible minimum of bad writing which would not have been there if the writer, however unintelligent, had had a good grounding in such education as was at that time available. He was, however, as we shall see, a good linguist, and was able to chatter fluently in French after very little practice.

On April 27, 1646, King Charles left Oxford on that journey which he concluded as a prisoner of the Scotch Army, and four days later Oxford was besieged by Fairfax. It was not until June 20 that the city surrendered, and by one article of the terms of capitulation it was provided that James should be placed at the disposal of Parliament. He was treated with some deference by the Parliamentary officers, who all kissed his hand (as he notes) except Fairfax, and none kneeled, as was proper, except Cromwell. For the few days he remained in Oxford Sir George Radcliffe was made responsible for his safe custody. James himself says that Sir George received an order from the Queen to take his charge to Ireland or France, but that he refused to obey any order of that sort without direct instructions from the King, but the story seems unlikely: there was no time for Henrietta Maria in Paris to receive news of Radcliffe's appointment and to send instructions before they were on the road to London, and moreover there was no means of making an escape, with the whole country in Parliamentary hands. In December 1645 Charles had had the intention to send James to Ireland, but the loss of Hereford and the siege of Chester had made the route to Ireland unsafe, and the plan was adopted, but not fulfilled, of sending him to his mother in France.[1] Sir George accompanied James and his personal staff to the suburbs of London, where the Earl of Northumberland met him by order of the Parliament, relieved Radcliffe of his charge and dismissed all James's servants, "not so much as excepting a dwarf whom His Royal Highness was desirous to have retained with him".

[1] James, from faulty recollection, no doubt, placed these projects after, instead of before, the capitulation of Oxford.

This Earl of Northumberland was Algernon Percy, the tenth Earl, a very moderate Parliamentarian; he had held chief command in the Navy and a very high command in the Army under Charles; in 1642 he took the popular side, but he was always in favour of settlement by negotiation, and in the House of Lords he headed the opposition to the trial of the King. He was already custodian of James's sister and brother, Elizabeth and Henry, and James was taken to join them at St. James's Palace. The three children (James says) received from Northumberland the treatment they would have expected if the King himself had confided them to his care; in a letter of intelligence of the time we read:

> The Earl of Northumberland hath presented His Highness with a very rich French embroidered coach and six excellent coach horses, wherewith His Highness and the rest of the King's children here have appeared *en princes* like themselves in Hyde Park.

One incident only seems to have marred the good relations of James and his custodian: a letter written in January 1648 relates:

> The imprisonment of the King had been concealed from the Duke of York. But two or three days since, one of his attendants, a servant of the Earl of Northumberland, told him of it: to which he replied, "How durst any rogues to use his father after that manner". The man told him he would inform his Lord what had been said; whereupon the Duke took a long bow then in the place, to have shot him, had not another behind him held his hand. For this, it is reported, the Earl of Northumberland will have the Duke whipped; but whether it has yet been done I know not.

Shortly after James's removal to London the King at Newcastle heard of a proposal to induce him to abdicate in favour of his second son; no doubt the Parliamentary leaders, having James in their power at a tender age, hoped to be able to mould him into a king to their liking.

On June 2, 1647, Cornet Joyce, acting for the Army against the Parliament, seized the King at Holmby House and conducted him to Newmarket. Later in the month he was taken to Hampton Court, and James was sent under escort to Maidenhead to meet him on his journey. From that time until Charles's escape to Carisbrooke in the following November father and son had several interviews at Hampton Court; Northumberland was very accommodating in this respect, and he even planned to move the children to his own house, Sion House, so that they should be nearer their father, but this the authorities would not permit. These interviews were overshadowed in the King's mind by the thought of his present condition and by the apprehension that his liberty would be more and more restricted and that he might never again be a free man. In these circumstances the conversations assumed the nature of death-bed valedictions and advice. To all the children he counselled loyalty and obedience to their oldest brother Charles, and James in particular he advised to take what opportunity he could to escape, and to find a refuge in Holland with his sister Mary, the Princess of Orange.

This last advice was superfluous. Within six months of his arrival in London, James had begun scheming to escape, and his father's friends had been scheming for him; the House of Lords in December 1646 took notice of the first attempt that was made and appointed a Committee to inquire into it. In February 1647 a letter to James from his mother was intercepted, and about the same time he was found to have written a letter to his father in cipher under pretence of writing to his brother-in-law, the Prince of Orange. What followed is described in a news-letter of the time:

> Upon discovery of this, my Lord of Northumberland, Sir William Ermyn and another of the house were appointed by the Parliament to examine the Duke who would confess nothing but that he wrote to the King to let him know the Queen and his brothers and sisters were in health; they demanded the key of the cipher which he told them was burnt as soon as he write the letter, which was all they could get out of him. Whereupon the House of Commons, taking the quickest and readiest way, fell upon the debate of sending him to the Tower, which he having notice of (wisely) wrote a letter of submission and sent it to the Parliament with the key of the cipher, confessing the whole truth, and begged that he might be continued with my Lord of Northumberland and not sent to the Tower, which was granted; though some of the House being very much incensed against him opposed it saying, "You see what a brood there is of them, like father, like sons, there is no truth in any of them";

and the writer concludes his narrative with a suggestion that James had been trapped by a woman *agent provocateur* into writing the letter and had been betrayed by her. (James's biographer gives the same story, except that he makes no mention of the letter of submission, in which no doubt he considered that James had compromised his dignity.) A year later a Committee of both Houses considered various attempts at escape that had been made, and James was constrained to write letters to the two Speakers "by which he engaged his honour and faith never to engage in such businesses". After his successful escape he was excused for his breach of faith on the ground that he was under age and should not have been put on oath; but Parliament took his promise seriously and made it a ground for exculpating Northumberland.

It was not, however, until April 1648 that success was achieved, and by an excellent piece of staff work on the part of one Colonel Bampfield. James was instructed to prepare for the attempt by playing hide and seek at dusk with his sister and brother, and this game he played with them every evening for a fortnight; so expert did he become at hiding himself that it was often half-an-hour before he was found. On this particular night he went off on pretence at hiding, and slipped down a back stair. Unfortunately he struck his foot violently against a door and made a clatter; no one took notice of the noise, but James retired to his bedchamber and pretended to be reading. When he found all was quiet he slipped down the stair again and across the grounds to "the door by the tiltyard-end" which opened on St. James's Park and of which he had previously obtained the key. Outside this door he found Colonel Bampfield, who provided him with the temporary disguise of a periwig and patches, and they made their way—no doubt at a leisurely pace so as to avoid notice—to Spring Gardens, "as gallants come to hear the nightingale". At the exit from Spring Gardens they found a hackney coach which had been engaged by a friend of Bampfield's of the name of Tripp. In this coach the three of them went along the causeway which is now the Strand as far as Ivy Lane, and there the coach was stopped, James and the Colonel got out on pretence of paying a call, and Tripp went on in the coach, so as to lay a false scent in case the chase was up. The other two slipped down to the river and went by boat to the neighbourhood of London Bridge, where they entered the house of a surgeon of the name of Low; there they found Bampfield's fiancée, Anne Murray; she had had a costume made to James's measurements by a woman's tailor, and she reports the tailor's remark, "that he had never seen a woman of so low a stature have so big a waist". Anne has left a very vivid (though ungrammatical) account of her part in the escape: Colonel Bampfield had told her that if they were not at Surgeon Low's house by ten she would know they had failed and must shift for herself. But they came a little later:

> The first that came in was the Duke, who with much joy I took in my arms. His Highness called "Quickly, quickly, dress me," and putting off his clothes I dressed him in the woman's habit that was prepared which fitted His Highness very well, and was very pretty in it. After he had eaten something I had made ready while I was idle lest His Highness should be hungry, and having sent for

> a Woodstreet cake (which I knew he loved) to take in the barge, with as much haste as could be His Highness went cross the bridge to the stairs where the barge lay.

At Billingsgate they engaged a barge to take them to Tilbury-Hope, where a Dutch pink was cleared and only waiting for "Mr. Andrews and his sister", who was going to join her husband in Holland. The barge-master was not quite satisfied with his passengers from the first—for one thing, no fewer than five persons had embarked with them to see them off, and for another, they appear to have had no luggage—and when they were under way, "peeping through a cranny of the door into the barge room, where there was a candle burning before the Duke, he perceived his Royal Highness laying his leg upon the table, and plucking up his stocking in so unwomanish a manner, that he concluded his former surmises of him were undoubted truths." (Another account says that Mr. Andrews was tying his sister's garter.) This was a bad break on the part of Master James: he was only fourteen-and-a-half, and no doubt was very self-conscious and uncomfortable in his unaccustomed costume. There was nothing to do but to take the barge-master into their confidence, and for a little time there was fear that the scheme had miscarried. The barge-master had no scruples of conscience; on general grounds he was quite willing, though by no means eager, to help James to escape; but he was a family man, and if he were detected as an accomplice—as he was likely to be by the guard-boats at Gravesend—he would be ruined. He yielded at last to James's promises to provide for him if he got into trouble, and without lights or oars the barge drifted on the tide undetected in the dark by the guard-boats and found the pink without mishap. The crossing to Flushing was uneventful, but their troubles were not quite over, for a vessel which they erroneously took for an English frigate followed them into the harbour, and the captain of the pink decided to proceed to Middelburg, a journey which was risky, with the tide as it then was. However, James's luck held, and "at Middleburg the Duke slept that night, and gave much wonder to the hostess, that a young gentlewoman would not let the maids help her to the bed, but be served by a pretended brother, in the same chamber in another bed". James finally arrived at the Hague on April 30.

Thus James's early boyhood had been spent in the atmosphere of the Civil War. He was a spectator at its two earliest episodes, and at Oxford, where he spent almost four years, he was at the centre of the resistance to the insurgents. There the talk of his seniors was entirely of the war and of the means to bring it to a successful conclusion. This atmosphere was, there can be no doubt, charged with an intense hatred of the Parliamentary leaders, coupled with an eagerness to swallow any sort of gossip against them. As in all civil wars, both sides claimed to be the national and patriotic party, and at Oxford it was treason to admit any virtues in the enemy: he would have been a courageous man who hinted that there was the least tincture of justice in the Parliamentary point of view. Later he was to see his father a prisoner in the hands of the Army—a father with whose moral and religious ideals he was in later life to have little sympathy, but for whom at that time, as we may assume from the scanty records, he had a deep affection. Later again he was to hear in Paris that his father had met his death on the scaffold. The impressions received in those years persisted in his mind through life. In maturity his outlook on life became fixed, immutable; these early impressions became fundamental truths which no experience or contemplation could modify; the subsequent twelve years, spent as they were among the exiled cavaliers, served only to deepen these early impressions, and we shall find James forty years and more later, still voicing the ideas, ideals and aspirations of the Cavalier party of 1642, and expecting a repetition of the events of that year.

CHAPTER II

EARLY YEARS OF EXILE, 1648–1651

JAMES spent the remainder of the year 1648 with his sister Mary and her husband, William II, Prince of Orange, at their mansion at Honslaerdyke, near the Hague. The position of William requires some notice. He was the grandson of the famous William the Silent, who had been the mainspring of the resistance of the Dutch to Philip II of Spain and of the establishment of the United Provinces as an independent State; this independence, however, had not been effectively recognised until the Twelve Years' Truce of 1609, twenty-five years after the death of William the Silent, and it was not legally accomplished until the Peace of Münster in 1648. The office of Stadtholder, or Governor, in several provinces had been held by William under the King of Spain, and, by a curious anomaly, he retained the title after the provinces had broken away from Spain. Actually no Prince of Orange was Stadtholder in all of the seven provinces, and there was no Stadtholder for the United Provinces as a whole; his chief strength lay in the fact that he was Captain-General and Admiral-General of the forces of the State and was also Stadtholder of the province of Holland, by far the most important of the provinces; for it contained both the commercial capital, Amsterdam, and the meeting-place of the States-General, The Hague, and contributed to the central revenues more than the other six provinces combined. Already in the middle of the seventeenth century the State as a whole was beginning to be known by the name of this single province.

In 1631, by the Acte de Survivance, the Stadtholdership had been made hereditary, and William II's father, Frederick Henry, had become virtually a constitutional monarch, though he did not assume royal state and his powers were closely limited under a republican, but by no means democratic, constitution. The seven provinces which had successfully revolted against Spain had been part of the seventeen provinces which had constituted the Spanish Netherlands, and they formed in essence a military league of independent States; each province clung to the privileges which it had enjoyed under Burgundian and Hapsburg rule and which Philip II had attempted to destroy. In the result the States-General, the body in which, according to unenlightened foreign opinion, sovereignty resided, more closely resembled the League of Nations than the central government of a federal State like Canada or the United States of America. Each province had a single vote in the States-General, and its delegate had to refer every fresh question back to the provincial estates, and to vote as directed by them; moreover, the States-General could take action only on a unanimous vote, and a single province could prevent action by the other six.

In the provinces there was a similar obstacle to decision, for the provincial estates consisted of a delegate of the nobles and one delegate each from a number of municipalities, and the municipalities, with rare exceptions, were in the hands of a few families; so that in theory in the last resort the representatives of these families in any one municipality could paralyse the States-General. In practice the constitution did not work so badly as that: the Dutch were strongly united in national sentiment, and they were in general inclined to accept the leadership of the province of Holland and its Stadtholder, and, during the minority of William III, that of John de Witt.

James was very soon brought into active interest in the Civil War. In June 1648 a mutiny on board some of the Parliamentary ships in the Downs, who put their officers ashore, provided the Royalists with a small fleet which was moored at Helvoetsluys. James, for whom the sea had an instinctive attraction and who had rights as Lord High Admiral, went on board the fleet and sent a messenger to Charles at Saint-Germain suggesting that he should join him. Charles accordingly arrived early in July via Calais, where a warship had been sent to meet him. He found the fleet in a state of faction in default of officers and through the intrigues of James's servants, acting nominally under James's orders. He decided that the only way to restore discipline was to give the seamen something to do and to take them away from pernicious influences ashore; he accordingly took the fleet for a cruise in the Downs, but left James, to his intense disgust, ashore. Charles returned to Helvoetsluys about the middle of September, where the fleet was threatened by the Parliamentary fleet under the Earl of Warwick. The attack was prevented by the action of Van Tromp, the Dutch Admiral, but the Parliament men were able to come ashore and to fraternise with the Royalist seamen; the result was that several of Charles's ships passed voluntarily over to the enemy, while others were allowed to be captured after a show of resistance. In October Charles went down with an attack of smallpox, and James, to avoid infection, had been moved to Mr. Henflet's house at Tylling. Charles recovered in time to superintend the refitting of what ships remained to him after the Parliamentary fleet had left on November 21, and to make the necessary appointments of admiral and captains. Prince Rupert was the obvious choice for admiral, but the seamen were prejudiced against him and would have preferred James, as the only other available person of sufficient rank. But James as admiral at the age of fifteen would have been a ridiculous choice, and Rupert was appointed. It was arranged that James should sail with the fleet, but when he heard that its destination was Ireland he refused to go. Thus early had he conceived a prejudice against that country.

King Charles had placed his younger children under the guardianship of the Queen, Henrietta Maria, and early in January 1649, in obedience to her commands, James set out from The Hague to join her in Paris. He passed through Brussels to Cambray, and there he received fresh instructions: his mother wrote that disorders had broken out in Paris and that her nephew, the King of France, had had to go to Saint-Germain; she advised him to remain where he was. A timely invitation enabled him to avail himself of the hospitality of the Benedictine monastery of St. Armand, where "he was nobly entertained by the Monks" for the space of three or four weeks; this was James's first serious contact with Roman Catholic discipline and practice. In the middle of February he was able to join his mother in Paris, and a few days after his arrival there he heard of his father's execution. In the course of the summer his brother Charles, who was now titular King of England, arrived from Holland, and the widowed Queen and her two sons took up their residence at Saint-Germain. James had previously been received with royal honours at the French Court.

We have a picture of James in the spring of this year from the pen of Henrietta Maria's niece Mademoiselle, the daughter of the Duke of Orleans:

> I have found staying with the Queen of England her second son, the Duke of York. . . . He is a young prince of thirteen or fourteen years of age, extremely good-looking and well made, and of fair complexion; he speaks French well and this gives him an advantage over the King his brother, for nothing in my opinion goes more against a man than lack of words. The Duke spoke to the point and I was much edified by the conversation I had with him;

and the young lady goes on to say how much she has enjoyed taking walks with James.

Charles was now nineteen years of age, and while he was at The Hague he had evidently decided that the time had come to dispense with petticoat government. Accordingly within a few days of his arrival at Saint-Germain he made it clear to his mother that as long as his father was alive and he himself was under age she had rightly been in a position to control his actions; but that now that he was King and grown up, the situation had entirely altered: for the future he was willing to be a good son to her, but he would not consult her on matters of policy. Poor Henrietta Maria had hoped to be able to play the same havoc with her son's plans as she had played with her husband's, and it was with no good grace that she outwardly accepted the situation: she continued until the Restoration to intrigue for a return to power, and she made a party for herself, with Lord Jermyn at its head, which added considerably to Charles's troubles by its incessant quarrels with his own servants.

Charles's journey to Paris was only en route for Ireland. During the early spring after the news had arrived of his father's execution, Charles's council had been divided between two schemes for the recovery of his kingdoms, one via Scotland and the other via Ireland. In March Charles wrote to Ormonde congratulating him on the peace he had recently made with the Catholic Irish, which had considerably brightened the Royalist prospects in Ireland, and announcing his intention of proceeding there without delay. In the same month arrived commissioners from Scotland making offers of assistance, but on condition that he should take the Covenant and "entertain no other persons about him but such as were godly men"; but Charles was not yet reduced to such extremities as to submit to this humiliation, and he had no hesitation in holding to his plan. But much time was wasted in raising funds and making other arrangements, and before everything was ready there was bad news from Ireland: in confirmation of previous rumours, Ormonde wrote that he had been defeated on August 2 by General Michael Jones at Rathmines, and he advised Charles to delay his voyage until the seas had been cleared by the autumn storms of the Parliamentary ships which were blockading Rupert's fleet in Kinsale Harbour.

The advice was excellent, but where was Charles to spend the intervening time? He was very unhappy in Paris; his mother made their relations impossible by offering him advice on his affairs, and he was forced in self-defence to make a practice of rising and leaving her abruptly when she ventured on forbidden topics; besides, the French Government were passively hostile: since one splendid entertainment which they had given him at Compiègne on his way from Holland they had entirely ignored his existence. The only part of his dominions which was still in his possession were the Channel Islands; he had spent two months in Jersey in 1646, he had most pleasant recollections of the loyalty and hospitality of the islanders, and it was conveniently situated as a base for the projected expedition to Ireland. It is not surprising therefore that he decided to make it his headquarters for the next few months.

On September 2 Charles and James left Saint-Germain for Coutainville, the port on the French coast nearest to Jersey. They passed through Caen, where they saw the Marchioness of Ormonde, and they were magnificently entertained by the Bishop of Coutances at the headquarters of his diocese. They embarked at Coutainville at noon on the 27th, in "the Prince's own pinnace" of eighteen oars, which he had had built during his previous visit, and which had provided him with a great deal of diversion. Charles was at the helm, the place which he always reserved for himself, and at about four o'clock the little flotilla arrived at Elizabeth Castle. At Coutainville James had given, in the eyes of his admirers, a proof of his natural flair for the sea: for when it was proposed to put off the departure until it was ascertained whether or not the passage was clear of enemy craft, he pointed out that as the wind then lay the enemy ships off Guernsey were wind-bound and could not intercept them. After some discussion his advice was followed, and it was justified by the complete safety of their passage, and by the fact that the baggage-ships, which followed them next day, when the wind had shifted, narrowly escaped capture.

Charles and James took up their residence at Elizabeth Castle, built on a rock and connected with St. Heliers by a causeway which was covered by the sea at high tide. They were accompanied by a train of no fewer than three hundred persons; among those who accompanied Charles or joined him later in Jersey we may notice Lord Byron, the Duke of Buckingham, Sir John Berkeley, Sir Edward Nicholas, Sir Edward Herbert, Sir Bernard Gascoigne, Sir Marmaduke Langdale, Stephen Fox, James's secretary, Henry Bennet, and his chaplain, Dr. Richard Stuart. The castle could hardly accommodate them all, and subsequent arrivals had to be accommodated in St. Heliers and elsewhere. Considerable state was maintained: Charles and James had each six well-matched horses for his coach, and there was a third coach-and-six for the Privy Council. There was some activity in strengthening the defences of the island, notably by an addition to Elizabeth Castle, and in increasing and training the militia, and there were many public ceremonies to attend; but mostly the royal brothers devoted themselves to such amusements as the island afforded, shooting, and sailing about in Charles's pinnace. Charles, however, was not allowed to feel at ease in Jersey; his servants were perpetually squabbling, and their squabbles led to duels, and there was an increasing fear that the Parliamentary fleet might blockade Jersey and take him in a trap. Ormonde, indeed, wrote from Ireland on September 27 urging him to go there, in a last desperate hope that his presence might put heart into his followers and regain that kingdom; but the letter arrived too late to determine his plans, and when, in October, the Scots commissioners followed him to his retreat and renewed their offers, Charles had to swallow his pride and what scruples he had about signing the Covenant and dismissing his "godless" servants—that is to say, all his servants except such as were prepared to assume godliness; he made an appointment to meet the commissioners in Breda in the following March. He accordingly left Jersey on February 13, after a parting with James (tearful on the part of both the brothers), and met his mother at Beauvais on the 21st. They parted on March 5, Henrietta to return to Paris, Charles to continue his journey to Breda and thence to Scotland on the quest which was to end at Worcester.

Charles's apostasy from Cavalier principles caused dismay among the Cavaliers both in England and Scotland; Lord Hatton reported that "the sweet Princess Elizabeth" away at Carisbrooke Castle "hath wept daily ever since". Sir Edward Hyde's letters from Madrid at this time express in admirable literary form the views of the best among the Cavaliers; they provide an abiding testimony to the moral integrity of the writer. He reproved Berkeley's flippancy in saying that Charles could not be cheated by the Scots because he had nothing to lose:

> It is no wonder if men are shy of trusting those who have not the reputation of being honest, and we can never be so low but we may again be deceived. When all is lost we may be cozened out of our innocence and misled into a partnership of mischief; therefore let us not think that we ought not to stand at guard, how undone soever we are.

And to the Countess of Morton he wrote:

> I pray God this treaty may prove prosperous to the King; the Scots methinks deal with him like honest men and tell him plainly that they will never do him good, and yet we are so mad as to believe that they will do better than they promise. . . . It is an excellent expedient to draw God's blessing upon us to have no other excuse for taking an oath than that they resolve not to keep it at the same time they take it.[1]

It was asserted in after years that the "*jure divino* episcopacy" were so incensed against Charles that there was a movement, connected with the name of Dr. Morley, for deposing him and substituting James as titular King, and that James knew of the movement and did not dis-

[1] It may be remarked in passing that the pretence of accepting Charles as a sincere Covenanter was as disgraceful to the Kirk as was Charles's hypocritical assumption of "godliness" to himself.

courage it. It is certain that he disapproved of the negotiations with the Scots and vehemently opposed Charles's journey to Breda; but he was not of the enlarged council which decided the matter and had no official right to express an opinion. Sir John Berkeley and Lord Byron were, however, consulted (though Berkeley was not of the Council), and James took revenge on them for the favour they had shown to the Scots by dismissing them from his household. Berkeley wrote to Hyde:

> My Lord Byron and myself as we were put into my master's bedchamber without our desires so we are put out at His Highness's instance without our consents; we could guess at no other reason but that we were lately for that treaty which our master passionately opposed and voted against it when His majesty voted for it.

But a very few months brought a change of mind: on August 24 James wrote from Jersey to the Earl of Argyll:

> My Lord
>
> I have sent this gentleman to congratulate to His Majesty the hopeful condition his affairs are put into now in his kingdom of Scotland, which I cannot remember without making some acknowledgements to you for that part you have contributed thereunto, which knowing to be a very considerable one, you may assure yourself of a proportionable share in my affection and friendship, and that I am always ready to give you the best proofs I can thereof as
>
> Your affectionate cousin
>
> James.

This is the third letter of James of which we still have the text. The two earlier letters, one written from The Hague in September 1648 and the other from Saint-Germain in July 1649, are letters of compliment addressed to the Marquis of Montrose when the Scottish cavalier party, of which he was the leader, was in favour with Charles. Within a year the two brothers had pledged themselves to Montrose's bitterest enemy.

Lord Jermyn held the office of Governor of Jersey and was entitled to the revenues of that position, though he rarely if ever visited the island; Sir George Carteret resided there as Lieutenant-Governor and carried out all the duties of the Government—an expensive but not uncommon arrangement in that and the following century. When Charles left for France he bought the governorship from Jermyn for £3000 (it is unlikely that the money was paid before the Restoration), and conferred it upon James. The circumstances are thus interpreted by the agent of the Parliament, who had been in Jersey and had followed Charles to Beauvais:

> He hath also done it to lay some obligation on the Duke to continue in the Island, where indeed he is no better than a prisoner to his brother's jealousy, which is very great towards him. Before our coming from thence he gave Sir George Carteret (in whom he reposeth very great trust), a very great charge to have a very strict eye, but withal secretly, over his person and actions, very much fearing that, being very active and of a stirring nature and good parts, and withal being more plausible, may be like enough at one time or another to create him trouble enough.

This is the first of several records of Charles's jealousy of James, and in this instance at any rate the evidence appears inconclusive. Charles clearly did not want James at Breda because he would have complicated matters by opposing the treaty, and in pure kindness and to lessen his disappointment at being left behind—there could have been no other reason—he made James governor; Charles's instructions to Carteret were, from their nature, secret, so that the latter part of the information is pure conjecture. Charles certainly on two or three occasions before the Restoration showed a jealousy of his brother, but it is not necessary to believe that this jealousy developed into a settled habit of mind. Three years before Charles died James wrote:

> The King was far from being jealous, for besides that the Duke had never given the least occasion for such a mistrust, it was not in the King's temper to be so;

and from what we know of the character of Charles we must agree with this verdict.

James was not at all satisfied with his situation in Jersey: he naturally felt that he was being left out of all the schemes that were on foot to restore his brother. No sooner had Charles left than he sent Berkeley (not yet dismissed) after him to suggest various alternatives: that he should join the fleet under Prince Rupert, that (for some obscure reason) he should go either to the Duke of Lorraine or the Queen of Sweden, or that he should return to his mother in Paris. But Charles did not approve of any of these plans, "so that (as Berkeley put it) my master seems to me to have the full liberty of the Island". There were rumours that the Scots would compel Charles to command James's attendance on him in Scotland, and would thus make him an additional hostage for his brother's good behaviour, but they proved to be without foundation.

There is a brief sketch of James as he appeared to a Jersey diarist, too slight, perhaps, to be worth reviving:

> The Duke of York, who had completed his fifteenth year (*sic*), was tall for his age and slight in figure but remarkably lively and pleasant in his manner. His Highness was attired in an entire suit of black, without any other ornament or decoration than the silver star displayed upon his mantle. He also wore a purple scarf across his shoulders.

The costume was, of course, that appropriate for the period of mourning for his royal father.

The Cavaliers who accompanied or followed Prince Charles in his flight from England were not on the whole the best of their class. They were soldiers without troops, squires without lands, lawyers without occupation, courtiers without more than the semblance of a Court, all without money, and they carried with them to the Continent the jealousies and animosities that had wrecked what chances they had had of defeating the Parliamentarians. A very few of them rose above their dismal surroundings. Of such was Edward Hyde, Charles's trusted counsellor, whose character at this time of his life shines singularly clear; he was hated by the courtiers both on account of his lack of claim to gentle birth, and for the favour which his devotion had won from Charles, but his disinterestedness and loyalty were in eminent contrast to their self-seeking. But many years before the Restoration Hyde had contracted the habit of ungraciousness which was so great a factor in his ultimate downfall: he was well aware that he was the intellectual superior of everyone who could compete with him in giving advice to the King, and he was at no pains to conceal this knowledge or to gain popularity by affecting to take advice; Lord Hatton said that he was aiming at "a viziership in Christendom to the height of that in Turkey", and it is easy to imagine how galling such an attitude must have been to the cavaliers of the Court, even if we make some allowance for exaggeration by one whose information was not always so accurate as his friends desired.

Of a very different hereditary and social background, but with the same political outlook, was the Marquis of Ormonde—to be known to history as the "great" Duke of Ormonde—owner of ancestral acres, accustomed to command, a great gentleman, a true Church-and-King man. He was perhaps a little inclined to dramatise himself: "as I am most clear from an itch to be meddling and from the faction of siding with parties, so I would be thought to aim at serving the King honestly and plainly without crotchets or lies"; in the same letter he complains of those "that reject advices barely upon dislike of those that give them". In another letter he wrote, "Though it hath pleased God to lay us flat upon the ground for our sins, he hath not forbidden us to look about how we may rise. I depend much upon your belief of my constancy to myself and the principles of our late blessed master. I hope I shall be found as little to swerve from them as anybody." Nearly thirty years later he was to write to the King that he would continue to serve him "with all the vigour time hath left me, and with all the faithfulness no time can alter or take from me". Unfortunately Ormonde was not at first at the centre of things: Charles apparently did not require his presence, and the rival Court of the Queen at the Louvre was too poor to support him. He and Hyde agreed in all things; they were much of an age—about twenty years older than Charles—and from their correspondence it is clear that they took a semi-paternal view of the young Princes and of the bickerings of their entourage. From his dignified poverty at Caen, from which he made only very rare visits to Paris, Ormonde exerted what influence he could in favour of sanity and decent living. His high station made it possible for him to speak to royal persons with a candour and freedom which were forbidden to Hyde, and there is envy as well as amused admiration in a passage in one of Hyde's letters to him:

> I am very glad you have made that journey to the Queen [Henrietta Maria] in which the King hath discharged his obligation, though methinks Her Majesty was sharper in her reflections than she had reason to be; however you were not a very good courtier in your reply, when she said that if she had been trusted the King had now been in England, that if she had never been trusted he had never been out of England.

With Hyde and Ormonde we may perhaps associate "Secretary" Nicholas, who was for four years Charles's representative at The Hague. He had served Charles's father with steady faithfulness for many years before the Rebellion and had incurred the violent animosity of the Parliamentary party; he was not a man of brilliant gifts, but his industry and common-sense made him a valuable public servant.

Henrietta Maria's counsels at the Louvre were ruled by Henry, Lord Jermyn, who had an infinite capacity for intrigue, but no other ability. So closely did he identify his interests with those of his royal mistress that it was confidently asserted that he was married to her; he contrived to live in affluence and splendour when the rest of the exiled cavaliers were near starvation. Before the expedition to Scotland in

1650 he had been a rival to Hyde in Charles's confidence, and his advice to accept the terms of the Scottish commissioners at Breda had been followed when Hyde was absent on a mission to Spain. But after Charles's escape from Worcester, Hyde became his chief adviser, and Jermyn, jealous on account of his loss of influence, became Hyde's implacable enemy. The Queen Mother took Jermyn's side, and the antipathy which she showed on all occasions for Charles's Minister seriously widened the breach which had appeared between mother and son. In this animosity against Charles's advisers Nicholas was included; he was accused of encouraging Charles in his resistance to his mother's influence; but Ormonde was too safely entrenched in rank and dignity to be attacked.

Henrietta's first duty after James's arrival at The Hague was to provide him with servants. She had no sense of economy, and there were plenty of people about her with nothing to do, so she appointed them all to various posts about James's person and sent them off to The Hague; and James, without money, had to provide for a staff in excess of what his father would have provided for him if he had been at liberty and in full possession of the royal revenues. The result was as could have been anticipated: a number of courtiers surrounded the boy prince; they had no money to procure such amusements as the place afforded, and they commenced a competition for James's favour and a series of squabbles among themselves; these squabbles lasted for nine years, and at certain periods became the chief topic of the letters which passed between the exiled Royalists.

An excellent choice had been made for the post of governor to James —Lord Byron, a distinguished soldier, well educated, and a thoroughly loyal and disinterested man; unfortunately he was not immediately available, and he was not able to impose discipline upon the household before the factions had got entirely out of hand. Sir John Berkeley was appointed to hold the post during Byron's absence. The accounts of Berkeley all agree: he was a hectoring, self-assertive, domineering man of moderate abilities and no real strength of character; he had fought well in the Civil War, but he over-valued himself and could not endure to be in any but the first place; when he had gained James's favour he fomented jealousies between him and Charles in order to increase his own importance. He had at first Bampfield to reckon with. Like many successful plotters, Bampfield could not cease plotting even when his plots had achieved success. It was natural that James should be grateful to him for the assistance he had given him in his escape, and he wanted him to have the governor's place; but when Bampfield had attempted to get up a Presbyterian faction in the household, and also to promote a sort of mutiny in the Royalist flotilla, it was clear even to James that he was impossible. He was dismissed with such pecuniary gratifications as funds would allow. He returned to England, and was there arrested and examined by the Council, but he escaped from the Gatehouse prison the night before he was to have been brought to trial for his share in James's escape. He subsequently, after the manner of his kind, passed over to the enemy; when next he visited the Continent it was as a spy in Cromwell's pay, and a number of his letters written in that capacity are to be found among the Thurloe State Papers.[1]

James's household not only bickered among themselves, but made trouble in the establishment of their host, the Prince of Orange, who had to bear "the reproaches to which his council was every day made liable by the impertinence and insolence of that train"—the old story of untravelled, aristocratic Englishmen treating foreigners as they thought they ought to be treated—and he was not sorry when James set out for Paris with his "uneasy family". There and in Jersey the presence of Charles seems to have driven faction underground—he had insisted on the dismissal of no fewer than twenty-two of James's servants in November—but no sooner had James returned to Paris (in September 1650) than the bluster and ineffectiveness of Berkeley and Henrietta Maria's open hostility to certain of James's other advisers produced a crisis. A faction consisting of Sir George Radcliffe, Sir Edward Herbert, the Attorney-General, Dr. Stuart, the chaplain, and Dr. Henry Killigrew, another divine, acquired an ascendancy over James and convinced him that he ought to strike out a line for himself. Charles IV, Duke of Lorraine, had been driven from his duchy by Richelieu: he was now at Brussels as a soldier of fortune fighting against France in the service of Spain. The conspirators filled James's mind with stories of this Duke's virtues and grievances, and prevailed on him to go to him at Brussels "as a pattern and example for all unfortunate princes to follow". They also told him that Charles had arranged for money to be paid to him at Brussels. There was no suggestion whatever that the Duke had expressed a wish to see James, and only James's youth can excuse his readiness to fall in with the scheme. Nor in fact could Lorraine claim to be "a pattern and example" for James to follow: he was a man notoriously unstable and fickle; his one steady ambition was to obtain from the Pope a blessing on the "marriage" which he had contracted during his own wife's lifetime and the legitimation of his children by

[1] At the Restoration Bampfield went into exile, and at the end of Charles's reign he was still repeatedly writing to Ormonde protesting that he had never betrayed the King and begging Ormonde to use his influence to obtain a pardon.

that "marriage". There can be little question that the ultimate object of James's advisers was to get the chief posts about his person in case Charles's expedition ended fatally to himself and James succeeded to the titular crown. In fact, there were rumours that Charles was already dead.

Henrietta Maria was strongly opposed to the plan. She had no intention of relaxing the hold she had over James as the sole source of his means of support, and she was also in a strong position, in that she had been appointed his guardian by his brother Charles. Radcliffe and the others had managed to raise funds from somewhere, and James was able to show his mother Charles's letter ordering him to leave Jersey, in which were "some ambiguous expressions which seemed to intimate that he desired that he would go to Holland". The Queen enlisted the assistance of her son-in-law, the Prince of Orange, and he wrote to James offering him an annual pension of 2000 pistoles if he would remain in Paris, and informing him that if he came to The Hague he must inevitably be shipped off to Scotland under a treaty which the Prince had made with the Scots.

But Henrietta Maria had very little influence with or control over James. She appears to have antagonised him from the time of his first arrival in Paris. She made to her ladies damaging comparisons between his character and that of Charles, and these remarks were repeated to him. He was probably already at this early age more stubborn and intractable than Charles, and she on her side maintained an "austere carriage" towards both her sons. Some instinct of family honour (which, however, he subdued later) may also have made him resent the intimate relations that existed between his mother and Lord Jermyn. In the present case she was helpless. She might storm and rage, as no doubt she did, but James had the means of disobeying her, and he used them. The best she could do was to prevail upon him to attach Lord Byron and Henry Bennet to his party as a measure of control over the hotheads into whose hands he had delivered himself (Berkeley characteristically declined a part in the act when he realised that he could not play the lead).

James left Paris on October 4 and arrived at Brussels on October 13, 1650. The Duke of Lorraine received him with courtesy, and even gave him small sums of money towards his expenses, but James's presence was an embarrassment: James was only a younger son of the English royal line, that line had small hopes of being restored, and even if it were restored, Charles was only twenty, and it was very unlikely that he would die without direct heirs. There were negotiations conducted by Viscount Taaffe, apparently without authority from Charles, for the marriage of James to the Duke's illegitimate daughter and for the provision of a jointure out of Irish revenues; but these and other more direct negotiations for Lorraine's assistance in the reconquest of Ireland came to nothing, nor does it appear that Lorraine on his side entered into them seriously.

After two months in Brussels without tangible results, James's advisers began to quarrel among themselves. The Spanish authorities were passively hostile, for they were anxious to remain on good terms with the revolutionary government in England; funds were so low that James ceased to have formal dinners and had to be content with "two dishes a meal in his chamber"; Henrietta Maria in Paris refused to send supplies. She was determined to get James back to Paris, not because she wanted him near her, but in order to vindicate her authority: as Nicholas put it, "that they may have the new modelling of him and teach him to bow to the Baal of the Louvre, which is the Idol which hath ruined our Israel". In these circumstances James determined to try The Hague again. Lord Byron had already been there to persuade the Prince and Princess to receive him, but the Prince died early in November, and his posthumous son, William, who was to play so disastrous a part in James's life, was born on December 4. Furthermore, Henrietta, though James had written to her asking her to use her good offices with the Prince and Princess, laid her positive commands on her daughter not to receive him. Consequently when in the first days of December the party sent a messenger in advance to announce that they were on the way, the Princess, "who was wholly governed by the Queen", replied that the visit was inconvenient ("which unkindness these Boers do wonder at", says Nicholas). They therefore turned east and spent a month at Rhenen, where James's aunt, the unfortunate Elizabeth, Queen of Bohemia, had a house.

Meanwhile Henrietta Maria had invoked the aid of Charles, and from Scotland Charles sent Henry Rainsford to James with a letter scolding him for leaving France without orders and commanding him to return to Paris and to reduce his household; these instructions end, however, on a kindlier note, expressing sympathy for James chafing at a life of inaction and admitting his right to choose his own servants, but at the same time they threatened with dire penalties any of those servants who should dare to advise James not to obey Charles's present orders. James did not obey them, but sent Richard Fanshaw to his brother and excused himself on the ground that his conduct had been misrepresented by his mother, who, indeed, had no great reputation for truthfulness. About the same time or a little earlier Jermyn, without the Queen Mother's knowledge, paid a flying visit to Rhenen, staying only one night, and vainly tried to effect by personal negotiation what other methods had failed to achieve; he might have been more successful if he had stood higher in James's favour.

Henrietta Maria now changed her tactics. Thinking, no doubt, that the Princess of Orange, who was entirely in her interest, might ease the situation, she withdrew the prohibition of James's visit to The Hague and he arrived there in the middle of January. This plan very nearly succeeded, for after only a fortnight at The Hague James was reported to be preparing to return to Paris; but unhappily Paris was again in an unrestful state, and his mother could not advise him to pursue his journey. Late in March a great reception to the new English ambassadors was announced at The Hague, and James retreated to Breda for a time to avoid being present; he returned to his sister when the festivities were over. Finally, however, his presence at The Hague was resented by the English ambassadors, and he had to shift his headquarters permanently to Breda. In May James had abandoned hope of profiting by his expedition and was begging his mother to recall him to Paris.

Now there was nothing to be done; no one had anything to suggest, and everyone cast the blame on everyone else—all except Sir Edward Herbert, who sulked solemnly by himself. At the beginning of June a further peremptory message came from Charles ordering immediate return to the Queen Mother, and Hyde arrived from Paris; there was a general feeling of relief, and the return journey was made without delay. Henrietta Maria controlled herself and confounded the prophets by refraining from undue heat at the first interviews. But there was conflict between them on the religious question: it was generally supposed in later years that the conversion of James to Rome had been due to his mother's influence, and as late as 1680 in the debates on the second Exclusion Bill there was mention of this widely held opinion, but she appears to have made no direct effort to convert him to her own faith. Of this fact there is almost conclusive proof in the postscript to a letter from Charles to his mother written in his own hand in December 1654—the subject of the letter itself is connected with Henrietta's attempt to convert Henry, Duke of Gloucester. Charles says:

> Your Majesty cannot forget how often you have pressed the keeping your promise to the King my father concerning myself and my brother the Duke of York as an argument to me not to fear any attempt would be made by Your Majesty to change my brother Henry.

These words constitute an admission that Henrietta had kept her promise as far as Charles and James were concerned, and that she had made no attempt to convert James—up to the end of the year 1654, when he was twenty-one years of age. The words also dispose of the rumours that reached Nicholas at The Hague shortly after Charles's return to Paris after the Battle of Worcester that there was a plan afoot at the Louvre to convert both Charles and James; at that time Charles was more inclined to listen to his mother's advice on public matters than he had previously been, and this change may have given rise to these rumours.[1]

But if Henrietta did not try to convert James, she placed difficulties in the way of his exercise of the Protestant rites, and he had to appeal to the Queen Mother of France for permission to set up a private chapel in the Louvre. Henrietta also treated him with such systematic contempt that Nicholas, writing to Ormonde, expressed a fear lest, strong as was James's loyalty to his brother, such conduct would undermine it:

> I see already that whatever the Duke doth that is not suitable to the Queen's mind and to the little designs of those about her is presently interpreted and reported to be a factious plot. And I may tell your Excellency I am very sorry to find so great and causeless jealousies endeavoured to be raised of the Duke, who (I assure you) hath in my opinion most dutiful affections for the King, but I cannot say that I believe he doth conceive that the Queen or any about her esteems him or hath much kindness for him. I do not discern any disposition or inclination in the Duke of York to do anything that may in the least manner distaste the King, but I very much apprehend that if he shall find that his great desire to merit by his obedience shall be still misrepresented, and that his person (being now past a child) shall be by the Queen and her sycophants rendered contemptible in their table discourses, it may (I doubt) make him give ear to counsels and persons that may put other things into his head than his natural good disposition inclines him to.

[1] In the compilation known as the *Memoirs of Sir Stephen Fox* occurs the passage:

> no sooner was the Royal Family arrived in France but Her Majesty by the means of her confessor and other priests, her domestics, was not only urgent with the King for the education of the Duke of Gloucester but were (*sic*) assiduous with the Duke of York to embrace their communion.

But this was written long after the event, when it had become an article of popular belief that Henrietta had influenced James in his religion; and so inaccurate is the work that in the passage from which this extract is quoted it is implied that the Duke of Gloucester had arrived in France with "the Royal Family", and not, as was actually the case, six years after James and nearly eight years after Charles.

Moreover, she strongly objected to certain members of his household, and in the last letter James had received from Charles there had been a definite command to dismiss Dr. Killigrew, and to reduce Sir George Radcliffe, as it were, to the ranks, so that James would be in no danger of following his advice. Henrietta Maria would have liked to dismiss Herbert, who at this time undoubtedly began to exercise an undue influence on James's mind, and she was so furious with Dr. Stuart that she sent word that if he came to Paris with James she would consider his action as a personal affront and "would use him accordingly". In this little quarrel she herself was not entirely blameless. She snubbed Herbert heavily, and then objected that he avoided her presence. James was closeted for long hours with Herbert, and though the conversations were not and could not be of any importance, his mother was itching to know what they had been talking about. The matter was brought to a head by James's pecuniary necessities. At the end of July 1651, when the royal apartments had been made uncomfortable for everyone during the five weeks since James's return, Byron wrote to Ormonde:

> Not long since the Duke went to Chaillot (where the Queen continues still) to desire Her Majesty's advice how he might better his condition here, his pension being so small that he was not able to live of it; to which she replied that she would not at all meddle in his business, nor advise him in anything, so long as he suffered himself to be so governed by the Attorney [Herbert], and that she could not any longer conceal the offence she took at his so frequent repair to him, without even acquainting Her Majesty or anybody else entrusted by the King in His Highness's affairs with the subject of his long discourses, and that she took the entertainment of such a person (who seemed to stand in open defiance with her) as a great disrespect and affront. . . . The Duke had little to answer to this so true a reproach and made what haste he could away, being much discontented for a day or two after; neither does the Attorney come so frequently to him, but so long as my Lord Gerrard does it is still the same thing.

To this humiliation followed a contest between Herbert and Gerrard on one side and a new alliance between Berkeley and Jermyn on the other for the chief place in the counsels of the young Prince. The best man on the spot for this position was probably Lord Byron, but he was too large-minded to fight for his own hand, and there was no body of disinterested opinion to support him. As will appear later, victory lay with Berkeley and Jermyn. Radcliffe was unable to reinstate himself, and it appears that the chaplaincy was taken away from Stuart and given to James Crowther, who continued with James until after the Restoration and who conducted the marriage service with Anne Hyde.

James had heard at Brussels of two tragedies in the family, the defeat of the Scots at Dunbar on September 3, 1650, and the death at Carisbrooke in October of his sister Elizabeth. In the autumn of 1651 it was proposed that he should be attached to the French Court, as part of his education, but the news arrived of the Battle of Worcester, and no one knew what had become of Charles until he had actually landed in France. In this state of uncertainty Henrietta Maria preferred to keep James with her. However, Charles landed at Fécamp on October 16, and James went as far as Magny to meet him.

We get a glimpse at this time of James—a few weeks before his eighteenth birthday—as he appeared to Sir Richard Browne: "The sweet Duke of York doth here subsist upon the allowance of one thousand crowns a month paid him from this State, being esteemed by all for his comeliness and personal dexterity, in behaviour and exercises."

In the winter of 1651 to 1652 there was a scheme to negotiate a marriage between James and the daughter of the Duke of Longueville, one of the greatest heiresses of the time. Berkeley apparently originated the scheme, at any rate he took a keen and unauthorised interest in it and intrigued with the women who were about the young lady's person. But when the matter came to the notice of higher authorities, Henrietta Maria linked it up with a scheme which had long been on foot for the marriage of Charles to his cousin, la Grande Mademoiselle, daughter of the Duke of Orleans; and when this other scheme failed to materialise she vetoed James's marriage on the general ground that it was not fitting that he should be married before his brother, the King. On the other hand, James's marriage project seems to have been looked upon with little favour by the French Court, for they thought it preferable that the heiress should marry a Frenchman and keep her money in the country.

CHAPTER III

THE MILITARY CAREER

THE actual circumstances in which James joined the French Army are a little obscure. He was negotiating for a troop of horse as early as July 1651, at the time of crisis in his relations with his mother, as an alternative plan to that of joining the French Court, and it is asserted that he was in action on Christmas Day of that year, when he distinguished himself by leading a forlorn hope against Condé's troops and having a horse shot under him.[1] He says in his memoirs, and he is supported by Clarendon, that the question of his joining the Army was a matter of keen debate in the royal counsels in the spring of 1652, that he himself was very anxious to go and that his only ally at first was Sir John Berkeley, but that in time he persuaded both Charles and his mother to give consent. Possibly the earlier adventure was undertaken without their previous knowledge. Even in 1652 he joined only as a volunteer, though soon after joining he was given a regular commission in command of the Switzers. He had great difficulty in raising funds for equipment, and when he left Paris it was with very few attendants, the faithful Berkeley being one, and "without so much as a led-horse in case of necessity".

It is not possible to give here more than the briefest outline of the circumstances in which the French Government and people were in the spring of 1652. Richelieu, who had been virtually dictator, had died over nine years earlier, when France was still engaged in the final stages of the Thirty Years' War. Richelieu, like many dictators, had lived too much in the present, he had made no provision for the continuance of his system of government after his death, he had neither trained able subordinates to succeed him nor created permanent institutions through which the royal will could operate. His successor, Cardinal Mazarin, an Italian, and for that reason unpopular with the French nobles, was a very able diplomatist, but he entirely lacked the necessary ruthlessness in home affairs; Mazarin's two great assets were the possession of the person of the boy King and of the entire confidence of the Queen Mother, Anne of Austria. In 1648 the Thirty Years' War ended in the Peace of Westphalia, and the French nobles, whose power it had been

[1] According to Aumale (*Les Princes de Condé*, VI, 116), Condé was not in action on Christmas Day 1651, but was manœuvring in the valley of the Charente.

Richelieu's life-work to curb, were set free to look after their own interests and to attempt to recover the ground they had lost in the previous thirty years; by 1652, after several minor movements had been suppressed, the country was in a state of civil war. This war was known as the Fronde, a name which it derived from the *Frondeurs*, the gamins of Paris who amused themselves by throwing stones at passers-by from the disused moats and who ran away when the authorities appeared; and the name aptly describes the frivolity of the combatants. For they were fighting for no political principle—unless a common dislike of Mazarin can be considered a principle; every leader fought for his own local independence or for a share of power in the central government, and there were frequent changes of side. The Civil War was complicated by the continuance of the war with Spain, for France and Spain had not come to terms at the time of the general pacification of Europe in 1648, and the opponents of Mazarin did not hesitate to ally themselves with the national enemy. In 1654 the war of the Fronde came to an end, but the war with Spain went on, and the Prince of Condé, one of the most famous of French generals, fought for Spain against his own country.

No attempt can be made to trace the course of the war or the particular experiences of James. He himself has left a long and somewhat dull record of the movements and actions in which he took part, a record so unboastful that we have to look elsewhere for the high esteem in which he was held by his brother officers, and there is an illuminating aside at one point by his biographer when describing the action before Étampes: "His Royal Highness (though he never mentions his own danger) was present in the places where the service was hottest." James had to leave Paris secretly, and did not bid farewell to his and the King's uncle, the Duke of Orleans, for the Duke was a Frondeur, and there were plenty of others in Paris. At first he had considerable difficulty in getting recognised as a combatant on the royal side—he was on one occasion turned back by sentries—but on April 24 he found himself at headquarters at Chartres. His departure for his second campaign was made publicly and without restriction of expense—James had evidently prospered in the first year of his military life.

> The Duke of York parted hence Thursday last with bag and baggage to the field where Turenne is in Champagne, and said at his going out of Palais Royal to his brother the King that now since he is forced to fight for his bread that he hoped soon to fight for his countries lost by his enemies; which made his brother very melancholy and many others. Both his brothers went with him

two leagues off, as also Ormonde, Inchiquin, Taaffe and three or four more. He had four mules to carry his baggage and a quantity of good horses.

From the first and throughout his four campaigns he was on Turenne's staff and was in constant touch with that great general. No better school for a young soldier could have been devised; he learnt at first hand the methods of the greatest captain of that age, possibly of any age. The high opinion, amounting almost to worship, which he formed of the Marshal's military capacity and of his thoroughness is testified in very many passages in James's memoirs, and may here be illustrated by a single extract:

> M. de Turenne went in person to view all the ground about Mousson, taking with him M. de Castelnau, when as in another army, I have seen the generals trust a *sergent de battaille* or some inferior officer to do it, so that they were wholly guided, and in a manner governed by the eyes and advice of other men: but M. de Turenne made use of his own judgment, where he thought it most proper to break ground, and which way to run the trenches; when night came, he himself was present at the opening of them, and continued there almost till break of day: besides it was his constant method, during the whole siege to go into the trenches both morning and evening, in the morning to see if the work was well performed, at evening to resolve what would be the work that night, having in his company the Lieutenant-General and some of the chief officers who that night were to command in the trenches, to instruct them himself what he expected to be done. Again after supper he went to see them begin their work, and would continue with them more or less, as he found it necessary for the carrying on of the present design.

There was, of course, considerable personal risk to the general in these inspections, and these risks were in all cases shared by James; for example, at the action of the Barricades in July 1654 Colonel Werden, who was one of his attendants and was close to him, was severely wounded; at the siege of Mousson in September 1653 James was struck on the foot by a spent bullet. The evidence is overwhelming that James at this time of his life was exceedingly brave—so brave as to be outstanding in an army in which courage was not exceptional: Burnet says that Turenne "magnified" him for his courage; Sir George Radcliffe wrote in 1652, "The Duke ventures himself, and chargeth gallantly, when anything is to be done", and, "The Duke of York hath gotten a very great reputation and power in the French army, he is bold and active"; Hyde wrote in May 1652, "In which action [at Étampes] the Duke of York behaved himself with extraordinary courage and gallantry", and in December 1653 from Paris, "The Duke of York is returned hither full of reputation and honour"; and one of Thurloe's spies, a hostile witness, wrote from Paris in November 1653, "The Duke of York is much esteemed in the French army". In September 1654 Jermyn wrote to Charles from Paris, in a description of the gallant feats of both French and English at the relief of Arras:

> It is most certain the general officers did all their duties excellently well in their general posts and most undoubtedly none better than the Duke of York, if any so well.

Bennet wrote from camp at Cateau Cambresis in the following month:

> His Royal Highness has an extraordinary esteem and kindness from this whole country, but most especially here in the army, where application to learn his profession and his behaviour in it is everybody's wonder; but I presume you know this already.

Simultaneously Hyde was writing from Cologne:

> The Duke of York hath received no wound though in all actions he hath been so forward that he hath got much honour among the French and even with the Spaniards.

When in June 1657 James was about to enter the Spanish army, Ormonde wrote to Hyde:

> The Duke of York will take exceedingly in the army, he is brave and little troublesome as a prince can be.

And Hatton joins this chorus of eulogy with, "The Duke of York is a most glorious young Prince".

In 1654, when he had served only two years and was still under twenty-one, James achieved the singular honour of promotion to the rank of Lieutenant-General; the promotion was no doubt in part due to his royal birth, but he would not have been promoted if Turenne had found him incompetent, and we may be confident that he had proved himself efficient. At the same time it may be noticed that the rank gives him no certificate of generalship; he was never tested in an independent command, and all that can be definitely claimed for him is that he was a dashing cavalry leader and that he could be trusted to carry out the Marshal's orders exactly and intelligently. A Grub Street panegyrist of the time of James's return to popularity in Charles's last years does credit to his own inventive powers by relating a story to the effect that at one time Turenne was ill and not likely to live, and that Louis (who, by the way, could only have been fifteen or sixteen years of age) asked him to nominate a successor to command the French Army: "To which he answered that if His Majesty would have his affairs prosper, he should make choice of a noble, valorous and fortunate general; the which if His Majesty empowered him to choose he could make choice of no fitter person than the thrice renowned and heroic Duke of York." As a matter of fact, as he himself records as a sort of jest, he was once in command of the French Army—for about a week, after the end of the campaign of 1655, when Turenne had to go off to a consultation with Mazarin and there was no other lieutenant-general available. During this time he accomplished the feat of marching the Army from Mouy to Mondêcour, a distance of about forty miles—a feat comparable to that attributed in song to a later bearer of his title. In all this it must be remembered that James was only twenty-two when he was for the last time in the field with the French Army.

During his service in the French Army, James was away from Paris for the whole of the summer, and only in the winter was he with his mother and Charles. Family broils continued incessantly; a period followed Charles's return to Paris after his escape from England in which he was so submissive to Henrietta that his counsellors feared that she would entirely dominate him. But this *rapprochement* had only transitory effect, and mother and son resumed their habit of hostility. James's biographer says that "it was very difficult for the Duke so to fashion his behaviour, that he might equally perform his duty both to the King and to his Mother", but we may be certain that it was to Charles's side that James constantly leaned: his loyalty to his brother was very steady, and any other attitude would have been inconsistent with his strong monarchical convictions. But Charles's presence had had some effect in easing James's position: he had induced him to moderate his hostility to Lord Jermyn, and though his direct relations with his mother remained difficult, she was able to keep in touch with him through this intermediary. Sir John Berkeley was now James's companion in arms throughout the year, he achieved complete ascendancy over his mind; Sir Edward Herbert had faded out of the picture and Berkeley had formed a close alliance with Jermyn. Another important person in James's household was his secretary, Henry Bennet, who had been placed on James's staff at Charles's suggestion and at the instance of his patron, the restless and intriguing George Digby, Earl of Bristol.

In the spring of 1654 Mazarin had entered into negotiations with

Cromwell, and in consequence of these negotiations and for many other reasons Charles left Paris in July, and after a short period of indecision went to live at Cologne. As long as Charles was at the Louvre, Berkeley and Jermyn had to conceal their jealousies of Bennet, but as soon as he had gone they were able to make Bennet's position almost intolerable. Bennet's abilities were considerable—far greater than those of his rivals in James's favour—but they were not in themselves great enough to have secured for him the very long tenure of high office which as Earl of Arlington he enjoyed in Charles's reign; this success was due in the main to his pre-eminence as a courtier. Though he was James's secretary, Bennet's chief object was to give satisfaction to Charles, and he succeeded so well that Charles, when he left Paris, wrote in his "Instructions" to James:

> You must be very kind to Henry Bennet and communicate freely with him, for as you are sure he is full of duty and integrity to you so I must tell you that I shall trust him more than any that are about you and cause him to be trusted at large in those businesses of mine which I cannot particularly write to you myself.

In other words, Bennet was more in Charles's confidence than James was, and it is not surprising that James, though he knew himself to be innocent of disloyalty, felt that he was being watched. Jermyn was entirely in Henrietta's interest, and Berkeley desired to exalt James at Charles's expense, so that each had a separate reason for disliking Bennet, and between them they encouraged James's distrust of him. Bennet was so unhappy in his isolation that he wrote to Charles asking to be allowed to join the King at Cologne, but Charles replied that, glad as he would be to see him, he was more useful where he was.

At this time Sir George Radcliffe was making a determined effort to get back into favour, but James had no ears except for Sir John Berkeley; to him he gave his devotion and subordinated his judgment, and with him and his close ally Lord Jermyn James spent all his leisure when he was in Paris. (It is interesting to note that Lord Hatton already suspected James of an inclination to Romanism and Berkeley of influencing him in this direction.) In his youth and in late middle age James was very prone to submit himself to complete domination by another man, to surrender to him all his freedom of judgment and to listen to no criticism of his mentor from any source whatever. During his brother's reign, certainly after the death of Charles Berkeley and the estrangement of Sir William Coventry, he appears to have had no such exclusive attachment. At about this time a nephew of each of these men comes into prominence, Charles Berkeley and Henry Jermyn the younger, both of whom were near James in age. The two uncles and two nephews formed a solid party in the Louvre factions, a party steadily hostile to Hyde, frowned upon from afar by Charles and doubtless regarded with complacence by Henrietta.

Before Charles had reached Cologne he received information of a widespread Royalist plot in England and Scotland (known after its collapse as Penruddock's Rising), and he conceived the intention of going to Scotland to lead the movement there, while James took charge of operations in England. For some time the exiled cavaliers with very few exceptions did not know where the King was, though Cromwell through his spies was well aware that he was at Middelburgh preparing for his descent on Scotland. At this time he sent to James (or perhaps only drafted) a paper headed "Instructions for my Brother", bearing as date July 1654. The Instructions are under seven heads, the most important being the fourth:

> Let nobody persuade you to engage your own person in any attempt or enterprise without first imparting the whole design to me, which will be easily done whilst there is no sea between us. And when that comes to be the case assure yourself I will desire nothing more than to have you with me or in action in some other place, but to deal freely with you till I am myself in action in some part of my dominions which I will endeavour as soon as possible, I should be sorry to see you engaged before me, and let no man persuade you to it under what pretence soever.

In short, Charles did not want people to be able to say in after years that he had been replaced on the throne entirely by his brother's efforts and, though he trusted James to do nothing of his own volition which would bring him into prominence at his brother's expense, he did not trust him to resist the malign influence of Berkeley.

The sixth "instruction" is also of importance, concerning as it does the very significant attempt by Henrietta Maria to convert her youngest son, Henry, Duke of Gloucester, to her own faith.

> I have told you what my Mother hath promised me concerning my brother Harry in point of his religion, and I have given him charge to inform you if any attempt shall be made upon him to the contrary; in which case you will take the best care you can to prevent his being wrought upon since you cannot but know how much you and I are concerned in it.

Henry had been released from imprisonment by Cromwell early in 1653, and had first gone to his sister at The Hague. It had been impossible to resist the demands of Henrietta that she should be allowed to see her son, whom she had last seen as a two-year-old child, though it was suspected from the first that she would use every endeavour to make him a Catholic. For more than a year before Charles left France, Henry had been living with him, his mother and his younger sister Henrietta. In November 1654 Charles at Cologne heard that Henrietta had broken all her solemn promises to him and to his father, and was making a direct attack upon Henry's religious beliefs, with the help of her attendant priests. Henry showed spirit, surprising in a boy of fifteen, in opposition to his mother's efforts—no doubt he had a good deal of James's obstinacy. Charles, however, considered that he needed the backing of the authority of an older brother and of a King; he wrote Henry a vigorous letter:

> Your letters that come from Paris say that it is the Queen's purpose to do all she can to change your religion, in which if you do hearken to her or anybody else in that matter, you must never think to see England or me again, and whatsoever mischief shall fall on me or my affairs from this time I must lay all upon you as being the only cause of it. Therefore consider well what it is to be not only the cause of ruining a brother that loves you so well, but also of your King and Country.

Charles had already written to James in July on the same subject, and James took up the matter very strongly, and we are told he wrote "a very good letter" upholding Charles's attitude; after his return to Paris in November his mother was so angry at his opposition to her plans and so apprehensive that he would stiffen Henry's resolution not to be converted that she forbade him to speak to Henry except in her presence. Charles ended the matter by summoning Henry to Cologne. It is not safe, especially as James's "very good letter" has been lost, to draw the conclusion that he was at this time, and at the age of twenty-one, a devoted son of the Church of England, backed though that conclusion is by his own testimony. All we know for certain is that he was opposed to the conversion of Henry by his mother, and the grounds of his opposition may have been either the same as Charles's or more strictly religious.

The following letter written to Charles by James in May 1655 shows that the writer did not rise above his contemporaries in their approval of assassination—of regicides, at any rate—as a political weapon.

> There is a proposition has been made to me which is too long to put into a letter, so that I will as short as I can, let you know the

> heads of them (*sic*). There are four Roman Catholics that have bound themselves in a solemn oath to kill Cromwell, and then to raise all the Catholics in the City and the Army, which they pretend to be a number so considerable as may give a rise for your recovery, they being all warned to be ready for something that is to be done, without knowing what it is. They demand 10,000 livres in hand, and, when the business is ended, some recompense for themselves, according to their several qualities, and the same liberty for Catholics in England as the Protestants have in France. I thought not fit to reject this proposition, but to acquaint you with it, because the first part of the design seems to me to be better laid and resolved on than any I have known of that kind; and for the defects of the second, it may be supplied by some designs you may have to join it. If you approve it, one of the four entrusted by the rest will repair to you, his charges being borne, and give you a full account of the whole matter. In the meantime he desires in his own name and theirs that you would let but one or two whom you most trust know it and enjoin them secrecy.

This plot was one of many against Cromwell's life, and James was willing to be in it without scruple. We do not know how Charles received this letter, but it was generally understood that it was unwise to communicate such plots to him, and in particular that he would not offer a reward to a would-be assassin.

From the spring of 1654 there had been signs that Cromwell and Mazarin were seeking for an accommodation, and the prospect of a definite alliance with the revolutionary Government on the part of France contributed largely to Charles's determination to leave that country and to seek another asylum. The negotiations were slow, and it was not until October 24, 1655, that a treaty was signed. Under that treaty France bound herself not to permit Charles and James and seventeen of their adherents, specified by name, to reside within her borders. This provision was a serious blow to James;[1] his position in the French Army suited him perfectly, and he had excellent prospects: Madame de Sévigné stated in after years, on the authority of a distinguished brother-officer of James, that if he had continued as he had begun he would soon have been a Marshal of France; he was probably

[1] At the same time James had the breadth of mind to see that Mazarin could not have acted otherwise: "I cannot but do the memory of the Cardinal that right to affirm that he had been a very ill minister if he had not made the treaty with Cromwell in such a juncture of affairs; and the King of France would have had just reason to be ill-satisfied with him if he had missed that opportunity."

happier and more popular than he was at any other period of his life. Mazarin was anxious not to lose him, for apart from his own military prowess he had been able to attract to the French Army a number of Irish troops who had formerly served with Spain, and there was a probability that these men, as well as the English cavaliers fighting with France, would follow him if he joined the Spanish Army. Cromwell, on his side, was very willing to encourage dissension between the Stuart brothers and to wink at the continued employment of James by France when there was every prospect of Charles's allying himself with Spain. There was, however, the difficulty that it was not possible to send an English ambassador to Paris as long as James was there, for there was a fear that he might be assassinated by James's friends, as Dorislaus at The Hague and Ascham at Madrid had been assassinated by English royalists a few years earlier. In these circumstances no step was taken during the ten months that James remained in France after the treaty to remove him from French soil; he was treated with courtesy by the Court, but the people of Paris naturally regarded him as an enemy alien, and made his residence there uncomfortable. He took no part in the campaign of 1655; when the negotiations with Cromwell were in an advanced state it was clear that he could not continue indefinitely to fight for France in Flanders. A compromise was suggested: Charles Emmanuel II, Duke of Savoy, was the ally of France, and it was proposed that James should command the joint forces of France, Savoy and Modena in North Italy; an additional consideration that attracted James to the scheme was that Charles Emmanuel was his first cousin, for his mother, Christina, was Henrietta Maria's sister. But nothing came of it. The proposal received no encouragement from Savoy; in fact Bennet wrote to Charles as early as April 1655 that it was "flatly refused".

In March 1656 Charles left Cologne for Brussels with very few attendants. There he was an embarrassment to the Spaniards, and he was forced to withdraw to the neighbouring village of Vilvorde. However, on April 2 he was able to induce the Spaniards to sign a treaty promising military aid for his restoration to the English throne as soon as he could secure a port in England at which they could be landed, he on his side promising, in the event of his restoration, naval aid to Spain against Portugal and, in secret clauses, great concessions to the English and Irish Catholics. Charles had specifically refused to allow James's name to be mentioned in the treaty, in the hope that he would be able to secure better terms for him after the treaty was signed. A week later he established himself at Bruges, where he was joined by his tatterdemalion Court—or rather such of them as could evade their creditors at Cologne—and by Henry Bennet.

But though Charles had kept James's name out of the treaty and possibly had not even made a verbal promise of his services to the Spaniards, he had no intention of allowing James to remain in the French Army, for clearly his transfer to the Spanish side would consolidate Charles's relations with his new allies. James failed to appreciate his brother's interests at this time, he was anxious above all things that his promising military career should not be interrupted, and he was piqued by the absence (as far as he knew) of any demand on the Spanish side for his services; he proposed to Charles a fantastic secret plan, which he had discussed with Turenne, that Charles should publicly send him an order to join him in Flanders, and, while privately conniving at his disobedience, should satisfy the Spaniards by pretended anger at it. But Charles had few enough people to command as it was, and it was not likely that he would wish to advertise to the world his lack of control over his own younger brother.

Charles began to demand James's presence with him as soon as the treaty between England and France had been signed and before his departure from Cologne. As early as December 21, 1655, Jermyn wrote that James would be back in Paris in a few days and would make speedy preparations for the journey; but a fortnight later James in a letter to Charles said that he was not being pressed to leave France and did not expect such pressure for some time, that the arrival of the Princess of Orange on a visit to her mother would delay him, that Mazarin had promised to continue his pension after he left France but had not given him a definite contract, and that all things considered it would probably be the end of February before he could be with his brother. At the end of January and again in the middle of February he wrote saying that his plans were unsettled and that Mazarin was detaining him by dilatoriness over the pension. Meanwhile, as he wrote, he was having a very gay time in Paris:

> This place is full of divertissements, there being no night that there is not some good ball up and down the town. I believe you have heard of that at the Chancellor's on Sunday last where there was the greatest supper I have ever seen since I have been in this country and the best collation at the ball; and ever since we have not gone to bed till four in the morning.

During the next months James was evidently playing for time, for in May Charles wrote to Ormonde that his brother was pleading "that if it consists with my affairs it will be as much for his advantage as ever to go into the field", but that he would reply "as I resolved before you parted" (from Bruges). There was an absurd rumour at this time that

James was to have a command in, or the command of, the English republican troops which were being landed at Calais to co-operate with the French Army.

Thurloe's spies reported in the middle of June that James had told Charles that unless he could give him a definite offer from the Spaniards he would go to the French Army, as he had been very much pressed to do. At this Charles lost patience; he sent Bennet forthwith to Paris with a peremptory order to his brother to lose no time in setting out for Bruges. But still James did not hurry—in August Charles was still sending orders; but by this time James had given up hope of remaining in France, and was only troubled by the necessity of paying his debts before he left. He had now a reason of his own for wanting to see Charles: he had been accused, no doubt by Bristol or one of the other mischief-makers, of conducting a correspondence without Charles's knowledge with one Tuke,[1] a royalist agent in England, and he was anxious to clear himself of that charge. Bampfield reported to Thurloe that he had tried to get into touch with James, but that James had told him that Charles had strictly forbidden him to have anything to do with him; Bampfield said that he did not believe that James had any correspondence with people in England, and he added unkindly, "neither his humour nor his parts rendering him capable of the management of it himself".

Charles had suggested that, in order to expedite his journey, James should leave Berkeley behind to make what other arrangements had still to be made consequent on his final departure from Paris. James saw in this suggestion a plan to remove Berkeley permanently from his service, and he determined to frustrate it; he disregarded all hints that Berkeley would not be *persona grata* at Bruges, made a great effort to clear up his affairs in Paris, sent off most of his servants with his baggage in advance, and left for Bruges on September 10, with Berkeley and one or two more. His journey was marked by one pleasant incident: at Clermont, where he had proposed to make a halt, he found the English ambassador, Lockhart, installed in the best inn. James drove up to the front door of the inn in his coach, got out, put on his boots, mounted a led horse and rode off on the Abbeville road, all under the eye of Lockhart, who was standing at a window. He was "very civilly entertained", no doubt under instructions from Mazarin, until he crossed the Flemish frontier, and Charles and Henry came as far as Furnes to meet him. Of the part of his journey which lay through the Spanish Netherlands Thurloe's spy at Bruges wrote on September 19, "The

[1] No doubt Sir Samuel Tuke, a colonel of horse in the rising in Essex in the Second Civil War.

Duke of York is come accompanied with 120 horse and 3 coaches as they say and special order was given in all places for his reception as if the King of Spain (forsooth) had been there in person."

At Bruges James found himself at a disadvantage. He was no longer, as he had been in Paris, a considerable person, smiled on by the Court and with the prestige of military command. Charles treated him kindly, but kindness was second nature to Charles; it did not extend to protecting his brother from the insolence of his servants, nor does it appear that James was admitted to the inner council of Charles's advisers. Moreover, Charles had long harboured an antipathy for Berkeley, and his servants, with the connivance of Bennet, found a favourable opportunity for making his position in James's household untenable. The motives of the conspirators were mixed. Bristol, who was most prominent in the intrigue, was impulsive and irresponsible,[1] Bennet had a long score of slights and snubs to repay, and others, like Radcliffe, had an ambition to succeed Berkeley and his nephew and the younger Jermyn in their posts in James's "family". Charles could not openly take part in the contest, for James had admittedly a clear right to choose his own servants: he was in the position of Queen Mary in 1692 with regard to Princess Anne and the Countess of Marlborough—he could only hint that James, in employing a confidential servant who was strongly disliked by himself, was acting disloyally.

The contest raged furiously for three months, and all James's latent obstinacy was roused by the persistence of Berkeley's enemies. He found himself in a dilemma of conflicting loyalties—loyalty to Charles and loyalty to the man with whom he had lived for five years. For the one and only time in his life he decided to act in direct opposition to the King, his brother, a decision which must have cost him serious pain. He pretended to bow before the storm, he ostensibly dismissed Berkeley, but told him privately to wait for him at Flushing. Two days after he had gone, James arranged to go shooting with a party including Gloucester, Charles Berkeley and Henry Jermyn; when they were near Sluys he told Gloucester that he had a private call to make there, and said that if he did not return by a certain time he should make his way back to Bruges. From Sluys he crossed to Flushing with his two friends, and rejoined Sir John Berkeley.

The breach between Charles and James was for the moment complete. Cromwell was delighted; he hoped that James's well-known obstinacy would prevent a reconciliation and that the quarrel would still further

[1] Hyde's mature judgement on Bristol was that he "always concluded that that was fit to be done which his first thoughts suggested to him, and never doubted the execution of anything which he once thought fit to be attempted".

lessen the Stuarts in public estimation. He attributed it entirely to the influence which Mazarin at his instigation had brought to bear on Berkeley and which, as he thought, had made that self-confident, blundering man unwittingly the tool of his intrigues. He wrote to Mazarin:

> I did fear that Berkeley would not have been able to go through and carry on that work, that either the Duke had cooled in his suit or condescended to his brother. . . . If I am not mistaken in his [James's] character, as I received it from Your Eminency, that fire which is kindled between them will not ask bellows to blow it and keep it burning. . . . I distrust not but that party which is already forsaken of God as to outward dispensations of mercy and noisome to his countrymen will grow lower in the opinions of all the world.

At Bruges meanwhile the royal Court were in dismay: they learnt, to their astonishment, that even the most fervent loyalty is not proof against strains such as those to which James had been subjected, and clearly it was not to Charles's interest to be permanently alienated from James: if for no other reason, he was valuable to Charles as a skilled and popular leader, whose services and whose influence with the English and Irish volunteers were a valuable asset in his relations with the Spanish Government. But James was quite unrepentant. His first intention was to return to France, but the sea passage was obstructed by ice, and the route through Flanders was for obvious reasons impossible. The States General, however, consented to wink at his residence incognito at Swillistine.[1] Charles sent Ormonde after him to try to induce him to return, but instead of complying, he addressed to Charles a dignified letter of remonstrance in which it is difficult to trace the hand of James, so high does it rise above any other of James's letters that are preserved for us.

> Sir,
>
> This is the first time that I have had any need to make an apology to your Majesty, having concurred absolutely and implicitly hitherto in all your commands and desires; and if some violent persons had not induced your Majesty to press that upon me that was never proposed to anybody else, I had still remained without the necessity of any; nevertheless I beseech your Majesty to believe that though they be able to disturb my peace, they shall never shake my zeal and affection to your person and service, nor

[1] Possibly this is James's corruption of Vlissingen (Flushing).

hinder me from sacrificing all interest but that of my honour to your Majesty, and I hope you will excuse me if I am somewhat tender therein, since I have little else left, and that without it I shall never be able to be of use and service to your Majesty, which is the greatest ambition I have in the world; and whatever ill men shall tell you to the contrary, I can and do assure your Majesty, that as I have the honour to be the first, so I have affected nothing more than the glory of being the best of your subjects; and God that knows my heart, discerns that if I had never so many lives, I would throw them all at your Majesty's feet, as I do myself, begging that you would believe me to be what I truly am.

Sir, your Majesty's most obedient Brother and most humble Subject and Servant,

JAMES.

Charles's reply to this letter was an offer of conciliation, in spite of Bristol's demands that James should have no quarter. He sent a Mr. Blague [1] to James offering to receive him back with all his servants except Sir John Berkeley, and proposing, alternatively, that he should state his grievances by letter or in a personal interview at any place near Bruges or Brussels. James replied in a portentous document—"The Duke of York's Instructions by Mr. Blague "—in which, in descending to particulars, many of them trivial, he also falls below his previous dignity of style. James's complaints are arranged under ten heads, and the first five are devoted to the misdeeds of Bennet: Bennet had accused him, pretending instructions from Charles, of carrying on a clandestine correspondence with Tuke—in essence, of making a party for himself in opposition to the King; he was so lacking in respect that he seemed to be a spy rather than a servant; he was for ever grumbling about the meanness of his allowance, though he got more than twice as much as anyone else; that Charles had ordered James to employ Bennet on a mission to the Spanish commander, Don Juan, "which I knew he would not execute well", that Bennet had induced James to leave Paris by gross misrepresentations of Charles's intentions with regard to his employment in the Spanish service. James next turns on the Earl of Bristol, who had been instrumental in getting him out of France, but had provided no money for the journey, so that Sir John Berkeley had "procured his friends to be engaged for near £40,000,[2] upon his assurance of having it paid out of my allowances either in France or in

[1] Probably to be identified with Colonel Thomas Blagge, who was at this time in Charles's employment as a sort of King's Messenger.

[2] So printed but the meaning intended may be 40,000 *livres*—*i.e.*, about £3000.

Flanders, which debt he will be liable to if his enemies can prevail over him"; further stating "that the Lord of Bristol said to Sir John Berkeley in my presence that if I concurred not with His Majesty's sense in all things it would be imputed to him, which was to tell me fairly in my face that I had no sense of my own", and that Bristol had falsely accused Berkeley of having disclosed confidential information to James. So far there is little that can be classed as worse than petty annoyance, though the implications of the last two complaints are serious enough; but two of James's grievances deserve more than a passing mention: he objects strongly and with reason to being placed in such a position that he may be compelled to fight against Turenne, "who is one of the men in the world I am the most obliged to and have the greatest value for", and finally, if a servant who is truly loyal to Charles is to be torn from James's side, he has little credit with the King, and if he does not "protect so faithful, so eminent and so innocent a servant", then there is "little sense of justice or honour" in him. The paper concludes with proposals of accommodation to the effect that Berkeley shall continue on James's staff and that he and the others shall be granted an indemnity for helping James to escape, that Charles shall endeavour to control the relations of his and James's servants, and that, if in future he finds anything to complain of, he will speak to James directly, and not through intermediaries.

The effect of this memorial was surprising. Charles gave way on all points that concerned James's household, and Ormonde was again sent to James, this time to bring him back to Bruges on his own terms. One cause of complaint had been removed before James's flight by the appointment of Bennet as Charles's envoy at Madrid, and Charles set himself to remove another by being so gracious and affable to Berkeley that he ceased to swagger and bluster; in fact, so high did he rise in his sovereign's esteem that in the following year he was raised to the peerage as Lord Berkeley of Stratton. Radcliffe, with his aspirations still unsatisfied, died in 1657, and six months after James's return Bristol was able to write to Ormonde:

> The Duke of York's gracious usage of me continues and improves daily so far as to have removed all shyness of employing me in business of his particular interest, and truly Sir John Berkeley carries himself towards me very handsomely and generously.

And to the King he wrote about the same time in similar terms. The incessant skirmishes of nine years round the person of James had suddenly terminated in a general amnesty. James, on his side, when he had time for reflection, was filled with remorse at having disobeyed

Charles; nine years later he was reported still to have so kept the incident in mind that he held off from any communications that might "lessen his awe for the King".

But nothing could save James from swallowing the very bitter pill of selling his sword to Spain. The Spaniards, it is true, were at war with his father's executioners, and in serving with them he was contributing something to his brother's chance of restoration; but these considerations weighed little against what he felt to be a betrayal of his honour. In France he had been among his mother's people, he had been accepted by his brother officers as one of themselves; in Flanders he was a foreigner and compelled to fight against his friends, and in particular against Turenne, by whose side he had fought four campaigns and from whom he had learnt all he knew of war.

Nor did his early experience in the Spanish service serve to mitigate his distress. He found himself in difficulties at once: he was surrounded by jealousies—the Spaniards jealous of the number of his English and Irish troops, and therefore not paying them regularly; Condé jealous on his own account; Bristol, not yet reconciled to him, interfering in appointments on his staff. Moreover, the Spaniards observed strict ceremonial in their army: the co-generals Don Juan and the Marquis of Caracena kept themselves carefully aloof from any sort of operation not amounting to a pitched battle or a siege; Don Juan in particular could never forget that he was a "son of Spain"—he was, in fact, an illegitimate son of King Philip IV—and "he observed the same forms of gravity and retiredness in the field as he used when he was at Brussels, and it was fully as difficult to get access to him abroad as at home". It was his habit when he arrived at a new camp to go straight to his tent, and generally to bed, whatever time of day it was, and he stayed there for days perhaps, leaving to his under-officers the inspection of the ground, the placing of sentinels and, if they were close to the enemy, the viewing of his lines; so that if the camp was unexpectedly attacked he had no knowledge, except at second hand, of the disposition either of his own army or the enemy's. Nevertheless he kept the command rigidly in his own hand and allowed no one under him to take advantage of unexpected opportunities. On two occasions on reconnaissance James found himself in a position to cut off a French convoy, but his next superior officer both times refused to move without orders from Don Juan or Caracena, and in one case further informed him that if anyone was to make the attack it was his own Spaniards, as having the precedence, and not James's men.

The only military episode worthy of record in the two campaigns which James served in the Spanish army was also his last—the famous

Battle of the Dunes, fought on June 3, 1658—which was also his last land battle until his final disaster at the Boyne more than thirty years later. In this battle, which was fought by the Spaniards to cover Dunkirk, James was in command of the right wing, and found himself opposed by the French left wing, consisting of Cromwell's troops. With his brother Gloucester at his side he charged the English infantry, and was beaten off, and then charged again with greater success; but, when he looked for his own infantry to make good this second attack, he found that they had followed the example of the Spanish troops on their left and were in full retreat. The two royal Princes did not join in the *sauve qui peut*, but with a small body of horse continued on the field to see if there was anything still to be done, and when they found the rout was complete they went off in good order.

After the battle York and Gloucester found themselves heroes: pæans of praise rose on all sides. From three separate quarters Nicholas received glowing accounts of their exploits. "I have heard and rejoiced at the gallantry of our brave dukes." "Their Royal Highnesses gave so brisk a charge that had they been seconded with one hundred horse that wing (which consisted entirely of English) had been totally routed" (this from Captain Peter Mews, of whom we shall hear again as Bishop of Winchester at Sedgemoor), and, "The Dutch speak very honourably of our dukes, especially the Duke of York, who, they say, did wonders in rallying the broken forces several times when the army was very much broken". In after years Sir William Coventry told Pepys that "no man ever did braver things, or was in hotter service at the close of that day". Our Grub Street biographer is here again at hand with his inventiveness: he describes either James or Henry (for his English is obscure) "exposing his Royal Person to the greatest hazard imaginable, in fighting among the thickest squadrons, where leaden thunderbolts like hail sung round his princely head, and heaps of slain like ramparts hemmed him in, whilst all the field was covered with the slain".

When the Spanish were in retreat a rumour spread among the French officers that James had been taken prisoner by the English. They at once determined to set him at liberty and, forming themselves into a troop, they demanded to see the prisoners the English had taken. James was not among them; had he been, they were determined if necessary to deliver him by force. A curious testimony to James's popularity with the French Army three years after he had left it.

The Spanish Army had not remained long enough on the field to have sustained heavy casualties. Dunkirk passed to the French, to be by them handed over to Cromwell; but Don Juan was able to rally his army and to take up a line of defence a few miles to the north-east. James was in command at Nieuport when he heard of the death of Cromwell on September 3. He at once arranged with Don Juan to be relieved of his command, and joined Charles at Brussels, where the brothers discussed new plans in view of the altered situation.

In the early summer of 1659 there was a plot in England, of which the details are obscure, to pass over Charles and to place James on the throne. There appears to be no evidence that James either countenanced this plot or was given any opportunity of discountenancing it. The longest reference to this affair is in a letter to Charles from Sir Allen Broderick, a royalist agent in England.

> I have been long since commanded by those for whom I did first negotiate to signify to your Majesty their joint resentments of the injuries your Majesty receives by the Duke of York's agents, and boldly to declare to your Majesty that, though they honour him as the best and worthiest of their fellow subjects, yet will they rather be traitors in abetting these people than any other who shall presume to stand in competition with your Majesty. . . . There is great opportunity used to procure some public invitation of the Duke of York hither, which I humbly refer to your Majesty's well-weighed considerations, since his arrival without your Majesty will give some colour of truth to the unequal character they have delivered.

The obscurity of parts of this passage (due no doubt partly to the fact that it was written in cipher) does not seriously matter, its general meaning is clear: that, while the general body of the active royalists in England are sound for Charles, there are certain "agents" of James who are trying to promote his candidature for the throne. The use of the word "agents" is unfortunate, for it implies that these men were acting for James with his knowledge; if that had been the case there would have been direct references to James's guilt in the nine or ten letters on the subject which have been preserved. The nearest to such an accusation is in a letter to Hyde from a royalist agent: "I have no other motive than my duty to the King in reporting anything that may have reflection on the Duke of York", which leaves the matter as open as it behoves us to leave it.

In these letters the chief name mentioned is that of Father Peter Talbot, the older brother of Richard Talbot, James's friend, whom he was to create Earl and subsequently Duke of Tyrconnel; Father Peter was a Jesuit who in James's reign became titular Archbishop of Dublin. It was, in fact, a Catholic plot, and it is very significant that even before the Restoration the English Catholics looked to James as a patron, if not something more; one of Hyde's correspondents refers to "that foolish generation of priests and Catholics", and continues, "I hope you do not think any man of that religion so kind to the King as to the Duke of York and his servants." It seems also to have been the work of a very few hot-heads and to have died from lack of support.[1] In any case, in August Father Talbot was in Paris and Fuentarrabia, protesting his loyalty to Charles and trying to induce everyone to believe that he had never wavered in that loyalty. Charles was very angry with Talbot, who had already annoyed him by officious intervention in the negotiation with the Spaniards when Charles was about to leave Cologne, but he does not appear to have suspected James of complicity in any of Talbot's intrigues.

In the confused politics of the eighteen months preceding the Restoration, Charles and James took no effective part, though the failure of all alternative governments produced for them a favourable and unexpected result. During this period there were two projects for achieving the Restoration by the help of foreign arms, both of which happily failed, and the Restoration, when it came, was not complicated and embittered by the presence of foreign troops, but was the result of an almost unanimous revulsion of feeling on the part of the English people. In August 1659 Sir George Booth attempted a Royalist rising in Cheshire, and Charles planned a descent on the south coast of England if the attempt should succeed and be followed by a general rising. James was on a visit to his sister Mary when he received a sudden summons to Brussels. When he arrived there Charles had already started for Calais. James followed him, and caught him up at St. Omer; they were on enemy territory, and disguise was necessary, and it was arranged, for greater safety in avoiding detection, that Charles should make his plans to start from Calais, while James operated from Boulogne. Charles from the first had no illusions about Booth, but for some reason known to himself he completely hoodwinked James; he passed through Boulogne, pretending to choose a new base of operations further west; for some time no one knew where he was, and he was supposed to be in Wales or the west of England. Actually he had determined to go to Fuentarrabia, on the Franco-Spanish border, where Mazarin was negotiating the Treaty of the Pyrenees with the

[1] This plot is typical of the turbulent and sanguine spirit of a small minority of Catholics, who thus rendered a very great disservice to the main body of their fellow-churchmen. This tendency to plot on the part of a few added considerably to the odium with which the Catholics were regarded and may easily have been a considerable factor in the belief accorded to Oates's Plot.

Spaniards, and where he vainly hoped to be able to get some promise of joint assistance from France and Spain, and he had travelled there incognito via St. Malo, Toulouse and Saragossa.

Meanwhile James was very busy. So certain was he that the expedition would take place that he arranged for transport for himself, Charles Berkeley and a handful of devoted followers. At this point his mother in Paris sent to tell him that Turenne had expressed a desire to see him. Not wishing to assume undue responsibility, he searched the coast for Charles, but, failing to find him, he went to Turenne at Amiens. Turenne accepted him as Charles's plenipotentiary, and with or without the connivance of the French Government made him a liberal offer of assistance—namely, Turenne's own infantry regiment to be made up to twelve hundred men, and the Scottish gendarmes, spare arms for three or four thousand, six field-pieces with ammunition, a liberal provision of meal, shipping to convey the force to England and, in addition, money personally raised by himself by pledging his plate and his credit. But this scheme was short-lived; Booth was defeated and taken prisoner by Lambert at Warrington on August 19; early in September James's principal officers were back in Brussels, and he himself followed a few days later. In November we still find him corresponding with John Mordaunt in England about the state of public feeling there and the possibility of a fresh descent, and declaring, "I will venture myself with the same readiness and alacrity as if the King were here, having authority from His Majesty so to do", but inclining to the view that the King at Fuentarrabia "is like in a short time to procure such an assistance and declaration from the two crowns as may make the work at least less difficult", and that it is better to wait on events.

But Charles had not only not gained anything by his journey to Spain, but had been subjected to humiliation. Mazarin regarded his presence in his neighbourhood as an embarrassment, and refused to see him, and from the Spanish side he achieved nothing better than fair words. He was no longer even a pawn in the game of international politics, and the Royalist cause was at its lowest ebb. He returned to Brussels, but he had no longer an assurance of a permanent asylum on Spanish soil. The winter passed miserably; news from England was eagerly scanned, but all men of influence there appeared to be as determinedly republican as ever. Early in the new year James was offered and accepted the post of High Admiral of Spain, a post of high dignity and (on paper) considerable emoluments. It was evident that he contemplated permanent exile.

Then suddenly in March General George Monck, who had been Cromwell's right-hand man in Ireland and in Scotland, who had until six months previously been ruling Scotland for the Parliament and who was regarded as the staunchest of Commonwealth men, opened a secret negotiation with Charles by means of Sir John Grenville. Monck advised a transfer of the Court to Breda, where he could not be suspected of being under French or Spanish influence (nor a great deal of Dutch), and the issue of a Declaration setting forth Charles's intentions in the event of his restoration to the Crown of England. The transfer to Breda was made, and the Declaration was dated April 4. Events now moved rapidly. The Long Parliament had dissolved itself on March 16, after an existence of nearly twenty years, and a new "free" parliament was summoned for April 25; the House of Lords reconstituted itself, and on May 1 received Grenville with deference as the King's representative, and the Commons followed suit and voted unanimously an address of loyalty and duty to His Majesty.

There remained only the business of preparing for a return to England on an adequate scale. On May 14 the English fleet under Admiral Montagu cast anchor off Schevingen and received James as Lord High Admiral, and on the 16th Charles gave audience to a deputation from the Parliament with a formal request for his return. Almost as important was the arrival of Sir John Grenville with £50,000 for Charles, £10,000 for James and £7000 for Henry. They had none of them seen so much money before, and Charles called in his sister and James to gloat over his share as it lay in a portmanteau. The money was badly needed, if only to enable the royal persons and their entourage to make a decent public appearance, for they had fallen so low that they were literally in rags, "their clothes not being worth forty shillings the best of them". But the local tailors, who no doubt had not previously allowed the exiles to run up accounts, were so stirred to activity by the prospect of ready money, that James and Henry when they went on board the fleet appeared to be "very fine gentlemen", less than a week after the money arrived. In the triumphant journey to London, first in command of the fleet, then in the progress to London and finally in the feasts and demonstrations in the capital, James's place was second only to that of his brother, the restored King.

CHAPTER IV

THE RESTORATION

THE years following the Restoration were the most disjointed in James's life. In a general survey of the condition of England furnished by the Venetian Senate his occupations are given small space:

> This prince applies himself but little to the affairs of the country and attends to nothing but his pleasures; but he is a young man of good spirit, loving and beloved by the King, his brother, and he discharges the office of Lord High Admiral.

In short, he lived the easy life of a prince of the Blood. If we are to believe Antony Hamilton, his sole occupation was the seduction of the wives of the nobility and gentry; but the Count de Grammont was a very old man when he gave Hamilton the materials for his memoirs, he had forgotten a great deal, he was chiefly anxious to place on record the amorous exploits of the gay companions of his youth, and there can be little doubt that he allowed himself considerable latitude of exaggeration in detail. Our other chief authority for James's life at this period is Pepys, and caution is no less necessary in accepting his testimony; Pepys had an enormous appetite for scandal about his betters, but he was mainly dependent for his information about the great upon his gossips—his Pierces and Poveys, who had only backstairs knowledge of what went on—and it is in the nature of such men to make their stories worth the telling; moreover, they themselves were for the most part only repeating what they had heard from others. Where Pepys reports what has come under his own eye, however, or what he has heard from Lord Sandwich, who moved in courtly circles, he is a good authority. But though we may reject most of the unsavoury and unedifying details as unsubstantiated, there is sufficient agreement between de Grammont and Pepys, as well as corroboration from other authorities, notably his own confessions in his *Memoirs* and in his *Advice to his Son*, to warrant the conclusion that at this period of his life James sowed a plentiful, if late, crop of wild oats. Apart from transitory amours, he had in succession three mistresses—Goditha Price, the Countess of Southesk and Lady Denham. His pursuit of the Countess of Chesterfield was so open and flagrant that her husband the Earl remonstrated with him; James in reply "fell to commending the lady", presumably not comprehending that the Earl was justly aggrieved; in consequence Lady Chesterfield was packed off to the country and kept there out of harm's way. There can be little question that his reputation in the matter of women was as low as that of his brother Charles—"that known enemy to virginity and chastity, the monarch of Great Britain", as his friends described him—but whereas Charles was a gourmet, James was a gourmand: he was "very amorous, and more out of a natural temper than for the genteel part of making love, which he was much a stranger to"; "perpetually in one amour or another, without being very nice in his choice, so that the King said once he believed his brother had his mistresses given him by his priests to do penance"; in 1677 Charles said to Courtin, the French ambassador, "I do not believe there are two men who love women more than you and I do, but my brother, devout as he is, loves them still more." James had nothing in common with the literary rakes—Rochester, Sedley, Buckhurst, Etherege and the others—his chief companions were Charles Berkeley and Dick Talbot.

From other vices James appears to have been free. He was reputed to be parsimonious, he was certainly careful of money; in the only case in which his debts became a matter of common knowledge the fault was imputed not to him but to his wife, and there is no evidence that he squandered money on his mistresses—the two who are best known, Arabella Churchill, perhaps, and Catherine Sedley, certainly, had money of their own. Gambling and thrift rarely exist in the same person, and it is unlikely that James was a gambler: there is no record of his playing cards except in the family circle during the period of enforced idleness in Scotland; and his interest in horse-racing—if indeed he had any interest and did not attend races merely because Charles was there—did not apparently extend beyond small bets. He was not a hard drinker. There was one occasion on a hunting expedition when the Court was entertained at Cranbourne by Sir George Carteret and there was a drunken orgy, "being all maudlin and kissing one another, the King the Duke of York and the Duke of York the King, and in such a maudlin pickle as never people were"; but such a lapse was very exceptional. Burnet in his earlier (and more reliable) account of James's character says that "he abhors drunkenness, he never swears or talks irreligiously"; there is nothing in the records to suggest that James was ever the care-free boon-companion, the midnight roysterer; and when he came to the throne he declared that anyone who was drunk at Court should be excluded from it and should lose his post if he had one.[1] It is a remarkable fact that at Faversham in December 1688,

[1] Ailesbury says that when in 1685 there was discussion on the best sources of supply from customs and excise, James showed himself an advocate of influencing morals through taxation. " 'Lay it', said he, 'on luxury as chocolate, tea, coffee, East India commodities are not necessary for the life of man, and

when James was under more acute mental strain than at any other period of his life, and in circumstances in which even the most temperate man might be expected to take liquor to fortify his courage, the seamen who were his captors were astounded at his abstemiousness; they supplied him plentifully with drink, for their experience of the quality (which was no doubt local and unfortunate) gave them to understand that all gentlemen drank hard, but James would not drink except with his meals, and very little then. In connection with James's temperate habits it is interesting to note that he (or perhaps his Duchess) was a tea-drinker barely twenty years after the leaf had been introduced into this country and when its use first became fashionable.

One obsession James had which amounted almost to a vice, and that was hunting—an obsession which, together with an autocratic temper, was one of the few qualities which he shared with his nephew and son-in-law William. In the late years of his brother's reign hunting no doubt furnished James with an escape from his troubles of mind at a time when he was excluded from public activity and when nothing he could do could serve to improve his position in the country; and people who suspected him of subversive intent could hardly believe that he was plotting with France for the overthrow of the English Constitution in Church and State on the two or three days a week on which he hunted. But before the Test Act of 1673 excluded him from employment, and when he held important administrative posts, there is clear evidence that he neglected business to satisfy his craving for the chase, and even in later years he frequently failed to interview Charles on important matters for the same reason.

In this connection it is interesting to find that James was one of the earliest, if not the earliest, aristocratic fox-hunter. The quarry for gentlemen up to his time, and for many years afterwards, had been stags and hares, though foxes had been hunted on horseback by yeomen and lesser gentry for a hundred years.[1] James appears to have taken to

(with warmth) on wine (for he was a most sober prince). Who obliges people to make themselves drunk? But if they will drink, let them pay for it.' "

[1] As late as 1781 a writer of a letter found it necessary to state that "Fox-hunting is now become the amusement of gentlemen; nor need any gentleman be ashamed of it".

It is generally accepted that fox-hunting began among yeomen and farmers in Elizabethan times; the first use given by O.E.D. of the word fox-hunter is 1692; but the name William le foxhunte appears in Patent Rolls, 1258–66 (quoted by Weekly, *Adjectives and Other Words*, p. 127). But William was almost certainly not a sportsman, but a destroyer of foxes as vermin; he was in fact a todhunter (see *The Romance of Words* by the same author, p. 112).

Mr. Aldous Huxley states (*Grey Eminence*, p. 154) that Louis XIII was addicted to fox-hunting; possibly James was made familiar with the sport during his sojourn in France.

fox-hunting soon after the Restoration, for in 1664 he already had two separate packs of hounds; in July of that year there is an entry in the book of his household showing that James Carlile, gentleman, Serjeant of the Hounds of His Royal Highness, was in receipt of a salary of £250 a year, "for the maintenance of the Duke's foxhounds and also for the maintenance of the same James Carlile and horses suitable for him as a huntsman"; in the same year there is mention of a Mr. Edward Sanders, foot-huntsman, who was given £25 a year for attendance on the buckhounds and £30 for attendance on the foxhounds. Fifteen years later a Mr. Hilliard was Master of the Foxhounds, and a number of huntsmen were employed to whom particular horses were assigned. The locality in which the hounds were usually kept is unknown, but James ordered the whole hunt to be sent on two occasions to his temporary place of residence—in 1679 to Brussels and in 1682 to Newmarket. Simultaneously the Duke of Monmouth and his friend Lord Grey of Werk each had a pack of foxhounds at Charlton near Goodwood. No doubt when Monmouth told the Prince of Strassburg in December 1674 that he had been "for some days hunting with the Duke of York in Sussex", it was at Charlton as the guest of Monmouth that James hunted and the fox was the quarry. James, as we have seen, had a pack of foxhounds[1] when Monmouth was only fifteen years of age, so that Monmouth must have learnt fox-hunting from his uncle. After the Revolution the Charlton hounds passed to the Duke of Bolton, and from him early in the eighteenth century to the second Duke of Richmond, and thus the aristocratic tradition of fox-hunting was preserved unbroken to our own day. What became of James's hounds is not known.

Whether pursuing stag or fox there can be no doubt that, as became a distinguished and intrepid cavalry officer, James was a hard rider to hounds. At a buck-hunt in 1663 in Enfield Chase no one but James, Sir John Reresby and one of James's equerries was in at the death; in 1684 a deer gave the Duke of York and his suite a tremendous run through Beaconsfield and Amersham well into Oxfordshire, the Duke and Colonel James Graham being among the few who were in at the death; and in May 1686, when he was nearly fifty-three and in popular estimation had lost his great physical courage, he outrode everyone in a two days' stag hunt in Essex: "His Majesty kept pretty near the dogs, though the ditches were broad and deep, the hedges high, and the way and the fields dirty and deep; but most of the lords were cast out again, and amongst them the Duke of Albemarle."

[1] It seems unlikely that James's foxhounds were of the same breed as that of the foxhounds of the present day.

Burnet's estimate of James's character, written at a time before he had fallen under James's displeasure, is very near the truth. (When Burnet revised his history and gave it the form in which it was published he cut this character down to the barest outline.[1])

> The Duke would pass for an extraordinary civil and sweet-tempered man if the King were not much above him in it, who is more naturally and universally civil than the Duke. . . . He has not the King's quickness but that is made up by great application and industry, insomuch that he keeps a journal of all that passes of which he shewed me a great deal. . . . He has naturally a candour and a justice in his temper very great, and is a firm friend but a heavy enemy, and will keep things long in his mind and wait for a fit opportunity. He has a strange notion of government, that everything is to be carried on in a high way and that no regard is to be had to the pleasing the people, and he has an ill opinion of any that proposes soft methods and thinks that is popularity; but at the same time he always talks of law and justice.

Other characteristics are, that "he receives enemies that submit, but tries to ruin those that stand out and cannot tolerate half submission"; that "he thinks everyone a rebel that opposes the King in parliament"; and "that he is very brave and abhors a coward".

Before the Restoration James's "inclination to the sex" had involved him in serious trouble. His roving eye had fallen on Anne Hyde, the only daughter of Sir Edward Hyde, Charles's trusted counsellor and Lord Chancellor. She was a maid of honour to James's sister, Mary, Princess of Orange, and he probably met her first at Breda in the winter of 1657–8. In the spring of 1659 he paid his sister a visit of considerable length, and it was then perhaps that Anne "indeed showed both her wit and her virtue in managing the affair so dexterously that the Duke was overmastered by his passion and gave her a promise of marriage some time before the Restoration". This is James's own story (or his biographer's), but there was more than a promise: both James and Anne after they were married subscribed formal declarations to the effect that they were contracted on November 24, 1659; Sir Edward Hyde had the matter fully investigated by the judges, and it was decided that though they were not fully married they were so strictly contracted that

[1] It has been frequently asserted that Burnet revised his draft for publication —particularly the passages dealing with the characters of persons—from interested and not quite honest motives. But in the interval between the draft and the revision it is not possible that he should not have modified his views on the characters of persons with whom he had been in contact.

any child of the union would be legitimate under English law without further marriage ceremony.

As long as James was a penniless exile the question of the propriety of his marriage to a girl without claim to noble birth did not seriously arise—though such a match could not bear comparison with the alliances previously suggested with the daughters of the Dukes of Lorraine and Longueville—and if there had been no restoration the marriage would no doubt have been acknowledged without hesitation or delay. But the return to England made James the first subject of the King, a grandee whose suit would be welcomed in any Court in Europe. James seems to have been genuinely attached to Anne, but, in spite of his subsequent denial of it, the fact appears to be that he determined to listen to the advice of his cynical friends and to repudiate her.

Charles Berkeley[1] showed his friendship in a peculiar way: he invented a story of his own successful intrigue with Anne and urged James not to ally himself with a woman of loose morals. (He subsequently had the grace to apologise to her father for having perjured himself and slandered Anne.) Anne's father, the Lord Chancellor, entirely lost his head: he was overwhelmed simultaneously by the thoughts of his daughter's frailty—for she was obviously with child—and of her aspirations to greatness, and he roundly declared that he would rather she were James's mistress than his wife. But Charles took a line of his own: in any other case he would no doubt have conformed to the conventions observed at the time, under which it was undesirable that men should marry their mistresses, shrugged his shoulders, ignored the previous contract and found a subservient courtier who would be willing to take James's place as Anne's husband. But Charles was well aware of his dependence upon Hyde, and would do nothing to weaken his loyalty to his service. He therefore gave James his orders in private (though he still thought that his brother had "played the fool"), and James, as at many other times, obeyed him without question and with a public appearance of alacrity. He was married to Anne very late at night on September 5 by his chaplain, Dr. James Crowther, and in the presence only of Ormonde's son, Lord Ossory, and one of Anne's maids—the circumstances were peculiar, and in any case a royal marriage was not at that time made an opportunity for pageantry. Their first child, one of many that died in infancy, was born on October 22. The marriage was registered by the Privy Council on February 18,

[1] Grammont says that Lord Arran, Richard Talbot, Henry Jermyn and Henry Killigrew conspired with Berkeley to give each his own fantastic story of a disgraceful personal incident in which Anne Hyde was concerned; but Clarendon is the better authority here.

1661, after the evidence of Crowther, Ossory and Anne's maid, Ellen Stroud, had been taken.

Thus was Anne Hyde, daughter of a lawyer of outstanding abilities but of no pretensions to gentle birth, raised to be the first lady in the kingdom, a position which she relinquished to Queen Catherine eighteen months later. Precedents might be adduced in the marriages of Anne Boleyn and Elizabeth Woodville among others, but in more recent years it had been the invariable rule for princes of the blood royal to ally themselves with the near relations of ruling princes. The social distance in those days both between the royal family and the nobility and between the nobility and the people was far greater than it is at the present time, and at once the new Duchess was forced into a very peculiar position with regard to her nearest relatives. The Earl of Ailesbury, whose testimony on other matters is of uncertain value, is here a high authority:

> It is well known that when Kings and Princes of the Blood make an alliance with a subject, their arms are not put into the royal escutcheon, nor did ever the late Duchess of York call the Lord Chancellor Clarendon father, nor did ever the late King James call the Earls of Clarendon and Rochester [Edward Hyde's sons] brothers, nor the Princess Mary and Anne term them as uncles. Indeed the late Chancellor, when he wrote letters of advice to the late Duchess in relation to her changing her religion, made use of the style of Daughter which in truth he ought not to have done.

Pepys, five years after the marriage, had an illuminating experience which corroborates Ailesbury's account:

> And so walked to Whitehall and there I showed my cousin Roger the Duchess of York sitting in state while her own mother stands by her.

And John Locke, the philosopher, relates that Sir Anthony Ashley Cooper (later Lord Ashley and still later famous as Earl of Shaftesbury), whose secretary he then was, even before the marriage was announced, was certain that it was a fact because "a concealed respect, however suppressed, showed itself so plainly in the looks, voice and manner wherewith her mother carved to her, or offered her of every dish". But Anne's father did not so easily forget the parental relation: he "always with the respect that was due to her quality preserved the dignity of a father very entire", and in the letter of remonstrance on the subject of religion which Ailesbury mentions, the Earl of Clarendon (as he became in April 1661), writing from his exile in France, says:

> No distance of place that is between us, in respect of our residence, or the greater distance in respect of the high condition you are in, can make me less your Father or absolve me from performing those obligations which that relation requires from me;

and Pepys was amused to notice that the Lord Chancellor when he inquired for his grandchildren,

> did ask not how the Princes or the Dukes do, as other people do, but "How do the children?" Which methought was mighty great, and like a great man and grandfather.[1]

The new Duchess of York had suddenly to accommodate herself to her exalted position. Charles, who was above all things a realist, and it may be added a gentleman, treated his sister-in-law kindly and with deference; but matters were not so easy with James's other near relatives. The graceless Duke of Gloucester declared that he could not bear her; she always carried about with her the smell of her father's green bag. James's mother was furious: apart from the unsuitability of the match on grounds of birth, she had a long-standing grievance against Anne Hyde: for in 1654 the Princess of Orange had taken Anne into her household at a time when Henrietta was hating Anne's father even more than usual, and the appointment had occasioned a violent quarrel between mother and daughter. In one of the little intimate notes which Charles in the early years of the Restoration was in the habit of writing to Hyde we find:

> My brother hath spoken with the Queen yesterday morning concerning the owning his son, and in much passion she told him from the time he did any such thing she would never see his face more

and he adds, "My brother tells me he will do anything I please." The Princess of Orange, too, had her special grievance in that she had to yield precedence to her former maid of honour. But Gloucester died a week after the marriage and the Princess before the end of the year; and Henrietta Maria was reconciled to her daughter-in-law before she went

[1] The social distance between the Hydes and their royal relatives did not (in spite of what Ailesbury says) extend to the second generation. Mary and Anne were both more intimate with their uncles Clarendon and Rochester than they were with other noblemen.

to France in January 1661,[1] and when she returned seven months later she found a new outlet for her energies in instructing her in the deportment suitable to royal princesses. In this voluntary task she succeeded in the opinion of most people only too well, and there were complaints of haughtiness unbecoming one who had had little time in which to forget her humble origin. But more discriminating persons gave Duchess Anne credit for playing well the big part for which she had been cast: the courtiers whom James brought to present to her as soon as a decision had been made about the marriage, were amazed to find her already lofty and gracious; and three years later the French Ambassador was able to tell his master that she "is a woman as gallant—the word 'genteel' is not strong enough—as I have seen in my life; she holds her position with as much dignity and certainty as if she had been of royal blood, or at least of that of a Guzman or a Mendoza".

Only a single voice proclaimed that Anne Hyde was handsome; the others agree with Pepys that she was a plain woman ("and like her mother, my Lady Chancellor", he adds maliciously); her portraits provide a conflict of evidence;[2] but she had wit and vivacity. She had some pretensions to literary ability, and she devoted some time to putting James's memoirs into narrative form, and after her death Gilbert Burnet refused James's invitation to continue her work. It seems probable that some papers of her writing were kept with the memoirs and were used by the compiler of the *Life of James*, but it is idle to attempt to ascribe particular passages to her.[3] Anne was much given to the exercises of religion, and passed for something of a prude in the gay Court, but she did not, as James's second wife did, look askance at the royal mistress of the time, for she was on easy terms with Lady Castlemaine. Of the marital relations of James and his first Duchess we know very little. The *Life of James* indeed says, "It must be con-

[1] Beresford (*Gossip of the Seventeenth and Eighteenth Centuries*, p. 118) states without giving reference that Mazarin made reconciliation with Anne a condition of Henrietta's welcome back to France. Evelyn (October 7, 1660) says that Clarendon mollified her by offering to arrange a composition with her creditors.

[2] The best-known portrait of Duchess Anne is that in the National Portrait Gallery (ascribed to the school of Lely); it represents her as somnolent, sensuous, rather fat and entirely unattractive. The portrait by Lely at Hampton Court, on the other hand, is very charming indeed. A group at Ditchley with James and the two Princesses, however (or so it seems from the reproduction), was not so kind, for she appears as moderately handsome but with a grim and determined mouth.

[3] Cf. Mr. Godfrey Davies (*Introduction to Papers of Devotion of James II*, p. xv), "It is obvious from the comments that it [*i.e.*, the undocumented portion of the *Life of James*] was composed some time after the events narrated". It is not easy to believe, for example, that the account of her marriage was written by Duchess Anne herself.

fessed that what she wanted in birth was so well made up by other endowments that her carriage afterwards did not misbecome her acquired dignity." Such a statement, however, is of no value even if it originated from James himself, and there is always the possibility that Anne wrote it. But it was quite impossible for James to be technically faithful to any wife; and the first years of their marriage tried her very sorely; she complained to the King and to her father, and by constant nagging reduced James to such a state of obedience that Charles nick-named him Tom Otter—of whom it was said in the play, "Mistress Otter corrects her husband so he dares not speak but under correction"—and mentally compared her to his own poor Queen, who had made one vain stand against the appointment of Lady Castlemaine to a post about her person, and had then sunk into silent acquiescence in whatever affront or neglect Charles cared to inflict upon her.[1] Unfortunately Anne's own married life was not entirely free from scandal: at Oxford (or perhaps York) in 1665 she developed an attachment, probably quite innocent, for Algernon Sidney's brother Henry—"handsome Sidney", her Master of the Horse. James either believed or affected to believe his friends' comments on the relationship, saw the advantage to himself as excusing his own irregularities, and dismissed Sidney.

Perhaps the least pleasing side of Anne's character lay in her extravagance, a natural outcome of her desire to be adequate to her position, but carried, as people thought, to immoderate lengths. James himself had few expensive tastes, none that his ample income could not have easily covered, but in 1667 he and Anne were said to be spending £60,000 a year on an income of £40,000.[2] This is the only occasion

[1] In the last year of Charles's life it is reported: "This day the Queen being at dinner the Duchess of Portsmouth as a lady of the bedchamber came to wait on her (which was not usual), which put the Queen into that disorder that tears came into her eyes, whilst the other laughed and turned it into jest."

[2] It is not easy to determine James's income even approximately, but there can be no question that he was one of the richest, if not the richest, subject of his brother. Two contemporary guesses are £100,000 and £150,000: roughly equivalent in purchasing power to a half and three-quarters of a million respectively of our money. We know that he received £16,000 from the Post Office and £24,000 from the Excise and the duties and licences on wines. But Pepys, when he gave the figure of £40,000 as his income, took no account either of the investment value of the two grants to him by Parliament (£10,000 in 1660 and £120,000 in 1665) or of his landed property. Charles settled on him a portion of those estates, both in England and Ireland, of the regicides and of other men convicted of treason. A transcript of uncertain authority in the Bodleian gives the names of his English manors and states their annual value at £13,000. In Ireland his agents, acting by all accounts very unscrupulously, made good his claim to no less than 100,653 plantation acres, the equivalent of 163,038 acres English statute measure. In addition, he was relieved of certain expenses—*e.g.*, his lodgings at Whitehall were repaired at public expense and some of his servants were paid out of the grant for the royal household.

after the Restoration when we hear of James's running into debt, and the fault may probably be justly imputed to Anne. Another serious accusation mentioned by Pepys may have a basis in fact:

> Mr. Povey do tell me how he is like to lose his £400 a year pension of the Duke of York. He tells me the Duchess is a devil against him. And do now come like Queen Elizabeth, and sits with the Duke of York's council, and sees what they do; and she crosses out this man's wages and prices as she sees fit for saving money: but yet, he tells me she reserves £5000 a year for her own spending; and my Lady Peterborough by and by tells me that the Duchess do lay up mightily jewels.

Povey had been removed three months earlier from the post of Treasurer and Receiver-General to the Duke of York and had been succeeded by Sir Allen Apsley.[1] Povey found a patron in Henrietta Maria, and by her intercession he was able to compound for the loss of his place for £2000. His evidence against Duchess Anne is suspect as that of a man who had by his own admission fallen under her displeasure; but she was a masterful woman, and we may be sure that, if she wanted to come to James's council (which was merely a meeting of the administrators of his private estate), nothing he could do would keep her away.

In general politics the early years of the Restoration were for James a period of apprenticeship, and for his instructor he took his father-in-law, the Earl of Clarendon, the Lord Chancellor. Clarendon relates that James used to sit beside him in the House of Lords on the Woolsack "that he might the more easily confer with him upon the matters that were debated and receive his advice how to behave himself". James was from the first a very firm supporter of Clarendon—his loyalty to the King would naturally lay on him an obligation to support the first Minister, and his personal connection with the Minister and his agreement with his father-in-law's points of view were contributing factors—"the Duke did not only profess a very great affection for the Chancellor, but gave all the demonstration of it that was possible, and desired nothing more than that it should be manifest to all men that he had an entire trust from the King in all his affairs, and that he would employ all his interest to support that trust"; and it was remarked that James was always eager to concur with the Chancellor when motions in the

[1] Sir Allen Apsley was of better social standing than Povey: he had served the King throughout the Civil War and was to prove a very faithful adherent to James.

House of Lords were put to the vote, and that "all parties that are sure of the Chancellor are sure of the Duke of York". James's attendances in the House of Lords were very regular, though it does not appear (of course) from the Journals whether or no he sat through the debates on all occasions when he put in an appearance.

He had been a Privy Councillor before he was sixteen; he does not appear ever to have been sworn, but he attended his first Council on August 31, 1649, at Saint-Germain, and he was present at meetings subsequently in Jersey and at intervals when he was not on campaign down to the Restoration; for some reason neither his name nor that of the Duke of Gloucester appears in a list of councillors inserted in the register in 1658. After the Restoration he took his duties as Privy Councillor for some time very lightly: in the year 1660 his absences largely outnumber his attendances, in 1661 he was more assiduous, and from December of that year he missed very few meetings except those at which Charles himself was not present. The most important matters were not, however, discussed in the Privy Council, but in the Committee for Foreign Affairs, which in the first years of the reign was an informal body summoned at need by the King, and of which no minutes were kept. It does not appear whether or no James was summoned as a matter of course to that Committee in the early months of the reign.[1]

To these years belong the most important part of James's activities in connection with the Navy. It cannot be doubted that his interest

[1] Miss Barbour, *Life of Arlington*, and Christie, *Life of Shaftesbury*, say that James was not at first summoned, but they quote no authority.

C. M. Andrews (*British Committees, Commissions and Councils of Trade and Plantations, 1622–1675*; Johns Hopkins University Studies, 1908) supplies a good deal of information regarding James's public activities in the first half of Charles's reign. He was not on the Committee for Trade and Plantations constituted under Order in Council of July 4, 1660 (Cal. S.P. Col. 1514–1660, pp. 82, 483; P.C. Reg. Charles II, Vol. II, p. 63; New York Colonial Documents, III, 30), nor on the Council of Trade, the Council of Foreign Plantations or the African Company. On January 31, 1668, regulations were issued for four standing Committees: for Foreign Affairs, naval and military affairs, trade and plantations and petitions and grievances, and it was stated that "His Royal Highness . . . is understood to be of all Committees where he pleases to be" (we may safely conjecture that this proviso was not a complete innovation, but that it was to some extent a recognition of existing practice, and that James had for some time had a seat on these Committees). Under the regulations for the Committee for naval and military affairs it was provided that "His Royal Highness may preside if he so please, or else the Lord General" (Egerton MSS. 2543 ff., 205–205b). A commission issued on April 13, 1669, established a Council of Trade, and the Duke of York was the first member named (Rawlinson MSS. A 478 f. 77; Cal. S.P. Dom. 1668–1669, pp. 224–225). A Commission issued on July 30, 1670, constituted a Council for Plantations; of this Council James was not an original member, but he was appointed to it the following year.

in the Navy, as was that of Charles, was great and persistent; he has given himself, and he has been given, great credit for this work, but it is doubtful if he took the initiative in any of the reforms which have been connected with his name. At the same time, he deserves full credit for giving effect to these reforms; for without the support of his great position, and without also his decision of character, the vested interests and the conservatism inherent in all public services would have defied all attempts at reform. A typical instance is given by Pepys: on July 24, 1668, Pepys called James's attention to "the weakness of our office", due apparently to lack of definition of the duties and responsibilities of individual functionaries, and James asked him to put his proposals in writing; on August 14 James reminded Pepys about these proposals; on August 23 Pepys read over to James the letter which he had prepared for him to address to the Board, and James "did hear it all over with extraordinary content"; on August 27 James had had the letter copied by his Secretary and had signed it "in my very words without the alteration of a syllable"; on August 28 James read the letter to the Privy Council as his own. Pepys claims to have taken the same initiative in, and in detail to have been to the same extent responsible for, the Instructions to Commanders, the basis of modern naval discipline; there is good reason to believe that the Duke of York's Sailing and Fighting Instructions were the work of Sir William Penn. Now, it is a matter of common knowledge that in all Government offices documents for which heads of departments and Ministers of the Crown assume credit and responsibility have been prepared for them by subordinate officers. But there is a degree observed in these matters: the documents have in most cases originated with instructions from above, and, even when the first suggestion has come from a subordinate officer, his superior generally makes at least verbal alterations.

It is clear from the Diary—due allowance being made for the diarist's own interest to make it appear so—that the administration of the Navy in the seven years following the Restoration was in the hands of Pepys and Sir William Coventry, and that when in 1667 Coventry was replaced by Matthew Wren as James's secretary the same sort of control continued—in one place Pepys mentions "the Duke of York and his master Mr. Wren". Thus James may be regarded as a royal patron whose chief merit was that he appreciated ability and industry when he found them and used the authority of his rank to uphold his best subordinates against the intrigues of interested parties. One of the very few surviving letters of James which has any subject but his own interests was written to Charles in May 1679, when James was in exile at Brussels, urging the appointment of Pepys to the Admiralty Commission. James can therefore claim no credit at first hand for the reforms which made the British Navy during two hundred and fifty years the greatest single factor in international affairs. But he showed both intelligence and steady loyalty in recognising the outstanding genius of Pepys and in consistently supporting him. Without this recognition and support the Navy would undoubtedly have fallen into the deplorable condition in which Pepys found it on his return to official duty in 1684. From the inefficiency and corruption which prevailed at the Admiralty Pepys only, with the support of the King and James, could save the Navy, and had not this combination of powers been in operation it is difficult to see how Britain could have survived the wars of the eighteenth and early nineteenth centuries. James was undoubtedly devoted to the Navy, and he showed his devotion in his very frequent visits to naval dockyards, but his administrative work extended little beyond presiding at a weekly meeting of the Navy Board, and even there his attendance was irregular; early in his career as Lord High Admiral there was a proposal to appoint a Vice-Admiral of England so that he might be relieved of these light duties. Out of twenty-two meetings mentioned by Pepys, six only were held quite regularly; on five occasions James kept the meeting waiting while he rose and was dressed; twice he had shifted the venue without previous notice; and nine times the other members of the Board arrived to find that there was no meeting—five times James had had other public engagements and four times he had gone hunting. But once in the chair, there was nothing perfunctory in the performance of his duties; he was most anxious to understand the business before the meeting and very patient in listening to all sides, even when his advisers, Sandwich and Coventry, thought they had made up his mind for him beforehand. Curiously enough, in spite of his merits, Sir William Coventry thought meanly of James's usefulness to the Navy, and in the autumn of 1665 urged him to retire when he was at the height of his popularity after the Battle of Lowestoft and when retirement would give no appearance of disappointment or pique.[1]

Macaulay's statement that James "loved the details of naval business and would have made a respectable clerk in the dockyard at Chatham" is very wide of the mark. Quite apart from the fact that he disliked above all things being kept indoors and had no capacity for sedulous

[1] J. R. Tanner (*E.H.R.*, XII, 19) has adduced a number of examples of the interest taken by both Charles and James in details of naval administration, but he fails to prove that this interest was more than spasmodic; as regards James, the important part of his article is his insistence (pp. 21n, 44–45) on the value to the Navy of having a Lord High Admiral with the authority of high rank.

and detailed office work, he had no exact knowledge. D'Usson de Bonrepaus, who had spent his life in the office of the French Admiralty and had risen to be Intendant-General, was in 1686 and 1687[1] sent by Louis to settle certain outstanding colonial and commercial questions and to report on the condition of the English Navy. During his first visit he reported that he learnt more in detail about the English Navy from conversations with James than he would have learnt by spending three months at Chatham. But eighteen months later he accompanied James on a visit to Portsmouth Dockyard and his report is more discriminating:

> It appears to me that the King of England is very ill-informed on the subject of the management of, and of the details of work in, naval arsenals. He was very much astonished at what we saw of the forging of the arms and flukes of anchors. I gave him my estimate of what a certain anchor weighed, he had it weighed at once and I was only six pounds out. Then he asked me several questions about cables and pieces of wood which we saw lying about. He told me laughing that I must have sat up all night weighing anchors, counting the ply of cables and measuring up wood. But if the King is ignorant about such things he is by no means ignorant about navigation. He often talks to me and enjoys talking, and I have an infinity of things to learn from him.

The inference from these reports appears to be that James, apart from the few months he had spent at sea acquiring personal experience, had lost no opportunity of conversing with practical seamen—indeed, he wrote to Sandwich (Sir Edward Montagu as he then was) before the Restoration "offering to learn the seaman's trade of him"—and by this means acquired at second hand a thorough knowledge of the practice of navigation; but that his many visits to ports and dockyards had been partly ceremonial and partly to receive verbal reports of the progress of work, and no doubt also to hear complaints and to use his authority to restore discipline where friction had arisen, and that he had made no effort to study the details of the building and equipment of ships.

The most pressing problem in connection with the Restoration Navy lay in the appointment of officers. The best captains of ships were unquestionably the men who had served under Blake and had ample sea experience. But although these men had made their submisson at the Restoration, James found in them "a deep tincture of their education: they both hated popery and loved liberty"; at the same time,

[1] Bonrepaus made a third visit to England in the autumn of 1688.

"they were men of severe tempers, and kept good discipline". It was natural that both Charles and James should prefer to appoint men who had always been loyal to the Crown; it was an easy way of rewarding service and it was important, in the state of perpetual fear of revolution in which the Court lived, that the Navy should be in the hands of men who could be trusted to support the monarchy if an outbreak occurred. Charles was not, however, at first of this mind: in November 1664 he took the French ambassador down to the fleet, introduced him to a number of Cromwellian officers and told him in their hearing that "these gentlemen had all had the plague, but they were entirely cured and were now less susceptible to the malady than the others".

In Cavalier officers, both military and naval, there were grave defects of character, defects which persisted in the Army until English troops were employed side by side with Continental troops in the wars in Flanders, and in the Navy to a much later date. These officers firmly held the opinion that they fulfilled the whole of their duty in getting themselves killed in action; and it may be admitted that in support of this opinion they gave many striking proofs of personal courage. But they were far from thinking that their duties included any preparation for war in time of peace: in their view, an officer when not actually fighting was free to enjoy himself. As late as 1689 Schomberg in Ireland bitterly complained of the lack of a sense of responsibility of English military officers; they would neither instruct their men in the art of war nor provide against sickness by looking after their bodily needs. The introduction into the Navy of men of this temper and of very short sea-experience engendered a plentiful lack of discipline in the ships they commanded, for no sooner was a ship in harbour than her captain left her, and it was frequently difficult to get him on board again in time for her to proceed to another destination with the rest of the fleet. In the higher command also endless difficulties occurred because of the jealousies between the "old" and the "new" officers. James in 1667 admitted that discipline was bad, but he claimed that as long as he had been in command at sea he had been able to preserve it and that he would find means to restore it. But he persisted in the policy of appointing Cavalier captains, without, however, entirely discarding the "tarpaulins", lest they should form themselves into a discontented party, and he made no secret of his intentions: for Pepys, in answer to an inquiry, said openly that "both the King and Duke were for commanding ships of war by gentlemen", a view which Pepys himself did not share. James, however, appears never to have been quite satisfied with the policy he was pursuing, for when he was King he had a conversation with Bonrepaus in which he expressed his admiration for the

French system of training naval officers and a desire to inaugurate a similar system in this country.

The work of naval administration was interrupted in 1665 by the Second Dutch War. The cause of this war was the deep jealousy which had long existed between two nations competing for commercial supremacy. Its occasion was a number of high-handed acts committed in distant seas by Dutch seamen and merchants. Possibly if we knew more of the Dutch case, it would be found that the English were not entirely blameless, but complaints appear to have been made only from the English side, and these complaints were ignored by the States-General; it was currently reported that their opinion was that this country was far weaker than it had been under Cromwell and that Charles would not dare to resort to war.

James was of the war party from the first; he thought, however, that there would be no war and that the Dutch would give way as soon as they realised that the English were in earnest. His sentiments at that time were strongly unfavourable to the Dutch, his name for them in moments of heat was "insolent republicans"; he had a strong aversion from their form of government, he had a personal grievance in the treatment he had received in the Netherlands during his exile, and the States-General, in spite of their repeal of the Act of Seclusion, by which his young nephew William had been deprived of the stadtholdership which was hereditary in his family, had refused to reinstate William in the civil and military posts which were the perquisites of that office. Moreover, both he and Charles had financial interests in the two companies which had suffered most from the depredations of the Dutch, the East India Company and the Royal African Company. It is safe to conjecture that, in addition to these overt excuses for his warlike attitude, James looked forward to some advantage to himself in being in command of the English fleet: directly he could gratify his desire for glory, particularly naval glory, indirectly he hoped to reinstate himself in favour with the English people by a great naval victory and to overcome his increasing unpopularity—an unpopularity for which it is not easy to account, but to which contributed his wife's haughtiness and his own close association with his unpopular father-in-law; in this hope he was justified by the event. James was already gaining influence in Charles's inner councils, and there he was supported by the Duke of Albemarle against the peaceful counsels of his father-in-law Clarendon, Lord Treasurer Southampton and the Duke of Ormonde. In September 1664 he had a conversation with the Dutch ambassador, Van Gogh, in which he conducted himself in a characteristically truculent manner; he told the ambassador that if the Dutch did not cease their provocation the King would not be able to resist the national desire for war, and that if war came he himself at the head of the English would show them that we were in earnest and that "he did not doubt but to live to see the Dutch as fearful of provoking the English under the government of a King, as he remembers them to have been under that of a Coquin".

When in October war became inevitable, James displayed great activity. He visited the dockyards of Chatham and Portsmouth and spent the whole of his days and the greater part of his nights with that part of the fleet which was being equipped in the Thames. Early in November the ships which were ready, forty-one in number, were assembled at Spithead, and on the 9th James travelled down to Portsmouth. Further delays occurred, and it was not until the 27th that the fleet set sail. The voyage was only in the nature of a trial trip, a few inconsiderable prizes were taken[1]—one of several acts of piracy committed by the English navy in this year—no Dutch men-of-war were seen, and after a voyage of only three days, in which the farthest point reached was Cape de la Hague, James and Rupert, who was second in command, returned to St. Helens and left four days later for London. This was the total extent of James's sea experience before the commencement of the Second Dutch War. As a boy in Jersey he had had a good deal of desultory sailing in Charles's pinnace, an excellent preparation for serious training; but during his exile he never sailed with the royalist fleet, and when he crossed the Channel it was as a passenger. Since the Restoration he had had a pleasure boat of his own on the lower Thames, and he had twice been a few miles to sea—to meet his sister in 1660 and Queen Catherine in 1662. The fleet was not in those days kept "in being" in time of peace, but was laid up and the men were paid off; the only naval operations were unofficial and in distant seas, and we know too much of James's life from day to day to admit that any cruise extending beyond a few days has escaped us in which he took part.

War was declared on March 4, 1665, and on March 31 James, "attended by several eminent persons and volunteers of the first quality", left London for the Gunfleet where the fleet was assembled. He travelled as far as The Hope with Charles and the Duchess of York on Sandwich's ship, the *Prince*, and finished the journey in his own yacht. In spite of his exertions of the previous autumn it was more than five

[1] Meanwhile, however, Rear-Admiral Tyddeman with a small squadron had been patrolling the Channel and had captured the greater part of the Dutch fleet from Bordeaux, and one estimate gives a total of 150 sail of all sizes brought into ports between Dover and Plymouth before December 10.

weeks before he was ready for sea. The fleet consisted of ninety-eight ships of forty guns and upwards, besides fireships and minor craft; James on the *Royal Charles* led the Red Squadron, Prince Rupert as Vice-Admiral was Admiral of the White, and the Earl of Sandwich was Rear-Admiral and Admiral of the Blue. On James's ship as Great Captain Commander (a title which afterwards became First Captain and still later, Captain of the Fleet) was the veteran Admiral Sir William Penn. This appointment bred jealousies in two quarters: the crowd of courtiers on the flagship, led by the Earl of Falmouth (James's old friend Charles Berkeley), despised Penn as a "tarpaulin", or perhaps rather as a Commonwealth man, and strongly resented having to submit to his orders; while the other admirals in the fleet, notably Sandwich, realised that whatever orders James gave them would be virtually dictated by Penn, whose seniority to themselves they did not admit.

For over a fortnight the English fleet hung about the Dutch coast; they succeeded in capturing a convoy of ten merchant ships, but the enemy refused to leave their harbours; then a storm disabled a number of ships and James had to put back to the Gunfleet to refit. On May 29 they were at sea again, and on June 1 they were lying in Southwold Bay when the Dutch fleet hove in sight. James had detached some ships to make up their complement of men from a fleet of colliers in the neighbourhood; but the Dutch did not take advantage of the dispersal, notwithstanding their superiority in numbers—113 men-of-war with eleven fireships and seven yachts—and it was not until the dawn of June 3 that the fleets got into touch with one another; they were then some eight leagues east of Lowestoft. Manœuvres and counter-manœuvres followed until ten o'clock, when the wind changed favourably for the English and the battle was fairly joined. James's own ship, as was proper, engaged that of Opdam, who commanded the Dutch in chief, and the two ships pounded one another for no less than four hours. Then the Dutch flagship blew up. The battle elsewhere had been going against the Dutch, and this fatality was the signal for a general retreat on their part; they crowded on sail and made for the Texel. James collected his fleet, made arrangements for the safety of such as were disabled and followed in pursuit.

He remained on deck until nightfall, and at about eleven o'clock he gave orders that the chase should be kept up at full stretch through the night, and lay down fully dressed in his cabin to snatch a few hours' sleep. During the night occurred a mysterious incident. Henry Brouncker, an officer of James's household, appeared on deck, represented to the officer of the watch the risk to James's person if they overran the Dutch in the night and were surrounded, and ordered him to shorten sail. The officer properly refused to admit the right of a volunteer to vary the orders of the Duke. Brouncker then went below for some minutes, and when he reappeared on deck he reported that he had seen the Duke and explained the situation to him and that his orders were to shorten sail. These orders were carried out, the speed of the English fleet was reduced and the Dutch were able to increase their lead. At dawn, when it was found that the enemy were several leagues ahead, sail was crowded on again, and James when he came on deck had had no information about Brouncker's action and concluded that he had been out-sailed. The delay enabled the Dutch to reach their own waters, and the English ships, which drew more water, were unable to follow them—or so it appeared from the English fleet, for, had James but known, the Dutch had to wait outside the Texel for four hours before the tide served to allow them to enter; a few stragglers were picked up, but the opportunity of destroying at a blow the naval power of the United Provinces was lost. There appears to have been no plausible motive for Brouncker's conduct; he himself was a man of vile reputation—it was said that his sole virtue was that he was a good chess-player—and it is quite possible that he was actuated by fears for his own personal safety; popular opinion was that the Duchess of York had convinced the Duke's household that their paramount duty in the action was to preserve the Duke, and that Brouncker interpreted her orders in his own way. This view was expressed by Sir John Denham in a passage describing the farewells at The Hope in his satire, *Instructions to a Painter concerning the Dutch War*, commencing:

> O Duchess! if thy Nuptial Pomp was mean
> 'Tis paid with interest in thy Naval Scene

and concluding:

> She therefore the Duke's person recommends
> To Brouncker, Penn and Coventry, her friends.

When James heard how Brouncker had betrayed him he was for having him tried by court-martial, but though Brouncker had to endure the humiliation of expulsion from the House of Commons, he managed to abscond to the Continent.

Though the English fleet had been robbed of further success on the second day of the battle, the victory on the first day had been complete: the Dutch had lost over twenty ships, sunk or taken, and upwards of 5000 men; the loss on the English side was under 1000 men and one small ship. The Dutch lost Opdam, their Commander-in-Chief, and three other admirals, the English lost two distinguished seamen in Sir

John Lawson, Vice-Admiral of the Red, and Robert Sansum, Rear-Admiral of the White. But James had to suffer a bitter personal loss: the Earl of Falmouth was killed on the quarter-deck when he was standing so near to James that James was bespattered with his blood (the cannon-ball which carried him off killed also the Earl of Muskerry, an old companion of arms with James in Flanders, and Richard Boyle, a younger son of the Earl of Burlington). As Charles Berkeley, Falmouth had been a close friend of James in France and Flanders, and after the Restoration James's devotion to Lord Berkeley was transferred from the uncle to the nephew and developed into a strong personal affection. Charles, too, showed an unwonted strength of sentiment towards Falmouth, and there had been a contest between the brothers for his services, marked on James's side by an abject expression of his submission to the royal will and of his love for Falmouth. Both Charles and James were more genuinely affected by Falmouth's death than by any other bereavement in either of their lives. James had a very high opinion of his abilities, particularly as a soldier, and held that once he had shed the follies of youth—for he was a notorious libertine—he would have developed all the qualities of a statesman; the general view was that James was in this instance merely giving additional proof of his lack of knowledge of men. But Sir William Coventry, who as James's private secretary had been in close touch with Falmouth for five years, who had taken the side of Sir William Penn against Falmouth's faction and must be regarded as an impartial witness, told Pepys three years after Falmouth's death of his "generosity, good-nature, desire of public good, and low thoughts of his own wisdom; his employing his interest in the King to do good offices to all people, without any other fault than the freedom he do learn in France of thinking himself obliged to serve his King in his pleasures". So that James and Charles may not have been at fault in their extraordinary affection for him. Falmouth's virtues were, however, known only to a few. Sir John Denham was expressing what was generally thought of him when he wrote:

> Falmouth was there, I know not what to act;
> Some say 'twas to grow Duke too by contract:
> An untaught bullet in its wanton scope,
> Dashes him all to pieces and his hope.
> Such was his rise, such was his fall, unpraised;
> A chance-shot sooner took him than chance raised:
> His shattered head the fearless Duke distains,
> And gave the last first proof that he had brains.

The victory put new heart into the English people; James had one of his fleeting moments of popularity and was acclaimed as a hero. Dryden addressed to the Duchess of York a fulsome ode which ranks far below his best work: it contains the absurd lines,

> How powerful are chaste vows!—the wind and tide
> You bribed to combat on the English side.

How far James deserved everything that was said and done is another matter. It is not easily conceivable that a young man not yet thirty-two years of age, trained it is true in the best available school of land warfare, but with next to no sea experience, and it may be added not a genius, can have done more than to have been lucky in the seasoned seamen whose advice he took. Of his personal bravery there can be no question, the death of his friends by his side is proof of the risks he himself ran. In his memoirs he claims to have been the inventor of the "line ahead" formation and to have used it for the first time in this battle; but he makes no mention of Sir William Penn.

In connection with the Battle of Lowestoft an incident occurred which shows James's character in a favourable light. The captain of an English ship on scouting duty had sighted two Dutch vessels which were bearing down upon him; he called his crew together, represented to them the unequal nature of the contest and signified his intention of taking action which "showed discretion, the best part of valour". Instead of obeying his orders, however, the crew mutinied, put him in irons, attacked the Dutch and captured one ship and put the other to flight. The Council of War to which the matter was referred overlooked the mutiny (as a modern Naval Court-martial would hardly have done), and condemned the captain to death for cowardice. When the matter was brought to James's notice he sent for the captain and pardoned him, but gave him a musket and made him a soldier, saying that English captains were "obliged to resist several enemies", but "seeing that he had not the courage to fight more than one", he might pass the rest of his life in the ranks. Such incidents (and, as will be seen, there were several of the kind in Scotland) give some ground for the contention on the part of Ailesbury and others that James was by nature inclined to mercy. By far the greater body of testimony is on the other side: "he was not born under a pardoning planet"; "though it was in his power, it was not in his nature to pardon". The explanation of this conflict of evidence lies in James's political views: James was the most complete Royalist that it is possible to conceive; he regarded rebellion as a crime so heinous as to be past forgiveness, and he not only denied mercy to traitors, but was disinclined to allow justice to persons accused of treason. On the other hand, where his worship of royalty and his fear of a repetition of the events of the Civil War were not concerned, he did sometimes pardon people whom his friends would have condemned. Such clemency was not, however, exercised on a fixed principle, but uncertainly and whimsically, after the manner of an Oriental potentate—his chief regret (as we shall see) after the loss of the *Gloucester* in 1682 was that he had missed the opportunity of hanging the pilot who had run her on to a sandbank.

The tangible result of the victory as far as James was personally concerned was the vote by Parliament of a gift to him of the princely sum of £120,000, "in token of the great sense they had of his conduct and bravery in the late engagement". They followed up this vote, however, by a humble address to the King asking him not to allow James to risk his life again. To this appeal Charles readily acceded: the death of Falmouth at James's side had brought home to everyone the risks the monarchy would have run if the cannon-ball had taken a slightly different course; Charles had been married for three years, there was no sign of a direct heir, and the probability that James would succeed had very much increased; in default of James, his daughter Mary, a child of three, would be heir presumptive. Henrietta Maria added solicitations that James should not be separated from her during the short time that she could expect to be with him, for she was contemplating a return to France, and no doubt James's Duchess thought that he had done enough for glory. To James's dismay, Charles ordered him ashore, and it was nearly seven years before he went to sea again. He retained his post of Lord High Admiral and he was very active in visiting ports and dockyards. For the disaster at Sheerness in June 1667, when the Dutch fleet sailed up the Medway, burned three ships at their moorings and carried off the *Royal Charles*, James was only in part responsible. He had strongly opposed the foolish policy of laying up the great ships and carrying on a defensive war by means of the third- and fourth-rates; but what he should have ensured, and did not, was that the land defences of Chatham were of adequate strength and in good repair.

James claimed to have been a great patron of trade, but this claim does not rest on very firm foundations. As early as October 1660 he was in consultation with the Earl of Pembroke with a view to forming a company to dig for gold "somewhere in Africa"; this idea may have been the germ of the Royal African Company, of which he claimed to be the founder. He also claimed to have furthered the interests of the East India, Turkey, Hamburg, and Canary Companies, and it is probable that he invested money in all of them; in the autumn of 1663 James fitted out a frigate at his own expense and for his own profit to trade with Guinea; he also had a financial interest in the Hudson Bay Company. In March 1664 Charles made a grant to him of a large tract of land in North America between Connecticut and the Delaware; James borrowed two men-of-war and sent them under the command of Colonel Richard Nicolls to take possession of his own territory and to make terms with or to dispossess the Dutch who had established trading-stations on the Hudson River. This expedition, with the assistance of local contingents, captured in August 1664 the Dutch settlement of the New Netherlands with its capital, New Amsterdam, and in James's honour both the captured province and the town were renamed New York. To him also was given the credit of refounding the Royal African Company after it had been dissolved at the end of the Third Dutch War. But, on the other hand, James appears to have taken no part in the long negotiations which resulted in the treaty with France of February 14, 1677, a treaty of vital importance to English merchants, as defining the rights of English ships in the war between England and France; nor did the deputation of sixty merchants which waited on Charles in June 1676 to represent to him the hardships inflicted on them by the French Navy seek James's mediation, as they certainly would have done if they had regarded him as a patron of trade. From the rather meagre evidence at our disposal it seems probable that James's interest in foreign trade was that of a director and shareholder rather than that of a statesman, and that it was his own (quite legitimate) financial advantage that he had in mind, and not the prosperity of the country as a whole.

Domestic matters occupied James's attention in these early years of the Restoration. In September 1660 his sister Mary, Princess of Orange, started on a visit to the English Court. James went in a ketch to meet her, but he was recalled to London by the news of the death of the Duke of Gloucester. He was said, after his death, to have been a prince of great promise, but he was only twenty-one, and it is idle to speculate on the sort of character he would have developed. Certainly if he had lived out the century with James he would have altered the whole course of English history—especially if he had remained a Protestant: he was by birth a far less exceptionable candidate for the throne than was Monmouth, and it is not probable that he would have proved less adequate to a distinguished position. In December 1660 James's sister, Mary, Princess of Orange, died of that prevalent scourge smallpox; and in February 1662 a remarkable cycle of deaths in the royal family was completed by the death of his aunt, Elizabeth, Queen of Bohemia, mother of the Electress Sophia and grandmother of George I. In the winter of 1661–1662 Henrietta Maria, accompanied by her daughter Henrietta, paid a short visit to England. She returned from

France for a longer stay in August 1662. In May of that year there had been a ceremonial reception of a still more exalted lady, Catherine of Braganza, Charles's new Queen. James, as Lord High Admiral, with a crowd of courtiers, took ship at Portsmouth, met the English squadron which had brought her from Lisbon a few miles out at sea and escorted it back to Portsmouth.

In June 1665, immediately after his return from his victory over the Dutch, James assisted Charles in the duty of speeding their mother on her way back to France. It is unlikely that Henrietta Maria was happy during her residence in this country. She had no voice whatever in public affairs, and to a woman of her temperament that was an unbearable deprivation. Among those whose memories went back to the previous reign she was for opposite reasons unpopular both with the old Cavaliers and the old Roundheads, and her religion was offensive to the growing anti-Catholic sentiment. The ostensible reason for her departure was fear of the plague; what she really feared was popular tumult against her, "which conceit of Her Majesty is the more confirmed of late by certain libels thrown out on Christmas Eve [1664], menacing the extirpation of Popery and Mass in her chapel".

When Charles and James returned to London they found the Great Plague raging there, and the Court took fright and moved to Hampton Court; but even there they did not feel themselves safe, and after a few days they transferred themselves to Salisbury. In August Charles found it expedient to send James to York; there was a rumour of trouble in the North, and the Court were still under the apprehension of a recurrence of the civil war; there was also in Charles's mind the same consideration which had actuated Charles I, when in 1646 he sent the heir to the throne to Bristol—if Charles and James were together they might both succumb to the plague, and the monarchy would have been in jeopardy.

Fresh from the glory of the naval victory, the Duke with the Duchess made a triumphant progress through the Midlands; Sir George Savile gave them splendid entertainment at Rufford Abbey, and when next he saw Charles at Oxford, James in requital vainly endeavoured to get Savile made a viscount—an honour he achieved three years later, when he became Viscount Halifax. The reception at York left nothing to be desired: all the nobility and gentry were present, there was a good display of troops, and the Mayor, after making a very long and courtly speech with all due emphasis on James's heroic exploits, presented each of the royal visitors with a purse containing a hundred pounds in gold. The seven weeks' stay in York was devoid of public duties, and James occupied himself with outdoor sports; he appears not to have found the neighbourhood suitable for hunting, and shooting and "flying" (that is to say, contests of speed and dexterity between falcons and other birds of the chase) had to take the place of his favourite diversion.

At York occurred the well-known incident of the riding accident to Arabella Churchill. James had amused himself by teaching this plain seventeen-year-old maid of honour to ride, and had found her an awkward and inapt pupil; but one day her horse ran away with her and she fell off in a position which she no doubt considered ungainly; not so James, for he at once fell in love with her, and, after a period of courtship which from the date of the birth of her eldest child[1] appears to have extended over some years, she became his mistress. Very little is known of Arabella Churchill, but she has two claims to notice by the historian and biographer: she was no doubt the means of giving her younger brother, John Churchill, the great Duke of Marlborough, his first step, as page in James's household, on the ladder by which he climbed to eminence, and she also provided the chief argument against those of James's contemporaries who held that the sexual excesses of his youth had rendered him incapable of begetting healthy children; for four of her children by James grew up in normal health: James Fitzjames, Duke of Berwick, who rose to be a Marshal of France, Henry Fitzjames, the Grand Prior, Henrietta, who married Sir Henry Waldegrave and became the ancestress of all the famous Waldegraves of the eighteenth and nineteenth centuries, and another daughter who became a nun.

In the middle of September 1665 James was suddenly summoned to Oxford, where the Court was then assembling and whither Charles had prorogued parliament. James travelled post, leaving the Duchess to follow at her leisure; he arrived at Oxford on September 25, almost simultaneously with the arrival from Salisbury of Charles and his stripling son Monmouth; the King and his brother took up their residence at Christ Church, and Monmouth and his wife were lodged next door at Corpus; the following day the Queen arrived, and set up her Court close by at Merton, and on October 5 the Duchess of York joined her husband at Christ Church. Every arrival was made by the dons an excuse for a fresh outburst of loyalty, and odes distinguished alike by their lack of originality and inspiration, and by their correctness in metre, diction and sentiment, were recited in the posture of homage to the royal visitors. The session of Parliament was short—October 10

[1] James Fitzjames, afterwards Duke of Berwick, born in 1670. There may, however, have been older children who died in infancy.

to 31—but the Court stayed on over the New Year, busy, after the manner of the "best people" of all ages, in entertaining one another, but giving great offence to their hosts by the insolence of their manners, an offence which was not lessened when they departed and it was found that they had left their lodgings in a filthy and insanitary condition.

In September 1666 occurred the fire which destroyed the greater part of London. Charles and James laboured incessantly and directed operations to prevent the fire from spreading. As one observer stated:

> All that is left is wholly due to the King and the Duke of York, who, when the citizens had abandoned further care except to preserve their goods undertook the work, and rode up and down, blowing up houses with gunpowder, to make void spaces for the fire to die in, and standing to see their orders executed; exposing themselves to the multitudes, the flames and the falling buildings, and sometimes labouring with their own hands to give example to others, for which the people now pay them all reverence and admiration.

Charles's conduct earned universal praise, but among the public some, who entertained the double suspicion that the Catholics had started the fire and that James was "a favourer of the papists", affected to see a certain levity in James's demeanour.

At the beginning of September 1669 Charles and James went to the New Forest to hunt, and there they had news of the death in Paris of their mother. James's obituary notice of her, "She excelled in all the good qualities of a good wife, a good mother and a good Christian", does credit to his filial piety, but (as Dr. Johnson says) "in lapidary inscriptions a man is not upon oath".

CHAPTER V

THE CONVERSION

DURING the year 1668 an entire change took place in the character of James. In the autumn of 1667 the fall of Clarendon and its attendant circumstances had brought him suddenly into prominence in public life, and his almost simultaneous conversion to the Church of Rome introduced a new seriousness into his outlook, gave him a higher sense of his political responsibilities, and in his private life (though it would be dangerous to be dogmatic on a question on which the evidence is scanty) introduced a certain modified regularity: he ceased, except for occasional lapses, to make the pursuit of women one of the main activities of his life and was content with a single mistress; this new strictness of life and its cause, as also James's liability to fall from grace, were evidently matters of common talk, for we find in a lampoon of a few years later the remark, "Though devotion has given his Highness a new turn, the bowls will still to their bias".

Clarendon's long service to the royal cause weighed as little with James as it did with Charles—gratitude of this description was not a Stuart characteristic—but James was always *plus royaliste que le roi*, and it was Clarendon's high sense of the royal prerogative which made James his consistent, almost blind, supporter during his ministry and which kept him faithful to him when Charles had abandoned him. Quite certainly also James was too much under the thumb of his Duchess to do other than to give her father his fullest support even if his political views and his personal predilections had run counter to those of the Lord Chancellor. There had been a party forming against Clarendon for five years before his fall: at first the leaders of the opposition were the irresponsible Earl of Bristol and James's own secretary, Sir William Coventry. Coventry always maintained that he had no personal animus against the Chancellor, but that he regarded him as an incapable minister, and James appears to have been unaware of his attitude until as late as the autumn of 1665. In July 1663 Bristol had launched in the House of Lords a premature attack on Clarendon, in spite of James's attempt, at Charles's instigation, to head him off; but Clarendon's unpopularity grew with the years—possibly the support of his princely son-in-law was disadvantageous as tending to increase his haughtiness and aloofness—until he had no friends left except James. He was attacked simultaneously from three sides, by serious statesmen like Sir William Coventry because he failed to recognise the changed conditions since the Civil War; by ambitious politicians because he snubbed them and stood in the way of their advancement; and by the riff-raff of the Court, including Lady Castlemaine, because he disapproved of them. Two politicians whose mutual rivalry vexed the politics of the reign—Henry Bennet, James' old *bête noire*, now Earl of Arlington, and George Villiers, second Duke of Buckingham—temporarily joined forces, and with the reigning mistress, Lady Castlemaine, made a concerted attack on the Chancellor. At last Charles himself turned against the trusted Minister of twenty years, and Clarendon had not only to give up the Great Seal, but to go into voluntary exile to escape the malice of his enemies. In the final eclipse of the Chancellor James was given the unwelcome task of breaking to him the news of Charles's decision, and later he wrote to his father-in-law strongly advising him to abscond.

When the blow fell James was laid up with a mild attack of small-pox, and except for a single speech in the House of Lords he was unable to vindicate his father-in-law in public. But he had previously talked freely in private, and Clarendon made no secret of his gratitude to him for his sympathy when "I have not many other friends to brag of". This sympathy was strongly manifested in James's purging of his own household of declared enemies of his father-in-law: at the end of August he dismissed Colonel Werden, a very old servant of his, who had fought at his side in the French Army and who was to live to be reconciled with James and to re-enter his service as private secretary; and a few days later James's secretary, Sir William Coventry, left his service. This last severance had been for some time in contemplation, and Coventry's activities against Clarendon had so much exasperated James that on one occasion he fairly lost his temper, he refused to sign papers that Coventry had brought him and told him that he could not bear the sight of him. A few days later, however, the incident was forgotten, and the parting was on good terms; in any case, it is unlikely that Coventry could have kept his post for long: he was a man of principle and ability, he would have seen through James's equivocations on the subject of religion and he would not have assisted him in his pro-Catholic plans. Sir William Coventry was succeeded as James's secretary by Matthew Wren, who had been one of Clarendon's secretaries, and who served James until he was killed in James's second sea battle in 1672.

In public James made many enemies by his devotion to Clarendon. Against Arlington James had a long account, and Buckingham was at once too clever and too unstable for James's taste.[1] They, with many others, sought to undermine James's influence with the King, for they feared that it might be used to procure the recall of Clarendon, and the return of Clarendon would mean their own ruin. Charles himself strongly resented James's opposition in a matter on which he had made up his mind. Up to this time the influence of James in the counsels of the King had been steadily growing. As early as April 1664 the French ambassador had been able to write that intrigues were afoot to create a breach between the brothers, but that these intrigues had merely recoiled on the heads of the plotters; for "I can assure your Majesty that I have never seen a union so close between two brothers: the King never comes to a decision on the most unimportant matter unless he has the approval of the Duke, whom he has consulted together with the Chancellor"; and Clarendon, after an account similar to that of the ambassador of the intrigues against James's influence, says that two years later Charles "had in truth a just affection for the Duke and confidence in him, without thinking better of his natural parts than he thought there was cause for; and yet, which made it the more wondered at, he did very often depart in matters of the highest moment from his own judgement to comply with his brother".

Charles had already shown resentment in public at James's presumption in aspiring to the favours of "La Belle Stuart", with whom he himself was infatuated, and the coolness which resulted had not been lessened when she escaped them both by marrying the Duke of Richmond. And now James's open opposition in the matter of Clarendon's dismissal created a very serious breach between the brothers, and it was nearly two years before a full reconciliation was effected; possibly Charles's anger was increased by some misgiving regarding his own behaviour. James was now more completely isolated than at any other time in his life: in the dark three years 1679–1681 he could rely, except for brief periods of pessimism, on the steady support of Charles, and in December 1688 a few sturdy royalists disdained to forsake him and many more would have rallied to his side if he had asserted himself; but in the year 1668 James had no support whatever among the courtiers and politicians who surrounded the King. Charles even encroached upon James's preserve of the Admiralty, for without consulting him he appointed Sir Thomas Osborne and Sir Thomas Littleton treasurers of

[1] Dryden's character of Buckingham which begins

> A man so various that he seems to be
> Not one but all mankind's epitome,

is too well known to require quotation in full. King Louis described him admirably in few words as "filling the air with the smoke of multiple plans, always unrealisable, which he supports with his loquacity and his grand airs".

the Navy, a slight which James felt so bitterly that he was reluctant to make recommendations to the King for the filling up of vacancies in the Navy office.

At this time appears the first movement to prevent the succession of James to the throne. The exclusion movement ten years later was a national expression of hatred of Catholicism and of fear of a Catholic sovereign. Buckingham and Arlington could pretend to no general and patriotic pretext for excluding James; they were actuated by the narrowest personal motives: rightly or wrongly they regarded him as utterly implacable, and they feared that once on the throne he would take his revenge upon them. They had two alternative schemes: to induce Charles to divorce Queen Catherine and to marry some other Princess who might give birth to an heir; and to get the Duke of Monmouth declared legitimate and heir apparent.[1] There was then pending in the House of Lords a Bill for re-marriage of the divorced Lord de Roos, and the promoters of Charles's divorce saw, or pretended to see, a resemblance between the two cases; they strongly supported the Bill, and made a major issue of what was a matter of private interest in the hope that the one divorce might form a precedent for the other—a striking and amusing example of the lengths to which Court intrigues were carried. But Charles could not be moved on either point: he would not inflict this last ignominy on the Queen whom he had already so grossly injured and insulted, and fond as he was of Monmouth, he knew he was a bastard, and his high sense of monarchy forbade him to tolerate the occupation of the throne by anyone labouring under that disability; moreover, angry as he was with James, he would not lend his ear to plots to deprive him of his birthright. Indeed, it seems probable that the intrigues to undermine James produced the same results that previous intrigues had produced, and caused a reaction in Charles's mind in James's favour. In any case, the attacks on James ceased as suddenly as they began: in November 1668 Arlington was asserting that James should not succeed to the throne, and less than three months later the Duke and the Minister were in solemn and secret conclave with the King and only two others, where they heard Charles's declaration of his adhesion to the Faith of Rome and agreed to adopt the Grand Design, whose purpose was the re-conversion of England to her ancient beliefs by the help of the money and if necessary the forces of France.

Thenceforward, for the next four years James took his place as the

[1] Evidence is not lacking that the legitimisation of Monmouth was in the air: Pepys, Oct. 27,1662; May 4, 14, 15, 1663; Dec. 16, 1666; Sept. 11, 14, 1667; H.M.C. Rep. X. App. Pt. 4, 114.

sixth member of the Cabal,[1] the inner circle of Charles's advisers, and Arlington was his constant ally, with Clifford as a third against the Protestantism of Ashley, Buckingham and Lauderdale. In 1674, however, when Arlington seemed to be unduly regardful of Monmouth, James's antipathy for Arlington revived, and he was not sorry to see him relieved of the seals and relegated to the post of Lord Chamberlain; in retrospect James wrote of him as a timorous Minister whose counsels had been the chief cause of the troubles of the middle years of Charles's reign. It is remarkable that James worked so long as he did in harmony with Arlington, for Arlington was an uncertain upholder of the royal prerogative and in foreign politics his long embassy in Spain had imbued him with strong anti-French prejudices.

The reconciliation with Charles was a slower business, but when once interested parties ceased to apply irritants the relations of the brothers gradually became easier, until in September 1669 James was able to tell his sister, the Duchess of Orleans, that "the King is much kinder to him than he used to be and uses him very well". From that time they lived together without serious difference, and it seems likely that if a day-to-day calendar were made of their movements, it would be found that when James was in England—that is to say, when he was not at sea or in exile—they saw and spoke to one another on five or six days a week. James drew more advantage from the relationship than did Charles; his pose was that of Charles's good angel, always at his elbow, urging him to forsake his pleasures and to adopt the strenuous life, the sort of life most repellant to him. It is difficult to see why Charles submitted to this persecution; he certainly writhed under it. James's second wife might boast that "he never leaves the King's side", and James's eulogist that Charles was "awaked by the daily admonitions of his brother"; but less partial observers were able to say that Charles feared and hated James though he was wholly governed by him, and there came a time when he complained to some of his intimates of James's "being so busy and giving him no rest".

James's steadfastness (or obstinacy) in the matter of religion was at the root of the major portion of Charles's difficulties, and Charles fully recognised this fact, and made no pretence at sympathy with or approval of such an attitude—he himself if he had found himself in James's situation would have known what to do. But though he showed great

[1] The word Cabal was applied to this quintet of advisers because the initials of their names, Clifford, Arlington, Buckingham, Ashley, Lauderdale, happened to make it up. But the word is of older origin, and it is unfortunate that it was used in this connection, for it conveys a suggestion of cohesion, which did not exist. There was almost complete political anarchy from the fall of Clarendon to the appointment of Danby as Lord Treasurer.

impatience with James, threatened to abandon him, and even offered concessions to James's enemies which appalled James, he never came near abandoning him, and the offers of concessions may easily have been a further example of Stuart promises, to be withdrawn or ignored when a favourable opportunity should occur. The whole situation presents a remarkable example of brotherly loyalty in a character in which loyalty was otherwise no conspicuous feature. The explanation is that Charles's loyalty was not entirely disinterested; he probably believed sincerely in James's rights—the right divine—but he also saw clearly that to abandon James to his enemies would be to remove one of the chief props of his own security. Two leading statesmen of the time expressed their views of Charles's sentiments towards James: Danby in May 1677, when he was still outwardly at any rate in James's confidence, told Sir John Reresby that though the King "denied almost nothing to the Duke, yet he did not really love him"; and Halifax, the most detached and the shrewdest observer of the time, wrote in his character of Charles, "His brother was a minister and he had his jealousies of him. At the same time that he raised him, he was not displeased to have him lowered."[1]

The foreign ambassadors, particularly the French ambassadors, had no doubt whatever about the special position which James enjoyed in his brother's counsels: from 1668 onwards they constantly employ in their despatches the words, "The King of England and the Duke of York", or, more shortly, "The King and Duke", and very often English ministers and ambassadors fall into the same phraseology; for example, the French ambassador writes to Louis in May 1668, "The King of England and the Duke of York continue to assure me that they will be glad to make a close union with Your Majesty"; in March 1675 we find in a letter to an English envoy, "I asked the King and Duke what commands they had for you"; Shaftesbury in March 1675 wrote:

> Besides there are none so likely as us . . . to give the only advice I know truly serviceable to the King, affectionate to the Duke, and secure to the country . . . no kind of usage shall put me out of that duty and respect I owe to the King and Duke.

In December 1677 Danby wrote to William of Orange that the news of the capture by the French of a town in Flanders "did so alarm us here (I mean the King and Duke themselves as well as others)"; and in July 1683 Jenkins, the Secretary of State, wrote to the same Prince bracketing

[1] A significant detail concerning the personal relations of Charles and James is that James made a practice of standing in the royal presence whenever affairs of state were under discussion, even when they were alone.

the names of Charles and James as holding a certain opinion. In January 1673 the French ambassador was much concerned because he feared that James and Arlington would be justly annoyed at not having earlier been taken into a discussion which had been held in secret with Charles; Sir William Temple in December 1677 wrote to William, "I hope your Highness will think fit to write particularly to the Duke, as well as to the King, in acknowledgement and applause of these late resolutions"; Sunderland in March 1680 advised William "to write kindly and submissively to the King and the Duke". These constitute a very small fraction of the instances which can be adduced of the prevalent belief in the very close association of James with Charles in foreign, and to some extent in domestic, affairs. The implication of those quotations, and of the many others for which space cannot be found, is clear: decisions in matters of foreign policy were an integral part of the royal prerogative, but Charles's decisions could not be regarded as final until James had signified his acquiescence in them and could be relied on not to use his influence to have them withdrawn. There is no parallel in English history to this tacit admission of dual responsibility in foreign affairs; the nearest is probably Wolsey's "ego et rex meus", but that was an encroachment by a powerful Minister, and not an association freely entered into by the King with the heir-presumptive to the throne.

But the opinions of observers, however numerous and however well informed, do not always represent the whole truth, and it is quite certan that James did not exercise in his brother's reign—in home politics, at any rate—the predominating influence which he was supposed by his contemporaries to exercise. A mere list of the measures which were taken by Charles in opposition to James's counsels, as we either know by the records or may justifiably infer, is very impressive. Among them are the withdrawal of the Declaration of Indulgence of 1672, the giving of the royal assent to the Test Act and the Habeas Corpus Act (if James had been king he would never have given his assent to these two Acts—he would rather have faced a revolution), the various proclamations putting into force the penal laws against the Catholics, for removing them from London and the suburbs and for expelling Jesuits and priests from the country—there were no less than twenty of these proclamations between 1663 and 1680—the recall of Sunderland to favour in 1682, and the refusal to dissolve Parliament in 1675 and 1676 (it may be doubted whether James had any influence whatever with Charles in the important matter of the regulation of meetings of Parliament). In matters of home policy, though their ends were identical, Charles and James differed entirely in method—James was always for taking the line of greatest resistance, and Charles made concessions which James considered confessions of weakness. Moreover, Charles's profuseness and negligence in money matters were a constant source of pain to James. Charles surrounded himself with a crowd of parasites, men and women, "who put great sums of money into his imagination"; and, as Ruvigny, the French ambassador, said, James saw the situation clearly, but did not dare to speak to his brother about it for fear of losing, through the intrigues of Arlington and others, such credit with him as he could still command. What probably misled contemporary opinion was the degree to which Charles gave way to him in the matter of appointments: in lesser appointments his patronage was certainly very great, and there were complaints from time to time that the Court was filled with his creatures; in major appointments also he claimed, and probably with justice, to have nominated two successive lords treasurer and a secretary of state, Clifford, Danby and Jenkins; and in 1677 he was successful in getting Sancroft, whom he supported against his stronger competitor, Compton, Bishop of London, appointed Archbishop of Canterbury. If it were necessary to sum up the relation of James to Charles in an analogy, it would be that of a nagging wife to a husband who loves quietness: she gets her way in lesser matters, and wastes her energy on them only to find that important decisions have been made without her knowledge. The analogy still holds for occasions when Charles and James were in agreement, for then James's constancy served to stiffen Charles's feeble resolution, an aspect of their mutual relations of which Louis and his ambassadors were fully aware. On the other hand, the nagging wife is very often a staunch upholder of her husband's interests against the world outside the family, and there is no lack of evidence that Charles appreciated James's unswerving loyalty and regarded him as a firm rock among the shifting sands of intrigue and corruption.

More extraordinary are the occasional extravagant outbursts in which he revealed a strong personal affection for his brother—no man ever kept his emotions more under control than Charles, and to James these outbursts must have brought a keen and almost painful joy. The most striking is reported by the Venetian ambassador in December 1674, when Charles was becoming increasingly aware of the trouble James was causing him in public affairs:

> I was at a dinner when His Majesty, divesting himself of all reserve, tenderly embraced the Duke several times, declaring that those men who sought their separation were rebels and that never would he do so great a wrong to himself as not to place full confidence in his dear brother; these expressions being accompanied

by tears of tenderness might have been attributed in others to weakness of head (*debolezza di testa*), but this free expression of heart was caused solely by the cheerfulness of the company, nor does anyone doubt the sincerity of the demonstration.[1]

By far the most important change which came into James's life in his middle thirties arose from his decision to abandon the State religion, for to that decision were due a new seriousness of outlook and a determination to lead a life more worthy of his new religious professions. In discussing James's conversion we are faced by a preliminary difficulty: he was a man of stubborn, fixed opinions who never yielded to argument on any subject on which he had made up his mind; how did he, on the threshold of middle age, when even men of more supple mind have ceased to speculate on religion, begin to listen to arguments against Protestantism? The answer is, though the evidence must be largely conjectural, that the change in James took place many years earlier than was generally supposed, and that what convictions he had held about religion he had held very lightly. Had Charles I lived and been in close touch with James while he was growing up to manhood it is probable that the father's influence would have kept the son in the Church of England; but he never saw his father after he was fourteen years of age, and his religious instruction in his early years on the Continent was entrusted to his chaplain, Dr. Richard Stuart, Dean of the Chapel Royal. This divine, from such letters of his as have come down to us, appears to have behaved more as a courtier than as a spiritual guide, and he gave James no impression of religion or example of the saintly life; moreover, he encouraged James, as did Radcliffe and other members of the household, to attend as spectator, when he was still a boy, at celebrations of the Mass. James's own accounts of the religious experiences of his boyhood are very vague: he mentions a nun who talked to him about religion, and who, when he said he was too young to enter into controversy with her, urged him to keep an open mind and to seek divine direction;[2] he records in an entirely different connection the solemn impression left on his mind by the religious exercises of the French Army before going into action; indeed, the atmosphere of the French Army, though Turenne himself was at that time a Huguenot,

[1] The Venetian ambassadors are not always first-rate evidence: it is unlikely that they knew any English or much French, and most of their information came from interpreters, probably priests. This anecdote may therefore be taken as accurate as regards the gestures, but not the words used by Charles.

[2] When he was asked if he had been in love with this nun he replied that "she was no desirable object"—five words which aptly illustrate James's coarseness of mind where women were concerned.

was entirely Catholic, and cannot but have had its effect in those impressionable years. The only evidence that James adduces, or has been given on his behalf, that before the Restoration he was a devoted son of the Church of England is his behaviour in the matter of the attempt by his mother to convert the Duke of Gloucester; and that, as we have seen, may easily have been inspired by the same secular motives as was Charles's behaviour at the same time. If we can safely generalise from a single incident observed by Pepys, when James and Lady Castlemaine "talked very wantonly" through the curtains of the royal pew at Whitehall Chapel, we should judge that he was during his Protestant days neither so devout nor so decorous a worshipper as he was in Roman chapels after his conversion.

He himself says categorically that he was a Protestant at the time of the Restoration, but in England he was reputed to be a Papist long before that. The "delight and glory" he took in hearing Mass was reported there as early as 1653—a report no doubt sedulously spread by the persons in power and growing in significance as the years went on and the offence was repeated. In the early summer of 1659, as we have seen, Father Peter Talbot and his fellow-Catholics thought that the substitution of James for Charles as King would be to the advantage of their Faith. In the spring of that year Dr. Morley, who later made other attempts to redeem James for his own Church, had an interview with James in which he frankly told him that he had fallen under suspicion of attachment to Rome and that the number of Romanists in his household gave excuse for the rumour; Morley put the matter on no higher ground than policy; he said that James's father had lost his head because he had been suspected of Papistry and that the rumours of James's conversion were very bad for the prospects of Charles's restoration. James replied that such of his servants as were Roman Catholics had been Protestants when they first entered his service, and that he had not encouraged them to change their religion, and added that he was resolved to continue in *profession and practice* a Protestant; it is very significant that he said nothing about his beliefs, as he did in later years when he was defending his attachment to the Church of Rome.

There can be little doubt, therefore, that at the Restoration the firmness of James's attachment to the Church of England was with reason under almost universal suspicion; shortly after the Restoration Pepys described James as "a professed friend of the Catholics", in 1663 a man was put on trial for having said that "the Duke of York had nothing but Irish rogues about him", and in the House of Commons in February 1671 a member spoke more truthfully than he knew when he said "that notwithstanding His Majesty's sincerity in the Protestant religion there were some eminent persons whose example gave encouragement to the contrary". It also appears to be a fact that he was early beginning to be unpopular; how far that unpopularity was due to suspicions about his religion and how far to other causes cannot be determined, but the sudden change from popularity in France and Flanders to unpopularity in England is very striking.

The distrust and hatred of the English people of the seventeenth century for the Roman Church and its priests was a very real and potent force. It has its origins long before the Reformation: in essence it was political, patriotic and anti-clerical rather than religious, and was based on an intense repugnance to the claim of the Papacy to the power to depose kings, and on the consequent belief that no Catholic could be a loyal subject without reservations in favour of the Pope. Incidentally this repugnance created the theory of the Divine Right of Kings as a counterblast to the Divine Right of the Papacy; but in the latter half of the century those who were at best lukewarm on the subject of the Divine Right of Kings held the papal claims even more strongly in abhorrence than their political opponents. It was this national sentiment which had made possible the severance by Henry VIII of the connection between the Church of England and the Papacy, and it had been intensified by the Marian attempt to reintroduce papal influence, by the excommunication of Elizabeth, by the long naval struggle with Spain, and, latterly, by the indiscretions of Queen Henrietta Maria. The Gordon Riots of 1780 showed how that spirit persisted long after there was any danger to the Protestant Churches, and even now it is a potent weapon in the hands of unscrupulous persons who wish to discredit those of the Church of England whose attachment to the ceremonial side of worship offends them. By a strange paradox the most ferocious opponents of the Church of Rome were frequently, in the seventeenth century as now, not very conscientious or reputable adherents of their own churches.

Very soon after the tumult and the shouting of the Restoration had died down, thoughtful men in Parliament and elsewhere began to have misgivings about several public matters, and among them Popery was the chief. Time after time the question was raised in the House of Commons. Charles himself fell under some suspicion, which his attempt at toleration in 1662 did nothing to allay; but gradually all the latent Protestant fury fastened itself on James; he became the embodiment of the menace of Popery, and it is hardly too much to say that, from about the year 1670, whenever Popery was mentioned either in or out of Parliament James's name was brought to mind. There can be no doubt that James himself was aware of what was going on and of the need for caution. When in 1668[1] he told Father Simon that he wished to be admitted to the Roman Communion, he asked him for a dispensation to enable him to make public appearances at the services and sacraments of the Church of England, and when Simon refused the dispensation he appealed to Rome. This appeal was refused, and James was with difficulty restrained from openly declaring himself a Catholic; but he continued for four years to take the Sacrament at the public celebration at Christmas and Easter, and it was seven years before he ceased to attend the services of the Church of England.

The crucial date was January 25, 1669, when Charles met in James's apartments a select gathering consisting of James himself, the Catholic Lord Arundel of Wardour, Sir Thomas Clifford, the Comptroller of the Household, soon to be a convert to Rome, and Arlington, the Secretary of State, who, like Charles, was to find Romanism a good religion to die in but was unwilling to make the sacrifices which would be involved in an immediate public confession of faith. To these four men Charles made a declaration of his adherence in principle to the Roman Church, and he asked them to advise him as to the time and manner of making his conversion public and the best means of "settling the Catholic religion" in England. This last question was the germ of the "Grand Design", the secret scheme for the redemption of England from her heresies and for her reconciliation to Rome. To what extent Charles believed in the "Grand Design" does not concern us here; but from now onwards James regarded the wholesale conversion of his countrymen as not only highly desirable and worth any effort or sacrifices that he could make, but, with divine assistance, by no means impossible of accomplishment. At that secret meeting, or at any rate about the time of that meeting, James found his mission in life; to that mission he devoted twenty years of unremitting toil, and for that mission he lost his throne.[2]

[1] The dates in the *Life of James* are inexact, for no allowance is made for the time necessary to communicate with Rome and for the delays of the Roman curia.

[2] Lord John Russell's conjecture regarding the attraction for James of the Roman Faith is probably near the mark:

> "He tells us himself that he was converted by reading Hooker's Ecclesiastical Polity. But, in fact, he could not fail to perceive that the Protestant religion was closely connected with freedom of opinion on other subjects, and that the Reformation was an example of resistance to ancient authority. Hence his preference for the Roman Catholic Faith. Passive obedience was, in his opinion, the simple and sole duty of a subject of a sovereign. Such a political doctrine was the fit counterpart of a religious creed which acknowledged the infallibility of a living head. His opinions, formed from books, were confirmed by experience. He observed when at Paris that the English Catholics were generally royalists, whilst the Protestants were friends of Cromwell."

James had to recognise from the outset that Charles was far from sharing his obsession. No doubt he would have preferred to see England Catholic, it is possible that he was experiencing a genuine religious crisis, and he was probably honest in launching the "Grand Design" at the private meeting, but when it came to a matter of action, of making his own public declaration, of altering the established religion and of commencing a campaign of wholesale conversion, he saw what an impossible task he had undertaken. To him "divine assistance" was a mere phrase, part of the jargon of the priests, and he saw that what would be needed would be the carnal weapons of military force. In such a contest there would necessarily be much expenditure of energy on his part, and he had no great store of energy; besides, there was more than a possibility that he would be defeated and sent again "on his travels", and that fate above all things he dreaded. Charles wavered and procrastinated, and whatever religious zeal he had had lost its intensity.

At this same secret meeting it was agreed in general that the chief need in promoting the "Grand Design" was the adherence to it of King Louis, and immediately what was in essence a purely domestic matter became involved in Charles's foreign policy. Chiefly Louis was to provide money, but in the last resort French troops might be needed to support the royal forces. Whatever was in the minds of the other men at the meeting, there can be no doubt that what James contemplated was a *coup d'état*, a spectacular announcement that the King had decided on an alteration in the State religion, with armed forces in readiness to suppress any sign of opposition. Already the strong places of the kingdom were in the hands of men in whom the King might confide—Fitzgerald at Yarmouth, Bath at Plymouth, Bellasyse at Hull, Widdrington at Berwick—while he himself was Governor of Portsmouth (here it is easy to recognise one of the earliest recollections of his own childhood, when Sir John Hotham refused his father entrance to Hull); above all things there were to be no concessions to the rebels—as he was constantly to say later, his father had lost his head through making concessions. James was fairly launched on his fatal voyage.

Charles had always had a desire for a close friendship with his cousin Louis. In October 1662 he had written to his sister, Henrietta Anne, Duchess of Orleans, "I consider nothing of greater value than the

---

James, who failed conspicuously in all secular undertakings, did not apparently succeed even in making himself a good Catholic; for Mr. Belloc alleges that there was "some tincture [of Protestantism] left in his mind after he had accepted the Catholic Faith", and adduces as proof that in his Papers of Devotion there is "no devotion of his to the Mother of God". Indeed, except for a single sentence (giving a list of objects of veneration, including the Virgin Mary), those papers contain nothing offensive to Protestant sentiment.

intimate friendship between my brother and myself", and from that time there had been continuous but desultory attempts to arrive at a satisfactory basis for a treaty. His conversion to Rome gave Charles a motive to revive these negotiations, for the interests of his religion were foremost in Louis's mind, and Charles would need his support if, as was confidently expected, the English people made their Sovereign's change of faith a pretext for rebellion. So afraid, indeed, was Charles at the opposition he might anticipate that he was at great pains to conceal not only the subject-matter of the negotiations, but also the fact that negotiations of any sort were in progress. His intermediaries were wisely chosen: Lord Arundel of Wardour, a Catholic, had been Master of the Horse to Queen Henrietta Maria, and he could carry despatches to France on the pretext of visiting his late mistress, while on the other side of the water Charles's sister, "Madame", Duchess of Orleans, with whom he had always corresponded, could have private interviews with her brother-in-law, Louis, without exciting remark. The intention was to prevent the organisation of opposition by presenting the nation with a *fait accompli* in the shape of a definite treaty, though in the event it was found possible to keep the treaty a secret.

In Louis's mind the necessity for an early attack on the United Provinces took priority over every other consideration. Charles was anxious that Louis should not employ the occasion by making such additions to his naval strength as to challenge English supremacy in the English Channel. He also had a desire to persuade Louis to bear the entire cost of the war, so that there would be no reason either to ask Parliament for money to further the ends of an alliance of which they did not approve, or to give them an opportunity to discuss that alliance. He made the proposal that he should publicly declare his change of faith before entering on the war with Holland. Louis was probably far more deeply interested in Charles's conversion than was Charles himself, but he realised the inexpediency of this plan and strongly opposed it; for anything which could create internal discord in England on the eve of a war was clearly to be avoided. It is difficult to account for Charles's attitude on any other ground than that he was using this plan merely as a lever to extract better terms for himself from Louis, for there is no evidence in his subsequent conduct that he had any intention of publicly declaring himself a Catholic either then or at any other time.

To what extent Louis was deceived by this manœuvre is doubtful, but James was completely hoodwinked. He had been admitted to the secret discussions almost from their commencement. He was valuable to Charles not indeed on account of any advice he had to furnish—in the whole series of letters which passed between Charles and his sister

James's name is barely mentioned—but because he was as anxious as Charles himself to prevent an increase in the French Navy and only too ready to take risks on behalf of the Catholic Faith. According to the French ambassador, however, James contributed little to the success of the negotiations: "Le Duc d'York . . . contribue d'autant plus a la ruine de l'alliance française qu'il temoigne plus de chaleur a la soutenir." James's temperament fitted him ill for delicate diplomatic exchanges. Ralph Montagu, Charles's envoy in Paris, had no inkling of what was going on, and it was only in October 1669 that Colbert de Croissy, the French ambassador in London, was let into the secret and was instructed to draft a treaty. On the English side Arlington and Clifford were the Ministers employed by Charles; Shaftesbury and Buckingham were kept carefully and successfully in ignorance.

The terms of the treaty were agreed upon early in 1670, but for reasons which are a little obscure it was decided to make the signature a formal occasion and to send Madame to England as Louis's representative. Whoever first proposed this visit, it was strongly favoured by both monarchs: by Charles because he was very much attached to his sister and had not seen her for a number of years, and by Louis because he hoped, through her influence over her brother, to persuade him to a strict adherence to the French interest. The visit was vetoed by Henrietta's husband, that very queer man Philip, Duke of Orleans, and Louis had to invoke the royal prerogative to obtain his consent. Even then the Duke was able to stipulate that Madame should proceed no farther than Dover, and that she should remain there only three days, a period which was subsequently, however, extended to nine days.

James's recollections of the circumstances of the treaty, as recorded in his memoirs, are very muddled. He says he was averse to the terms because the war with the United Provinces was given precedence to the declaration on religion, whereas up to Madame's arrival the contrary had been agreed. As a matter of fact the text of the treaty remained exactly as previously, and by the second Article the time of the declaration was left entirely to Charles's discretion. The key to James's dislike of the treaty may perhaps be found in the jealousy which he confesses of Henrietta's influence over Charles; there was a danger, he said, that she might decide to settle in England, in which case her aim would be "to govern all things here", and, we may add, keep James out of his brother's inmost counsels. Behind these objections there was a latent antipathy between James and his sister: she had lived with her mother up to her marriage and from time to time after it, and had probably imbibed a good deal of that lady's dislike of James; certainly in March

1669, at the very beginning of the negotiations, Charles had found it necessary to apologise to Henrietta for making James a party to them. Nor would it be a wild conjecture to ascribe to James the wider principle that he objected to the intrusion of women into public affairs; such anti-feminism would have been in accord with his amorousness. That James wrote to Monsieur asking him to allow Madame to make the journey is of small importance, for the letter may easily have been written at Charles's command.[1]

A year later James appears to have taken the opposite view on the relative importance of the Dutch war and the declaration on religion, for he told the French ambassador that nothing should be allowed to stand in the way of a war with Holland. In that same conversation he revealed an attitude of mind which persisted throughout his political life. He said that the affairs of the country had reached such a crisis that he did not believe that a king and a parliament could exist together, and that he was opposed to the summoning of Parliament until both the Dutch war had been brought to a successful conclusion and the Catholic Faith had been established in England; when that happy consummation arrived "they would be in a condition to obtain by force, what they could not obtain by mildness".

In the summer of 1670 James fell ill and went to Richmond for a change of air. His biographer (who for this period may have been Duchess Anne) says that "it showed signs of turning to consumption" (a word of comprehensive meaning in those days) and that "he did not recover until almost the end of the summer". But one independent witness described him in the middle of July as being "well and at Richmond", and stated that he had not had "anything to confine himself to his chamber except a cold", and the Venetian ambassador called the complaint merely a low fever. The matter is important in a biography of James, for this is the only illness—apart from trouble with his eyes in France, the attack of small-pox in 1667 and a couple of hunting accidents—from which he suffered after his childhood.[2] The opponents of

[1] According to James's biographer he did not arrive at Dover until Madame had been there three or four days, during which time agreement on the provisions of the treaty had been reached; but the facts are otherwise. May 15 was the first Sunday on which the meeting-houses were to be closed under the second Conventicle Act; riots were feared, and Charles ordered James to remain in London with the troops which were held in readiness at the Tower. But he was able to be in Dover in time to put out to sea at dawn the following day, in company with Charles, Prince Rupert and Monmouth, in order to meet the flotilla which was accompanying Madame. He was again in London for several days the following week-end, and that fact may account for the confusion in the biographer's mind.

[2] Long after James's death his widow, Mary Beatrice, told the nuns of

Exclusion sometimes hinted that Charles was the better life and was likely to survive James, but facts were against them, for Charles had had at least two illnesses which had been considered dangerous.

James claimed to have been opposed to the Third Dutch War on the grounds that it would unavoidably run Charles into debt, that to recoup himself he would have to appeal to Parliament and that Parliament would not be likely to be in a good humour or to provide funds for a war entered into without their advice and in alliance with France. But the evidence to the contrary is sufficient. He certainly accelerated the declaration of war by his action in despatching Sir Robert Holmes in 1672 to intercept the Dutch Smyrna Fleet. This act of piracy—which achieved only a partial success—perpetrated in European waters and in time of peace, naturally exasperated the Dutch, and in March 1672 war was declared.

Again James was placed in command of the English fleet,[1] but this time he had the assistance of a French squadron under D'Estrées. For a second time he allowed himself to be taken by surprise in Southwold Bay, and this time he blames his flag-captain, Cox, for advising him against his own better judgement—an admission which seems to strengthen the view that James was not in effective command, but had to submit to the advice of men with more experience. De Ruyter, who was in command of the Dutch fleet, did not commit Opdam's mistake by giving James time to form line and to get out to sea, but attacked at once. The result was a confused battle which left neither fleet in a condition to pursue the other back to its ports, but the general view abroad inclined to the belief that De Ruyter had the better of the day. English opinion concentrated on the behaviour of the French squadron, which, for reasons that must remain obscure, took no active part in the battle. This apparent betrayal of the alliance seriously increased the hatred of the opposition in Parliament and their supporters for the French alliance and decreased the popularity of the war; but in favour of D'Estrées it may be urged that he was successful in neutralising part of the Dutch fleet, for De Ruyter detached the Zeeland Squadron to watch the French, and moreover James in his account of the battle lays no blame on D'Estrées.

James himself was again in the thick of the battle. He fought his flagship, the *Prince*, until "her main-top-mast was shot by the board,

Chaillot "that during the twenty-eight years of their married life he had always been in perfect health, that nothing upset him and that he was proof against every sort of fatigue".

[1] He again showed commendable activity in getting the fleet fitted out.

her fore topsail, her starboard main shrouds and all the rest of her rigging and fighting sails shot and torn to pieces and above two hundred of her men killed and wounded". He took boat and shifted his flag to the *St. Michael* and fought his new ship till she had so much water in the hold that she became unmanageable: then finally he transferred his flag to the *London.* There were murmurs that James had been too careful of his own life in leaving ships that were sorely pressed by the enemy; but the general opinion in England was that he had acquitted himself well and that if he had been properly supported by the French he would have achieved a signal victory. A year later, after Rupert's unsuccessful battle of June 7, it was said that if James had been there things would have gone better. Later again he had the high honour of a compliment from Van Tromp (son of Blake's famous antagonist), who is said to have told Charles in addition that "if the French had fought like the English the Dutch fleet had been wholly ruined".

James returned with his fleet to the Nore, refitted it and vainly hung about the Dutch coast in stormy weather, daring De Ruyter to renew the engagement; then in August, sadly battered and with much sickness on board, he returned to the River and hauled down his flag for the last time. In the following January Charles sent Arlington to the French ambassador to inform him that he had decided to appoint Prince Rupert to the command of the fleet, adding with regard to James "that he has no better nor more affectionate subject, that the close union which exists between them is sufficient to smother any factions or cabals that may break out in the kingdom", that if anything happened to James he would be exposed to great risks, and that if both brothers died the next heir would be William of Orange, "taking no account of the Duke's two daughters".[1]

The Test Act prevented James from taking part in the naval campaign of 1673. But he was still in control at the Admiralty, and he cannot escape all blame for the dispersion of the fleet which gave victory to the Dutch.

But now affairs at home became for James even more important than the war. In March 1672, during a parliamentary recess, tactically prolonged to keep opposition silent, Charles had issued his Declaration of Indulgence, suspending all penal laws against Protestant Dissenters and Popish Recusants and providing for the licensing of places of worship for the former, and for the latter the celebration of their rites in private houses. When in February 1673 Parliament reassembled they

[1] In some quarters James was thought to have been dissatisfied with his achievement in this battle and to have been anxious for an opportunity to retrieve his reputation.

were naturally incensed: only eighteen months previously they had re-enacted the Conventicle Act and stiffened its terms, and the growth of Popery they had made it their business to watch and to frustrate by every means in their power. Charles put up a good fight, but Arlington saw that if the King persisted there would be no supply, while Louis feared that the dispute would endanger the success of the Dutch War. They advised Charles to give way, and the Declaration was accordingly withdrawn on March 7, in spite of James's advice to adhere to it even at the risk of civil war. But Parliament were not content with this partial victory; they proceeded immediately to make the position both of the Protestant Dissenters and of the Catholics worse even than it had hitherto been by passing before the end of the month the famous Test Act, an Act which was not repealed until 1828, and which, by imposing on all holders of office the duty of taking the Sacrament according to the rites of the Church of England and of making a declaration against transubstantiation, kept the administration in the hands of churchmen or of Protestant Dissenters whose scruples did not inhibit them from occasionally taking the Sacrament, for a hundred and fifty years. Immediately after the passing of the Test Act, and as a compensation for what the Protestant Dissenters had lost by that Act, a Bill passed the House of Commons to grant them freedom of worship; this Bill was, however, lost in the Lords by the action of the bishops.

James took an active part in the debates on the Test Bill in the House. For him the Act was a major disaster: he was not yet a professed Catholic—indeed, during the reign of his brother he never made such open profession—but he had, on grounds of conscience, ceased to take the Sacrament in the English Church, and he could certainly not subscribe to a declaration against transubstantiation. He had perforce to lay down all his offices—Lord High Admiral, Governor of Portsmouth and Warden of the Cinque Ports—and not only that, he was compelled to make a tacit admission of his change of faith. He wept when in June he returned his commissions to the King, but Charles betrayed no emotion; he also ceased to attend Council, affected to be so disgusted with public life that he had resolved to take no further part in it, hunted frequently, and was so often seen displaying his melancholy visage in St. James's Park that people flocked to see him there. He was popularly known as Squire James, and there were rumours that he had taken a house in Suffolk and was going to live there in seclusion with a company of priests and fellow-papists. Actually he was biding his time: there was no interruption in his attendance at Charles's inmost councils; Clifford, the Lord Treasurer, had resigned with James in obedience to the Test Act, but James had a great deal to do with the appointment of his successor, Sir Thomas Osborne;[1] within seven months of the delivery of his commissions he was openly summoned to consultations by the King; and a new Board of Admiralty was appointed consisting entirely of his friends, so that his control of the Navy was in practice undiminished. In the interlude of enforced abstention from public activity he was engaged on a personal enterprise which decreased still further his depleted stock of popularity—his second marriage.

[1] Sir Thomas Osborne was immediately given the Scottish peerage of Lord Osborne of Aunblane, entered the English peerage as Lord Latimer, and very shortly afterwards became Earl of Danby.

CHAPTER VI

THE SECOND MARRIAGE

ON March 31, 1671, died Anne Hyde, Duchess of York. She had been in poor health for a considerable time, and her death appears to have been due to the not uncommon cause that, feeling temporarily better, she gave her appetite full rein. The most circumstantial account of the pathetic deathbed scene is as follows:

> By the best and truest intelligence she did not die as a Papalina, but she made no profession or confession either way. Her last acts were here:—She dined heartily at Burlington House on Thursday before, and that night according to custom she was about three-quarters of an hour at her own accustomed devotions, and at her return from Burlington House she called for her chaplain, Dr. Turner, to pray by her. The Queen and Duke were private with her an hour or more on Friday morning and no priest, but Father Howard and Father Patrick were attending to their duty on the Queen in the next room. The Duke sent for the Bishop of Oxford out of the chapel, who came, but her senses were first gone. In the meantime the Duke called, "Dame, do you know me?" twice or thrice; then with much stirring she said, "I" (*sic*). After a little respite she took a little courage, and, with what vehemency and tenderness she could, she said, "Duke, Duke, death is terrible, death is very terrible," which were her last words. I am well assured she was never without three or four of her women, so that it was impossible a priest should come to her.

Such an account in a private letter and with no motive for deception demands respect, but there is ample evidence elsewhere that Anne died a Catholic, and had been a Catholic for a year or more before her death; and that Charles, when he heard of her conversion, was troubled for the reputation of the royal family for sound churchmanship, and demanded that she should keep it a secret. She also set the precedent which Charles followed of leaving behind her a paper giving her reasons for preferring the Church of Rome to the Church of England. Her conversion was of later date than James's, but it is not necessary to conclude that she yielded to his influence, though such was the contemporary belief: she had always been a religious woman, and there is slight evidence that up to the time of his conversion James had felt strongly the claims of religion; in these circumstances, and apart from Anne's undoubted independence of mind, she would not have been inclined to listen to the little that he would have to say—he himself admitted his incompetence in religious argument. It is probable that Anne took the step from Anglicanism to Rome of her own volition.[1] Such a conjecture is in accordance with her own statement, in the paper on religion which she left behind her, that no one had attempted to induce her to change her religion; but, on the other hand, that statement has small value, for "to withdraw any subject to the Romish religion" was high treason, and she would naturally have been anxious that James (or some other person) should not suffer on this account.

In spite of the attempts at secrecy the air was full of rumours, and Anne's father and her two brothers, all three stout Churchmen, were dismayed: Clarendon wrote expostulatory letters both to James (whose own conversion to Rome he did not suspect!) and to his daughter; Henry, Lord Cornbury, was so upset that he refused to visit his sister on her deathbed, and Laurence Hyde brought an Anglican divine with him and vainly tried to have him admitted to the death-chamber.

It was now James's clear duty to marry again, and reasons of state may be held to excuse the haste which was shown in providing Anne Hyde with a successor. There was no prospect of issue by Catharine of Braganza. James's only surviving children were Mary and Anne, and it was to the public interest that there should be a male heir. James's first flight of fancy showed that he had forgotten the troubles and scandals of his first marriage, for he made his addresses to the widowed daughter of Lord Belasyse, and actually proposed marriage to her. The lady seems to have been—like Anne Hyde—in every way a suitable match except in the important matter of her birth; the great point in her favour was that she was a strong Protestant, though her first marriage had been into a Catholic family. Charles made short work of this match: he sent for James and told him that he had played the fool once and was not going to be allowed to do it a second time. James sighed as a lover and obeyed as a subject; he had loved Lady Belasyse well enough to endow her with an annuity of £2000 a year out of his Irish estate, but he promised Charles to submit "his fancy and liberty in the choice of a wife to His Majesty's judgement and election".

To supply details of the negotiations for a bride for James throughout

[1] At the same time anxiety to consolidate her influence over James may have been, if not, as Burnet asserts, the main reason, at least a contributory cause of Anne's conversion.

the Courts of Europe would require more space than their historical importance warrants. They provided a comedy whose richness was not lost on Charles, though James preserved entire seriousness—he was not given to laughing at himself. The quest is admirably summed up by a modern French historian:

> The despatches of Croissy on the choice of the future Queen of England are like the chapters of Rabelais on the marriage of Panurge. The Duke decides, draws back, changes his mind; shall it be a German, a French woman or an Italian? This princess is suitable but she is very ugly; another is accepted but he suddenly learns that she had red hair, and he hates red hair; the Princess of Wurtemburg might have been chosen, but she has a harridan of a mother, and "it would have been necessary to obtain a promise that her mother would go into a monastery and never come to England, very rough conditions to make with a mother-in-law . . ."

Charles had no tolerance for James's insistence on beauty (perhaps he felt that James was taking the sting out of his famous *bon mot*); he told him that:

> the more or less of beauty that a wife has, contributes nothing to, and takes nothing from, the happiness of marriage, and in a week one gets so accustomed to her face that it neither pleases nor displeases one.

But he was very anxious to get James safely married to someone of suitable rank; he did not know what sort of new sister-in-law James would produce for him if left to himself. He delivered himself at great length to the French ambassador, he told him that he recognised two prominent weaknesses in his brother—on religion and on marriage—that the first had already produced effects enough, and that he had reason to fear worse effects from it in the future; that he had found him since Anne's death strongly inclined to a second marriage, and that he had proposed to him all the princesses whom he believed to be friendly to Louis's interests, knowing well that his brother's temperament would inevitably lead him to a complete subordination to whatever lady he might take for his wife. The Duchess of Portsmouth was also very active; she was for a French match; this would please Louis, and she supported successively a Guise and an Elbeuf princess: but James thought his cousin of Guise ugly and begged Louis not to compel him to take a wife for whom he had an aversion, and the Elbeuf heiress was of the Lorraine faction, and also too poor and too young—the last objection appears inconsistent with his final choice. The lady whose name was for a long time at the head of the list was Claudia Felicitas, Archduchess of Insprück, and protracted negotiations were carried on in regard to her with the imperial Court, for the Emperor was her feudal superior and had the disposal of her hand; orders were actually issued for the completion of the proxy marriage. But these negotiations came to an unsatisfactory end through the dilatoriness of Hapsburg diplomatic methods, and eventually the Emperor lost his own wife and married Claudia Felicitas himself; so near was this country to having a queen of that euphonious name.

At last the choice of Louis, with the acquiescence of Charles and James, fell on Maria Beatrice, sister of the young Duke of Modena. The Earl of Peterborough, who had been causing amusement by his activities on the Continent as James's matrimonial agent, furnishing him from time to time with reports on the personal qualities of the candidates for his hand, was ordered to proceed to Modena and to make a proposal in due form. But there were unforeseen difficulties: the Princess was averse to marriage and wished to take religious vows and to become a nun; she was then "but fifteen years old, and so innocently bred that till then she had never heard of such a place as England, nor of such a person as the Duke of York", and she was scared at the prospect of great place; she was also apprehensive lest in Protestant England she would not have full facilities for worshipping God in the manner to which she was accustomed and which she believed to be the only acceptable manner. From Rome also came the objection that James had not yet been received into the Church, and Louis was asked to use his good offices with the Pope to procure the necessary dispensation, and also with the dowager Duchess of Modena to convince her that the dispensation was a mere matter of form and need not delay the completion of the marriage contract. But the personal objections were over-ruled and a promise was made to the bride that she would have a public chapel in which she could arrange everything to her liking; it was also decided to proceed with the marriage, in which Peterborough acted as James's proxy, without waiting for a formal dispensation from the Pope, who had, however, sent a "hortatory breve" (elsewhere called an "honorific breve"), which we may understand as a permission to proceed in anticipation of formal sanction.[1]

[1] The secret was well kept, for Lady Russell, who was in a position to get the latest news, wrote to her husband on September 23, 1672: "I will tell you the news came on Sunday night to the Duke of York, that he was a married man; he was talking in the drawing-room when the French ambassador brought the letters in and told the news; the Duke turned about and said, 'Then I am a married man.' It proved to be the Princess of Modena; for it was rather expected to be Canaples' niece."

Immediately on Mary's arrival at Dover on November 21, 1673, Nathaniel Crewe, the Bishop of Oxford, conducted what is surely the most casual ceremony that has ever been dignified by the title of marriage service under the laws of England.

> The Bishop of Oxford first asked His Royal Highness if he had the King's consent to marry Mary d'Este, Princess of Modena, to which the Duke answered, "Yes". The Bishop then asked Lord Peterborough if he had authority from His Majesty and power from the Duke to contract the said marriage, and if his lordship had observed all the instructions given him in that behalf. His lordship answered, "Yes". The Bishop then asked the Duke if he were content to marry Mary d'Este, Princess of Modena. The Duke answered, "Yes". The Bishop then asked the Duchess if she were content to marry James, Duke of York; she said "Yes" (in French). The Bishop then declared them Man and Wife in the name of the Father and of the Son and of the Holy Ghost.

In effect the pliant Bishop was content to recognise the proxy marriage in a Catholic church as a true marriage; his reward was the rich See of Durham, where he continued to serve James faithfully as long as James was able to be of use to him; he was among the first to go over to William after James's flight. Objections were made to the inadequacy of the ceremonial, but there were few alternatives: Mary would possibly have refused to be married in an English church, and a private, indeed a secret, wedding in one of the authorised Catholic chapels—that, for instance, of the Queen at Somerset House—would hardly have been of sufficient dignity for the occasion. Moreover, there was need for haste: it had been intended to get the marriage completed before Parliament assembled and could raise objections; this plan had been foiled by an indisposition in Paris which had delayed Mary's arrival, but it was important that no more time should be lost.

The news of the proxy marriage was received with dismay throughout England. Not only was the bride a Catholic, but it was suspected that French influence had brought about the match and that the dowry and jointure were to be furnished by Louis. On October 30, while Mary Beatrice was on her journey through France, the marriage was taken into consideration by the House of Commons. Charles tried to cut short the debate by a sudden prorogation; but either by accident or design proceedings were delayed in the Lords, and the Commons were enabled, before they were summoned by Black Rod, to agree on an address to the King against the consummation of the marriage. To this address Charles's answer was inevitably that things had gone too far for withdrawal. The Commons, on their reassembly, unabashed by Charles's reply, presented a second address in much the same terms as the first; to this Charles gave no answer. The behaviour both of Charles and of Parliament in the matter of this marriage requires explanation. The marriage of James to a Catholic was contrary to Charles's policy of providing for the ultimate succession of Protestants to the throne;[1] in pursuit of this policy he had forbidden James to influence the religious education of Mary and Anne, under a threat that they would be taken away from him, and was later to insist on the baptism in an English church of Mary Beatrice's children as children of the State. The dilatoriness of the House of Commons can be accounted for only by the lack of co-operation between individual members when the organisation of parties was in its infancy and there were no recognised leaders. At any time during the two and a half years in which James's remarriage was discussed, and when it was clear that none but Catholic candidates would be considered—for instance during the session February 4 to March 29, 1673—it was open to the Commons to address the King in general terms against a Catholic marriage. It is possible that Charles would have rejected their address, but he could hardly have had so good an answer to give them as he had when it was obviously impossible to control events.

To James, now a man of forty, this marriage with a girl of fifteen appeared, in view of her personal attractions, entirely suitable;[2] Peterborough, who was nearly fifty, was more than half in love with Mary Beatrice himself. In his memoirs he wrote:

> She was tall and admirably shaped; her complexion was of the last degree of fairness, her hair black as jet, so were her eyebrows and her eyes, but the latter so full of light and sweetness, as they did dazzle and charm too. There seemed given to them by nature a power to kill and a power to save; and in the whole turn of her face, which was of the most graceful oval, there were all the features, all the beauty, that could be great and charming in any human creature.

This is the language of infatuation, but others more critical found little in her person that was displeasing, except certain gaucheries to be expected in so young a girl and one who had spent most of her life in a convent; and she was found to be intelligent. Nor are later opinions less favourable: her chief fault was religious bigotry, and we may be

[1] Charles's own marriage was, of course, at variance with this policy.

[2] But Mary told the nuns of Chaillot that at first she could not love the Duke of York: she wept whenever she saw him.

certain that on religious questions she never exercised her influence over James in the direction of restraint and caution. The expressed doctrines of the Church of Rome with regard to members of other churches are on paper hostile and uncompromising; but some Catholics (regarded with disfavour by their stricter Brethren) are, and always have been, far more tolerant than they profess to be, and in practice they no more subscribe to those doctrines than do members of the Church of England to the implications of (for example) the Baptismal and Coronation Services; but Mary Beatrice, and it may be added James also, gave a literal interpretation to the doctrines of their Church and regarded Protestants of all denominations as heretics who were in open defiance of God. Danby once said that when the Archbishop of Rheims was in England he went into our churches and knelt during the time of divine service, but that James would not be persuaded so much as to come to the door. Mary was generally held to be arrogant and imperious during the four years in which she was Queen-Consort; she was prone also to the bourgeois solecism of making public "scenes" to achieve her private ends and to reprove James's infidelities. But her bigotry proceeded from a very real piety, and her haughtiness as Queen from her entire lack of understanding of English society and politics—a deficiency as marked in her as it had been in her mother-in-law, Henrietta Maria. She was at her best in adversity: during the troublous eight years which followed her marriage she showed admirable spirit, achieving a great degree of personal popularity by her wit and her gracious manners, and sharing her husband's exile and the long journeys involved—by land it was bad enough, jolting over the execrable roads and in constant danger of being held up by floods; but a sea voyage was torture to her, she was invariably sick, and a rough sea meant hæmorrhage and actual risk to life; during the final exile her pride and constancy provide a welcome contrast to the lethargy and imbecility to which James was reduced by the shock of the Revolution.

The reception by Charles and Queen Catharine of the new Duchess was all that she could have desired. Some of the ladies of the Court were affronted at the distinguished civility extended to her mother, Duchess Laura, in giving her a chair in the royal presence, and refused to attend functions at which she was present so long as she was accorded precedence to them. The poor woman had to keep her chamber during the remaining festivities. James and Mary failed at first to secure the favour of the reigning mistress, the Duchess of Portsmouth, who thought they did not treat her with sufficient respect; later on Queen Catharine objected that they showed too much respect to the Duchess. With James's daughter Mary, her junior by four years, Mary Beatrice struck up a warm friendship—in this instance she kept her religious fervour well in check—and this friendship survived Mary's marriage four years later with William of Orange; in October 1678, in charge of Lord Ossory and accompanied by the Princess Anne and the Duchess of Monmouth, she paid the Princess of Orange a visit at The Hague.[1]

Outside Court circles, however, the marriage was not popular: the Lord Mayor neglected to attend on the newly married couple with the customary compliments of the citizens of London and there were no bonfires. There was a spate of scurrilous lampoons which were issued secretly and were passed from hand to hand—Madame East was the vulgar Anglicanism of the name of Mary d'Este as Madame Carwell had been of that of Louise de Keroualle, Duchess of Portsmouth. In such an atmosphere it would have been madness to have observed the article of the marriage treaty which gave to the new Duchess the right to a public chapel, it would have been impossible to prevent the mob from disturbing the celebration of the Mass; Mary worshipped in the private chapel at St. James's Palace, far from the eyes of zealous Protestants, and she and James nursed a grievance at what they considered to be the perfidy of Charles.

James was undoubtedly fond of his new wife and shared this grievance of hers; but it was out of his power to be faithful to her: within a month of the marriage he was said to have renewed his relations with Arabella Churchill. It says much for Mary Beatrice's forbearance that James's lapses, which were not unknown to her, did not embitter their habitual relations; two years later the Modenese envoy wrote to his Court:

> The Duke her husband loves her tenderly, and does nothing without informing her. The King recognises her great spirit and esteems it highly;

the French ambassador found it wise to keep on good terms with her because of the power she wielded over James; and three years after the marriage it is recorded:

> The Duchess is much delighted with making and throwing of snow-balls, and pelted the Duke soundly with one the other day and ran away quickly into her closet and he after her, but she durst not open the door.

Such games are not played by couples who are living in strained relations.

[1] The Duchess was accused of undertaking this journey in order to cover the escape of "many priests, jesuits and plotters", who had been concerned in the Popish Plot.

The second marriage of James was an outstanding event in the growth of the national frenzy against the Catholics which was to find satisfaction five years later in the death of the victims of the plot of Titus Oates. Rumours of conspiracies by Catholics had been current not long after the Restoration: in October 1666 Pepys wrote in his diary:

> Some ugly knives like poignards, to stab people with, about two or three hundred of them were brought in yesterday to the House, found in one of the houses' rubbish that was burned, and *said to be* the house of a Catholic. This and several letters out of the country, saying how high the Catholics are everywhere and bold in the owning of their religion, hath made the Commons mad, and they presently voted that the King be desired to put all Catholics out of employment and other high things.

The following month he relates that James had himself told him that there were apprehensions at Court and elsewhere "that a fatal day is to be expected shortly, of some great mischief; whether by the Papists, or what, they are not certain", and simultaneously at Oxford Anthony Wood wrote in his diary that "the papists are very insolent in most parts of the nation; appear in public; contrive the massacring of many . . . frequent at Oxford, frequenting scholars' company at the coffee-house; I have mentioned their frequency here a year or more"; and in May 1668 Pepys mentions that "all the town is full of talk of a meteor, or some fire, that did on Saturday last fly over the City at night", and that "the world do make much discourse of it, their apprehensions being mighty full of the rest of the City to be burned, and the Papists to cut our throats".

Through all these rumours run two common characteristics: the flimsy evidence which in the popular belief connected the Catholics with anything that seemed dangerous or ominous—we have already seen them accused of the Great Fire—they even apparently went so far as to ascribe the Dutch raid on the Medway to Catholic machinations; the second point to be noticed is the dual accusation against the Catholics: they were insolent in owning their faith, and at the same time they were secretly plotting—if they showed themselves and made no secret of their religion, objection was raised that they were insolent, boasting of something of which they ought to have been ashamed; if they were not heard of, then they must be "working underground like moles". The anti-Catholics would have found great difficulty in producing a Manual of Behaviour suitable to Catholics; it was much easier to take exception to anything the Catholics did than to indicate a line of conduct which would give no offence to good Protestants. This phenomenon has had a parallel at many times and in many countries—the nearest is probably the Jews in Nazi Germany—where a religious or political creed is so obnoxious to the Government or the people, or to both, that the lives of the holders of it are rendered intolerable. The penal laws against the Catholics then in force, in addition to the prohibition of Catholic rites, can be summed up under four heads: to attribute jurisdiction to the Pope was praemunire in the first offence, high treason in the second; to harbour any Jesuit or priest was felony without benefit of clergy; to withdraw any subject to the Romish religion was high treason both in the withdrawer and the withdrawn, and a concealment of such withdrawal by a third party was misprision of treason; and to send a child abroad for education by papists, or to send money for this purpose, disabled the sender from any suit at law and from holding property.

Such were the inhuman laws which were still unrepealed and which were actually summarised in a royal proclamation on December 21, 1679. But there is no evidence that they were ever anything but a dead letter, and even the periodical royal proclamation that they should be put into force had no practical effect: Ruvigny, the Huguenot French ambassador, told Pomponne, "Such orders are often given but not carried out"; and Sir William Temple expressed the opinion that it would be an injustice to leave "priests to the law upon the accusation of being priests only . . . since the connivance had lasted now through three Kings' reigns"—that is to say, since the death of Elizabeth.[1] Nor is there any record that of the many priests who were known to the authorities to be in England during the reign of Charles II a single one was put to death merely for being a priest; indeed, during the trials of Oates's Plot the courts did not proceed against them under the penal laws, as they might have done with a great saving of trouble, but condemned them on other grounds. Nevertheless the continued existence of the Penal Laws and the reminder of their existence by royal proclamation placed the Catholics before the law in a position inferior to their fellow-countrymen and constituted a strong and legitimate grievance. Furthermore, and in part arising from their inferior legal position, there was a feeling in the courts that the testimony of Catholics was unreliable, so much so that Oates in his trial for perjury in 1685 contented himself with making the one point against each of the prose-

[1] There can be no doubt that the object of the Penal Laws was a general prescription of the Old Faith. But when the Queen died they fell to a great extent into desuetude. (See Clarendon's *History*, I 107, II 98, IV 353, V 56, 57.) Nevertheless, they were not entirely a dead letter. There were twenty-four executions of priests (*qua* priests) before the Restoration and a number of persons suffered death for harbouring priests.

cution witnesses that he was a Catholic and expected (though in this he was disappointed) that the jury would ignore their evidence. Sir Thomas Clifford wrote in his *Commonplace Book*:

> There is generally such a prejudice against Catholics that they are never heard: everyone from the cutpurse to the traitor speaks for himself, but they are not permitted, and when any fault was to be found with the Government in all revolutions the running verse was they endeavoured to bring in popery. If there be a storm they are likely to be thrown overboard and bear all blame, as Nero burnt Rome and put it on the Christians.

Even before James's second marriage the fear of the Catholics and the resentment against them had increased enormously. In May 1673 the Duke of Buckingham conducted a recruiting campaign in Yorkshire for the expeditionary force which was to be used against the Dutch.

> So jealous were the commonalty there of Popery that a man scarce would come into his Grace till he had gone and publicly took the sacrament at York. The whole town do nothing but pretend to jealousies of the growth of Popery, and have straight reports from divers parts of Wales of their numerous meetings and nightly trainings, and furnishing themselves with arms.

Shaftesbury in January 1674 tried to rouse the House of Lords by telling them that there were in London and its neighbourhood more than sixteen thousand Catholics ready to make a blow of despair and that no one could be safe as long as these men were at liberty, and urged the Lords seriously to take into consideration means to prevent a massacre which might happen any day. This appears to have been Shaftesbury's first venture into the field of anti-Catholic agitation; a year earlier he had been willing to support the King's Declaration of Indulgence which accorded to the Catholics a modified toleration, from 1674 onward he was their declared enemy, and he exploited the popular fears and antipathies as a means towards the exclusion of James from the succession to the throne. At one time he was, or affected to be, in such apprehension of assassination by the Catholics that he "caused his family to be armed, and kept constant watch all the summer, resolving to sell his life at the dearest rate". One symptom of the excitement prevalent in the month of the marriage was a great increase of activity on Guy Fawkes' Day, and on the birthday of Queen Elizabeth, when many "Popes" were burned.

At this distance of time it is easy to see that there was no real ground for these apprehensions: there were only about twelve thousand adult

Catholics in a population of over five million,[1] and most of them were desirous of nothing except to live quietly and in the full exercise of their religion, and those who were prepared to support even the most peaceful agitation against the penal laws were extremely few. Their numbers were negligible, but they were regarded as the spearhead of a great propagandist power overseas whose expressed intention was the subversion of the existing polity of the country: "If the Pope gets his great toe into England," said Sir John Knight in the House of Commons, "all his body will follow." The strength of the existing order rested on the strong anti-Catholic bias of the English people; without such a bias the incoming tide would have been irresistible. But in England in the 1670's not only were the Catholics socially important in proportion to their numbers—they were enormously over-represented in the House of Lords—but the King's brother and intimate adviser, who was also heir to the throne, was to the public eye a declared Catholic, as were the King's public mistress and a number of the habituées of the Court. The most prominent of these last—notably Richard Talbot and Father Patrick—yielded to popular clamour and went into obscurity in the autumn of 1673. But James and the Duchess of Portsmouth remained, James by his presence keeping alive the dread of danger from Rome, the Duchess personifying another and more real danger—from the immense growth of the power of France.

James, and Charles still more, realised the dangers of the situation. James affected not to understand what all the fuss was about; he declared that his conversion was his own affair and that he had no intention of interfering with the religion of anybody else—the Grand Design was momentarily out of his mind; and he was suddenly alive to his own unpopularity, which, hidden under forms and ceremonies, had hitherto escaped his notice:

> Before that time he was looked upon as the darling of the nation, for having so freely and so often ventured his life for the honour and interest of the King and Country, and for having been always

[1] Courtin says 12,000 Catholics, but it seems probable he meant adult males, see A. Browning, *Life and Letters of . . Danby*, Ch. x, quoted by Ogg. Brian Magee (*The English Recusants*, pp. 169 *et seq.*) states that from the Parliamentary Lists of Papists for 1680 that Catholic gentlemen were 7¼ per cent. of the total number of gentlemen; but he has found so many omissions among the lists of peers, baronets and knights that he conjectures that 10 per cent. would be a more accurate figure. It would be impossible to accept either percentage without careful scrutiny of his sources, and his further contention that the percentage for the whole nation was the same as that for the gentry is totally inadmissible. Amongst the gentry family tradition operated far more strongly than among the middle and lower classes to keep people staunch to their old faith.

> so active and industrious in carrying on everything either as to trade or as to navigation that might tend to their advantage: but no sooner was the alarm given of his being turned Papist, when all these merits were blotted out of their memory, and he set upon on every side as the common enemy.

After James had begun to absent himself from the public celebration of the Sacrament and had resigned his offices rather than declare against transubstantiation, his unpopularity had, as he says, greatly increased (though he never had been "the darling of the nation"), and it was with difficulty that he was restrained at this very time from reducing himself to extremity by making a public declaration of his change of faith;[1] the signatories of the Treaty of Dover agreed that he had ruined the Grand Design by his premature zeal.

To Charles James's adhesion to the hated Faith was a great nuisance, a frustration of his dreams of a time when the country would be quiet and contented, and he himself relieved of external control and free to live his own life in his own way. Already he had heard the first rumblings of the storm which was to rage so violently six years later—the demand for James's exclusion from the succession. To Colbert de Croissy, the French ambassador, Charles said in the presence of James and Arlington,

> that all that has happened from time past has so embittered every one against the Duke of York that there will be furious resolutions against him in the coming parliament, unless the peace [with the Dutch] is concluded before the time at which they must assemble; and that in all appearance they would go so far as to demand the exile of the Duke of York and an act which should exclude for ever all Catholic princes from the English crown;

and the ambassador goes on to say that he had already heard similar forecasts from other sources. Charles knew his brother too well to hope that he could be brought to conform to the National Church: two foreign Protestants who were in England about this time pressed Charles to do what he himself most desired to do, and received replies memorably phrased: to Schomberg, who was in command of the troops which had been raised for the Dutch war, Charles said, "You know my brother long ago, that he is as stiff as a mulet"; to Ruvigny, Colbert's successor, "if it were not for my brother's folly (*la sottise de mon frère*)[2]

[1] He had been barely dissuaded from this course of action two years earlier.

[2] An expression, according to Bolingbroke, used by Charles on many occasions.

I could get out of all my difficulties." This view of the situation was becoming increasingly obvious to everyone and it was frequently expressed by Charles to the French ambassador, the sole repository for confidences of this kind. About this time commenced the series of attempts by well-meaning persons to persuade James again to become a Protestant. The first attempt was made by Shaftesbury (not yet alienated from James), and among others who took up the vain quest were Burnet and Stillingfleet. Others of his friends advised him to withdraw from the Court and to live for a time in the country. But he felt himself unsafe from insult anywhere in England away from the King's protection; besides, the country was dull, there was nothing to do there except "to hunt and to pray", and he enjoyed his activities at the centre of government and regarded them as valuable to the State.

In the month of the completion of James's marriage, almost exactly in the middle of Charles's reign, occurred an event of tremendous importance—the dismissal from the Lord Chancellorship of the Earl of Shaftesbury. Thenceforward he was in opposition to the Court, an opposition which was based on a widespread hostility to James and the Catholics and which increased in intensity as time went on, and the troubles of the following years, in which James was the chief victim, were due almost entirely to Shaftesbury's skilful leadership of the anti-Court party.[1] As members of the Cabal administration James and Shaftesbury were in opposite camps; but their personal relations were, as far as we know, cordial, and as late as January 1673 Shaftesbury had, in order to oblige James, gone out of his way to support Colonel Werden's parliamentary candidature for the City of Chester. But since the withdrawal of the Declaration of Indulgence Shaftesbury had found himself increasingly at variance with the royal policy; a man of his acute intelligence could not but be aware that the King's real intention in pressing for toleration was to favour the Catholics—and whatever may be thought of Shaftesbury as a man of principle, he was at any rate a strong and unwavering Protestant; it was further alleged (on doubtful authority, however) that Arlington, to serve his own ends, had divulged to him the terms of the real Treaty of Dover, and if this allegation has good foundation, the resentment which Shaftesbury

[1] For a few months in 1679 Shaftesbury was President of the Council which Charles set up to take the place of the Privy Council, but in October of that year he was finally dismissed from public office. There is nothing new to be said on the subject of Shaftesbury's character. It is certain that he was a man of principle, especially on the subject of toleration to Protestant dissenters; it is equally true that he was unscrupulous in the means he employed to attain worthy ends.

felt at the deception which had been practised on him sufficiently accounts for, and to a great extent excuses, his subsequent conduct. There is a story—almost certainly invented in the years in which James and Shaftesbury were declared enemies, and when James had outlived his reputation for physical courage—to the effect that on one occasion when Charles was to appear officially in the House of Lords, Shaftesbury found his place as Lord Chancellor on the King's right usurped by James; there was some discussion, and "at length the Duke was obliged to submit, but said in a passion, 'My Lord, you are a rascal and a villain.' He with great composure replied, 'I am much obliged to Your Royal Highness for not calling me likewise a coward and a Papist.' " The story is very ingenious, hitting off exactly the characters of the two men, for James was liable to sudden bursts of anger, and Shaftesbury's reply accords with his reputation for self-command and ready wit; unfortunately it depends upon the fact that Shaftesbury was still Lord Chancellor, and the relations between the two men did not become strained until a later date. It seems not improbable that the story had its rise in an incident in the House of Lords mentioned by the Venetian Ambassador in January 1674:

> The Duke of York has been deeply hurt by the declaration of the peers that as heir presumptive to the Crown he must take the oath of allegiance like the rest; to which the ex-Lord Chancellor added that His Royal Highness must sit on the Duke's bench and not in the chair on the King's left hand, the place destined for the Prince of Wales.

On James's side Shaftesbury's steady Protestantism must have become increasingly irksome, and no doubt he felt Shaftesbury's unexpressed disapproval of his marriage. The cleavage between the two sections of Charles's inner council had grown so wide that the King called them together with the purpose of not listening to them and Ministers gave their opinion with the purpose of not being understood. Charles spoke to James of gaining time by these methods; James retorted that he was not gaining but losing time, and urged him to dismiss the Opposition leaders; James is also said to have sent for Shaftesbury and to have told him to his face that he was a madman. However, Charles was at last prevailed on to dismiss Shaftesbury.

When Clifford resigned the office of Lord Treasurer, because he could not take the oaths prescribed by the Test Act, James had a good deal to do with the appointment of his successor, Sir Thomas Osborne. He claimed to have raised Osborne "from insignificance to the height of power"—an extravagant claim when we remember that his first appointment as Treasurer of the Navy had been generally regarded as a snub to James—but it is probable that at the beginning of his career as Lord Treasurer he considered James as his patron and looked to him for support. At that time there was close association between the new Minister, James and the Duke of Lauderdale, who formed a triumvirate which governed Charles's counsels during the four years 1674–1677. They were all three ardent royalists, but Danby's royalism was of a very different stamp from James's: James was averse to parliaments of any kind. Danby's aim was to strengthen the monarchy by a parliament predominantly Anglican and Cavalier.

The two Ministers knew they were unpopular in Parliament—an address asking Charles to dismiss Lauderdale was presented by the House of Commons in January 1674—and that they derived their only support from the King; and James was by this time well aware that he had no party except in the Court. In foreign politics Lauderdale did not play a large part and, as far as can be known, had no settled convictions; but Danby, though he kept it in abeyance, had strong antipathy to the French. Both Ministers were at variance with James on the question of religion, for their sympathies were entirely Protestant. The triumvirate was, for purposes of foreign policy at any rate, in effect a council of four; for successive French ambassadors had constant access to the King, the Duke and the Ministers, and, as is evident from their despatches, were in possession of all the secrets of Government, even of those which Charles thought fit to keep from his other counsellors. This fact was not unknown to the party in opposition, and was one of their most legitimate grievances.

The divergence of principle on the question of religion threatened to break up the alliance when it had been in existence for little more than a year. In 1674 Charles issued one of his periodical proclamations putting into strict operation the penal laws against the Catholics. Immediately after the Council meeting at which it had been decided to issue the proclamation Danby and Lauderdale waited on James, and were given a hot reception: the two Ministers declared that they had done their best to prevent the proclamation from being issued, but James refused to believe them; he treated them to a harangue on the principles of toleration and the crime of persecuting persons of tender conscience, and told them that they had committed this crime for the sake of gaining favour in Parliament and that they had "so violently furthered a plan which placed the King among rocks and himself in the midst of precipices"; then, "with reproaches for their ingratitude and insincerity", he dismissed them. Ruvigny, the French ambassador, similarly reported to Louis that Danby and Lauderdale had been the chief promoters of this proclamation, that their action had given small satisfaction to James, and that the enemies of the Ministers, who had hitherto been James's enemies as well, were now courting him in the hope of depriving the Ministers of his support. Ruvigny was afraid that these intrigues would be successful, though he was not slow to remind James of his own principles—to depend upon the King and not upon Parliament, and to leave to the King the prerogative of dismissing Ministers; but, he says:

> It is to be feared that the resentment of this Prince, who cannot endure insults, will oblige him to revenge himself on these two lords and to abandon them to the passions of the parliament. . . . This Highness cannot disown this principle [the King's right to dismiss ministers] but he is so excited with the pleasure of vengeance that there is reason to fear that he will give his support to the plan to renew the accusations which have been made against Lauderdale and to commence them against Danby.

Towards the end of the following year there was a further breach between James and Danby (Lauderdale meanwhile having apparently lost importance) over the question of the dissolution of Parliament. James was strongly of opinion that Parliament should be dissolved, in the hope, perhaps, that a new Parliament would be more amenable than the present one, and, backed by Ruvigny's successor, Courtin, worked hard to that end. In opposition to him Danby was advising Charles to summon Parliament at an early date.[1] This time it was the ambassador, fearful lest a Parliament would force Charles to break with France, who was advising James to break with Danby; he told James that he should try to persuade Danby to his own way of thinking, and that if he did not succeed he should tell Danby frankly that he would not only cease to be known as his friend and to bear part of the hatred he had incurred, but would make use against him of the Parliament he was so anxious to have assembled by putting himself at the head of Danby's enemies; Courtin further advised James, if this threat was insufficient to frighten Danby, to communicate with "the chiefs of those who were known as the Confederates—that is to say, Shaftesbury and Hollis—and with all Danby's enemies, who were eager for a dissolution and for the election of a new Parliament" and to let them know what he had said to Danby.

But James's mind moved incredibly slowly: eighteen months earlier Ruvigny had, at great labour, convinced him of the unwisdom and dis-

[1] Burnet says that Shaftesbury was at this time endeavouring to widen the breach between James and Danby.

loyalty of the very same course of action as that to which Courtin was now urging him; at first, indeed, he promised Courtin to take his advice, but in spite of repeated reminders he failed to implement his promise, and after the scheme had been under discussion for over two months he told the ambassador that he would not enter into any intrigue contrary to the King's interests and intentions, adding, however, that he had no particular understanding with Danby and that he would always be ready to give the King the advice he thought best for his service. He continued until late in the year 1677 to work against Danby for the dissolution, but by February of that year he was no longer contemplating adopting Courtin's plan and was working with Danby in the management of Parliament, and in October Barrillon, Courtin's successor, said that James had several times spoken to him of Danby with esteem, and had said that Danby was exposed to the intrigues of Arlington, the most adroit courtier in England, and of others who had the King's ear, but that he was an able man, and if he were not crossed he would be an eminently successful Minister.

Courtin's plan, however, simmered in James's mind, and he attempted to put it into operation in April 1678—that is to say, he approached the leaders of the opposition to the Court behind Danby's back and without, as Courtin had proposed, trying to gain his ends by privately threatening the Minister. Danby had exasperated James in the late autumn of 1677 by promoting the marriage of Princess Mary to William of Orange, but what his fresh offence was does not appear; possibly he had continued to advocate war against France when James had already advised Charles to accept Louis's terms. By that time, however, there was evidence of a personal estrangement; Louis in his instructions to Courtin, when he took up his Embassy in the spring of 1676, noted signs in Danby of a desire to be independent of James, whose slow-moving mind must constantly have galled the Minister's quick intelligence; and towards the end of the same year Danby and Lauderdale began to be frightened at their own unpopularity: they began to realise that James as an ally was a liability rather than an asset, for he loaded them with the imputation of being lukewarm on the subject of religion. Courtin certainly thought they were looking for an opportunity to show themselves zealous Protestants, and even to save themselves by taking the lead in the coming parliamentary attack on James; in May 1677 Sir John Reresby had had a conversation with Danby in which Danby had spoken of James in disparaging terms, and in September 1677 it was said that "the Duke and the Lord Treasurer are far from being friends". There are two mutually contradictory accounts of the abortive negotiations between James and the opposition leaders.

Shaftesbury left among his papers a long confidential memorandum on the condition of public affairs in the spring of 1679; in the memorandum it is stated that James sent Sir Thomas Littleton and Sir John Baber to Shaftesbury and two of his associates (probably Lord Russell and Lord Hollis), offering to "procure the dissolution of this Parliament and the calling of a new one and the removal of the Treasurer, and thereupon desired to know what the King and he might expect in return for so great a benefit by him obtained unto the whole kingdom"; and that the reply was to the effect that the three lords agreed that what was proposed was eminently desirable, but that they could not fetter their liberty by entering into any engagement as to their future conduct. James's own version is preserved in his memoirs: he says that Lord Russell and others proposed to him that in return for his assistance in prosecuting Danby and getting him dismissed, "they would undertake to remove the incapacity under which he lay of being High Admiral or exercising any public office, and do anything else that might be for his satisfaction"; and that he replied in a lofty tone scorning the possibility of his "falling upon the King's Minister without the King's consent, unless he were visibly guilty of some great misbehaviour". The former account is contemporary and not, as far as we know, composed for publication, the latter is what James wished posterity to believe. It is very improbable that Lord Russell ever contemplated absolving James from the penalties of the Test Act, and quite impossible that Shaftesbury could believe that he could put such a proposition before his followers without breaking up the party. On the other hand, we shall see that a year later James thought that Shaftesbury might be won back to the Court party, and he was quite capable of believing that the principles of the country party were rooted little deeper than in personal animosity against Danby.[1]

In 1676 James, yielding no doubt to steady pressure exerted for over two years by Mary Beatrice, decided to cease to attend the services of the Church of England, as from 1672 he had absented himself from the Sacrament. He made a semi-public declaration that "he would never more come under the roof of Whitehall Chapel", and it was

[1] Osmond Airy, however (*Charles II*, pp. 305–306), without giving references, states that in the late summer of 1675 Shaftesbury and James had entered into a close alliance, which included Louis, to counteract Danby's scheme of Cavalier Anglicanism, and that James had received £20,000 from France for distribution at the end of the session, on condition that Parliament took no action hostile to France. "Louis had tricked both Charles and the Commons by this intrigue, which was carried out in the profoundest secrecy." In spite of this weighty opinion to the contrary, I hold that it was not in James's nature to pursue a line of policy secret from Charles and hostile to his interests.

generally known that at Easter he had taken the Sacrament in accordance with Roman rites. This action raised a fresh storm about James's ears: whatever slight doubt there had lingered in the public mind as to his change of faith had now vanished; nothing was discussed but the new situation, parsons all over the kingdom preached that the Church was in danger and that it was Louis's aim to ruin it; the prevalent sentiment was one of fear of what James might do if he came to the throne: "the whole of England apprehends that a Prince who is capable of exposing himself to the risk of losing a crown for the sake of his zeal for the Catholic religion, will carry things to all lengths in order to establish it". To Charles James's virtual declaration of his conversion was a severe blow: he showed his exasperation by telling his friends that James had ruined all his plans and that his misfortunes were entirely due to him; in an interview with Courtin he exclaimed with unwonted heat that his brother had got himself into a mess from which it would be a great trouble to extract him, and he repeated an opinion that he had previously expressed, that if he were to die James would not be able to remain a week in England.[1]

The suggestion was revived that James should voluntarily withdraw from the Court until the excitement had subsided, and Danby sent the Earl of Bristol to him to try to persuade him to that course. James was unwilling to go, and he received strong support from Charles in his refusal. In spite of his anger against his brother he could not do without him: he said that the religious question was only a pretext, and that the real object of Parliament was to separate him from James, "who is the only person in England in whom I can have entire confidence"—no one but James knew the whole of Charles's commitments with Louis, even Danby, who, Charles said, was a thoroughly honest man and who served him faithfully, and was in these respects "alone in England with the Duke of York", was not in complete possession of the secret. The ambassador strove to strengthen Charles in his resolution to keep James at his side, for James, besides being "the firmest support the King had within his kingdom", was very valuable to the French interest, he was as much attached to Louis as Charles was and had more firmness and application to business; Charles was ready to listen to his advice and was by him confirmed and maintained in the resolutions he had taken; moreover James was bound to France by his interests as a Catholic: "Nothing is so important for Your Majesty's interests," wrote Courtin to Louis, "as to prevent the withdrawal from public

[1] A considered judgement of Charles is reported that James would not be able to keep his crown for more than four years; but authority appears to be lacking. It is possibly a prophecy invented after the Revolution.

business of the Duke of York; if such an event took place the King of England surrounded on all sides by the enemies of France will be forced to follow the advice of his minister in order to get money from parliament and at the same time to please his subjects."

Meanwhile Danby was constant in his advice that Parliament should be summoned; the treasury was empty and the Navy had been allowed to fall into decay and must be refitted. "In order to shut his mouth", James, with equal constancy, urged on the ambassador the necessity of subsidies from France. Charles up to this time at any rate had visions of a day when he should come to that point of agreement with Parliament in which they would supply him with money sufficient for his needs, but experience had only hardened James in his conviction that Monarchy and Parliament could not exist together. The basis of government was to him (as far as he considered the matter on broad lines) that Louis should provide sufficient funds to supplement the King's hereditary income and the revenues granted to him for life; but it is difficult to believe that he was of opinion that such a temporary expedient could ever form part of a permanent system. Perhaps he did not look so far ahead.

CHAPTER VII

WILLIAM AND MARY

THE marriage of James's elder daughter Mary to his nephew William of Orange, son of his sister Mary, was the outcome of protracted negotiations. The first hint of the possibility of the match was made in the winter of 1670–1671, when William was twenty and Mary in her ninth year. By the autumn of 1673, when England was still at war with Holland, it had become a matter of common talk, and the anti-popish party had made it an object of policy. In February 1674 the Third Dutch War came to an end, and it was expected that negotiations for the marriage would immediately commence. Charles from the first regarded the match favourably; he had a high opinion of William and he thought that such a matrimonial alliance would tend to the stability of affairs in Europe; more particularly he hoped to render James less unpopular and so to diminish his own troubles and "to regain the authority he had lost and to reign peaceably for the remainder of his life". But he did not take Louis's point of view into account—neither Charles nor James appears to have come near to realising Louis's obsession with the northern frontier of France—and the thought that Louis hated William as an obstacle to his dreams of territorial expansion never entered their heads. James, however, saw that if the marriage took place while the French were still at war with the Dutch, Charles might be regarded as taking a side hostile to Louis, and he stipulated that peace should be concluded before there was any definite contract of marriage.

But James had another reason for wishing for delay. In 1673 Canaples, an attaché at the French Embassy, had hinted to him that a marriage might be arranged between Mary and the Dauphin of France; how far this suggestion was made seriously and how far it was merely a cynical attempt to play on James's feelings does not appear. But James seized on the plan eagerly: nothing could more fully satisfy his ambition than to see his daughter married to the heir to the crown of France, and the fact that she would of necessity become a Catholic no doubt added to the attractiveness of the project. In April 1674 Ruvigny, the French ambassador, had a conversation with James which he reported to Louis. James told the ambassador that he had not thought of the marriage with the Dauphin until Canaples had made the first overture, but it was clear to Ruvigny that he had since thought of it a great deal. James said that Charles had spoken to him of the match with William on the way to Newmarket and that there was a party at Court, headed by Arlington and Ormonde, who were trying to press it on; but he was doing all he could to prevent a decision so as to keep open the scheme for the French match. Ruvigny told James

> that he had other strong reasons to fear the conclusion of this marriage as he feared death, that he should regard the Prince of Orange as the idol of the English people, and that such a son-in-law would inevitably prove his ruin.

He said further, and James agreed with him, that Arlington in supporting the match was governed by ulterior motives, among them, no doubt, a desire to steal a march on Danby. James said that it would not be difficult to postpone decision, as Mary was not yet twelve years old. "But," says Ruvigny, "I knew that what he said to me was always in the hope of having the Dauphin, for he mentioned him from time to time." Ruvigny said he saw no reason for undeceiving James about the French match; indeed, it would have been difficult to undeceive him, so fixed was the idea in his mind; he did, however, go so far as to tell James that the match would be so unpopular in England as to lead to a revolution, "for the English would never expose themselves to the risk of seeing the heir to the throne of France reigning over them".[1] The ambassador concludes his letter with words of satisfaction at what he has done to counteract the persuasions of Charles. What seems clear from this account is that James had kept his ambition for his daughter as a secret locked in his own heart and known to no one except the French diplomatists, and that in particular he had not discussed it with Charles; he probably knew all about it, saw through the artifice and was convinced that James had been played with. On receipt of Ruvigny's report the French Court suggested a match between Mary and Francis Louis, Prince of Conti, Condé's nephew, but Ruvigny dared not broach the project to James, for he knew that he would have rejected it in a rage as a poor substitute for what he had hoped for.

In November 1674 Arlington, with Ossory as his companion, was sent on a special mission to The Hague. The object of the mission was the settlement of a number of questions arising out of the peace which had been concluded at the beginning of the year, but Charles

[1] As late as the eve of the marriage of William and Mary, Charles said that certain opposition members of Parliament had made their peace with him on the news of the marriage, "for they had been persuaded that a resolution had been taken to marry the Dauphin to Princess Mary" and that England would become a province of France.

was aware that the question of the marriage might arise. He said that he was willing to do anything to secure William to his interests, that the marriage was "the only thing capable of helping the Duke" and that he had spoken to James, who, as became one "who professed to be his brother's first and most obedient subject", had given his consent "upon the Prince of Orange's desiring it". When Arlington and Ossory had returned to England, James, through a misreading of Ossory's report, concluded that he had been over-eager and had made an offer of Mary's hand; Ossory was able to point out the error, but James refused to be convinced. William had mentioned the scheme of the marriage only to lay it aside; he was at that time in no haste to take it up: he had been captain-general of the United Provinces since the early spring of 1672 and became Stadtholder of the province of Holland four months later, and the assassination of the brothers De Witt in August of that year had left him in a predominant position in the country; the English Court was known by the Dutch to be in friendly relations with Louis, with whom the Dutch were still at war, and William no doubt felt that the proposed matrimonial alliance would create misunderstandings in the minds of his fellow-countrymen.

The next move in the projected marriage was made by Sir William Temple, who had a rather cryptic exchange of remarks with James on the subject when he was starting for The Hague in the spring of 1675 and a year later had a two hours' conversation with William in the gardens of Honslaerdyck. William stated his public objection to the match, which was that as things were in England he hesitated to ally himself with Charles and James lest he should be thought to support their domestic policy and should incur unpopularity; on the personal side he said that he himself might be difficult to live with, but he could not contemplate marriage with "one to give him trouble at home", in view of the immense public troubles that he saw ahead of him. Temple reassured him on both points: he said that Charles was very safely seated on the throne and that it was necessary only to satisfy the Court (Temple had no great understanding or facility in home affairs), but that if circumstances should alter, "the most seditious man in England would be hard put to it to find an ill side in such a match". And he could give perfect reassurance with regard to Mary's character: his wife and sister knew Mary's governess intimately, and, from what they had learned from her and from what he had himself observed, he had formed the highest opinion of the young Princess.

These arguments seem to have sunk into William's mind, for when, in the autumn of the following year, he paid a visit to England, he was fully determined to marry Mary if he could get her on his own terms, a determination which was strengthened by seeing her for the first time since she had left the nursery. William's position in the United Provinces had altered for the worse in the three years which had elapsed since the embassy of Arlington and Ossory. The lack of striking success in his struggle with Louis had disappointed the Dutch, and he had offended their republican susceptibility by ill-judged and premature action to improve his political status, which had been suspected as an attempt at monarchy. He was yet far from the position he achieved at the end of his life, when it could be said of him (with, however, only an approximation to the truth) that though he was only Stadtholder in England, he was King in Holland. He was more inclined than formerly, therefore, to any course which might strengthen the Dutch externally and raise his prestige at home.

James was suspected of a strong dislike to the match, but there can be no doubt that he liked William; when his visit was determined on he sent him a very cordial letter of welcome, and when he arrived he installed him in his own lodgings at Whitehall. He had also probably rid himself of the illusion that he could marry Mary to a Catholic, and if she was to have a Protestant husband he was quite content that William should be the man. Louis was strong in opposition to William's visit; he was anxious to secure an advantageous peace with the Dutch, but he did not think that a personal discussion between the Stadtholder and his uncles would serve that end, and under his instructions Barrillon did what he could to have the invitation cancelled. The ambassador also tried in vain to sound James as to his personal views: James told him that he would take no important step without consulting Louis, but he avoided saying that he had any aversion to the match.

William arrived at Newmarket on October 9, and it was nine days before he began to discuss the marriage or any other business; but he paid great court to James and was present regularly at his *coucher* and very often at his *levée*. Barrillon began to think that his object in coming was not the marriage but an alliance with England to provide for the future, though he could hardly expect to engage the King and Duke to declare against Louis. But on the 18th William abruptly approached James on the subject of the marriage; James was shocked, as was Charles also, at William's brusque methods, and told him that there were many things to be discussed before the question of the marriage could be raised. To Barrillon James declared with heat that his nephew was "a self-opinionated man, who took advice from no one and had been badly brought up", and that there could be no question of the marriage until peace had been concluded; James also reiterated his promise to take no step without Louis's advice. But the ambassador was again disappointed that James had not taken the opportunity to state a personal view against the marriage.

Charles and James had hoped to use the marriage as a bribe to induce William to accept Louis's terms of peace. William had no motive for conciliating Louis, he knew nothing of the secret treaty of the previous year, and he wanted the marriage to take place at once so that his declared friendship with the English Court should give him an advantage in the negotiations for peace. Temple was called in to mediate: he found William rigid in his determination to marry Mary before the peace or not at all, and in despair when he learnt that the royal brothers were equally determined on the other side, Temple said, "He was in the worst humour ever I saw". But Danby saw in the marriage a great opportunity to diminish his own unpopularity, on grounds of policy he was attracted by a project adverse to the French interest, and he advised Charles to give way; there was also a danger, amounting almost to a certainty, that, if William were allowed to return home without at least a contract of marriage, Charles would be forced into it by popular clamour, and so lose the access of popularity that would follow action on his own initiative. Charles sent Temple to James to inform him that he had decided to accept William's terms; James was shocked, but he recovered himself sufficiently to say, "The King shall be obeyed, and I would be glad all his subjects would learn of me to obey him: I do tell him my mind freely upon any thing; but when that is done, and I know his pleasure upon it, I obey him." Temple returned to the Prince, who at first refused to believe him, but when he was convinced that he was speaking the truth he embraced him "and said I had made him a very happy man".

This was on October 20, 1677, and the following afternoon James took Mary aside and told her what Fate had in store for her, "whereupon her Highness wept all that afternoon and the following day". In the evening the Privy Council were informed of the decision, James made them a little speech to the effect that his chief end in all his actions was the security of the kingdom and that he would never interfere in the religious education of his children, and the news and the speech were well received; a few days later he made a similar speech in the House of Lords. The marriage was solemnised on November 4 at nine o'clock at night in Mary's bedchamber, only James, Mary Beatrice and the King being present; Charles punctuated the service with small jests, and "at eleven o'clock they went to bed, and His Majesty came and drew the curtains, and said to the Prince, 'Now, nephew, to your work! Hey! St. George for England.' "

The marriage, which in the long run was to turn out happily, and incidentally was to be fatal to James, commenced under the shadow of William's boorishness. Once married, he saw no necessity for behaving to his bride in public kindly, or even with courtesy; he thought only of getting back to Holland and to the business of his life, and he chafed bitterly at the contrary winds that delayed him. In the end he insisted on putting to sea when it was almost impossible to beat up against the wind. There is an amusing contemporary description of the farewell scene and of William's reaction to it:

> There was a very sad parting between the Princess and her father, but especially the Duchess and her, who wept both with that excess of sorrow that the Prince, though the wind still is so bad that they can tug but eight miles a day, will not return again as he says to make a second scene of grief.

And he held to his resolution in spite of cordial letters from Charles and James begging him to come to them to wait in London for a change of wind.

James could make capital in England out of his daughter's marriage, but placating Louis was a more difficult matter. Barrillon was shocked to learn on October 22 that negotiations for the marriage were far advanced, and when Charles had unburdened his mind to him he saw that it was "a matter resolved on". Charles said:

> I consider it very useful to my interests, and I believe I shall get very considerable advantage from it immediately and still more advantage in the future. This alliance will put a stop to my subjects' suspicion that the close touch I keep with France is based on a change of religion. It is my brother's conduct that has given rise to all these suspicions. All the jealousy and animosity that there is in this country against the prosperity of France springs from what he has done.

James when he next saw Barrillon was much embarrassed: he said that Charles had insisted on his submission against his will and that Danby had worked for the marriage behind the scenes in order to fortify himself against his enemies; he hoped that Louis would excuse him, "for he valued his esteem more than anything in the world". Three days later James told Barrillon that the marriage would bring the peace nearer because the anti-Orange faction would suspect that it was part of a plot to make William absolute in the United Provinces by English help and they would work for peace in order that William's army might be disbanded—a curiously accurate forecast.

Louis was furious; he had no knowledge of the course of the negotiations in England and he was unwittingly unjust to James: "he spoke of the King's part in it more decently, but expostulated severely on the Duke's part, who had now given his daughter to the greatest enemy he had in the world", and to Ralph Montagu, the English ambassador in Paris, the French King "spoke very hardly of the Duke for consenting to it, and not at least acquainting him with it". It was rumoured in Paris that as soon as he realised the danger of the conclusion of the marriage contract, Louis formed the project of reviving the plan for a French husband for Mary, but Danby heard the rumour after the decision had been made in favour of William, and it does not appear that even tentative proposals were ever received by the English Court.

In England there was general rejoicing at the marriage; in London "the whole night was spent in the ringing of bells and bonfires and the greatest expressions of joy which I believe were ever in England, except at the King's Restoration", and in many provincial towns there were similar demonstrations of joy. It was said that in England only Barrillon and Arlington were dissatisfied at the news, Arlington because he had professed to be deeper in William's confidence than any other Englishman, had failed to rob Danby of the credit of the match, and had been totally unaware of what was going on. From Holland masters of ships brought the news that the generality of the people of Holland received the news of the intended marriage joyfully; but the marriage did William no good with the ruling classes, for the Stuarts were not popular with them, and they dreaded, as James had said they would, a family compact to subvert the liberties of the English and Dutch. A Dutch pamphlet alluded to "the ambitious spirit of the Prince of Orange supported by his future father-in-law the Duke of York"; and the Danish Resident at The Hague wrote to his Court: "The joy here at the marriage is neither complete nor universal, and the celebrations are for the most part conducted in a hypocritical spirit."

William during his short stay in England did more than acquire a wife: he used his great diplomatic talents to such purpose that he succeeded in undermining the fervent and blind loyalty with which Charles and James had for the previous seven or eight years served Louis, and in making them, for a few months only, it is true, critical and distrustful of French policy; incidentally he achieved a signal triumph by leaving James with the impression that the honours of the diplomatic exchanges had remained on the English side, and that Charles and he had persuaded William to accept their proposals for a peace. There can be little doubt that it was William who convinced Charles and James that Louis's conquests in the Spanish Netherlands were a threat to the security of England, thus bringing them into line with the traditional English policy of keeping Antwerp and Ostend out of the possession of a first-class Power. "He who holds Antwerp", said Napoleon, "holds a pistol levelled at the heart of England," and this maxim was part of our political creed in the time of Elizabeth and earlier, and still underlay British strategy in the wars of the present century.

On his return to the United Provinces after his marriage, William announced to the States-General that, either a speedy peace would be concluded on reasonable terms through the good offices of the King of England, or a close union would be formed with that Prince; and the hope of English assistance reanimated the Dutch war-party. On November 22 the Earl of Feversham was sent to Paris on a mission to Louis to propose certain terms of peace which had been formulated by Charles at William's instigation; these terms would, it was thought, by the restoration to Spain of a number of Flemish fortresses which the French had taken, provide a sufficient barrier to protect the United Provinces against aggression, and at the same time satisfy English susceptibilities regarding the Flemish ports. But William had overrated Louis's dependence on Charles's goodwill; Louis was indignant that Charles should have had the effrontery to propose such terms as would (he wrote to Barrillon) "rob me not only of a great part of the conquests I have made in a war declared against me by Spain, but of the chief places which I acquired under the Treaty of Aix la Chapelle". He did not condescend even to consider or discuss Charles's suggested terms, but told Feversham in his first interview that he might tell the King of England "how surprised he had been at receiving such proposals and how little inclined he was to accept them".

Charles was now embarrassed to find himself at the head of a nation bent on a war with France of which he himself, from long habit of mind, strongly disapproved. But for the moment his fear of popular tumult outweighed his fear of Louis's displeasure, and to Barrillon he made no secret of the unpleasantness of the dilemma in which he was; the news that Parliament was to meet, coming so soon after the long-desired marriage, caused an outbreak of enthusiasm, and it was believed that war had already been declared against France. Charles was forced to assume a bellicose attitude, and in his speech on January 28, 1678, at the opening of Parliament he stated that he had failed to make an honourable and safe peace by negotiation, and had been driven to make war in alliance with the Dutch, and he demanded supplies sufficient to equip ninety ships and thirty or forty thousand soldiers.

The House of Commons replied to the King's speech by an address in which they urged him not to agree to any treaty of peace with France which did not reduce the boundaries of that kingdom to the limits prescribed by the Treaty of the Pyrenees of 1659—that is to say, that Louis should be compelled to renounce the gains made by the Peace of Aix-la-Chapelle of 1668 as well as his conquests since 1672. Charles whispered to Barrillon, "They seem to have lost heart: you must have bribed them into making such an extravagant proposal"; to which the ambassador replied drily, "I do not think that money would have been well employed in making them pass a resolution of this sort." Later Charles told Barrillon,

> that this demonstration had been indispensible to appease the English, where fears had outrun all reason; that in his heart he did not want war and that he would do anything he could do avoid it;

and when Barrillon called attention to the activities of James and to his proposed departure for Flanders to take command of the English troops, Charles replied:

> I tell you frankly that my brother's talk pains me. We have not yet a penny for the raising of troops and he speaks as if we had an army. The idea of being a general has gone to his head, but for my part I have no belief in these war plans. I am not persuaded that anything can be done in alliance with the Spaniards.

Charles sent a few troops to Ostend—sufficient to alarm the Dutch but not enough to cause disquiet to Louis—but he did not declare war on France, and the continued residence in England of Barrillon, and the close touch which he kept with Charles and James, contributed more than any other single cause to the preservation of peace between the two countries.

But William had been more successful with James: he was a whole-hearted convert to the war-party, and in concert with Danby he drove on the preparations with all the great zeal of which he was capable. The motives of Danby were simple: his natural bias was anti-French, and that bias had not been weakened by long suppression in the course of serving Charles's pro-French policy; he was also anxious, by heading the popular movement against France, to avoid the attack which the opposition in Parliament were preparing to launch against him. James's motives were more complex and doubtful: as a patriotic Englishman (as he undoubtedly was), he had been impressed by William's arguments and alarmed at the situation which would be created by a French occupation of the Spanish Netherlands—even before Louis had rejected the terms conveyed to Louis by the hand of Feversham, Danby wrote to William that, at a discussion with Charles and James on the situation in Flanders,

> to my great admiration the Duke said very briskly that in case they do not agree to the propositions sent by my Lord Feversham, the King ought to let the King of France know that, unless he would forbear any further conquests in Flanders, he could not hinder England from coming into the war;

and a few days later James told Barrillon that Charles could not possibly have done otherwise than to enter the war; had he not prevented the occupation of Flanders, all his subjects, with no exception but James himself, would have rebelled. James had quite as much reason as Danby for attempting to reinstate himself in popular favour by taking the lead in a popular movement; and he certainly had an aspiration (in spite of the Test Act) to command the English army which was being raised or even, it was hinted, the whole allied army.

What is doubtful is his ultimate intention with regard to that army: did he intend to allow it to be disbanded at the end of the war, or to do his best to persuade Charles to keep it in being as a standing army, and to use it for the abolition of parliamentary government and for the accomplishment of the Grand Design? Barrillon at any rate had no illusions about his intentions; on April 18, 1678, he wrote to Louis:

> The Duke of York believes himself lost because of his religion, if the present opportunity does not serve to bring England into subjection; it is a very bold enterprise and the success very doubtful. I believe they have persuaded this Prince that a war is more proper to accomplish his design than peace. He thinks that by declaring strongly against France he will diminish the animosity against himself. This does not appease his enemies; he is more suspected than ever and not less hated; his change with regard to your Majesty does not add to his reputation; many persons believe he will return to his former engagements with the same lightness with which he has quitted them. The King of England still wavers upon carrying things to extremity; his humour is very repugnant to the design of changing the government. He is nevertheless drawn along by the Duke of York and the Lord Treasurer; but at bottom he would rather choose that a peace should leave him in a condition to remain in quiet, and re-establish his affairs, that is to say a good revenue, and I do not believe he cares much for being more absolute than he is. The Duke and the Treasurer know well with whom they have to deal, and are afraid of being abandoned by

> the King on the first considerable obstacles they meet with to the design of enlarging the royal authority in England.

In short, the ambassador believed that James and Danby, acting in close association, were plotting the overthrow by a *coup d'état* of the historic constitution of the kingdom; it is not easy to believe that Danby was wholeheartedly in this plot; he was certainly a Tory (to anticipate a nickname that became current a couple of years later) and worked to uphold the prerogative, but there is no evidence that he at any time in his career showed a belief in absolutism on the French model, and he was not such a fool as to embark on so hazardous an enterprise with James as his single ally; it is much more likely that for his own purposes he deceived James, and that Barrillon in his turn was deceived.

But whatever James's motives and intentions, the scheme for a war with France ended in a complete fiasco. The House of Commons in great haste and eagerness voted that ninety ships should be put into commission and a force of thirty thousand men raised, but when they should have followed up this vote by voting supply and imposing the necessary taxes they did nothing: the votes for the Army and Navy were passed on Feburary 6 and 8, but it was not until March 8 that they passed a poll bill, calculated to bring in £600,000 out of the required million, and there they stopped; a parliament which had shown such zest for the war refused to furnish the means for carrying it on. James showed his impatience in a series of letters to his son-in-law William: "those who seemed most zealous for a war with France last session are those who obstruct most the giving of a supply"; "it is now near a month that the parliament have sat, and yet not so much as a money bill got ready"; "truly the temper of the House seems not to be good, and looks as if some of them minded more how to get the power from the King than anything else"; "they have such groundless jealousies in their heads that they make no advances in providing the rest of the money."

From the meagre accounts that have come down to us of the debates in the House of Commons during the Session January 15 to March 8, 1678, we gather no impression of a body representing a nation which was entering on a life-and-death struggle with the greatest military Power of the time: there was nothing like the continuity of effort which was displayed upon the subject of exclusion by the Parliament which met on October 21, 1680. They discussed many things—the irregular conduct of the Speaker in adjourning the House, the recusancy of a member, the granting of improper protections by a member to his servants, the resumptions of Crown lands—and only incidentally did they deliberate on the necessities of the war. But French intrigue had been busy among the members. At the end of January arrived in England Henri de Ruvigny, son of the late ambassador; he was first cousin of Rachel, Lady Russell, wife of the eldest son of the Earl of Bedford, and his visit was ostensibly to his relations; actually his intention was to get into touch with the leaders of the Opposition. To Russell and his friends Ruvigny furnished arguments, to less scrupulous members of the party he gave bribes; the argument which appealed most to his hearers, since it strengthened suspicions already in their minds, was that Charles had no intention of making war and that any funds which Parliament might supply would be used for other purposes; they may have been a little sceptical when he told them that Louis had no interest in making Charles absolute in England and that he had never been in treaty with him to alter the religion of this country. Russell promised to help Shaftesbury to prevent any increase in the subsidies voted by Parliament, and to have such conditions attached to the grants already made that Charles would rather give up the war than consent to them. The dilemma in which the Country party was placed was well expressed in the House of Commons by Sir William Coventry: "If a war really be, he must be a madman who will not give money; and if it be a peace no Englishman will be for keeping up the army"; for the rule of Cromwell's major-generals was still fresh in memory, and "No Standing Army" was second only to "No Popery" as a rallying cry for all except the extremists of the Court party.

The outburst of popular indignation in England at Louis's threat to annex the Spanish Netherlands, carrying Charles with it on its flood and zealously encouraged by James—whose fidelity had been the one certainty in England on which the French interest could rely—had no doubt considerable effect in inclining Louis to peace and in moderating his demands. The Dutch were financially exhausted by the war and were thoroughly tired of it, though William's spirit was not curbed, and he had renewed his courage by his matrimonial alliance with England and by the treaty which had been signed with that country on December 31, 1677. But it was not to William that Louis made his overtures: the Dutch people and their representatives, the Municipalities, the States, and the States-General, had been alarmed at the possible consequences to their republican institutions of the marriage of William and Mary, and when they saw English troops landed at Ostend, and heard that they were forerunners of a large army, they felt that their worst fears had been confirmed. A situation arose similar to that which had arisen in England, and it was generally believed, as Danby had previously warned William that it would be, that the alliance had not been made for the purpose of resisting the aggression of Louis, but "that the King of England and the Prince of Orange had laid their plans for the subjection of the two countries". Modifications of Louis's demands, and the plea that what he proposed to leave to Spain would provide an ample barrier to the Dutch, disposed the leaders of the States-General to an accommodation; by May William himself was in favour of peace, at the end of that month full agreement upon all points appeared to have been reached between the French and Dutch, and in June letters were exchanged, effusive on William's side, reserved on Louis's, between the two great antagonists.

Simultaneously the delay in England in the preparations for war gave Barrillon full opportunity to exert pressure upon Charles and James. Charles had been ready to be persuaded from the first, and he must have experienced considerable relief when he realised that the House of Commons had lost its eagerness for the war and that he was free to take his own line. James's change of mind is more difficult to explain: as late as April 16 he wrote to William about "good and vigorous resolutions for carrying on the war", and "that he did not know what may happen if the war does not go on, considering the temper of the nation"; a month later, as a culmination of discussions which must have occupied several weeks, James helped Barrillon to persuade Charles to sign a new secret agreement with Louis:

> I pressed the King and the Duke of York [says Barrillon on May 17] very warmly to conclude or to break off the treaty—The Duke of York took up the affair with warmth, and made the King give me his positive word that the business should be concluded today. The Duke of York appears greatly desirous to deserve the same share of Your Majesty's good graces which he had heretofore; he conducted himself in the negotiation as I could wish.

The terms of the agreement were, in brief, that Charles in exchange for six million *livres* (£450,000) should prorogue Parliament for four months, should disband his new army, and should use his influence with the Dutch to persuade them to accept Louis's terms.

Four days after Barrillon's letter James wrote to William:

> You see how little is to be expected from hence by what passed the other day in the last session. And now they are to meet again on Thursday, and I fear they will be very disorderly and that it will be all we can do to keep things quiet here at home; for now the ill men in the House strike directly at the King's authority, and

> should we have been in a war now, they would have so imposed upon the King as to leave him nothing but the empty name of a King and no more power than a Duke of Venice. . . .
>
> You see I speak my mind freely to you, I am obliged to do it out of the kindness and concern I have for you. I know such a peace as is offered is a very hard one for you and us to submit to; however I see no remedy, and do not exasperate France that may be of use to you. Pray let nobody see this letter, it is only wrote for you and not fit for anybody else to read or know. I say so much to you; 'tis only my kindness has made me write it, and you may be sure I shall always continue it to you.

This letter is a curious combination of diplomatic craft and family affection. He and his brother thought that they had sold William to France, and he was anxious to advise William to do the best for himself possible under the circumstances of the secret treaty. But William was already negotiating, or preparing to negotiate, behind the backs of his uncles.

Louis at the last moment raised a fresh point in the negotiations with the Dutch: he decided that he would not restore to Spain the barrier fortresses which he had promised to restore unless and until the Elector of Brandenburg had restored Bremen and Pomerania to Sweden. This was a condition which had no bearing on his differences with the Dutch and which they had no means of fulfilling. The Dutch resumed the war, and Charles and James were furious. This time Charles did not dissemble; he genuinely felt that Louis had played him false. He kept Parliament in session, he did not recall his troops from Ostend, and on July 16 he concluded a fresh treaty with the Dutch. To Barrillon he declared "that all he had done went for nothing in France, that he had persuaded the States-General to make peace, and that, if he disbanded his army and Louis took considerable fortresses in Flanders, he would be in danger of being driven from his kingdom for having betrayed national interests". James was even more violent, "he expressed himself with great heat, and did all that he could to persuade everybody that war was inevitable". However, one of the Swedish ambassadors intervened with a suggestion of a compromise; this compromise was accepted by Louis and by the States-General and peace was signed on July 31. The only result for Charles of his intervention in the rupture of negotiations was that he lost the six million *livres*.

To James the result was even more serious. He had built up a reputation with Louis as a steadfast adherent of the French interest, and, while

Louis was resigned to Charles's vacillations, he looked to James to keep his brother loyal to his engagements. On this occasion James had not only gone astray himself, but had carried Charles with him, and after having been forgiven he had repeated the offence. Louis was already angry with James over Mary's marriage, and it was many years before he fully forgave him; indeed, the distrust with which Louis treated James after his accession may have had its roots in the resentment of this time. James on his side made repeated efforts to recover his place in Louis's good graces, but without success. In September 1679 he wrote to the French King, "It is from you I expect all, and by you alone I can attain my re-establishment in this country"; and at the end of the following year he wrote to Barrillon:

> I received your letter with a great deal of satisfaction, because you give me fresh assurances of the King your master's goodness to me; I will endeavour to deserve the continuance of it, whereof I beg you to assure him;

and there are other similar expressions in the correspondence. But Henry Savile, who succeeded Ralph Montague as envoy in Paris, wrote in May 1679 to his brother, Lord Halifax:

> I am very confident the Duke of York remains under the same displeasure with this King that he has done ever since the marriage of the Prince of Orange and the zeal he shewed last year to enter into the war; but I will not doubt but when you have made him desperate in England, upon the least application he will make here he shall be received into favour as a proper instrument to hurt England with.

This reinstatement actually took place when James was in Scotland in 1681; but it was only temporary then, for in September 1683 Lord Preston, the new resident, wrote from Paris to Halifax:

> I am sorry the Duke thinketh that France is firm to him. If I see anything, not withstanding all promises, the old rancour remaineth.

Sometime in the years 1678 to 1680 James severed his relations with Arabella Churchill and adopted a new mistress in the person of Catherine Sedley. John Evelyn had met this lady in 1673 and had pronounced her "none of the most virtuous but a wit"; in 1677 Catherine was proposed as a wife successively for John Churchill and for Sir Edward Hungerford, and in April 1678 she became a maid of honour to Mary

Beatrice. Two years later the fact that she was James's mistress was public property; for the Dowager Countess of Sunderland wrote to Halifax on July 1, 1680, "Some say that the Duchess of York is with child, others that she is melancholy, not for Mrs. Sedley, but greater matters"; and again on July 8, "The Duchess of York is not with child. She prays all day almost. She is very melancholy, the women will have it for Mrs. Sedley. She looks further than that, if she has so much wit as is thought by some"; and in October Henry Sidney wrote to William of Orange, "The Duchess is very melancholy, but whether it proceeds from the apprehensions of making another journey, or seeing the Duke so publicly own Mrs. Sedley, I cannot tell."

From that time until the Revolution, after which, as far as is known, James and Catherine never saw one another, the mistress exercised over James a fascination from which from time to time he vainly attempted to free himself. As a woman she seems to have been a sort of Nell Gwynne in high life: like Nell Gwynne, her greatest asset was an impudent wit; especially was she prone, as Nell was, to describe her own status in a coarse monosyllable. Of both women it is true that they never had a chance in life: Nell's account of herself was that she was "brought up in a brothel to fill strong water to the gentlemen"; Catherine's father, one of the minor Restoriation poets, was a byword among the rakes—"worse than Sir Charles Sedley" is the worst that Pepys can say of another member of the fraternity. Catherine is best remembered by her sayings or rather the sayings that have been imputed to her: of James's attachment to her she said, "It cannot be my beauty because I haven't any, and it cannot be my wit because he hasn't enough of it himself to know that I have any"; to Queen Mary she is said to have retorted, "If I broke one of the Commandments *with* your father, you have broke another *against* him"; and when, after the accession of George I, she met simultaneously William III's mistress Elizabeth Villiers and the Duchess of Portsmouth, then a very old woman, she exclaimed, "Fancy we three * * * meeting like this."

CHAPTER VIII

THE POPISH PLOT: THE FALL OF DANBY

In the summer of 1678 James's prospects were not bright. He had done nothing in two years to mitigate the access of unpopularity which he had incurred by his abstention from attendance at church. He had hoped to have gained some credit from the marriage to William of Orange of his daughter Mary; but the manner in which that marriage had been brought about had given the impression, not entirely false, that he had unwillingly acquiesced in it. The only way in which he could have used the marriage to his advantage would have been to have appeared beforehand enthusiastically in favour of it; in his speeches to the Privy Council and to the House of Lords after the marriage agreement had been completed he was naturally held to be trying to acquire merit for a proceeding which he had opposed. His bellicose attitude against France in the winter and spring of 1677 to 1678 had done him harm rather than good in the public eye, for no one believed that this attitude was more than a cloak for designs on the national religion and liberties.

Any increase in James's unpopularity, and in the certainty of his conversion to Rome, of necessity brought with it an increase in the suspicion and hatred with which his fellow-Catholics were regarded, and by the time that Titus Oates launched his charges against them the public mind was in a condition to accept without examination the wildest accusations. Oates did not create the national fear and abhorrence of the Catholics: he merely exploited it and raised it to a frenzy. Though he was the chief criminal, the entire nation must share the blame in the greatest of our national crimes; for there were few, except the Catholics themselves, who had any doubts about the truth of Oates's stories, and it was the popular ferment that drove on the judges and juries to inflict death on innocent victims, and not pressure from above—Charles certainly would have stayed the effusion of blood if he could.

James's conduct was thus the indirect cause of Oates's pretended revelations. He was also directly responsible for bringing them to public notice. On August 13 Oates's advance guard, Kirkby, informed Charles that there was a plot against his life; Charles thought so little about it that he went off to Windsor next day with James, leaving with Danby instructions to investigate this plot and to keep the matter a secret even from James. At Windsor Father Bedingfield, James's confessor, received a parcel of clumsily forged letters directed to himself and presumably intended to incriminate him; he showed these letters to James, and James took them to Charles, and, not daring to conceal accusations against the Catholics, and secure, as he thought, in the innocence of the accused, demanded an investigation by the Council.

The Bedingfield forgeries gave James the first intimation that anything was afoot, and when he showed them to Charles, Charles may well have told him of Kirkby's warnings and made him realise that an attack on the Catholics had been organised. He probably learnt at the same time that one of the persons named by Oates was Edward Coleman, a man very well known to him. The characteristic of Coleman that most impressed contemporaries was his vanity, and that characteristic is very prominent in his letters. For example, he writes:

> When it happened that what I foresaw came to pass, the good Father was not a little surprised to see all the great men mistaken and a little one [Coleman himself] in the right, and was pleased to desire a continuance of my correspondence;

and his account of affairs of the previous two years, written in September 1675 to Père la Chaise, Louis's confessor, abounds in claims that if his advice had been taken fewer mistakes would have been made. Coleman had been secretary to the Duchess of York, but he had had many other duties: he had been in close touch with successive French ambassadors and had been employed by them as a link with the House of Commons, on the one hand as a reporter of each day's proceedings, and on the other as a distributor of bribes. He had incurred considerable suspicion and had had to leave London for a time and to give up his post as secretary. But he had returned, and in the autumn of 1678 he was again unofficially in the service of Mary Beatrice.

James was well aware that Coleman had been corresponding with Jesuits and others at home and abroad and that the object of his correspondence was the promotion of the Grand Design—the recovery of England to the True Faith by means of a close alliance with France. As soon as he knew that Coleman's name appeared in Oates's deposition he realised that this correspondence would be a dangerous weapon in the hands of the fabricators of the Plot, and he urged Coleman to destroy it. But Coleman's vanity was too strong for such a sacrifice; without these letters he had no proof of the important rôle he had played in international affairs; he destroyed a large number of letters, but he so ineffectively concealed the remainder that they were discovered when he was arrested. There was nothing in these letters which could be made to suggest a plot to assassinate the King, and such a plot was the essence of Oates's accusation against Coleman and against the other men who had been arrested at Oates's instigation. Oates and Bedloe gave evidence that Coleman had been privy to a plot of assassination, but it was on the evidence of his own letters that he was convicted: according to the law in force at the time it was treason to endeavour to subvert the religion of the kingdom, and the sentence was just. James had before the trial no doubt that the evidence of the letters was sufficient to bring him to the scaffold and, though he thought that the other Catholics who suffered the death penalty had all been innocent, he admitted Coleman's guilt.

For James the discovery of Coleman's letters was extremely awkward. Coleman had made very free use of his name, and had in many places stated that he was acting as his agent:

> His Royal Highness is at present surrounded with infinite perplexities (Southwell wrote to Ormonde), which all good men must lament. He has been always present at the Committee of the Lords while the papers of Coleman and Sir William Throgmorton have been read. Each of them have dared to name and interest His Highness in their dangerous contrivances, which he hears with indignation, and appeals to the improbability of his confiding either to the folly of the one or the madness of the other. And yet this does not satisfy the warm spirits of that House and much less is it likely to do that of the Commons.

Another danger to which James was liable was,

> if Mr. Coleman finds himself in extremities and has quite abandoned all hopes of protection from the Duke, that he may then run into much liberty of discourse in order to save his life.

But though according to one observer Coleman was confidently expecting a reprieve up to the time when he mounted the scaffold—or perhaps because he was expecting it and missed the opportunity—he did nothing to incriminate James.

For there can be no doubt that, though James probably did not see Coleman's letters before they were sent, he was sufficiently responsible for their contents to be seriously implicated in Coleman's guilt. The Commons resolved that the letters should be printed, but in the Lords James pleaded that they contained many unsupported calumnies against himself which should not be made public in England and abroad, and secured the rejection of the resolution. If a certain letter (which indeed from internal evidence does not appear to be a forgery) had come to light which James wrote to Père la Chaise in September

1675—the time at which Coleman was conducting that part of his correspondence which he allowed to be seized—there can be little doubt that the House of Commons would have made an attempt to impeach James and that Charles would have had to resort to successive prorogations to save him. In that letter (which is in effect a request for money to promote the Grand Design) occur such passages as:

> All was transacted by the means of Father Ferrier, who made use of Sir William Throgmorton, who is an honest man and of truth, who was then in Paris and hath held correspondence with Coleman, one of my family, in whom I have great confidence;

and

> As to anything more I refer you to Sir William Throgmorton and Coleman, who I have commanded to give an account of the whole state of the affair and of the condition of England.

Coleman, in the course of an examination by a Committee sent by the Lords, said that he had on one occasion gone to Brussels "with the Duke's allowance" to see the Internuncio, and James in the House of Lords explained that

> poor Father Patrick, bringing over some broken story or message from the said Internuncio, he had let Coleman go over to know what it meant;

a sufficiently lame excuse, and one which would naturally have led to a question as to the nature of James's correspondence with the Internuncio; good manners, presumably, restrained the Lords from pressing a royal duke so closely. The House of Commons, however, ordered an inquiry by a secret committee on the evidence of the letters into the part played by James in Coleman's intrigues. But this was so late as the end of April 1679, and there is no record that the Committee reported before the prorogation of May 26. Though James escaped direct attack, the suspicions which Coleman had aroused added enormously to the strength of the attack on James in the debates on the two Exclusion Bills.

The discovery of Coleman's correspondence was very fortunate for Oates: he had accused Coleman at a venture, and his letters had revealed a plot of which Oates had been completely unaware; Coleman's plot bore no relation to the plot which Oates had fabricated, in fact the letters broke off before the earliest date mentioned in Oates's allegations, but an uncritical public regarded them as a confirmation of Oates's statements. Another piece of good fortune (it is barely possible that he contrived it) was the murder of Sir Edmund Berry Godfrey: no sooner had Oates accused the Catholics than by this murder they provided evidence against themselves—or so the public thought.

It is necessary to enter in some detail into this celebrated murder mystery, because some years ago a very ingenious attempt was made to lay it at the door of James or of James's Jesuit friends. Sir Edmund Berry Godfrey, a London magistrate of known probity, left his house near Charing Cross on the morning of Saturday, October 12, 1678, and was missing for five days. On Thursday, October 17, his body was found in a ditch near Primrose Hill, in the open country about three miles from Charing Cross; his neck was broken, his sword had been driven through his body (after death, for there was little sign of effusion of blood), and his money and other valuables on his person were intact. It is possible to suggest suicide only on the supposition that his relations had found his body hanging and, in order to prevent the forfeiture of his estate, had attempted to create a presumption that he had been murdered.

Godfrey's connection with Oates was in his official capacity as a magistrate: on September 6, Oates, Tonge and Kirkby had come to his office for the purpose of registering an oath that certain written information was true—Godfrey was not at that time allowed to see the information; on September 28 Oates came again with two copies of the information which he was laying before the Council; on one of these copies he caused Godfrey to witness his affidavit and the other he left with Godfrey. On the same day Godfrey had a long interview with Coleman, an intimate friend of his, who was to be arrested two days later. Several of his remarks between the dates of his interview with Coleman and his disappearance show that he was apprehensive of a murderous attack, and he told a Mr. Wynnel that he was in possession of a dangerous secret which would be fatal to him; "Oates", he said, "is sworn and is perjured."

Now, Oates's accusation against the Catholics was based on what he stated he had heard and seen at a meeting of the Jesuits held on April 24, 1678, at the White Horse Tavern in the Strand. It was proved in his trial for perjury that Oates was at the Jesuit College of St. Omer on this date and could not have been present at the meeting. As a matter of fact he had got the date right: there *was* a provincial meeting of English Jesuits on April 24, a routine meeting of no political significance, and Oates could easily have heard of it at St. Omer and made a bad guess at the venue. For, as James told Sir John Reresby some years later, the meeting was held at James's official residence, St. James's Palace, and if that fact had become known a very potent weapon would have been put into the hands of James's enemies, and it is possible that he would have had to answer a charge of high treason. The theory of the complicity of James or his friends in the murder of Godfrey rests on the supposition that, at his meeting with Godfrey on September 28, Coleman sought advice as to the best way of meeting Oates's accusations and that he pointed out Oates's mistake about the place of the Jesuits' meeting as a possible means of invalidating his testimony, thus inadvertently putting Godfrey in possession of a secret which he would rather not have known; that in the two days remaining before his arrest Coleman made known his indiscretion to his Jesuit friends; and that they decided that it was not safe, considering the risk to James of the secret coming out, to let Godfrey remain alive: a chain of evidence with several very weak links.[1]

James had been expressly exonerated by Oates in his original deposition from all suspicion of connection with the Plot, but the revelations in Coleman's letters, the damaging evidence which was given to the Commons' Committee, and the apprehension that he might use his influence with his brother to stifle investigation of the Plot led to a personal attack upon him in both Houses of Parliament. On November 2 Lord Shaftesbury in the Lords, and on November 4 Lord Russell in the Commons, moved an address to the King to remove his brother from his person and counsels. On November 4 James

> made a declaration in the House of Peers that he would withdraw himself from all places where any affairs of the nation were agitated, and would no more be present at the Committee of Foreign Affairs or the Admiralty;[2]

and in the House of Commons on the same day Henry Coventry, the Secretary of State, made a similar statement on his behalf. He himself admits, however, that this withdrawal was not voluntary on his part, but that "the King could not persuade the Duke to abstain from Council to prevent an address for removing him from his presence. The Council was forced to order him to do so."[3] Possibly James's unwillingness

[1] For a full discussion of this theory see Sir Chas. Firth's review of Pollock's *Popish Plot* in *English Historical Review,* XIX, 789.

[2] According to Barrillon, James said that his withdrawal was in order to give satisfaction to those who believed that his counsel to the King was harmful. Shaftesbury moved that James's declaration should be embodied in a royal proclamation, but the motion was lost, the House was content with James's verbal promise.

[3] James had not been officially a Privy Councillor since the summer of 1673, nor does his name appear in the Register. It must be inferred that he had been allowed to attend unofficially. Possibly the "Council" to which James referred in his memoirs was the Committee of Foreign Affairs.

became known and there was a fear lest he would return to the inner counsels of the King as soon as parliamentary pressure was withdrawn; whatever the reason, these declarations did not interrupt the course of the debate.

Nothing has been preserved of what was said in the Lords; from the summaries of speeches in the Commons it appears that the supporters of the motion were very careful to say nothing that could give personal offence to James. Lord Cavendish (who as Earl of Devonshire was to be so harshly treated by James as King) said, "I have an extreme veneration for the Duke, for I think the Duke had not the least hand in the Plot. I think his loyalty to his brother is without example; but his being next of blood to the succession of the crown, and what encouragement that may give the Papists to take away the King"; Sir Robert Sawyer, "I can assign no other cause for this dismal attempt that has been discovered, but the hopes the Papists have of the Duke's religion"; Mr. Harwood, "I respect the Duke as Duke, but as he is a Papist let every man lay his hand upon his heart whether his being a Papist has not given encouragement to the Plot"; and so on throughout the debate: variations on the theme "if James had not been a Catholic there would have been no Plot". There is a well-known story to the effect that James, returning in his coach from hunting with a great train of attendants, met Charles scantily attended, and remonstrated with him on the risk he ran of assassination; and that Charles replied, "No kind of danger, James, for no man in England will take away my life to make you King." Clearly the opinion of the House of Commons was that Charles's retort might be true of Protestants, but that many Catholics would be glad of an opportunity to substitute a Catholic for a Protestant king, and would not be very scrupulous about the means they employed.[1]

Charles bowed before the storm: on November 8 Danby informed Reresby that "the King would be content that something were enacted to pare the nails (to use his own phrase) of a popish successor; but that he would not suffer his brother to be taken away from him nor the right line of the succession to the Crown interrupted". The following day, while the debate on the Address was still in progress, Charles addressed both Houses, saying that he would give them full support in any measures they found good to take to secure the Protestant religion both in his own time and after his death, "so they tend not to impeach the Right of Succession, nor the descent of the crown in the true line; and so they restrain not my power, nor the just rights of any Protestant

[1] There is a sentence in the *Life of James* on the authority of one of James's letters which shows that James had taken Charles's *mot* to heart: "The King was sensible that his chief security lay in having a successor they liked worse than himself."

successor"; the suggestion that James should be removed from his person and counsels he ignored.

On October 28 the Commons had sent up to the Lords a Bill to disable Catholics from sitting in either House of Parliament. Barrillon reported that James's name came up constantly in this connection, that Shaftesbury, Buckingham, Essex and Halifax were irreconcilably opposed to his interests, fearing the revenge he would take on them if and when he had the power, that some of the Opposition were already talking of substituting William for James as heir-presumptive, but that they saw small prospect of making a breach between James and William. On November 21 the Bill came back from the Lords with an amendment[1] exempting the Duke of York from the necessity of taking the oaths of Allegiance and Supremacy and from making the Declaration against Transubstantiation. The proviso was thus carefully worded so as to avoid forcing James to a declaration of his religious beliefs, and in the debate upon it in the Commons this intention was made very clear; and the desire to avoid branding James as a Papist—joined to a very real loyalty to the Crown—resulted in agreement with the Lords by two votes.

The House of Commons next fell upon Danby. In the previous March he had written to Ralph Montagu, the English ambassador at Paris, regarding the six million livres that Charles was to receive as the price of his withdrawal from the treaty with Holland and of the postponement of the meeting of Parliament. The draft of his letter had been personally endorsed by the King, and had contained instructions to Montagu to refrain from communicating its contents to the Secretary of State; Montagu, actuated by private pique against Danby, and at the instigation of Louis, communicated this letter to the House of Commons. The position of Louis in the matter is made quite clear in a letter addressed to him by Barrillon on October 14, 1678; after giving details of the intrigues into which he had entered with Montagu, he writes:

> As your Majesty has commanded me to do everything that is possible to raise troubles to the King of England, it does not appear to me that anything could possibly happen more disagreeable to him than to see the man accused in parliament in whom he has reposed the care of affairs, and the government of his kingdom for two years. The Treasurer's enemies, who are very numerous, will take courage, and it is not impossible that the Duke of York will turn against him.

[1] According to Barrillon this amendment was passed by a majority of twenty; Mazure quotes in *oratio recta* part of a speech by James, but fails to give the reference in Barrillon's despatches. Elsewhere Barrillon states that James achieved the result through his friends.

This letter is a remarkably frank statement of the attitude of Louis to Charles at a time when Charles had every confidence in the good will of the French King; this attitude was constant in the relations of Louis both to Charles and James, and can be illustrated by a large number of extracts from the correspondence of the French ambassadors; it must be borne in mind throughout the reign of James and in his final exile. Louis's foreign policy was, of course, entirely concerned with French interests, and, though on occasion he could show himself disinterested when the Catholic Church was concerned, he had no motive for interference in the domestic problems of England except in so far as these problems affected the relations between the two monarchies. He was beginning to see in the young William of Orange a formidable obstacle to the achievement of his main object in the early years of his reign, viz., the creation of a strong barrier on his northern frontier for the protection of Paris. The popularity of the marriage of William with Princess Mary had taught him that the English people would never be brought to fight on his side against William, and the events of the spring and summer of 1678 made him apprehensive lest circumstances should arise which might bring England into alliance with Holland against him. If he could not have Charles as an ally, the next best thing was to secure his neutrality, and the obvious way to that end was to keep him in perpetual conflict with Parliament.

The Opposition in Parliament seized eagerly upon Danby's letter, and in their factious fury ignored the complicity of Ralph Montagu. James was by this time completely estranged from Danby: there had been friction over the marriage of Princess Mary, a matter in which James thought Danby had shown officiousness and had over-reached him; but the irritation was momentary, for the Duke and the Minister fell at once to working in concert in furthering the plans for the war with France. Indeed, James in February 1678 made in Danby's interest one of his rare remonstrances to Charles: when it began to appear that Charles's attachment to his chief Minister was weakening, Nell Gwynne essayed to amuse the Court by mimicking Danby's personal peculiarities, as Buckingham and Henry Killigrew had mimicked Clarendon before his fall in 1667; James "with all his power dissuaded and exhorted therein", but Charles declared that "he would not deny himself an hour's divertissement for any man".[1]

The chief grievances that James had against Danby were of more recent date: he had, James thought, shown excessive zeal in the prosecution of the Popish Plot, and he had advised Charles to deliver to Parlia-

[1] Danby was said to have incurred Nelly's enmity by refusing to support her aspiration to be made a Countess.

ment the speech of November 9, the speech in which a promise was given of a restriction of the prerogative of a popish successor. In November James told Barrillon that Danby was in close alliance with James's declared enemy, the Bishop of London, and was bent on ruining him, and Barrillon reported to Louis that Danby had no longer any fear that James could injure him; he added that James did not know which side to take in the attack on Danby in the House of Commons. But James was well aware that, in spite of the loyal sentiments expressed by almost all the speakers in the debate on the resolution to impeach Danby, the attack on the Treasurer was a covert assault upon the King and his pro-French policy, and he took the side of Danby not on personal grounds, but because Danby was the King's Minister. On December 20 he wrote to William:

> I believe you will be surprised to hear what Mr. Montagu has done; for being yesterday accused in council of having had secret conference with the Pope's nuncio at Paris, he to revenge himself of that produces letters written to him by the Lord Treasurer by His Majesty's command when he was ambassador in France, and shows them to the Commons, who upon it order an impeachment to be drawn up against the Lord Treasurer upon the matter contained in those letters and other things they had against him. I am confident there was never so abominable an action as this of Mr. Montagu's and so offensive to the King, in revealing what he was trusted with when he was employed by His Majesty; all honest men abhor him for it, and tomorrow I believe the impeachment will be brought up to our House, then we shall know what the articles will be. I make no doubt but that the Lord Treasurer will defend himself very well; I am sure His Majesty is bound to stand by him.

In order to save Danby, or at least to give him time to prepare his defence, the King prorogued Parliament on December 30 and dissolved it on January 24; it had been in existence since May 8, 1661. The new Parliament met, after a short prorogation, on March 15, 1679, and betrayed no less rancour against Danby than its predecessor had done. Charles had dismissed him from office and granted him a pardon; the Commons addressed the King, maintaining that a royal pardon in bar of an impeachment was illegal, a declaration which was later embodied in a formal resolution of the House; this resolution affected James eighteen months later. Danby went to the Tower, where he remained for five years; as soon as his interests were separated from those of the King, James resumed his hostility to him, a hostility which he retained to the end of his life. Several letters passed between the two men in the spring of 1679—by that time Danby had added to his list of crimes that of advising James's exile—and from these it is clear that each thought the other an unprofitable ally and one whose stock was so low that the quicker he was dropped the better.

In August 1679 Sir Henry Goodricke reported to Danby from Paris an interview which he had had with James at Brussels (where he was then in exile), in which James had recounted various grievances he had against Danby and had alluded to him as "one that was his friend once"; Goodricke concluded from the interview that Danby could expect from James "nothing save a cold indifference" until misunderstandings were removed. When in February 1684 Danby was at last released from the Tower it was in spite of James's opposition; the ex-Minister waited on James in the hope of regaining his favour, but the result was unsatisfactory, and thereafter they met no more.

> Lord Danby told me [says Sir John Reresby] what had passed between the Duke of York and him at his late visit to him after he had been with the King, whereby I found him disgusted with that prince; and that upon his telling the Earl that he had something of slight he should say concerning him, the Earl should reply that it was true he had often been so unfortunate as to differ from him in opinion and had not yet found reason to repent of it, but that he had never said anything against his person, and, if anybody had told him that, they were but whispers and lies, and should be glad to know who were his informers (but the Duke avoided that).

CHAPTER IX

THE SECOND EXILE: THE FIRST EXCLUSION BILL

BEFORE Danby had been sent to the Tower, James was in exile in Brussels. There was nothing new in the proposal that he should be withdrawn from Court; as long as he was there, though he had no official status, there was always the suspicion that he was influencing policy and promoting the interests of the Catholics. In the winter of 1673 to 1674, as we have seen, certain of the Duke's friends advised him to withdraw voluntarily, and when it was found that he would not absent himself without a direct command from Charles, an influential deputation, including the Duke of Ormonde and the two Secretaries of State, Arlington and Sir William Coventry's brother Henry, waited on the King and tried, but failed, to persuade him to banish James from the Court and from public business until the excitement raised by his marriage had subsided. In the early spring of 1679 Charles had his back against the wall: Parliament had forced him to dismiss Danby, the hue and cry after the Papists started by Oates was gaining strength, and though he was convinced of their complete innocence, he could do nothing for the victims; and there could be no doubt that opinion in favour of the exclusion of James from the succession was hardening and would at no distant date lead to definite motions in Parliament. James, as always, was for strong action; Charles knew well that his only chance was to wait on events and to hope that there would be a turn for the better: there is no reason to suppose that he anticipated what eventually happened—he was not master of the situation at this time—but he saw enough to realise that the more conciliatory he could appear without making any real concessions, the better chance he had of ultimate victory. The ostensible reasons for sending James away were that his presence lent colour to the suspicion that the King was following his popish counsels and that as long as he remained in view he would be a mark for attack; but Charles had undoubtedly the further motive of relieving his counsels of an adviser who persisted in giving the wrong advice. James fought hard against being sent away, but when he received a direct command he said to his friends, "What can be done, since it is the King's pleasure?"

Accordingly at very short notice James left for Brussels on March 3, 1679, "not without many tears shed by him at parting, though the King shed none"; two months later Lord Conway was able to write that

Charles was no more concerned for Danby "than for a puppy-dog, nor for what becomes of the Duke of York neither". Before he sailed James had to repel a strong direct attack on his religious faith by Sancroft, Archbishop of Canterbury, and Morley, now Bishop of Winchester, who had in 1659 come to him on a like mission. James received them courteously, but told them he was very angry with the people who had sent them, for his failure to comply with their wishes would do him harm in the debates then pending in Parliament. For the rest, he said he was not learned enough to argue with them, but that he had made his change of faith after due deliberation, and could not now change again. He dismissed the Bishops on the plea of pressure of business, but he took care to soften this seeming discourtesy by writing to Sancroft as soon as he got to Brussels, giving him an outline of the experiences that had led him to embrace the Roman Faith.

James travelled via The Hague; he spent some days there with his daughter and son-in-law, and on March 17, 1679, he arrived at Brussels and took up his residence in the house which Charles had occupied twenty years earlier. During the five months he spent at Brussels (including a short visit to The Hague at the end of April) he wrote a vast number of letters. His chief correspondents were Colonel George Legge, who had been his Lieutenant-Governor when he was Governor of Portsmouth and is better known by his subsequent title of Lord Dartmouth; his son-in-law, William of Orange; and his brother-in-law, Laurence Hyde, who two years later, after a few months as Viscount Hyde, was to add to the extraordinary confusion of titles of nobility in this period by assuming that of Earl of Rochester, twelve months after its extinction at the death of the son of John Wilmot, Earl of Rochester, the poet and rake. To Charles also he wrote, but all the letters save one have been lost; we can guess their contents and, with no great stretch of imagination, supply Charles's reasons for not considering them to call for immediate reply. For James had two objects only in his mind: his own immediate recall, and the restoration of the power and prestige of the Crown; he was quite incapable of realising that the two objects were incompatible and that his best chance of success in his ultimate object was to remain quiet and out of the public eye. On the larger issue he was almost in despair:

> I wish in England some considered the good of our family so much as I do. I have but a very dismal prospect of our affairs in general, and I do not see without a miracle how they can be mended, for His Majesty has so given up himself into the hands of his new counsellors, that I can see nothing but the ruin of the

monarchy; and that which I think is a very bad sign, is, that His Majesty is not so sensible as he should be of the ill condition he is in.

And truly the events of the summer of 1679 gave Charles and James little cause for hope. The new Parliament which assembled on March 6 was overwhelmingly in opposition to the Court. There was an initial deadlock caused by the refusal of the King to accept the Speaker elected by the Commons, and Charles had to get out of it by a short prorogation, which wiped out all the previous proceedings. When Parliament reassembled, the question of the Speakership was settled by a compromise. Immediately after Danby had gone to the Tower, Charles announced to Parliament that he was embarking on a new constitutional experiment: he was about to appoint a new Council of thirty members to take the place of the old Privy Council, and when the names of the new councillors were announced, it was found that not only was Shaftesbury, the leader of the party in opposition to the Court, appointed President of the Council, but that a majority of the members were of that party. James was dismayed, but he was always ready to clutch at straws, he seriously thought that the new arrangements might mean that Shaftesbury had been persuaded to be reconciled to the King, and he commissioned Legge to prepare the way for an understanding between Shaftesbury and himself; the French ambassador thought that Charles had capitulated to the Opposition and that James was ruined. But James and Barrillon were the only two people deceived: Charles had had no intention of giving the Council any real power; his private view was expressed to the Earl of Ailesbury: "God's fish, they have put a set of men about me, but they shall know nothing"; the House of Commons saw through the gesture; to them the Council was a Greek gift, and they even neglected to give Charles the customary address of thanks for his gracious message, but fell at once on the business for which in their view they had come together.

On Sunday, April 27, after several attempts had been made by the small Court party to divert attention in other directions, the House entered on a general and diffuse discussion about the danger from the Papists and from the succession of a Papist to the throne. They unanimously passed the following resolution:

> That the Duke of York being a Papist and the hopes of his coming such to the Crown hath given the greatest countenance and encouragement to the present conspiracies and designs of the Papists against the King and the Protestant Religion;

in other words, "If the Heir-presumptive had not been a Papist there would have been no Popish Plot". The resolution was carried to the House of Lords, where it was softened by the addition of the word "unwittingly"—" . . . hath unwittingly given the greatest countenance". On the 30th Charles came down to the House; he instructed the Lord Chancellor to declare the concessions he was willing to make in the interests of public security. These concessions, if they were honestly meant, were more than sufficient to satisfy all moderate men: in the event of a Papist succeeding to the throne, he should have no control over ecclesiastical preferments; he should be disabled from unreasonably preventing Parliament from assembling; privy councillors and judges should be appointed by Parliament and only Protestants should be Justices of the Peace; and all military and naval appointments should be made either by Parliament or by persons deputed by Parliament to make them. Charles also promised to take into favourable consideration any further limitations of royal authority that Parliament might see fit to suggest.

But the House were in no mood to listen to talk about compromise. They were determined to exclude James from the throne, and they were convinced that no statutory limitations of the prerogatives of a Papist king could prevent him from favouring those of his own faith and from subverting the Established Church. "For us to go about to tie a Popish successor with laws for preservation of the Protestant Religion is binding Sampson with withes; he will break them when he is awake." Moreover, though no one in the House was so impolite as to express it openly, there was an undercurrent of mistrust of Charles's sincerity; for his part in the proceedings that had led to Danby's fall—his acceptance of subsidies from Louis on condition that Parliament should not meet—was fresh in everyone's mind. From the extracts from speeches in the debates on Exclusion that have been preserved it appears that no one attempted to answer in the negative the constitutional question propounded by William Sacheverell six months earlier, "whether the King and the Parliament may not dispose of the succession of the Crown"; nor, except for a half-hearted plea by Sir Leoline Jenkins, promptly brushed aside by Colonel Birch, did Charles or his advisers raise this issue. (It must be noted in passing that this issue was very different from that raised at the Revolution—whether Parliament alone may not dispose of the Crown and dispossess the holder of it; there can be no doubt that Parliament, in so disposing of the Crown, committed a revolutionary act.)

On May 11, again on a Sunday, the debate was opened on the Lord Chancellor's speech, and as a fortnight earlier vain attempts were made to lead the House into other paths; four days later the First Exclusion Bill was read a first time, providing that James, Duke of York (by name), should be declared incapable of inheriting the Crowns of the three kingdoms; that on Charles's decease the Crown should pass to the next successor, just as if James were dead; that it should be high treason on James's part to perform any act of sovereignty after Charles's death, and on the part of anyone else to take measures calculated to assist him to the throne; and that James should be perpetually banished from the kingdom. (It is curious that, though in the preamble to the Bill the reason for the exclusion is shown to be that James had been traitorously seduced by the emissaries, priests and agents of the Pope, no provision was made in the Bill for his succession if he again changed his religion and became a Protestant; probably, as James was to say later, it would have been argued that such a reconversion would have been insincere and under dispensation.) On May 21 the second reading was passed by the substantial majority of 79, 207 to 128, but further proceedings upon the Bill were prevented by the prorogation of Parliament on May 26, on the ostensible ground of dispute between the Houses, and by its subsequent dissolution.

James was not greatly concerned at danger to himself from the Exclusion Bill; he was confident that the King and the House of Lords would prevent its passing. But he was distressed to hear from his correspondents of the growth of what he considered to be the anti-monarchical temper of the House of Commons. He heard that on May 11 the Commons had passed a not very worthy resolution that they would stand by the King with their lives and fortunes, and that if he was assassinated they would assume that it was by the Catholics and would take revenge on them, and he at once wrote Charles a letter which deserves study on other grounds than the matter immediately in hand:

> I can never sufficiently acknowledge the sense of gratitude I have for Your Majesty's goodness to me, I do assure you I can bear any misfortune with patience so long as you are so kind; I have but one life to lose and I shall always be ready to lay it down in your service, and at the rate the things now go there is too great a probability an occasion may not long [be] wanting. They will never be satisfied unless Your Majesty unking yourself, and if you deny them anything they ask, I am confident they will fly out, especially if you permit the militia of London and parts adjacent to draw together. I know there is danger and hazard in making those steps that are necessary to keep your Crown, and more than would have been some months ago, but you are utterly lost if it is any longer deferred.

> Let not therefore knaves and mean-spirited people flatter you into an opinion that you may be safe by yielding and temporising, for nothing less than the destruction of your family and the Monarchy itself will content them. Now therefore is the time to break in upon them before they are formed or have a man to head them; and the only person capable (I think) of that employment (pardon me for naming him) is the Duke of Monmouth, for I am sure the same reasons and persuasions that has prevailed with him to behave to you and me as he has done will make him stick at nothing that favours his ambition; and therefore I beg your Majesty will have a watchful eye upon his actions for your own security, and that you will please to give some signal mark of your displeasure to Sir Thomas Armstrong and young Gerrard, who were such earnest agitators against me in the House; for unless something of that nature be done, many will not think you in earnest. Suffer not Ireland or Scotland to be put in other hands as they are at present; you may count upon their assistance, and the Prince of Orange too has given me all imaginable assurance that he will stand and fall by you. Wherefore I beg Your Majesty to make use of those parts and courage God has given you, and not rely upon concessions already made or to make any more. Be pleased to use all possible diligence in providing your forts and garrisons; and certainly the speediest way of breaking their measures is to break the parliament itself and proportion your way of living to your revenue, rather than to lie any longer at the mercy of those men, who, by that villainous vote to revenge your death upon the Papists, can have no other meaning than to expose your life to the bloody hand of any desperate fanatic who shall think fit to attempt so inhuman an act.

Perhaps the most interesting side-light that this letter throws on James's character is his conviction that the rebels, as he would have called them, can only be dangerous if they have a leader of royal blood: clearly here he is taking his analogy not from the Civil War, but from the Fronde.

James followed up this letter with one to Legge urging him to see the King and to endeavour to make him see that "now or never is the time to save the monarchy", and enclosing "Heads you are to discourse with his Majesty upon, so as to let him know they are reasonable". These heads add emphasis and point to what James had written to Charles, especially with regard to Monmouth:

> That His Majesty ought not to apprehend but that he is strong enough to deal with and punish his enemies if he will but be resolute and stick to himself and countenance his friends. The fleet is yet

> his, urge the consequence and advantage of that, the guards and garrisons are also his, except Hull which might easily be made so. Scotland and Ireland yet his if he continue Lauderdale and Ormonde in them, them two kingdoms will make men of estates consider well before they engage against the King. The Prince of Orange has given me all the assurances of his serving His Majesty. . . . If he will bestir himself now they are not quite prepared, want a head, he must have a care the Duke of Monmouth does not head them, for he is the only dangerous man that can do it; if he does not, no man of quality will dare.

And to William he wrote in the same sense and in very similar words, with the addition:

> Firmness and good husbandry may carry him [Charles] through all his difficulties, and I am very apt to believe that whensoever he shows he will no longer be used as he has been and that they see he will be a King, there will be a rebellion.

But Charles was both wiser and less resolute than his father, and James's plan of a *coup d'état* was not put to the test.

In addition to the passages just quoted, there is abundant evidence in the correspondence from Brussels of the strengthening in James of a sentiment which had been latent for some years, his jealousy of James, Duke of Monmouth, Charles's eldest son.[1] Of Monmouth it is safe to say that no man who appeared so attractive to his contemporaries figures in history as so worthless and contemptible. He had a good reputation as a soldier, he had won golden opinions fighting at John Churchill's side at the siege of Maestricht in 1673, and he had no doubt the dash and courage of his Cavalier relations and associates; but it has never been suggested that in the campaign of Sedgemoor he showed any of the qualities of a general. For the rest, he was so weak as to let himself be "made the cat's foot" by any politician who thought he could make use of him, and so vain that he thought that a brave carriage and popular manners could lead an aristocratic society to overlook the defects of his birth. "The Booby Duke" he was called by Rochester (the poet, not James's brother-in-law), and the title fits him so well that it is curious that it did not pass into common talk;[2] Dryden wrote more politely,

[1] If, as seems likely, we can reject the legend of James la Cloche. See Arthur Bryant, *Charles II*, p. 47.

[2] "Rochester's Farewell", in which this appellation occurs, appears not to have been published for some years after the poet's death in 1680, but it was no doubt freely circulated in manuscript.

> The ambitious youth, too covetous of fame,
> Too full of angel's metal in his frame,
> Unwarily was led from virtue's ways
> Made drunk with honour and debauched with praise.

Charles did not take his paternal duties very seriously, nor during the first ten years of his son's life, spent as they were in exile, were there facilities for education and discipline. Monmouth showed some precocity as a swashbuckler, for before he was fourteen he had conceived the notion that his bastardy could be annulled by a sufficiently bold denial of the fact, and he threatened to be the death of anyone who said that his father and his mother had not been married; at the age of seventeen he was reputed to be the complete rake. Charles was so fond of him that there were persistent rumours before he was eighteen that he would be legitimised, and the King appears to have done nothing to counteract these rumours or to prevent illusions from taking root in the boy's mind. James had his jealousies of his nephew at this early period, but they did not strike very deep, and the intrigue of Buckingham and Arlington in 1668 to have Monmouth declared legitimate caused no breach, for James was not aware of it at the time. Monmouth was married at the age of seventeen to the young heiress of the Earl of Buccleuch, and James was for a long time in close relations with both husband and wife. In 1669 occurred the ludicrous incident of the Abbé Pregnani, which conveys an impression of easy relations between Charles, James and Monmouth. This French ecclesiastic had a reputation both in regular science and in the science of forecasting events, and he was sent over ostensibly to help Charles in his hobby of chemistry, actually to influence him in the French interest. Monmouth, who was very superstitious, got hold of Pregnani and tried to find out from him whether he or his Uncle James would be successful in an amorous intrigue in which they were competitors. Charles was then at Newmarket with James, and when he heard of Pregnani's powers he said he was the very man to help them to back horses, and he told Monmouth to bring the Abbé to Newmarket. The result was disastrous for Monmouth: he put entire faith in Pregnani, who proved to be inefficient as a tipster and was wrong on every race, and who returned to France entirely discredited.

There is considerable evidence that the good relations between uncle and nephew continued unbroken until 1674. In July 1673 we read:

> Yesterday His Royal Highness dined at the Duke of Monmouth's, who were together most of the afternoon; it being observed by those that are near His Royal Highness that he has a particular kindness and affection for His Grace, upon whom, indeed, all the world now looks as a rising sun.

Monmouth was evidently anxious at that time to do nothing to rouse James's jealousy:

> The King proffered my Lord Duke to make him Commissioner of Scotland in the place of my Lord Lauderdale; but His Grace modestly refused it, telling His Majesty that he desired to appear in action while the war continued, and in a time of peace he feared that employment would draw upon him the envy of the Duke. The King commended him for his prudence and told him he was of the same opinion.

A considerable breach occurred, however, in the summer of 1674. James relates that on July 17 he had occasion to warn Monmouth that Arlington was attempting to make trouble between them. Monmouth replied that "he could not believe he had such evil intentions, else he would have nothing to do with him". The same evening Monmouth told James that he was thinking of applying to the King for the post of General, and asked for his support. Now, James had in 1670, on the death of George Monck, Duke of Albemarle, advised Charles not to appoint a successor: the English Army was so small that it did not need a general. But it is quite clear that in giving this advice James felt that he was performing an act of self-abnegation, and that he had no doubt whatever that if a general were appointed there could be no choice but himself. Monmouth's application was therefore a shock to him, although since the passing of the Test Act he himself could no longer be considered eligible. He told Monmouth that his present priority in the Army as Colonel of the Guards gave him all the powers of General and that "he was not to expect my friendship if ever he pretended to it or had it". He was dismayed to learn a few days later that Charles had appointed Monmouth Lieutenant-General. About the same time Monmouth began to take exception to James's intimacy with his wife—whether he feared that James would seduce her or would convert her to his own Faith does not appear—and by September there was open feud at Court between uncle and nephew. The majority of the courtiers took the side of Monmouth—Charles was at this time inclined to favour him at James's expense—and James got the worse of a verbal encounter with Arlington (who made a special study of Charles's mind and knew who was the favourite of the moment):[1] he told Arlington that if Monmouth did not desist from interfering in regimental appointments he would lose his friendship, "to which that dexterous Minister replied

[1] The temporary *rapprochement* between James and Arlington in 1669 had been ended when in 1672 Arlington and Clifford were candidates for the Treasurership and James strongly supported Clifford's claims.

something haughtily, that the Duke of Monmouth could not need his favour more than His Highness needed the King's, which he might hazard to lessen by thus crossing his inclination for so beloved a son".

The final alienation of James and Monmouth was, however, delayed some years; apart from their hunting together in December 1674, there are several references which show that there was no great mutual antipathy and that each was willing to help the other in little ways. As late as August 1678 James wrote to William:

> I am glad my nephew, the Duke of Monmouth, has been with you. He has done justice to your troops and gives the highest commendation to your footguards and dragoons which can be and which they deserve.

As early as November 1678 Barrillon reported that Monmouth had begun to have hopes of the succession and that he had allowed his health to be drunk as Prince of Wales; but his followers were few and most people laughed at his pretensions.[1] But when Shaftesbury began to encourage those pretensions, Monmouth's head was completely turned, and for the first time he took himself seriously as a politician. When James went to Brussels, the fact that Monmouth remained behind basking in the royal favour was a grave addition to his troubles; Charles, however, the day James left made a formal declaration in Council "that he was never contracted to any other woman but only to his present wife Queen Catherine", a gesture calculated to convince James that there was to be no tampering with the succession. But two months later insurrection broke out in Scotland, and James was confident that had he been in England he would have been appointed to the command of the troops sent to suppress it. Instead, at the very time when James was warning Charles about Monmouth's political activities, Monmouth was given the appointment, and he conducted the short campaign with complete efficiency; not only that, when he returned to London he "left a mighty reputation behind him in Scotland for the clemency and indulgence procured by his means". James, who never wasted pity on rebels—or on persons suspected of rebellion—regarded Monmouth's mildness after Bothwell Brigg merely as an effort to gain popularity and a sure way to encourage the fanatics to another rebellion.

James had little hope of being speedily recalled from Brussels, and he lost no time in making arrangements for comfort and amusement. One

[1] Sprat accuses Shaftesbury of deliberately "inflaming him (Monmouth) with imaginary suspicions of the Duke of York's irreconcilable hatred of his person, which was . . . far from having any real foundation".

of the first things he did was to instruct Legge to send over some of his coaches and coach-horses, "as also two pads and four of the summer hunters, whereof Windsor and Griffin to be two"; the coaches might be sent direct to Antwerp, but the horses should be embarked at Dover to avoid a long sea passage. These instructions were supplemented by others, including a demand for "some of the Hulks spaniel to shoot withal". Finally, the day before he unexpectedly left for England he sent orders for Hilliard, the Master of his Foxhounds, to bring with him the foxhounds and the huntsmen and their horses: "I now begin to have good sport stag hunting, and the country looks as if the fox-hunting would be very good."

James and the Duchess kept a small court at Brussels and, in addition to his large personal staff, visitors from England and elsewhere were from time to time welcomed, among them the Earl and Countess of Peterborough and the Duchess's mother, Duchess Laura. James, however, was not very happy in Brussels: fear of Shaftesbury's spies kept him from making an open profession of his religion, though he had, no doubt, his own private oratory, and this abstention made the Spaniards,

> not only uneasy, but even scandalised; that instead of seeing him at Mass (which none of them ever did), there were two ministers in his family reading prayers constantly twice a day, and sermons twice on Sundays to the Protestants that belonged to him.

Moreover, James's isolation from the Court left him open to an attack from which he would otherwise have been protected: at the time when he and Charles were bent on removing the suspicion that he had designs on the existing polity of England, Catholic malcontents, mostly Irish, flocked to him with hare-brained schemes for a rising in Ireland which should lead to an invasion of England in the Catholic interest; James was glad to see these people, but they embarrassed him. In particular, one Colonel Fitzpatrick was sent over by the Irish Catholic bishops to concert a plan with the Papal Internuncio at Brussels, and expected to be countenanced by James. James very wisely refused to have anything to do with him, and he "was forced to remove thence by His Royal Highness's commands, which he obeyed not without much regret and murmuring". These intrigues gave point to the objection raised in the Exclusion debates that James in exile would be in a position to plan an invasion. James was unpopular with the Spaniards because he showed discretion in not appearing publicly at Mass and because he had Protestant clergy in his household for the benefit of his servants; on this account, and because of the unjust suspicions his conspiratorial visitors brought upon him, he thought seriously at one time of transferring his residence to the Protestant town of Breda, and made the suggestion to William that accommodation might be found for him there.

The day James had sent for his foxhounds his stay at Brussels was suddenly cut short by alarming news from England: Charles at Windsor had been suddenly laid low by a serious attack of illness (as usual, poison was suspected). Monmouth was on the spot and at the head of the armed forces of the kingdom, and the moderate politicians, Viscount Halifax and the Earl of Essex, who had not followed Shaftesbury's lead in supporting Monmouth's pretensions to the succession, realised their responsibility as Charles's Ministers and the danger to the country if Charles died, and sent an express to Brussels urging James to come over without delay; at the same time—August 27 and 28—he had letters containing similar advice from Sunderland, Feversham and the Duchess of Portsmouth. He left Brussels on August 29, his Duchess alone being informed of his departure. Lord Longford's account of the journey in a letter to Lord Arran, written four days after James's arrival at Windsor, contains much illuminating detail.

> He left Brussels in a disguise of a black perruque only and a plain stuff suit without his Star and Garter, rode post to Calais with my Lord Peterborough, Colonel Churchill, Mr. Doyley and two footmen, but not in their livery. He then took ship, and it was so bad a sail that though he had no ill wind he was nineteen hours at sea before he landed at Dover. He went immediately to the post house where Churchill like a French officer in his scarf represented the best man in the Company, and being known to the postmaster, he welcomed him, took him by the hand, said he was glad to see him, but swore by God he should be much gladder to see a better man than he, and at an instant looked full in the Duke's face, when he knew it would not seem to take notice of him, because he saw him in disguise. Churchill was mounting upon the best horse, and just as the Duke was mounting, another man who belonged to the post office went to the other side of the Duke, looked full in his face, and whispered so softly to himself that nobody could have heard him, but the Duke took no notice, but rode on. These were the only persons that knew him upon the road, and yet they kept his secret. My Lord Peterborough and Doyley were outridden so that only His Highness and Churchill with one footman arrived on Monday, September 1, in the evening at seven of the clock at the Barbican at Smithfield, where they took a hackney coach and drove to the law office in Lombard Street, where Churchill alighted and went to see if Phil Froude was at home, but he being abroad, Churchill left

> a letter for him to follow him to Sir Allen Apsley's when he came home, not acquainting him that the Duke was come. At Sir Allen's the Duke supped and went to bed there, and at three in the morning took coach for Windsor, where he arrived about seven, and came into the King's withdrawing room at the moment my Lord Sussex, who was then in waiting in the bedchamber, opened the door; at which the Duke entered, and when he came to the King's bedside he with great submission threw himself upon his knees, asking the King's pardon for his coming into England and into his presence without his leave, saying he was so confounded at the news of His Majesty's illness that he could have no satisfaction or content in his mind until he had seen his Majesty. And since that now he had that happiness to find him past all danger (for which he blessed God) he was ready to return again that morning if it was His Majesty's pleasure; for he came with resolutions to be absolutely governed and disposed of by His Majesty in all things. Upon this His Majesty cast his arms about him, kissed him and received him with all kindness imaginable and 'tis said by the standers-by that they both shed tears of joy at the interview.

Charles was very anxious that no one should know that he had had any previous knowledge of James's visit to England, and he had stipulated that James should give out that he had come of his own accord and without an invitation, "so fearful His Majesty was of giving the least disgust (said James), and that if any fault was found, it might fall upon the Duke's shoulders which were more accustomed to bear such burdens, and this he knew would make no great addition to what he already bore". And the chief thing in the King's mind after the raptures of reunion had subsided was how best to get James out of the country before public notice was taken of his presence. James wrote to William four days after his arrival at Windsor saying that he had more friends in England than he had thought and that the rebellion which Charles had expected on his return had not materialised. He was therefore confirmed in his view that Charles had been unduly apprehensive, and he was quite certain that now he was back in England he could safely stay there. But Charles would not yield to his arguments: Parliament had been summoned for October 7, and there was no time to be lost. Two concessions, however, James did achieve: Charles was impressed by the occurrences of the past few days, he had no intention of letting Monmouth take advantage of James's absence abroad in the event of his own sudden death; and within ten days of James's arrival Monmouth was deprived of his rank as Lieutenant-General and ordered abroad; Charles also reiterated before the Council his declaration that he had not been married to Monmouth's mother. Charles appears to have made public no reason for this harsh treatment of his favourite son, but it was "variously reported": that he had incurred displeasure by his own open opposition to James, by his intimate relations with the Opposition leaders in the City, by an amorous intrigue with the Duchess of Southampton and, most serious of all, after his successful campaign in Scotland, by "laying the foundation for the succession in that kingdom and making himself popular by the industry of his agents and friends". There was apparently open conflict at Court between the partisans of the two Dukes while Monmouth's fate was in the balance: Henry Savile (Halifax's brother, whose jests were sometimes too pointed even for Charles) wrote from Paris that he was so ignorant of what was passing in England that "I knew not from those I intend to shout with whether I was to cry 'a York' or 'a Monmouth' ". Monmouth went to The Hague, and James found occasion to remonstrate with William on the kind reception his nephew was given. The disgrace of Monmouth was followed on October 15 by the dismissal of Shaftesbury from the Council.

The second concession which James obtained was permission to change his place of exile from Brussels to Edinburgh, a change which, together with other advantages, still further improved his hold on the succession. Charles allowed him only three weeks in England, and on September 24 he was on his way back to Brussels to rejoin the Duchess and to make arrangements for his departure to Scotland. He made the same time as he had taken on the homeward journey, and he was in Brussels on the 27th, and he took so short a time over his preparations there that he was at The Hague with Mary Beatrice five or six days later. There he found ships to convey his retinue and belongings to Scotland, and he embarked, after bidding farewell to his daughter and son-in-law for the last time. His intention was to go to the Downs and wait for Charles's permission to go to London; but he was driven by stress of weather to the Norfolk coast, he missed the message Charles had sent to the Downs, and putting Churchill ashore with a letter to Charles, he waited for the reply. Poor Mary Beatrice suffered acutely; they eventually arrived in London on October 14.[1]

During the fortnight of this stay in England James was on October 21 entertained at a banquet at Merchant Taylors' Hall by the Artillery

[1] Miss Foxcroft (*Life of Halifax*, I, 191) says, without giving references, "A treacherous understanding took shape between the Heir-Presumptive and Sunderland, according to which James, while ostensibly on his way to the North, should halt with his family in London, his stay being insensibly prolonged with a view to his permanent settlement."

Company,[1] as he was frequently entertained throughout the reign. James chose to regard the occasion as a spontaneous expression of affection and loyalty to himself; but it was alleged that the Artillery Company was a close preserve of James's own, that when some years earlier he had been Chief Leader and Captain of the Company he had nominated as stewards a number of his friends, such as Lord Ossory, the Earl of Feversham, Colonel Legge and Sir Robert Holmes, and that it was these stewards, and not the general body of the Company, who organised this banquet, paid for it and issued the invitations; it was also stated that James himself had to contribute £200 towards the cost, that the Lord Mayor was present but less than half the aldermen, and that menbers of the Company who were given tickets in many cases either tore them up or sold them for what they would fetch. There was great enthusiasm over the drinking of the healths of the King and James, and James accepted this enthusiasm as evidence of renewed popularity; he made a speech in which he said "that he would always maintain the laws and liberty of the subject, but yet he would not be catechised by any"; and as he was leaving the Hall he remarked "that this was pretty well for a poor banished man, so little while since". But signs were not absent that the warmth of feeling in the Hall was not reflected outside: anti-popish bills had been stuck on the doors and in the approaches, and in Cheapside, when James and his retinue were returning on horseback to St. James's, there was a large and hostile crowd. At one point where Oates and some of his friends were in a balcony overlooking the street "the rabble about them cried, 'a Pope, a Pope', as the Duke passed, whereat they were threatened by one of the Duke's guard, who cocked a pistol at them, and the rabble began to cheer, 'James' ".

About this time James received from the Pope a letter which shows how little James's tactless zeal for his religion was appreciated at Rome:

> Most beloved son in Christ, we send greeting. It has been reported to us that, on the occasion of the illness into which the King your brother fell, you hastened to visit him and that you possibly have had thoughts of remaining with him. News of this nature has filled us with very grave anxiety, for we have considered that, bearing in mind the state of things in that realm, the hatred of abandoned persons towards you and the manifest plot against you, that it was inopportune for you to subject your safety, the hopes of the Orthodox Faith, and also the welfare of the realm itself, to such

[1] Founded under royal charter in the reign of Henry VIII, and since 1770 known as the Honourable Artillery Company, under which name it still flourishes.

a risk. Wherefore we strongly urge you to consider the matter seriously and to put off to a time when Divine Providence shall have shown more clearly a way of success a plan no less dangerous than courageous. You will acknowledge in these fatherly exhortations the power of the affection in which we embrace you; and desiring that everything will turn out fortunately for you our best beloved son in Christ, we bestow our apostolic benediction upon you from the very bottom of our heart.

CHAPTER X

THE FIRST VISIT TO SCOTLAND

THE new Parliament met on October 7, 1679, but only to be prorogued for ten days; on the 17th it was adjourned until the 30th, and it was then and afterwards successively prorogued seven times before it met for the despatch of business on October 21, 1680. Charles II has several parliamentary records to his name, but none more remarkable than this: a parliament not even permitted to elect a Speaker until more than a year after the date for which it was summoned. When James arrived in London on October 12, 1679, Parliament was not sitting, for Charles had no intention of permitting a continuance of the debate on Exclusion. The main reason for James's absence from England had therefore disappeared, and he fought hard to be allowed to remain at Court. But Charles would give way only to the extent of promising that his absence should be a short one—only to the middle of the following January.

James on his long journey on the Great North Road was accompanied by his Duchess. In his memoirs he commends Mary's constancy in taking this journey so soon after her sea-sickness and vomiting of blood and in spite of the short time they were to be in Scotland, "and though she was not then above twenty years old, chose rather even with the hazard of her life, to be a constant companion of the Duke her husband's misfortunes and hardships, than to enjoy her ease in any part of the world without him"; but perhaps Mary had other reasons for keeping him under her eye. They travelled in state, for Charles had arranged that troops of horse in three relays should accompany them on the road (it is interesting to read that Captain Piercy Kirke, subsequently to achieve notoriety at Tangier and after Sedgemoor, commanded the second troop and was with the Duke and Duchess from Grantham to York); and they had an excellent send-off, for they were entertained by the City of London at the Artillery Garden, and a very considerable train of nobility and gentry conducted them to Hatfield, their first stopping-place.

At Hatfield House there was a setback, for the Earl of Salisbury absented himself; he sent his son to James with excuses, but he had made no provision for his entertainment. Progress was slow: the daily journey was only from twenty to twenty-five miles; the Marquis of Atholl travelled with James in his coach, and his Marchioness—much to the envy of ladies left behind in London—in that of the Duchess. James was so well satisfied with the company of the Marquis, and of the other gentleman who no doubt from time to time took his place, that he made no use of the led horses that had been provided, though occasionally he stretched his legs in a walk of a mile or two. The second night was spent in an inn at Biggleswade, and there he was waited on by the Earl of Ailesbury and other local gentry. The third stopping-place was Sir Lionel Waldron's seat at Huntingdon; then, after sleeping the nights of October 30 and 31 at Stamford and Grantham, they arrived at Newark, where they remained for the week-end. The night of Monday, November 3, was spent with the Duke of Newcastle at Welbeck; the following morning they passed into Yorkshire, and were received on the border of the county by the High Sheriff and a number of the local magnates; others joined the procession on the way to Doncaster. Pontefract was reached on November 5, the following day between that town and York they were received at Tadcaster by the Archbishop of York, and five miles farther on by the Cathedral clergy and by the Lord Mayor, aldermen and sheriffs of the City. The Deputy Recorder made a speech of compliment to the Duke and Duchess, and the deputation was honoured by James, who himself led them to the Duchess to kiss her hands.

At York they spent four days, but their experience there was disappointing. The loyal gentry made a great effort, but they were small in numbers, and the large following of Shaftesbury conspicuously absented themselves; the city fathers apparently considered that their duties had ended with the official reception, for James was so displeased with their conduct that he moved Charles to send them an official reprimand. It was possibly chagrin at this neglect that caused James to omit the most ordinary courtesies to the few gentlemen who had behaved seemingly: Sir John Reresby, the Governor, reports that, "I had presented His Highness with venison and wines, and entertained some of his favourites at my house in York, but it was not worthy of his notice".

On November 10 the northern progress reached Norton Conyers, the seat of Sir Richard Graham; then, after a halt at Richmond, they arrived at Durham, where they had what was probably the most splendid reception this side of the Border. The obsequious Nathaniel Crewe, now Bishop of Durham, had been on his way to London, five days on the road; as soon as he heard James had left London he turned back and prepared for his entertainment. For three days the Duke and Duchess and their train enjoyed the Bishop's hospitality before they set out on the last bleak stage of their journey to Berwick. Long before the end of the journey James and Mary were so bored with travelling that even Mary vowed she would never take that way again, but would travel by the dreaded, but far quicker, sea route; besides, at sea there were no stopping-places where one might meet with rebuffs.

James can have had no expectation of the tremendous enthusiasm of his reception in Scotland. A very full account was sent by a Catholic priest to a friend in Paris, and this letter is preserved among the remnants of the Stuart papers at Blairs College, near Aberdeen. James's progress from Berwick was a veritable triumph; the whole Council met him at the Border with two thousand nobility and gentry and the King's troop of horse; James alighted from his coach, and those of sufficient dignity kissed his hands and passed on to kiss the Duchess's hands as she sat in her coach. Claverhouse and his troop of dragoons joined the procession a few miles on, and a stop of two days was made at Lethington, the Duke of Lauderdale's mansion, where they were nobly entertained. There was further hand-kissing at Lethington, and the enthusiasm of the populace, of which he had recently experienced little in England, seems to have gone to James's head, for we read that "he remained with an open table, where all the lords sat with him; his discourses were very free, especially concerning his own pretensions and the Parliament of England"—the sort of indiscretion to which he became increasingly liable as he advanced in years.

The progress continued on the same scale to Leith, where James left his coach for his entry to Edinburgh on horseback; at the water-gate of the city at three o'clock on Monday, November 24, he was met by the provost and the bailiffs, "then the cannons of the Castle went off for a considerable time, and bonfires were made throughout all the town and the ringing of bells continued until ten o'clock at night". In fact there there was a reception comparable in spontaneity and good-will, if not in magnificence, with that of Charles at the Restoration.[1] A good deal of this enthusiasm may be ascribed to other reasons than that of James's personal popularity; the Scottish people knew little about James except that he was of the lineage of their ancient kings, and it was the return of the dynasty rather than the visit of the individual that they welcomed; moreover, they had hopes that the tyranny of Lauderdale, under which they had groaned for so many years, was at last coming to an end. James, however, continued popular with the common people throughout his stay in Scotland. In October 1681, when he had been there altogether a little over a year, he paid a visit to Glasgow, and there he

> was welcomed by all the soldiers with volleys and by the townsmen who went out to meet him with Archbishop Ross with acclamations of joy, and by the town itself with bonfires and ringing of bells;

[1] The writer of the letter was, of course, biased in James's favour, but it is unlikely that he would have exaggerated more than a little to a private friend.

and when he went to Dumbarton the following day there were similar demonstrations. It is fairly safe to say that in no town in England would James at that time have been given more than a perfunctory welcome.

Holyrood House was placed by Charles at James's disposal as a residence; in the order for the preparation of the palace for his occupation it is stated that he has allowed James "to reside in Scotland during his royal pleasure", a clear implication that he held no official position.[1] He had always held the honorary status of Privy Councillor of Scotland, and he now proposed to take his seat on the Council; but the difficulty arose that he could not take the necessary oaths. Reference was made to Charles, and he replied that it was "our pleasure that he continue to act as a privy councillor, in that our ancient kingdom, without taking any oath".

All accounts agree that James made a very good first impression in Scotland. Lauderdale had governed by a faction and had excluded from office and favour everyone who refused to accept his principles of administration and to submit to his commands; James made overtures to many of the nobility who had been in opposition and established himself as above party. His own account of his policy is probably very near the truth.

> I live here [he wrote to Legge] as cautiously as I can, and am very careful to give offence to none and to have no partialities, and preach to them laying aside all private animosities and securing the King his own way. None shall have reason to complain of me, and though some of either party here might have hoped I should have showed my partiality for them, and some of my friends have been of opinion it had been best for me to have done so, and by it have secured one side to me, yet I am convinced it was not fit for me to do it, it being no way good for His Majesty's service.

The Scottish Constitution, more aristocratic than that of England, and the absence in the Scottish Parliament of any tradition of opposition to the monarchy, suited James very well. He appears to have made some little study of the condition of Scotland and he was able to arrive at the conclusion, obvious to a newcomer, though obscured by use to natives of the country, that the state of the Highlands was entirely unsatisfactory; and before leaving for England at the end of his short visit he strongly urged the Council "to devise some measure for enforc-

[1] Major Hay (*Enigma of James II*, pp. 11–13) protests against Mr. Winston Churchill's statement that James was "marooned" in Scotland; he has apparently not seen this official statement. Burton and Mr. Ogg say that James went to Scotland as High Commissioner; apart from the evidence here adduced there could be no Commissioner when Parliament was not sitting.

ing the law in those disorderly districts, without which he conceived the King is not entirely King of the whole kingdom". It is odd that he did not pursue this matter when he returned to Scotland for a longer stay and with increased powers. Had he done so with success he would, however, have done much to ruin in advance the Jacobite cause; for, besides Claverhouse in his own lifetime, his son and grandson, after he was dead, drew what strength they possessed from districts in which royal authority had never been made effectual.[1]

On January 28, 1680, Charles announced to his Council his intention of recalling James, saying that his exile had not had the good effects on public life that had been anticipated and that it was only just that James should be near at hand when his affairs were being discussed. Leave to return was accordingly sent to James, and he prepared for his departure from Edinburgh. His popularity had not waned during his stay there, and the ceremonies of farewell were on the same scale as those of his arrival. His private behaviour appears to have given no opportunity for scandal, for we read (from a Catholic source, however) that "all persons, even fanatics, are forced to love him because of his virtuous and exemplary life". He left Edinburgh by sea with Mary Beatrice on February 17, 1680, after a stay of twelve weeks, and arrived at the Privy Stairs at Whitehall a week later. Charles received him with unwonted cordiality and declared that they would never be parted again. Part of his good spirits may have been due to the address he had received from twenty-eight members of the Scottish Privy Council: in very fulsome terms this address set forth the great benefits that James's stay among them had brought to the country, and declared their loyalty to his royal person and "to your royal successors in the ordinary degrees of succession according to the unalienable right of blood". More surprising, as bearing no element of sycophancy or courtly compliment, was the behaviour of the London (or perhaps only Westminster) mob: on February 24 Sir Robert Southwell wrote to Ormonde

> The Duke and Duchess of York arrives this day at Whitehall, both very well, and received with all demonstrations of joy. But the King did forbid any expression to be made in the City by my Lord Mayor. Yet at this end of the town the bells are ringing and the bonfires numerous.

Well might the Dutch ambassador write to William at the end of this year, "Les mouvements de cette nation sont souvent extrêmement brusques".

But not only was there this unofficial rejoicing at James's return;

[1] See Miss Cunningham, *The Loyal Clans, passim.*

official bodies also gave him welcome. Two days after his arrival the Lord Mayor, the Recorder and eighteen aldermen of the City of London waited on him, and on March 8 he and Charles were entertained in the City at a great supper, where they stayed until one o'clock (incidentally it was rumoured that the wine was bad, for some of the retinue had headaches next day, "though I heard the Duke commend it exceedingly"); in May the Mayor and Corporation of Bath in a loyal address mentioned the great benefits they had enjoyed, "particularly by the recall of His Royal Highness".

After the fall of Danby,[1] Charles had entrusted the administration to three men who in their subsequent and very diverse careers proved themselves to be of outstanding ability, though it is doubtful if any one of them could claim to be a statesman: Robert Spencer, second Earl of Sunderland; Laurence Hyde, James's brother-in-law, the younger son of Lord Chancellor Clarendon; and Sidney Godolphin. At the time of their appointment they were young—Sunderland, the oldest, was not yet forty—and unknown; the wits laughed at them and called them "the Chits"; but Charles had in a supreme degree one quality which was absolutely denied to James, a knowledge of men and an appreciation of ability. All three men showed great industry and devotion to business. Sunderland from the first stood out as the King's chief adviser; he was a man of great administrative capacity, but entirely lacking in principle, and so short-sighted that he was unable to recognise at any crisis which side it would be to his interest to take. Hyde, better known as the Earl of Rochester, was the one man of principle of the three, a thorough-going Church-and-King man, prepared to go to any lengths in defence of the royal prerogative, but as consistent an opponent of Catholic aspirations as was his far weaker brother, Henry, second Earl of Clarendon; he was the only one of the three who remained faithful to James during the Exclusion crisis. Godolphin, until the reign of Anne, when events forced him into political prominence, was pre-eminently the unobtrusive public servant: as Charles said, "never in the way, and never out of the way". He took small interest in faction fights or even in dynastic struggles; when they were over he was always ready to place his first-class financial brain at the disposal of the victor. If he had a principle it was that the most important consideration was that the work of the Treasury should be well done.[2]

[1] There was an interval of some six months in the summer of 1679 in which the "triumvirate" of Halifax, Sunderland and Essex (with Temple as a timid and doubtful fourth) had jointly the chief place in the King's counsels.

[2] There is an illuminating passage in one of Godolphin's letters to William, written in 1694, when faction was at its height and he himself was classed as a

The summer of 1680 was a very uncomfortable period in James's life. Of actual events there were few of importance—Parliament was not sitting—but there was intense political activity all over the country. Shaftesbury was now at the height of his power, and through the organisation of the Green Ribbon Club he kept up the excitement which had been engendered by the Popish Plot. Both he and the King realised that the Opposition was helpless as long as the Parliament elected the previous autumn was in abeyance, and in consequence he devoted his energies to promoting petitions for an early meeting of Parliament. These petitions poured in to Charles from all sides, and he strongly resented what he considered to be an attempt to interfere with his right to control the meetings of Parliament; he was justified in his resentment in equity, if not in law, for though subjects have a right to petition the King, an organised bombardment of petitions comes near to an attempt at coercion. When Charles's irritation became known, the Court party presented loyal addresses abhorring the methods of those who had presented the petitions, and the two contending factions became known as "Petitioners" and "Abhorrers", names which were very shortly afterwards exchanged for "Whig" and "Tory", both in their origins terms of abuse invented by opponents. James underrated the strength of the support which the petitioners had from public opinion: he wrote to William:

> There has been some endeavours used in several countrys [counties] by some few gentlemen to have got petitions for the speedy sitting of the Parliament, but they were rejected everywhere, and really the generality of the nobility and gentry are very loyal, and it is but a few, and those not considerable, that make all the noise.

From the day of his return from Scotland, James, to outward seeming, took up again the commanding position in the King's counsels which he had enjoyed a year earlier. Immediately after his arrival the Dutch ambassador reported to Henry Sidney that "the Duke governs all", and a month later Reresby writes of him as "having now the application of all men, being fair with the King". The royal brothers resided for the most part at Windsor,[1] and went to London every Wednesday for the

---

Tory: in that letter he expresses himself, as First Commissioner of the Treasury, delighted with a new Treasury Board which had recently been appointed, because the new men "love despatch in business as the others did trifling"; as a matter of fact a board exclusively composed of Tories had been displaced to make room for a board exclusively (with one doubtful exception) composed of Whigs.

[1] Where (said Mary Beatrice) Charles "did not care to be spoken to on business".

day, Charles to attend a Council meeting, James to amuse himself as best he could; for he was not a member of the Council and was only called to its meetings rarely and for particular purposes. James hunted two or three times a week, and he wrote to William on one occasion that he had had so long a run that he did not return to the Castle until midnight.

But James's condition was not happy: he enjoyed neither the power nor the peace of mind with which he was credited. At first, indeed, all went well; there had been some apprehension that he would make trouble by trying to divert policy from the lines which Charles and his advisers had followed during his year of exile, but he was in an accommodating mood, and agreed to everything; he was also in a mood of optimism, but it was only because he lacked the facility of looking beneath the surface of things. By April he was beginning to have misgivings; early in that month he told Barrillon that he was in a condition to maintain himself and could rely on the support of Ministers, but that he was not free from apprehension that his enemies would prevail; he added that he was convinced that the monarchy would be in danger if Parliament were allowed to meet, and that he would do everything possible to prevent its meeting. A week later he expressed himself dissatisfied with his influence in affairs, though he still stood fair with the Ministers; Barrillon's private opinion, which he confided to Louis, was that James had no power in home or foreign affairs, that he was unaware what danger he would be in if Parliament met, and that Charles and his Ministers were deceiving him by simulating optimism. At the same time James wrote to William

> As for the temper of the several countries [counties], the judges and all that are come to town do say they find, within these two or three months the greatest alteration for the better that can be imagined, and what His Majesty hath done in purging the Commissions of the peace of all disaffected people to him, has contributed much to it by encouraging his old friends, the Cavalier or Church party, and truly I am persuaded, if he do but continue steady to the grounds he has now laid down to himself (as I make no doubt but he will) that within some time he will be more master and in a better condition than he has been these many a year; so that except the Duke of Monmouth do some hot-headed thing, which I think him capable of, all things are likely to be very quiet here.

What James did not see was that Monmouth was only part of the trouble, though a very important part, as providing a rallying-point for the Opposition. He had returned to England in the previous November without Charles's permission, and had behaved in his usual self-confident manner. He went to his lodgings at the Cockpit at Whitehall and sent across to Charles to ask for an audience; Charles refused to see him, and ordered him abroad again; Monmouth refused to go, and dared his father to prosecute him. Charles's prerogative did not extend to having his son arrested and deported, and he took the only step open to him and deprived him of his places of profit and trust, "so that the Duke is like to have little left but his wife's estate to live on". Monmouth left the Cockpit and went to live at his house in Hedge Lane (now Whitcomb Street), repeatedly sending vain requests to the King for an audience and at the same time forming relations with the leaders of the Opposition.

In May a rumour came to light to the effect that Cosin, the late Bishop of Durham, had had in his possession a Black Box containing papers which proved that Charles had been married to Lucy Walter, Monmouth's mother, and that the Bishop had bequeathed the box to Sir Gilbert Gerrard. The Privy Council questioned Gerrard, and he denied all knowledge of the Black Box; Charles told the Council that he knew how much it was to his interest to have a legitimate son, but

> that his conscience and his honour would not permit him to tolerate such a shameful belief as that he had married or promised to marry the Duke of Monmouth's mother and that he would do everything possible to prove its falsity,

and he followed up this statement by making a fresh declaration that he had never been married to any woman but Queen Catherine, and he had this declaration registered in the Court of Chancery.

In June occurred an incident which had no immediate results, but which furnished an indication of the growing audacity of Shaftesbury and the Exclusionists. Barrillon thought they were going to indict James for high treason and that James would go to the Tower and never leave it, but their attack took a different form. The Earl and some of his friends among the nobility and gentry appeared in the King's Bench before Chief Justice Scroggs and presented an indictment against James as a popish recusant—if he had been convicted he would under the existing law have had to forfeit two-thirds of his property—and against the Duchess of Portsmouth as a common nuisance. Scroggs acted with firmness and deliberation, though with little legality: he put the indictment on the list for the grand jury, proceeded with the other cases for several days, and then dismissed the jury before it could consider the cases of James and the Duchess—an action for which he was called to account by the House of Commons at the end of the year. James was justly indignant at this purely personal attack, but even while the grand jury was still sitting and no one could foretell the issue, and while Charles and the Ministers were terribly upset, James showed no embarrassment; he told Barrillon that he hoped the incident would open Charles's eyes.

The Duchess of Portsmouth was thoroughly frightened; hitherto she had been working in close association with James, and it had been the general opinion that they, with Danby and Barrillon, were in effectual control of the royal will. She now went over to the Exclusionists, and it is possibly by her influence that Sunderland eventually found himself in the same camp. The Duchess at this time appears to have conceived a new idea: with a mother's infatuation, she believed that if James could be set aside, her own (and Charles's) son, the Duke of Richmond, now eight years old, might by a declaration of the King be placed next in the succession. James later described her defection as "a dog trick" and declared he could no longer rely on her word: at the time, however, they preserved an outward appearance of amity, though Barrillon was aware that they were at cross-purposes and he suspected that for a time James and Hyde tried to set up the Duchess of Mazarin [1] as a rival in the favour of Charles to the Duchess of Portsmouth.

James could show courage during the crisis before Scroggs had dismissed the grand jury, but there was a reaction as soon as the crisis was passed; he had to recognise that Shaftesbury would not have come into the open as he had done unless he had relied on considerable support in the country and even had had some hope that Charles might give way on the subject of Exclusion. Thenceforth until the dissolution of the Oxford Parliament in the following March, James was, with occasional deviations into optimism, in deep trouble of mind; this was not the despair of eight years later, when he abandoned hope and left everything he cared for in the hands of his enemies; but a soldier's feeling of helplessness among politicians whose methods he distrusts, and a strong desire to get to physical grips with his enemies.

> The Duke of York's design [wrote Barrillon] is that his affairs shall be brought to an extremity and produce an open rupture. He is persuaded that the royal authority cannot be established except by a civil war. He believes that by that he may escape the peril with which he is threatened.

[1] The Duchess of Mazarin, Hortense Mancini, one of the nieces of Cardinal Mazarin and a famous beauty, had been domiciled in England since 1676. She was a great favourite with both Charles and James, though in James's case the affection was platonic. In May 1676 he and Mary Beatrice jointly bought a new house in St. James's Park and presented it to her. On his accession James gave her lodgings at Whitehall.

In this conflict he desired above all things the help of France, he kept urging Barrillon to convince Louis that without his support the English monarchy would be lost. He was unaware of Louis's point of view—that he had no motive of kindness or of gratitude to Charles or James and was quite content to see England in the toils of civil conflict and innocuous in foreign policy; as Barrillon cynically remarked, Charles deserved no help from Louis, and James's good intentions could be of no use to him.

James steadily lost ground in the country. As early as July, Lady Sunderland informed Sidney that people were more exasperated with him every day, and Charles about the same time began to be aware of the fact. Shaftesbury openly boasted that he had the Duke in his power and that it was too late for him to save himself even by the desperate expedient of going to church, receiving the Sacrament and abjuring transubstantiation. This was also Barrillon's opinion: he told Louis that great efforts were being made to persuade James to change his religion and that (surprisingly enough) Mary Beatrice was not opposing those efforts because she dreaded a further period of exile; but that if James became a Protestant the opposition would have to find some other pretext for excluding him from the succession—a clear implication that James's unpopularity was due only in part to his religion.

In August Monmouth started on a tour through the Western Counties, where he was entertained by a number of gentlemen of the country party and, though the Court party stood aloof, he was everywhere received by the common people with acclamation, and was met and accompanied by large troops of horsemen at the entry to all the towns he visited. As late as October 3, James wrote to William, "His Majesty, notwithstanding all their endeavours, continues very firm to me, and yet, if he will be resolute and show favour to his old friends all will do well". But Charles had in August declared in Council that Parliament would definitely meet on October 21, and at a Council held ten days before that date James met with a serious disappointment: there was numerical support for his plea that he should be allowed to remain at Court, to face the worst that Parliament could do to him and to rely on Charles to save him in the last resort by a dissolution or prorogation: this party included Finch, the Lord Chancellor, the two Hydes and Jenkins; but on the other side were Sunderland and Godolphin, who had at that time more influence with the King than any other Minister. James was particularly angry with these two Councillors, "those whom I expected to be most my friends are no more so now, for they would have me go away", a remark which excludes the possibility that such advice might have been tendered by his friends and for his benefit.

But he still thought he might avoid exile, he represented to Charles that those who advised him were either biased in their judgements or men of depraved character—that Halifax, for example, was an atheist—and that, as he constantly maintained in his correspondence, the attacks on him were in essence attacks on the monarchy.

On October 16 James had a conversation with Barrillon in which he expressed his hopes and his fears: he said that he did not yet despair of being able to save himself, that Charles had not definitely decided to abandon him to his enemies, and that the advice of Sunderland and the Duchess of Portsmouth that he should be sent away had not yet been and might not be followed; but that notwithstanding all this he would not be surprised if the King made him depart in two days. In this anticipation he was not much at fault, it was actually four days.

Charles would no doubt have preferred that James should go voluntarily, but when he found that persuasion was of no avail he gave him a direct command, softening it, however, with kind expressions of regret. This time also he was not merely "permitted to reside in Scotland", he was entrusted with a definite commission: he was to hasten the settlement of the new model of the militia in Scotland, and to use his influence "for the general settlement of the peace of that our ancient kingdom". But one grievous disappointment James had to endure: he requested Charles to give him a public pardon for all his past offences, and Charles refused. The case of Danby was not forgotten, and to grant a pardon in existing circumstances would have been merely to invite the House of Commons to repeat the assertion of their right to overrule royal pardons and to proceed at once with the impeachment of James.

CHAPTER XI

THE SECOND VISIT TO SCOTLAND

JAMES embarked at Woolwich with the Duchess on October 20, the day before the meeting of Parliament, and after a stormy voyage landed at Kirkcaldy on the 26th. Holyrood House was undergoing repairs, and they spent three days at Leslie before crossing over to Edinburgh. There their reception gave them entire satisfaction, though it was marred by an unfortunate and possibly ominous incident.

> A little after their arrival, having visited the Castle of Edinburgh, and for a testimony of joy the gun called Mons Meg, being charged by the advice of ane English cannoneer, in the shooting was riven; which some foolishly called a bad omen. The Scots resented it extremely, thinking the Englishman might of malice have done it purposely, they having in England no cannon as big as she.

James was fully aware, as he had been at Brussels, that he could not be recalled within a short time, and he settled down for a long stay. At the end of September Charles had decided to make a paper concession to Lauderdale's enemies and had formally terminated his appointment as Secretary for Scotland; his successor was the Earl of Moray, but it was understood that the administration should remain in effect in Lauderdale's hands.[1] This device could not, however, continue to operate while James was representing the King in Scotland, and Lauderdale's long control of the affairs of that kingdom came to an end; he was still a member of the English Privy Council, but he had ceased to have influence in the royal counsels, he lost one by one all his offices and when he died in August 1682 he was virtually in disgrace. The Commission which Charles had given James was interpreted in the widest possible sense and, though he still held no definite post in the administration, he was from the first for all purposes the King's representative.

The main business of the Scottish Government was the suppression

[1] Hume Brown alleges that "in the course of the year 1680 a quarrel had arisen between Lauderdale and the Duke which had made it impossible for them to sit at the same board". W. R. Mathieson and Andrew Lang ascribe this quarrel to the vote which Lauderdale gave in the House of Lords against Lord Stafford. Lauderdale resigned the Secretaryship in September and gave this vote on December 7, so that there is a clear discrepancy. In any case the breach was not final, for the two men corresponded amicably in the following year.

of rebellion in the south-west, a rebellion which had commenced with the Restoration and continued ever since, and had been scotched but not killed by Monmouth's victory at Bothwell Brigg. The rebels, known as the Covenanters from their adhesion to the Solemn League and Covenant of 1638, and as Cameronians and Cargillites after successive leaders, boasted that they were the only people remaining faithful to the Truth after the numerous defections to the side of the Stuart Government; into minds formed by their narrow lives entered no conception of other people of faith and practice similar to their own, and they conceived themselves to be, like the Children of Israel, the only true worshippers of God and followers of His rule of life in a world given over to wickedness and abomination. For their belief they were prepared to die in battle or on the scaffold, or, in the event of victory (in the true Israelite tradition), to submit their enemies to wholesale massacre—at Bothwell Brigg, for example, they erected gallows behind the lines for the despatch of prisoners. They refused submission to Government by "ungodly" men—that is to say, by men who did not share their peculiar views—and in effect they declared war without quarter on the existing Government of Scotland. Nor does it seem probable that any government to their liking could have been devised, for they were such thorough-going anti-Erastians that they repudiated control by government of religion in any of its aspects, and these aspects were often held by other people to be secular; perhaps their ideal was a theocracy—a rule of the saints in which the State would be controlled by the Church.

The Government, on their side, tried to keep the Covenanters in check by a series of harsh laws, and terrible crimes were committed under these laws both by the high officials who issued orders from Edinburgh and by soldiers on the spot, like John Graham of Claverhouse. No one can claim that in his dealings with the Covenanters Charles II through his deputies—that is to say, for the greater part of his reign through Lauderdale—displayed either wisdom or moderation; but the problem was one which would have baffled the wisest and most humane government. Individually these Cameronians and Cargillites were men of low education, but of keen but narrow intelligence, exemplary in their private lives and selfless in their devotion to the Cause; but from the point of view of the Government they were *mauvais sujets* who could be neither softened by compromise nor tamed by coercion; their one virtue was that they gave little trouble to the judges, for when they were on trial for treasonable utterances they made no defence, but repeated their treasons in open court, or even improved upon them. Their most voluminous early apologist has prefaced an account of their sufferings in the year 1681 in words whose moderation is very remarkable:

> Against them it was alleged, and indeed it was all that could be said, that they committed treason in face of the Court before which they were staged; but if we consider their circumstances, the views they had of matters, and the hardships they were brought under, certainly great charity must be exercised towards them; and although, according to the present laws, they were found guilty of treason, yet their bloodshed will, by after generations, be reckoned innocent blood; and the courses taken with, and inhumanities exercised towards them, must certainly be abominated by all sober persons.

James's conduct in regard to the Covenanters has no bearing on the question of his attitude to religious toleration. There is no doubt that he regarded them as blasphemous fanatical schismatics, but there appears to be no evidence that this opinion influenced him in the least in his dealings with them. On the other hand, he did not try to placate them by measures of moderation and religious tolerance on the lines suggested by Archbishop Leighton a few years earlier. He dealt with them as rebels, not, he must have admitted, as immediately dangerous rebels, but as people who denied in their hearts and by word of mouth the right of Charles Stuart to reign in Scotland; such pernicious doctrine might spread and, lest it should become universal, those who held it must either repudiate it or be exterminated. There is evidence that James was not entirely happy about the methods which were being employed to suppress sedition: those who had appeared in arms against the Government at Bothwell Brigg and refused to come in and make submission he pursued with a relentless severity which was a fitting prelude to the Bloody Assizes four years later; but for those, particularly women, who were condemned merely for their spoken beliefs he exhibited real compassion; he claimed (as has been seen) to have converted many from the error of their ways, and to others he offered reprieve if only they would pronounce the words, "God save the King"—it was his misfortune that he could not understand that such an utterance would have been a betrayal of the faith for which they were prepared to die, a faith as dear to them as James's was to him. The year 1681 was one of the worst in the history of the persecution of the Covenanters, but it would be unjust to ascribe the increased activity on the part of Government entirely to James. He is reported to have said shortly after his second arrival in Edinburgh that the plotters "deserved a Bedlam rather than a gallows"; Burnet, who in this case may be regarded as a hostile witness, says that he made a very real effort to prove himself a just and clement ruler in Scotland; and Halifax, who was neither biased in James's favour nor inclined to condone harshness, and who had supported a movement to remove Lauderdale on the ground of his undue severity, said that James "did a great deal of good in Scotland by his influence and watchfulness in that mutinous kingdom".

One of the gravest general charges that has been brought against James is in connection with his administration of Scotland. It was first propounded by Burnet in the following words:

> When any are to be struck in the boots, it is done in the presence of the Council and upon that occasion almost all offer to run away. The sight is so dreadful, that without an order restraining such a number to stay, the board would be forsaken. But the Duke, while he had been in England, was so far from withdrawing, that he looked on all the while with unmoved indifference, and with an attention, as if he had been to look on some curious experiment. This gave a terrible idea of him to all that observed it, as of a man that had no bowels nor humanity in him.

This statement of fact may be true, but it need not bear the implication that Burnet places on it: James was not a man of acute sensibility, and he could easily have forgotten the sufferings of the victims in his concentration on the evidence. But even that degree of truth is denied by the annotators of Burnet, who point out that many of James's inveterate enemies had written accounts of this very period, and had made no mention of a circumstance which they could hardly have overlooked if they had known of it.

But Macaulay, ignoring the commentators, although their notes appear in the edition of Burnet which he habitually used, not only accepted the story, but gave it currency in an improved form:

> The Duke of York, it was remarked, seemed to take pleasure in the spectacle which some of the worst men then living were unable to contemplate without pity and horror. He not only came to Council when the torture was to be inflicted, but watched the agonies of the sufferers with that sort of interest and complacency with which men observe a curious experiment in science;

and, as if he felt he had not sufficiently misused his authority, he improved on his first effort on a later page.

> He who had expressed just indignation when the priests of his own faith were hanged and quartered amused himself with hearing

> the Covenanters shriek and seeing them writhe while their knees were beaten flat in the boots;

and in support of this latter statement he adduces as an authority in addition to Burnet a book in which occurs no statement more damaging than that James was present in council when a certain prisoner was tortured. He reverts to the subject again in connection with the condemnation of Argyll after the failure of his rebellion.

> . . . James, was doubtless sorry that he could not feast his own eyes with the sight of Argyll in the boots. . . .

Nevertheless there is no doubt that James approved of the Scottish judicial procedure in which there was provision for the use of torture in eliciting evidence.[1] Writing to Queensberry in August 1682 after his return to London, he says, "I find by yours the boots had done no good upon Spence, and believe him so stubborn he will not own what he knows"; and again ten days later, "By yours of the 7, I was glad to find that Spence began to speak. I hope to hear soon he has been ingenious (*sc.* ingenuous) and will discover all he knows." These passages are isolated, but they are in keeping with what we know of the attitude of James to the law—in common with Jeffreys and most of the judges and Crown lawyers—in criminal cases in which the Crown was concerned: they did not conceive the possibility that the prisoner could have been wrongly suspected and arrested, and if he did not confess his crime they held that any method of procuring evidence and any interpretation of the rules of procedure were justified. If James had been capable of detached thought, the application of this principle in the Popish Plot trials would have made him less certain of its validity.

After an intermission of nine years Charles decided that it was time that his third Scottish Parliament should meet; he appointed James Commissioner, and convened it for July 28. Five weeks before that date James wrote to Lauderdale, who had been Commissioner in the previous Parliaments, asking for information and advice. Lauderdale replied at length; he said that in all the sessions in which he had been Commissioner he had had to pay particular attention to the means of getting well-affected members returned, but he added significantly, "I hope Your Royal Highness shall not need such precautions seeing it may in reason be thought impossible there should be any opposition made or storm raised against such things as you shall in your wisdom

[1] As Andrew Lang points out (*Mackenzie of Rosehaugh*, pp. 194–5) the use of torture was not condemned by the most enlightened of James's contemporaries.

propose"; for the rest, he advised James to consult the Duke of Rothes and the lawyers on the spot. James took great pains over the opening ceremony, and he was anxious that his clothes and the housings of his horse should be correct and that his own coaches should be in order for the procession to the House; on the opening day he gave a great dinner to the members.

James was pleased with the political complexion of his Parliament; indeed, he could hardly have been otherwise when the prevailing circumstances of parliamentary elections are taken into account. For the elections were in no sense free, even to the small degree that they were in England: the Lord Advocate in course of a debate was able to remark that "if the burghs had liberty to choose whom they pleased to represent them, factious and disloyal persons might prevail to get themselves elected"; a voter was actually prosecuted for having "voted against the Duke and the Court faction in the election of the commissioners to Fife". Moreover, legislation was strictly controlled by the Lords of the Articles, a Committee of members nominally elected by the House but actually appointed by the Royal Commissioner; no legislation could be initiated except by the Lords of the Articles, and they had at command various devices to prevent discussion, such as rushing controversial measures through the House late in the evening when members were tired.

The proceedings opened with the reading of the letter from the King, in which he urged the members to provide for the security of religion and recommended to them "our most dear and most entirely beloved brother, James, Duke of Albany and York", whom he had named as his Commissioner. James's speech followed; he outlined the programme of the session: the maintenance of the government of the Church by archbishops and bishops, the suppression of seditions and rebellious conventicles, the declaration of the rights of the Crown in its natural and legal course of descent—but he was careful to say nothing about popery. In their reply the Parliament were not so scrupulous: their address did indeed affirm in the strongest terms attachment to the hereditary principle, but it described "the usurpations and disorders of popery and fanaticism" as the chief dangers against which provision must be made. Legislation followed on these lines: by the first Act of the Parliament all existing laws for the protection of the Church were re-enacted; the second declared the Crown of Scotland to be "transmitted and devolved by a lineal succession, according to the proximity of blood" and that "no difference of religion, nor no law nor Act of Parliament, made or to be made, can alter or divert the right of succession"; it further declared it to be treason to attempt in any way to vary the succession from the direct line. There was clearly from the start a confusion of intention in this single-minded and subservient assembly: the habit of twenty years made them support the Protestant episcopal Church against the sectaries on the one hand, whom they regarded historically as typifying the rule of the saints and the Cromwellian conquest, and personally as rebels and outlaws, and on the other hand against the papists, dangerous upholders of a faith alien to their national habits of thought; but at the same time they were not only willing but anxious for the succession of James to the Scottish throne, in spite of the patent fact that he was a devout and uncompromising Roman Catholic.

After granting a supply the Parliament proceeded to pass a very savage Act by which landowners were forbidden, under very heavy penalties, to allow Covenanters to be their tenants or servants, or to hold field Conventicles on their land; the Covenanters were thus to be deprived of their livelihood and became for all intents and purposes fugitive outlaws. But the Act which caused the greatest controversy was the Test Act. This Act, after commanding all public officers, judges and magistrates to put to full and vigorous execution all the existing laws against papists and "fanatic separatists", prescribes an oath which shall be taken not only by all civil, ecclesiastical and military officers (excepting "the King's lawful brother and sons"), but also by all persons exercising public functions, such as clerks to boroughs, advocates in the courts and teachers. Two main objections were made to the Act: the first was that by implication it expelled from their professions large classes of people who could not conscientiously take the oath, the second was the wording of the oath itself. The oath was in two sections: by the first the person sworn affirmed adherence to the Confession of Faith recorded in the first Parliament of King James VI,[1] and disowned popish or fanatical doctrines inconsistent with it; by the second he promised allegiance to "the King's Majesty, his heirs and lawful successors", and undertook not "to endeavour any change or alteration in the Government". There was a definite contradiction between the Confession and the Oath, for the Confession stated that Christ was the only Head of the Church. Incidentally it was alleged that it was understood between the Government and the magistrates that the Act, as had been the case with the two previous Acts against popery and fanaticism, should be put into full force against the Protestant sectaries, but should be of no effect against the Catholics. Indeed, it was given out among the

[1] This phrase was said to have been introduced on the motion of Sir James Dalrymple in the hope that it might cause misgivings among the bishops and result in the defeat of the measure. Andrew Lang attributes this statement to James himself, but I do not find contemporary corroboration.

Catholic priests that if the Papists kept quiet the Church would do them no harm.

The seventeenth century was the age of oaths; whatever party was in favour tried to perpetuate that power by solemn affirmations of loyalty to itself or to the religious or political principles which it represented. In the House of Lords in 1690 the Marquis of Wharton said he was a very old man, that he had taken a multitude of oaths in his time, and that he hoped God would forgive him if he had not kept them all, for truly they were more than he could pretend to remember; the Earl of Macclesfield, an old Cavalier, said he was in much the same case as Lord Wharton, though they had not always taken the same oaths. Such must have been the case with almost everyone in public life: if those only had been employed who had taken no oath inconsistent with his loyalty to William and Mary, their Government would have been carried on by men who had previously lived in obscurity. No oath can bind any but the most scrupulous when entirely new and unforeseen circumstances arise—such, for instance, as those caused by the flight of James II—and it is only the most scrupulous who on grounds of conscience refuse to take oaths. The unscrupulous take oaths and break them with equal complacency; the moderately conscientious take them in good faith, and they have sometimes, perhaps after many years have passed, to decide whether or not it is in the public interest that they shall continue to hold themselves bound; and unfortunately it is not given to man entirely to separate in his mind the public interest from his own private interest.[1]

There was little disturbance of men in office on account of the Scottish Test Oath: some were, no doubt, honest in their adherence to the Episcopal Church and a popish succession, others took it as a matter of course; some, like the Marquis of Queensberry, hesitated; but all the chief officers of State took the oath, with one exception. That exception was the most powerful noble in Scotland, the Earl of Argyll. He, indeed, took it, but with a verbal reservation:

> I have considered the Test, and am desirous to give obedience as far as I can. I am confident the Parliament never intended to impose contradictory oaths, therefore I think no man can explain it

[1] Many cavaliers adopted during the Interregnum the principle that oaths taken under durance were not binding. One of them is reported to have said, in reply to an assertion that Parliament had unlimited power and could do anything, "that they could not make an oath as he could not swallow".

Halifax is reported to have said, "As no man would even sleep with open doors though all the town should be sworn not to rob, so the state gained no security by oaths; and their only effect was to disturb or exclude some honest conscientious men, who would never have prejudiced the government".

> but for himself. Accordingly, I take it as far as it is consistent with itself, and the Protestant religion; and I do declare I mean not to bind myself in my station, and in a lawful way to wish and endeavour any alteration I think to the advantage of the Church or State, not repugnant to the Protestant religion and my loyalty; and this I understand as a part of my oath.

He was permitted on November 3 to take the oath before the Privy Council with this explanation, and after taking it he was admitted to his usual seat at the Council board. Many of the Councillors had, no doubt, had the same mental reservations, and regarded him as unnecessarily scrupulous in declaring them. But after the Council meeting his enemies (of whom there were many, for between the Campbells and most of the other clans feuds had existed for centuries and Argyll had been very harsh and unscrupulous both with his creditors and his tenants) thought they saw a chance of laying him in the dust. They went to James and represented to him that Argyll's criticism of an Act of Parliament was an offence which might be made to appear treasonable. James, too, had a grudge against the Earl: he had shown far more independence of judgment than the other Councillors, and in particular he had shown himself strongly anti-papist by insisting on the insertion in Bills which were to be laid before Parliament of phrases which placed the papists in the same position before the law as the Protestant sectaries; in addition, both Charles and James distrusted Argyll: he was an "over-mighty subject" who might easily turn the balance against the monarchy in case of civil war. The lawyers when they were consulted gave the conspirators little hope that a charge of treason could be upheld on the slender grounds suggested. However, James and his subservient Council decided to proceed; the oath was again tendered to the Earl as Commissioner of the Treasury; he made the same explanation, but this time he was held not to have taken the oath, and he was excluded from the Council. The following day he was arrested on a charge of high treason and confined in Edinburgh Castle. In the letter which the Council sent to the King reporting their action, they stated his crime to be that, when he was commanded to take the oath without equivocation,

> he refused to do so, but gave in a paper the only sense in which he would take it; which paper we all considered as that which had in it gross reflections upon that excellent act of parliament, making it to contain things contradictory and inconsistent, and thereby depraving your Majesty's laws, misrepresenting your parliament and teaching your subjects to evacuate and disappoint all the laws and securities that can be enacted for the preservation of the government.

Halifax told Charles, when he consulted him about the matter, that he knew no Scots law, but that in England one would not hang a dog on such a charge, and Lauderdale exerted himself on Argyll's behalf.

Charles, however, wrote to the Council approving their procedure, but ordering that in the event of a conviction the court should not pronounce sentence until they received a communication from him. It was not the intention of the royal brothers to bring Argyll to the scaffold: when it was suggested to James before the trial that "it was hard measure upon such a foot to threaten such a person with a forfeiture of life and fortune", he answered "Life and fortune, God forbid!" and he always maintained that all that was intended was to get the Earl at the mercy of the Crown so that the power which he exercised through his vast estates and his hereditary jurisdictions might be reduced. But if this was the aim, there were methods easier and less open to objection ready to their hands: the Council need only have declared Argyll not to have taken the oath within the meaning of the Act, and he would automatically have been deprived of his jurisdictions; this was the procedure followed in the case of twenty-two jurisdictions which were in the hands of persons who neglected or refused to take the Test.[1]

Argyll's trial began on December 5, with long pleadings by the lawyers on both sides, and it was not until the 12th that he appeared before his judges. On the 13th James wrote to Colonel Legge,

> Lord Argyll's trial began yesterday, and their forms in the Justice Court are so tedious, that they could not make an end of it then, but will as I believe this evening, and have reason to believe the jury will find the bill, and not Ignoramus, and that that Little Lord will be once again at His Majesty's mercy.

It would not perhaps be unduly straining the meaning of this passage if it is suggested that James had reason to be satisfied with the composition both of the Bench and the jury, and that he was confident that, in contradiction to the best legal opinion, they would find the verdict which he desired. Nor was he disappointed: the Earl was found guilty of the major charge of treason, though, to save their faces, the jury acquitted him of the charges of perjury which had been included in the indictment. The verdict was communicated to Charles, but before the royal pleasure could be made known Argyll had escaped from the Castle; it is possible that it was James's intention that he should escape and that orders had been given to the guards not to watch him too

[1] Ranke (IV, 239) quotes from a letter of Charles who requires an opinion "how to dispose of those superiorities and offices which he thought too much for one person".

closely; in any case there appears to be no evidence that disciplinary measures were taken against the guard, as was usual in cases of escape of important political prisoners. After lurking for a short time in London, the Earl passed over to Holland, and in his absence the Court pronounced sentence of death. James had made his first essay in converting a powerful and loyal man into a rebel.

There was one pleasing incident in connection with Argyll's escape. His step-daughter, Lady Sophia Lindsay, had obtained permission to visit him in the Castle, and he had escaped by changing clothes with her footman. Some of the Council proposed that she should be whipped through the streets of Edinburgh; but James replied that they were not used to dealing so harshly with ladies in his country—thus in one sentence disappointing them of their revenge and disavowing his Scottish nationality.

James had set out for Edinburgh in a very truculent mood. Barrillon told Louis that he had had a conversation with him immediately before embarking: James gave the ambassador an account of the deplorable condition into which his affairs had fallen:

> to this he added, in terms full of rage, that if he were pushed to extremity, and saw himself like to be entirely ruined by his enemies, he would find means to make them repent it, to revenge himself on them by giving Your Majesty also your revenge for the conduct they had held here with regard to you; the meaning of which is that he hopes to excite troubles in Scotland and Ireland, and he even alleges that he has a party in England more considerable than is thought of.

To this letter Louis replied that, if James thought of setting himself up independently in Scotland, secret supplies would be available from France, and he followed up this offer by sending an agent to James at Edinburgh.[1] It appears therefore that James succumbed temporarily to the Stuart fallacy (he reverted to it in 1689), and had thoughts of the conquest of England by the assistance of a section of the Scottish nation. But wiser counsels prevailed, and at the end of January Barrillon reported that Churchill in a conversation in London had frankly admitted that James could not maintain himself in Scotland without Charles's support. Meanwhile Shaftesbury had got wind of this intrigue—or

[1] A newsletter emanating from London reported that the Scottish Council had permitted James to add 3000 French to his guards. But there is no record of such a decision in the Register of the Privy Council of Scotland, and on general grounds the statement cannot be believed.

perhaps he had the inspiration to invent a similar plot: on December 23 he made a speech in the House of Lords (the Lords so strongly disapproved of it that they had it burnt) in which he said:

> In the meantime where is this Duke that the King and both Houses have declared unanimously thus dangerous? Why, he is in Scotland, raising forces upon the *terra firma* that can enter dry-foot upon us without hazard of winds and seas. . . . We all think the business is so rife that they have the garrisons, the arms, the ammunition, the seas and soldiery, all in their hands. They want but one good sum of money to set up and crown the work.

This project of military action temporarily improved James's relations with Louis. In the autumn of 1679, just after his sudden appearance at Windsor from Brussels, James had addressed to the French King a letter in which he had expressed the warmest sentiments to France and his strong approval of the treaty which was then under discussion between the two monarchs, and concluded, "It is from you I expect all. And by you alone I can attain my re-establishment in this country." A month later Barrillon wrote that James was so anxious for the conclusion of the treaty that he was prepared to pledge his personal credit if the necessary funds could not be obtained elsewhere. (He presumably meant that he would be surety for any loan that Louis might offer.) In December 1680 James was in the same posture of a humble suppliant; he wrote to Barrillon of Louis's goodness to him and of his aspirations to deserve the continuance of it. In the same month, however, Barrillon reported that he had told Ralph Montagu—with what sincerity we cannot tell—

> that to what regards the Duke of York, his past conduct frees Your Majesty from all you might have done for him, if he had persisted in the first engagements which he had made; that at present Your Majesty had too much prudence to charge yourself with the protection of a prince against whom all England seems to be united.

Louis at the same time was instructing his ambassador to employ all his energy to supporting whatever faction in England appears to be weakest:

> If you see even that the Duke of York's party is likely to succumb, let me know at once and advise me how best such a fatality may be averted;

for, as he said in another letter, he had no interest in the affairs of England unless the Crown was unable to maintain itself in the precarious state in which it was, and England did not degenerate into a republic while preserving the name of a monarchy. Nevertheless, Louis instructed his ambassador to urge on Charles the necessity of recalling James to his counsels; and in February Barrillon told Churchill that Louis considered James's interests and his succession to the throne of the first importance, and was of opinion that the preservation of the monarchy was bound up with James's safety. Throughout the year the ambassador and his master continued to advocate the termination of James's exile; in spite of his vacillation of three years earlier, they both regarded him as the more reliable of the two brothers.

Of James's private life in Scotland during his second and longest stay there we have glimpses from his letters to his young niece, the Countess of Litchfield, a natural daughter of Charles by Lady Castlemaine. In these letters, stilted in style and bald in matter as they are, James appears in a new and more human guise than he does in other letters of his that have been preserved. On the whole we find that, though he is longing for Charles's permission to return to England, he finds Scotland a good country to live in. In particular the political atmosphere is calmer and more pleasant there than in England:

> Here false witnesses dare not come, perjury being death; if it had been so in England so many innocent people had not suffered and things would have been quieter than they are.

And again:

> You must wonder if I have not sooner answered yours of the 2nd since I have had so much business upon my hands ever since I received it, by reason of the sitting of the Parliament, for although a Parliament here be not so troublesome as the English ones have been of late, yet it takes up all one's time.

Princess Anne, now fourteen years of age, arrived on July 17, 1681; she and her step-mother settled down to a routine of simple pleasures, and in these James joined when he had time and inclination. Out of doors they rode and indoors they played basset, Anne took part in private theatricals, she and the Duchess danced country dances and James occasionally condescended to join them; the Duchess unfortunately had a fall from her horse, she escaped serious injury, but it was some weeks before she could dance again with Anne. A troop of Irish actors had come to Edinburgh and were "pretty tolerable"; at first James and the ladies went to the theatre from time to time, later the players performed twice a week at Holyrood House. James lamented that the neighbourhood of Edinburgh was not good hunting country; he apparently tried hunting once or twice, but he wrote to William:

> I find you hunt almost every day, and that it is a place very proper for it; this country affords no such kind of hunting, for where the stags are there are such hills and bogs as 'tis impossible to follow any hounds, so that hare-hunting and shooting are the only sports one can have here; after June is once over there will be very good shooting at heath-pouts [grouse], of which and partridge there are great store here.

Apart from shooting when the weather was fair, he was "abroad every day and playing at 'Goffe'", and in bad weather he patronised the Scottish winter sport of curling, but bad weather was "a great mortification to me, that love best the diversions without doors than those within".

The domestic felicity of the household at Holyrood House was sadly disturbed in March 1681 by the news of the death in London, in her fifth year, of Isabella, the little daughter of James and Mary. James wrote to the child's great-uncle, Prince Rinaldo of Este,

> The loss which I have sustained by the death of my youngest daughter Princess Isabella, whom it pleased God to take from me a few days ago, afflicts me so acutely that I have great need of the consolation which I expect from your friendship, knowing as I do that you have enough of that to be with me in spirit in anything of that nature which touches me. The subject of this letter is too sad for me to discuss it further.

CHAPTER XII

THE SECOND EXCLUSION BILL AND THE TORY REACTION

DURING the whole period of his exile, and particularly during his residence in Scotland from November 1680 to March 1682, more than half James's attention was devoted to the English political scene. By his correspondents—principally Legge and Laurence Hyde—he was supplied with a constant stream of news, and twice he despatched to London Colonel John Churchill to intrigue on his behalf and to report the situation to him on his return.

The proceedings of the Parliament which was elected in September 1679, and met on October 21, 1680, were of supreme interest to James. They opened with an extraordinary and disgraceful episode: Dangerfield, perhaps the most disreputable of the informers, appeared at the bar of the House of Commons to make an accusation against James; briefly, he alleged that it was at James's instigation that he had engaged himself in the so-called Meal-Tub Plot—a clumsy attempt to fabricate a Presbyterian conspiracy to assassinate the King. Other informers followed Dangerfield on similar lines. James's friends were not in a position, even if they had been given opportunity, to repudiate the charges, and the House settled down to discuss Exclusion in the atmosphere of prejudice against James for the creation of which this preliminary scene had possibly been staged.

On October 26 Lord Russell moved to take into consideration how to suppress popery and to prevent a popish succession, and on November 2 Colonel Titus moved for a Committee to draft a new Exclusion Bill, and from the debates on that motion and on the subsequent stages of the Bill we can obtain a very clear picture of the state of feeling on both sides of the House. The supporters of the Bill were on the whole very scrupulous in abstaining from anything like a personal attack on James,[1] but there runs through almost all their speeches a strong belief in the Popish Plot, an impatience of any doubt of its existence, and a sense that the two questions of the Plot and the Succession were intimately associated; "I am satisfied that, as long as the Duke has any prospect left of coming to the Crown, the King cannot be safe"; "the Duke being

[1] *E.g.*, Sir Francis Winnington said, "When I speak of this great Prince, whom I have a great respect for, and had once a relation to, I do it with great reluctance".

looked upon as Heir-apparent to the Crown, the King's life is still in danger"; "Can the King be safe as long as the Papists know that there is nothing but his life stands in their way of having a King to their mind?"; —such remarks occur with only slight verbal differences in many speeches, and in many others the same meaning is expressed or implied. Perhaps the most interesting contribution to the debate was that of Sir William Pulteney, who prophesied what actually occurred when James came to the throne.

> I cannot foresee how the excluding of one person, who hath a right to the succession depending upon contingencies upon such an account as this, should occasion a civil war; but rather do think there is a great deal more danger, not only of a civil war, but of our religion and liberty too, if we should not do it, and so have a popish king. For I do believe that such a king would soon have a popish council. For if there be eleven to seven now for the interest of a popish successor what may you not expect when you have a popish king? And should you not then soon have popish judges, justices, deputy-lieutenants, commanders at sea and land; nay, and popish bishops too? . . .

But two speakers were not so careful in their language, and no doubt they expressed the opinions of many members who were too timid or too decorous to speak out: Henry Booth, who had forsaken the royalist principles of his father, and as Lord Delamere in James's reign was one of the most violent opponents of the Court, not only argued that by the laws of England James had no right to the succession, but accused him of corresponding "with the Pope and the French King to subvert our religion and laws"; he absolved him of any inclination to shorten his brother's days, but continued, "Though he be averse to it, yet in obedience to the Pope and his Priests, it must be done either by himself or some other hand, and then how long may we expect His Majesty's life?" Booth's peroration is interesting as revealing the enormous gap which separated at this time the views of the extreme Whigs and the extreme upholders of passive obedience.

> If kings were good men an absolute monarch were the best government; but we see they are subject to the same infirmities with other men, and therefore it is necessary to bound their power; and by reason that they are flesh and blood, and the nation is so apt to be bad for their example, I believe was that wherefore God was averse to let the Jews have a king; till they had kings they never revolted so wholly from him: when their kings were good

> they were obedient to him; but when they were idolatrous, then the people went mad for idols. I hope it is no regis exemplum that makes our nation so lewd and wicked at this day.

Goodwin Wharton, a cadet of a famous Whig house, but an irresponsible and weak-minded person, went farther: he belittled James's naval services, hinted that he or his friends had protected the men who had originated the great fire, and, without actually employing the unparliamentary word, brought several instances forward to show that James was a liar; so offensive was he that Lord Castleton interrupted him, "To hear a prince thus spoken of, I am not able to endure it".

The opponents of the Bill for the most part sat silent, and the few who spoke did so with no apparent conviction. Their chief argument was that James was being condemned unheard: Laurence Hyde, the best of them, saw that in the temper the House was in there was no chance of defeating the Bill except by offering the compromise of limitations,

> I am of opinion that the Duke, for deserting his religion, deserves a great many mortifications from the nation; and I believe the Duke is convinced that it cannot be reasonable for him to expect to come to the Crown upon such terms as if he had not given those apprehensions and jealousies.

So disheartened were the supporters of hereditary right that they did not even challenge a division at any stage of the Bill. It was carried by Lord Russell to the Lords on November 15.

This, as a contemporary describes it, "was one of the greatest days that was ever known in the House of Lords". The hero of the day was George Savile, Earl of Halifax; he had hitherto been classed among the Whigs, and the general temper of his mind inclined him to their principles. But he was not a party man, he was temperamentally averse to the violence of faction, he had a hearty contempt for the stupidity of politicians and he took pride in standing alone against the flowing tide. He had no sentiment of personal loyalty to James, but he had a strong conviction that the principle of hereditary monarchy must be supported. This position he defined in a letter to Sir Thomas Thynne on October 5:

> For my own part I neither am nor will be under any obligations that might restrain the freedom of my opinion concerning him [James]; but yet if there is any possibility of making ourselves safe by lower expedients, I had rather use them, than venture on so strong a remedy, as the disinheriting the next heir to the throne.

He was also influenced by two apprehensions of a more immediate nature: that James would not passively accept exclusion but would involve the country in civil war in defence of his rights; and that exclusion would affect adversely the interest in the succession of the Prince of Orange. Nor were personal considerations entirely absent: he distrusted Shaftesbury's principles and methods and could never sink to being a mere member of his party. It is possible also that he suspected Shaftesbury of an intention to make Monmouth heir-presumptive; but though Monmouth undoubtedly had aspirations of that sort, and though Shaftesbury may have encouraged those aspirations, it is doubtful that he seriously supported his candidature.[1]

Halifax had no support in the debate: single-handed he met all the arguments of Shaftesbury and of his followers, such as Essex and Sunderland. The opponents of the Bill had been daunted by its easy passage through the Commons and were disinclined for a contest with the other House in which they saw little prospect of victory; but Halifax put new heart into them; he actually achieved, in the opinion of his contemporaries, that rare feat of influencing votes by his oratory, and secured defeat of the Bill on its first reading by 63 to 30.

James for the moment was saved, but Halifax hastened to show that his action on the Exclusion Bill did not free him from all apprehensions regarding the succession of a Catholic to the throne. The day following that on which the Bill was thrown out he introduced in the Lords a scheme for stringently limiting the prerogative in the case of the succession of a papist to the throne, and for the banishment of James during Charles's lifetime or for a period of five years.

During the few weeks that intervened between the rejection by the Lords of the Exclusion Bill and the prorogation of Parliament on January 10, the Whig majority in the House of Commons lost all sense of moderation and proportion. They addressed the King asking him to remove Halifax from his counsels for ever, on the pretext that he had advised the dissolution of the last Parliament, but quite obviously on account of his opposition to the Exclusion Bill; for the same real reason, but on a different pretext, they drew up articles of impeachment against Sir Edward Seymour; they attacked Jeffreys and Chief Justice North for hindering petitions for a new parliament and Scroggs for discharging the grand jury when Shaftesbury had made his presentment against James and the Duchess of Portsmouth; and they concluded their proceedings with a series of thirteen resolutions in which they bound themselves not to grant supply until an Exclusion Bill was passed, made

[1] For a full discussion of Halifax's attitude to Exclusion before Parliament met see Foxcroft, I, 233–45.

a list of persons whom they regarded as James's friends and wished to have removed—the Marquis of Worcester, the two Hydes, Lord Feversham and Sir Edward Seymour—and contemplated addressing the King in favour of Monmouth. Meanwhile they had brought Lord Stafford to the scaffold, on evidence that would not have convinced an impartial court, by unscrupulous management of his case in Westminster Hall. They also discussed at great length limitations as a substitute for exclusion, and speaker after speaker gave his opinion that no laws could be sufficient to restrain a popish king. Perhaps the happiest simile of this debate was that of Colonel Titus

> to accept of expedients to secure the Protestant Religion after such a King had mounted the throne, would be as strange as if there were a lion in the lobby and we should vote "That we would rather secure ourselves by letting him in and chaining him than by keeping him out"

which was versified:

> I hear a lion in the lobby roar;
> Say, Mr. Speaker, shall we shut the door
> And keep him out?—or shall we let him in,
> To try if we can turn him out again.

The stage was set for a conflict between King and Parliament which could hardly have ended except either by the acceptance by the King of the demands of the Whigs or in civil war, when Charles ordered a prorogation on January 10, 1681, and a dissolution a few days later.

The progress of the second Exclusion Bill was followed by James with the greatest anxiety. Unfortunately the earliest letter on the subject which we have is to Colonel Legge in reply to Legge's letter of November 16, which had conveyed the news both of the defeat of the Bill in the Lords and of Halifax's motion for limitations on the following day:

> You will easily believe yours of the 16th was very pleasing to me, to find by it the bill was thrown out of the Lords' house at the very first reading, but it was as bad as a stab with a dagger to me to hear, after Lord Halifax had spoken so handsomely for me, and managed the whole debate, he should make such a proposition as he did next day, what shall I say to it? I would willingly not be thought of of not being very sensible of kindnesses done me, and I am as sensible as possible of his doing his part so very well at the rejecting of my bill, but can I or anybody think him really my friend, that would have me banished from His Majesty's presence, for he moved it, so that I am in a strait as to him, and know not almost what to do.

James was always in "a strait as to" Halifax. The early relations of the two men had been cordial: Halifax, as we have seen, had entertained James magnificently on his way to York in 1665, and James was influential in getting Halifax his first step in the peerage. But there could never have been anything approaching intimacy between them: Halifax was altogether too intelligent for James's liking; he disliked his "refined arguing" and said he was "always for cleaving a hair in his advice". Moreover James had a tidy mind and liked his world divided into those who were Tories and honest men and those who were Whigs and scoundrels, and he had no use for a Trimmer—a man who might, as far as James knew, appear on either side on any given question; nor, it must be admitted, was James alone in this attitude: Halifax was respected for his intellectual abilities and powers of oratory, but the Whigs, after what they considered his apostasy on the Exclusion question, hated him worse than they hated the Tories, and the Tories, though they accepted his leadership on that occasion, suspected his cleverness much as James suspected it. By the end of 1675 it was an open secret that James hated Halifax,[1] and when Halifax was dismissed in January 1676 James was delighted; when he was in Brussels he wrote that he thought Halifax was no true friend to the monarchy and admitted that he had once told him that he looked on him as one of the "dangerust" men he knew. After the mingled gratitude and resentment that the proceedings in the House of Lords on November 15 and 16 had produced, James conceived the notion (which was probably well grounded) that Halifax had been instrumental in getting him sent both times to Scotland and was advising Charles to keep him there, and the references to Halifax in his letters during the ensuing winter and spring are invariably hostile. Then suddenly in June there is a change of attitude, owing apparently to "the assurances Lord Hyde gives me of Lord Halifax's being my friend". But the mood was short-lived, for in December James writes:

> I never could understand his politics, and I am sure they were never calculated for the meridian of a monarchy. And though he be such a hero in a House of Lords, and has a tongue which makes him to be considered there, he is less than other men out of his sphere, and will I doubt run the King into those inconveniences that I fear will be fatal to the Crown, and even to His Lordship too, though he does not think it.

And by February 1682 James was convinced that it was impossible

[1] Burnet ascribes the cleavage to two events in 1673: Halifax's opposition to the Declaration of Indulgence, and a witticism of his in which he played with the oriental compliment, "O King, live for ever" and hinted that he did not trust James.

things could go well if Halifax were at the head of affairs. It is probable that in the course of these months it dawned on James's slow mind that Halifax had no personal respect for him.

James was very angry with two lords who had voted for Exclusion, Sunderland and Essex, and he could not understand why Charles had not dismissed them immediately after they had recorded their votes. Godolphin, too, was in temporary disfavour with him, presumably because he had not spoken in the Commons against the Bill. He envisaged an administration composed entirely of anti-exclusionists—Clarendon Secretary of State instead of Sunderland, Finch at the Board of Treasury instead of Godolphin, and Peterborough and Craven brought into the Privy Council. These were the men to be at Charles's ear when James could not be there to urge on him the necessity for strong action, but it would be far better if James could be recalled to stiffen the King's resolution. Strong action and the necessity for his recall were the themes of all James's letters from Edinburgh; the majority of these have been lost, but his biographer mentions a number to the King, to Laurence Hyde, to Edward Seymour and to a certain mysterious "Doctor",[1] and there is frequent mention in the letters which have survived—those to Colonel Legge—of letters sent and received by James. But the loss of those letters is no great historical calamity: it is easy to guess their contents from the extracts given in the *Life of James* and from the dreary repetitions in those other letters which have been preserved. One quotation (from a letter to Legge of January 16, 1681) will serve as typical of James's persistent attitude to Charles's problem and of his contempt for the "temporising counsels" of his Ministers:

> [Your letter and the one] I had from Mr. Hyde made me resolve to send Churchill to press my being sent for, which I look on as essentially necessary for His Majesty's service, as my own good and satisfaction; now is the time or never, for if I be not called home now, I shall have little hopes on't, and must expect sooner or later to be ruined, for absent my friends cannot long support me and my enemies will be the more encouraged to persecute me. I have instructed him so fully as to this and what concerns me that I need not say much more to you about it, having charged him at large to discourse and advise you upon it, His Majesty must now take bold and resolute counsels and stick to them, and who dares advise him to them without I be with him to help to support them.

On March 21 Charles's fourth and last Parliament met at Oxford. The Whig leaders arrived there in a thoroughly assured and, as the

[1] Probably Sir Alexander Fraizer (or Fraser), physician to Charles.

Tories thought, insolent spirit. They were confident that they would now have no further difficulty with their Exclusion Bill. But recently one Fitzharris, an Irish Catholic, had been indicted in the King's Bench for fabricating a story of a plot against the King's life. The Whigs thought that they could make political capital by transferring the case to their own jurisdiction, and the House of Commons brought a formal impeachment against Fitzharris; but the House of Lords refused to concur in this attempt to interrupt the ordinary course of justice, and a quarrel arose between the two Houses. The Whig leaders made a gross error of judgment in prosecuting this quarrel, for they gave Charles the excuse he had been looking for for dissolving Parliament. Both Houses fell to discussing a scheme put forward by the Council for allowing James to succeed to the throne with such severe limitations that he could hardly be said to retain any legal powers, but this plan was rejected by the Whigs, and it was clear from the course of the debate that they would be satisfied with nothing short of Exclusion. Charles, however, recognised that by their ill-advised persistence in the quarrel over the Fitzharris case the Whigs had played into his hands; he was now confident of victory, and in private he declared that he had no intention of yielding. Taking pains to conceal his intention, he appeared suddenly in the House of Lords on March 28, summoned the Commons, and, to the dismay of the Whigs, dissolved Parliament on the ground that they were wrangling among themselves and were unlikely to do any good by sitting longer. James was delighted; quite naturally he drew the moral that this was what he had been advocating all along, and that if Charles had acted earlier on his advice he would haved saved himself a great deal of worry and anxiety. But James saw Legge's point that the Opposition by raising a quarrel between the two Houses on the Fitzharris case made a fatal mistake. He wrote on March 31, 1681:

> I am much of your mind in what you say in yours of the 26th, and think we are very much beholding to the folly of our enemies. . . . For my part I look on this whole affair of Fitzharris as the hand of God, for you see what was so cunningly designed and laid with so great malice, and so securely as they thought and not to be hindered, is turned upon them, and may prove their ruin if the right use be made out, but I hope it will.

James had no doubt that now that Parliament was dissolved the Exclusion question was dead and that there was no longer any reason for keeping him in Scotland. We now know that not only was the Exclusion question dead, but that the question of limiting the prerogatives of a popish king had died with it; but no one in England in the summer of 1681 was aware of the revolution that had occurred. Charles, it is true, had won a considerable tactical success in dissolving the Oxford Parliament, and the Whig leaders were discredited; but it was not supposed that they had sustained more than a temporary check or that they would not be able to rally their forces and to return to the attack on James with undiminished energy. Charles certainly did not realise the extent of his victory and he had no intention of giving the enemy a fresh pretext for attack by bringing James back into personal contact with himself. In any case, he had no motive for recalling James: his personal affection for him was at best spasmodic, and he never seems to have missed him when he was away, James was on bad terms with the Duchess of Portsmouth, and Charles feared that their bickerings would disturb his domestic peace, and he did not value his brother's advice in public matters. Nor were there many among Charles's advisers to advocate James's recall, probably Laurence Hyde and Jenkins alone favoured that course.

The two chief events in England of the year 1681—the conclusion of the secret treaty with France in March, and the visit to England in July of William of Orange—took place in James's absence. Charles had not seen fit to inform him of the negotiations which were in progress with France, but independently James instructed Churchill to see Barrillon and to represent to him the necessity of a fresh treaty, and a few weeks later he wrote a violent letter to the ambassador urging him to see Charles immediately and to arrange a treaty.

> It is time now or never to conclude this bargain, for otherwise the King will be obliged to put himself into the hands of parliament [this, of course, was previous to the dissolution of the Oxford Parliament] and of the Prince of Orange; it will then be too late, and the Duke infallibly ruined. . . . You may be sure the Duke of York will do his duty to press the King for if it is not concluded now and without loss of time, the Duke is lost. . . . Let the King your master know that, if he has any goodness or consideration for the Duke of York, it is time to show it.

To the visit of William, James's reactions were entirely hostile. Two years earlier, during the debates which preceded the introduction of the first Exclusion Bill, and when he was in Brussels, he had advocated a visit of William to England, presumably as a *persona grata* to the Opposition who was also in his interests and whose mediation would be valuable. In 1681, however, though he still trusted him to do what he could for him, he had formed the opinion that William had been listening too much to Henry Sidney, the English envoy at The Hague, and had acquired an entirely erroneous view of the condition of affairs in England, and that he would therefore be inclined to encourage the Whigs to demand more than James was willing should be granted them; moreover, that now that the victory was won the presence of a mediator would be worse than useless.

It would not be out of place in a biography of James to discuss the vexed question of the date at which William formed the definite intention of attempting to succeed to the throne of the three kingdoms at the expense of James. Macaulay's view seems to have been that William had no ambition for the Crown for its own sake, and that he accepted it with reluctance as the only means of securing the alliance of England with Holland in the struggle against Louis XIV. Such a view represents him as more than human: it is not conceivable that any man could have placed no value whatever on the prestige of being the second or third personage in Europe. The other extreme view is more common.

> How few have ever heard of the long course of cold-blooded treachery and intrigue by which, from the very day of his marriage, William of Orange planned the ruin of his wife's family; . . . how eight years before the Revolution he was preparing to support an insurrection in England.

And James's biographer, writing after the event, is of the same opinion. Certainly James at the time had no suspicions of his son-in-law, but that is not to say there were no grounds for suspicion. James's mind was not speculative and he did not harbour vague suspicions; it was not difficult to deceive him by a pretence of friendship, and he was not on his guard against a man whom he had considered a friend until that man had committed a very overt act of hostility.

William never in words gave any encouragement to this second view, but he was above all things discreet in his conversation and correspondence, and his words by no means conveyed all that was in his mind. It is more than likely that he allowed his mind to play from a very early age on his proximity in blood to the royal line and on the chances of death, and that he was fully aware that the chances had been improved by his marriage to Mary; such imaginings are a natural outcome of the hereditary principle, even in matters of less moment than thrones and crowns. It is also true that at the time of the Exclusion Bills William's name was freely used by those exclusionists who kept their heads and realised the impossibility of the substitution of Monmouth for James. William and Mary were also nominated as regents in the schemes for a regency, and there is no evidence that William discouraged this use of his name. Henry Sidney in November 1679 formed an opinion that James suspected William of an intention "to set up for himself"; Charles during William's visit in 1681 apparently ascribed to him ulterior motives in wishing to dine with his old friends in the City and took the very extreme step of commanding his attendance at Windsor; and the Modenese ambassador reported to his master that "the King of England has severely reproved the Prince of Orange for having attempted to supplant the Duke of York in the succession to the Crown". But the ambassador does not disclose the source of his information about what was clearly a private conversation, nor does Charles's reprimand, if indeed it was given, prove William's guilt; it may easily have been inspired by an indiscretion of one of William's English partisans. In March 1681 William had written a letter which Laurence Hyde understood to convey the opinion that Charles should agree with Parliament on the subject of Exclusion; worse than that, he mentioned William's letter to Charles and gave him the same impression of it; Charles, who might justifiably have been annoyed at William's supposed officiousness, remarked mildly that,

> there never can be a good accommodation without bringing both the parties to some tolerable abatement of the demands, but this that is hinted at by that part of your letter and hath been so long insisted on here is entirely yielding on one side, and is therefore not an accommodation but a submission.

William was very angry with Hyde:

> I do not know why you put explanations upon my letters when I do not explain myself on a matter so important and delicate as that of the Exclusion, on which I have neither explained myself nor pretended to do it; moreover I am very much surprised that you have spoken of my letter to the King and had drawn from it the implication that I was of opinion that His Majesty should submit to the will of Parliament. The opinion which I expressed to you and which I still hold is merely that, unless some expedient is found for bringing together the King and his Parliament, the affairs of the King, of the Kingdom, and of all his allies, are in a very bad condition. What remedy there may be to escape such great evils, I do not know; nor if I did know should I take the trouble to write to you about them, since you draw inferences from my letters.

Hyde's reply was a full and frank apology, and though he was an anti-exclusionist, it is not necessary to accuse him of an intention to do injury to William, but only of blundering. But it does not appear that he took steps to disabuse Charles, and the impression left on Charles's mind must have been that William favoured Exclusion as a means to the satisfaction of his own ambition.

But from William's own recorded remarks it would be difficult to argue any such intention: for example, he told Sidney in September 1679 that all he desired for the present was that he might be considered the third (should it not have been fourth?) heir to the Crown; in August 1680 he was said to be giving out that he would not accept the Crown if Parliament should exclude James; in November he told Sidney that he regarded excluding the Duke an injustice and that he would not advise the King to do it for all the world, adding that he would be the first to be undone if the Exclusion Bill became law; in the same month he wrote to Jenkins, "I am vexed to learn with what animosity they proceed against the Duke. God bless him! and grant that the King and his parliament may agree"; in December he again wrote to Jenkins deploring the proposal to limit the prerogative of a popish king, on the ground that, once imposed, these limitations would be continued against a Protestant successor—thus implying that he regarded himself as a possible successor of James, and not his supplanter; finally, when in February 1685 James obtained peaceable possession of the Crown, William wrote in the same month to the Prince of Nassau-Dietz—from whom he could not possibly expect advantage by concealing his real feelings—and expressed his joy at seeing that James had "mounted the throne in such tranquillity".

Throughout the period of James's second residence in Scotland he was subjected by his friends to persistent advice that he should abandon the Catholic Faith and be received again into the Church of England. In January 1681 Laurence Hyde was sent by Charles to Edinburgh charged with the special mission of converting his brother-in-law; James was very indignant at what he considered an attempt to induce him to act against his conscience, and he was still more indignant when he heard that there had been a rumour that Charles had written him an ultimatum saying that if James did not go to church the Exclusion Bill would be allowed to pass, for he concluded that the only way in which such a rumour could have started was by a violation of confidence by Charles's advisers. Had James been able to bring himself to follow the advice of Hyde and his other friends and to convince the world of his sincerity in making the change, Charles's troubles would have been at an end;[1]

[1] Or so Charles thought; but the conflict between Charles and his parliaments went far deeper than the Exclusion question, and Parliament would not have given way until something in the nature of the Revolution Settlement had been achieved.

for the question of the succession would have been solved, and with it nearly all the other differences between Charles and his Parliaments.

James did not realise all the difficulties, he still thought that they could be overcome by more resolute behaviour on Charles's part; but he did see that his position was one of extreme danger and that his religion was the chief, indeed the only, reason for that danger. In these circumstances he rose to a pitch of moral heroism to which we cannot but pay respect, and which would have struck a chord of sympathy in the hearts of the Exclusionists themselves if they had not been blinded by political and sectarian passion:

> Yet I look on my condition as very bad [he wrote to Legge] and do not flatter myself with the hopes of being sent for in haste and so am arming myself with as much patience as I can, and shall, as I have done these many years, prepare myself for the worst that can happen to me; and, pray, once for all, never say anything to me again of turning Protestant, do not expect it or flatter yourself that I shall ever be it, I never shall, and, if occasion were, I hope God would give me grace to suffer death for the true Catholic Religion as well as banishment.

This was from Brussels; two and a half years later he wrote from Edinburgh:

> Now, because others have brought things to the pass they are, I must be pressed to sacrifice my conscience and my honour and be thought a knave by all the world. . . . You are a man of conscience as well as honour, do but think what a base mean thing it would be in me, besides the sin of it, to dissemble and deny my religion; I have by God's grace never to do so damnable a thing, and let my friends take their measures accordingly.[1]

But, matters of conscience apart, he realised that it was now too late for him to make the desired change. As he said in his memoirs:

> If he should conform they would say it was by virtue of dispensation,[2] and so imagine him a more dangerous enemy, for by entering into all his employment they would fancy his power greater and his will the same to do mischief.

[1] There is in this passage a distinct echo of the words James's father wrote from Newcastle in October 1646: "I have long ago resolved rather to shipwreck my person than either my conscience or honour."

[2] Cf. Sir Thomas Littleton's speech in the Commons on April 30, 1679: "If a Prince will say, I am no longer a Papist, and will go to Church and have a dispensation from the Pope to do it, there is an end of it."

When in July 1681 James as Commissioner opened the Scottish Parliament for the first time for five years he was present when prayers from the English liturgy were read, for they were part of the ceremony; he also, as we have seen, concurred in the passing of Acts of Parliament which imposed penalties upon the Catholics. Hence arose in England rumours similar to others that had previously arisen that he was wavering in his adhesion to the Catholic Faith. Seeing, as he thought, a new opportunity, Charles in September again sent Laurence Hyde to make a still more violent onslaught upon James. James's story is that he and his brother-in-law discussed the situation in all its bearings for three full days: we may be sure that Hyde, with his strong attachment to the Church of England, did not refrain from theological argument, but it was the interests of James's King and beloved brother that were his main theme; when he found that all his pleadings were in vain, Hyde took from his pocket a holograph statement from Charles to the effect that if James would consent merely to attend the services of the Church of England, without making any profession of change of faith, he would be permitted to return to England. Halifax also wrote to him and told him frankly "that except he became a Protestant his friends would be obliged to leave him, like a garrison that one could no longer defend"; to which James replied "that then his case was more desperate than he understood it to be before, for that he could not alter his principles". These persistent attempts to persuade James to forswear his settled convictions in his own interests and in those of Charles and as a condition of his return from exile "mortified him very much", and he considered the compulsion under which he continued to reside in Scotland was a confession of weakness on the part of Charles; he urged also that Charles should send for him, if only for a short time, so that they could discuss together the affairs of Scotland. He had for a time the fear that Charles was jealous of him: he complained that, as Halifax had warned him, his friends were all slipping away from him, and he had an uneasy suspicion that his brother was attaching them to himself. But he appears to have been misinformed, for it was reported that at Court "nobody hath any credit but the Duke's creatures".

James began to despair of ever returning to England, and his depressed state of mind may well have been a factor in a decline in will-power and mental grip which set in about this time. It has been suggested that there is evidence of this decline in the naïvety of the letters which he wrote to William of Orange from the year 1686 onwards, but it is difficult to detect a change in this respect, for his letters had always been naïve. What is significant is that about this time James, who, since he emerged from boyhood, had, apart from his subservient submission to the royal will, shown great firmness and independence of mind, now for the first time begins to be accused of submitting to the counsels of worthless favourites. Halifax told Reresby that James

> had a host of hungry servants about him that were still pressing for his return, and would never let him alone till, out of interest to themselves, they would put him upon that which would turn to the prejudice of their master by the ill timing of it

and at another time:

> that those which belonged to the Duke of York made him mad for there were few among them that had common sense.

To this period also belongs Sir John Lauder of Fountainhall's devastating statement of the impression James gave in Scotland:

> Some wise men observed that the Duke of York might have honesty, justice and courage enough, and his father's peremptoriness, but that he had neither great conduct [*sc.* ability] nor a deep reach in affairs, but was a silly man.[1]

But Halifax's statement of the case was incomplete: it is true that at this time James's counsellors began to take a more prominent place in his life, but they were counsellors only by courtesy. For James's mind, by the impetus of its previous energy, kept on its way without deviation, and the only advice he took (except from his priests) was such as conformed to his own intentions. In these circumstances the wisest counsellor was he who most intelligently anticipated the operations of James's own mind.

[1] The *Oxford English Dictionary* gives an interesting history of the meaning of the word "silly": at this time it had not its full modern significance, but it was far from being a synonym for "simple".

CHAPTER XIII

CHARLES'S LAST YEARS

JAMES owed his escape from Scotland to the last person from whom he could have expected such a boon. The Duchess of Portsmouth, now completely estranged from James, wanted to take the waters at Bourbon, and for the expenses of the trip she wanted money, for any surplus she had had from her ample income had been spent on repeated demolition and re-erection of her lodgings at Whitehall. She tried to borrow money on the security of her pension from the hereditary excise, but found that it was not a negotiable security; it then occurred to her that if she could exchange with James £5000 of her income from the hereditary excise for £5000 of his from the Post Office, she would be able to give security for the necessary loan. She communicated with James, who behaved with great astuteness: he had no love for the Duchess and he had no intention of making her a present by exchanging £5000 on good security for £5000 on not so good security; moreover, he was well aware that his income from the Post Office was a parliamentary grant and that it could not be alienated except by Act of Parliament, that Charles was not likely to call a Parliament for such a purpose and that if the question had been brought up in Parliament they would be more likely to endeavour to reduce him to a bare subsistence allowance than to do anything to oblige the Duchess of Portsmouth. James affected, however, to be agreeable to the mistress's scheme; but he pointed out that it would not be possible to complete the transaction unless he was present in person in London. James's return to Court was the last thing the Duchess wanted; but she calculated from Charles's insensibility to James's requests for recall, that she would have no difficulty in procuring his return to Scotland as soon as he had served her purpose. She applied to Charles her well-tried arts, and Charles, with reluctance, but finding it less trouble to yield than to resist, sent George Legge's brother William to Edinburgh with letters permitting James to join him at Newmarket.

James lost no time in making use of this permission; leaving the Duchess and the Princess Anne at Holyrood House, he took ship on March 6 at Leith with a small escort of yachts which he had collected there.

> His Royal Highness the Duke of York arrived at Yarmouth in one of His Majesty's yachts the 10th [of March] and was entertained

> by the magistrates of the town at dinner; and that afternoon he went to Norwich, attended with a great number of gentlemen, where he came that night, and was splendidly entertained by the Mayor and aldermen; the next morning he parted thence for Newmarket, accompanied by many gentry, where he arrived that evening and was received by His Majesty with all the expressions of kindness imaginable, and since his arrival there hath been waited on by most of the nobility to pay their respects to him.

Another report says that the crowd at Newmarket was great at his arrival because everyone came to wait on him; and when Charles and James arrived in London from Newmarket on April 8 they were visited by the nobility and gentry and there were public rejoicings. An extraordinary revolution in James's favour had occurred from the time, only a few months back, when James thought he had no friends in England except Jenkins and Hyde, and the change must have been as pleasant and surprising to him as had been his reception at the Artillery Dinner in September 1679 and the bells and bonfires in London in February 1680. But while those two outbursts of enthusiasm were temporary and bore a partisan character, the welcome accorded to James at Yarmouth, Norwich and Newmarket was a prelude to a period of nearly four years in which James kept his popularity among almost all people who had the means to express their feelings; the only exceptions were those who during the succeeding eighteen months gave Monmouth an ovation whenever he appeared in public.

In May James paid a flying visit to Edinburgh for the double purpose of winding up his public affairs there and making appointments in the highest offices and of bringing back his wife and daughter. On his way north the *Gloucester*, the ship in which he was a passenger, was, by the negligence of the pilot, wrecked on a sandbank off the Norfolk coast. James's own account of the occurrence, written to William three days later from Edinburgh, gives a very painful impression of callousness:

> Before this gets to you you will go near to have heard of my being safely arrived here, though the frigate in which I was in (sic), was cast away upon a sand called the Lemon, which lies some eight leagues from the coast of Norfolk. It was on Saturday morning the ship was lost, and by Sunday night I landed at Leith, and so was here by nine o'clock that night. We lost a great many men, and, considering the little time the ship was above water after she struck first, 'twas well so many were saved; of lords there were drowned Lord Roxborough and Lord O'Brien; of gentlemen, Lieutenant Hyde, who was lieutenant of the ship, and Captain

> Stuart, a reformade, both English; of Scots, Hopton, Sir Joseph Douglas and one Levington a physician; several of my under-servants were drowned, and of 250 seamen, which was the ship's complement, 110 were lost; 'twas to the too great presumption of the pilot and his mistaking both his course and distance that was the cause of the loss of the ship; he was esteemed one of the ablest pilots we had for these northern seas; he was saved among the rest, by one of the yachts-boats, which had I then known, I had caused him to have been hanged up immediately, according to the custom of the sea, but now he must receive his doom by a court martial, so soon as I shall arrive in England, which I hope will be some time the next week, for I intend to embark with the Duchess and my daughter about Monday next on board the Happy Return, a fourth-rate frigate; 'twas the Gloucester, a third-rate, was lost.

In short, his regrets were for the escape from sudden death of the pilot rather than for the death of a number of gentlemen, and of over a hundred seamen, who (as James says in his memoirs) gave "a great huzza" when they saw that he was safe.

John Churchill was among those saved, and his account of the wreck was written down by his wife sixty years later, and is probably not exactly as he gave it to her. But among a mass of incompatible details which are given by other eye-witnesses concerning James's conduct at this moment of sudden crisis, one point emerges from the story told by the Duchess of Marlborough which is borne out by all the other accounts—the fatal delay owing to James's fussiness and irresolution. The clearest of these accounts is one written by the son of Colonel George Legge to a friend a few months after the accident:

> This is only in answer to the last paragraph in yours of the 21st. My father was on board the Gloucester, but so litte deserved to have the drowning of 150 men (which the bishop has so liberally bestowed upon him) laid chiefly to his charge, that it was in great measure owing to him that any escaped after the ship had struck. He several times pressed the Duke to get into the boat, who refused to do it, telling him that if he were gone nobody would take care of the ship, which he had hopes might be saved if she were not abandoned. But my father finding she was ready to sink told him if he stayed any longer they should be obliged to force him out: upon which the Duke ordered a strong box to be lifted into the boat, which besides being extremely weighty took a great deal of time as well as room. My father asked him with some warmth if

> there was anything in it worth a man's life. The Duke answered that there were things of great consequence both to the King and himself that he would hazard his own rather than it should be lost.

There can be no doubt that the James of ten years earlier would have taken charge of the situation at once, have improvised a plan and have put it in operation with a few sharp words of command; the next best thing he could have done would have been to have allowed himself to be expeditiously put over the side into a boat—for his was to everyone the most important life, and nothing could be done until it was known that he was safe—so as to leave the ship's officers free to save the rest. As it was, he hung about and refused to be hurried while valuable minutes were being wasted. At the last moment his chief thought was not for his priests and his dogs (as some alleged), but for a great box of papers, no doubt containing his memoirs—a less hidebound and egotistic man would have left them in London on this short trip—which he insisted on having in the boat with him. The closing picture which we form in our mind's eye is that of a calm sea with a couple of yachts standing by and several boats, not daring to approach the *Gloucester* for fear of being swamped when she goes down, and James, with his great box by his side and surrounded by his courtiers, waiting for the ship to slide off the sandbank and to founder as the tide falls.

James arrived in Edinburgh on May 7, and left again on May 15 with Mary Beatrice and Anne, having in the meantime made fresh appointments to the chief Scottish offices. They had a tedious voyage, and did not arrive in London until May 27. The King and Queen received them at Arlington House, the residence of the Earl of Arlington, and after dinner set out for Windsor. James and his Duchess went to St. James's and, to their delight, "at night were ringing of bells and bonfires in several places and other public expressions of joy". For more than a year life was uneventful; James remained in close contact with Charles and went with him on his journeys between London, Windsor and Newmarket. In July Sunderland's miscalculation in the matter of Exclusion was forgiven him by Charles at the intercession of the Duchess of Portsmouth, and in spite of James's opposition he returned to Court; of this reinstatement James wrote, "Many honest men are alarmed at it, but not I". Sunderland wrote to William of Orange:

> The King has received me very graciously and so has the Duke, much beyond what I ought to have expected from His Royal Highness, whose proceeding has been such to me in this whole matter

> that I must forever acknowledge to owe more to him than I can hope to deserve, though I will always endeavour it.

Sunderland was reappointed to the Privy Council in September and resumed his duties as Secretary of State in the following January, a post which he held continuously for nearly six years. In August James received a more surprising offer of reconciliation—from the Earl of Shaftesbury:

> The Duke made him a wise and no unkind answer, that he had been an open enemy, and when he had reconciled himself to the King, he would be the first that would take him by the hand as he had done my lord Sunderland.

James now felt himself strong enough to take revenge upon his enemies. He had a weapon ready at his hand in the medieval statute *De Scandalis Magnatum*—Libel against Great Persons—under which peers of the realm who could prove that words had been spoken against them by Commoners could demand damages in a criminal action and no plea of justification could be admitted. During the previous three years when Exclusion was in the air wild talk about James had been universal, and there were not wanting informers who were willing to secure James's favour now that it was worth having. A typical instance is that of a Mr. Arrowsmith, an apothecary, who had invited to dinner a customer from the country, which customer brought a friend with him. In the course of the dinner someone suggested drinking James's health, and Arrowsmith objected to the toast and gave his reasons. Information was laid by the customer's friend, and James entered an action for *Scandalum Magnatum* against Arrowsmith. Narcissus Luttrell mentions in his diary no fewer than eight actions by James under the Act, and there may well have been more; the bearer of the honoured name of Sir Francis Drake, and the anti-Catholic informer Dangerfield, absconded, Sir Scroope Howe succeeded by submission and apology in having the action against him withdrawn; but four of the accused who stood their trial—Alderman Pilkington, John Dutton Colt, Nicholas Covert, and the notorious Titus Oates—were each cast in damages for the enormous sum of £100,000.

In September 1682 Monmouth started on his second progress. The visit to the West two years earlier had had no definite political object, though he visited the Whig gentry and took delight in the personal popularity which was expressed in his reception by the people. Now he travelled in state with a retinue of more than a hundred horsemen. Wherever he stopped he dined in state and the populace were admitted to pass through the dining-room. On the former occasion he had given no direct provocation to the susceptibilities of the Court party, but now there was considerable opposition to the displays of welcome; in particular, attempts more or less successful, were made to extinguish bonfires. The progress came to an abrupt end at Chester on September 20 with the arrest of Monmouth by royal warrant. He was conducted to London, examined by Sir Leoline Jenkins, the Secretary of State, and released on giving sureties. In February 1683 he went down to Charlton to hunt with Lord Grey and arranged a demonstration at Chichester similar to those of his second progress.

In June 1683 occurred the discovery of the famous Rye House Plot: a plot to assassinate Charles and James at a farmhouse in Essex—the Rye House—on their way to London from Newmarket. Unfortunately for the conspirators a fire occurred at Newmarket, and in consequence the royal brothers returned safely to London a fortnight earlier than they had intended. A number of the plotters saved themselves in the manner common at the time by turning King's Evidence. James was very active in tracking down the fugitives and examining such as were taken, and he betrayed no regrets when one of the most lovable personalities and one of the greatest minds of the time—Lord Russell and Algernon Sidney—were condemned and executed as accessory to the conspiracy.[1] Of Russell he wrote:

> This day Lord Russell was beheaded. He behaved himself like a stout man, but not like a good Christian; said little, but left a most seditious paper signed by himself, to be sent to the king, which just now is brought to me in print, which has been published by some of his factious friends. When you see it you will say there cannot be a greater libel on the Government;

and,

> when the trials are printed all the world will see with what disingenuity and little Christianity Lord Russell died, and what damnable designs these conspirators had.

And of Algernon Sidney:

> Yesterday Algernon Sidney was beheaded; he died stoutly and like a true republican. . . . Algernon Sidney's speech is come

[1] The impression given by the evidence is that Lord Russell was guilty at least of misprision of treason; during the Exclusion crisis Russell advocated the impeachment of James in the hope of a capital sentence, and this fact may explain James's personal animosity against him. Sidney was convicted for private opinions expressed in unpublished writings, and few people, even of his own time, can be found to uphold the justice of his sentence.

> out in print, and his trial will I believe be out this week; by both which you will see what a fine principled man he was, and of the same trampe [*sc.* temper] are all those the Duke of Monmouth was to have headed; and I think 'twas a great mercy he discovered himself so soon not to be a true penitent.

Even before the trials James had assumed Russell's guilt; in his eyes a man who confessed to republican—that is to say, to liberal—principles was capable of any crime, even of assassination.

On November 24, 1683, the Duke of Monmouth made his last appearance—but one—at Whitehall. He had been excluded from the Court for four years, and had been continuing to live at his house in Hedge Lane, and his country house, Moor Park in Hertfordshire, in close touch with Shaftesbury and the other Whigs and Exclusionists. His objects were variously reported—James thought he aimed at a republic with himself as Stadtholder, for James could not imagine a King who was at the same time a Whig—but he probably had a vague plan of being ready to take what opportunity might serve to seize the Crown if Charles died. At the end of June 1683 a proclamation was issued ordering his arrest, together with a number of Whig leaders, on suspicion of complicity in the Rye House Plot, and he went into hiding for five months. On November 24 he suddenly reappeared, surrendered himself to the Secretary of State, and requested to see the King and James alone. The request was granted, and Monmouth made a humble submission to his father and craved James's pardon for everything he had done against him; he admitted that he had been deep in all the Whig conspiracies, but denied that he had any knowledge of the assassination plot. After the interview he was allowed to go to his own lodgings in Whitehall in custody of a serjeant-at-arms, and next day he appeared before the Council and was released and received a royal pardon. He had requested that he should not be called as a witness against his friends, and Charles promised that he would not make use of his confession in that way, received him back into favour and ordered James to be reconciled to him. But as soon as he had got his pardon Monmouth returned to his old friends (from whom presumably he had been separated while he was in hiding), and they convinced him that he had done a base and unmanly thing in making submission.[1] When Charles demanded that he should sign a confession confirming his oral statement, he not only refused, but gave out that he had never made any such statement. He was therefore repudiated by Charles, who caused a copy of the declaration which he should have

[1] There was nothing in the written confession which could incriminate any of Monmouth's associates.

signed to be entered in the register of the Privy Council;[1] if he had been given time he would no doubt have got back into his father's good graces, for he could never be angry with him long; he remained for a few weeks at his private residences and then crossed to Holland. There he was well received by William and Mary; a house was assigned to him at The Hague and another at Leyden, and he lived in some state. James wrote two letters to his daughter Mary expostulating with her at the hospitality given to a man who was under Charles's displeasure and was his own "mortal enemy".

The discovery of the Rye House Plot was a piece of great good fortune to Charles and James: nothing could have served better to complete the discomfiture of the Whigs, to secure to Charles for the last eighteen months of his life that ease and tranquillity for which his soul yearned and to confirm to him and to James the popularity they had recently acquired—for assassins have never been popular in England. No one dared to show opposition to the Court for fear of being implicated in the Plot; of the Whig leaders, four—Shaftesbury, Russell, Essex and Algernon Sidney—were dead, and the rest scattered and without hope or plans. James in particular benefited exceedingly. Burnet, after animadverting on "the shedding of so much blood upon such doubtful evidence", describes

> the strange change that appeared over the nation with relation to the Duke, from such an eager prosecution of the Exclusion to an indecent courting and magnifying him, not without a visible coldness to the King;

then, after recording the spate of loyal addresses, he has a dig at his own cloth:

> The clergy struck up a higher note, with such zeal for the Duke's succession as if a popish king had been a special blessing of Heaven to be much longed for by a protestant church.

With the Duchess and Princess Anne, James had paid a visit of five days to Oxford in the previous May, and had been received with great enthusiasm by the local gentry, the University and the individual colleges; as an outcome of this visit and of the discovery of the Plot, the University on July 21 issued a manifesto repudiating a portentous list of Whig doctrines, among them: "Birthright and proximity of blood

[1] The fragment of Monmouth's diary which has been preserved states that his submission had been arranged beforehand with his father in order to deceive James.

give no title to rule or government, and it is lawful to preclude the next heir from his right and succession to the throne"; on September 9, which was set apart as a day of thanksgiving for the preservation of the King and the Duke from the fate which had been prepared for them,

> the smart lads of the city marched down the streets with cudgels in their hands, crying for the King and the Duke of York, and all people had "York" in their mouths, and his health was drunk publicly in most halls at dinner.

James's next visit to Oxford was not so fortunate.

Apart from his personal popularity, James recovered his old position as Charles's most intimate adviser, and even improved upon it. From the time of his return from Scotland he had remained in virtual control of that kingdom. During his second stay in Scotland he had formed attachments with a number of men, and his second visit in 1682 was for the purpose of placing the administration in the hands of men he could trust. The Commission of the Treasury was discontinued, and William Douglas, Marquis of Queensberry, was appointed Lord High Treasurer; Sir George Gordon, who as a Scottish Judge held the title for life of Lord Haddo, was made Chancellor; and James Drummond, Earl of Perth, succeeded Queensberry as Lord Justice-General. The Earl of Moray remained in his post as Secretary of State; he resided in London and was in constant attendance upon James. Perth's brother, John Drummond of Lundin, subsequently to achieve a sinister reputation as the Earl of Melfort, and the evil genius of James's later years, was also in London; in August 1682 he was appointed Treasurer-Depute under Queensberry.

It was said that Lundin had first attracted the favour of Duchess Mary when she was in Edinburgh by his handsome figure and his grace and skill as a dancer; throughout his life she remained convinced that so attractive a man and so assiduous a courtier must be a reliable counsellor. James rated him no less highly, and though he was twice—in 1689 and in 1694—compelled by Melfort's detractors to dismiss him, he submitted with the greatest reluctance. Melfort's career belongs mainly to the period after the accession of James; here it is sufficient to say that in character he resembled Sunderland, for he had no principle except self-interest; he resembled Sunderland also in his method of dealing with James, always giving the advice which most nearly conformed to James's own opinions. In one respect, however, there was a vast difference between the two men: Sunderland was one of the ablest men in public life in his time; Melfort, except in intrigue, was one of the most incompetent.

No sooner had the new administration been formed than Queensberry and Perth commenced a joint intrigue against Lord Haddo. The Chancellorship had in the past always been given to a great noble, and the appointment of a Commoner was regarded as an affront; his elevation in 1682 to the hereditary peerage as Earl of Aberdeen did not wipe out the obscurity of his birth; there can be little doubt that Perth coveted his post, though there is nothing in Lundin's letters to Queensberry to support such a surmise. In these letters from August to November 1683 there is a complete record of the writer's persistent efforts to poison James's mind against Aberdeen. Never was there less material on which to build a charge and never was better use made of such slight material, and the frank avowal of rascality in the letters—for he admits that some of his accusations are false—stamps Lundin as one of the basest of men. Most men in such circumstances are at pains to convince themselves that they are actuated by zeal for the public good or the King's service, but no doubt Sunderland, if he had had an intimate friend as Lundin had in Queensberry, would have written in similar terms about his intrigues against Rochester in 1685 and 1686. The two points against Aberdeen upon which Lundin insisted were that, in contrast to Queensberry, he was a poor man and must therefore strive to advance his relations, and that he was inclined to leniency to the Covenanters. It was most important to the conspirators that Aberdeen should not be permitted to come to London to justify himself, and in due course Aberdeen wrote to James complaining that he was being persistently maligned and was given no opportunity of refuting his accusers. James showed his letter to Lundin, but Lundin protested that he had done no more than to answer as truthfully as he could questions about Aberdeen and others, and he had no difficulty in convincing James of his entire disinterestedness. So easily was he deceived by those to whom he gave his confidence, the very persistence of the attack on Aberdeen should have put him on his guard.

Lundin's perseverance was at long last rewarded when on June 23, 1684, Aberdeen was dismissed. The persecution of the Covenanters had by this time reached the stage known as "the killing time", in which Queensberry and Perth took an active part and Lundin gave assistance from Whitehall; it was not difficult to represent Aberdeen's comparative humanity as lack of zeal in the royal service, and he himself unwisely courted popularity by gestures of moderation and played into his enemies' hands. Queensberry and Perth also secured the good offices of the Duchess of Portsmouth by a bribe of £27,000,[1] which Queensberry had the effrontery to furnish from public funds. Queensberry had been made a Duke in the previous February, Perth succeeded Aberdeen as Chancellor, on July 16 Queensberry and Perth made a triumphal entry into Edinburgh, and in September Lundin was made joint Secretary of State with Moray. At the close of the reign Queensberry and Perth had the whole Scottish administration in their hands, and the two secretaries in London, Moray and Lundin, were entirely in their interest. Charles did not concern himself with Scottish affairs. James wrote to Queensberry every week; in this correspondence the phrase "King and Duke" appears frequently, and in general Burnet was very near the truth when he said Scotland was so entirely in his dependence that the King would seldom ask what the papers imported that the Duke brought to be signed by him.

Burnet's estimate of James's importance in England during the years after his return from Scotland is also probably fairly accurate, though Burnet was not in England for the whole of the three years.

> In England the application and dependence was visibly on the Duke. The king had scarce company about him to entertain him, when the Duke's levees and couchees were so crowded that the antichambers were full. The King walked about with a small train of the necessary attendants, when the Duke had a vast following; which drew a lively reflection from Waller, the celebrated wit. He said the House of Commons had resolved that the Duke should not reign after the King's death; but the King in opposition to them was resolved he should reign even during his life.

Burnet's information is corroborated by Sir John Reresby, who was on the spot, and who says in January 1684, "The Duke of York did now chiefly manage affairs, but with great haughtiness". From July 1683 James had been in constant attendance at the Committee of Foreign Affairs, or Cabinet Council as Jenkins calls it, and in May 1684 James was readmitted to the Privy Council, and in the same month he was virtually reinstated as Lord High Admiral: that is to say the Admiralty Commission was abolished and Charles signed all papers on James's advice.

This latter appointment was extremely popular, for the Admiralty

[1] Perth signed a bond for half the amount in case the payment should be disallowed at a subsequent examination of accounts. The matter came up in July 1686, and the Duke of Hamilton was for disallowing it; it does not appear whether or no Queensberry and Perth were made to refund the money to the Treasury.

Commission had justly acquired a reputation for incompetence. Louis expressed his satisfaction at James's return to the position he had previously enjoyed:

> The King of England could have taken no resolution more agreeable to his prosperity and reputation than that of reestablishing the Duke of York in all his offices.

James declares in his memoirs that when he returned from Scotland he promised Charles that when once he had reported on the affairs of Scotland he would meddle no more in the public business of either kingdom, great as would be the personal sacrifice involved; James's biographer, however, having transcribed this passage from the memoirs, imples a few pages later that the promise was not kept, for he mentions among the blessings which Charles enjoyed at the end of his life,

> the Duke his brother at his side, whose indefatigableness in business took a great share of that burden off his shoulders, which his indolent temper made uneasy to him, and this His Royal Highness performed with such a perfect conformity to His Majesty's inclinations and obedience to his will, as made his services as free from jealousy and unsuspected as they were affectionate and useful, both to confirm his happiness at home and establish his reputation abroad.

In view of this and other passages in the biography and of the independent evidence above quoted, James need not be believed when he states elsewhere in his memoirs that the long conversations he had with Charles, and which caused pangs of jealousy to the Duchess of Portsmouth, were entirely upon the subject of religion. Be that as it may, the Duchess was undoubtedly jealous of James at this time, and it was a galling thought to her that she had been the means of bringing him back to the chief place in Charles's counsels, to be forced herself into the background. The outcome of her jealousy was a plan for sending James back to Scotland, and so persistent was she (helped also by Charles's weariness at James's constant company) that had Charles lived a few months longer the plan would have succeeded and James would have found himself again in exile, though this time, no doubt, on more honourable terms than previously. The decision to make the journey was taken as early as November 1684, but no date was fixed; on January 17 James's departure seemed imminent, but a week later he told Melfort that he would not go until he had been to Newmarket with Charles, an excursion planned for the first week in March.

The last public event of importance of the reign of Charles II was the marriage on July 28, 1684, of James's younger daughter Anne to Prince George of Denmark, a marriage, as events were to prove, of no political or dynastic significance. It is characteristic of the subservience to France of Charles and James at this late period that they took the greatest pains not to repeat their error of the marriage of Mary, and made quite certain that this marriage had Louis's approval. The secret of their correspondence with the French King was not well kept, for Burnet was able to say, "The marriage did not at all please the nation, for we knew that the proposition came from France". James wrote to Queensberry before the event:

> My daughter's being married to the Prince of Denmark will now be no news to you, and I am the better pleased with it because I find the loyal party here do like it, and the Whigs are as much troubled by it;

a significant passage. James was guilty of two errors to which men of his stamp of mind are liable: he thought that everyone who opposed the Court on any point—in this case the French connection, for no objection could be taken to Prince George as a husband for Anne—was a Whig, and that not only were the Whigs not to be placated by concessions, but that there was a virtue in irritating them.

The death of Charles II was very sudden. On February 2, 1685, he had an apoplectic fit when he was preparing to be shaved, and though he rallied and gave hopes of a recovery, he had a second fit and died at mid-day on February 6. The French ambassador Barrillon wrote a long account of the final scenes to his master, and its reproduction here is fully justified by the consummate command of narrative style shown by the ambassador—anyone who compares the story as he told it with Macaulay's paraphrase of it must be struck by the distance the historian fell below his original.[1]

> The letter which I have the honour this day to address to Your Majesty, is solely to transmit to Your Majesty an exact account of the most important events which took place at the death of the late King of England. His illness which began on the morning of Monday, February 12, took different turns during the following days; sometimes he was thought to be out of danger, but afterwards some circumstance happened which gave reason to believe his disorder was mortal; at length, about noon on Thursday, February 15,

[1] It must be remembered that Barrillon's dates are new style, so that February 12 should read February 2 according to the old style which we are observing.

I was informed from a good quarter that there was no longer any hope and that his physicians did not think he could survive the night. I immediately after went to Whitehall; the Duke of York had given orders to the officers who kept the door of the antechamber to allow me to pass at all hours; he remained constantly in the King's chamber, except when he came out to give orders respecting what was passing in the town. The report was several times spread during the day that the King was dead. As soon as I arrived the Duke of York said to me, "The physicians think the King is in the greatest danger; I beg you will assure your master that in me he will always find a faithful and a grateful servant". I remained in the King's antechamber till five o'clock; the Duke of York invited me several times into the room and conversed with me about what was passing without-doors, and of the assurances he had received from all quarters that everything was very quiet in the town and that he would be proclaimed King the instant his brother should expire. I retired for some time to the apartments of the Duchess of Portsmouth; I found her overwhelmed with grief for the physicians had deprived her of all hopes. Nevertheless, instead of speaking to me of her sorrow and of the loss she was about to sustain, she led me into a closet, and said, "Monsieur l'Ambassadeur, I am going to tell you one of the greatest secrets in the world, and if it were known it would cost me my head. At the bottom of his heart the King is a Catholic, but he is surrounded by Protestant bishops, and nobody informs him of his situation or speaks to him of God. I cannot with decency again enter his room, besides the Queen is always there. The Duke of York is busied with his affairs, and these are too important to allow him to take that care which he ought about the conscience of the King. Go and tell him that I have conjured you to advise him to think on what can be done to save the King's soul: he is master of the King's room and he can cause to withdraw whoever he pleases. Lose no time, for if there be the least hesitation it will be too late."

I immediately returned to the Duke of York. I begged him to pretend to go to the apartment of the Queen who had quitted the King's room; she had just been bled because she had fainted; the room communicates with both the apartments; I followed him to the Queen's and told him what the Duchess of Portsmouth had said to me. He roused himself as it were from a profound lethargy: "You are right," he said, "there is no time to lose. I would sooner hazard everything than not do my duty on this occasion." He returned to me an hour after, under pretence of again visiting the

Queen, and told me he had spoken to the King his brother and that he had found him determined not to receive the sacrament to which the Protestant bishops were pressing him; that this had very much surprised them; but that some of them would always remain in the King's room, unless he found a pretext to cause everybody to retire in order that he might speak to the King his brother with more freedom and induce him to make a formal abjuration of heresy and to confess himself to a Catholic priest.

We discussed various expedients: the Duke of York proposed that I should ask to speak with the King his brother, as if to communicate something in secret to him from Your Majesty, and that everybody should be ordered to withdraw. This I offered to do, but I represented to him that, besides the noise such a proceeding would make, there was no colourable pretext to justify my remaining in private with the King of England and him alone so long a time as was required for the accomplishment of what we had to do. The Duke next thought of bringing the Queen, as if to take a last farewell of the King and to beg his forgiveness if she had disobeyed him in anything, and that he should perform the same ceremony. At last the Duke of York determined to speak to his brother before all that were present, but in such a way that no one should understand what he said, because this would remove all suspicion and it would be imagined that he was only consulting him about State affairs and what he wished should be done after his death; therefore, without any more precaution, the Duke, after having forbidden anyone to come nigh, stooped down to his brother's ear; I was in the room, and more than twenty persons at the door which was open; what the Duke said was not heard, but the King said aloud from time to time, "Yes, with all my heart." He made the Duke sometimes repeat his words because he did not hear very well; this lasted about a quarter of an hour. The Duke of York then left the room as if to go to the Queen, and said to me, "The King has consented to my bringing him a priest; I dare not send any of the Duchess's, they are too well known; send quickly and seek one". I told him I would do it with pleasure but that I thought too much time would be lost, and that I had just seen all the Queen's priests in a closet near to her chamber. He replied, "You are right". He perceived at the same time the Count of Castelmelhor, who warmly embraced the proposition I made him and took upon him to speak to the Queen. He returned in an instant and said "Though I were to endanger my head in this business I would do it with pleasure, but I know none of the Queen's priests who understands and speaks English". Upon this we resolved to send in search of an English priest to the Venetian Resident's, but as the time admitted no delay the Count of Castelmelhor went to the room where the Queen's priests were and found among them a Scotch priest named Huddlestone, the man who saved the King after the battle of Worcester and who had been excepted by Act of Parliament in all the laws enacted against the Roman Catholics and the priests. They gave him a wig and cassock to disguise him and led him to the door of an apartment which communicated by a small flight of steps with that of the King.

The Duke of York whom I had informed that all was ready sent Chiffinch[1] to receive and conduct Mr. Huddlestone; he said next aloud, "Gentlemen, it is the King's wish that everybody should retire except the Earls of Bath and Feversham": the former is First Lord of the Bedchamber and the latter was this week in waiting. The physicians withdrew into a closet the door of which was shut when Chiffinch brought in Mr. Huddlestone. In presenting him the Duke of York said, "Sire, here is a man who saved your life and who comes at this moment to save your soul". The King replied, "He is welcome". He then confessed himself with sentiments of great piety and repentance. The Count of Castelmelhor had taken care to have Huddlestone instructed by a Portuguese bare-footed Carmelite what he was to say to the King on such an occasion, for of himself he was a man of no great acquirements. But the Duke of York told me he acquitted himself very well and made the King formally promise, in case of his recovering, to declare himself openly to be a Catholic. The King next received absolution, the Communion and even the extreme unction. All this lasted about three-quarters of an hour. The persons in the ante-chamber looked at one another, but nothing was expressed except in looks or whispers. The presence of the Earls of Bath and Feversham, who are Protestants, has somewhat removed the apprehensions of the bishops, but nevertheless the Queen's women and the other priests saw so much coming and going that I do not imagine the secret will be long kept.

After the King had received the Sacrament he had a slight respite of his illness. It is certain that he spoke more intelligibly and had more strength; we had already begun to hope that God was willing to work a miracle in curing him, but it was the opinion of the physicians that his malady was not diminished and that

[1] William Chiffinch had succeeded his father Thomas Chiffinch in 1666 as closet-keeper to Charles II.

he could not survive the night. However he appeared much easier and talked with more feeling and understanding than he had yet done from six o'clock in the evening till eight o'clock next morning. He spoke several times aloud to the Duke of York in terms full of affection and friendship, he twice recommended to him the Duchess of Portsmouth and the Duke of Richmond, as also all his other children. He made no mention of the Duke of Monmouth, neither good nor bad; he often testified his confidence in God's mercy. The Bishop of Bath and Wells, who was his private chaplain, said some prayers and spoke to him of God; the King moved his head to show he heard him. The Bishop was not over-officious in telling him anything particularly nor in proposing to him to make a confession of his faith: he was apprehensive of a refusal, and feared still more, as I think, to irritate the Duke of York.

The King retained his senses throughout the whole of the night and talked of several things with great calmness; at six o'clock he asked what hour it was and said, "Open the curtains, that I may once more see the day". He suffered great pain, and at seven o'clock was bled under an idea that it would alleviate his sufferings; at half-past eight he spoke with great difficulty, about ten was senseless, and calmly expired at noon without any convulsions. The new King retired to his chamber, was unanimously acknowledged and afterwards proclaimed.

I have thought it my duty to send Your Majesty an exact account of what passed on this occasion, and I esteem myself very happy that God has bestowed upon me the favour of having a part therein.

Barrillon's account contains almost all that it is necessary to know of Charles's last twenty-four hours—except perhaps the two well-known remarks: "Gentlemen, I am an unconscionable time a-dying",[1] and "Don't let poor Nelly starve" (poor Nelly died two years later, leaving a large fortune to her son, the Duke of St. Albans—some people said a million pounds!). Of James's part there is little more to be said: all authorities agree that he was very assiduous at the bedside and that Mary Beatrice was also constantly present. Ten years or so later Mary Beatrice told the story in James's presence to the nuns of Chaillot, and James wrote another account for their benefit. In neither of these accounts, nor in the account in James's memoirs, is there mention of the part taken by the Duchess of Portsmouth and by Barrillon in the deathbed conversion of Charles, and in all three of them James is given

[1] I am unaware whether or no there is good authority for this oft-quoted saying.

credit for a spontaneous impulse (assisted perhaps by hints from the Queen and Mary Beatrice) to have a care for Charles's spiritual necessities. It is not conceivable that Barrillon invented this part of his account, but it is not necessary to assume that James was consciously lying: he was in such a state of strain after three days' watching that Barrillon's intervention may have left no impression on his mind. Nor from Barrillon's narrative does it appear that James was ever aware that the original motion came from the Duchess of Portsmouth—he would in any case have had a delicacy in giving before the nuns such credit to his brother's mistress. These two accounts, however, fill one gap left by Barrillon: the whispered conversation between James and Charles which Barrillon failed to overhear was on the subject of the risk that James would incur by assisting at his brother's conversion, Charles very anxious that the risk should be avoided if possible, James insisting that any risk was negligible when Charles's salvation was in the balance.

It would be easy to exaggerate James's preoccupation at the deathbed with his own concerns and with the precautions to be taken to secure his own peaceful accession. In spite of Shaftesbury's insinuation that James had for thirty years been looking for an opportunity to supplant his brother on the throne, there can be no doubt in the mind of anyone who has studied the evidence that he had a genuine affection for Charles, and, in addition, that his royalism was of so extreme a type that it cannot be conceived that he ever allowed a desire for Charles's death to enter his mind. On these grounds alone, and without noticing the entire absence of positive evidence on the other side, the Whig libel (or unjustifiable suspicion) that James poisoned his brother may be brushed aside. The psychology of succession presents an array of normal cases: a son unaffectedly grieved at his father's death and at the same time not a little pleased at coming into his father's estate. There can be no doubt that James was immensely gratified at being King—if for no other reason than that of finding himself in a position to strike a blow at heresy and schism—but it does not follow that he did not keenly regret the fatality which had given him the Crown. James might in all sincerity have given to the dying Charles (with the alteration of a single word) the farewell address that Prince Hal gave to his father

Thy due from me
Is tears and heavy sorrows of the blood,
Which nature, love and filial tenderness
Shall, O dear father! pay thee plenteously;
My due from thee is this imperial crown,
Which, as immediate from thy place and blood,
Derives itself to me.

To James's mind his brother's reign had on the whole been a complete success. The Test Act and the Habeas Corpus Act had it is true found their place in the Statute Book, but Charles had by resolute action triumphed in the end and now there would be no looking back. We in our day are accustomed to the "swing of the political pendulum" (a pendulum so oddly constructed that the movements to the left are consistently of greater range than the intervening movements to the right); James without our experience was unaware of this phenomenon and had no apprehension that the next swing would be the most violent in our history and would sweep him from his throne. He entered upon his reign under the fixed delusion that there would be no longer any restriction to arbitrary arrest and no more judges who would refuse to pronounce judgements which were in effect royal decrees.

In every generation in modern England there has been either an individual or a group of prominent politicians who have refused to believe that the advance of constitutional liberty in their own day has served the highest interests of the country and have nursed the illusion that a recovery can be made of the ground lost in recent years by conservative forces. When the group has thrown up no acknowledged leader it has been known as "the Old Guard", "the Last Ditchers" or "the Die-hards"; if there was an acknowledged leader he was to his contemporaries "the Last of the Tories". Names which spring to the mind in the nineteenth century are Lord Eldon, Lord George Bentinck and Henry Chaplin; in the eighteenth century there was Lord Bolingbroke, but he lacked three important qualifications: he was insufficiently sincere, he had too much imagination, and he was without following; in the present century there have been many claimants to the title. But of all claimants in all generations no one has a better title than James, Duke of York; in none of his letters and in none of his reported words can there be found a hint of a liberal idea, in the Exclusion debates no one was found to support his extreme view of the rights of the Crown, he steadily maintained that any concession to parliamentary demands would reduce the King to the position of a "Duke of Venice", and when he left England in 1688 he was, except for the insignificant men who accompanied him, entirely alone in holding those views. He had no predecessor, but a number of successors; we must remember always that he specifically and wisely declined to attempt to form a party, but with that reservation we can accord him the unique honour of being the first of "the Last of the Tories".

PART II

KING JAMES II

The two brothers, Charles and James, became . . . infected with popery in such degrees as their different characters admitted of. Charles had parts and his good understanding served as an antidote to repel the poison. James, the simplest man of his time, drank the whole chalice. The poison met in his composition with all the fear, all the credulity, and all the obstinacy of temper proper to increase its virulence and to strengthen its effect; . . . drunk with superstitious and even enthusiastic zeal, [*he*] *ran headlong into his own ruin while he endeavoured to precipitate ours. His parliament and his people did all they could to save themselves by winning him. But all was in vain: he had no principles on which they could take hold. Even his good qualities worked against them, and his love for his country went halves with his bigotry.* Bolingbroke.

The most dangerous use which supreme authority can make of law and public institution is to attempt to make them express consequences contrary to their natural end. To the scandal to public conscience thus despised is joined the tacit admission of the artifice which is the refuge of weakness. People respect force, even when used unjustly, if it is displayed with courage, but they have the sense to give it its true value when it is only borrowed. They despise it and it falls. Mazure.

[*Reproduced by permission of the National Portrait Gallery*

KING JAMES II
(Studio of John Riley)

CHAPTER I

THE ACCESSION

James II ascended the English throne better equipped by experience for the task of kingship than any other English monarch. For nearly the whole of his brother's long reign he had been the most prominent subject, and though it is easy to over-estimate the influence which he exerted on policy, he had been, except on rare occasions, in the King's most intimate counsels. It is true that he had spent nearly two years in exile, but during the greater part of that time he had resided in Scotland, in effect though not in name Charles's deputy, so that he should have gained an intimate knowledge of the affairs of that kingdom; while his six months' residence at Brussels should have enabled him to correct, by acquaintance with the Spanish point of view, his prepossessions in favour of France. Charles, partly by natural indolence, partly by an intuitive knowledge of possibilities, had avoided direct conflict with Parliament on the constitutional question; he was content with the reality of power and he was not anxious to have that power exactly defined. James had no conception of a monarchy which was not absolute; from a principle of loyalty, which we must believe to have been perfect and without flaw, he had obeyed his brother implicitly in everything (except his personal religion), but he had not approved of his temporising policy; he had repeatedly urged him to assert his authority, even at the risk of civil war, but when Charles had refused to take his advice, James had loyally preserved silence.

James's mind resembled in many ways that of his father: he desired, not only that the power of the King should be real, but that it should be manifestly real; while, however, the father sought power for its own sake, the son, in addition, valued power as a means to the accomplishment of the passionately desired object of his life: the conversion of England to the Roman Church. As long as his brother was alive James had no hope of making progress in this ulterior object, and in the ten years between the popular realisation of his conversion and his return from Scotland in the spring of 1682 he was fully occupied in defending himself against attacks of various kinds; but his endeavours to extend the power of the Crown were unremitting, and he regarded the Tory reaction which followed the dissolution of the Oxford Parliament in March 1681 as a final triumph for the monarchy. This misconception is but one of many examples of his incompetence in political judgement and his inability to gain knowledge from experience; his political and religious obsessions blinded him to the dangers which he had to avoid; he was firmly convinced that Charles's victory at Oxford might have been achieved many years earlier, and that if necessity arose it could be repeated at any time and in any circumstances.

There can be little doubt that at the time of his accession James was suffering from premature mental decline, a decline which had set in some four years earlier when he was in Scotland. He had never been given credit for superior mental equipment, but he would probably not have been noticeably inferior to his neighbours if he had lived as a country gentleman—the nickname "Squire James" which he acquired at about the age of forty reflects the popular view of his abilities—but he had declined even from that low standard. In February 1685 he was little more than fifty-one years of age, and should have been at the height of his mental powers; and it is difficult to avoid a suggestion that in the sexual excesses of his youth he had incurred infection which had resulted in a fairly common mental disease.[1] In recent years this disease in many cases yields to treatment, but apparently there is no instance known in which it has cured itself by the passage of time, leaving, as in James's case in December 1688, the patient's mind in a condition of extreme senility but his bodily strength unimpaired.[2] Be the reason what it may, the chief symptom of this disease was present in James in a very marked degree: extreme haughtiness and arrogance, an exaggeration of his kingly office which was even more than an application to his own person of the veneration he had felt for Charles, a total absence of misgiving, amounting to foolhardiness, in regard to the consequences of his actions; the Greeks would have said that he was in the grip of ὕβρις, and the Scotch that he was "fey"; of no man can it be more confidently said that the gods made him mad before destroying him. He did indeed control his natural impatience at the beginning of his reign, especially in the first three months, but before he had been on the throne a year he had lost all sense of proportion and balance.

Barrillon, the French ambassador, and Bonrepaus, whom Louis sent over on three occasions during the reign on diplomatic missions,

[1] It was commonly held by his contemporaries that the death in infancy of so many of James's children was due to his diseased condition. Modern medical opinion is contrary to such a conclusion; moreover, infant mortality was terribly high in the seventeenth century, and the proportion of survivals among James's children, legitimate and illegitimate being taken together, was low, but not phenomenal.

[2] The health and vigour which James had enjoyed before his accession continued unbroken throughout his reign and to within a few months of his death. He hunted up to his sixty-sixth year, and his incredulity and annoyance when he was told he had gout are quite in character with a man who did not know what it was to be ill.

were in the same confidential relations with James as Barrillon had been both with Charles and James in the previous reign;[1] James told his Ministers very little about his ultimate aims, but to the French envoys he opened his mind completely. The reports which these envoys made to their master were strictly confidential and were based on a thorough knowledge of James's character, and they had no motive for reticence or dissimulation.[2] The quality of James which is most frequently mentioned in their despatches is "*hauteur*", and they found him very impatient of advice and criticism: "He suffers very impatiently the least contradiction", wrote Barrillon; and at another time:

> The King of England openly expresses his joy at being in a position to exercise his authority boldly; he is very pleased at being complimented on these displays of power,

and Bonrepaus thus sums up the King's character:

> It is quite certain that this King is neither so self-controlled nor so great a man as has been supposed. He has all the faults of the King his father, but he has less sense and he behaves more haughtily in public.

The Earl of Ailesbury, who suffered forty-five years of exile as a Jacobite, left an almost unqualified panegyric of James's public life, but he admits that he "had the misfortune to be snappish for the moment, and wholly resembling his royal father". In a contemporary letter ascribed to William Penn, but repudiated by him, we find:

> Every mechanic knows the temper of his present Majesty, who will never receive a baffle in anything that he heartily espouseth.

Finally, Roger North in his *Life of Lord Guilford* relates that the Lord Keeper

> knew the King's humour, that nothing he could say to him would take place or sink with him. So strong were his prejudices and so feeble his genius that he took none to have a right understanding that were not in his measures, and that the counsel given him to the contrary was for policy of party more than for friendship to him.

These last sentences are very significant: James could not understand

[1] Barrillon wrote to Louis on May 28, 1685, "This prince treats me exactly as he did when he was Duke of York, and he has several times told me to address him with the same openness as previously".

[2] It is, however, very important to employ great caution in accepting the dicta of both ambassadors, and especially those of Barrillon, on any matter outside the verge of the Court. They both show great ignorance of the English character and of the political forces which were working beneath the surface.

that unpalatable counsels might be given him in good faith by Ministers who were entirely in his interests, and that to advise moderation was not necessarily to betray Whiggish tendencies; "he accounted every body disloyal that disputed or demurred at any of his commands". He told Guilford and Halifax on one occasion that their advice was not wanted, and that their duty as Ministers was not to turn him from his fixed purpose, but to find legal justification for his actions. In these circumstances it is not surprising that James was unable to command the services of the best and ablest men in his kingdom. His most strenuous defenders admit that he was a poor judge of men; he supplemented this constitutional disability by refusing to employ in the highest offices of State anyone who did not at least pretend wholeheartedly to support his policy—a policy the success of which no one of sagacity could desire or expect. In the result he retained in his service two able but unscrupulous men, Sunderland and Jeffreys, together with the three Catholic lords who had been acquitted of complicity in the Popish Plot, Lord Arundell of Wardour, Lord Belasyse and the Marquis of Powis, men of good character, but all three well past the ordinary age of retirement—Lord Arundell was nearly eighty in 1685—and among them only Belasyse had more than moderate ability, and he was an invalid and an unwilling co-operator in James's schemes.

It was notorious at the time that James was increasingly throughout his reign under the influence of zealous and sanguine priests of his Church, who were wholly lacking in political common sense, and the statement that a priest-ridden king is an unsuccessful king is one that needs no reinforcement from anti-religious prejudice. Another influence hardly less disastrous was that of his cousin, King Louis XIV of France. For him he had the warmest admiration, and, had he been able to remould England nearer to his heart's desire, he would have achieved a polity on the French model and have been in England in all things what Louis was in France: James never said, "L'état c'est moi", but it was his aim to be able to say it. In more personal matters he made Louis his pattern. It is difficult to believe, indeed, that he ever thought of rivalling the magnificence of the French Court, for parsimony and splendour cannot cohabit: Bonrepaus, with less than perfect diplomatic tact, on one occasion informed him that "there were more candles burning in a single antechamber at Versailles than there were in the whole of Whitehall", and on another that Louis had "for his personal use, his coaches and other conveyances, more than a thousand horses in his stables". But James no doubt had the French Court in mind when he reformed in his own Court the easy-going manners of his brother's time. A typical innovation was in the etiquette of the reception of foreign envoys: the Tuscan ambassador reported:

> His Majesty receives all the foreign representatives who come to compliment him on his accession seated, with his hat on and in a special room; not, like the late King, standing in his own bedchamber and with his hat in his hand.

This procedure was copied from Louis's behaviour to Lord Churchill when he went to Versailles to announce James's accession; Barrillon's comment is that the King's intention is "to observe every formality and to preserve exactly all the externals of the royal dignity", and he himself, though he retained his confidential relations with the English King and could in practice choose his own time for an informal conversation, received an official order to request an audience whenever he had business with the King.

James's determination to have a large standing army—in April 1685 he told Barrillon that he was determined to raise it to 20,000 men or more—was mainly political, and the fear that it was to be used to support arbitrary power was justified, but there can be no doubt that James regarded the possession of a well-equipped army, quite apart from its practical use, as an addition to his royal splendour; his frequent attendances at reviews, at first in Hyde Park and later at Hounslow, show a liking for military display for its own sake. In August 1685 he wrote to William:

> On Saturday last I saw some of my troops at Hounslow, they consisted of ten battalions of foot of which three were of the guards and the other seven new-raised regiments; of horse there were twenty squadrons, one of grenadiers on horseback and one of dragoons; and really the new troops were in very good order and the horse well mounted. *I was glad that the Mareschal d'Humières saw them for several reasons.*

In one respect James observed decorum with more strictness than did his model, Louis, for he had no public mistress. Indeed, within a few days of his accession he announced his intention of severing his relations with Catherine Sedley, his mistress of several years' standing; he ordered her to vacate her apartments at Whitehall, offered her an additional pension if she went abroad and vowed he would see her no more. But she went no farther than St. James's Square, and after a short time her connection with the King was resumed. In other ways also he reformed the manners of the Court: he declared himself emphatically against duelling and drunkenness and, what is even more important, he put a stop to the waste on expensive pleasures of the money of which his brother had been in such need. James has no claim to financial talent, but he was by nature parsimonious, and he had one virtue which was not until recent times common in royal princes, financial morality: he exerted himself throughout his reign to pay off Charles's debts and to keep his own expenditure within the limits of his income.

It is not possible to impute to James any fault in his intention, not only to remove the disabilities under which the Catholics suffered and to throw open to them all posts in the public services, but to make England, Scotland and Ireland Catholic kingdoms. As a convinced Catholic not only was it excusable to entertain such aspirations, but it was his clear duty to do all in his power to realise them. In this regard James's faults were of the head and not of the heart: the methods he employed brought him in effect no nearer to a permanent improvement in the position of the Catholic religon in England, but by increasing the fears, and consequently the antagonism, of the Protestants, he rendered a reaction certain: and this consummation was anticipated by almost every Catholic in the country except the Jesuit priests at the Court.[1] Whether a wise, and above all a patient, Catholic king could in James's circumstances have done anything for his religion is very doubtful, so deep was the national prejudice; but it is possible that, by building up for himself a reputation for justice and moderation and by removing all suspicion that he had ulterior aims, he might in a period of years have persuaded Parliament to repeal the more sanguinary of the penal laws, and even to permit the celebration of Catholic rites in private chapels by a few licensed priests. But James was neither wise not patient: he was incapable of taking a detached view of his situation and of formulating in his own mind the most fitting course of conduct for the Catholic head of a Protestant State; at his accession he saw clearly the difficulties he would have to contend with, but as soon as he saw how easy it was to make the penal laws and Test Act a nullity in particular cases, he became "an old man in a hurry"; he set no bounds of discretion to his actions, took no account of consequences, and as a result found himself (though he did not know it) politically bankrupt long before the expedition of William of Orange had been thought of; and he had done more harm to the cause he had at heart than any Protestant king could have done.[2]

In one sense no doubt James, as was said by the Archbishop of Rheims, "lost three kingdoms for a Mass", but such a statement is an unwarrantable simplification: James lost his crown not because he was a Catholic, but because he took unwise measures for the benefit of his religion and because he gave ample ground for suspicion that he was

[1] It was James's "unfortunate destiny" (as Dickens said of Buffer) "to damage a cause by espousing it".

[2] Voltaire alleges that it was a joke among the Cardinals at Rome that James ought to have been excommunicated for losing for Catholicism the slight influence which had remained to it in England.

resolved to make it the dominant, if not the only, religion in his kingdoms. Further, James was regarded by the Catholic Jacobites as a Martyr to the Faith, as one who, as it were, by definite choice abandoned an earthly for a heavenly crown. But the facts furnish no support to such a thesis: up to the time when his earthly crown was irretrievably lost James had no doubt that he could keep the one and attain the other—in fact he persistently identified his authority as king with the cause of religion—and it was not until, by the Peace of Ryswick, his hopes of regaining the crown of the three kingdoms were finally dashed, that he devoted himself unreservedly to the salvation of his soul.

No discussion of James's character as king would be complete without some mention of his conception of loyalty. Like the sentry in *Iolanthe*, he thought that everyone was born into this world with an immutable political character; they were either loyal or disloyal at birth, and so they continued through life: that a man whom he had thought loyal turned against him was to James merely a proof that his loyalty had been only a pretence; he could not understand that loyalty, even when it is a plant of robust growth, cannot survive more than a certain degree of rough treatment. It is very remarkable that James, who was so careful about money, should have been so lavish in squandering his friends. In so doing he added enormously to the number of his personal enemies and left himself without support in the time of crisis: but he might have survived as king had he not also squandered the loyalty of the most powerful institution in the kingdom, the Church of England. There is a parlour game with affinities to experimental psychology in which a person is given a word and required to produce another word associated with it; if James had played that game, and the clue given to him at any time before July 1688 had been "Church of England", he would without hesitation have replied "loyalty". It may be broadly said that never did he mention the Church without either praising it for its loyalty or upbraiding it for not living up to its own principles of loyalty. It was his failure to realise that there may be a conflict of loyalties, and that the men of the Church of England might cease to be loyal to their King when, as they thought, he was directly attacking their Church, that in the main cost him his throne.

Immediately after the death of Charles, the Privy Councillors who happened to be in London assembled in the Council Chamber in order to agree upon the form of proclamation of the new King and the ceremonial to be observed in that connection. They had nearly completed this work when James came into the chamber, and after making some fitting and no doubt sincere remarks on the loss which he, both as a brother and in common with the rest of the kingdom, had just sustained, he was moved to make the following speech:

> My Lords,
>
> Before I enter upon any other business I think fit to say something to you since it hath pleased Almighty God to place me in this station and I am now to succeed so good and gracious a King as well as so very kind a brother I think fit to declare to you that I will endeavour to follow his example and most especially in that of his great clemency and tenderness to his people. I have been reported to be a man for arbitrary power but that is not the only story that has been made of me: and I shall make it my endeavour to preserve this government in Church and State as it is now by law established. I know the principles of the Church of England are for monarchy and the members of it have shewed themselves good and loyal subjects, therefore I shall always take care to defend and support it. I know too that the laws of England are sufficient to make the King as great a monarch as I can wish, and as I shall never depart from the just rights and prerogative of the Crown, so I shall never invade any man's property. I have often heretofore ventured my life in defence of the nation and I shall still go as far as any man in preserving it in all its just rights and liberties.[1]

Vague and non-committal as these words appear on a sober reading, the Councillors were surprised and delighted at their tone; a cynic might have detected an implied threat in the terms on which the King regarded himself as bound to support the Church of England, but it is most improbable that James had anything of the sort in mind; he had had very little sleep since Charles's first seizure, and he would have been wiser to have postponed his declaration until he was in a condition to weigh his words. However, if he spoke on impulse, it was on a very good impulse, and it may well be that if he had given himself time to consider he might have produced a declaration more exactly in accordance with his real intentions, and less calculated to remove apprehensions. What actually happened was that the Councillors prevailed on him then and there to authorise the publication of his speech, which among them they were able to reproduce in the words he had employed, and thus to silence those whose interest it was to show that there was danger to religion and law, and to give James and his Ministers a breathing space in which to prepare their plans. These promises for the

[1] According to the Brandenburg resident, James also said that "as regarded his private opinions no one should ever perceive that he had any", but he struck these words out of the draft.

preservation of the Protestant religion gave very great satisfaction and were "preached in every pulpit". After the matter of publication of the speech had been settled the Councillors present were sworn members of the new Privy Council and a proclamation was authorised retaining in office all public servants "until His Majesty's further directions".

The same afternoon the ceremony of the proclamation of the new King was performed at Whitehall, at Temple Bar and at the Royal Exchange, and subsequently in other parts of London and throughout England, Scotland and Ireland. Burnet remarks on the occasion:

> It was a heavy solemnity: few tears were shed for the former, nor were there any shouts of joy for the present king. A dead silence, but without any disorder or tumult, followed it through the streets.

But Burnet was not in England, and in this instance he was unfortunate in his sources of information; for there is ample evidence that the proclamation was received with applause throughout the three kingdoms. Thus the Modenese envoy wrote to his master that the announcement of Charles's death was received with fitting grief and the proclamation of James "with universal applause and shouts and demonstrations of joy greater than could have been hoped for"; Barrillon says that in London "the people made the acclamations usual on such an occasion"; Evelyn was present at the proclamation at Bromley, and he refers to the "many shouts of the people"; the Mayor and Corporation of Newcastle informed Sunderland that "the two proclamations [the death of Charles and the accession] were proclaimed in our usual solempnityes with all the demonstrations and expressions of joy and thankfulness and all matters here are in great peace and quiet and nothing but gladness in every man's countenance"; at Lincoln, "after His Majesty was acclaimed as aforesaid, the Mayor, Aldermen, etc., went to the Guildhall, where a banqueting was provided at the City's charge, and then they went to some bonfires and drank the King's, Queen's, and royal family's healths, and the night concluded with bonfires, drums beating, ringing of bells, etc."; at Reading also "the proclamation was attended by the clergy and abundance of gentry and the inhabitants, with great acclamations, the bells ringing, drums beating and trumpets sounding"; Ormonde wrote that the King was proclaimed with great joy in Dublin, and all other parts of Ireland of which he had heard; and the high sheriff of Northumberland assured the Minister that "there is no county in England would proclaim him with more acclamation of joy nor express more entire resolution to serve him with their lives and fortunes".

The most elaborate account comes from Oxford, where the conduit at Carfax ran claret, and there were great shouts and acclamations when the mace-bearer of the city read the proclamation. At night there were bonfires before all the colleges; at Merton "two barrels of beer were drunk at the bonfire by the junior scholars and several of the parish boys and neighbours and servants of the house. The gravest and greatest seniors of the house were mellow that night as at other colleges." But perhaps most striking is the reluctant testimony of two zealous Whigs, James Welwood and Edmund Calamy, the famous dissenting minister. Welwood says:

> All the former heats and animosities against him and even the very memory of a bill of Exclusion seemed to be now quite forgot amidst the loud acclamations at his accession to the Crown,

and Calamy as an eye-witness:

> Never did I see so universal a concern as was visible in all men's countenances at that time. I was present upon the spot at the proclaiming King James II at the upper end of Wood Street in Cheapside—and my heart ached within me at the acclamations made upon that occasion, which, as far as I could observe, was very general.

It is not difficult to organise demonstrations of joy, and some of those mentioned may have been of an artificial character; in London, however, the time was too short to allow of preparations, though no doubt the liquor which was freely distributed in the streets for the purpose of drinking the King's health was (as three years later when the Prince of Wales was born) provided out of public funds. But the entire absence of disturbance in any part of the three kingdoms is very remarkable and was not anticipated by those who were in the best position to form a judgement. James himself a few days later spoke of the time of Charles's death as critical, "a time when King Louis did not know whether or no there would be a rising in London and the King would be driven out". Rochester wrote to Ormonde on February 10, "Everything is calm and quiet to a wonder"; the Tuscan envoy informed the Grand Duke that James had taken peaceful possession of the Crown to the extreme astonishment of the disaffected; that they are living in such fear that they are hiding their goods and thinking how best to secure their persons; and that there appears to be great restraint in political discussion. The French ambassador wrote that James had been proclaimed in York and in all the towns of England, in Edinburgh and in Dublin, and that there was no disturbance anywhere, even in such ill-disposed towns as Bristol and Chester; Ormonde wrote from Ireland that he had been apprehensive of "endeavour to raise disturbance", but that he had little doubt that things would continue in the calm in which they were; and he was later able to say that he had been correct in his judgement.

Sunderland, as principal Secretary of State, had taken elaborate precautions against disturbance. Peter Shakerley, the Governor of Chester, wrote on February 7, before he had heard of Charles's death, that he had taken the precautions Sunderland had instructed him to take —for example, he had stopped all arrivals and departures of shipping at the port and had arrested all suspected persons; there are letters from Bristol, Deal, Harwich and Newcastle that all passengers on incoming and outgoing ships had been searched and questioned, and it may safely be surmised that similar steps had been taken at the Secretary's instance at all the ports; in London and York troops were held in readiness to suppress disorder during and after the proclamation. But in the event there was no attempt at disturbance and no necessity for all this activity; there were many thousands of people in England who looked on James's accession as a national disaster, but they were isolated in small groups and without organisation. Four years earlier Sir William Jones in the House of Commons had said without fear of contradiction:

> I take it for granted that it is impossible that a Papist should come to the possession and quiet enjoyment of this Crown without wading through a sea of blood;

and in the same debate Laurence Hyde, the ablest of James's advocates and the one most in his confidence, had admitted that James could not hope to succeed without strict limitations on his prerogative. Perhaps at no time in the history of England, except at the Restoration, has there been so sudden and unexpected a victory in so short a time of one school of political thought over another.

The most urgent business of the Government was the disposal of the body of Charles, and the new Privy Council on February 6, after making arrangements for the proclamation, appointed a Committee to consider this matter and to meet at six o'clock the same evening. The funeral took place on February 14, and there is an extraordinary divergence of authority on the degree of pomp attending it. Oldmixon quotes the Bishop of Salisbury—Seth Ward—who was probably present (though advancing to senile decay)—as saying:

> He did not even lie in state, no mournings were given and the expense of it was not equal to what an ordinary nobleman's

> funeral will rise to. Many upon this said that he deserved better from his brother than thus to be ungratefully treated;

and Evelyn says that Charles was "very obscurely buried under Henry VII's chapel at Westminster, without any manner of pomp and soon forgotten after all this vanity". But the body lay in state in the Painted Chamber for several days, and there is ample evidence that the procession from the Painted Chamber to the Abbey lacked nothing in dignity. Luttrell says:

> The body was carried under a velvet canopy attended by the servants of the nobility, their royal highnesses, their present Majesties, &c. . . . The Prince of Denmark was chief mourner, the supporters to him were the Dukes of Somerset and Beaufort; the assistants to the chief mourner were sixteen Earls . . .

And in the Public Record Office there is a draft of "The proceeding to the private interment of the Most High . . . Most Excellent and Most Mighty Monarch Charles the Second", which, from the erasures and interlineations, had evidently been the subject of detailed discussion by the Committee; this document corroborates Luttrell's account and adds the interesting details that the bishops took their place in the procession as peers and that the Archbishop of Canterbury walked with Norroy, King of Arms, immediately in front of the coffin. But the actual interment was private, and for the very good reason that James and very few others knew Charles had died a Catholic and that it was not expedient that this fact should be known before the country had settled down after the accession; it is probable also that James was anxious not to be under necessity to be present at a Protestant rite. The coffin was received at the door of the Abbey by the Dean and prebendaries of Westminster, and after the burial service the officers of the household (who were probably the only persons present in addition to the officiating clergy) broke their staves of office over the grave according to custom.

In the meantime the Council were compelled to consider a very urgent financial question. By a curious oversight, or possibly by design, the two chief contributions to the public revenue, the Customs and the Excise,[1] had been granted to King Charles for life and without continuance for a specified number of months to his successor. When Charles died the Commissioners of Customs were in a quandary: legally the parliamentary grant had lapsed and no duties could be

[1] That is to say, that part of the Excise which was not hereditary.

levied, but if the law were strictly observed the result would be not only a loss of revenue, but a flooding of the market with cheap foreign goods, to the injury of the merchants who had stocks in hand on which duty had been paid. A little comedy was enacted between the Customs Commissioners and the Treasury Commissioners, who were asked to give a ruling in the matter, and who declined to allow themselves to be drawn into a trap, and replied that the Customs Commissioners could read the law as well as they could and that they must act on their own responsibility. The Privy Council quite properly solved the question by issuing a proclamation that the duties should continue to be levied. But the wording of the proclamation was disingenuous: when Parliament is not sitting it is the duty of the Executive to provide for an emergency such as had arisen, but they are bound to seek indemnity from Parliament on reassembly; the proclamation regarding the Customs mentioned, indeed, that a Parliament was "speedily to be assembled", but that seems to have been only to deceive the public, for the implication of the proclamation taken as a whole is that the King was entitled to the Customs by right, Parliament or no Parliament. There was no difference between the King's advisers as to the propriety and expediency of continuing the Customs, but Lord Keeper Guilford made the puerile suggestion (which was over-ruled) that the duties when levied should be hoarded pending a decision by the King in Parliament as to the disposal of the money.

The Excise was on a different footing, for it was not collected by Government officers, but by farmers, and a new contract for three years for the farm of that part of the Excise terminable at the King's death had been signed the day before Charles's death, the amount in question being about £550,000. The judges were consulted as to the legality of this contract, and decided by a majority that it was legal, whereupon the Council authorised the continuance of the collection of the Excise. Sir Thomas Jones, Chief Justice of the Common Pleas, and Justices Levinz, Montagu and Atkins dissented from the judgement of their brethren, and there was a rumour that they would all be dismissed—for the public accepted the doctrine that judges must not pronounce judgements unpalatable to the King. No such action was taken at this time, but they were all, except Atkins, dismissed in the following year. By the time the farm of the Excise should have been renewed on February 5, 1688, James had provided his subjects with so many other grievances that the necessity of this step was overlooked.

In one very important matter James lost no time. He had for nine years been a Papist recusant—that is to say, he had refrained from attendance at the services of the Church of England—and for thirteen years it had been known that he had absented himself from public celebrations of the Sacrament. Suspicions which had arisen long before the Restoration had by the time of the Popish Plot grown into a certainty in the public mind that James was a Catholic, and it was only in deference to Charles's wishes that he had refrained from an open declaration of adherence to the old faith. Now that he was a free agent he determined, no doubt with the full approbation of Queen Mary, to make an end of all concealment. Two days after his accession he attended Mass publicly in the chapel of St. James's Palace, where the Queen had worshipped, and he with her, for a dozen years. This was the first public evidence of his change of religion.[1] The following Sunday he had service at Whitehall. He did not invade the Chapel Royal—there Dr. Tenison preached to the Household—but he opened an oratory attached to his own lodgings as Duke of York, which Charles had closed for fear of scandal, and this oratory became for all practical purposes the Chapel Royal. It can have been of no great size, but no expense was spared to make the services magnificent, and six months later Barrillon told Louis that they were like those for a cathedral, and that the Protestants observed them through the open door with respect and reverence. In the following year James demolished the Privy Gallery near the Banqueting House at Whitehall and built on its site a range of buildings, including apartments for the Queen, lodgings and offices for public servants and a magnificent chapel. Wren was the architect, and Grinling Gibbons, Verrio, Gennari and other artists contributed to the embellishment of the chapel. It was opened on Christmas Day 1686; at the Revolution it was dismantled, and it disappeared in the fire which destroyed Whitehall in 1698. All that remains of James's single considerable venture in building are the organ-case, which went to St. James's, Piccadilly,[2] and some panels of the altar at the church of Burnham, Somerset. The annual charges of the services amounted to over £2000 and included the salaries and wages of twenty-two persons.

Louis thoroughly approved of James's conduct in appearing openly at Mass; he said it was not fitting that a great king should dissimulate in so important a matter, and thought this step was more likely to inspire respect and fear in his subjects than to play into the hands of the malcontents: King James's Ministers advised him to temporise until he was more firmly seated on the thone. James himself in a conversation

[1] It is only fair to James to state that on two occasions he had determined to make a declaration of his adherence to the Church of Rome, but had been restrained by Charles.

[2] By a very happy accident this valuable organ escaped damage when the church was destroyed by a bomb.

with Barrillon gave grounds for his action which will commend themselves to every impartial reader: he contended

> that everyone should act according to his own temperament; that dissimulation in religion was opposed to his way of life; that if he had shown fear the people ill-disposed to him would have had him at a disadvantage; that though he took some risk in his action his conscience obliged him to make open confession of his religion; . . . that he hoped God would protect him and that since Louis supported him and bore so sincere a friendship to him he had nothing to fear.

In the event James and Louis were proved to be right and James's Ministers wrong. There was a great deal of talk, and the dissenters murmured that James should have worshipped in private, as they were compelled to do; Evelyn, who was in some ways a Victorian born out of his time and who minded abuses little if they were wrapped up in decent parcels, was horrified; the London mob was very angry, and agitators tried to make them believe that the public exercise of the King's religion was a first step to the establishment of Catholicism, the proscription of Protestantism and a revival of the Marian persecutions. But men of sense were unmoved: they could not see how the King could be denied the full performance of the rites of his religion; and, indeed, it was inconsistent that the people who had so enthusiastically acclaimed the accession of a Catholic King should make any sort of objection to his appearing openly as a Catholic. After a very few weeks, when the novelty of the sight had worn off, opposition was silenced.

As Easter drew near a fresh problem arose. Hitherto James had had an informal escort of such members of his household as had no strong prejudices and were even in some cases willing to join in part of the worship in order to please the King. But he decided that the celebration on Easter Day must be accompanied by the pomp and ceremony of a full procession to and from the chapel not only of the officers of the Household, but also of the chief Ministers of State. Rochester, who as Lord Treasurer held the highest office, was in a quandary: apart from his religious convictions (which were undoubtedly sincere), he was anxous not to lose his position as head of the Church party; at the same time he could not afford to displease the King. He told James that he would not attend unless he was formally ordered to do so. James behaved very well in the matter, and told him that he respected his scruples and that he might spend Easter at his country house. Rochester's was apparently the only defection, for all the other great lords took their places in the procession. In the following year not only Rochester but also Sunderland and Jeffreys were out of London during Easter; so that it appears that James was sincere in his expressions to Rochester, and that Rochester's abstention fom the Easter procession was not a factor in his fall from favour.

At the time of Charles's death the chief Ministers were Lord Guilford, Lord Keeper; Rochester, Lord President of the Council; Halifax, Lord Privy Seal; Sunderland, Principal Secretary of State; and Godolphin, First Commissioner of the Treasury. After the fall of Danby, Rochester, Sunderland and Godolphin had shared the chief place in Charles's counsels, but latterly Rochester had fallen from favour, and his place had been taken by the King's mistress, the Duchess of Portsmouth, whose close alliance with Sunderland was regarded by James as hostile to himself. Halifax occupied a peculiar position: Charles enjoyed his society and delighted in his cynical wit, and there was something like personal friendship between the King and the Minister. Halifax had been on excellent terms with Rochester, but at his instigation Rochester had, because of certain irregularities in his accounts, been removed from the Treasury, where he had been First Commissioner, and made Lord President, and was to be sent into honourable exile as Lord Lieutenant of Ireland in succession to Ormonde. It is evidence of Rochester's essential goodness of heart that he bore Halifax no grudge.

The Duchess of Portsmouth by the death of Charles naturally lost all claim to public importance. James had been very angry with her at the time of the Second Exclusion Bill, but he had latterly been outwardly on good terms with her. On James's accession she was in some apprehension that he would not treat her well, an apprehension which was confirmed when James took away from the Duke of Richmond, her thirteen-year-old son by King Charles, the post of Master of the Horse and gave it to Dartmouth, and she appealed to Louis to intervene on his behalf. But James, as was his habit of mind, was thinking more of the recipient of the favour than of the loser by it, and intended no harm to the boy. As to the Duchess, he was quite indifferent whether she remained in England or took with her to France the wealth she had accumulated in fifteen years, but he stipulated that before she went she should pay her debts.[1]

Of the others, Rochester was the Minister most deserving of James's favour. Not only was he the brother of James's first wife, Anne Hyde,

[1] It is a curious instance of the presumption of royal mistresses that both the Duchess of Portsmouth and Nell Gwynne attempted to decorate their horses and coaches in mourning for Charles in a manner exclusively reserved to the royal family.

but he was by far the most influential man in the kingdom who had been uniformly a supporter of James's interests; he had spoken strongly against the Exclusion Bills (though he had admitted that it might be necessary to limit by Statute the prerogative of a Catholic King), and he had visited James twice at Edinburgh in an attempt to arrange an accommodation between Charles and James on the question of James's religion. When Rochester had been under a cloud at the end of the late reign, James so clearly identified their interests that he considered that he himself was involved in the loss of Charles's favour. Rochester cannot have been a very pleasant man: it was generally agreed that he had a violent temper, particularly when he had been drinking, that in that condition he spoke indiscreetly, and that he had the common faults of a bully of being haughty in prosperity and unduly humble in adversity. But in those days of lax political principles he was one of the few prominent men who pursued a consistent line of conduct; he was a strong royalist and an equally strong Churchman, and it was probably his influence which kept the King within the bounds of moderation during his first four months; but he was much to blame for remaining in office when his advice was no longer listened to and when the ultimate aims of the royal policy were no longer in doubt. Within ten days of his accession James revived the post of Lord Treasurer and gave it to Rochester; but, though the Minister had for the time being a predominant position in the royal counsels and was in effect Foreign Minister, he was not given a free hand in his own department, but was subject to close supervision by the King.

Sunderland had every reason to fear that the death of Charles would put an end to his political career. It is idle to search Sunderland's actions for any underlying principle: on the Exclusion question he had made one of his many miscalculations; he had not expected that James would come to the throne and he had taken a leading position in what he thought would be the victorious party. James had been very angry at his desertion. But Sunderland need have been in no apprehension; three days after the accession Barrillon wrote to Louis (after recounting James's favours to Rochester):

> Lord Sunderland has also a large share in the King's confidence; he has spoken of him to me in terms of the highest esteem, and as he regards him as a fitting instrument to serve him in the plans which he has in mind, His Britannic Majesty has endeavoured both before and since the death of the late King to establish a close relation between Lord Rochester and Lord Sunderland;

and he added that recently James had not had much success in this endeavour, for Sunderland had allied himself with Godolphin and the Duchess of Portsmouth in an endeavour to undermine Rochester. This alliance was broken up by Charles's death and the Duchess's relegation to obscurity, and for some months the Treasurer and the Secretary of State worked together without friction, though Barrillon noticed that no sooner had Sunderland recovered from his fear of dismissal than he began to be jealous of the predominance which his high office gave to Rochester. Sunderland quickly gained with the King: already in March the French ambassador formed the opinion that he was "entirely informed of the plans of the King his master", and in July James himself told the ambassador that he had spoken to Sunderland on the subject of religion with less reserve than to other Ministers. James seems always to have found discretion in conversation a very irksome discipline, and Sunderland no doubt provided an outlet for opinions and projects which could not yet be made public. Louis saw in Sunderland a tool ready to his hand, and he instructed Barrillon to exert all his influence in Sunderland's favour and even to "let it be known that his retention in office will be very pleasing to me". Sunderland, on his part, continued until the Revolution to be faithful to the French alliance, though there came a time when Louis found it wiser to pay him for his services.

Godolphin was another exclusionist who was kept in office at James's accession; but he lost his position at the head of the Treasury Commission on Rochester's appointment as Lord Treasurer and was mortified by having to accept the minor post of Chamberlain to the Queen. This transfer must be accounted a success for Rochester, for Godolphin kept up his alliance with Sunderland. Godolphin consoled himself by indulging in a sentimental affection for his royal mistress, and no doubt contributed, in his unobtrusive manner, to Sunderland's success in obtaining her favour. Moreover, he was, in these first few months, very much in the King's confidence; for with Sunderland and Rochester he made up an inner Cabinet of three which was in almost permanent session in James's closet, and which either together or singly conducted the greater part of the long negotiations between James and the French ambassador.

Henry, Earl of Clarendon, Rochester's elder brother, displaced Halifax as Lord Privy Seal, and Halifax succeeded Rochester as Lord President of the Council—a position of dignity, but without great influence on affairs. The second Earl of Clarendon was a man of whom none of his contemporaries had a high opinion; he was a great friend of the bishops and a consistent royalist and Churchman; after the Revolution he was among the very few prominent men who refused to take the oaths to William and Mary; but he was essentially a weak man, and in the previous reign his relationship to James had secured for him no higher advancement than that of Privy Councillor. James treated him very badly, but nothing could lessen his spaniel-like attachment to his master. Halifax James disliked on both personal and public grounds. His wit and subtlety of mind, which had commended him to Charles, were to James a bewilderment; he disagreed with James in the three cardinal points of his policy, for he was against the French alliance, he was against unconstitutional and unprecedented extensions of the royal prerogative, and, if he was not too wise and too tolerant a man to be in favour of the continuance of the proscription of the Catholics in its extreme form, he was certainly against the repeal of the Test Act. He had earned James's gratitude by his stupenduous oratorical effort in the House of Lords by which he had, single-handed, procured the rejection of the Second Exclusion Bill; but he had followed up that effort by proposing limitations to the powers of a Catholic king which James had regarded as worse than exclusion. At the accession Halifax expected immediate dismissal, but the new King received him graciously, and told him, with truly royal courtesy, that he would remember nothing with regard to him except his services in the Exclusion debate. But to Barrillon James used different language; he said that the continuance in office of Halifax and others was only a gesture of moderation, and

> that he knew him and could never trust him, that he let him into no real secrets of business, and that his post of Lord President would serve to show him how little credit he had;

and he added that his chief motive was to avoid frightening his opponents into a belief that they were entirely ruined and that they could not by moderate conduct advance in his favour.

The reconstruction of the Ministry, together with a similar discretion in the distribution of posts in the Household, caused grave disappointment to Catholics and to others who thought they had a claim upon James's favour. Richard Talbot and the younger Henry Jermyn (shortly to be known respectively as the Earl of Tyrconnel and Lord Dover), who had been James's close friends ever since they were young together, were very much put out at not being made Lords of the Bedchamber. But James thought he saw a means to keep the loyalty of those who were in office and to gain the loyalty of those who sought to displace them. He told Barrillon

> that those who remained in possession of their posts feared to lose them and the others were in hopes to take their places; that all this

> would produce a good effect when Parliament met; and that there would be time to make changes when he saw how the men behaved whom he had retained in office.

The Earl of Guilford continued to be Lord Keeper, albeit on sufferance, and James did not even displace the Lord Chamberlain, the Earl of Arlington, with whom, except for a brief period about the time of the Treaty of Dover, he had been in antagonism for the whole of his life; he said (with a magnanimity of which it is difficult to find other examples) that Arlington was a very old man and that it would be unduly harsh to deprive him of the short enjoyment of office that remained to him.[1] Talbot and Jermyn received a sort of compensation for their disappointment by being made members of a new council which looked after the interests of the Catholic religion and of its adherents, the other two members of this council being Lord Arundel of Wardour and Lord Belasyse.

No sooner had James, two days after his accession, decided to gratify his people by promising an early election and meeting of Parliament, than he bethought himself that perhaps Louis would take it amiss that he had made the promise without previous consultation with the French King. The same day he saw Barrillon and explained his action in terms hardly becoming one whose ambition it was to be a great and independent monarch. He said that he had resolved to call a Parliament to meet in May, and that he had not thought fit to continue to collect the Customs duties without the promise of a Parliament. When Parliament met they would either put him in legal possession of his brother's revenues and he could dissolve them if he found it convenient, or they would refuse supplies and he would have to find other expedients.

> Many people tell me I have been too hasty in summoning Parliament; but if I waited longer I should lose all the credit of the action. I know the English; one must not show them at the start that one is afraid of them. If I delay I shall give the malcontents an opening for commencing an agitation in favour of a Parliament and that would be such a popular cry that they could easily damage my interests with it.

He added that he was well aware that it would be embarrassing to Louis if the Parliament took up an attitude hostile to France, but he would see to it that they did not meddle with foreign politics, and would dissolve them the moment they showed signs of ill-will.

[1] James may, however, have known of Arlington's leanings to the Roman Church.

> It is for you [he told Barrillon] to explain what I am telling you to the King your master in order that he may have no cause to reproach me for having taken this important resolution so promptly without consulting him as I ought to have done and as I wish to do in all things; but I should have ruined everything if I had postponed decision even for a week.

Not content with these servile messages to Louis, James sent Rochester to Barrillon the following day—the day of the announcement of the decision to call a Parliament—to reiterate his arguments and excuses and to add that there had been a danger which it had been necessary to anticipate, that Halifax and Guilford would have pressed him to call a Parliament, and that he wished to avoid any imputation that his action was not spontaneous, but the result of external pressure.

Barrillon himself, in conveying this news to his master, was apprehensive that Louis would not be pleased to hear it: he said that he had not thought fit to protest against a decision which had already been taken and which could not be revoked, and that he had not wanted to compromise Louis's dignity by any suggestion that he was afraid of an English Parliament. To Rochester, Barrillon said that he was not afraid of the name of Parliament, and that he had every confidence in James's power and firmness, but that the hopes of the old enemies of the Duke of York would be raised and that they would use every artifice to prevent supplies being voted to the King except on very hard terms. But Louis was not annoyed, but, on the contrary, commended James's decision. He replied to Barrillon:

> I approve also of the resolution which he has taken to call a new Parliament to assemble in May and the reasons which he has given convince me that he could not have done better: I have too good an opinion of his wisdom to doubt that nothing can happen which can loosen the bonds between us.

James expressed to Barrillon the greatest joy at Louis's approval of his action.

The elections took place in April and early May, and there was no long time for preparation. Every endeavour was made by the Court to secure the return of members well affected to the King, and in the whole history of Parliament it is doubtful whether the Crown on any other occasion put forth such an effort or interfered so universally and systematically in a parliamentary election. The organisation of victory was in Sunderland's hands, and within ten days of the accession[1] he

[1] One letter—to the Earl of Plymouth—went out on February 13, the remainder, as far as can be ascertained, on February 17.

sent to all corners of the kingdom letters which he had written to local magnates upon whose influence in the royal interest he could rely. Only one of these letters appears to have survived, but it is no doubt typical of the rest; and there are extant a large number of replies addressed to Sunderland and mentioning his letter of February 17. His letter to the Earl of Rutland runs:

> His Majesty being well satisfied of your Lordship's zeal for his service, and not doubting but you will use your utmost endeavours and employ all your interest that good members may be chosen for the approaching Parliament, commands me to tell you that he would have you take care of the Leicestershire elections, so as to prevent all intrigues and disorders which ill-affected persons may endeavour to set on foot: and therefore His Majesty thinks it necessary you should be present at the County Election and at as many of the borough elections as you can, and to take all possible care that persons of approved loyalty and affection to the government be chosen.

Such a vast body of material exists regarding the details of what happened in the constituencies that it is difficult to make a representative selection. From Hull, for example, the Earl of Plymouth wrote that he had persuaded the Corporation there to oppose the election of anyone who had voted for the Exclusion Bill and to elect members nominated by himself; he was also confident that his nine nominees in the county of Worcester—two for the county, the remaining seven for various boroughs—would be successful; the Duke of Newcastle believes that "the eight that goes from this county (Notts) will be very honest gentlemen"; the Earl of Winchelsea writes that he is assured that the county and various boroughs of Kent "will make loyal members their representatives" (he hopes at the same time that he will not be forgotten at Court while he is rendering this service in the provinces); the Earl of Derby promises diligence in Lancashire; Sir Charles Holt, Lord Brooke and Andrew Hacket write long and amusing letters about what they have been doing in Warwickshire: while Lord Chief Justice Jeffreys writes to Sunderland regarding the Bucks County election:

> Pardon me (my most honourable Lord) for giving you this trouble. I thought for His Majesty's service that you should know that this day I have had several gentlemen of the county hereabout with me who are resolute in the affair to oppose Wharton and Hampden. But they have been very industrious to spread false reports. [It is certain] Hampden will assign his interest to Sir

> Roger Hill who now sets up a horrid Whig: his father was one of the murthered Martyr King Charles the First judges and this spark a fierce exclusioner. . . .

In the boroughs the Court had little difficulty, for the corporations had been, or were in process of being, remodelled in the Church and Tory interest, or were afraid of royal displeasure and consequent loss of their charters,[1] and in the counties the local magnates were either honestly in the King's interest or were timid in declaring themselves on the other side. So strongly were the constituencies in the Tory interest that many prominent Whigs declined to stand.[2] Very significant is the appearance on the Court side in the election of certain names which in the course of a very few years figured prominently as those of James's opponents. Sir Cresswell Levinz, who lost his seat on the Bench in 1686 because he would not support the dispensing power and who was subsequently one of the Counsel for the seven bishops, was working for Sunderland at Salisbury, and the Earl of Shrewsbury and Henry Compton, Bishop of London, who were two of the famous seven who signed the invitation to William, were very active on the same side; Shrewsbury, as Lord Lieutenant of Staffordshire, managed the elections in that county together with Sir Francis Lawley, Lord Ferrers and Lord Dartmouth;[3] while Compton wrote to Strype, the ecclesiastical historian, who was one of his clergy:

> You will likewise now have an opportunity to give a real evidence of your professed fidelity by using your utmost interest among the gentry and other freeholders where you are acquainted to give their voices for such sober and prudent men as will seek the peace of the Church and State by promoting the King's and kingdom's service. I need not warn you of the great diligence used by the enemies of both to make choice of factious and turbulent spirits, and I hope the truth and justice of your cause will make you no less industrious to prevent such wicked and pernicious designs, which bear so fatal an aspect upon all honest men. Thus, praying God to direct you in so good a work, I remain . . .

A King's party which included such leading figures as Shrewsbury

[1] The Mayor of Bridgewater, however, wrote, "I am informed that notwithstanding Sir William Portman and Mr. Samford intended to stand for Taunton this damnable crew will set up Mr. Trenchard and William Stack; they are birds of one feather."

[2] One conspicuous exception was Charles Gerrard, son of the Earl of Macclesfield, who had sat for Lancashire in the last parliaments of Charles II and was nearly to lose his life for complicity with Monmouth. A tremendous and successful attempt was made to prevent his re-election.

[3] James's old friend, George Legge.

and Compton was indeed comprehensive, and it is not surprising that at the conclusion of the election James was able to say that there were not forty members[1] of the House of Commons that he would wish elsewhere. But Barrillon was not optimistic: he said that the elections had indeed gone well for the Court, but no one knew what might happen to the best-affected members when they got together; they were well aware that when they had given the King his revenues he might have no further use for them and that by granting supplies they may be signing their own death-warrant.

> It is true that members of the old factious party have not been elected; but the elected members may easily become factious themselves; they have almost all of them a rooted aversion to the Catholic religion and the greater number are enemies of France and are jealous of Your Majesty's glory.

And he doubted if it would be possible for James to propose even a relaxation of the penal laws.

For some obscure reason James was very anxious to get himself crowned before the meeting of Parliament. If Barrillon has correctly reported him, he had a very curious conception of the legal significance of the coronation. The ambassador says:

> It is regarded in England as a ceremony absolutely necessary for the establishment of the royal authority, for after it has taken place everything done or said against the King is high treason;

and a little later he returns to the subject and says that according to a law dating from the time of the Wars of the Roses the title of a king, once he is crowned, cannot be disputed, and he refers to the precedent of Cromwell. Clearly what he has in mind is the distinction in constitutional law between a king *de jure* and a king *de facto*. In another matter connected with the coronation James showed himself an indifferent lawyer: he told Barrillon that the Catholic peers would take part in the ceremony according to their rank, and that this concession would be a step towards getting them back into the House of Lords. He forgot that the Test Act of 1678 deprived Catholics of the capacity to sit in Parliament but of no other dignity or privilege.

The coronation took place on St. George's Day, April 23—a fitting date for the installation of a patriot king. Nothing was omitted that could enhance the splendour of the occasion, except that James and his Queen spent the previous night at St. James's Palace, and not, as

[1] Barrillon said there were only five or six malcontents.

was the traditional practice, at the Tower, so that the citizens of London were deprived of the sight of the procession. It was suggested that James chose St. James's Palace because there was a Catholic chapel there and he wished to pass the eve of his coronation in vigil. A Committee had been appointed two months in advance to regulate the procedure so as to satisfy the King's conscience without omitting any essential feature. In the event the entire ceremony was performed by the Archbishop of Canterbury, assisted by other bishops, with the single omission of the Communion.[1] Everyone seems to agree that the acclamations of those present left nothing to be desired, but there were two unfortunate incidents which contribute to James's reputation for lack of dignity in his public appearances: the first was that, by the awkwardness of the barons of the Cinque Ports, who carried it in procession, the canopy fell over the King, and the second that he had trouble with an ill-fitting crown; of this latter there are two contradictory accounts: Burnet (who was not present) says that the crown was too large and that it descended over the upper part of James's face; the Queen (who regarded the incident as an omen of evil) and Henry Sidney that it slipped sideways and nearly fell to the ground, and Sidney adds that he himself put a hand to it to steady it, remarking to the King "that it was not the first time a Sidney had supported the crown".

The religious part of the coronation gave complete satisfaction neither to Protestant nor Catholic casuits. Some Protestants said that without the Communion the ceremony was incomplete, others that the King and Queen had taken part in the Protestant forms of prayer with mental reservations and had been given a dispensation by the priests. With the Catholics the points at issue provided subject for controversy for months, and not only in England, whenever two priests met. On the one hand it was urged that the prayers, with the omission of the Mass, were merely a translation from the Latin of those which had been in use since pre-Reformation times, and that James's decision to submit to receive the crown from the Archbishop was a supreme example of his respect for the civil rights of the Church of England, and on the other that everything about the ceremony was heretical, and that the King and Queen committed mortal sin in giving it countenance.

On May 24, two days after the assembly of Parliament, when James had been more than three and a half months on the throne, Reresby wrote in his journal, "All things seemed now to look very auspicious,

[1] It appears that the original intention was that James and Mary should both take the Communion, for provision was made for a silk towel each "to be held before them at the Communion".

the King not giving the least token to change the religion but much to the contrary". Reresby moved in Tory circles, and it may well be that the Church and King men, who had no incentive to look below the surface for reasons to suspect the King whom they had done so much to bring in, were satisfied that their own predominance and the quiet state of affairs which had existed for the past four years would continue. Reresby, however, discounted the apprehensions of his friend Halifax, who was not given to accepting things at their face value and who saw in James's beginnings in the Irish army, where he had already begun to give commissions to Catholics, signs of trouble to come. In England, too, Halifax scented danger in James's indiscreet and repeated statements, from the first month of his reign, that he would insist on obtaining from Parliament the revenues for life, and without conditions. A further event of great significance, though no notice was taken of it at the time, was the issue on May 11 of the first of many orders in favour of loyal (sc. Catholic) recusants.

But meanwhile James, though he was certainly indiscreet about his aspirations towards arbitrary power, was in other respects successfully concealing his intentions. Until Sunderland arrived at a full participation in his secret plans it was to the French ambassador alone that he could speak freely about his projects for the benefit of his Church. A few days after his accession he first broached the subject to Barrillon, and at that time he took a very reasonable view of the situation: he limited his aspirations to the repeal of the penal laws, and he fully admitted the necessity for caution and patience; he showed, however, characteristic simplicity in expecting the co-operation of the Tories.

> This Prince [wrote Barrillon] has thoroughly explained to me his intentions with regard to the Catholics, which are to grant them entire liberty of conscience and the free exercise of their religion; this is a work of time and it can be brought about only step by step. His Britannic Majesty's plan is to achieve it by the assistance of the episcopal party which he regards as the royalist party.

A week later James was more sanguine; he derived confidence from the fact that even the declaration of his faith had been insufficient to disturb public calm or to rouse suspicions of his intentions in the minds of responsible persons. He persuaded Barrillon to believe that Parliament would consent immediately to put a stop to the persecution of the Catholics and to permit them to worship in their own houses, and that objection would be raised to the employment of Catholics in military and civil posts (other than those in the royal household) only from fear that eventually none but Catholics would be employed. But before the end of April his success in the parliamentary elections had gone to James's head; he was no longer so insistent on the necessity for caution nor so moderate in his expectations from Parliament; he told Barrillon that he was confident that he would obtain in the first session not only the revenues for life and the abrogation of the penal laws against the Catholics, but the repeal of the Habeas Corpus Act, an Act which he had consistently held to be incompatible with monarchy.

Foreign affairs was one of the subjects which James kept strictly in his own hands, and Sunderland in this, as in other fields, entered wholeheartedly into his master's plans. There was here no inconsistency, for the whole of Sunderland's previous ministerial career had been in an atmosphere of subservience to France; simultaneously, in common with all the leading politicians of the time, he endeavoured to insure his future by keeping on good terms with William of Orange, the husband of the heir-presumptive; thus in effect the Minister's predilections and interests coincided, and he was able to avoid in foreign politics the imputation of time-serving which he incurred in other connections.

In spite of some inconsistencies, we may safely ascribe to James certain general principles of foreign policy: by temperament he was haughty, and for that reason he valued his own independence, but he had long ceased to dream of personal military glory and he had no desire to extend his dominions by war. He certainly aimed at an extension of England's prosperity by trade and at an increase of her strength by land and sea; but this power was desirable merely as an enhancement of his own regal magnificence and of his security at home, and not as a pretext for aggression. If he had any ulterior aim, it was to be the arbiter of Europe. What he failed to realise was that he could not be respected abroad unless his power at home rested on the strong foundation of the support of his people.

One undisputed principle of the English constitution of the time was that foreign affairs were exclusively the concern of the King, and Charles II had been on firm ground when in 1677 he reprimanded Parliament for addressing him on this subject. But apart from the general difficulty of pursuing an unpopular foreign policy, the King's power was in practice limited by the control of Parliament: he could not enter a war of which Parliament disapproved, for they would refuse to vote him the supplies necessary for carrying it on. Of this fact James was well aware: he could deceive himself into thinking that his Tory Parliament would consent to remove Catholic disabilities, but he knew that their prejudice against France was so deep that if England was involved in a continental war he might be forced to take up arms against France. At the very least he would find himself in conflict with Parliament, and if he was to obtain from Parliament the religious measures which he sought, it was essential that there should be an atmosphere of conciliation. These considerations were in his mind when he told Barrillon that he would go to any lengths to prevent any discussion of foreign politics in Parliament. Sunderland, with characteristic cynicism, told Barrillon that Parliament was so attached to the interests of Spain and the Prince of Orange that it would be impossible to separate them, but that after the revenues had been granted it would be easy to "raise the mask"—but Sunderland was not aware at that time that the revenues were only part of what James required from Parliament.

In these circumstances it was a profound shock to James to receive a report five weeks before the date for the meeting of Parliament that Louis was likely to be involved in war with Spain. It was said that Spain intended to cede the Spanish Netherlands to the Emperor, and that Louis, who regarded the Dauphin, through his mother, Maria Theresa, as heir presumptive of the whole Spanish dominions, was prepared to defend his son's interests. James said that it would be disastrous for him if a rupture occurred between France and Spain when Parliament was sitting, for they would make every endeavour to force him into taking a side:

> His enemies (he said) would take the opportunity either to embroil him with Louis or to antagonise his subjects, who would be persuaded to believe that he had abandoned the true interests of England.

James was delighted to hear that this rumour was without foundation, as also he was shortly before the reassembly of Parliament in November to learn that a difference with regard to the Palatine succession had been amicably settled.

James was not the chief object in Europe of Louis's attention; that position was occupied by William, and Louis's relations with James were important to Louis mainly as they affected James's nephew and son-in-law. For Louis not only regarded William as his chief public enemy, but hated him with an intense personal hatred. A more generous soul would have conceived some respect and admiration for the young patriot who had for six years withstood with greatly inferior resources the might of the French armies; but Louis had the common defect of autocrats, he had no sense of chivalry for his opponents; to him William's resistance had been an insult to his personal honour, a sort of *lèse-*

majesté to be expiated only by defeat followed by abject submission.[1] One of his first thoughts when James came to the throne was to oust William from the succession and to work for that end by persuading Princess Anne to adopt her father's faith so that she might be preferred to her elder sister. In this Louis showed his usual lack of understanding of English politics and of the impossibility of tampering with the succession in the Catholic interest; James appears to have given little encouragement to the scheme, though Louis's envoys had hopes from time to time of persuading him to agree to it.

When Louis and William were not openly at war they were persistently engaged in creating difficulties for one another; there was no possibility of cordial relations between them. While William was taking the first steps for the formation against French aggression of the defensive alliance which developed into the League of Augsburg, Louis was busy creating trouble for William by encouraging, through his ambassador, Avaux, anti-Orange sentiment in the United Provinces, especially in the city of Amsterdam, and by endeavouring, through Barrillon, to embitter William's relations with James.

It is true that for a few weeks after his accession James was not at all pleased with his son-in-law. The trouble was chiefly about Monmouth. William had known that (notwithstanding the fact that he was officially in disgrace) hospitality extended to Monmouth would be pleasing to Charles, and in spite of James's protests Monmouth had lived at The Hague in intimate relations with William and Mary. When Charles died the case was entirely altered; for James, not without reason, nursed an implacable hatred against Monmouth, and regarded him as the natural leader of any trouble that might arise in England. James was also aware that Monmouth had influence with some of the officers in the English regiments in Holland who were suspected of entertaining sentiments hostile to the English monarchy. A number of letters passed between James and William in the first month of the reign. James wrote in an exceedingly arrogant tone. He made three demands: that William should entirely cut himself off from communication with Monmouth, that he should dismiss the ill-affected officers, and that he should improve his relations with Louis. William had already anticipated the first demand when he had finally parted from Monmouth, after giving him excellent advice, on the very day on which the news of Charles's death arrived; and he proceeded to remove from the English regiments the officers to whom James objected. The submissiveness of William's

[1] Louis's unchivalrous attitude to William was not however that of some of the French people: Mme. de Sévigné, for instance, wrote on March 1–11, 1688–89, "What a deuce (*diantre*) of a man this Prince of Orange is, when one thinks that he puts the whole of Europe in motion! What a star!"

replies to James's hectoring letters is very remarkable: he avoided the awkward demand that he should shape his foreign relations according to James's will by sheltering himself behind the States-General; he said that he would satisfy James in all things except what was contrary to his oath to the States, but added that he was wholeheartedly in his interests save only in the matter of religion.

Meanwhile Barrillon was actively engaged in sowing distrust of William in James's mind:

> The King of England knows well, it seems to me (he wrote on February 12), that the greatest danger he runs originates from the Prince of Orange; he says he is strongly on his guard and is prepared to anticipate every move of the party of the Prince.

Four days later he wrote that he was persistently warning James of William's evil intentions, and in particular advising him not to permit the visit which William proposed to make. And when later in the month William decided not to come himself, but sent Overquerque with very submissive messages, the French ambassador wrote:

> I shall miss no opportunity of representing to him (King James) that the submission and respect of the Prince of Orange are not sincere and that he will continue to behave in his present manner only as long as he is forced to do so by circumstances.

Louis commended Barrillon's conduct and told him that he himself had no faith in William's protestations.[1]

James, for his part, fully satisfied Louis that he did not take these protestations at their face value. When first William's proposed visit was mentioned he said that if William offered to come it would be difficult to refuse permission, for such a refusal would give an impression of fear. A few days later James had changed his mind; he told Barrillon that he had determined to disallow the proposed visit, in obedience to

[1] It is clear, from Louis's correspondence with his ambassadors at St. James's and The Hague, that this distrust of William on the part of all three men was genuine and not a mere diplomatic fiction; Avaux, for instance, wrote to Louis on February 19:

> I am persuaded that the Prince of Orange will act against the King of England. . . . I have told Mr. Skelton who is going to England that the submissions which the Prince of Orange and the Duke of Monmouth have made are not to be trusted. They were surprised by a sudden blow before they had time to lay their plans; they dare not make any move for fear of delivering up their most zealous partisans without achieving anything; but there is every indication that when they have had time to look around they will make trouble for the King of England.

Louis's wishes. He also said that he was keeping up an appearance of friendship with William so as to avoid providing his domestic enemies with a leader. He gave Barrillon an account of the first audience of Overquerque, and said that he told him

> that he would always be glad to see the Prince of Orange mindful of his duty and remorseful for his past misdeeds, but that he could not accept his submission or believe in the sincerity of his professions unless that submission was complete and without exception; that he (James) and the late king had established a friendship with the King of France to which the Prince of Orange had always been opposed; that it was not enough that he was willing to alter his attitude to affairs in England, but his behaviour to the King of France must also be very different from what it had been in the past; and that this last condition must be fulfilled before he could place the slightest confidence in what Overquerque had to say on behalf of the Prince of Orange.

But James's relations with William were far more cordial than he allowed Barrillon to suppose. To his courtiers he revealed the true state of his feelings under a pledge of secrecy. The Earl of Moray, the Secretary for Scotland, wrote to Queensberry on February 26:

> All the news I shall tell you is that the Prince of Orange will be right with the King, and will do some things to convince the world that it is so, but this is only to yourself, for the King told us of it this night only, and not to be made known.

A few days later Ormonde learnt from one correspondent:

> It is said for certain that the King and the Prince of Orange are heartily reconciled and that there is created a perfect understanding between them, and that the King has declared that he will henceforth look upon him as his successor and concert with him all those things which shall be for the common good of the nation.

And from another:

> In Holland the Prince of Orange gets ground apace since the reconciliation and that His Majesty has declared in his favour.

In the middle of March it was a matter of common knowledge in Holland that William had received from James a letter full of cordiality and affection:

> In this letter (Avaux reported from The Hague) His Britannic

> Majesty calls him his son, assures him that he will always consider him as such and that he will in time see that he is given satisfaction for what hath been done against him in France;[1] but that he must have patience and not embroil himself with Louis; that he regards the Princess of Orange as his eldest daughter and loves her tenderly; with many other expressions stronger and more affectionate.

This is apparently the letter which James wrote to William announcing Charles's death, and which he described to Barrillon as containing certain conventional phrases of friendship which William had interpreted as genuine expressions of goodwill.

Before the end of March, Barrillon was forced to recognise that his efforts to make trouble between James and William had been entirely unsuccessful, but he comforted himself with the thought that what he had been unable to effect would come about of itself: it was to the interest of each to be on cordial terms with the other, but their other interests clashed at many points, and James pursued his own way, and took no account of what might please William. William's friends, said Barrillon,

> want the King of England to enter into the sentiments of the nation and that he should endeavour to please them by giving them all possible assurances on the maintenance of religion and law; but this Prince shows a firmness on anything that touches his authority which astonishes everyone who is capable of reflecting on it.

As late as July, Sunderland spoke to Barrillon of the reconciliation as only a rumour which he himself hardly credited, for William was impatiently expecting the English crown, and there was always present the fundamental difference on the subject of religion.

And, indeed, it is inconceivable that between these two men, both of autocratic temper and with interests so opposed, friendship could be anything but precarious. Apart from their diverse attitudes to Louis, William was anxious that his wife should succeed to the throne of a kingdom prosperous and at peace within itself and with the royal prerogatives unimpaired; and he saw that James's blinkered pursuit of autocracy and Catholic ascendancy in the State could lead only to civil commotion, and ultimately to the victory of liberal ideas and a decline in the power of the monarchy. Moreover, William had taken an early opportunity of warning James that though in all other matters he would not only not oppose but do all in his power to promote James's interests, he reserved to himself freedom of action in the matter of religion—a

[1] No doubt a reference to the occupation by French troops of William's principality of Orange.

warning of which James took little notice at the time, and which he chose to forget later when he attempted to persuade William to give his moral support to the repeal of the penal laws and the Test Act.

James, on his side, made no attempt to conciliate William even in matters in which his own personal interests were concerned. Shortly after his accession he recalled Chudleigh, the English ambassador at The Hague, and appointed in his place Bevil Skelton, who, apart from his absolute incompetence,[1] was personally disliked by William and was regarded with suspicion and hatred by the Dutch people, on account of his conduct in Holland on a previous occasion. James disregarded William's spirited protest against the appointment and, as was inevitable, Skelton's embassy was unhappy. At the same time James recalled Henry Sidney, who commanded the six British regiments which were in the pay of the States-General. Henry Sidney was Sunderland's uncle and, if reports were true, the lover of Sunderland's Countess. William protested strongly against his recall, and testified to his ability and to his loyalty to James:

> I cannot dissemble with Your Majesty (he said) that I could have wished Your Majesty had thought proper to have left him here, since I can assure you that there never was a minister[2] in this country who succeeded better or who did you more faithful service, it is also impossible that any person can be more zealous for your service for which I can answer.

Whether or no Sidney's loyalty to James was as deep-seated as William represented it to be, this is the last time anything was heard of it. He continued to be a great friend of William's, he was constantly at The Hague, and he was one of the earliest and staunchest supporters of the Revolution.

[1] Avaux, who as French ambassador at The Hague worked with Skelton in the Anglo-French interest, had a very low opinion of his abilities; in one place, for instance, he describes him as "Le Sieur Skelton . . . un homme fort léger et fort inconstant". Four years earlier Charles had proposed to supersede Sidney by Skelton but had withdrawn the proposal, though regretfully, on objection being taken to it by William.

[2] The use of the word "minister" in this letter is extraordinary, for it is clear from James's letter to William of March 6, 1685 (in Dalrymple), that Chudleigh had been the English Minister at The Hague. Another odd thing about this letter is its date, June 25, which, from allusions in it to the appointment of Skelton, is about three months later than would be expected.

CHAPTER II

THE PARLIAMENT OF 1685: MONMOUTH'S REBELLION

It is not difficult to read in James's actions and sayings his conceptions of the functions of Parliament. He certainly had no intention of consulting it and, according to the ancient formula, acting by its advice. For him Parliament existed to fortify the King's will, not to modify it, still less to oppose it. The proper procedure was the introduction by the King's Ministers of measures embodying the King's intentions, followed not by a debate, but by a series of speeches of cheerful and loyal acquiescence. James, as is evident from his pathetic and persistent endeavours to get together a Parliament which would endorse the Declaration of Indulgence, fully appreciated the enhancement of authority which was given to a statute by the forms of parliamentary procedure—the impressiveness of the three readings of the Bill in both Houses, followed by the formality of the royal assent. But privilege of Parliament—the rule of freedom of speech under which a member could express himself in any terms whatever, within that degree of decorum which the House itself prescribed—James held in the greatest abhorrence; and he had no compunction in punishing, by any means open to him, members who voted or spoke against motions of which he approved, or who addressed the House freely on constitutional questions. He was himself impervious to argument, he knew he was right on every subject, and it is at least unlikely that he could conceive that an opinion contrary to his own could be honestly held; anyone who expressed such an opinion was *ipso facto* dishonest, for he pretended, for purposes of his own—and these purposes were probably subversive of the monarchy—to hold opinions which no sane man could hold. The behaviour to the Catholics and to himself of the English Parliament in the years 1678–81 in the debates on Oates's Plot and on Exclusion had raised in him a frenzy of impotent rage, but part of the blame he imputed to his brother's neglect to assert himself. He had no doubt that not even the most Whiggish of parliaments would have dared to brave the king's displeasure if that displeasure had been sufficiently plainly shown. All through his reign he continued to hope, in spite of overwhelming evidence that the quest was hopeless, to realise the Parliament of his dreams, and it was not until his flight that he admitted, possibly only in the mood of the moment, that independence of mind is the badge of an elected assembly—his outburst, "All Commons are alike", in reference to the

Dublin Parliament of 1698, conveyed an acknowledgement that his hopes had been vain.

It was in accordance with his view of his constitutional position that from the time of the proclamation that a Parliament was "speedily to be assembled" James began to formulate in his mind, to discuss with Barrillon and to make known to the world what he expected Parliament to do for him. The most urgent and important question was that of the revenue; he foresaw clearly at this time, though later he wavered from that opinion, that he could not avoid coming into conflict with the Houses if he endeavoured to do anything to relieve the Catholics, and that frequent meetings of Parliament for the purpose of voting the revenues, and with the constant opportunities for criticism of his actions, would be inconvenient and unpleasant. At first James said he would be content if Parliament voted supplies for three years, because he hoped that by the end of that period he would be in such a strong position that he could continue to draw the revenues without further grant. But that moderate mood lasted for only a few weeks; Charles had had the revenues for life, and James felt that anything less would be tantamount to an abatement of his royal dignity. At the beginning of March, Barrillon reported to Louis that James and his Ministers made no secret of his intention to dissolve Parliament if they refused him the revenues for life which Charles had enjoyed, and that he would not even accept a term of thirty years; the ambassador said further that the King knew how important it was to show firmness at the commencement of his reign, and that he was afraid of no one so long as he had Louis's support. From that time until the meeting of Parliament the matter of the revenues was uppermost in James's mind: on March 30 Barrillon wrote that the King "continued to act with great firmness and haughtiness" and that he said he would insist on having the revenues for life, and ten days later he explained his attitude at greater length but unfortunately not very clearly: he told the French ambassador,

> that Parliament might grant him money only under conditions hard and damaging to his authority and that this was the artifice of those who wished to prevent him from establishing the full exercise of the Catholic religion; that the subsidies which he needed were not for the purpose of resisting his subjects or of constraining them by force to obey him, but in order to maintain himself by legal methods and to have measures passed in parliament which would give sanction to the proceedings he proposed to take; that therein consisted all the advantage which he intended to get from this assembly of parliament; that if he was obliged at the start

> to act timidly and irresolutely he might expect to have to submit throughout his reign to contradictions and difficulties; whereas if his affairs took the right direction at the beginning it would be easy to keep them in the same condition and to act according to his own inclinations and interests.

Barrillon suggested that it might be necessary to bribe members in order to obtain the revenues for life and without conditions, and to get laws passed according toleration to the Catholics; but James would have nothing to do with such a policy: he pointed out how miserably it had failed in Danby's hands. Shortly before Parliament met he had decided that, if Parliament proved intractable in financial matters, he would dissolve it and collect the revenues by force.

James's unofficial declarations did not pass without comment; as soon as he began to deliver them, Halifax, undeterred by the possession of high office, expressed the constitutional view, and, in terms which did not fail to arouse James's anger, he observed:

> that it is an innovation for the King to explain beforehand what he expects from Parliament; that the threat of breaking it if it does not carry out his intentions will still further embitter those who are already discontented and will make everything more difficult; that the prosperity of the reign depends on these beginnings and that for his part he wanted nothing less than that Parliament should be apprehensive of dissolution if it did not immediately comply with what was demanded of it.

Parliament duly assembled on May 19, and the Commons were summoned to attend the King in the House of Lords and sent back to choose a Speaker. The Earl of Middleton, colleague of Sunderland as Secretary of State, proposed the King's nominee, Sir John Trevor; two names had been put before James—the Lord Keeper, Lord Guilford, had suggested Sir Thomas Meres; Jeffreys had recommended Trevor; as in all other matters, James accepted the advice of the Chief Justice against that of the Lord Keeper. The nomination by the King's representative was an innovation and an invasion of the privileges of the Commons; heretofore they had chosen their own speaker, and their choice (except on a single occasion) had been accepted by the King. But this was the King's Parliament, and no voice was raised in protest.

After two days spent in swearing in, the members of the Commons were again summoned to the Upper House to hear the King's Speech. After the usual preliminaries he said:

> What I said to my Privy Council at my first coming there I am desirous to renew to you; wherein I fully declare my opinion con-

> cerning the principles of the Church of England, whose members have showed themselves so eminently loyal in the worst of times. There is one popular argument which I foresee may be used against what I ask you of from the inclination men have to frequent parliaments, which some may think would be the best secured by feeding me from time to time by such proportions as they shall think convenient; and this argument (it being the first time I speak to you from the throne) I will answer once for all: that it would be a very improper method to take with me and that the best way to engage me to meet you often is always to use me well.

He then informed the Houses that Argyll had landed in rebellion in the Western Isles. It is evident from the wording and from the extremely truculent tone of this speech that it is of James's own unaided composition. It is doubtful whether any Parliament on its first assembly has been addressed by the sovereign in such terms; the tradition was for the King to request, if not humbly, at least politely, for such supplies as he required from his faithful Commons; James's speech is a demand accompanied by a hardly veiled threat: Give me my revenues for life, else you are in danger of incurring my displeasure. The speech also implies an intention to put an end for all time to the parliamentary practice of withholding supplies pending the redress of grievances, a practice which James no doubt held to be a violation of the unwritten law against "capitulating with the King". Moreover, the custom had been for the Lord Chancellor (or Lord Keeper) to supplement the King's Speech with a long harangue of his own enlarging upon the points made by the King. These speeches—some of them must have taken a couple of hours to deliver—were, as far as one can judge, a mere waste of time and a sore trial to the patience of the members (especially the Commons, who were standing the whole time), but they were a recognised part of the ceremony of opening Parliament. Guilford had come prepared with a speech, and he was naturally affronted when James, without previous warning, cut the proceedings short and prevented him from delivering it. James had no liking or respect for Guilford, and he had no compunction in snubbing him, but it is unlikely that he would have been so deliberately offensive if he had had no other motive. It appears probable that he thought his own abrupt speech was best left in the circumstances without comment, that nothing but misunderstanding could result from an attempt to explain and expand the reference to the Church of England, and that members were more likely to vote the revenues quickly if they had his menaces ringing in their ears.[1] But in nothing did the King displease the members: at every period of his speech the House gave loud shouts.

The Commons also proceeded, with unparalleled expedition, to carry out the first part of James's programme; "Such was the eagerness of the House to comply with the Crown" that they were impatient of the customary procedure. The same day they went into Committee on the revenue, and as a House resolved that James should have for life the same revenues as Charles had had for his life. This resolution was embodied in a Bill which was read a second time in the Commons on May 25 and carried to the Lords after the third reading on May 26; the Lords passed it through all its stages on that and the following day. In all this there is little that is surprising: every member who accepted the nomination of James or of his election agents—and such members were in an overwhelming majority—was well aware beforehand what was expected of him, and most of them had no doubt pledged themselves to vote the revenues for life. The minority saw no point in opposing the Bill, for their opposition would have been ineffectual.

The harmony of the proceedings was disturbed by a violent speech from Sir Edward Seymour bitterly attacking the Government for the way in which the elections had been conducted; he said that he did not oppose the grant of the revenues, but he urged that the question should be postponed until it was ascertained whether those present were in point of fact members of Parliament: "The complaints of the irregularities are so great that many doubt whether this is a true representative of the nation or not". He alleged that the elections had been carried out by "intrigue and authority" and that the established principle of free election had been violated. He also complained that the remodelling of the Corporations, commenced at the end of the late reign, and still in progress, had resulted in the return of the wrong kind of member:

> For there had never been a time when it was more necessary to have a Parliament composed of members of good-will, who were attached to the laws of England; the people of England were strong in their aversion to the Catholic religion and were attached

[1] The text of the speech which Guilford was to have delivered, and which no doubt James had perused beforehand, gives support to this surmise—*e.g.*, "You may look upon the gracious promises you but now received from His Majesty as concessions made in full Parliament, as laws which His Majesty hath given himself, which will be more binding and effectual than any that can be proposed to him. Never therefore let our Church of England fear to want support when he hath said he will defend it. Never let any man entertain the least jealousy of arbitrary government when His Majesty hath declared against it."

to their laws; these laws could not be altered except by Parliament and alterations could easily be made when there was a Parliament dependent on those who had that end in view; there was already talk about the repeal of the Test Act and the Habeas Corpus Act, the one a bulwark against the establishment of Popery at the expense of Protestantism, the other the firmest foundation of English liberties.

Seymour admitted that he had small hope of getting a motion for enquiry carried in a House in which the great majority were interested parties—"Little enquiry is expected on petitions where so many are too guilty to judge justly and impartially". Indeed, the motion was not even seconded, for he had apparently not troubled himself to secure support beforehand, and though many members approved of his speech, no one was ready to follow it up for fear of revealing their numerical weakness. It was a fine and timely speech, but Seymour cannot on the strength of it be hailed as a single-minded defender of constitutional liberties: in recent elections he had exercised great influence in many constituencies in the West of England, and Sunderland's manœuvres had undermined that influence. He may also have harboured the thought that he would have been elected Speaker if the election to that office had been conducted in the traditional manner. The irregularity of the elections was again made the subject of a motion by Sir John Lowther a few days later. This motion was supported by several members, but it led only to an inconclusive debate.

In the matter of the revenues James's success had been complete and swift, but this success was immediately followed by a serious rebuff. Right up to the meeting of Parliament he had hoped that so loyal a body could be moved to do something for the King's religion, and the action of the House of Lords while they were waiting for the Revenue Bill to pass the Commons may have given him encouragement: the Lords rescinded a rule by which impeachments were carried over from Parliament to Parliament, and in consequence the Catholic lords who had been victims of Oates's plot and were on bail—Powis, Arundel of Wardour and Belasyse—were released and were no longer liable to be condemned on the evidence which had been produced against them.[1] But the Lords had been moved by principles of abstract justice and not by any new kindness for the Catholics, and it was in the Commons that the shock was felt. On May 26, the very day on which they had sent the Revenue Bill up to the Lords, the Commons went into Grand Committee to consider that part of the King's Speech which referred to

[1] Danby also benefited by the action of the Lords.

religion. Two resolutions were passed: the first a rather colourless Church-and-King composition directed against Argyll; the second a recommendation to the Throne "to make an humble address to His Majesty to publish his royal proclamation for putting the laws in execution against all dissenters whatsoever from the Church of England". Resolutions in similar terms had been passed from time to time by the Parliaments of Charles II, and had been followed as a matter of course by royal proclamations. No doubt the majority in the Commons had some slight compunction at their own servility to the royal demands in the matter of the speakership and the revenues, and remembered that they were not only a King party but a Church-and-King party, and in this recollection they were assisted by the few Whigs in the House and the many outside, who lobbied and met members at taverns and coffee-houses.

James was very much upset: not only had he failed to get a Parliament which would give concessions to the Catholics, but he had saddled himself with one which took the initiative in attacking them. He sent for

> the leaders of the Lower House . . . and those whom he believed to be in his interests; he lectured them severely on their conduct in allowing themselves to be seduced and dragged into a resolution so dangerous and so unacceptable to him; he declared that if they held to their intention of presenting him with such an address he would reply to the Commons in such firm and decisive terms that they would never so offend again.

The result was very surprising: the following day when the recommendation of the Committee came before the House it was rejected, and it was resolved *nemine contradicente* "That this House doth acquiesce, entirely rely, and rest wholly satisfied in His Majesty's gracious word and repeated declaration to support and defend the religion of the Church of England as it is now by law established; which is dearer to us than our lives". The unanimous resolution of the members had on the following day been by the same members unanimously rejected. James had achieved a singular personal success, and he felt that he had moved a great way towards making the Commons amenable on the subject of religion—in the address which he made to Parliament three days later, and in which he thanked them for the "readiness and cheerfulness" with which they had passed the revenue Bill, there is no sign that he harboured any resentment. Louis wrote in high approval of his conduct, but with slight knowledge of English conditions: "It may be said that no

King of England has ever acted with more authority in his Parliament".[1] But Barrillon was not sure that James had acted wisely or had secured anything beyond a temporary advantage; for it was in Committee that the members had shown their real opinions, and their subsequent recantation was merely a concession to the King. Moreover, their Whig friends had a good opening for mirth at their discomfiture—their abject fear of royal displeasure, for instance, presented a sorry contrast to the resounding phrase, "dearer to us than our lives"—and he was inclined to agree with James's opponents that the parliamentary majority were so ashamed at yielding to browbeating by the King that on a future occasion he would be "neither able nor willing to exercise authority"—that is to say, that James had got his way this time by high-handed methods, but that he could not expect the same methods to succeed a second time. His quarrel with his Parliament did not become acute for some months after this incident, but it can hardly be doubted that from this time onwards his hold over Parliament was loosened, a fact which he himself tacitly acknowledged, for we hear no more of his intention to induce it to grant relief to the Catholics. The resolution of the Committee had placed him in an awkward situation, but he made the mistake of employing direct and not temporising methods. His brother Charles would have acted very differently: he would have allowed the Address to pass the House, and then by delay and possibly a short prorogation he would have passed it by without a direct affront to the House.

These ultimate effects were not realised at once, but the browbeating by the King had the immediate effect of taking all life out of the Parliament. They would have welcomed prorogation or adjournment, "for they saw that they could not pass any resolution unless it was to the King's liking". However, they still had work to do on supply: when James on May 30 thanked Parliament for granting the revenues for life, he asked for a grant for special purposes—namely, stores which were very deficient for the Army and Navy, his brother's debts, the cost of suppressing Argyll's rebellion and to make good anticipations of the revenue. This was a very reasonable demand; in essence it was merely a plea that the new reign should commence free of debt. But instead of meeting it by voting a lump sum of, say, £2,000,000, they granted an additional revenue for eight years amounting to about £400,000. Never before or since has there been a Parliament so lavish of public money, and they had not the excuse that they were working in the dark:

[1] Louis's attitude to Parliament is illustrated by his remark in his memoirs, "This subjection which puts the sovereign to the necessity of taking the law from his people is the last calamity into which a man of our rank can fall".

they were well aware that Charles had had to do his best with a supply calculated to yield a revenue of £1,200,000, and that if it had not fallen short of the estimate he would have had almost enough; they knew also that the present charge of government was not more than £1,300,000, and yet they gave the King four millions at once and a revenue little less than two millions.

Parliament was still sitting when news was received of the landing of Monmouth at Lyme on June 11. The Commons at once took steps to ascertain the truth of this news, and when they had satisfied themselves, they brought in a Bill of Attainder against Monmouth for high treason; this Bill passed both Houses within three days. They also hastened to vote an extraordinary supply of £400,000 for the expenses of suppressing the rebellion, and put a price of £5000 on Monmouth's head. The friction between King and Parliament was immediately forgotten, and every member who wished to keep it alive was well advised to remain silent.

This reaction of feeling carried the Houses to dangerous lengths. In London, as was notorious, there were a great many people who were cognisant of the plot and many more who sympathised with it,[1] and a good deal of loose talk had no doubt come to the ears of members and had been keenly resented by them. It was decided to bring in "A Bill for the Preservation of the Person and Govt. of His Gracious Majesty King James the Second", the main purport of which was to extend the definition of high treason to include "anything said to disparage the King's person or government". If this Bill had become law no one in the kingdom would have been free from a constant danger from informers; the most harmless remarks, even if they were correctly reported, could by a court anxious to show its loyalty be construed to come under the Act, and as in Nazi Germany, no one would have dared to discuss public questions. These considerations were urged in speeches of great ability and gravity, but the only concessions which could be wrung from the Houses were that preaching or teaching against the errors of Rome should be excepted from the provisions of the Act and that all informations should be laid within forty-eight hours of the alleged offence. The former amendment was not at all to James's liking, and Queen Mary was very much upset by it, for by implication it encouraged the delivery of those very sermons which it was James's intention to prohibit. This may have been his real reason for suspending the session (on July 2), and for doing so by an adjourn-

[1] The Lord Mayor told James that he could not answer for the City, "for if there was one for there were three against him", and James threatened to turn the guns of the Tower on the city if there was any disturbance.

ment and not by prorogation, so that Parliament could resume the Bill at the stage it had reached and might perhaps be induced to drop the objectionable clause. But Parliament reassembled in November in a very different mood, and nothing more was heard of the Bill. The House of Commons had so far shown itself entirely irresponsible in matters of finance and blind in its attachment to the interests of the Crown; but in the vital matter of religion, in which James had hoped for so much from it, it had entirely discouraged him from promoting legislation.

The sudden death of his father was a cruel blow to Monmouth: as long as Charles was alive he could harbour hopes of being recalled from exile[1] and received back into favour, but he was convinced that James was implacable. He was at The Hague when the news arrived, actually at William's house; he left at once, but returned at ten at night and was closeted with William until midnight. He later left his own house secretly and was at first thought to have left The Hague, but Bentinck had taken him in. As a result of the good advice which he got from William and Bentinck, Monmouth drafted a letter to James,

> which was conceived in very respectful terms and in which he professed most perfect obedience and entire fidelity and asked pardon for everything he had done.

He showed this letter to William, who entirely approved of it. That James would have accepted the letter at its face value is not probable; he conceived himself to have too long a score against his nephew to trust him again without solid and tangible proofs of change of heart and after a period of probation. But James was never put to the test: Monmouth decided not to send the letter, but trusted to his Duchess—who could have no motive of kindness for him—to use her good offices with the King. He drifted away from The Hague and from the orbit of William's good influence, and into the influence of the Whig exiles; they, like Shaftesbury before them, filled his vacant head with glorious aspirations and led him on to an enterprise which could result only in the ruin of himself and his followers.

The expeditions of both Argyll and Monmouth were organised at Amsterdam and with the connivance, if not the assistance, of the burgomaster of that city; and the incompetent Skelton failed to prevent

[1] There appears to be no evidence that Charles communicated with Monmouth in the last months of his life. Orders were issued to the king's representatives abroad to abstain from recognising Monmouth in any way, and Charles reproached both William and the Elector of Brandenburg for receiving him. This official attitude may have been due to pressure by James and may not have reflected Charles's real feelings.

either fleet from putting to sea because he had not taken the trouble to master the intricacies of the administrative system of the United Provinces, and because in each case he applied so late to the Admiralty of Amsterdam that they were able to reply that the ships had sailed and were no longer within their jurisdiction. William could have saved Skelton from these errors, and Avaux was convinced that William had deliberately avoided doing anything to frustrate the plot; he wrote to Louis saying that Argyll could not possibly have organised his conspiracy and collected arms without the connivance of William, that William had not shown a proper eagerness in James's interests when the plot became known, and that he had insisted on certain modifications in the memorial which Skelton was going to present to the States-General, these modifications being in the interest of the principle of right of asylum, and hence in that of the English rebels; Avaux was also firmly convinced that Bentinck was deep in the plot and that he would not have kept his activities a secret from William.[1]

At first glance, it appears that Avaux was in this instance justified in his suspicions, and it is almost incredible that William did not know what was going on and that he might not have taken more active steps in James's interests. The key of the mystery is probably in the character of Skelton: he appears not only not to have asked William to advise him, but to have been so confident of his own powers that he gave William no chance of offering advice. For the evidence against William's complicity is complete. Barrillon, indeed, wrote on May 11 that he had done all he could to increase James's suspicions that William had not behaved well about Argyll's expedition, that James had agreed, but had said that he must for the present conceal his opinions, and that he had declared in Council that if certain persons had in the late reign done their duty in respect of the exiles in Holland they would not now be discussing measures to resist their invasion—a plain hint at William's former relations with Monmouth. But James was deceiving the ambassador, and his remark in Council was a rather indiscreet allusion to a grievance which no longer existed. The whole tone of James's correspondence with William is that of perfect confidence on the one side and eagerness to help on the other. William used all his influence to persuade the States-General to send to England first the Scottish and later the English regiments which were in Dutch pay, and made repeated offers of his personal services and of those of his officers; and on June 25 his friend Bentinck embarked for England with most

[1] Avaux wrote on July 5, the day before Sedgemoor, that one could judge by the whole conduct of the Prince of Orange that he was not displeased that Monmouth had made trouble in England, but that he had not given him sufficient help to ensure success—a curious example of diplomatic subtlety.

cordial messages for James. James's replies to these approaches are also extremely cordial; on June 2 he wrote:

> I take very kindly of you what you offer concerning yourself; but besides that you cannot be spared from where you are, the rebellion of Argyll is not considerable enough for you to be troubled with it. However I am as much obliged to you as if I had accepted of the offer you made as to yourself.

On June 30 and July 3 he repeated his thanks for William's offers of service and for what he had done in the matter of the despatch of the regiments, and on July 19 Queen Mary wrote:

> The kind message you sent to the King by Mr. Bentinck, and your good wishes, I believe brought us good luck, for, God be thanked, here is the end of all troubles and in such a manner as that we may never hope to see the like again as long as we live. I have desired this bearer to give you a thousand thanks for all the marks you give of your friendship both by him and in your letter. I am extremely pleased with it and desire nothing more than the continuance of it, of which I will not doubt being resolved to show myself upon all occasions truly and sincerely yours.

More direct evidence of William's fidelity to James is not wanting. In Monmouth's letter to James after he had been taken in the New Forest appears the significant passage:

> The Prince and Princess of Orange will be witness for me of the assurance I gave them that I would never stir against you.

A number of letters passed between William and Bentinck in June and July 1685, when Bentinck was on his mission to James. These were naturally of a confidential character, but they could have been shown to James without furnishing excuse for suspicion. Throughout the correspondence William shows himself eager for the defeat of Monmouth[1] and actuated by no other motive than to secure the assistance of James in the impending struggle with Louis; Bentinck's letters show clearly his conviction that the interests of James and William were identical.[2]

[1] *E.g.*, "We have heard the good news of the capture of Argyll; God grant that we may soon have the same news of the rebels in England".

[2] A curious point which emerges from this correspondence is that Bentinck says that James suspected Louis of having assisted Monmouth; this suspicion had been in William's mind a month or more earlier, and he had mentioned it to Skelton; it is, of course, open to William's detractors to say that his suspicion was simulated.

James himself was no more unduly apprehensive of the results of Monmouth's expedition than he had been of Argyll's: four days after the landing at Lyme he wrote to Queensberry, "I shall do well enough with the rebel Monmouth". But he did not lay his plans with efficiency and circumspection. The chief muddle was in the matter of the command-in-chief. The original intention apparently had been to give this to Churchill, and to him Sunderland wrote on June 15 that certain orders given to Kirke are not to his prejudice, "for His Majesty will give particular orders to the troops which shall follow that they obey Your Lordship".[1] Again on June 18 Sunderland wrote still more definitely to the Duke of Somerset, "The King . . . commands me to let you know that he has appointed Lord Churchill to command his forces which are marched down to the West. . . ." But the following day the Secretary wrote telling Churchill without preamble or excuse that he had been superseded by Feversham:

> The King commands me to acquaint you that he has made the Earl of Feversham Lieutenant-General. . . . He also thinks it for his service that the Earl of Feversham should command in chief, wherever he is, as well the militia as the King's forces.

It seems clear that, while Churchill was employing his unmatched military talents in the West of England, Feversham and his friends had been busy at Whitehall, and that James, in Churchill's absence, had been led to believe that Feversham had superior claims to the command. It is true that James had been Churchill's first and only patron and that Churchill had owed his rise in great part to James; but, on the other hand, he had given James single-minded service for a number of years, and he should not have been suddenly laid aside in this callous manner for another favourite. A great deal has been said of Churchill's disloyalty to James at the Revolution, but little about James's flagrant disloyalty to Churchill: another example of the Stuart tendency to accept personal service as something due to themselves for which no gratitude need be paid.

Monmouth had chosen his place of landing well, for the West of England was at the best lukewarm in James's interest, and the militia, which was the only military force available in those counties at short notice, was neither efficient nor anxious for the defeat of the invader. But as soon as regular troops could be brought into the field the result was not in doubt, and the rout of Sedgemoor on July 6 placed Mon-

[1] Churchill had been raised to the peerage as Baron Churchill at the coronation.

mouth and all his followers at James's mercy.[1] Monmouth wrote to the King, and to everyone else who could be expected to influence the King, in a vain hope to save his life. But there could be no mercy for him; for not only had he waged war against the King, but he had taken upon himself the name of King, and was doubly guilty of high treason. Monmouth begged James to grant him a personal interview, saying that he had information to give him which was for his ear only, and James very weakly granted the request—which, as his biographer naïvely admits, "he should not have done unless he had been disposed to pardon him". There were many alternatives: he could, for instance, have offered him a choice of any one of those in the royal confidence as an intermediary. James does not appear to have been unduly distressed by the interview; he was no doubt disappointed to find that Monmouth had offered information merely as an excuse for getting an opportunity to plead for his life; but he should certainly have had a finer sense of the consideration due to a man condemned to death, for he allowed himself (or so it appears) to lose his temper. Sir John Bramston, who is in general a reliable witness, with a lawyer's dislike for unsupported rumours, says:

> I have been told the King asked him how he could expect pardon that had used him so, "To make me a murderer and poisoner of my dear brother, besides all the other villainies you charge me with in your declaration". To which Monmouth replied, "Ferguson drew it and made me sign it before ever I read it". That so angered the King that he said, "This is trifling: would you sign a paper of such consequence and not read it?" So he turned from him and bid him prepare to die.

James's own account of the interview is given in a letter to William of July 14:

> I have yours of the 17 (7th), and now the Duke of Monmouth is brought up hither with Lord Grey and the Brandenburger. The two first desired very earnestly to speak with me as having things of importance to say to me, which they did, but did not answer my expectations in what they said to me; the Duke of Monmouth seemed more concerned and desirous to live, and did not behave himself so well as I expected nor as one ought to have expected from one who had taken upon him to be King. I have signed the warrant for his execution tomorrow. For Lord Grey, he appeared more resolute and ingenious [ingenuous] and never so

[1] James very surprisingly commends highly Monmouth's generalship in the campaign of Sedgemoor "he had not made one false step".

> much as once asked for his life; his execution cannot be so soon by reason of some forms which are requisite to be complied with.[1]

In his memoirs, touched up no doubt in the light of subsequent events, James said that he had heard from one of their intimates that Monmouth and William had been working together and that he expected from Monmouth at the interview information which would establish William's complicity.

The suppression of Monmouth's rebellion was followed by the orgy of judicial massacre known as the Bloody Assizes. Horrible as the carnage was, it does not seem to have awakened public reprobation at the time. The many pamphlets which recounted the names and sufferings of the victims were published in the winter of 1688–9 (concocted mainly by Tutchin and Danton and sponsored by Oates), and were part of the revolutionary propaganda; it was not until many years later that English public opinion would have disapproved of any degree of severity against rebels taken with arms in their hands. The contemporary diaries place very little emphasis on the assizes which Jeffreys conducted in the West; Sir John Reresby does not mention them at all, Bramston gives them a short passing reference, Anthony Wood gives the numbers and in another place says without comment that 700 of the prisoners were transported and forty or fifty pardoned, "the rest have been executed in several places of the three counties to terrify others from doing the like hereafter", and Evelyn appears to have thought that the "severities" of Jeffreys in the West were of small account in comparison with those he had previously committed in Westminster Hall. Perhaps the most striking remark known to have been made at the time was that of Sir Edward Seymour in the House of Commons:

> This last rebellion has contributed to our future peace, and those engaged in it have sung their penitential psalms and their punishment rejoiced at by all good men;

and Seymour, though he was usually classed as a Tory, was by no means a hearty royalist; moreover, his home was in the West, and he must have been acquainted with some of the victims. In the same vein Sir Charles Lyttleton wrote to Lord Hatton on October 7, 1685, after describing the disgusting sight all over the countryside of the rotting heads and limbs of the victims:

[1] Forde Lord Grey of Werk and created by William Earl of Tankerville was son of a regicide and suspected of complicity in the Rye House Plot; he was second in command to Monmouth, and his general of horse; he was allowed to compound for his life by the forfeiture of his estates. If he had been put to death, his fortune would have gone to his brother.

> Those who suffered here were so far from deserving any pity, at least most of 'em and those of the best fashion . . . that they showed no show of repentance as if they died in an ill cause but justified their treason and gloried in it.

James and Jeffreys subsequently attempted to shift responsibility for the Bloody Assizes upon each other, but they would have done better to have kept quiet: their disclaimers were entirely unconvincing, and the current opinion after the Revolution, except among the relatives and friends of the victims, was that, though the punishments had been excessive, there was nothing much in them to complain about: "for though the executions were by law just, yet never were the deluded people all capitally punished"; Jeffreys gloried in his butchery; when his campaign was drawing to a close he wrote to James from Bristol:

> I will pawn my life and that which is dearer to me, my loyalty, that Taunton and Bristol and the County of Somerset too shall know their duty to God and their King before I leave them;

and on the previous day, in his charge "at the City of Bristol . . . in his return from his Western Campaign", he had employed similar language.

James was so little concerned at the time that he left London on September 14 to visit Winchester and Portsmouth. He wrote two letters to William in which he alluded to the trials of the rebels as a mere matter of routine. On September 10 he wrote:

> Lord Chief Justice is making his campaign in the West and when the parliament meets some of the peers which are in custody will be tried;

and on September 24:

> As for news there is little stirring except that Lord Chief Justice has almost done his campaign; he has already condemned several hundreds, some of which are already executed, more are to be and the rest sent to the plantations.

His defence as stated in his memoirs reads:

> The punishment of Monmouth's followers raised discontents. A Commission of oyer and terminer was issued to the Lord Chief Justice Jeffreys to go down into the West and inflict such punishments as the example of former reigns and the security of the present seemed to require. But imprudent zeal, or some said avarice

> carried him beyond the terms of moderation and mercy, and he drew great obloquy upon the King's clemency, not only in the number but in the manner too of several executions and in showing mercy to so few . . .

and he goes on to say that he had attempted to balance the "imprudent zeal" which he had expected Jeffreys to show by sending with him four other judges as well as the Whig Pollexfen as solicitor, and concludes:

> After all this care and foresight His Majesty had reason to acquiesce in what had been done, though it was a great disservice to him at bottom.

The Jesuit Father d'Orléans, to whom James supplied information, wrote in similar terms:

> Many others were punished and a great many more than the King had intended. . . . It is said . . . that punishment or pardon was not meted out according to the greater or less gravity of the crime, but that those who had least means to buy themselves off paid most dearly and that if many lost their lives it was because few had enough money to preserve themselves. The King was informed of the irregularity too late, but no sooner had he learned of it than he showed his indignation; and if he was obliged to spare, on account of the services they had rendered, those who had been accused of it, he repaired, as far as he could, the injustices they had committed by a general pardon to those of the rebels who were still able to profit by it.

Apart from his letters to William already quoted, there can be no doubt that James was fully informed of the details of the Assizes and could at any time have put a stop to the carnage. Letters to him from Jeffreys are extant from Dorchester on September 5 and 7, from Taunton on September 19 and from Bristol on September 22, and these appear to be only part of a regular correspondence. Churchill was a spectator of the trials at Taunton, and went straight from there to the King; it is unlikely, from the well-known mildness of his nature, that he expressed to James anything but disgust at what he had seen.

Nor can there be any doubt that at the time James furnished positive evidence of his approval of the Bloody Assizes. Sir John Bramston records that he was present on October 3, when he saw "the Western judges come all together to the King and kissed his hand and had His Majesty's thanks". The elevation of Jeffreys to the peerage took place before Monmouth's rebellion, and his appointment as Lord Chancellor had no doubt been decided on immediately on the death of Lord Keeper Guilford, and before the Assizes opened, so that neither can be regarded as a reward for his services in the West. But the entire absence of any record of James's disapproval at the time of the excessiveness of the punishments is significant: it is hardly conceivable that if he had expressed himself in this sense the fact would not have been mentioned in one or more of the contemporary memoirs, diaries and letters which have come down to us.

But those who indiscriminately condemn the inhumanity of the Bloody Assizes are lacking in historical perspective: the events of the seventeenth century must not be judged by the moral standards of the twentieth. The humane outlook of the modern Englishman dates from the end of the eighteenth century; no doubt James was callous and insensible and Jeffreys sadistic and corrupt, in comparison with their own contemporaries, but it is idle to blame them for not being a hundred years ahead of their time. Throughout the eighteenth century the death penalty and transportation were inflicted for what we should call venial offences, and no one can call rebellion a venial offence. Sixty years after the Bloody Assizes such of the rebels as were taken after the Battle of Culloden drew lots; one in twenty was hanged and the rest sent to the plantations. Monmouth had about 6000 men at Sedgemoor, and the estimate generally accepted of the number hanged is in the neighbourhood of 300;[1] nearly 1000 were transported, and a number were flogged and otherwise punished. In both rebellions a very large number of the rebels evaded capture, and with this fact in mind it may be admitted that statistically Jeffreys was less merciful than his successor, but the same principle was observed in the two cases.

What we are also apt to forget is that, except among the small minority of the population who still kept alive the political ideas of the Commonwealth, high treason was accounted the greatest of sins and the greatest of crimes; the sovereign was next to God, and violence against him came near to being the sin against the Holy Ghost. If James had kept his crown until his death in 1701 we should have heard far less about the Bloody Assizes. But in 1689 everyone was anxious to justify the Revolution, and the Bloody Assizes provided an obvious objective

[1] The latest biographer of Jeffreys, Mr. Montgomery Hyde, says (p. 223): "In the light of the Gaol Books [reprinted by F. A. Inderwick in *Sidelights on the Stuarts*, pp. 398–427] and the official returns to the Treasury in the shape of Judges' Lists [reprinted by J. G. Muddiman in *Bloody Assizes*, pp. 195–225], . . . the total number of executions in the four counties, including those which took place after Jeffreys' departure, was . . . less than 200—probably between 160 and 170."

for an attack on James; the high-handed behaviour of Jeffreys in court, his browbeatings of witnesses and juries, which had already earned him the hatred of the people of London, gave additional point to the pamphlets which were produced. There was an opening for an answer to this form of propaganda if anyone could have been found bold enough and open-minded enough to write it; such an answer would have pointed out that recent rebellions—Penruddock's rising in 1654, Venner's revolt, the northern plot of 1664—had been punished with no less severity and that there had been browbeating judges before Jeffreys—Scroggs, for example, in the trials of Oates's plot.[1]

By the defeat of Argyll and Monmouth and the dispersion and massacre of their followers James had entirely rid himself of active enemies. For better or worse, it was the turning-point of the reign. A wiser man would have consolidated his position and rendered it impregnable by rallying round the throne the best elements in the nation. But James considered his position already impregnable, and was confident that he could embark without hesitation on the policy on which he had set his heart. The hour of his greatest apparent prosperity was also the hour when he choose the path which led to his destruction; during the first months of his reign he had, with occasional lapses, been very careful to avoid giving offence; now that he had, as he thought, gained the hearts of the nation, he grew prodigal and wasteful of loyalty, and the remaining years of his reign provided a succession of injuries and insults, to individuals and to categories of men, which led eventually to his almost complete isolation.

His first trouble was with the Army. To the regiments raised to meet Monmouth's rebellion he had appointed Catholic officers. He could not plead that they possessed qualifications which could give them preference over the many Protestant gentlemen who were ready to serve; for, except for the very few who had served abroad, they had been excluded both from the King's troops and from the militia, and had had no military experience. It was clear to everyone that the innovation was in the interests of the Catholics and at the expense of such Protestants as could look to the Army as a career. James was not unaware of the

[1] Macaulay devotes some space at the end of his chapter on "The State of England in 1685" to showing that "our ancestors were less humane than their posterity"; but when he comes to treat of the Bloody Assizes the difference of outlook of the English people of 1685 and of 1848 is entirely ignored: the bestial cruelty of the punishments is regarded as the personal crime of Jeffreys, connived at by James, and not, as it should have been, symptomatic, to a great extent, of the age. All this is in accordance with Macaulay's historical method: he had consigned James and Jeffreys to his Chamber of Horrors, and he was not concerned with palliating their crimes.

opposition he was arousing. On the day the Battle of Sedgemoor was in progress, Barrillon described two interviews he had had with James: James told him that the equality he aimed at between Catholic and Protestant officers had annoyed a great many people, that he had not intended to move in the matter so early, but Monmouth's rebellion had given him a good opportunity which might never occur again. In the second interview he gave the ambassador more details: he had armed the Catholics in Ireland; in Scotland Lord Dumbarton and the Duke of Gordon, both Catholics, were in command of the army and of the militia; in England he had placed military commands in the hands of Catholics as far as possible; this was to a certain extent to "raise the mask", but, as he had said previously, he could not let so good an opportunity pass; he knew that he had shocked a great many people, "but he would march straight forward, and nothing would make him turn from the road he had chosen, if only the King of France would assist him in so grand and glorious a plan"; Hamilton's regiment of dragoons were all Catholics; he had given troops of irregular cavalry to Bernard Howard and to other important Catholics; he was gradually attaining his object, and what he was now doing involved the free exercise of the Catholic religion, and this liberty would be established in practice before it was legally authorised by Parliament; James added that Barrillon would agree that the eligibility for public employment would make more Catholics than would the permission to celebrate Mass publicly. Louis for his part thoroughly approved of James's measures and plans for the future: he said that he could never expect such concurrence from the nation as during the outburst of loyalty following the defeat of the rebellion;[1] what neither monarch saw was that James's action was the best possible means of ensuring that the outburst of loyalty should not develop into a steady attachment to the Crown.

James now thought himself strong enough to dispense with Halifax. He had hoped that love of office (which indeed the Marquis had in a strong degree) would incline him to support the royal policy in Parliament, or at any rate to refrain from active opposition, but it had never been intended to keep him in office indefinitely, for James distrusted him, and had retained him at first merely to preserve a sense of mildness and security and of continuity with the previous regime. Halifax was not a party man, but he was immovable on certain principles which James would have designated Whig; though he was not opposed to a reason-

[1] The first open defection from James was that of George Monck's son, the second Duke of Albemarle, who claimed the right to the Command-in-Chief of the Army by a patent of Charles II, and was so incensed at the continuance of Feversham in that office after the rebellion was crushed that he resigned all his commands in the army.

able exercise of the prerogative, he had a great respect for law and the rights of Parliament, and he was anti-Catholic and anti-French. At the beginning of the reign James had given as a reason for taking the initiative in summoning Parliament the certainty that Halifax and Guilford would have pressed such a step on him—a clear indication that James had no hope of his support in his absolutist intentions. According to Burnet (who is on the whole a reliable guide, though two witnesses are always better than one), Halifax gave James occasion for dismissing him by moving in Council "that an order should be given to examine whether all the officers in Commission had taken the test or not"; he did not find a seconder, and the motion dropped; but James could not pass over so bold an expression of opposition on the part of one of the highest officers of State. He did not, however, dismiss Halifax at once, but adopted a device which he was to employ very freely later in his reign—he put him to the question: he asked him in private audiences whether he was prepared to support the repeal of the Test Act and of the Habeas Corpus Act, and in effect threatened him with dismissal if (as he expected) he gave a negative reply. But the audiences passed off without heat on either side, and James did not exhibit the irritability and asperity which marred so many of his acts of State; and in this the credit must go in part at least to Halifax, who no doubt carefully avoided saying anything to arouse the royal displeasure. He wrote to the Earl of Chesterfield:

> I am very satisfied with my own method of not turning away my master, but rather chose to receive his commands for my dismission, which I did after two several audiences I had upon that subject in which I received a great many kind words and took leave of him very well satisfied in these two respects: that I neither had anything laid to my charge, not so much as any hard words to mortify me, nor any obligations laid upon me to lay any greater restraint upon me than that which shall arise from my duty. . . . I will only tell you in short that I have had a fair fall and am turned away because I could not prevail with myself to promise beforehand to be for taking away the Test and the bill of Habeas Corpus.

Halifax had no suspicion that his dismissal had long been determined on, and James on this occasion showed himself a competent actor, good enough to deceive the most astute of his contemporaries.

Halifax's post of Lord President was promised to Sunderland in addition to his Secretaryship of State, though the new appointment was not officially announced until some weeks later. This advancement was the outward and visible sign of the progress which Sunderland had since the beginning of the reign been making in the royal favour. As early as the middle of March, Barrillon had told Louis that Sunderland "seemed to be entirely informed of the plans of the King his master"; in July the ambassador noted that the Minister appeared to be *au courant* with the discussions on religion which he had had with James, and a little later James himself confirmed this surmise by telling Barrillon that he had spoken on the subject of religion with less reserve to Sunderland than to his other Ministers. Simultaneously the decline of Rochester had commenced. Rochester told Burnet (no doubt some years later) that the day of Monmouth's execution was the end of the King's confidence in him: up to that time James had spoken to him every morning about the business of the day, but subsequently the conversation had been confined to Treasury business. Four months later Barrillon found the first direct evidence that there was a connection between the rise of the one Minister and the decline of the other; it is probable that Sunderland commenced his attack on Rochester soon after James's accession, when he found he could remain in office without Rochester's assistance, but he kept his own counsel. In the middle of November, Barrillon wrote to Louis a long letter mainly devoted to Sunderland. He said that even the least observant people now recognised that Sunderland had the chief place in the Ministry, that Rochester was employed merely as a useful Treasury official, but that even there James interfered freely in matters of detail, that Sunderland had given proof of his attachment to the French King, in contrast to Rochester, who had a liaison with the Prince of Orange founded on interests which could not change, and that Sunderland had told him a story, which it was difficult to disbelieve, to the effect that Rochester had advised William, through Henry Sidney, to come to England at any cost and in spite of any objections James might raise, and had told him that this was the only possible means of diverting the English Government from the disastrous course which it was pursuing. Barrillon believed that Sunderland's only possible motive for telling him this story was to persuade Louis that Rochester was taking William's side against him; it is more than possible that Barrillon was not Sunderland's only confidant and that this story was effectual in undermining James's confidence in Rochester. Barrillon said further that whereas Rochester annoyed the Catholics by his zeal for the Protestant religion, they had openly declared for Sunderland, and that the Jesuit Father Petre, "who is very much in the King's confidence", has pointed out to James "how important it is to honour and to reward a Minister who serves him more faithfully and courageously than the others". Sunderland's policy henceforward was to work in close contact with the extreme wing of the Catholic party led by Petre, with whom the Earl of Tyrconnel and Lord Dover were associated; we hear nothing of direct dealings between him and the moderate Catholics, the Capuchins, as Ailesbury calls them (no doubt having in mind James's confessor, Mansuete), whose leaders were the three Catholic lords who had narrowly escaped death in Oates's plot: Powis, Arundel of Wardour and Belasyse. For two years Sunderland was able to drift with his allies and to secure himself in James's confidence; but when he saw disaster ahead and attempted to save the ship of State from ruin by adopting more cautious methods, they turned on him and prevailed on James to dismiss him. James owed Sunderland a great debt of gratitude, for without Sunderland's able support the collapse of his plans would have occurred far earlier than it did.

Foreign politics occupied a great deal of James's attention during the last six months of 1685. In August he renewed with the States-General the defensive treaty which Charles had concluded with them in 1678, omitting, however, the guarantee for the Spanish Netherlands: this renewal came to Louis as an unpleasant surprise, for it had been conducted behind his back and neither Avaux nor Barrillon had heard more than a rumour that negotiations were proceeding; he was annoyed that a treaty which had been avowedly aimed against France should have been renewed when he and James were acting in concert. What caused him the greatest anxiety was the possibility that James would make a fresh treaty with Spain, and even that he would be drawn into the league which William was forming to resist French aggression; he had, however, the consolation of believing that James and William could never be close friends. James did not seem to think that Louis had a legitimate grievance; he said that the renewal of the Dutch treaty was a mere formality, and that it was a contribution to the general peace. Barrillon, though he told Sunderland that it was rather a plan for war than a defensive treaty, reassured Louis on the other points: he said that James showed no inclination to include Spain and Brandenburg in the agreement with the States-General, and that he was hostile to the league against aggression. In September Barrillon reported that James had annoyed the Dutch ambassadors by maintaining at Court, in a voice loud enough to be overheard, that the Calvinist princes were opposed to his interests and were the enemies of all monarchy. Early in October he told Barrillon that the Minister of the Elector of Brandenburg was endeavouring to make an alliance between the Elector and the States-General, that the Northern Powers and certain of the German princes would be invited to join this alliance, and that there was thus every appearance of a project for a Protestant league, hostile to France, which the House of Austria would regard with favour. When the League of Augsburg was formed in July 1686, James was not a member, nor, in spite of Louis's apprehensions, had he ever had the least intention of joining the League.

Skelton's uneasy embassy at The Hague was ended by an incident in October 1685 which brought to a head William's persistent dislike of James's envoy, and which exhibits James's entire lack of personal sympathy and inability to appreciate another man's point of view. William intercepted a letter in cipher to Skelton from Dr. Covell, Princess Mary's chaplain, in which he described William's household in very scandalous terms, alleging among other things that "none but pimps and bawds must expect tolerable usage here"; and on enquiry it was found that other members of the household were engaged with Covell in supplying Skelton with information. Now, it may be admitted that Mary was made unhappy by William's intimacy with Elizabeth Villiers, one of her maids of honour, but it cannot be maintained that he was dissolute according to the standards of the time, or that Dr. Covell, in his anxiety to earn his pay as a spy, was not guilty of gross exaggeration. But apart from the truth of the allegations, there can be no question that James's conduct in receiving secret reports from one of William's servants was quite indefensible. He, however, could see no validity in the strong protest which William made; Barrillon represents him as incensed by this protest and as saying:

> The Prince of Orange shows clearly his bad will towards him when he is so much upset by the knowledge that his minister is informed of what goes on in the house of his daughter and son-in-law.

Nevertheless he consented to withdraw Skelton as soon as he had wound up the business of his embassy. There was difficulty in finding a successor who would be acceptable to William but who would not attach himself to William's interests, and it was not until ten months later that the post was filled by the appointment of Sir Ignatius White, Marquis d'Albeville.

James had great hopes of the Parliament on its reassembly after adjournment, and in this opinion he was supported by Louis, but these hopes merely provide further evidence that neither of them had even a rudimentary knowledge of the psychology of Parliament. Barrillon was a little less sanguine, but he had no contacts outside the narrowest Court circles, and he saw little that was not on the surface; he wrote:

> Although the greater number of Members of Parliament appear to be well-intentioned to His Majesty, the Test and Habeas Corpus Acts are regarded by all the English as the ramparts of the Protestant religion and of the privileges of the nation. The King hopes to succeed in getting them repealed; but unless he can hope to succeed it will be imprudent to make the attempt and to find himself obliged to dissolve parliament without getting what he considers necessary for the consolidation of his authority.

In the event, in the short period of ten remaining days of the session the Habeas Corpus Act was not even mentioned and the Test Act only by implication, and the only subjects which came up for discussion in the House of Commons were the necessity for a standing army and supply for its support, and the employment of Catholic officers.

On November 9 James opened proceedings with a long speech: he congratulated Parliament and himself on the suppression of Monmouth's rebellion, but he drew the moral that Monmouth's early successes had revealed the necessity for the strengthening of the defences of the nation and he asked for a supply for the purpose of increasing the standing army; he was very explicit and uncompromising on the subject of the Catholic officers; he recognised, no doubt, the advantage of having the first word on a question that was certain to be raised:

> Let no man take exception that there are some officers in the army not qualified according to the late tests for their employments; the gentlemen, I must tell you, are most of them well known to me, and having formerly served with me on several occasions and always approved the loyalty of their principles by their practice. I think them now fit to be employed under me; and I will deal plainly with you that after having had the benefit of their services in such a time of need and danger I will neither expose them to disgrace nor myself to the want of them if there should be another rebellion to make them necessary to me. I am afraid some men may be so minded to hope and expect that a difference may happen between you and me on this occasion, but when you consider what advantages have arisen to us in a few months by the good understanding we have hitherto had, what wonderful effects it hath already produced in the change of the whole scene of affairs abroad, so much more to the honour of the nation and the figure it ought to make in the world, and that nothing can

hinder a further progress in this way to all our satisfactions but fears and jealousies amongst ourselves, I will not apprehend that such a misfortune can befall us as a divison or but a coldness between me and you, nor that anything can shake you in your steadiness and loyalty to me, who by God's blessing will ever make you returns of all kindness and protection with a resolution to venture even my own life in the defence of the true interest of this kingdom.

The debate on the Address opened on November 12, and it was clear from the outset that the opposition had grown in courage and in numbers and were no longer afraid of challenging divisions. Their first spokesman was Sir Thomas Clarges, who sketched the earlier history of their Parliament: the King had promised to preserve the government as established by law in Church and State and to maintain the nation in its rights and privileges, and, acting on this promise, they had hastily granted to the King a special supply and a revenue far in excess of his needs—four millions at once and £1,900,000 a year, when the whole expenses of government, including the cost of the Army on its present footing, was only £1,300,000; he then reverted to the debates on the Exclusion Bills, and reminded the House that what was then feared was already coming to pass—that a popish successor would have a popish army. In spite of this plain speaking and of the obvious lack of necessity for the money, the House decided that they had better attest their loyalty by granting supplies before discussing the more questionable parts of the King's Speech. After suggestions ranging from £200,000 to £1,400,000, a compromise figure of £700,000 was accepted;[1] in the intervals of other business Grand Committee proceeded to apportion the sum among various new taxes, and immediately after this vote it was decided, by 183 votes to 182, to postpone further discussion on supply until the question of the retention of the Catholic officers had been discussed. By implication the House accepted the principle of a standing army, though (as Seymour pointed out) there was no more need for it than there had been in the previous reign, and in spite of a vigorous effort to get over the difficulties and dangers which the King had mentioned by improving the militia.[2]

But in the matter of employment of Catholic officers in the Army

[1] Even this moderate sum was voted only by 213 to 193, so great had been the increase in the number of the opposition from James's original estimate of forty.

[2] No one seems to have detected the fallacy in James's argument: Monmouth's early success was due not to the small numbers of the King's troops, but to their distance from his place of landing.

both Houses were uncompromising.[1] To many, no doubt—to Halifax and to Compton and the other bishops, for example—the question was purely one of principle—not a very high principle as it appears to the modern observer—the preservation of the rights of the Church of England. The motives of others were mixed: they were either themselves officers in the Army or had sons or other relations in the Army, and they had a vested interest in preserving commissions to churchmen. This consideration did not appear in the debates, and it is one which the members themselves would not have admitted, and the mention of which they would have keenly resented; but it certainly contributed to the acrimony of some of the speeches. The situation was comparable to the indignation roused recently in the House of Lords when in the debate on the Coal Bill (1938) the Lord Chancellor

> urged their lordships to be very sure before they voted against the second reading of the Bill that their own personal interests did not influence that course.

In both cases there was a higher principle than personal interest behind the action of the members, but in both cases, unconsciously perhaps, the attitude of some of them was in part due to personal considerations. Certainly James's House of Commons was more vehemently opposed to the employment of Catholic officers than to the establishment of a standing army, although a standing army would have increased the demand for officers. On the other hand, it was generally understood in the House that members who were officers in the Army who voted against the Court interest would forfeit their commissions, and this apprehension no doubt decreased the opposition vote.

The King's Ministers were unable to resist the evident desire of the House that an Address to the King regarding the Catholic officers should be drawn up; all that was open to them was to endeavour to make the Address as mild and innocuous as possible. A proposal that the House should acquiesce in the continued employment of those Catholics who already held commissions, on the understanding that no further unqualified officers would be appointed, was rejected, but a certain success was achieved by the alteration of the uncompromising words "that His Majesty would be pleased not to continue them in

[1] Indeed, here James failed to carry with him moderate Catholic opinion. The Earl of Ailesbury in his memoirs recalled the consternation with which the news of James's speech was received by Lord Belasyse: "That evening, according to custom, I went to visit my worthy friend and kinsman the Lord Belasyse, who seldom stirred out, being so infirm in his limbs. My Lord Belasyse, who was in a great chair, took me by the hand saying 'My dear Lord, who could be the framer of this speech? I date my ruin and that of all my persuasion from this day.' "

their employments" to "we therefore do humbly beseech Your Majesty that you would be pleased to give such directions therein that no apprehensions or jealousies may remain in the hearts of Your Majesty's good and faithful subjects"; another concession was that to those officers who had accepted commissions without taking the oaths an act of indemnity was promised.

It then appeared to the promoters of the Address that its weight would be enormously increased if it went to the King as an Address of both Houses, and not merely of the House of Commons; they accordingly moved that the Address should be sent up to the Lords and that they should be invited to join in it. The Court party had no doubt whatever that the feeling against the Catholic officers was even stronger in the Lords than it was in the Commons, that the Address would have an easy passage in the Upper House, and that a joint Address of the two Houses would be less easy to reject than one which came from the Commons alone. By a skilful effort of parliamentary finesse they secured the rejection of the motion by 212 to 138.[1] The following day, November 17, the Commons went in a body to present the Address to the King, who was at no pains to conceal his annoyance at their presumption.

James had not the excuse which he had later when the bishops presented their petition, that he had been taken by surprise: he was well aware of what had been going on in the Commons and he should have been prepared to behave with dignity and courtesy. But his impetuous self-confidence drove him on, and without giving himself time for reflection, he went next day to the House of Commons and delivered an outrageous speech; he said:

> I did not expect such an address from the House of Commons, having so lately recommended to your consideration the great advantages a good understanding between us had produced in a very short time and given you warning of fears and jealousies amongst yourselves. I had reason to hope that the reputation God had blessed me with within the world would have created and confirmed a greater confidence in you of me and of all that I say to you; but however you proceed on your part I shall be steady in all my promises I have made to you and be very just to my word in this and all my speeches.

This abrupt and undignified utterance does not bear examination. The least the Commons could expect was a reasoned and courteous

[1] These are the numbers given by the Commons Journals, which should be the best authority; but Cobbett's *Parliamentary History* gives 216 to 204.

reply; what they received was an injunction to acquiesce in whatever measures the King was pleased to take, followed (if the report of the speech is correct) by a jumble of words conveying no sense. No more gross affront could have been given to the representatives of the nation, and the offensiveness of the words was enhanced by the haughty and angry tones in which they were delivered.

On the King's withdrawal "deep silence and demur" fell on the members, and "each in others' countenance read his own dismay, astonished". Then followed an incident of great interest to the student of the psychology of deliberative assemblies, and particularly of this unique Parliament. Thomas Wharton rose in his place and moved that on the following Friday (November 20) the House should take His Majesty's answer into consideration; he was seconded by John Coke, the approved royalist member for Derby and a captain in the Army, who added to the formal words of a seconder the famous statement, "We are all Englishmen and we ought not to be frighted out of our duty by a few high words". Now, it can hardly be doubted that this little speech exactly represented the private sentiments of the majority of the members; but that House of Commons, nominated as it was in the main by the King, could by no means tolerate anything which savoured of personal disrespect to the sovereign—"every man that spake did it with great tenderness and reverence to the King". Poor Coke obtained no support whatever; he made a half-hearted attempt to deny that the words attributed to him were correct, and Sir John Talbot proposed that he should be made to ask pardon of the House and to receive a reprimand from the Speaker; but the sense of the House was for severe measures and, at the suggestion of Lord Preston and Lord Middleton, Coke was sent to the Tower. His outburst brought about a reaction of feeling in the House disastrous to the cause which he was supporting, for though Seymour and Clarges tried to revive the resentment engendered by James's speech, the heart was taken out of the opposition; they did not even press for a division on Wharton's motion, and the House, after an adjournment, returned to the business of providing the supply of £700,000 which they had voted. But for Coke's ill-advised intervention it is possible that the House would have postponed the grant of supply to the redress of grievances, and the stage would have been set for a struggle similar to those of Charles I with his Parliaments, with the difference, however, that James was financially much better placed than his father, and would not have hesitated to silence opposition by prorogation or dissolution.

Meanwhile James was attending the debates in the House of Lords with slight enjoyment. To a man of his hot and impatient temperament it must have been a great strain to keep silent while one lord after another, under forms of deep respect, lectured him (by implication) on his failure to obey the law—"he was much concerned at the plainness which was used in this debate". The Court party had hurried through the House an Address of thanks for His Majesty's gracious speech on the reopening of Parliament, and had hoped by that manœuvre to prevent discussion upon it. Halifax replied caustically that giving the King thanks for his Speech was a matter of common courtesy:

> They had reason to thank His Majesty that he would speak to them at all, but they ought (with) greater reason to thank him when he spake plainly to them;

and the courtiers were overruled. A debate opened on a motion to appoint a day to consider the King's Speech, and in that debate many grave and weighty speeches were made. It was moved in a maiden speech by Lord Mordaunt, that brilliant, unstable Whig who failed as a politician because he could never serve loyally with a party but turned against his friends and tried to betray them, but who as a general (and as the third Earl of Peterborough) was to achieve a striking (if lucky) success in the capture of Barcelona in 1705. He was followed by the most responsible among the peers, Halifax, the Earl of Nottingham—whose Toryism was as sound as Rochester's—the Earl of Anglesea, the Marquis of Winchester, and others; on the other side were Clarendon and some peers whose names have not come down to us, and even they had no word to say in favour of the King's Speech, but spoke only of the irregularity of considering it when they had already given their thanks for it. The speech which carried the greatest weight was that of the Bishop of London, Henry Compton, who "spake long, calmly, and with great respect and deference to His Majesty, yet very full and home; and when he ended he said he spake the sense of the whole bench, at which they (the rest of the bishops) all rose up". Compton said, as was the feeling throughout the kingdom, that the appointment of the Catholic officers was merely a prelude to the introduction of Catholics into the higher posts of the civil administration and the transformation of England into a Catholic state; the laws of England were like the dykes of Holland, he said, and universal Catholicism like the ocean—if the laws are once broken, inundation would follow. Jeffreys made a speech which he had cause to regret; he attempted the same course with the lords that he had taken in the courts; but the lords were not to be brow-beaten, and the Earl of Devonshire replied to him in such plain terms that he wept tears of mortification; the sentimental side of his bullying nature came to the top, as it did in his last days in the Tower when he professed penitence for his sins and plentifully deceived the divines who visited him.

This was on Thursday, November 19, and it was decided to enter on an examination of the King's Speech on the following Monday, but James had heard enough about the popish officers; besides, it had been proposed that the judges should be called in to advise upon the legal aspect of the King's actions; James had had no opportunity of interrogating the judges and of supplanting such as would not give an opinion in his favour, and the result might have been fatal to his plans if they decided against his recent exercise of the prerogative. On Friday, November 20, Jeffreys was sent to convey without speech or explanation the royal will that Parliament should be prorogued to February 10. By this sudden action James lost the grant of £700,000, an Act for which the Commons were on the point of completing, but he could not bear any more talk which implied that he himself was under the law and which insisted on the irrevocable privileges of the Church of England; Barrillon was of opinion that he might have got the money and yet have prorogued Parliament in time to prevent the Lords coming to a decision, but James considered the risk too great. In any case, he was in no real need of money; as Louis had told his ambassador, James was richer than any of his predecessors.

The prorogation of Parliament James regarded as a personal triumph to himself: Barrillon reported to Louis three days later:

> The King of England is in excellent spirits and he congratulates himself on having taken a dignified and firm part, which he thinks should enhance his reputation at home and abroad.

He had no doubt that he had made both Houses feel the weight of his displeasure and that when they reassembled they would be in a more submissive mood. In a letter to William (accommodated to that Prince's more democratic views) he said:

> I am as sorry as you can be that I was obliged to prorogue the parliament; I hope when they next meet they will be in better temper and consider the true interest of the nation, and not be deceived by some ill men who fill their ears with fears.

Louis, as usual, approved of James's high-handed dealings with his Parliament; he thought that the mortification he had given them by the prorogation would make them more amenable in a future session, and he added:

> However that may be, his firmness in retaining the Catholic officers, and in refusing to suffer his co-religionists to remain

> exposed to the penal laws, can produce none but good effects for his reputation and for the security of his government.

But Barrillon's view was the more correct one: he had been doing his best (which in this case was not very much) to foment dissension between the Parliament and the King, and he rejoiced that the prorogation had confounded, at any rate for a time, the hopes which some people had of an agreement between them. He said also that the members of Parliament were not remorseful at having put James in a position to do without them, and that they were pleased at being able to pose before public opinion as strong upholders of the Protestant faith, and had decreased their earlier unpopularity. There was, however, more of the spirit of John Coke among the members than Barrillon was aware of: the members cannot fail to have been outraged by the successive brow-beatings which they had endured, and James's refusal, at the expense of a large subsidy, to permit the question of religion to be freely debated left them in no doubt as to his intentions in that regard. James had rendered it impossible that as long as he was King the same or another Parliament could sit, even a Parliament elected by the methods of the first months of his reign. The only immediate effect of the debates in these last days of James's only Parliament was the dismissal from civil and military posts of a number of members of both Houses whose conduct had displeased the King; the most important sufferer was Compton, who was dismissed from the Privy Council and ceased to be Dean of the Chapel Royal.

For a brief period at the beginning of the year 1686 James's mistress, Catherine Sedley, was of political importance for the only time in her life. On his accession James made the gesture of dismissing her, but he had not been able to keep his pious resolutions, and it was well known to those about the Court that he had been visiting her surreptitiously for some months. On January 19 it suddenly became known that he had created her Countess of Dorchester. The Queen (who may have been unaware of the resumption of her relations with James) was highly indignant, and made no effort to conceal her distress in public. Attempts were made to convince the Queen that the Sedley affair was of no importance, that the title was merely a farewell gift from James:

> But when [writes Barrillon] it was known that she was to be a countess and that she intended to appear at Court the Queen was in great distress. She loves her husband sincerely and she is very proud. . . . She declares she will under no circumstances suffer the public scandal which it is proposed to perpetrate and that

> she will never receive the new countess; and that, if the King does not give her up, she will retire to a Convent.

James's Catholic advisers were also dismayed, for they not only regarded with horror the scandal in the private life of a prince who had made himself so conspicuous a champion of their Church, but they apprehended that the new Countess would assume the position held in the last reign by the Duchess of Portsmouth and influence James in the Protestant interest[1]—a baseless fear, for there is no evidence either that James ever in public matters availed himself of female counsel, or that Catherine had any ambitions beyond the ordinary feminine desires for wealth and consequence. James was subjected to two concerted attempts to compel him to break with Catherine. On one occasion Mary asked him to come to her apartments, and when he entered he found her surrounded by priests; the priests all fell on their knees and the Queen "broke out into bitter mourning for this new honour, which they expected would be followed with the setting her up openly as mistress". James was troubled; his experience of his wife had not led him to expect so determined an attack; he pretended that the honour had been conferred on Catherine as a parting gift, and promised to see her no more; and when Mary said she had no belief in his promises, he undertook to send Catherine out of the country. At another time the initiative was taken by Father Gifford, later to be made one of the four apostolic delegates and President of Magdalen; he went to the King in company with three Catholic lords, Tyrconnel, Dover and Arundel of Wardour,

> who all told him the advantage it gave to the enemy to retain a Protestant mistress and desired him to set a mark on those men who encouraged her and persuaded him to keep her. The King's answer was that Father Gifford had spoken to him about the Countess of Dorchester and that he took it very kindly from him, being a very religious man and one who by his function was obliged to take notice of it; but for their parts he said this was the first time he took them for divines, and that he was sure they spoke not out of religion but some private piques, and bid them for the future not concern themselves with things that did in no way relate to them.

In short, James chose to regard the matter as one exclusively of morals (as indeed it was), and saw through the artifice of Sunderland and Tyrconnel to use the occasion as a means of getting Rochester dismissed.

[1] Catherine had also exasperated the priests by making them the butt of her jests.

For there can be little doubt that Sunderland, though he did not initiate the agitation, carefully nourished it, and by working on the feelings of the Queen and of the priests, succeeded in discrediting Rochester in James's eyes; for James, though he had occasional flashes of insight in which he was aware that the constant hints against a Minister made by a confidential servant had a definite personal motive, yet at the same time was unable to resist the cumulative effect of these hints. Later in the same year, when Tyrconnel was dissatisfied with what Sunderland had done for him, he blackmailed Sunderland by threatening

> to expose to the King his league with Lord Dover and himself and upon what promises it had been founded, the turning out of Lord Rochester, that he himself was to be Lieutenant of Ireland, Lord Dover to be a captain of the guards in England and a Lieutenant-General . . . (and to the Queen) that the true motive of removing Mrs. Sedley was to weaken Rochester and gain herself to their party, and not the honour of religion; for that Sunderland had assured them there was no leading the King, their main interest, but by a woman, a priest, or both; that Her Majesty was pitched on for the one and Father Petre for the other, who was promised to be made a cardinal.

And Sheridan, who furnishes this account and by whom Tyrconnel's message was conveyed, adds that Sunderland changed colour and said that Tyrconnel must be mad, but made no attempt to deny the charges. What evidence there is that Rochester supported Catherine or proposed to make use of her influence with James probably originated with Sunderland, and is therefore of no value, but Rochester appears to have played into the hands of his enemies in keeping aloof at the time of crisis and in failing to express his sympathy with the Queen by waiting on her.

The new Countess made as much trouble as possible; she could be persuaded to leave the country only by a threat of the forfeiture of her pension, and she refused to go to any country where there were convents, for fear that she would be kept in confinement in one of them,[1] and when at last she was induced to choose Ireland, she made excuses for delay. The one thing she was bent upon was being received as a countess by the Queen, and Mary Beatrice was equally determined not to receive her.

[1] She no doubt had in mind the fate of the Duchess of Northumberland, whose husband, one of Charles's sons, took her to Flanders and immured her in a convent; he produced a paper in her handwriting in which she said she had taken the step of her own free will.

> You may easily imagine [writes someone unknown on January 28] what disorders and transports of passion such an unexpected message would raise in her who was preparing for the Drawing Room the next day and had everything in order as to clothes and dress befitting her rank whilst she appeared before the Queen to pay her humble duty and respects to Her Majesty.

And he adds:

> All imaginable arguments were made use of to bring the King to this resolution and the victory obtained does fill the hearts of all virtuous ladies and honest wives with inexpressible joy, because so solemn an act does generously attest all their matrimonial privileges and liberties . . . [the Countess] is very well pleased to live in her great house in the Square [St. James's] where she is visited by the greatest lords and ladies in town, which makes the Queen show her dislike of it to such ladies as come to her and visit the Countess.

On February 17 the Countess of Dorchester set out for Ireland with an equipage of four coaches and six, and arrived in Dublin on March 2.[1] There the Earl of Clarendon was at great pains to avoid reproach by treating her with the barest courtesy: as Lord Lieutenant he could not entirely ignore the presence of a person with the rank of a countess. But Queen Mary was not in a mood to make allowances, and she nursed an additional grievance against the Hydes. The Countess when she left London had made no secret of her intention to return in three or four months, and as early as the first week of April she was reported to be making arrangements for permanent residence in London by having her house in St. James's Square sumptuously furnished and by booking a seat in the newly consecrated St. Anne's Church. She actually left Dublin on her return journey on August 17. The Queen was naturally indignant that the only result of all her trouble had been a short respite, but James assured her that he would never see Catherine again, and this time he convinced the Queen of his sincerity. But if he held to his resolution, it was only for a few months, and Catherine Sedley was not the only woman admitted to intimacy. In May 1687 Bonrepaus found that the King's promiscuous amours were known to a number of people about the Court; he was said to be seeing women in his closet at Whitehall and at St. James's where he went without the Queen. In July

[1] She appears at this time to have prepared for a final severance from James by making her peace with the respectabilities; in Dublin she conspicuously arrived first at Church.

Bonrepaus, after naming a particular lady who was seen to enter the King's room secretly, related an incident that had happened at Windsor:

> Three days ago he [James] went to London on the pretext of visiting the Queen Dowager. It was known that he had constantly seen this Countess of Dorchester during the past year. I was in company with the Queen on the terrace and she was in a gay mood, but when the hour had passed at which the King usually returns she appeared distressed and tears came into her eyes, she was unable to hide her suspicions. The King arrived very late, he saw at once what the situation was and did all he could to appease the Queen. Those who are accustomed to this sort of trouble know that there will be no peace unless the Queen has her own way in everything. She has not naturally great penetration but she is jealous and sometimes she finds more than she is looking for. She often speaks of her jealousy which she says is common among people of her country.

Mary Beatrice's jealousy must have been a constant worry to James—she was even jealous of his two sons by Arabella Churchill, whom he brought to Court in September 1685 and acknowledged under the names of James and Henry Fitzjames. She had also degenerated from her behaviour as Duchess of York when, by her gracious manners, she had done much to mitigate her husband's unpopularity, for she was now remarkable for her haughtiness.

She made, moreover, undue use of her position to promote the interests of her family, particularly of her uncle, Prince Rinaldo d'Este: after having succeeded by her importunity in inducing the Pope to make him a Cardinal, she obtained for him, an Italian, the salaried post of Cardinal-protector of England and Scotland, and displaced that excellent man Cardinal Howard, who had been looking after the interests of English Catholics in Rome for eight years with universal satisfaction, and against whom she could allege no fault.[1] Another foible which caused some scandal at Court was her ungovernable temper:

[1] See the letter of her secretary Caryll to Cardinal Howard:

> "I have a particular command from the Queen to acquaint your eminence how much Her Majesty is concerned lest you should attribute to her any unkindness upon the account of transferring the Protectorship of England to Cardinal d'Este. . . . I can assure you that Her Majesty has at present no less kindness for your person than ever formerly she had. . . ."

Queen Mary's real grievance against Cardinal Howard was that in common with the Pope, Adda and the majority of English Catholics he had counselled moderation in James's religious policy.

she was said on one occasion to have boxed Lady Peterborough's ears, and on the eve of the Revolution, when there was indeed some excuse for rising passions, it was reported that when an officer told the King that there would be no peace in the City until the Roman Catholic chapels were abolished,

> The Queen up with her hand and gave him a box on the ear and then he went away, and she did the like to the Princess of Denmark in her chamber,[1] which the King is troubled at.

But up to the time when he was convinced of William's intention to invade England James's chief troubles were within himself. Of the sincerity of the belief that attached him to the Church of Rome there can be no question, and he was well aware that whenever he was with a woman he was committing mortal sin; it is not possible to believe that he achieved even temporary satisfaction. In a moment of expansiveness he told Bonrepaus how much he envied King Louis's conquest of his passions: "He is younger than I am, and yet I have not as much control over my desires as he has". In the writings of his later years—in the *Advice to his Son*, the Prince of Wales, and the *Papers of Devotion*—remorse for his incontinence is a persistent theme; but it was not the usual remorse of the reformed rake. At about the age of forty, Burnet, greatly daring, had pointed out the inconsistency of his religious professions with his manner of life, and James had replied angrily, "Must a man be of no religion unless he is a saint?" but that remark does not represent his attitude when he came to the throne; by that time remorse had become a habit of mind and, whatever face he showed the world, in the secret places of his heart he was a very unhappy man.

[1] Princess Anne had, of course, left London before James returned from Salisbury, so that the part of the story that refers to her is untrue. But these stories would not have occurred casually in contemporary letters unless the Queen had had a reputation for such outbursts.

CHAPTER III

THE MIDDLE YEARS

THE two-and-a-half years following the prorogation of James's only Parliament was a period of small events and apparent repose. Every single action of James tended to the same end: the improvement of the position of the Catholic Church and of its members, and, though he did not cease to encroach upon the civil privileges of the kingdom and to use every endeavour to increase his prerogative, arbitrary government was no longer merely an end in itself, but must also be regarded as a means of realising his religious aspirations. The success which the King achieved in securing liberty of worship to the Catholics and in putting the administration into their hands was very considerable, but the cost at which this success was achieved was great out of all proportion, and the tranquillity of the country was entirely illusory. Every step that James took in favour of his religion either offended the personal interest of an individual and increased the number of his personal enemies, or outraged the Protestant prejudices of the nation. Of the former there are innumerable instances; and James's inability to see that when loyalty is rewarded with disgrace it ceases in most cases to exist is very remarkable, nor could he learn by experience and refrain from repeating his mistakes: it was a perpetual surprise to him that loyal subjects whom, as he said, he had loaded with benefits should suffer, after insult or dismissal, a decline in loyalty. Of the outrages to Protestant susceptibilities there can be few contemporary proofs, for Parliament was in abeyance.[1] And, a few pamphlets printed in Holland notwithstanding, there was no expression of public opinion through the Press; but it is not possible that the successive attacks on the Church of England would be regarded with equanimity, that the demonstrations in favour of the Seven Bishops could be other than a culmination of the resentment gradually increasing in the previous years, or that the outburst of hostility to James at the Revolution can have been due to a sudden and violent revulsion of feeling.

By the beginning of the year 1686 Sunderland had established himself in power to the exclusion of all rivals. James had signified his increasing reliance on his services by appointing him in December 1685 Lord President of the Council while retaining the post of principal

[1] There are plentiful references from the first months of the reign in the correspondence of the foreign envoys, particularly Barrillon and Terriesi, with their Governments to these unexpressed and unco-ordinated discontents.

Secretary of State. For two years he held a position in the State even more preponderant than any of his predecessors as chief Minister—Wolsey, Burleigh, Clarendon or Danby—for he had complete control of the King's sources of information: no public functionary could approach James without Sunderland's permission, and James would listen to no criticisms of his Minister. At the same time except in certain departments in which the King took small interest—Ireland, for example—Sunderland had very little real power: on the one hand he was obliged to keep the favour of Father Petre and others, James's religious advisers, and on the other he had to admit himself beaten at all points by the King's obstinacy—James wanted not advice but obedience, and he employed Sunderland's abilities merely to devise means for effecting what he had determined to do. Small heed need be paid to Sunderland's contention after the Revolution that he had consistently worked for the Revolution by advising James to take courses which would inevitably ruin him; but he was no doubt sincerely drawing on his own experience when he said (as reported) "that he wondered anybody would be so silly as to dispute with kings". Of James's complete confidence in Sunderland there is some little doubt. Queen Mary, writing to her brother in August 1687, describes him as "prime minister and favourite with the King above all others" and as "my great friend", and Barrillon gives no hint that James did not trust him completely; but Bonrepaus, who endeavoured to look below the surface,[1] thought that he was aware of his Minister's failings.

> The King of England [he wrote in May 1687] well knows the character of the Earl of Sunderland, that he is ambitious and capable of sacrificing everything to his ambition, and although he has not great confidence in him he makes use of him because he is more devoted to himself than others are and that he gives his entire support to his master's sentiments for the Catholic religion, though for his part he professes no religion.[2]

The figure of Father Petre dominated the reign of James II; he worked behind the scenes and left no letters; but his character, although it depends mainly on the evidence of hostile witnesses, can be safely conjectured. He is said to have laid the foundations of his immense influence at Court two years before James's accession, but it was not

[1] Bonrepaus, however, was not infallible: as late as March 1686, when Rochester's stock had sunk very low, he wrote, "I have not so great an idea of Lord Sunderland's credit and I always believe that there is more solidity in Lord Rochester's fortune".

[2] Macaulay quotes only the last sentence of this passage: "for his part he professes no religion" and ignoring what has gone before concludes that in the opinion of Bonrepaus James was entirely Sunderland's dupe.

until the summer of 1686 that his name appeared prominently in diplomatic and private correspondence. At that time he was said by the Tuscan ambassador to dominate the King's mind and to be a man to act without reflection and to aim at what could by no possibility be achieved—an accurate estimate of the sort of counsel which led James to his ruin. Shortly after his flight James stated that Petre had never given him any but good advice, but his considered opinion when he wrote his memoirs was that he "was indeed a plausible but a weak man, and had only the art by an abundance of words to put a gloss upon a weak and shallow judgement". In July 1686 it was apparently James's intention to appoint Petre to the Privy Council at the same time as he appointed the four Catholic lords. Petre declined the honour, but before the end of the year James gave him the lodgings at Whitehall which he himself had occupied as Duke of York and promised him the charge of the new chapel which was approaching completion. Sunderland found Petre a necessary and useful tool: it was easy to play upon his vanity and he was flattered with the notion that he would be made a Cardinal and Archbishop of York.[1] Barrillon credited Petre with an ambition to be a second Wolsey, and to add the dignity of Lord Chancellor to those in the ecclesiastical heirarchy which he notoriously coveted. But Petre seems to have been afflicted with a timidity which frustrated his ambition: he was very much the poor cat in the adage; Barrillon describes him as mortified by his obscurity, but he had not the courage to appear openly. Besides, Sunderland was not at all inclined to enable Petre to become his rival, and his backing of his pretensions had little sincerity and was calculated rather to secure his support than with a view to their success.

Petre's domination of James's mind was consummated by his success in substituting the Jesuit Warner for the Capuchin Mansuete as Confessor to the King. An intrigue against Mansuete had been on foot in March 1686, but it was not until a year later that he was removed. It was given out that the King thought it fitting that his Confessor should be an Englishman: Barrillon says that the true reason for the change was that Mansuete was suspected of immoral relations with his housekeeper; but French intrigue was said to be behind the change, and little heed need be paid to the accusation. It is more than likely that

[1] It was widely suspected that James intended to make Petre Archbishop of York, but the suspicion lacks confirmation. It is unlikely that he could have contemplated so gross an affront to the Church of England; he would in any case have had to prepare the way for it by the appointment of Catholics to northern bishoprics. He did indeed keep the Archbishopric vacant from the death of Dolben in April 1686 to the appointment of Lamplugh in November 1688, but the vacancy can be explained by the fact that the Treasury benefited by about £1000 a year.

Mansuete counselled moderation and that his dismissal, following close on that of Rochester, signified James's determination to get rid of everyone near his person who was not prepared to support his forward policy in religion.

James's first action in favour of the Catholics was taken when he had been on the throne barely three months. On May 11, 1685, he issued a royal warrant to the Lord Treasurer to supersede and stay until further orders all process against a number of loyal recusants—that is to say, those loyal recusants were for the present not to be fined for absence from church; on June 1 there was a similar order, with the addition that all fines still in the receivers' hands and not yet paid into the Treasury should be refunded, and this was followed on December 1 by a list of over 100 persons to be similarly treated. On February 24, 1686, a warrant was issued in general terms for a stay of execution of all fines and other punishments of loyal recusants until the King's pleasure be known, and there was again on November 23 a long list of names of those exempted.

The use of the adjective "loyal" in all these warrants is not very ingenuous; the obvious implication is that exemption from recusant fines should be a reward for service to the royal cause in the Civil War, but with very few exceptions (or with none) the Catholics had fought for Charles I and the Protestant Dissenters for the Parliament,[1] so that the exemptions were a boon only to the Catholics. This distinction is still further brought out by two warrants of March 7 and March 8, 1687. The former is in general terms of restoration and exemption for "all recusants who have certificates of loyalty for themselves or of their relatives"; the latter reads:

> . . . The King . . . does hereby order the restoring, paying and discharging to all and every of his subjects who (by the certificates made in 1681, 1682, and 1683 made by the Receivers of Recusants' Forfeitures) shall appear to be of the Roman Catholic religion, all moneys grown due and that grow due to the King thereon, and all moneys levied and received thereon and not yet answered to the King, and, further, all process against the said persons touching the premises is hereby to be superseded: all whether such certificates of loyalty . . . be produced or not;

a clear indication that in the previous warrants the use of the word "loyal" was a mere subterfuge. And this tacit admission was openly

[1] Clarendon's statement (*History of the Rebellion*, VI 75) that there were no officers and few common soldiers in the royal army who were papists applies only to the first year of the Civil War and is probably not accurate even with this limitation.

acknowledged in a warrant of March 15, "The King being well satisfied of the loyalty of his Roman Catholic subjects", and by a warrant of April 21, 1687 (the first Declaration of Indulgence having been issued on April 4), which repeats this last warrant with the addition:

> His Majesty having declared that his grace and favour should extend to all his subjects as well Protestant Dissenters as Roman Catholics.

Finally, in addition to orders for exemption of particular persons, on June 3, 1687, in temporary forgetfulness of his grace and favour to the Protestant Dissenters, the Treasury Lords wrote to the Barons of the Exchequer:

> The King has signified to us his pleasure that all recognizances against Roman Catholics be totally discharged.

Thus had James quietly and without drawing undue attention to his action relieved the Catholics of their most pressing burden, the fines for recusancy. Repugnant as these fines are to modern judgement, they were part of the law of the land, and were regarded by the people in general as one of the chief safeguards of their religion.

It has been held by James's advocates that he was very much in advance of his time in the matter of religious toleration and that his efforts to promote toleration, which culminated in his two Declarations of Indulgence, were the outcome of a settled conviction that no one should be made to suffer for his religious convictions. It is important that the arguments for this view should be stated fairly and at length, but at the same time great precision in a discussion on human motives cannot be expected. One of James's remarks in 1669 to a certain Dr. Owen, a nonconformist divine, is quoted from his memoirs to the effect that he

> had no bitterness against the nonconformists, he was against all persecution merely for conscience sake, looking upon it as an unchristian thing and absolutely against his conscience;

this report is unfortunately not contemporary and may only represent what James wished posterity to think of him. They also bring forward the address to James of the Quakers on the release from prison of 1600 of their number in 1687 (they had been in jail for two years since his accession!), in which they say:

> Though we entertain this act of mercy with all the acknowledgements of a persecuted and grateful people, yet we must needs say,

> it doth the less surprise us since it is what some of us[1] have known to have been the declared principle of the King, so well long before as since he came to the throne.

In addition may be adduced a remark of James's friend Coleman to a parson in Norfolk who persecuted "the fanatic nonconformists",

> that the Duke (of York) was very much troubled that any persons should be troubled for serving God that was within their conscience they thought they ought to do.

Furthermore, it must be admitted that this general opinion in favour of toleration with which James's name was associated was expressed in spite of his prejudice against the Protestant Dissenters as the murderers of his father, and as republicans and potential rebels.

Nevertheless we are bound to recognise that James as a Catholic had a personal interest in toleration, and he may easily have perceived many years before his accession that the Catholics could not hope for relief from their disabilities except as part of a general toleration; and this knowledge may, consciously or unconsciously, have influenced his opinion. Nor, unfortunately, was he invariably so discreet in his utterances that he did not sometimes reveal a different opinion. The day after his accession James met the bishops, and the following account is given by an anonymous reporter who is supposed to have been the chaplain of Francis Turner, Bishop of Ely:

> His Majesty again repeated what he had before declared; and said moreover he would never give any sort of countenance to dissenters, knowing that it must needs be faction and not religion if men could not be content to meet five besides their own family, which the Law dispenses with.

(It may be noted that he said nothing about their liability to fines for recusancy.) And to Barrillon at the very beginning of his reign he gave the impression that he had no intention of favouring the Dissenters;[2] indeed, he said that he would do nothing for them until he had established himself by means of the episcopal party and had nothing to fear from the others.

The Quakers achieved toleration in advance of the other Protestant

[1] Major M. V. Hay in *Winston Churchill and James II* has misquoted this address, substituting "most of us" for "some of us".

[2] Three days after his accession, for example, Barrillon reported, "Le Roi d'Angleterre . . . me dit . . . qu'il ne serait jamais en sûreté que la liberté, de conscience pour eux [clearly from the context meaning the Catholics] ne fût entièrement établie en Angleterre."

Dissenters, but in the early part of his reign James viewed them with distrust. In July 1685 he wrote to Queensberry:

> Though I have not great reason to be satisfied with the Quakers in general yet I look on this bearer, Robert Barclay, to be well affected to me.

But meanwhile James was consolidating the extraordinary, indeed inexplicable, friendship with William Penn. Penn's father, the admiral, and James's shipmate in the naval campaign of 1665, had on his death-bed commended the younger William to James's patronage; but that fact would explain a close acquaintance, but not a friendship which was known and commented on far beyond the verge of the Court, a friendship, too, which survived the Revolution and made Penn risk a charge of high treason rather than abandon his personal correspondence with Saint-Germain. With Penn liberty of conscience was a passion; in 1683 he wrote to Ormonde:

> Of all that falls under thy administration, in the love of God and the sincere affection of a friend, let me prevail with thee to avoid troubling conscientious and quiet living dissenters. . . . I cannot think that God will damn any man for the errors of his judgement . . . 'Tis what I ever told both the King and Duke, and that at parting; if God should suffer men to be so far infatuated as to raise commotions in the kingdom, he would never find any of that party [the Quakers] among them, at least not of note or credit. . . . I am for the just and merciful thing, whoever gets or loses by it, as ought all men of truth, honour and conscience to be.

This credo went far beyond anything that James ever said, but there were not many people outside the Quaker community who were sincerely desirous of a general toleration, and Penn was no doubt attracted to James by his profession of a tolerant spirit. What in Penn attracted James is more difficult to see, as it is in that other great Christian who enjoyed James's friendship, Bishop Ken; all he had to say on the subject was that he enjoyed Penn's conversation, of which, indeed, that very great Englishman was profuse. We can almost certainly trace to Penn's influence James's rather belated kindness to the Quakers; he was no doubt able to reinforce his entreaties for mercy on his brethren by the concrete argument that the Quakers had been only at their beginnings at the time of the Civil War and had taken no part in it, and that by their beliefs and practices they were politically harmless. They were relieved of the penalties for recusancy in March 1686, and in the following November Rochester wrote to Sir Daniel Fleming saying with regard to the meetings of Quakers that the King's pleasure "is not to have those people so troubled upon the account of their being Quakers only".

Among the most curious documents of the period is the diary left by Thomas Cartwright, Bishop of Chester. Cartwright was said to have owed his elevation to the Bench to a grossly sycophantic sermon, in which was a passage to the effect that "the King's promises are donative and ought not to be too strictly examined and urged, and that we must leave to His Majesty to explain his own meaning in them"; and throughout the reign he formed, with Nathaniel Crewe, Bishop of Durham, and Samuel Parker, Bishop of Oxford, with the ineffective support of the Bishops of Lincoln and Lichfield and the more circumspect adhesion of Thomas Sprat, Bishop of Rochester, a minority party among the bishops which followed the King wherever he might lead. His diary (which clearly he did not intend to publish) is a record of a series of actions calculated to increase the King's favour to him, but to no degree governed by the interests of the Church of which he was a prominent member; in particular it reveals him as an intimate acquaintance of Father Petre, a declared enemy of that Church. There is a passage in this diary which, coming from such a source, appears to furnish conclusive evidence that James's convictions about toleration were a late growth: it is an entry under April 20, 1687, describing a meeting at the Lord Chancellor's, attended by Sunderland, the Bishops of Durham, Rochester and Oxford, Cartwright himself and, oddly enough, Thomas White, Bishop of Peterborough, who in the following year was one of the Seven Bishops. The object of the meeting was to draw up an address of thanks to the King for the first Declaration of Indulgence. During the discussion White and Sprat raised the objection that "they could not choose but remember how vehemently the King had declared against toleration and said he would never by any counsel be tempted to suffer it"; Sunderland admitted the fact, but reproached them for calling to remembrance an opinion which James no longer held, "for other men as well as the King had altered their minds upon new motives".

Perhaps the strongest argument against James's claim to a sincere desire for religious toleration for its own sake lies in his behaviour with regard to Louis XIV's action in revoking the Edict of Nantes, in October 1685, and to the previous and subsequent persecutions of the Huguenots; we must, however, carefully distinguish between two views, neither of them identical with his private opinion—namely, those which James wished to have known in England as his own, and those which he expressed in private to Barrillon as suitable for the ear of Louis. As early as August 1681 he wrote that he can hardly believe "the reports of the ferocities, or rather barbarous cruelties, used in France against the Protestants . . . against all common sense and reason, as well as against charity and justice", and after his accession he told the Spanish and Dutch Ambassadors that

> he abhorred the employment of "booted missionaries" in France as impolitic and unchristian . . . although he wished to see his own religion embraced, he thought it contrary to the precepts of Holy Writ to force conscience; he expected only to see his Catholic subjects enjoying the freedom of other Englishmen, not treated as if they were traitors.

In his conversations with Barrillon on this subject James no doubt expressed himself more warmly than he would have done to an English Catholic, for it was always his aim to stand well with Louis, but his whole-hearted enthusiasm for the work Louis was doing for the Catholic faith is, even with this allowance, obviously very real. On September 21, 1685, Barrillon wrote to Louis :

> His Britannic Majesty has heard with joy what I have told him about the marvellous progress with which God blesses the efforts of Your Majesty in regard to the conversion of your subjects and says that in no country nor at any time have there been such results in so short a period. His Majesty well believes that so important a work will not remain imperfect and that God will favour Your Majesty by completing it entirely.

In letters of October 1, 8 and 19, Barrillon reports further expressions on James's part of delight at the conversions of the Huguenots. On the last date James had had an advance copy of the Edict by which the Edict of Nantes was to be revoked:

> I have given the King of England (Barrillon writes) a copy which he has asked for of the Edict which Your Majesty is to execute immediately. It is not possible to show more joy than this prince did to see the measures which Your Majesty is taking to destroy heresy in his kingdom. He has spoken of it to me several times in the last three days in terms which make it evident that what he says comes from the bottom of his heart. He is very grateful for the confidence which Your Majesty has placed in him by letting him know of so important a matter before it is made public.

It may be noticed in passing that James had no respect for the Edict of Nantes as a royal charter; royal charters were to James documents which could be torn up at the royal pleasure—those of Magdalen College, for example. At one time, it is true, James had misgivings about the excessive violence of the *dragonnades* and suggested to Barrillon that it would be better to conduct the business a little more gently; but that was merely a temporary reaction to the violently hostile feelings which the persecutions had raised in England, for a fortnight later Barrillon reports:

> The King of England is convinced in his heart that nothing is so glorious and so beneficial as the work which Your Majesty has undertaken. He sees that the success has exceeded what could have been humanly conceived possible.

But he adds that James has to be very careful not to allow his opinions to be known:

> He is obliged to keep in mind the people by whom he is surrounded and not to say everything that is in his mind.

And indeed the indignation in England was very intense and genuine, assiduous as were both James and Barrillon to ascribe the expression of it to ulterior and unworthy motives:

> Many zealous protestants and others who wish to be considered such (Barrillon wrote) are speaking with great heat about what is happening in France with regard to the Huguenots. His Majesty knows that those who are behaving in this manner are not well affected to him. He told me yesterday that Halifax is one of the worst and that he is not actuated by conscience and religion.

Barrillon's own view was that the principal motive of the critics was jealousy of France:

> It is easy to believe that an event so advantageous to the Catholic religion and so glorious to the person of Your Majesty excites the jealousy of the English and increases their bitter hatred of France.

He continues, however, in a more convincing strain:

> The English read all the news they can get about the conversions and deplore their inability to help their co-religionists. In the coffee houses there is a lot of wild talk and they say that the same thing will happen in England under a Catholic King. At Court the King has to put up with a certain amount of talk, less extravagant it is true, against the Catholics.

The extensively held opinion that James lacked only power to introduce Louis's methods in his own kingdom received great encouragement from an indiscreet speech of the Bishop of Valence, widely circulated in England, in which it was more than hinted that when Louis had completed his glorious work in France he would assist James to a similar success in England. James was seriously embarrassed by this conjecture of what he might do if he had the power and by the anti-French and anti-Catholic propaganda which it evoked; he made a feeble effort to counteract the propaganda by representing the Huguenots as republicans and rebels. One piece of propaganda he took serious notice of, though Louis protested that by doing so he was giving it unnecessary advertisement. Jean Claude, one of the refugee Huguenot ministers, had written a book on the persecutions which seemed to reflect on the French King, and this book had been translated into English; both books were publicly burnt by the common hangman. According to the notions of the time the action was justified; James was perpetually complaining about libels against himself published in Holland, and he could not fail to take notice of an attack on a monarch whom he held in such reverence as Louis.

Meanwhile the French Protestant refugees were pouring into England:[1] most of them arrived in a state of destitution and, from motives both of protest against the persecution and of common humanity, a clamour arose for the establishment of a fund for their support and for a public collection to support that fund. According to the laws of the time no subscription could be raised for charitable or other purposes unless with the permission of the King in Council,[2] and early in November 1685 the Privy Council, still a strictly Protestant body, approved in principle of the issue of permission with two restrictions: that the beneficiaries should conform to the Church of England, and that the fund should be administered by the two Archbishops. Barrillon entirely approved of these restrictions, for he thought that they would discourage subscriptions from the dissenters. He devoted his energies, however, to co-operate with James in postponing the actual issue of the "brief" in the vain hope that he would be able to prevent it altogether; there is ample evidence that James expressed himself to be just as anxious as Louis or Barrillon that no assistance should be organised

[1] They had been arriving in considerable numbers since the autumn of 1681.

[2] I have been unable to trace the history of this law, but it crops up from time to time—*e.g.*, in the examination of Bishop Ken by the Privy Council in 1696, when he was accused, among other things, of inviting subscriptions for the non-jurors without the necessary "brief". On November 13, 1665, the Mayor, Jurats and Constabulary of Rye petitioned the Privy Council for a brief to enable them to collect £5000 for the repair of their parish church.

for the refugees. Three months after the Privy Council had taken the first move in the matter Barrillon wrote to Louis:

> It will be difficult to prevent much longer the execution of the resolution passed by the Council for the fund for the French protestant refugees. The King of England always speaks of them as ill-disposed and he is resolved that the money subscribed to this fund shall not go to anyone who cannot satisfy the authorities that he has joined the Church of England or is suspected of being mixed up with faction. The delay in the institution of the fund has grieved and mortified the French refugees here; they see clearly that the King of England is disinclined to favour them and that they can hope for no more from him than he can avoid doing.

And a week later he says that James

> expresses a strong aversion for them and would be very glad to avoid having to give permission for the collection, but he does not believe that such a course is possible. It is anticipated that such a collection will give occasion in all parishes for sermons full of revilings against the Catholic religion and of calumnies about what has happened in France,

and James is seriously thinking of having the subscriptions raised through the Archbishop of Canterbury, and that the Archbishop should issue orders to the clergy to refrain entirely from exhortation or explanation in announcing the opening of the fund to their congregations. In the middle of March Bonrepaus (who had been sent by Louis to England on a special mission, among other things to induce the Huguenot refugees to return to France) wrote that Barrillon and he had exhausted their pretexts, and that it was no longer possible to prevent the appeal for subscriptions, that James had created as great a delay as possible, and that, if he could have been made to see the deplorable consequences when the question was first raised, he would have prevented the Council from passing their resolution.[1]

The brief for the collection was dated March 5, but the reading of it in the London churches was delayed until March 29;[2] James thought it worth while to conceal his real feelings by heading the list with a subscription of £500. Early in April 1686 there was a meeting of the Commissioners of the fund, including Sancroft, the Archbishop of

[1] The delay in the issue of the brief and the difficulties the refugees experienced in obtaining benefit from the contributions are illustrated in letters of Rachel, Lady Russell, January 15, 22, April 14, 1686.

[2] Barrillon objected to the wording of the first draft of the brief as reflecting upon Louis, and the brief was accordingly redrafted.

Canterbury, at which Jeffreys endeavoured to discourage subscriptions by speaking of the Huguenots in very offensive terms. He said that great care would be exercised against carelessly distributing the money to people for whom it had not been raised, and that it was not His Majesty's intention that any of it should go to anyone whose political conduct was not above suspicion or who was not known to conform to the doctrine and practices of the English Church. The Huguenots were very much hurt, but this speech had no effect in checking the enthusiasm of subscribers, for, apart from their sympathies for the oppressed, an admirable opportunity was provided for protesting their anti-Catholic zeal:

> His Britannic Majesty (wrote Barrillon) knows well that it would have been better not to have instituted the fund and that the people who are hostile to the Catholic religion and to him are taking this opportunity to advertise their sentiments, which otherwise they would have been obliged to conceal.

A year later there was a widespread desire for a second brief, and James again had to make a gesture of compliance; but Barrillon was successful in so limiting the scope of this second brief that it became merely supplementary to the first, and ordered a collection only in "such parishes wherein no collections have been made". No one was allowed to subscribe twice for the relief of the Huguenots.

During the Exclusion controversy James had found his staunchest allies among the bishops and clergy of the Church of England, and it was to them to a considerable extent that he owed his peaceful accession to the throne. But at his accession they were at great pains to insist that their loyalty to the Crown implied no weakening of their hostility to the Church of Rome. James himself was very far from recognising the Church of England as the religion of the State: his general attitude suggested that he tolerated it in view of its loyalty, and he could hardly blame the clergy for speaking in their own defence. In the month after his accession it was brought to his notice that anti-Catholic sermons had been preached in many London churches, and he sent for the Bishops and warned them that if the affronts to his religion were not discontinued he would have to withdraw his protection from the Church of England. This threat had so little effect that early in the following year he sent for the two Archbishops and demanded that they should order the discontinuance of afternoon sermons as being directed against his religion; the Archbishops consulted the Bishops, and their reply to the King was that they could go no farther than to remind the clergy that the King was a Catholic and to counsel them to avoid offensive expressions. James had been able to put a stop to the national anti-Catholic demonstrations on Queen Elizabeth's birthday and Guy Fawkes Day, but the congregations could not forego their pleasure in the anti-Catholic sermons at a time when the accession of a Catholic king had revived their fears of Rome. When the brief for the collection for the Huguenots came to be read in churches he was very apprehensive that the exhortations to subscribe would be reinforced by violent diatribes against the Catholics, and he did what he could to restrict the clergy to a bare reading of the brief. But he had no control over them in this matter, except that in a few cases he was able to show his displeasure by dismissing from posts in his gift clergy who offended him, and by stopping their pensions.

The matter was brought to a head early in the summer of 1686, by a sermon delivered by John Sharp at his church of St. Giles in the Fields. Sharp was a man of high character and attainments; in addition to his metropolitan living he held the Deanery of Norwich, and after the Revolution he became Archbishop of York. He had received an anonymous letter purporting to have been written by a man whose Protestant faith had been shaken by Catholic arguments, and the sermon in question was intended to solve the doubts of his correspondent. In the report which was made to the King it was alleged that Sharp had been less discreet than a man of his wisdom could be expected to be, and in particular that he had reflected on certain sheets in Charles's handwriting which had been found among the late King's papers and which summarised the reasons which had induced him to embrace the Roman Faith. James was furious, and he determined to make this a test case. Compton, Bishop of London, in whose diocese the sermon had been delivered, was peremptorily ordered by Sunderland to suspend Sharp; Compton replied with perfect propriety that it was not in his power to suspend anyone from his ecclesiastical functions unless and until he had been found guilty of offence by the appropriate ecclesiastical tribunal; at the same time he privately requested Sharp to desist from preaching pending a settlement of his case. But James had no respect for any law which interfered with the direct operation of his power: he determined to strengthen his hands against the clergy by instituting a Commission with summary powers, and he was no doubt influenced in this decision by a desire to settle his long-standing account with Compton.

In July 1686 he declared in Council his intention to set up this tribunal, and gave as his object "the prevention of indiscreet preaching". But he had much more in his mind than the pulpit attacks on Catholicism, and the powers of the Commission were actually so wide that it superseded all other ecclesiastical courts; by it he was enabled to make effective his powers as Head of the English Church, a position which as a Catholic he ought to have repudiated as an encroachment on the rights of the Pope.[1] These powers, as he told Barrillon and Adda, he determined to use for the subversion of the English Church and for the advantage of the Church of Rome. To Barrillon he said

> that God had permitted that all the laws which have been passed for the establishment of the protestant, and to destroy the Catholic religion, should now serve as a basis for what he wished to do for the re-establishment of the true religion and should give him the right to exercise a power still greater than Catholic kings in other countries exercise over ecclesiastical affairs,

and to Adda that

> the unlimited authority granted by Parliament over Ecclesiastical affairs can be employed with an aim contrary to what was intended, that is to say to the advantage of the Catholics.

If Parliament had been sitting, the Ecclesiastical Commission could never have come into being, for the Restoration Parliament when it re-established the other ecclesiastical courts had expressly and in unequivocal terms refused to reconstitute the Court of High Commission. It was recognised as what it was, an instrument in the King's hand for the exercise of arbitrary power over the clergy; Sancroft, the Archbishop of Canterbury, who ought undoubtedly to have been consulted before it was decided to set up the Commission, and whose name, by courtesy only, stood first in the Commission, refused to serve, though characteristically he did not, as he certainly should have done as representative of the Church, state that he considered the Commission illegal,[2] but excused himself on the grounds of ill-health and pressure

[1] Cf. Lonsdale Memoirs, p. 22, "They that defended the legality of this Commission said it was founded on the Statute of 1st Elizabeth, whereby in my Lord Coke's construction all the power the Pope had vested in the Crown. Which made many wonder that the King . . . should take the benefit of a law that was the highest violation of the rights of the Church."

[2] Mazure, however, states (without references) that Sancroft said to the King, "As Primate of the Church of England I cannot authorise, even by my silence, a tribunal in which the rights of dismissing clergy and bishops is put into the hands of laymen . . .". Ranke (IV, 300) and Lingard (X, 213n) make a similar statement, the former apparently on the authority of Barrillon. But whatever he may have said to James in conversation, his official letter asking to be excused the appointment merely states that he is nearly seventy years of age and begs that "Your Majesty . . . would be pleased to dispense with his attendance . . . to the end he may the better mind those things which belong to his peculiar care".

of other business. Rochester lost much of his prestige as the chief lay supporter of the Church by accepting a seat on the Commission—he could hardly have done otherwise if he expected to continue to be Lord Treasurer; he excused himself on the ground that he could in that position best serve the interests of the Church, an excuse rather specious than sound. Two other bishops consented to serve—Crewe of Durham, always servile to James, and Sprat of Rochester, a man of no violent religious principles, but who deserves to be known in the annals of literature as one of the chief precursors of the Augustan age of English prose. Sunderland represented the Catholic interest and Lord Chief Justice Herbert was one of the two legal members. The other was Jeffreys, who throughout dominated the Commission and expected silent acquiescence from his colleagues; such clearly was James's intention, for it was laid down in the rules that no quorum should be complete without him; indeed, it may be said to have been his own Commission, for, if Burnet is to be believed, the original suggestion came from him. It is significant that he never allowed himself to be drawn into argument on the legality of the Commission. The single virtuous act of the Commission was that it issued a decree regulating the procedure of weddings and putting a stop to the scandal of clandestine marriages, and thus anticipated Lord Hardwicke's Marriage Act by nearly eighty years. This decree was annulled at the Revolution, together with all the other proceedings of the Commission.

Jeffreys did not think it worth while to conceal the true occasion for the setting up of the Commission, but proceeded at once to the prosecution of Compton. Compton raised objections to the constitution of the Commission, but Jeffreys had no difficulty in overruling them; the Bishop would have been far better advised to have treated the Commission as an illegal tribunal and to have ignored the summons. He gained nothing by his attendance except a short delay for the preparation of his case, for the Commission could not allow itself to fail in the very case for which it had been appointed. If, however, Compton had deliberately absented himself and taken as his ground that the King had no right to set up courts condemned by Act of Parliament, the Commission would have been in a dilemma: they could either have compelled attendance by sending messengers to apprehend the Bishop, or have condemned him *in absentia*; in either case Compton could have sought his remedy in the civil courts. It is unlikely that as the Bench was then constituted a verdict hostile to the King would have been returned, but the arguments by which the Commission would have been upheld would not have convinced unprejudiced persons, and James's true aims would have been exposed. In the event Compton was suspended from his episcopal functions, but the Commission did not dare to expose themselves to action in the King's Bench by depriving him of the emoluments of his See.[1]

James had revived one of the chief grievances of his father's reign in this new Court of High Commission, and if necessary he would have revived the Court of the Star Chamber as well. But it was not necessary, for he was able by perfectly legal means to obtain from the existing courts all and more than all that the Star Chamber Court would have given him. His immediate need at the prorogation of Parliament was to obtain from the courts a justification of his conduct in giving military commissions to Catholics in defiance of the law. The only ground on which such action could be justified was that in such cases the royal prerogative superseded the law, and James's endeavour was to find lawyers who would take this view of constitutional law; he could then (as he was legally entitled to do and as Charles had frequently done before him) dismiss the judges who were not of his mind and replace them by those who were.

Thus commenced a political device invented by James and used systematically by him and by no other English king, the device later known as "closetting": an attempt by the King to secure the conversion of individuals to his own opinion in a personal interview and by means of argument and the awe of majesty. It does not appear that James received in audience all the twelve judges, but he certainly received Sir Thomas Jones, the Chief Justice of the Common Pleas, who, when James told him he was determined to have twelve judges who took his own view of the prerogative, made the famous rejoinder that His Majesty might find twelve judges of his mind, but hardly twelve lawyers. He was dismissed with three other judges in April 1686; two other judges had been dismissed in February, though possibly not for the same reason. James had now twelve judges pledged to return a verdict agreeable to himself, and the unsatisfactory position had been reached, by legal but unprecedented means, of an *ad hoc* tribunal, set up not only to try a particular case, but to find a particular verdict. The next move in the game was to provide a test case. Action was brought against Sir Edward Hales, by Godden his coachman acting as common informer, for having, in contravention of the Test Act, held a commis-

[1] Ranke, quoting Barrillon, says that Rochester was in favour of giving Compton time to institute a regular process against Sharp, that Jeffreys was inclined to agree, but that Sunderland opposed the suggestion as contrary to the King's will. Burnet says that Rochester, Sprat and Herbert were for Compton's acquittal, but that Rochester acquiesced in the conviction after an audience with the King in which he was threatened with loss of the white staff.

sion in the army for more than three months without taking the Sacrament. Hales admitted the fact, but pleaded that by the terms of his commission the King had permitted him to hold it notwithstanding the Test Act, and the judges with one dissentient, Street,[1] found for the defendant. Henceforward James was able with legal sanction to appoint Catholics to any public post.

The case of Godden *v.* Hales presents a number of interesting features. The fact that several judges left their posts rather than concur in the verdict which was ultimately found does not necessarily mean that the verdict was bad; there could be no doubt that it was unpopular, and it is likely that there was an element of fear of Parliament in the refusal of these judges to undertake in advance to uphold it. But whether or no the verdict was bad in law, the case is a typical example of Stuart failure, an inability (and it may be said a lack of desire) to carry public opinion with them. They found constitutional law in a fluid state and based on mutually contradictory precedents; they procured judicial decisions favourable to the Crown and congratulated themselves on their success; but these decisions surprised and exasperated the politically conscious part of the public, and their answer was in effect, "If this is the law, the quicker the law is altered the better". There can be no doubt that one of the first activities of a Parliament, if James had called one, would have been to attack the prerogative as it had been defined by the judges. In the absence of a Parliament this decision was, through the use the King made of it to appoint Catholics wholesale to public posts, one of the main causes of the Revolution.

But James, free as he was after this decision to override the penal laws and Test Act, and much as he had done by royal warrant to nullify the recusancy laws in particular cases, was not satisfied; he exerted all his energies towards procuring from Parliament a repeal of the anti-Catholic statutes. And here we have a conspicuous example of the confusion of his mind: it is exceedingly difficult to discover why he was so anxious to convert to his views the Parliament of 1685, and why, when, after successive prorogations, that Parliament was finally dissolved in July 1687, he took such infinite pains about getting another Parliament elected, pledged, as the former Parliament had been pledged in the matter of the revenue, to extend to the Catholics the same privileges as

[1] No satisfactory explanation can be found for Street's dissent. Macaulay's suggestion that he was "commanded to give his voice against the prerogative" does not carry any conviction, for clearly a unanimous verdict would have been better for James's purpose. Bramston (p. 223) says that he asked Street the direct question, but that he would not answer, and, further, that Street was subsequently a long time in the royal closet, but was not dismissed.

were enjoyed by his subjects of the Church of England. No individual Catholic could gain by a favourable parliamentary decision, for he had only to apply to the King to be free from the penalties attached to his faith, to worship how and where he pleased, and to be eligible for any post in the public service; moreover, James's political creed was purely royalist and autocratic, and the summoning of Parliament would have been a tacit admission that he was not all-powerful in the kingdom. Partly, no doubt, he was influenced by a natural feeling that the very existence of the anti-Catholic laws on the Statute book was a slur on his faith; for though the courts had decided that he could except individuals from the operation of particular laws, they had not given him the power to repeal Acts of Parliament; that question was to be raised later, in the trial of the Seven Bishops.[1] But James must have known by his unfortunate experience in November 1685 that a Parliament, however elected, however it might be pledged beforehand to support the royal policy on a particular subject, could not be prevented from raising other subjects—the standing army, for example. Besides, there was the House of Lords, over whose composition he had no control unless he had adopted Sunderland's jesting proposal and called up to the peerage Churchill's regiment of the Guards. Perhaps he hoped that they could be induced to repeal the offensive laws with the same expedition with which in May 1685 they had granted the revenues for life and that they could have been prorogued before they had time to raise awkward questions. But even that device could not have been successful, for by the nature of bi-cameral legislation both Houses are not simultaneously engaged on the same Bill, and it was not in his power to suspend the sittings of a single House.

Whatever may have been his reasons, "James may not inaptly be described as having been engaged in electioneering [2] from the beginning to the end of his ill-starred reign". When Parliament was prorogued in November 1685 James was convinced that his brow-beatings had been a success and that they would reassemble in a chastened and servile mood; he seems to have had a genuine intention to allow them to sit in February 1686, but something or other occurred to convince him that the occasion was not yet favourable, and they were prorogued again until August; then again he was not certain how they would behave, and they were

[1] The contract for the farm of the revenue was for three years from February 5, 1685, and could only be renewed by Parliament. There appears to be no evidence that James had this fact in mind when he schemed for a new parliament.

[2] "Lobbying and electioneering" would have been more accurate, for there was no question of electioneering between the election of the Parliament of 1685 and its dissolution on July 2, 1687.

again prorogued. At the end of the year James systematically began to apply to members of both Houses the methods which he had found so successful with the judges. He called them one by one into his closet, put to them his stock argument that the Test Act had been the product of a wave of rage and panic on the Catholic question, asked them to promise to support the repeal of the Test Act and the penal laws, and if they refused or demurred (as they did in most cases) he dismissed them from civil employment or from military or naval commands, had their names erased from the Commission of the peace or from the list of deputy lieutenants of their counties, or, if they had nothing tangible that he could take from them, put them on his black list. The policy underlying this action was clearly explained by Barrillon:

> The King of England is resolved to come to a definite understanding with all those who are in posts in his gift and to ascertain, before the reassembly of parliament, whether or no he can expect from them what he desires; this demand for personal statements and for explicit promises to consent to the repeal of the penal laws and the Test Act is without precedent and is considered by many an encroachment on their liberty and privileges.

A few of the actual dialogues between the King and members of the two Houses were also reported at the time; that with Lord Maynard will suffice as an example:

> I have been told that the Lord Maynard alleged his conscience would not permit him to part with the laws made for the preservation of the religion he professed. The King said there was no matter of conscience in it. "No Sir?" he replied, "is not conscience concerned in defence of religion? I pray, if the Test be gone, what hinders but you may bring whom you please, and as many as you think fit, into the House of Lords, and so having the majority you may make what laws you please, even against the religion established." To which the King made no reply, but bid his lordship think better and speak with him again;

and the result of the audience was that Lord Maynard lost his post as Controller of the Household and was succeeded by the King's son-in-law, Waldegrave.

This conversation illustrates the *impasse* at which James had arrived after he had been two years on the throne. In the first few months of his reign he had seen clearly the difficulties of the situation; he was well aware that in order to achieve the slightest modification of the penal laws, let alone the repeal of the Test Act, he would have to overcome the immense prejudice against the Catholics which had been accumulating in the minds of the English people for three generations. But when he saw that he could give commissions in the Army to Catholics without immediate disaster, and, still more, when he had the support of the law in such action, he ceased to view his problem clearly and as a whole, and he attempted the totally impossible policy of continuing to protest his faithfulness to his early promises to protect the Church of England, while at the same time he was breaking those promises and creating apprehensions about what would happen if his powers were increased. For, though we in the twentieth century may doubt whether the grant of freedom of worship to the Catholics and their admission to office was a legitimate grievance of the Church of England, they were certainly regarded as such at the time, and it was with the opinion of his own time that James was concerned.

Up to the summer of 1687 no great stir was caused by appointments of Catholics; the policy had rather been to prepare the way for their appointment by removing from office all who refused to support the repeal of the Test Act and to substitute subservient Protestants. In the summer and autumn of 1686 five Catholics—Lord Powis, Arundel of Wardour, Belasyse, Dover and Tyrconnel—had been sworn of the Privy Council, and in March 1687 Lord Arundel of Wardour had been appointed to one of the four chief posts in the administration, that of Lord Privy Seal. But the most striking change in the personnel of the administration had been the dismissal in January 1687 (December 1686?) of the Earl of Rochester. Rochester had been steadily losing ground since the summer of 1685, and for a year his activities had been confined to his own department. But he was still Lord Treasurer, and nominally, at least, the chief adviser of the King; he was also one of the chief (if not the chief) of the lay supporters of the Church of England, and, in spite of the blind eye which he had had to turn on some of the proceedings of the Government, it was felt that he was in a position to prevent the most serious breaches in the defences of that Church. In public James gave as his reason for the dismissal that he thought the Treasury too great a charge to be in the hands of one man—a sound reason, but one which might have occurred to him earlier than June 1686, when he first mentioned his intention; he further said in Council that he was not acting from "any dissatisfaction against the late Lord Treasurer, for he had served him very well both before his coming to the Crown and since"; but he weakened the value of his tribute by not appointing Rochester to the new Commission of the Treasury. He did indeed show gratitude and personal friendship by securing to him a considerable income—£4000 a year from the Post Office for ninety-nine years or two lives, in addition to the £16,000 granted him six months earlier out of the forfeited estates of Lord Grey—but he cut him off entirely from the royal counsels.

Rochester was put to a different test from that which was employed in the other cases. He was not asked whether or no he would support legislation in favour of the Catholics, but actually in his own person to join the Roman Church, and it was no doubt understood that his retention of the Lord Treasurership depended on his decision. In James's eyes the claims of the Church of Rome were so unassailable that it was only by a persistent refusal to listen to the arguments of the priests that Protestants were able to keep their faith; he was unaware that appeals to reason are of small effect in conversions, and he pressed Rochester to allow two priests to attempt to convert him. Rochester, who must have seen that such a proceeding could be no other than a solemn farce, could not frustrate the King in a harmless design on which he had set his heart, but he asked that two priests of his own Church should be present to uphold their own views. James agreed (characteristically, however, vetoing particular clerics), and there were two conferences, at the first of which James was present and took part. As is usual in religious controversy, there was no agreement on basic beliefs, merely assertion and counter-assertion, and Rochester was unimpressed. The expected result followed, and the new Commission for the Treasury was headed by a Catholic, Lord Belasyse, who was seventy-two years of age and a cripple, and comprised another Catholic, Henry Jermyn, a man of notorious incompetence,[1] who had been created Lord Dover; the three other Lords of the Treasury—Godolphin, Sir Stephen Fox and Sir John Ernle—were good appointments; they had all been on the Commission in the reign of Charles, and the presence of Godolphin in particular was a guarantee of efficiency.

Very shortly afterwards, to no one's surprise, the Earl of Clarendon was recalled from Ireland, and was succeeded by the Earl of Tyrconnel as Lord Deputy. Clarendon had hoped to be allowed to retain his post as Lord Privy Seal, the duties of which had been performed during his absence in Ireland by a Commission of three members; but the King relieved him of that also, and, what was worse, took no thought for him, as he had taken for his brother, to provide for his maintenance, and he fell into desperate poverty. But nothing could shake his loyalty; he alone

[1] See Etheridge's letter to Dover of January 31/February 10, 1687; Lauzun's complaints at the arrangements for his landing in Ireland, and the mirth of the French at Dover's assurance that his return to Ireland would restore efficiency there.

of those who had held high office under James in the early part of his reign refused to take the oaths to William and Mary.

James's relations with the Pope were never easy. The Pope during his reign was Innocent XI, who, though Burnet had a poor opinion of his education and intelligence, appears to have possessed considerable firmness and political wisdom. He was in perpetual conflict with King Louis, whose imperious temper could not bear to see the French archbishops and bishops deriving their authority from a power outside his kingdom. There were two particular matters of conflict: the succession to the Archbishopric of Cologne, for which Louis had a candidate, Furstemberg, distasteful to the Pope, and what was known as the franchises, the jurisdictions of foreign ambassadors in Rome in and about their embassies, which considerably curtailed the sovereignty of the Pope in the Holy City. It may be said on the whole that Innocent had a more bitter and continuous quarrel with Louis than any of his predecessors, since the Middle Ages, had had with any Catholic monarch in Europe: the Most Christian King was the least loyal supporter of the Head of his Church. The era of the Wars of Religion had passed before Louis came of age; his attitude to the Papacy made its revival impossible. James was Louis's friend and, though he himself would not acknowledge the fact, notoriously under Louis's influence; he tried to ingratiate himself with Innocent by ignoring the conflict with Louis or by ineffective mediation, but he could never induce the Pope to receive him as wholeheartedly in the interests of the papacy. Moreover, James had put himself into the hands of the Jesuits, and Innocent had no love for the French and English Jesuits; he saw clearly that their methods were unlikely to benefit the Catholic Church in England. He had already in 1679 written to James warning him against indiscreet zeal, and during James's reign he was in sympathy with the resident English Catholics, people like Lord Belasyse, who knew their fellow-countrymen and were aware that any strong attempts by the Catholics to better their position would recoil on their own heads, and in opposition to the new arrivals who had spent their lives in continental seminaries.

The unofficial representative at Rome of the English Catholics at the time of James's accession was that excellent person Cardinal Philip Thomas Howard, who was popularly known as the Cardinal of Norfolk. He was entirely of the Pope's opinion on James's religious policy, and for that reason not in James's favour. For the first few months of his reign James carried on an unofficial correspondence with the Roman Curia through Cardinal Howard, but in September 1685 he told Barrillon that he had decided to inaugurate regular diplomatic correspondence with Rome and asked for his advice on the etiquette of such correspondence. A few weeks later Barrillon had heard that the first ambassador was to be Roger Palmer, Earl of Castlemaine, and that rumour proved to be correct. James's choice was not without justification, for Castlemaine was a keen Catholic and learned in controversy, he had travelled in Italy, he was of good family and he had earned the respect of the English Catholics by standing his trial for his life in Oates's Plot. But the outstanding fact about him—the only fact which was known to the English public—was that he was the husband of a famous royal mistress and that he owed his title to his wife's infidelity to himself; for this reason he should have been disqualified for any public position, and it came near to being an insult to the Pope to send Castlemaine to him as James's representative; the Pope also doubtless mistrusted him as being under the influence of Petre and the English Jesuits. Moreover, Castlemaine was not the man to hide the misfortunes of his private life under a correct and dignified public manner: he was of so hot and violent a disposition that he could not restrain himself, even in audience with the Pope, when he was unable to get what he wanted, and to the Pope a direct affront from a foreign ambassador must have been a new experience; James actually after Castlemaine's return to England had to apologise to the Pope for his ambassador's conduct. Castlemaine's particular business in Rome was to secure a red hat for Queen Mary's uncle, Prince Rinaldo d'Este, and a red hat and an archbishopric for Father Petre;[1] both demands were contrary to papal policy, which was averse to making princes cardinals and to bestowing any ecclesiastical dignity upon Jesuits. Innocent gave way in the matter of Prince Rinaldo, but he could not be moved to do anything for Petre. After a few audiences he began to treat Castlemaine with contempt, and when the ambassador became importunate the Pope would terminate the audience by being "seasonably attacked by a fit of coughing". Castlemaine was in almost complete isolation in Rome, for in addition to his notorious disfavour with the Pope he had exasperated the English Catholics there by his treatment of their acknowledged leader, Cardinal Howard.

Castlemaine had left for Rome early in November 1685, and a few days after his departure James received the Papal nuncio, Ferdinand, Count d'Adda. No secret was made either of his presence or of his

[1] Lingard (X, 123), the *Life of Petre* in *Oliver's Collectanea*, and the Records of the English Province of the Society of Jesus (VII, i, 592), furnish reasons for believing that Petre, as behoved a good Jesuit, was not ambitious, and in particular did not desire the Cardinalate; Ailesbury (I, 128) and Barrillon, June 30/July 10, 1687, are of the contrary opinion and the facts appear to be on their side.

position, but he was not publicly recognised, and the fiction was observed that he was a foreign visitor of private station. Though Adda was in England for three years he never achieved such an important position as the Pope's representative might have been expected to hold. Partly, no doubt, his own character, which was gentle and gracious rather than forceful, did not fit him for the proud behaviour of his pre-Reformation predecessors, but still more, representing as he did the moderate papal view on Catholic policy in England, he incurred the violent hostility of the ruling Catholic clique, Petre and the extreme Catholics, latterly also of James and the Queen, who did not scruple to hint that he had been a traitor to their cause and the cause of the Church.

The mission of Adda was mainly important to James as furnishing two opportunities for spectacular affirmation of his adhesion to the Church of Rome and for creating the illusion of the return of England to her ancient allegiance. On May 1, 1687, in St. James's Chapel, Adda was consecrated Archbishop of Amasia (a Turkish village which he never visited), and two months later there was a splendid ceremony at Windsor on the occasion of his public reception as papal nuncio It had been James's intention from the first to give him a public character, but Adda had on various pretexts, which no doubt concealed the real objection on the ground of inexpediency, successfully eluded a decision.[1] James so far met his unexpressed misgivings by deciding not to hold the ceremony in London, where the mob could not have been prevented, except by the employment of a considerable military force, from turning the procession into a riot. James was able to escape this popular affront, but he had to endure one of his most unfortunate personal encounters, and his discomfiture was not kept a secret: he ordered the Duke of Somerset to introduce the nuncio in the public audience, and was met by an uncompromising refusal. James was anxious that a peer of the highest rank should perform the office of introduction, and he had no reason to apprehend that the Duke, who as gentleman of the bedchamber had attended him to his own public worship, would be scrupulous in the present instance. But Somerset had taken legal advice, and he refused on the ground that to recognise the jurisdiction of the Pope in England was high treason, and that a royal pardon given in advance was invalid:

[1] As early as February 1686 Adda wrote that he had been pressed by Sunderland to appear in the public character of nuncio and that he had objected on the grounds of his own unfitness and of the absence of orders from Rome. There can be little doubt that the true reason behind these objections was that the Pope recognised that in the existing state of public feeling in England more harm than good would be done to the cause of Rome by emphasising Adda's importance.

> He humbly desired of the King to be excused; the King asked him his reason; the Duke told him he conceived it to be against law; to which the King said he would pardon him. The Duke replied he was no very good lawyer, but he thought he had heard it said that a pardon granted to a person offending under assurance of obtaining it was void.

It was easy to punish Somerset by depriving him of his offices and to substitute for him in the ceremony James's nephew, the Duke of Grafton, but Somerset's action was widely applauded and the implication of the terms of his refusal was clearly seen—namely, that the Declaration of Indulgence was legally null and void: as Barrillon wrote to Louis, "The refusal of the Duke of Somerset to conduct the nuncio to the audience shows that the anti-Catholic laws are still in force".

When on July 2, 1687, Parliament was finally dissolved by proclamation it was James's intention to summon a new Parliament as soon as he could feel himself safe to have one elected to his liking. His closeting now had a different aim: instead of trying to influence the votes of existing members, he exerted pressure on everyone who possessed local influence in elections. He had already taken steps to revise the Commissions of the peace; in October 1686 a Committee was appointed with Jeffreys as chairman to revise the list of justices in every county, with the result that a very large number of changes were made; in the list of those "put out" may be noticed the names of Dr. Tillotson, Dean of Canterbury (Kent), Dr. John Sharp, Dean of Norwich (Norfolk) and Sir John Maynard (Lancashire); among those "put in" are Sir Edward Hales (Kent), the Dukes of Grafton and Northumberland and Lords Feversham and Churchill (Middlesex) and Lord Castlemaine (Radnor). It will be noticed that the first and last of the latter list were Catholics; indeed, it was alleged that nearly all the new justices were of that faith. In August 1687 James began to inquire into the attitude of the Lords Lieutenant to his proposed reforms and, where necessary—that is to say, in nearly every case—to replace them by persons more amenable. Now, the Lord Lieutenant was a man of very great local consequence indeed; he was the natural leader of county society and generally the largest landowner in the county; as commander of the county militia, it is true, he held military rank, but that was the extent of his dependence on the King; though he was as a matter of form appointed by the King, it could almost be said that he appointed himself by his natural predominance in the county; it had not been the practice to bestow lord-lieutenancies on successful courtiers, though there had been occasions in which the leading man in a county had been obnoxious to the King and another landowner from the same county had been preferred to him. It followed that when James dismissed a Lord Lieutenant and appointed another who had no local connection it was not the individual dismissed who suffered—in former times it had been held a disgrace to be dismissed by the King, but now dismissal was for a matter of conscience in which the county concurred—but the efficiency of the administration. In a smaller field the same was true of a dismissed justice of the peace or a dismissed deputy-lieutenant, for the efficient performance of these duties depended largely on the natural authority of the officer in his own immediate locality.

The occasion of the wholesale changes in the lord-lieutenancies [1] was an attempt by James to take what is called in America a "straw" vote of the whole country, and to ascertain in advance from prospective members of Parliament and from voters what support he was likely to get from a Parliament to his designs in favour of the Catholics. In the autumn of 1687 every Lord Lieutenant was ordered to go down to his county and to put three questions to deputy-lieutenants, sheriffs, justices of the peace, mayors and members of corporations, Government officials such as customs and excise officers, forty-shilling freeholders and any others who could influence or take part in an election, and to demand a separate answer from each individual. The questions were:

1. If in case he shall be chosen Knight of the Shire or burgess of a town, when the King shall see fit to call a Parliament, whether he will be for taking off the Penal Laws and the Tests.
2. Whether he will assist and contribute to the election of such members as shall be for taking off the Penal Laws and the Tests.
3. Whether he will support the King's Declaration for Liberty of Conscience by living friendly with those of all persuasions, as subjects of the same Prince and good Christians ought to do.

The majority of Lords Lieutenant refused to have anything to do with these questions and accepted dismissal; the questions themselves were without precedent, and an attempt to pledge Parliament in advance to a course of action was, constructively at least, a breach of the privileges of Parliament; besides, there was an implied intention that a Lord Lieutenant who put the questions was to use his influence to secure favourable answers to them. A few, however, consented to obey the royal command, relying on their local reputations to avoid suspicion of Catholic bias, but put the questions in such a colourless manner as to

[1] There had been a previous purge among the Lord-lieutenancies of considerable extent in August 1687.

discourage rather than to encourage affirmative replies. One of the few exceptions was Rochester, who lost whatever reputation he had gained from his refusal to continue in office at the cost of changing his religion by attempting to obtain by violent speeches the adherence of his county of Hertfordshire to James's views; according to Barrillon he had concealed his true feelings from fear of the royal displeasure, and there is no doubt that he was in danger of losing his pension of £4000 a year.

The device of the Three Questions could not have been conceived by anyone who had knowledge of the general currents of opinion in England. It is improbable that Sunderland, who was a man of the world and had opportunities of listening to the conversation of men, at any rate of his own class, had any hand in it. Either James himself evolved it or it emanated from the sanguine and ignorant brains of the Jesuit camarilla. In effect it attempted on a large scale what closeting had attempted on a small scale: to determine which of James's subjects could be relied on to follow him in his pro-Catholic policy, so that they could be employed to ensure the return of a Parliament which would repeal the penal laws and the Test Act. Such a device could only be justified by its success: it should not have been adopted unless after discreet local inquiry it had been ascertained that it would be successful; failure, as the event proved, left James's prospects of getting together the Parliament he wanted even less happy than they had previously been. There was, indeed, a fairly numerous minority which was willing to satisfy the King; in this minority were many in whom the lamp of loyalty burned undimmed, but there were many also who would sign anything rather than let their wives and children starve, and many who thought they could better their fortunes by a display of loyalty.[1] The majority—in some localities the whole body of those questioned—refused to give any pledge that they would assist in returning a Parliament of James's mind on the religious question. They took their stand on the sound theory (which, however, is not in accordance with the facts of democratic government) that members of Parliament should assemble with open minds and should give their votes to the side which produces the more convincing arguments. Their answers were identical in substance, though not verbally, and the inference is unavoidable that the opposition was concerted all over the kingdom, as it undoubtedly was in particular localities. Here is a typical answer:

> 1. If I be chosen a Member of Parliament I conceive myself obliged to give my vote according to the reason of the debate of the House and not otherwise.

[1] Brian Magee (*The English Recusants*, pp. 171–5) assumes that all those who gave favourable answers to the questions were "Catholics and those who were not ill-disposed to Catholicism".

> 2. If I shall concern myself in the election of any to serve as Member of Parliament I shall give my vote for such as to the best of my judgement will serve the King and kingdom faithfully and honestly.
>
> 3. I think it my duty to live friendly and peaceably with all men, as becomes a good Christian and a loyal subject.

A reply which a courtier at Whitehall characterised as a "civil and politic denial".

The effect of imposing on everyone of local importance—in some places on every parliamentary voter—the obligation to declare his opinion for or against the repeal of the laws against the Catholics was to reveal the overwhelming determination of the country to give the King no assistance in the matter: what had hitherto been a matter of conjecture had become a matter of fact; even the moderate men, who were averse to persecution for religion, disapproved of the means which had been taken to secure repeal, suspected James's ultimate aims and kept their principles in abeyance. Hitherto, moreover, everyone had been careful in declaring an opinion contrary to that of the King, not knowing on which side his neighbour stood and fearing lest indiscreet talk might be reported and distorted to the agents of the Government. As the Imperial Ambassador wrote in April 1688:

> So far from serving a useful purpose [the enquiry] has done more harm than one can express, seeing chiefly that nearly everywhere a negative reply was given; . . . before this enquiry . . . everyone suspected his neighbour of being a partisan of the King and people suppressed their disaffection, which now they express without fear.

James himself was entirely unaware that he had sustained a major disaster: he took his defeat philosophically and said he would go another way to work. He did not realise that he had consolidated the opposition and that his problem had been made far more difficult by the ill-conceived attempt which he had made to solve it.[1]

Simultaneously with the issue of the three questions James attacked the Corporations. In November 1687 a Commission, again headed by Jeffreys and including Sunderland and four Catholics—Lords Powis and Castlemaine, Father Petre and Sir Nicholas Butler[2]—was appointed

[1] A mass of material on this subject has been accumulated by Sir George Duckett in his *Penal Laws and Test Act*.

[2] Ailesbury's character of Butler is worth quoting as showing the contempt which the English nobility, even those who remained faithful to the end, had for James's tools: (he) "had been a stocking merchant and a bankrupt, a man that had wit and sense, but else of little or no morals and had publicly changed his religion".

to deal with them. In the last years of Charles's reign there had been a revision of the charters of towns and cities throughout England, and the process was still going on in the early part of the new reign; by the legal means of *quo warranto* the charters were forfeited and new charters granted, ostensibly because of irregularities committed by the Corporations (there can be little doubt that the Corporations were thoroughly corrupt bodies), but actually for the purpose of excluding Whigs and Dissenters from them and appointing Tories and Churchmen in their places. James had never respected even these new charters, for he frequently violated the right of local election by excluding aldermen and other members and substituting his own nominees. Hitherto the aim had been to man the Corporations with adherents of the old Court party; now James was concerned with the contemplated general election, and wanted Corporations which would influence the borough elections in favour of the principles of the Declaration of Indulgence, and, as Tories and Churchmen were in general opposed to those principles, the only people available were on the one side Catholics and on the other the far more numerous Protestant Dissenters. But this Commission differed altogether from that which had preceded it; there was no longer a question of revising the charters by legal process—indeed, legality had no part in the action of the Commission—but of purging the Corporations, as the Lord Lieutenancies, Commissions of the peace and the other local organisations, of all people who would not give a definite and affirmative reply to the three questions.[1] During the few months in which these revised Corporations sat, their meetings must have presented a ridiculous appearance: there was some slight contact between the Catholics and the "jure divino" churchmen and between the liberal churchmen and the Protestant Dissenters, but the Catholics and the Protestant Dissenters had nothing whatever in common except their grievances against the Church of England; the Protestant Dissenters hated the Catholics as subjects of the Scarlet Women of Rome, and as persecutors of the Huguenots, and the Catholics despised the Protestant Dissenters as fanatical schismatics, and probably also regarded them as socially contemptible.

In the autumn of 1687, as he had done on a smaller scale a year earlier, James made a royal progress in the West of England. He set out from Windsor on August 16 with the Queen, who left him early in the journey and went to Bath, while he himself proceeded to Portsmouth. There he inspected the fortifications, and after passing through Southampton and

[1] There are numerous instances in the Privy Council Register of the nomination of particular persons to Corporations.

Salisbury he rejoined the Queen at Bath. The progress was admittedly an electioneering device, an attempt to influence the electors in favour of "freedom of conscience"; on the whole the local gentry hastened to do their duty in receiving their sovereign with traditional hospitality and loyalty; but while their personal attitude to the King was unchanged, so was their devotion to the Church of England, and there is no record that James had any encouragement in his hopes of a favourable election. He touched for the King's evil at various places, and these exhibitions of Romish rites can hardly have been to the taste of the local gentry. At Bath in particular the healing was made the occasion of a gross affront to the Church of England, for in the Abbey there Huddlestone delivered a proselytising address to the multitudes who came to be touched. As the good Bishop Ken wrote to Sancroft:

> When His Majesty was at Bath, there was a great healing,[1] and without any warning except by a flying report: the office was performed in the Church between the hours of prayer. I had not time to remonstrate, and if I had done it it would have had no effect but only to provoke: besides I found it had been done in the Churches before, and I know no place but the Church which was capable to receive so great a multitude as came for cure: upon which consideration I was wholly passive. But being aware what advantage the Romanists take from the least seeming compliances, I took occasion on Sunday . . . to discourse of Charity . . . though we could not open the Church doors to a worship different from that we paid to God, yet we should always throw them open to a common work of charity.

From Bath James went to Gloucester, Worcester, Ludlow, Shrewsbury and Whitchurch, spending one night at each town; from Whitchurch he made a pilgrimage to Holywell; he arrived at Chester on August 27 and remained three days. There he met Tyrconnel, who gave him his own version of what was happening in Ireland and successfully prevented him from hearing an independent version from Thomas

[1] James took these healings, the touching for the King's Evil, very seriously, symbolising as they did the divine character of kingship. Before he had been on the throne a month an order was given for "an elbow chair covered with black for His Majesty to sit in at healings", and in April 1685 the mint was ordered to strike off 1000 healing medals "which will be made use of before Easter". Altogether during his reign he expended between £4000 and £5000 on healing medals. During the first year the healing ceremony was in English, no doubt in the form used in the previous reigns, and was conducted by bishops and clergy of the Church of England; in the spring of 1686, however, a Latin service was substituted and Catholic priests officiated. At Oxford in September 1687 James is said to have touched seven or eight hundred persons in two days.

Sheridan. Bishop Cartwright, more obsequious than Ken, put the Cathedral choir at the King's disposal for the healings, and 450 persons were touched; before leaving, James commissioned Cartwright to find accommodation for Roman Catholic worship—a curious duty to impose on a bishop of the Church of England and for a seventeenth-century bishop to undertake. From Chester James went to Newport, Lichfield, Coventry and Banbury, and arrived at Oxford for his last and most memorable visit on September 3. From Oxford he returned to Bath via Cirencester and rejoined the Queen; he passed through Winchester on his journey back to Windsor, where he arrived on September 17. James himself was well satisfied with his reception everywhere, and on the whole he was justified, for he could do himself no harm by showing himself to his people, though it is very doubtful if the true object of the progress was fulfilled or that he made a single convert to the cause which he had at heart. For the rest, he was probably unaware that a great number of leading gentry left their neighbourhoods so as to avoid having to kiss his hand; those who were sufficiently well-disposed to give him public welcome made a brave enough show to conceal the absence of the others.[1]

The systematic effort to concentrate the central and local administration in the hands of Catholics and complacent Protestants was accompanied by no corresponding attack on the Church of England. It is true that when a See fell vacant, as at Chester and Oxford, a bishop was appointed who could be trusted not to oppose the royal will in matters affecting the interests of the Church, and in one instance—at Putney—the incumbent was by royal dispensation permitted to retain his cure of souls in spite of his conversion to Rome. The civil appointments had been made entirely with a view to getting a Parliament which would endorse the Declaration of Indulgence and, though the influence of the clergy in elections was manifestly strong, it would have been idle to approach them by such a device as the Three Questions: for not only would their response have been overwhelmingly negative, but, secure as they were in their freeholds, there was no machinery by which they could have been replaced. There is no evidence that James had in view any scheme for substituting Catholics for Protestants in the rectories

[1] The opinion of Bonrepaus at the time of the conclusion of the progress was that James had so convinced himself that the disposition of the country was favourable to his plans that he determined to summon parliament; "But (adds the ambassador) the acquaintance I have made with the affairs of this country does not lead me to believe that he will find it easy to succeed in his principal object, the repeal of the Test Act. The party attached to the Prince of Orange is stronger than it is thought to be. Everyone of ability or position in the country is either openly in this party or is sympathetic to it."

and vicarages, but we may be sure that the sanguine and unpractical Petre dreamt of such a substitution. Be that as it may, it is very striking that in the list of grievances which the bishops presented to the King in September 1688 there appeared only two which concerned the Church of England directly: the suspension of Compton and the vacancy at York.[1]

But the Universities, which on the one hand were the sole recruiting-ground of the English clergy, and on the other were entirely staffed by clerics, and were therefore regarded as the Church's dearest possessions, had to endure a series of sharp attacks on their liberties. Cambridge, indeed, had only one conflict with the Crown, a conflict in which the Crown was not on the whole victorious: one Alban Francis, a Romanist missioner for the County of Cambridge, obtained a royal mandate for an honorary degree, exempting him from the rule that he should take the oaths; the University rejected the mandate as contrary to the statutes; the Ecclesiastical Commission thereupon deprived the Vice-Chancellor of his post (but not of his freehold as head of his college); his successor on taking office made a defiant speech declaring his determination not to suffer any invasion of the rights of the University, and was not reprimanded; nor does it appear that Francis succeeded in obtaining his degree. At Oxford, on the other hand, the religious controversy was kept well in the foreground. The Master of University College, Obadiah Walker,[2] declared his conversion to the Roman faith and was allowed by royal dispensation to retain his post; he set up an oratory in his college, and with the aid of three Fellows, two of University and one of Brasenose, and in spite of systematic persecution by the undergraduates, he managed to maintain a Catholic nucleus in the University. Further, the Deanery of Christ Church, which was in the royal gift, was bestowed on John Massey, a junior Fellow who had nothing to recommend him except his change of religion,[3] and by a royal dispensation he was installed without taking the oaths.

The affair of the Presidentship of Magdalen College was more protracted and important; it affords many opportunities for forming an opinion on James's character, on his state of mind at the time of his highest apparent prosperity and on his control of his Ministers. It also

[1] I have not overlooked the vacancies in the Irish Sees, but these are a matter apart from the present discussion.

[2] Dr. Walker was a scholar and a man of excellent character; his only fault, if fault it was, was his change of religion, but such a conversion in the heated atmosphere of the times covered a multitude of virtues.

[3] It is not quite certain that Massey was a declared Catholic at the time of his appointment in October 1686 (see Wood, III, 197; Burnet, I, 674), but when he was installed at the end of December there was no doubt that he was a Catholic (Wood, III, 201; Ellis, *Corresp.*, I, 210).

provides a second instance, the Ecclesiastical Commission being the first, of definitely illegal action on James's part.

On March 24, 1687, Dr. Henry Clarke, President of Magdalen, who had been on sick leave from the College since February 7, died at Gawthrop Hall, Lancashire, the house of his daughter, Lady Shuttleworth, and the College was officially informed of this occurrence on March 29. On March 31 the Vice-President, Dr. Aldworth, convened the Fellows, a meeting for the election of a new President was fixed for April 13, and the text of a letter was agreed upon to Peter Mews, Bishop of Winchester, the visitor of the College; in this letter the Bishop is asked "to patronise us in the choice of a President according to the direction of our Founder's Statutes", a form of words which was substituted for "to recommend us to His Majesty's grace and favour, and prevent any stranger's being set over us". On April 2 the Bishop's reply was received; he advised the College to proceed to an election at once, and suggested Baptist Levinz, Bishop of Man, as a suitable candidate.[1] On April 5, Sunderland signed a royal mandate to the College, ordering them to elect and admit Anthony Farmer to the place of President, "any statute, custom or constitution to the contrary in any wise notwithstanding, wherewith we are graciously pleased to dispense on his behalf"; the King also stated that he was well satisfied of Farmer's "piety, loyalty and learning", but it may be remarked in passing that there was no mention of the oaths in the mandate or that Farmer on election would have had to declare himself a good Protestant.

On April 8 the Bishop of Winchester wrote to Sunderland:

> I am informed that great endeavours are used with His Majesty to recommend one Mr. Farmer, who is not at present, nor ever was, Fellow of that College, to be President of it, which is directly contrary to the Statutes of the Founder, as I am confident some who promote Mr. Farmer's interest cannot be ignorant of;

and put forward the names of certain other persons of merit who did not labour under Farmer's disqualifications. The same day the Bishop wrote to the College advising them to petition the King against the mandate and, either on that advice or independently of it, the College on April 9 agreed on a petition representing "that the said Mr. Farmer is a person in several respects incapable of that character [*i.e.* of President], according to our Founder's Statutes". This petition was sent by the College post haste to London by the hand of one of their members,

[1] It was said that Levinz's brother—possibly Sir Cresswell Levinz—dissuaded him from risking himself in so hazardous an enterprise.

Captain Francis Bagshaw,[1] and on the following day he and Dr. Thomas Smith, another of the Fellows who was living in London, waited on Sunderland and delivered it to him. On April 12, Smith and Bagshaw again waited on Sunderland for news of the success of the petition; they were given an appointment on the next day, and Sunderland said to them:

> I have delivered the Bishop of Winchester's letter and your address to the King: the King has sent down his letter to the College, and expects to be obeyed.

Meanwhile this second mandate[2] had reached the College by the hand of Robert Charnock, the single Fellow who was a Catholic, and who was to be executed nine years later for plotting against the life of William III. The mandate was considered at a meeting on April 11, and it was decided to hold to their intention of proceeding to election on the 13th. The election was adjourned, however, until the 15th (a postponement expressly allowed by the Statute), when Dr. Thomas Smith, who had hurried down from London, moved for a delay to provide time for the despatch of a second petition to the King, but was over-ruled. In the election which followed the discussion on Dr. Smith's motion, and which was held according to the prescribed forms, Dr. John Hough was declared President; and the following day he went with the Vice-President to Farnham, where the Bishop as Visitor confirmed the election.

The various points on which more information up to this date are required are: (1) Had James any plan to interfere in the election in existence before the death of Dr. Clarke, when he was known to be very ill? Such a plan seems to be hinted at in the words deleted from the first draft of the petition of the College. (2) Did James see the petition which Smith and Bagshaw handed to Sunderland? Smith had his doubts at the time, and, from reports of conversations in which James took part when he was at Oxford in September 1687 and questions which were put to Smith by Jenner and Cartwright in November, we must very strongly suspect that Sunderland kept the petition in his own hands and that his answer to it was without authority. (3) Had James any previous knowledge of the candidate who was put forward in his name for the presidentship? If he had not, as appears likely, he must be convicted of acting very irresponsibly in failing to inquire into Farmer's suitability for so important a post.

[1] Bagshaw had earned his rank in the contingent raised by the University at the time of Monmouth's rebellion.

[2] There is no text of this document extant, but its existence and contents can be inferred.

For there can be little doubt that in the long history of the Universities of Oxford and Cambridge no person less qualified to be a Head of a House has ever been proposed for such an office. His qualifications began and ended with his tenure of a master's degree and with an alleged willingness to adopt or support the Catholic religion. Anthony Wood appears to have known something about him before his character had been fully investigated, for on April 9 he wrote in his diary:

> Was there ever such a ridiculous thing that a mandamus for such a person should come from the King? Sure if the King had a right understanding of things and men he would not have recommended such a person;

and it seems likely that Farmer was well and not favourably known at Oxford; indeed, the words of the petition, "a person in several respects incapable of that character", reveal that the Fellows of Magdalen knew something of him in addition to the fact that he had not qualified for candidature by becoming a Fellow of Magdalen or New College. His most obvious disqualification was that he was under thirty years of age[1]—a disqualification which could be ignored only if it were balanced by exceptional scholarship or strength of character. But the Fellows of Magdalen set to work, and with the zeal of modern detectives traced Farmer's record and unearthed a series of incidents any one of which (unless lived down by years of serious living) would have rendered him unfit for any position of dignity: he had, on his own signed confession, been expelled from Trinity College, Cambridge, for misbehaving at a dancing class; he had been usher to an unlicensed dissenting schoolmaster; he had been asked to leave Magdalen Hall because of the disturbances he caused there by his "troublesome and unpeaceable humour"; he had seduced undergraduates to debauchery and provided a naked woman for their entertainment; he had insulted an honest inn-keeper's wife; he professed himself willing to court Catholics or even to profess himself to be a Catholic in furtherance of his own interests; he was constantly drunk in public and in company with troopers and other mean persons, and as late as June 12, 1687, when he was still the King's nominee for the Presidentship, he had been drunk with a number of other men at Abingdon and had concluded a riotous evening by uprooting the town stocks and throwing them into Mad Hall's Pool. Such a list whets one's appetite, and it is disappointing to read that the College proved these misdeeds sufficiently and "as much more against him, even such things as are not fit to be heard or spoken".

[1] Farmer matriculated at Trinity College, Cambridge, in 1672 (*D.N.B.*).

The King took notice of Dr. Hough's election merely by a short letter of expostulation addressed to the Vice-President and Fellows and demanding an explanation of their conduct. To this letter a reply was sent couched in very loyal terms and enclosing a statement to the effect that they had been bound by their statutes neither to postpone the election nor to elect Mr. Farmer, who had never been a Fellow of their College or of New College "and wanting likewise such personal qualifications as are required in the character of a President"; that included in their oaths was an undertaking not to procure or accept any dispensation from their oaths; and that though in the past the College had on occasions obeyed royal mandates in their choice of Presidents, these Presidents had invariably possessed the statutory qualifications. No answer was made to this letter, and the College was left in uneasy security for over two months.

On May 28 the Vice-President and Fellows, or such as they should empower to represent them, were cited to appear before the Ecclesiastical Commission. They appeared on June 6, and were allowed a week to prepare their case; on the 13th they put in two statements, one of their legal position, the other containing their allegations against Farmer's character; on the 22nd the Commission declared the election of Dr. Hough null and void and suspended the Vice-President for contempt in not having obeyed the royal mandate, and another Fellow, Dr. Fairfax, for no stated reason, but actually for having put Jeffreys into a passion by questioning the legality of the Commission. On the 27th they considered the allegations against Farmer, and it was noticed by one of them that at the meeting their demeanour had changed: they no longer hectored the Fellows, but treated them with deference, for they had become aware of the weak position in which the King had put himself by offering such a man as President. Farmer had put in a written answer to the charges against him—he appears to have had some of the brazen effrontery of Titus Oates—but even he himself was unable to suggest that he had any positive qualifications for the post. The Commission determined to examine witnesses and,

> What was made out against Farmer was so scandalous that Obadiah (Walker) and his other friends being in Court could not say one word, the evidence of the College being most of them people of good report. The conclusion was that my Lord Chancellor told Farmer that that Court looked on him as a very bad man.

In short, Jeffreys, conscious as he was of his precarious position in the King's favour and willing to strain law and equity to any extent, was for once unable to override the force of the evidence, and had to admit that the man who had been in so public a fashion put forward as the King's candidate was an utterly worthless creature. No single action on the part of James exhibits in the same clear light his entire unfitness for kingship: for not only did he make no inquiry into Farmer's character before committing himself to his candidature, but after the event there is no record that anyone was reprimanded for having deceived the King in this matter. It is clear that Sunderland had a part in this deception, but it seems probable that Sunderland himself was deceived by the Jesuit clique led by Petre, for Petre was undoubtedly very closely in the counsels of the Commission of three which finally installed Dr. Parker, and it is not likely that he came into the affair then for the first time; James could not have broken with Petre without destroying the foundations of the system of government which he had erected.

The College had justified themselves as far as Farmer was concerned, and they persisted in refusing to acknowledge the validity of the declaration by the Ecclesiastical Commission that the election of Dr. Hough was null and void. But it was far from the nature of James to admit defeat; on August 14 a fresh mandate was issued, no mention being made of the previous mandate to elect Farmer, calling upon the Fellows to elect Samuel Parker, Bishop of Oxford, in the vacancy which the Commission had declared to exist. After a fortnight's delay the Fellows replied, submissively in form but stubbornly in essence, that "they humbly conceived the place of the President to be full". James determined to try to overawe the Fellows by his personal presence. He arrived at Oxford on his Western progress on September 3, and was met on the Woodstock Road by the University and the City and conducted to his lodgings at Christ Church, through streets decorated with green boughs and amid cheering crowds, in a procession of great magnificence and solemnity; and he no doubt accepted this expression of loyalty as a sign that he could make his will prevail.

The following afternoon James sent for the Fellows of Magdalen, and in the Dean's lodgings was enacted a scene in which he exhibited to the full that lack of royal dignity which his most extravagant contemporary eulogist, the Earl of Ailesbury, admits to be his gravest fault. After obtaining the admission of Pudsey, the Senior Fellow, that they had received his mandate to elect Dr. Parker, he addressed them as follows:

> Then I must tell you and the rest of your Fellows that you have behaved yourselves undutifully to me and not like gentlemen; you have not paid me common respect; you have always been a stubborn and turbulent college, I have known you to be so these six and

> twenty years myself; you have affronted me, know I am your King and I will be obeyed. Is this your Church of England loyalty? One would wonder to see so many Church of England men got together in such a thing. Go back and show yourselves good members of the Church of England. (Here all kneeling Dr. Pudsey offered a petition, which the King refused saying) [I am] hearing nothing from you, get you gone, I command you be gone, go and admit the Bishop of Oxford, Head, Principal, or what do you call him (one that stood by said "president") as President of the College. Let them that refuse it look to it. Go and obey me or you shall feel the weight of your sovereign's displeasure.

As they were going out James called them back to reprimand them afresh for having confirmed a probationary Fellow in contravention of a royal mandate to elect no new Fellows, and when they attempted to justify their action he cut them short by a fresh outburst.

Even when it is read in cold print this exhibition of temper gives an impression of gross want of self-control and of regard for the elevation of majesty. The effect on those who stood round him further heightens that impression. Bonrepaus, the French agent, says that the King's anger prevented him from continuing his speech for some moments; a correspondent of Pepys informed him that "His Majesty chid them . . . with a much greater appearance of anger that ever I perceived in him"; another eye-witness says:

> The King put himself into so great passion that he changed colour and faltered in his speech, but Lord Sunderland stood by his elbow with much sedate malice in his face.

And the worst of it was from James's point of view that with only two dissentients the Fellows persisted in their view that it was not in their power to elect Dr. Parker. They restated their position in a paper which was left for James at Christ Church, and when he returned from University College, where he had been attending vespers with Obadiah Walker, he received this paper, "Which answer perusing (says Antony Wood) he said he was misinformed of the matter".

But if he actually made such a remark it represented only a passing phase of mind. The next morning, Monday, September 5, he attended a collation prepared for him in Bodley's Library,[1] and later he held discourse with the Vice-Chancellor and complained of the conduct of

[1] "None did eat but he, for he spoke to nobody to eat", and after he had finished he watched with interest the spectators scrambling for the remains of a gargantuan feast.

the Fellows towards him.[1] The Fellows on their side appear at this point to have been horrified at their own temerity in opposing the royal will. They sent to James at Bath by the hand of Sunderand a very obsequious address, expressing themselves as "being deeply afflicted with the late sense of Your Majesty's heavy displeasure", and offering "to obey your royal pleasure in any instance that does not interfere with and violate our conscience". This latter expression Sunderland chose to interpret as meaning that if the King were to put Dr. Parker into the presidency by royal mandate, and excuse them from the form of election, they would be satisfied and would acknowledge and obey him. There followed a short period of surreptitious bargaining, the Fellows holding that they could not elect Parker, even if Hough made way for him by resigning,[2] without violating their oaths and committing perjury, and that perjury, being a *malum in se*, could not be covered by royal dispensation;[3] the King hesitating to create a new precedent by making the direct appointment. Whatever scruples he had had, he overcame them by the middle of October, when he appointed as "Lords Commissioners for visiting Magdalen College" Cartwright, Bishop of Chester, Chief Justice Wright and Baron Jenner. These commissioners sat at Magdalen from October 21 to 28; they repeated the old arguments with the Fellows and, finding them still obdurate, they forcibly entered the President's lodgings on October 25 and left in possession there one of the chaplains of the Bishop of Oxford as proxy for the Bishop. On the afternoon of the same day they received a declaration by all the Fellows except Dr. Fairfax (Dr. Hough having previously been dismissed from his fellowship) that they would obey Dr. Parker as President "so far as is lawful and agreeable to the Statutes of the said College". Dr. Fairfax, who was already under suspension, was thereupon dismissed; but James was not satisfied with this qualified submission: on October 27 Sunderland conveyed peremptory orders that the Fellows must address the King "asking pardon for their late offences and obstinacy and acknowledging the jurisdiction of the Court", and that any Fellow who refused to join in this address should be expelled. The Fellows had already incurred odium in Oxford for their qualified offer to accept Dr.

[1] This conversation is too long to quote, but it is an interesting example of James's controversial methods: he made a statement, waited until the reply was concluded, but took no notice of the reply and proceeded to another statement on the same or another subject.

[2] Hough does not appear to have been at any time willing to resign, nor was pressure put upon him to do so.

[3] This legal point does not appear to have been raised directly but it is inherent in all the pleas of the College; Aldworth, a Fellow, came near to raising it when he propounded the curious paradox, "As long as they obeyed the statutes they obeyed the King".

Parker; they stiffened their attitude, and with three exceptions—Robert Charnock, Jasper Thompson and Thomas Smith—they refused. On November 15 the three Commissioners returned to Oxford, and on the following day dismissed the twenty-five recalcitrant Fellows. On November 28, Sunderland moved at a meeting of the Ecclesiastical Commission that the expelled Fellows should be "incapacitated"—that is to say, that they should not be allowed to earn the means of subsistence by accepting ecclesiastical preferment. Unexpected opposition was met from Lord Chief Justice Herbert and Thomas Sprat, Bishop of Rochester, who both said that in their opinion Dr. Hough's election had been regular. On December 10 this vindictive resolution was passed by a single vote. On December 31 James wrote to Dr. Parker ordering him to admit twelve new Fellows; six of these are known to have been Catholics, and it is probable that the remainder were of the same faith, for they were not to be called upon to subscribe the oaths. On March 21, 1688, Parker died; by that time there were no Protestant fellows except Dr. Thomas Smith and perhaps Jasper Thompson, and a few days before Parker's death a confidential servant of his was witness of an extraordinary scene in which he worked himself into a passion,

> he walked up and down the room, and smote his breast and said, "There is no trust in man, there is no trust in Princes. Is this the kindness the King promised me? To set me here to make me his tool and his prop! To place me with a company of men which he knows I hate the conversation of."

But from a conversation Parker had with Thomas Smith as early as March 28, when he said that "the King expected that the person he recommended should be favourable to his religion", it is clear that he was deceived not in the nature, but in the extent of James's intentions. On March 31 Bonaventura Giffard, one of the four Catholic Vicars-General, was admitted President of Magdalen in obedience to a royal mandate, and the process of converting the College into a Catholic seminary was complete.

As in many other cases, James's victory was less complete than it appeared to be. The College was indeed in Catholic hands and the Fellows had been driven to dependence on charity. But they had defied the royal will for nearly seven months; even at the end of that time the King had been unable to persuade them or to scare them into electing his nominee, and they had compelled him to use force to attain his ends.[1] But the worst feature of the proceedings was that it had des-

[1] As Hough said, "I see it is resolved that the papists must have our College, and I think all we have to do is to let the world see that they take it from us and that we do not give it up".

troyed the unanimity of the Ecclesiastical Commission, which up to that time had been willing to go to any lengths to further James's plans. There can be little question that, had the headship of another College at Oxford or Cambridge, not by statute in the royal gift, fallen vacant, James could not have entered on a second conflict of the same nature, and that Jeffreys would not have advised him to take such a step. Nor can he be absolved from personal responsibility or from acting in opposition to the advice of persons wiser than himself in thus undermining the loyalty of the Church of England; for the Earl of Ailesbury has left a record that he went on his knees to the King, begged him not to touch the freehold of Hough and the Fellows, urged that if he must have a Catholic College at Oxford it would be a less flagrant breach of the law to found a new one, and added that though he himself had no ready money, he would raise a thousand pounds on credit as a subscription to such a scheme.

The years 1686 and 1687 provide no outstanding events in James's foreign policy strictly so called. The chief interest abroad lies in the personal relations of James with his nephew and son-in-law, William of Orange; these relations, however, inevitably had repercussions on James's dealings on the one hand with the States-General, in whose employ William was, and on the other hand with William's personal enemy, King Louis. In general it may be said that during these years there was a steady decline in cordiality between James and William, and that in the spring of 1688 James was so angry with his nephew that, short of a breach which might have led to war, he would have done him any injury in his power; that this decline in cordiality was accompanied by a growing aversion to the States-General, who supported William in his opposition to James's plans, and by an increasing dependence on Louis, under whose domination he had shown restiveness towards the end of 1685.

James's disavowals notwithstanding, it can hardly be doubted that the renewal in July 1685 of the treaty with the States-General was a symptom of a desire on his part to pursue a foreign policy independent of France. In the following month Avaux, the French ambassador at The Hague, a far more active and reliable diplomatist than Barrillon, reported to Louis that James had told William and Fagel, the Grand Pensionary, "that he knew what measures to take with France, but that if he took such measures immediately the results might be disastrous".[1]

[1] James wrote seven letters to William in order to remove his apprehensions of a sudden attack on Holland by France, and promising to make every endeavour to maintain peace.

Early in December, Barrillon told Louis that there was a general impression in English Court circles that James was anxious to demonstrate that he was not a docile tool in the hands of the French King, but that he would henceforth stand on his own feet and conduct an independent policy.

> Most people think (writes the ambassador) that if there is a cooling off it is on the part of the King of England, who is not so amenable nor so tractable as the late King his brother, and who is believed to be more fanatical (*entêté*) about what is called the interest of England and the honour of the nation;

and he adds that James had no doubt allowed himself to be flattered, and that, since he has obtained from Parliament all the money he needed, "he has used such language and conducted himself in such a manner as to encourage those who wish to sever his relations with Your Majesty".

For the most part James was discreet and avoided any action or declaration which could give offence to Louis. On one occasion, however (as Barrillon reports), when the Dutch ambassador Van Citters showed him a pamphlet, "A Remonstrance made to the King of England by his Council", in whch he was accused, among other things, of subservience to France, he was moved to anger and said all that was in his mind:

> Today I possess the Crown in full right and I am determined not to dishonour it. I was born an Englishman and I want all the world to know it. . . . Never, no never, shall I do anything to put myself below the Kings of France and Spain. Vassal! Vassal of France! Sir, if Parliament had wished, if it still wishes, I would have carried, I will still carry, the monarchy to a degree of consideration which it never enjoyed under my predecessors. And your State may find in the English monarchy its own security.[1]

These brave words were, however, at no time justified by James's behaviour when he found himself at variance with Louis; in such circumstances he showed himself half-hearted and timorous, and Louis

[1] A modern French historian has said that Europe had been accustomed for twenty-five years to see England following the lead of France, but that James was far more national and independent than Charles; and he adds that probably if he had succeeded in making England Catholic he would have joined the European movement to curb Louis's ambitions. But even in 1678, when James was advocating war with France, he appears to have been unaware of the true object of that war, to limit Louis's conquests in the Spanish Netherlands; apart from the religious question, he had no sympathy with the territorial aims of the League of Augsburg, and we have no choice but to accept Ranke's dictum, "No prince has ever had less thought for the balance of power in Europe than James II".

treated his representations with scarcely disguised contempt. In September 1685 Sir William Trumbull succeeded Lord Preston as ambassador at Paris. To Louis the appointment was distasteful on two grounds: he was not a nobleman or even of gentle birth, and he took his Protestantism more seriously than his predecessor had done. Trumbull's tenure of the Embassy was troubled and unsuccessful. Two questions came to a head shortly after his arrival, both arising out of the Revocation of the Edict of Nantes. The first question did not concern James directly; from family interest he endeavoured to mediate between Louis and William in the matter of William's principality of Orange. The possession of Orange had been confirmed to William by the Treaty of Nimeguen in 1678, but after the Revocation it became a place of refuge for Huguenots fleeing from the dragonnades. Louis could not tolerate a Huguenot enclave in the heart of France, and in October 1685 he occupied Orange with his troops, levelled its fortifications and subjected its Protestant inhabitants to the rigours of persecution. Except by precipitating a European war, William had no means of redress against this high-handed proceeding. He did, however, persuade James to take up his case, and James made formal and half-hearted representations to Louis. But Louis refused even to discuss the matter: he said that the sovereignty of Orange was attached to the Crown of France, and that he could not believe that James could object to the extirpation of heresy in the town:

> I must believe [he wrote to Barrillon on November 19] that the King of England will not take up this question, especially as the interests of our religion do not permit that this town shall remain longer in heresy. You may . . . make it known that I have sufficient confidence in his friendship to believe that he will entirely abandon this solicitation.

Early in December, James told Barrillon that he could not refuse to take up the Orange question without offending William, and that what had happened had been so strongly resented in England that there would be discontent if he did nothing; Barrillon replied that both before and after the Treaty of Nimeguen the French King had held the sovereignty of Orange, and that Louis could not tolerate a place of retreat for Huguenots in the heart of his kingdom. Bonrepaus was then in England on a mission which included persuading Huguenot refugees to return to France, and his view of the matter was that James had intervened only because he could not help himself, and that he could be satisfied by a few polite words. Meanwhile Trumbull at Paris has been informed that the Orange question was closed, that the French troops had been withdrawn and the town restored to its former condition; nothing apparently was said about the refugees and the Protestant inhabitants. In January 1686 James wrote to William saying that he was sorry Trumbull had had no more success with the memorial on the Orange question which he had presented, "but", he added, "I shall still continue to do my part in pressing it". There is no evidence, however, that the matter was again raised either with Barrillon in London or by Trumbull at Paris.

The second question gave Trumbull constant trouble during a period of months: the question of the status of English Protestants domiciled in France. His instructions were that he should do nothing to facilitate the escape of French Protestants, but Protestant worship was prohibited in France, and the country had in many ways been rendered impossible for Protestants of any nationality. In consequence there was a general exodus of the English to their native country. There was endless conflict about particular cases. Louis took up a typical dictator attitude; he recognised no restrictions imposed on him by international law and made no pretence of reciprocity: he rejected all James's claims over Englishmen domiciled in France, while pressing his own claims over Frenchmen domiciled in England. In particular he insisted that the French wives of Englishmen living in France, and their children who had been born there, were his subjects and could not leave the kingdom without his consent, and on the other hand he committed the enormity of having certain French fishermen domiciled at Rye kidnapped, and refused to give them up. James protested that he was actuated by no desire to favour the "*prétendus reformés*", who had been his brother's and his own worst enemies; but the English people were sensitive about anything that concerned the sea, and for that reason he was bound to press for the return of the kidnapped men (he was unaware that Louis had no reason to desire political harmony in England). This was James's public attitude, but at the same time Sunderland gave Barrillon to understand that, as in the Orange question, Trumbull's representations might be quietly ignored. James's stock at Versailles at the beginning of the year 1686 was very low, and Louis could congratulate himself on having as completely neutralised the power of England as he had done in the previous reign, and at considerable less expenditure of money.

In September 1686 Bevil Skelton was succeeded as envoy by the Marquis d'Albeville.[1] Albeville came of a family of Irish adventurers,

[1] His official title was Sir Ignatius White, Baronet of England, and Marquis of Albeville in the Roman Empire. An account of Albeville and his brothers by Mr. E. S. de Beer will be found in *English Historical Review*, XLV, 397.

and his own record, if Burnet is to be believed, was not good. He was appointed on the recommendation of Barrillon, who, in conjunction with Avaux, also obtained for him a pension from King Louis on condition that he should model his conduct according to the advice of Avaux. But Barrillon, on second thoughts, and in spite of the solemn assurances which Albeville had given to him before leaving for Holland, was unwilling to guarantee his fidelity; he feared that William might offer him higher terms, and recommended that the pension should be contingent on satisfactory reports of his conduct from Avaux. Albeville was in fact miserably poor, and was willing to sell his services to the highest bidder. Avaux never trusted him, and a year after his appointment Bonrepaus stated that he had gone over to the Prince of Orange; but there is no evidence of any act of treachery on his part to James or Louis;[1] it seems probable that William, who had little patience with fools, made no effort to attach him to himself. His appointment was in itself an affront and a disappointment to William, for, apart from the fact that he was a Catholic, it had been understood that Skelton's successor would be a man of quality. This was among James's many bad appointments, and he was certainly not better served at The Hague during his last two years than he had formerly been; Burnet's explanation of the choice was that Albeville was entirely in the interests of the Jesuit faction at Whitehall and was the only man they could trust to further their designs.

The relations between James and William during the greater part of the year 1686 appear, from the few letters between them which have survived, to have been amicable. In May 1686, for example, James addressed three letters to the Prince on the subject of English refugees in Holland. In these letters he assumed that William would agree that it was undesirable that James's enemies should be allowed to congregate so near to the English coast; he also expressed himself aware that the matter was not in William's control, and he merely requested him to use his influence with the States-General to prevent the abuse of the right of asylum.

Towards the end of July, however, trouble commenced in a disagreement between the King and the Prince regarding the appointment of a commander to the six British regiments which were in the pay of the States-General. The existence of these regiments was an anomaly, and their status was not accurately defined. They dated from Elizabethan

[1] Dalrymple (V, 29), however, states that in Albeville's letters in the French archives there is evidence that he acted in the Dutch interest against his master.

times and derived from the English volunteers (among whom was Sir Philip Sidney) who had assisted the Dutch in their revolt against Spain. Only one attempt had been made to bring the regiments into direct contact with the English crown; this was early in 1678, when the English and Dutch were in league against France, and a proposal had then been made that the King of England should be empowered to recall them to England if in any crisis he had need of them. This proposal was the subject of correspondence between Charles and William, but no agreement had been reached, and certainly no such agreement had been ratified by the States-General. At the time of Monmouth's rebellion the regiments had been sent over at James's request, but this acquiescence was a free act of assistance and in no sense the acknowledgement of a right. Individually the officers and men remained English or Scottish subjects; collectively the King of England had no control over the regiments, but by courtesy he had been allowed to nominate an officer to command them, and hitherto there had been no conflict over the appointment.[1] The gallant Lord Ossory, Ormonde's eldest son, had held the post at the time of his death in 1680, and subsequently Henry Sidney had been in command, to the entire satisfaction of William and the States-General.

James had recalled Sidney in March 1685, and for eighteen months he had failed to nominate a successor. The motive for the delay must be a matter of surmise, but we may suspect that James's intention from the first was to put in a Catholic, but that he hesitated to take such a step until he considered himself sufficiently secure at home. On July 23, 1686, he at last wrote to William saying that he had long been unable to find a man of the necessary qualifications, but that he had now decided on Francis Taafe, Earl of Carlingford.

> 'Tis the Earl of Carlingford I recommend to you, . . . who so soon as you let me know that you approve of him, shall prepare himself to go over to you to receive his orders. . . .

The wording of this letter is significant in view of what subsequently occurred, for James at this stage made no claim to do more than to recommend, and by implication he admitted William's right to object to the appointment.

To William the recommendation was extremely embarrassing: the chief object of his policy was to avoid giving any sort of offence to

[1] In 1680–81 after the death of Ossory there was a prolonged discussion between Charles and William about his successor; Charles first suggested the Earl of Dumbarton, but William objected that he was a Catholic, and Charles withdrew the nomination.

James, but commands in the Dutch army were given by the Captain-General, and the appointment of a Catholic would seriously injure him with his own people.

> There is nothing in the world [he wrote to Bentinck] I desire more than to give satisfaction to His Majesty in everything that depends upon me. But as the Earl is a Catholic, it would hurt me extremely in this country if I gave the command of these six regiments to a person of that religion.

He added that in the previous reign the recommendation of the Catholic Earl of Dumbarton had been withdrawn at his instance, and he asked Bentinck (who was then in England) to make a verbal representation to King James so as to avoid the apparent disrespect of a refusal by letter. James replied by Sunderland in uncompromising terms, saying that Dumbarton's name had been withdrawn because of the agitation at the time of the Popish Plot and that his case could not be considered a precedent, that James had adopted the principle of employing competent Catholics, and that "he cannot but desire that my Lord Carlingford may command these regiments and thinks the alterations of times and persons ought to be considered". To this letter William replied on September 2 with a polite but stubborn refusal.

> It would not be decent [he wrote] and I have too much respect for His Majesty to enter further into reasonings on that matter, and therefore I have only to beg you will humbly intreat His Majesty on my part to have the goodness not to insist upon this affair.

James was in a quandary, and he took no further direct action until the winter of 1687–8. He would have liked to recall the troops, but his military expenditure had increased to such an extent that he could not afford to support the additional burden of these regiments. In the summer of 1687 he conceived the plan of persuading Louis to assist him in a project, to which the French King would have no general objection, to deprive William of part of his army. But six months passed and many letters were exchanged before agreement could be reached regarding the form which Louis's assistance should take. The simplest plan, and that which first commended itself to James, was that Louis should entertain the regiments on conditions similar to those under which they had been entertained by the States-General; but to this plan there were two insuperable objections: pay was higher in the English than in the French Army, and Louis could not treat foreign troops better than his own men; and, moreover, most of the men were Protestants, and since the Revocation of the Edict of Nantes Protestants could not live in France. Eventually Louis undertook to furnish the pay of 2000 men to be stationed in England, provided that every one of them had been taken from the regiments in Holland. Then in January 1688 James formally demanded from the States the return of the regiments. This demand was (according to Barrillon) discouraged by the moderate Catholics, notably Powis and Arundel of Wardour, on the grounds that it would create a rupture with the States-General and with William, and that it would cause, to such Tories as were still loyal, apprehension that the increase in the royal army was a menace to the Church of England. The States-General rejected James's demand as *ultra vires*, and he forthwith issued a proclamation commanding every one of his subjects who was serving in Holland to return to his native country. There was sufficient response to this proclamation to enable him to form six regiments, and those who returned were (naturally enough) "the Catholics and those who are not entirely won over by the Prince or Orange". They were the men of whom alone he had intended to make use when the negotiations with Louis commenced, but though he succeeded in getting much of his own way, it was at the price of any good will which the Dutch still retained for him, while William still kept the men who were most devoted to him. On July 16, 1688, Barrillon reported to Louis that he had made over to Godolphin 93,440 *livres tournois* as the first two months' pay of the three new regiments and had promised a similar payment after each succeeding two months. Thus a final settlement of the question was arrived at almost exactly two years after James had opened it.

In this controversy the States-General was involved equally with William. Simultaneously James was engaged in a second controversy which concerned William personally as husband of the heir-presumptive. From the beginning of the reign responsible English Catholics had realised that James's successor would almost certainly be a Protestant, and that in that case there would inevitably be an anti-Catholic reaction in which everything that James had gained would certainly be lost, and in all probability the Catholics would be in a worse position than they had been when James came to the throne. These moderate Catholics had no less than James the cause of their Church at heart, but they saw farther than he did. They had no vision of an England predominantly Catholic; they knew that, even if by a most unlikely event a succession of Catholic kings could keep the administration in Catholic hands, the results must be a revolution; and they were convinced that the policy best calculated for their ultimate benefit was to make no greater demands than the most humane and enlightened Protestants (such as Halifax and William himself) were ready to grant them, and to prove to the nation by consistent quiet behaviour over a period of years that it was possible for a good Catholic to be a good citizen. James's view of the matter was in accordance with his political principles; he entirely underrated the strength of English Protestantism, and believed that a succession of English kings pledged to continue his own policy would in the long run produce a Catholic England.

It was not until he had been on the throne for nearly two years that James realised that any concessions he could secure for the Catholics might come to an end with his life and be reversed by his successor. In November 1686 he sent to The Hague his Quaker friend, William Penn, on a special mission; this mission was to endeavour to persuade William and Mary to declare publicly in favour of the repeal of the penal laws and the Test Act. Burnet, who was then at The Hague and had conversations with Penn, alleges that, as the price of William's acquiescence, James offered to join the coalition against France. If Burnet's statement is accurate, the bait was tempting, but William, apart from his own convictions, was deterred from accepting it by the knowledge that he would by such a declaration forfeit all claim to the leadership of the English Protestants; he therefore replied that he

> readily consented to a toleration of popery, as well as of the dissenters, provided it were proposed and passed in Parliament, and he promised his assistance, if there were need of it to get it passed—but he looked on the tests as such a real security, and indeed the only one, where the King was of another religion, [and] he would join in no counsels with those that intended to repeal those laws that enacted them.

After the First Declaraction of Indulgence, Albeville was instructed to commend the royal policy to William and to endeavour to gain his approval and support; he was to argue that the Test Act was a restraint on the royal prerogative and that its repeal would be to the ultimate advantage of William and Princess Mary; he was to say that James had been led to favour the repeal of the penal laws by seeing what benefits the United Provinces had gained by religious toleration; he was also to express his master's abhorrence of Louis's religious policy. William had spoken freely to Penn, as to a private friend of his father-in-law, but he was embarrassed by being approached officially by King James's ambassador, and for some time he avoided giving a positive answer. When, however, he found the ambassador persistent he said

> that he would never consent to the repeal of those laws which had been enacted for the support and safety of the Protestant religion

> and that his conscience would not let him consent, even if by doing so he might gain not only the kingdom of England but the empire of the world.

Bonrepaus, who furnishes this uncompromising statement, adds that James was more incensed against William than he had ever been before.

The special mission of Dykvelt to England from February to June 1687 was of paramount importance in the history of the Revolution, for though he was nominally the envoy of the States-General, he was, as James was aware, closely in William's confidence, he carried instructions from the Prince (in which Burnet had had a hand), and he was the means of establishing William's position as head of the opposition to James's religious policy and of concentrating the hopes of that opposition upon the ultimate succession of William to the throne. William's instructions to Dykvelt were:

> to expostulate decently but firmly with the King upon the methods he was pursuing both at home and abroad, . . . to assure all the Church party that the Prince would ever be firm to the Church of England and to all our national interests, . . . to assure them [the protestant dissenters] of a full toleration, and likewise of a comprehension, if possible, whensoever the Crown should devolve on the Princess, . . . and to try all sorts of people and to remove the ill impressions that had been given them of the Prince.

To the Catholics only Dykvelt brought no message.

This is surely a unique document: never before or since has an envoy been accredited both to the King and to the opponents of his policy.[1] It would be a grave mistake, however, to exaggerate the scope of William's intentions at this time and to believe that Dykvelt was to work for a usurpation already planned;[2] William's immediate object was to contrast his own view of the religious situation with that of his father-in-law so as to gain popularity with the English people; his ultimate object was to prevent King James from tampering with the succession, as it was rumoured he intended to do, and to secure in due course Princess Mary's peaceful succession to the throne; and, it may be added, the pleas on which William demanded the suffrage of the English people were not adopted for immediate purposes, but were based on his sincere attachment to the principles which he professed.

[1] Dykvelt's instructions bear, however, a distant resemblance to many given by Louis to his ambassadors under which they were to bring pressure on Charles and James by encouraging Parliament to make trouble for them.

[2] Even the hot-headed Mordaunt, who early in 1686 proposed to William that he should make a descent on England, did not contemplate James's expulsion, but only a compulsion on him to rule by law.

Dykvelt returned to The Hague in June 1687 bearing letters to William from prominent men of all shades of political opinion—from Halifax, Danby, Nottingham, Compton, Admiral Herbert and John Churchill; it may be noted that of these Churchill alone was in James's employ, and that he wrote rather on Princess Anne's than on his own behalf. The letters are in general terms, and are merely expressions of regard and devotion to William; cumulatively, however, they imply something more than mere compliment, an acknowledgement of William's leadership, which at that time could only mean leadership of the opposition to James's policy, and possibly a hint of confidence that when William came to the throne in right of his wife he would redress the nation's wrongs and revert to strict constitutional practice. Nothing is said of immediate measures to be taken, still less can it be inferred from any one of the letters that the employment of force is in the writer's mind.

Upon James Dykvelt made not the slightest impression. At the final audience before his return to Holland the King showed himself still convinced of the justice and expediency of his policy and unshaken in his determination to continue it: William should not, he said, object to the arbitrary nature of the Scottish Declaration of Indulgence or to favour given to the Catholics, for both would ultimately benefit him as successor, the first as an assertion of the prerogative, the second as confirming in their loyalty a body consistent in their support of the throne; the Test had been invented to destroy hereditary right, and every Englishman who subscribed to it swore that Catholicism was idolatry and could not therefore without absurdity be a loyal subject to a Catholic king; if he had power to suspend the penal laws, it was only just that he should provide against their re-enactment after his death;

> he was aware of the rumours about the succession, but they had no foundation in fact but were invented by the factions in order to alarm the heirs; he was incapable of intention to interrupt the succession, such an intention would have been contrary to justice and to the affection he bore to his children, especially to the Princess of Orange. But neither she nor the Prince could oppose his unalterable plans without displeasing him; their duty was to deserve a continuance of his good will by an entire submission to his judgement.

Dykvelt replied that the Protestants were alarmed at the power which the repeal of the Acts would put into the King's hands: he could give the administration over entirely to the Catholics, he could create Catholic peers and swamp the House of Lords, and the Catholics, in their new ascendancy, would oppose the succession of a Protestant. He added that these fears were justified by the notorious Catholic maxims regarding royal authority, by the example recently given in France, by the existence of a large standing army and by his own action in arrogating to himself the right to suspend laws which Parliament alone could repeal. He told the King that his only means of regaining the confidence of his subjects was the abandonment of the repeal of the Test Act and, if indeed it was not already too late, the dismissal of his violent Catholic counsellors. Dykvelt further suggested that the only result of an agreement between William and James on the justice of the Catholic claims would be a revolution. James retorted that he had been talking to the extreme Whigs and had learnt his politics from them, and Dykvelt replied that he had had conversation with prominent men of all parties, but that he had formed no attachments prejudicial to James's interests.

Into the controversy between James and William there intruded in the autumn of 1687 a Scottish Whig, James Stewart,[1] a refugee at The Hague; he was either a sincere enthusiast for the principles of the Declaration of Indulgence or more probably saw an opportunity by a counterfeit enthusiasm to secure a pardon from King James. He appears to have been a man of good education and address, and he had sufficient ability to get himself made Lord Advocate in Scotland after the Revolution. Stewart made friends with Grand-Pensionary Fagel and wrote several letters urging him to use his influence with William to persuade him to accept his father-in-law's religious policy. It is not clear whether Stewart was acting in this matter on his own responsibility or as the agent of the English Court; but his letters were shown to William, who saw that they provided him with an excellent opportunity both of publicly defining his attitude to the religious question in England and of refuting a charge, which the Jesuit Cabal at Whitehall had been sedulously propagating, that his intention on the succession of Princess Mary was to extirpate the English Catholics. This charge had no repercussions in England, for the English people were so incensed against the Catholics that they did not mind what happened to them, but it was calculated to drive a wedge between William and the Catholic Powers of Europe. At William's instigation, Fagel replied to Stewart in January 1688; he stated at some length that William was personally in favour of the Dutch system, under which Catholics enjoyed freedom of worship but were not admitted to office, but that he had no intention of imposing this system on the English people, who must settle the

[1] Burnet says that Stewart had been disbarred by the Scottish Test Act of 1681 because he refused to renounce the Covenant.

question themselves through their representatives in Parliament. Fagel's letter was a carefully written document, and the English translation of it which Burnet made was widely circulated. James was so ill-advised as to give it additional publicity by publishing, under the name of Parlimentum Pacificum, a reply prepared by some of the Catholic clergy,[1] which alleged that the letter was a forgery or, alternatively, that Fagel had not correctly represented William's opinions: a ridiculous allegation, for James had already twice—through Penn and through Van Citters—privately sounded William and learned those opinions; but it was not possible for James to conceive that an opinion different from his own could be honestly held or could prove impervious to persistent contradiction. Fagel was very angry that his letter should not have been accepted as genuine, and that he should have been accused of mendacity; he told Albeville that not only did the letter represent the views of Their Mightinesses, but that it had been published by their command. This statement was also published and circulated.

In the course of these proceedings the Dutch people naturally began to take an interest in the religious controversy in England; they were under fewer restrictions than the English people and they published their opinions freely. James had always regarded the Dutch as "insolent republicans"; he forgot that he had himself encouraged them to take this interest in the internal affairs of England, and was incensed against them. The Imperial ambassador, in a long letter written at the end of January 1688, reviewed the various questions on which the English Court and the States-General were at variance: some of these, such as the claim of the English to Bantam, were old disputes revived; the chief bone of contention was that the Prince of Orange, the States-General and the Dutch people were taking

> an interest without precedent in the government of England and especially in the religious question, countering the King of England at every point, and speaking, writing, printing and generally being more active than the English themselves; all this (he adds) is very distasteful to the King, who is very sensitive and proud, at a time when the Queen is so bravely supporting the fatigue of pregnancy and is to bear a prince who will confound all the heirs-presumptive.

Another cause of conflict mentioned by the Imperial ambassador in the same letter was the protection afforded in Holland to Dr. Gilbert

[1] Hoffmann, the Imperial ambassador, says "some of the bishops", but the Anglican bishops were all on William's side in the controversy—except men like Crewe and Cartwright, who were incapable of sustaining such a correspondence. Possibly he means Leybourne, the vicar Apostolic, and the vicars-general.

Burnet. It is a remarkable fact that after the trials which immediately followed Monmouth's rebellion, James, with only two exceptions—those of Compton and Burnet—showed none of that vindictive spirit against his personal enemies which was so marked a feature of his character both before and after his reign. The probable explanation is that he was so certain in his own mind that he would succeed in making himself an absolute king, and so contemptuous of the efforts of those who tried to oppose him, that he could well afford to postpone retribution until he could deal with all his enemies at once. It may be added that he preserved this reputation for implacability which he had gained early in life, so that those who were dissatisfied with his methods were very careful not to give him opportunities for action against them; they were discreet in the expression of their dissatisfaction and circumspect in the company they kept.

Dr. Burnet had in the last reign been for a long period *persona grata* at Court, and he was so intimate both with the King and James that he was able without giving offence to expostulate with them about the irregularity of their private lives. He was of a singularly open, honest and generous nature, and his notorious lack of discretion was a natural concomitant of these virtues. He was famous as a preacher, and more than a little vain of his popularity with his audiences.[1] His humanity was shown at the time of the Popish Plot, when he was almost alone in protesting against the persecution of the Catholics. In 1684 he incurred Charles's displeasure; he was deprived of his appointments and was permitted to go abroad. He visited Paris, Rome, Geneva, Strasburg, Frankfort, Heidelberg and Utrecht, and in 1686 he accepted an invitation from William to visit him at The Hague, and there he remained until he sailed for England with William's expedition in 1688. Burnet was a man who could never be idle; he had already gained a great reputation by the publication in 1679 and 1681 of the first two volumes of his *History of the Reformation*, and he was engaged on his most famous work, the *History of My Own Times*. He also found time to write tracts on the political and religious situation in England and to translate French tracts on the same subject into English. By the beginning of 1687 this activity had become so well known to King James that he marked him down as a personal enemy, and, in the true dictator spirit,

[1] Johnson in his *Life of Thomas Sprat*, Bishop of Rochester, another famous preacher, thus contrasts his behaviour in the pulpit with that of Burnet: "When Burnet preached part of his congregation hummed so loudly and so long that he sat down to enjoy it and wiped his face with his handkerchief. When Sprat preached he likewise was honoured with the like animating hum, but he stretched out his hand to the congregation and cried, 'Peace, peace! I pray you peace'."

he yearned to get him into his power. In the course of the year Burnet added to his offences by publishing an account of his continental travels, in which he contrasted the misery of life in Catholic countries with the conditions prevailing in Holland and England.

Among the instructions of Albeville when he took over the Embassy at The Hague in January 1687 was a demand for the dismissal of Burnet from William's household. William complied with this demand, and, if we are to accept Burnet's own statement, he never saw the Prince again until a few days before they both sailed for England. James, however, suspected that Burnet was in regular communication with Bentinck, and that through him he kept in touch with William. James also at the same time demanded that Burnet should be extradited to England, or alternatively to Scotland, to stand his trial for high treason. This was a matter not in William's hands, and James found the States-General unexpectedly stubborn: they refused the demand for extradition on the general ground that Burnet was a political refugee, and also because he had further protected himself by adopting Dutch nationality; but they offered James facilities for having him tried in Holland, an offer which was naturally not accepted. There were two separate indictments: in Scotland and in England. The Scottish indictment charged him with communication with Argyll in 1681 and in 1687; it was embodied in "Criminal Letters" issued against him on April 19, 1687, and adjudged outlawry against him unless he surrendered before June 27. The second indictment was on his reply to the charge in Edinburgh, and was issued in London in June 1687 with citation for August 9; in this he was charged with having threatened to publish the secret history of the previous twenty years and with having transferred his allegiance from the King of England.

Burnet was very apprehensive that after his outlawry in Scotland he would be either forcibly removed or assassinated, and just before the outlawry took effect he "invited all his friends to dinner, and after that was over took his solemn leave of them, resolving to converse no more with them". Louis regarded Burnet's behaviour as an affront to monarchy, and he was prepared to co-operate in bringing him to the rack and the scaffold. At the end of the year he made it known that he would provide not only an asylum in France for anyone who came into conflict with the Dutch police in an attempt to kidnap Burnet, but also active assistance in the attempt.[1] It seems probable, however, that the publicity

[1] "Jai aussi ordonné . . . que qui que soit qui entreprenne de l'enlever en Hollande trouvera une retraite assurée et une entière protection dans mes êtates, mais aussi tout assistance qu'il pourra désirer pour faire conduire sûrement ce scelerat en Angleterre."

given to the intention roused the vigilance of the Dutch authorities, for no attempt appears to have been made. It is curious that James should have taken this refusal on the part of the States-General so much to heart—in all his conversations with the Dutch ambassador he mentioned it as a major grievance, and in February 1688 he is said to have stated that it would have furnished a pretext, if he had wanted one, for declaring war on the Dutch. To him, no doubt, the whole affair was an act of insolence and defiance by one of his own subjects, an experience to which he was not up to then accustomed; and his inability to punish the offender reduced him to a condition of impotent rage.

Enough has been said to show that in the spring of 1688 James was exasperated both against the States-General and also personally against William. As early as March 1687 Bonrepaus had written that James could hardly conceal his hatred and jealousy of the Prince of Orange, and subsequent events served to increase his irritation. Van Citters, the Dutch ambassador, found himself in an impossible position: if he kept away from Court it was a crime, if he appeared he was insulted; if he attempted to justify the States-General James lost his temper, if he kept silence he was held to have acknowledged their misdeeds.

In the spring of 1688 James might have boasted that he had accomplished almost everything that had been in his mind at his accession. Since the prorogation of Parliament in November 1685 he had for two and a half years enjoyed the same unrestricted power as his father had enjoyed between 1629 and 1640, and he had used that power unreservedly in the interests of the Roman Catholic religion and of its adherents. Catholics were able to worship in public (though in some apprehension of the mob) and were free from all disabilities under the penal laws; their priests were not only not proscribed, but were openly organised under four vicars-general; there were Catholics in every sort of public position in numbers far in excess of what they would have claimed under a general toleration—the Lord Privy Seal and five other members of the Privy Council, two Commissioners of the Treasury and a large proportion of the Lords Lieutenant, Deputy Lieutenants, Sheriffs, Justices of the Peace, members of corporations and revenue officers; there had as yet, indeed, been no attempt to put Catholics into livings or positions of dignity belonging directly to the Church of England, but at Oxford three Heads of Houses and a number of Fellows were Catholics, and the vicar of Putney had been allowed to retain his living after he had declared himself a Catholic. In one matter only had James been disappointed: at the commencement of his reign he had anticipated that converts would pour into the Church of Rome as soon as it was realised that Catholics were under no disability in public employment; but as a matter of fact conversions had been very few; two Earls—Salisbury and James's old friend Peterborough[1]—went over, but they were both so contemptible that their conversion served rather to deter others than to encourage them to follow. This absence of converts was, indeed, of supreme importance; it was the measure of James's real failure in spite of his apparent success. This success was entirely fallacious; by a singular paradox he had accomplished nothing; the structure he had raised had no foundations, and must inevitably have fallen in the course of a very few years if events had not hastened its destruction. James had not only failed to carry the people with him, but had antagonised them at every step; the politically conscious among them (and he had enormously spread political consciousness) were almost to a man against him, and there were very few to say that his system of government was superior to that which it had replaced. James, though he did not know it and was never to acknowledge it, was politically bankrupt.

A very remarkable series of letters was addressed to William of Orange from the commencement of the year 1687 down to the eve of the Revolution by opponents of James's policy. In these letters there is nothing which to a modern eye would appear treasonable—in particular there is not a vestige of a hint in any one of them that William's interest in England went beyond his legitimate desire that, when by right of his wife he should in due course have a direct part in the government, the kingdom should be in internal peace and predominantly Protestant. But no doubt the writers put no trust in the royal courts and feared that words might be twisted to support charges of treason, for there is evidence that the letters were not sent by the ordinary post but by "good conveyance"—that is to say, secretly by the hand of someone making the journey to Holland. The most striking, and the longest, of these letters are from the Earls of Halifax and Nottingham, and from them it is easy to infer the reasons which deterred those eminent and clear-sighted noblemen from taking an active part in the Revolution. For the burden of their story is that James's policy, which they abhor no less than the most violent revolutionary, is inevitably doomed to failure; that the farther the King advances along the road he has determined to take, the greater his difficulties become; that what appear at first sight to be successes are in truth disasters; and that misgivings as to the situation are producing divisions among James's chief advisers;

[1] The sincerity of Peterborough's conversion is illustrated by the following anecdote. "When the churchwardens of St. Margaret's Westminster asked his lordship if they might dispose of his pew in the church, 'No, no,' said he, 'one doth not know what may happen'."

so that all that is needed is to wait in patience for the inevitable *débâcle*; any form of violent action is likely only to heal these divisions and to unite the Court against the aggressors.

> The men at the helm are certainly divided amongst themselves, which will produce great effects if men will let it work and not prevent [*sc.* anticipate] the advantages that may be expected by being too unquiet or doing things out of season; the great thing to be done now is to do nothing but wait for the good consequences of their divisions and mistakes. Unseasonable stirrings or anything that looketh like the Protestants being the aggressors will tend to unite them, and by that means will be a disappointment to those hopes which otherwise can hardly fail. Nothing therefore in the present conjuncture can be more dangerous than unskilful agitators, warm men who would be active at a wrong time and want patience to keep their zeal from running away with them.

Thus wrote Halifax in April 1688; three months later Nottingham wrote:

> The birth of the Prince of Wales and the designs of a further prosecution of the bishops, and of new modelling the army and calling of a parliament are matters that afford various reflections. But I cannot apprehend from them such ill consequences to our religion or the just interests of Your Highness that a little time will not effectively remedy, nor can I imagine that the Papists are able to make any further considerable progress.

The Countess of Sunderland and the Earl of Shrewsbury were no less definite in their expressions of confidence in the future, though the latter, at any rate, saw salvation in revolution.

The crux of the whole matter was James's fixed determination, which he never abandoned until the night of his first flight, to have a Parliament which would repeal the Test Act and the penal laws. He saw clearly enough that it was hopeless to attempt to overrule the second Test Act of 1678 and to get Catholics into Parliament; for not only would the Electorate, however manipulated, have declined to elect them, but every Catholic candidate would have required a body of troops to protect him from the mob. He hoped, indeed, that the Protestant Dissenters might be prevailed on to help him, but their numbers were very small in comparison with the Churchmen, and even if the Catholics voted with them, their candidates would have small chance of election. Moreover, the Dissenters were not a united body, few of them had accepted the Declaration of Indulgence without misgivings, and any candidate who declared in advance that he was in favour of concessions to the Catholics would have had no support from his own people.

> It may reasonably be expected [wrote Nottingham] that such dissenters as shall be chosen will not in their present circumstances concur to the repeal of so much as the penal laws; for this has been their opinion in former parliaments, in which they would never give that ease to the Papists which they desired for themselves, and to do it now might encourage the Papists to greater attempts, and the dissenters would never recover the reproach of having been factors for popery,

and the consequence to themselves would be that they would not have "such reason to expect a like indulgence in other times".

Halifax had never the least doubt that James would not be able either to allow his first Parliament to meet again for business or, when that Parliament was dissolved, to have a second Parliament elected; William appears to have thought there might be a new Parliament, and Halifax as time went on was able to boast the superiority of his own foresight. In the first place, the converts to Romanism were very few, and the attempts to make converts and to persuade members of Parliament to change their views had had the effect of hardening the rest in their opposition,

> though there appeareth the utmost vigour to pursue the design which hath been so long laid, there seemeth to be no less firmness in the nation and aversion to change;

and again:

> Besides the considerations of conscience and the public interest it is grown into a point of honour universally received by the nation not to change their opinion, which will make all attempts to the contrary very ineffectual.

But the second objection to calling Parliament was still stronger: that there was no likelihood that they would confine their discussions to the subjects on which they had been called together to legislate, and that in addition to the negative danger of a disappointment to the royal hopes there was a danger, amounting almost to a certainty, that other questions would be raised which James was averse to submitting to public discussion:

> A Parliament can never be an indifferent thing, and therefore it is a very weak argument to say that it will be tried and if it doth

> not comply it shall be dissolved. Things of this kind are not so handled: the consequences may be too great to make the experiment without better grounds to expect success than at present appear,

and Nottingham, with perhaps less art, expresses the same meaning:

> And yet if this repeal of the penal laws would be granted, there are so many other things that will be taken into consideration by a Parliament, and of a nature so contrary to the present interest and humour of the Papist, that it will be next to impossible that there should be time to bring such a bill to perfection how zealously soever it may be prosecuted in the House of Commons or otherwise encouraged.

We may form a safe conjecture of the apprehension with which the assembly of Parliament was viewed by those about the King after Rochester was dismissed: Sunderland, Jeffreys, the Catholic lords, the judges. Not one of them was safe from impeachment; Sunderland and Jeffreys for having, among other things, given unconstitutional advice to the King and for having sat on the Ecclesiastical Commission, the judges for their verdict in the case of Godden *v.* Hales, and the Catholic lords for having acted on that verdict and continued in office without taking the oaths. Petre was in a somewhat different position; in common with the rest of the Roman priesthood, he was liable to the death penalty for breach of the penal laws, but as long as the magistrates failed to put those laws into operation Parliament could only send the King futile addresses asking that the abeyance of the laws should be terminated; in June 1687, however, Petre was sworn of the Privy Council, and three months later he could have been impeached for not having taken the oaths and made a declaration against transubstantiation. It is not surprising, therefore, that James got small encouragement from his court in his endeavours to have a Parliament.

Meanwhile all this talk of a Parliament, whose election was always vaguely promised but never accomplished, was very harmful to the King's party throughout the country. The opposition were well aware that (except by armed rebellion) it was only through Parliament that the King's policy could be defeated; they were confident that it would be impossible for Sunderland to pack a Parliament as he had done in 1685 —he himself admitted that an election was impracticable until more preparations had been made; to the moderate men who desired little more than to live at ease it became evident that Parliament alone could relieve the political tension, and as time went on the demand for a

Parliament was merged in the other aspirations of the opposition and swelled its numbers, so that James's prospects of getting support in a Parliament steadily decreased.

Confirmation of the judgement of William's correspondents on the discontents of the English people and on the insecurity of James's position is given by the despatches of the foreign envoys. All the Catholic envoys approved of James's aspirations, but all, except Barrillon, persistently decried his policy. Barrillon's letters are not on the whole of great value for this purpose; he lived too much at Court to see what was going on outside, and the best that can be said of him is that he was less blind to the consequences of James's policy than was James himself. But even Barrillon had his moments of insight: in the spring of 1686 he wrote:

> Discontent is great and general. . . . It is openly said that the people will not suffer the subversion of their laws and their religion.

The Tuscan envoy, Terriesi, was far more apprehensive. Four months after Monmouth's execution he wrote that it was already a matter of common talk that there would be a great revolution on account of the way in which the King was conducting the government. In May 1686 he enlarged on the same theme: he said that all the English except the few who are hoping for it were in daily apprehension of a great rebellion; that the chief grievances were the arbitrary manner in which the laws of the kingdom were over-ridden, the standing army and the King's subservience to France both in temporal and spiritual matters (the envoy, being a Catholic, avoids direct mention of the religious grievance); fortunately the malcontents are as yet without a leader, but on the other hand James has no one near him whose counsel is valuable, for the better men have been alienated or have been dismissed with little regard to their dignity. Finally the envoy exclaims, "God preserve the King when he realises that his troops will not be faithful to him, for they are English".

Bonrepaus in July 1687 informed his chief, Seignelay, that the Protestants who were closest to the throne—Sunderland, Churchill and Godolphin—were all keeping on good terms with William by correspondence with a view to securing their future in case of James's death, "the Chancellor (Jeffreys), a very violent man, is the only one who is not involved in intrigue"; and he added:

> The King of England is very unfortunate in having noone near him on whom he can rely, but he would be still more unfortunate if he saw all that the others see.

At the end of September he wrote:

> The King of England is very cheerful and he believes that he is succeeding in all his projects. His ministers do not disabuse him, but I have discovered that Lord Sunderland is not without misgivings. He does not dare to offer direct opposition to the zeal with which the King labours for the repeal of the Test Act but he tries to divert him from this aim by suggesting other schemes.

The influence of Bonrepaus when he was in England appears to have induced in Barrillon a mood of pessimism in which he realised the dangers of James's situation; from this mood he recovered when Bonrepaus returned to France, and during the spring and summer of 1688 he was as confident as James himself that the royal policy would succeed and the opposition be crushed. Towards the end of September 1687 Barrillon wrote two long letters to Louis. In the first he said frankly that the whole country was seething with discontent and that private prudential considerations alone prevented the precipitation of a general rising:

> There is a great deal of general excitement and there is considerable activity among the opposition groups in London; but the English are not easily moved to rebellion and they keep themselves within legal bounds so as not to run the risk of losing their property. This fear prevails in general over every other consideration in this country and their zeal for religion is not violent enough to lead them into enterprises which would make them liable to legal penalties. Hence opposition to the designs of the court expresses itself only in talk and in anonymous publications.

But he added if Parliament were summoned a means of expression would be presented to the malcontents:

> Every member can say freely and without fear of punishment all that is in his mind and he can vote for or against any proposal that is made.

Three days later he wrote that what might possibly happen was that James might summon a Parliament and that, if he found that they were unwilling to repeal the penal laws and the Test Act, he would repeal them by decree; in such a case he would need the support of his friends both at home and abroad, for he would encounter an opposition little different from open rebellion. He added that William was the true leader of the opposition and that everyone felt great bitterness at the size of the army and regretted that Parliament had, by granting the revenues for life, given away the only means of reducing it; and he concluded ominously, "It is difficult to see what will happen".

CHAPTER IV

SCOTLAND AND IRELAND

THE history of James's dealings with Scotland during the first year of his reign is largely concerned with the contest for power among the King's chief subjects. At the time of the accession the Duke of Queensberry was Lord High Treasurer and the Earl of Perth, Chancellor, in London the Earl of Moray and Perth's brother, Lundin, were joint Secretaries of State. These four men held the reins of power; they had seven months previously succeeded in ousting the Earl of Aberdeen from the Chancellorship, and still preserved the close alliance which had been formed to attain that end. Queensberry was an ally of Rochester, with whom he was connected by marriage,[1] and his character and his career during the reign were in some degree similar to those of Rochester; like Rochester, he was ready to go to any lengths in support of the royal prerogative, but his Protestantism was firm and not subject to change from motives of personal interest. Like Rochester, also, he held at the time of the accession James's chief confidence in the affairs of his country. Of Perth at this time little is known except that he was an unscrupulous politician and a violent persecutor of the Covenanters. Moray appears to have been respectable, and his loyalty to Queensberry when Queensberry's fortunes were declining does him credit.

Lundin is far the most important of the four in a biography of King James, on account of the important part he played, as Earl of Melfort, in James's life after the Revolution. At the accession Lundin was at the commencement of his career, but he was already revealing those characteristics which account for James's disastrous attachment to him and which made him one of the most unpopular men of his time. As late as October 1687 Barrillon described Melfort as Sunderland's tool,[2] and this description is probably true, for it was in the nature of Melfort to secure his own advancement by attaching himself to the most influential man in the Court; there are great similarities in the character and method of the two men, but it may be doubted if Melfort learned his statecraft from Sunderland. In October 1683, before Sunderland had acquired his ascendancy in James's counsels, Lundin wrote to Queensberry, "I will sound the Duke, and if I find it is his opinion I shall proceed"—an anticipation of Sunderland's technique in dealing with James. This

[1] The connection was not very close: Queensberry's son Lord Drumlanrig had married Lady Rochester's niece.

[2] "Milord Melfort qui a été menagé par Milord Sunderland."

technique was invariably employed by Melfort, and Avaux, the French ambassador with James in Ireland, found it his chief obstacle in getting James to listen to him. Like Sunderland, Melfort had a passion for power, and was quite shameless in his intrigues against his colleagues; both men were hard workers: no lazy man could have written the long letters Lundin wrote to Queensberry in the years 1682–85, or the still longer letters from Rome to Queen Mary Beatrice in 1689 and 1690.[1] But with these resemblances there was a fundamental difference: Sunderland was an extremely able man, while Melfort's incompetence was a byword. He was very plausible, and he had the ability to achieve high office and to keep himself in it, but no capacity whatever for administration. Another exasperating characteristic was his perfect self-complacency: on July 9, 1685, Moray wrote to Queensberry, "Melfort thinks he can err in nothing", and in July 1689 Avaux reports that, after Melfort had committed every possible blunder in Ireland and had organised nothing, he told Lady Tyrconnel "that if an angel had come down from heaven he could have done no better than he had done for the King his master".

Moray was for a time deceived by Lundin; at the time of Lundin's appointment as joint-Secretary of State he wrote to Queensberry:

> I wish him much joy, and as I know him a person loyal and firm to his friends, it will be none of my fault if we do not live well and friendly together.

Four months later, however, there were signs that Moray had begun to find him out, and early in James's reign he was to realise that he aimed not only at undermining Queensberry, but at discrediting his colleague and securing a monopoly of James's attention and favour. At the time of James's accession Moray was wholeheartedly in Queensberry's interest, Lundin expressed the most fervent loyalty to Queensberry, and these expressions were no doubt genuine at the time.

A month after the accession, Queensberry and Perth set out for London to receive James's commands on Scottish affairs. The immediate business was the assembly of the Scottish Parliament. James's experience in

[1] Avaux thought Melfort lazy, but his only evidence, except that as a result of incompetence his work was negligible, was that he saw Melfort walking with his wife at a time other men were working; but Melfort was very jealous of his handsome wife, and would not let her go out alone. No doubt he made up time when most people were at leisure. Melfort's own account (to Queensberry) is probably true: "I am confident hitherto there has been no cause to complain of my neglect, for I have been as diligent as it was possible to be, and I am sure, what ever the success may be, I shall never let want of application lose any business I have in hand. . . . I toil like a horse and have no hour my own." It would probably have been better for James if Melfort (and he himself) had been lazier.

1681 had taught him that the constitution of Scotland gave the King virtual control over both elections [1] to Parliament and legislation. The procedure was that a committee of Parliament, known as the Lords of the Articles, decided what measures should be introduced, and so tight a hold had the King, through his Commissioner, of the nomination of the Lords of the Articles that Lauderdale wrote to the King in 1669, "If they be amiss blame me for I wrote the lists and not a man was altered". The measures drafted by the Lords of the Articles were passed by Parliament almost as a matter of routine. James could therefore rely on the obsequiousness of the Scots Parliament, provided he did not openly attempt anything for the Catholic religion, and he determined that it should meet before the English Parliament, so as to set an example to the latter body, though its very lack of independence would, to a man of more subtle mind, make its decisions suspect in England. James since his accession had been as careful in Scotland as in England to do nothing to cause apprehension to good Protestants. Queensberry, as Commissioner to Parliament, carried with him back to Edinburgh a very elaborate set of instructions; the only measures proposed with regard to religion were an Act in favour of the Established Protestant religion and an Act making preaching in a conventicle or in the fields a capital offence, and imposing severe penalties for worshippers and for landlords and towns on whose land the proscribed services were held (James's toleration had suffered diminution in the previous four years). James did, however, privately instruct Queensberry "to suffer nothing to pass to the prejudice of the Roman Catholics more than was already". Parliament met on April 23, and behaved as it was expected to behave—that is to say, with complete obsequiousness; on the motion of the Duke of Hamilton, the King was granted excise for life, and all the measures he proposed were passed. On May 25 James wrote to the Secret Committee of the Privy Council suggesting that the members would be better employed in helping to stamp out Argyll's rebellion, and on June 1 to Queensberry ordering him to adjourn Parliament as soon as possible and to thank them "for their signal loyalty expressed in their humble offers to us", a reference, no doubt, to an Act (suggested by James himself) to place the lives and fortunes of all persons between sixty and sixteen at His Majesty's disposal. Two significant events

[1] In the Parliament of 1681 the Lord Advocate remarked in course of a debate that "if the burghs had liberty to choose whom they pleased to represent them, factions and disloyal persons might prevail to get themselves elected"; and a voter was actually prosecuted for having "voted against the Duke (of York) and the Court faction in the elections of the Commissioner to Fife". The certainty of the election of "loyal" members was still further increased by the Test Act of 1681.

occurred during the session of Parliament: the appointment to the Scottish Privy Council of the Earl of Dumbarton, a Catholic, without the necessity of taking the oath of supremacy—he was also appointed Inspector-General of the Forces; and the dispensations to Commissoners of Revenue who were Catholics.

The first sign of the breach which was to divide the Scottish administration into two hostile factions occurred on April 14, when Lundin, that day created Viscount Melfort, and no doubt intoxicated by his new elevation, delivered to Moray a violent diatribe against Queensberry, saying that he "carried now much higher than Duke Lauderdale did and pretended to be more absolute than ever he was".[1] Moray replied equally hotly in Queensberry's defence. Queensberry was still high in James's confidence, there was no intention during the whole of the year to remove him from his position as first Minister, and no word of a conflict between him and Perth appears to have reached the King's ears until several months later;[2] but the quarrel was so well known in Scotland that when, in June and July, the mail from London to Edinburgh was twice plundered at Alnwick it was thought that the robbery was a device of Queensberry's to get hold of Melfort's letters to Perth. There was hardly even a pretence on either side that the conflict involved any principle, it was avowedly a contest for power.

In the autumn this contest took a new colour on account of the conversion of Perth to Catholicism. Now, it has been until very recently an assumption among historians, among whom Burnet is the earliest, that the conversion of both Perth and Melfort was due to a cynical calculation of advantages and disadvantages and that it was a master-stroke in the struggle for power with Queensberry.[3] But recently there has appeared in French a book[4] which has all the external appearance of Catholic propaganda, but bases its arguments on quotations from papers at Drummond Castle, hitherto unpublished, and on other material to which sufficient notice has not been paid. Among these papers is Perth's own account of his conversion; according to the author of the book it is of a simplicity and naïvety which compel belief, and his conclusion is that Perth's conversion was "what it ought to have been, a

[1] Fountainhall, who was a neutral onlooker in the contest, supports Melfort's accusation.

[2] On May 8, James wrote to Queensberry, "You need not apprehend . . . it is anybody's power to do you ill offices with me. Nobody has gone about it, and if they had it would only have done them harm, not you."

[3] Thus Sir Charles Firth writes "Queensberry . . . was not disposed to turn Catholic himself. The two Drummonds . . . were not men to stick at such trifles. Both had abjured their creed, and had for some time been plotting to overthrow their rival."

[4] A. Joly: *Un Converti de Bossuet, James Drummond, Duc de Perth*; Lille, 1934.

purely religious matter into which politics did not enter". Perth says that when he was in London in March 1685 James gave him a copy of the famous papers on religion which Charles had left, and that they led him to the study of Bossuet's writings, that he wrestled in prayer for divine guidance, that he thought that if he became a Catholic he would not only have to give up his post as Chancellor but to go abroad and live as an exile, that he spent several weeks examining his conscience, and that when he had made up his mind he made the general confession and abjured heresy, to the great improvement of his health and spirits. There is extant a letter of resignation of the Chancellorship and of his other offices, but it is neither dated nor signed, so that it is not certain, therefore, that it was delivered to James. But in the memoirs of the famous Edinburgh doctor, Robert Sibbald, there is a passage which almost exactly corroborates the account which Perth put into writing several years after the event.

> The Earl [says Dr. Sibbald] had many times signified the aversion he had for some of the doctrines of the Church of Rome; . . . but, behold, . . he had declared himself of the Romish Faith and joined in their worship some two months before I knew it. . . . I thought there could be nothing more contrary to his interests than it was; he said he was sensible of it, and had offered with great earnestness to resign his place; but the King had commanded him upon his allegiance to continue his post.

Dr. Johnson said wisely about the almost contemporary conversion of Dryden, "That conversion will always be suspected that apparently concurs with interest", and it is not surprising that the popular verdict was unfavourable to Perth. Two circumstances made people less critical in their judgements than they might otherwise have been: the conversion was not made public until all danger that Perth would be disgraced had passed; in the inflamed atmosphere of the time none of James's friends, especially his Catholic friends, could expect impartial consideration. It is not necessary to defend Perth in other respects; he was apparently always a very religious man, but he was nevertheless an unscrupulous politician and an inhuman persecutor of the Covenanters; nor was his private life regular.

The conversion of Melfort is more open to suspicion: he was at first very angry with Perth for having gone over to Rome, and no doubt thought he had seriously compromised the fortunes of the family; he did not announce his own conversion until February 1686, four or five months after that of his brother—that is to say, when it had become clear that resignation of office would not follow conversion. On the other hand, it is interesting to find Perth writing to Bossuet and wishing that he could attain to Melfort's high standard of religious life.

In the summer of 1685 Perth's religious doubts were known only to at most one or two intimate friends, and his quarrel with Queensberry had no element of religion in it. On September 1 James wrote to Perth giving him permission to come to London to formulate his grievances against Queensberry who was already there. Barrillon wrote at the end of September that the conflict had ended in Perth's favour, but the news was premature; Barrillon added that Perth was waiting only for James's permission to declare himself a Catholic. Perth seems to have delayed his journey, for it was not until late in November that conferences began in which James tried to reconcile his chief Ministers, for it seems evident that he was impartial between Queensberry and Perth, and in spite of Perth's conversion, which was now known, if he inclined to either side it was to Queensberry's. Perth's first complaints he brushed aside as trivial, and Perth, writing to Hamilton on November 26, said that though James continued to give him kind words, he saw no results. It is probable that it was about this time that Perth had his meeting with Halifax and signified his apprehension, when, in Burnet' words:

> The Marquis answered him, he needed fear nothing, his faith would make him whole; and it proved so.

The conferences extended over several weeks and were entirely inconclusive. Queensberry had the support of Rochester and no doubt of Moray; Sunderland's name is not mentioned in the letters which Perth and Melfort wrote to the Duke of Hamilton (and which are our fullest source of information), but we may be certain that what influence he exerted was in favour of the Drummonds, for his conflict with Rochester was at that time coming to a crisis. Queensberry in his position of power could afford to be magnanimous; he went so far as to say that he loved and trusted Perth and Melfort and that he was hurt by their opposition to him. But the Drummonds, though they promised obedience to the King's commands to live at peace with Queensberry, said they could never trust him; and Perth was so unrestrained in his language (and, it may be added, so disrespectful to James in using in his presence such words about his first Minister) as to say that "Duke Queensberry was an atheist in religion, a villain in friendship, a knave in business and a traitor in his carriage to him". As late as February 2, 1686, after Queensberry and Perth had returned to Scotland, Moray wrote to Queensberry:

> It is the King's pleasure that Lord Viscount Melfort and I live well together, and be united in his service, which we have accordingly

resolved to do; but withal I told him I would not in the last abate the honour and friendship I have for Your Grace's person and family, which I must say he not only complied with, but said, whatever thoughts were entertained of him, he would still do just and equal things and give you no reasonable occasion for judging otherwise of him.

From these words we may gather that the campaign of Perth and Melfort against Queensberry had failed, and that the balance of power in the Scottish administration was maintained in the condition in which it had been the previous summer.

But this equilibrium was unstable, and it was disturbed by an unexpected incident. On January 31 there was serious anti-Catholic rioting at Edinburgh, the Countess of Perth was pelted with mud as she came from Mass at Holyrood, and on the following day the mob rescued one of the rioters who was being taken to be publicly whipped. James was highly indignant, and the Drummonds seized the opportunity of insinuating that Queensberry both as governor of Edinburgh Castle and as head of the civil government had been lax in suppressing the disturbance. On February 10, immediately after hearing accounts of the riots read by the secretaries, James wrote to Queensberry, "I will not let any suffer or be the worse for being of my persuasion", and to Perth he wrote, "As to you and all those where you are who share my beliefs I will support you and show everyone that that is my intention".[1] A fortnight later he wrote again saying that he had decided to put the Treasury into Commission (with Queensberry as a member but under Perth as first Commissioner) and to replace him as governor of Edinburgh Castle by the Catholic Duke of Gordon, "to make that town . . . civiller to the Catholics by seeing it in the hands of one of that persuasion". This letter was not in any sense a peremptory dismissal: he said that "nothing but my being satisfied upon long and mature consideration that it is absolutely necessary for the good of my service could have obliged me to do it"; that in his new posts as Commissioner of the Treasury and President of the Council Queensberry "may have the opportunity of serving me as well and as usefully as in the former station you were in"; and concludes with warm expressions of the continuance of his regard and esteem. But James, as so often during his reign, deceived himself in thinking that an officer with a sense of grievance—and Queensberry naturally regarded himself as being delivered up to his enemies—would keep his loyalty unblemished. His support of James was henceforth so lukewarm that in June 1686 he was

[1] These are not James's exact words, they are a translation of M. Joly's translation into French.

deprived of all his offices and was for the remainder of the reign in opposition.[1]

James now made preparations for the reassembly of the Scottish Parliament. He had "thrown off the mask" in England, and he proposed to do the same in Scotland. On March 4 he wrote to the Privy Council explaining his intentions: that the Catholics were no longer to be under the disabilities of the penal laws and of the Test Act of 1681, but that no relief should be given to the Covenanters. The reply of the Council was so unsatisfactory that James ordered three of them—the Duke of Hamilton, Lieutenant-General Drummond [2] and Sir George Lockhart —to attend him at Whitehall, where they arrived on April 8. They were all three zealous royalists and Protestants, and while they protested their loyalty and reverence for their sovereign, they were anxious that no injury should be done to their religion. In deference to James's wishes, they were willing to support a certain mitigation of the Catholic grievances, but they firmly held that the extreme Presbyterians should benefit equally with the Catholics in any scheme of toleration. According to Barrillon, James fought hard against any concession to the sectaries, and, if the ambassador is to be believed, he goes a long way towards showing that James was not at heart in favour of religious toleration and that he did not affect to be actuated by the principle of toleration when, as in Scotland, he felt himself strong enough to get his own way without using it as a pretext. Barrillon's words are:

> This question of giving liberty of worship to the nonconformists has been debated for several days. The King is very anxious that only the Catholics shall be granted the free exercise of their religious rites.

James also refused a demand that he should make a declaration securing the Protestant religion in its rights and privileges on the ground that it was a false religion—a position that he would hardly have taken up in the presence of a deputation of English Protestants. On the whole, the three Scots wasted their time by coming to London, for James had intended characteristically not to arrange a compromise, but to force them to adopt his point of view.

Parliament met again on April 29, 1686. The Commissioner was the

[1] Too much has, I think, been made of the refusal of Queensberry and Hamilton to turn Catholic. There is no evidence that pressure in that direction was put upon them and in any case the social ostracism which would have resulted would in itself have been a deterrent. Hatred of Catholicism was even more fanatical in Scotland than it was in England.

[2] Macaulay erroneously states that Drummond was a younger brother of Perth and Melfort; he was a rather distant cousin.

Earl of Moray, who had followed the example of Perth and Melfort and gone over to Rome.[1] In Moray's speech at the opening of Parliament the most significant passage was:

> His Majesty believes that none will wonder if he desire, by the advice and consent of this his Great Council, to give ease and security to some of his good subjects of the Roman Catholic religion, who have in all times been firm to the monarchy . . . so that His Majesty, who perfectly understands the loyal and dutiful temper and genius of Scotland, rests fully persuaded of your ready and dutiful compliance with his royal desire and inclinations. . . .

In return for acquiescence the King was ready to make certain concessions for the benefit of Scottish trade, including some measure of free trade with England and a return of the material benefits of the Cromwellian occupation of Scotland;[2] he also attempted to satisfy the House by declaring that he wanted no more money. But James achieved no success in overcoming the rooted Scottish prejudice against his religion. In the Scottish Parliament there was neither the machinery for, nor the tradition of, opposition to the Crown; members are reported to have said in private that they had been reproached with having sold their King, but that no one should be able to say of them that they had sold their God; in Parliament they were in the main content with passive resistance to James's demands. Though a contemporary observer complained that "the Parliament was like to do nothing thoroughly and so neither please God nor man", and, though the constitution did not permit an excursion into the enemy's country by protests against Catholic encroachments or by anti-Catholic legislation, this passive resistance was as effective as the more spectacular resistance in England. A Toleration Act was drafted, far milder than what James had hoped for, not touching the Test Act nor abrogating the penal

[1] There seems to be some doubt about Moray's conversion. Burnet, I, 679, and the Ellis Correspondence (I, 46–7, 57) are the authorities for it, and it is accepted by Rait (*Parliaments of Scotland*, p. 88) and the Editor of *H. M. C. Buccleuch and Queensberry*, II (p. 6); but W. L. Mathieson (*Politics and Religion in Scotland*, II, 323n.) disagrees with these authorities. Woodrow (IV, 365) states that Ramsay, Bishop of Ross, wrote to Moray telling him that "a project was already laid to turn his lordship out of his post as secretary as soon as parliament [*i.e.*, the parliament of 1685] was up and put a papist into it".

[2] W. L. Mathieson (*Politics and Religion in Scotland*, p. 324) has a very good note on Moray's speech: "James VII, like his father, was an adept in what Adam Smith calls 'the higgling of the market'. All these things were to be done, not because they were good in themselves, but because the King wanted something in return; and, that something being refused, nothing more was heard of the intended reforms . . . the Stewart kingship, when stripped of romantic illusions, was a very prosaic affair."

laws, beyond permitting Catholics to worship in their own houses, but it passed the Lords of the Articles by only eighteen votes to fourteen, and was defeated in the House by a majority of nearly two to one. A still milder Act was drafted, backed by a strong disclaimer of any intention to repeal the Test Act, but the prospects of its passing were so hopeless that James ordered a prorogation in order to avoid a second rebuff. He showed his indignation, as he had done in similar circumstances in England, by dismissing from the public service those functionaries who had opposed him; against others he instituted proceedings for high treason on very slight evidence.

James now determined to effect by his prerogative what Parliament had refused to sanction: in successive messages to the Scottish Privy Council in September and November 1686 he ordered them to protect Catholics in their worship in their own houses and to disregard the Test Act in making appointements to civil and military posts, and even to Church livings. A Declaration of Indulgence was issued on February 12, 1687, and was so badly drafted that it was necessary to issue a second Declaration on July 5 in order to correct certain misapprehensions which the first declaration had caused. These declarations were similar in scope to the English declarations, but in Scotland James was under no necessity to excuse his exercise of the prerogative, but based his action on "the unlimited authority in ecclesiastical matters which the Scottish legislature conferred on the sovereign" by the Act of Supremacy of 1669.

James did not despair of getting a Parliament together which would confirm the principles of the Declaration of Indulgence, and to that end he introduced innovations in the royal burghs; he violated their rights by nominating provosts and town-councillors, and attempted to persuade the Convention of Royal Burghs to change the qualifications of candidates for Parliament by declaring eligible non-residents and Catholics. He did in fact succeed in getting Catholics made eligible, but there was small chance of getting Catholics elected; as in England, he was hampered by the remodelling of the burghs in the previous reign, which had put them into the hands of men loyal to the Crown but hostile to the Roman Church, and he never summoned a second Parliament.

James's difficulties in what in Scotland corresponded to "closeting" —that is to say, the attempt to threaten or cajole influential men into lending their support to Catholic relief—are well illustrated by the correspondence between Melfort and William Douglas, Duke of Hamilton. Hamilton was at heart a Presbyterian, and in 1681 he had signified his dislike of the Test Oath by an ostentatious delay in taking it, but when at last he had in form adhered to the Episcopal Church,

James looked on him as one of the chief props of the Scottish throne, and he wrote to him in March 1685 a holograph letter accepting his offers of service. In the controversy of the winter of 1685–6 Hamilton took sides against Queensberry and was the recipient of confidences from Perth and Melfort. In March 1686 Melfort wrote from Whitehall that the King was depending on Hamilton to further his plans, and later in the same month he was more explicit in his demands, and asked the Duke "how he should think it consistent with the King's honour to suffer those of his opinion to be murdered or forfeited for their opinions". When, in the following month, Hamilton, together with Lieutenant-General William Drummond and Sir George Lockhart, was summoned to London, James exerted himself to persuade Hamilton to give his promise to support the projected legislation. But Hamilton would go no farther than to undertake not to be active in opposition, and he demanded time to make up his mind; James could understand no answer except a plain yes or no, and he construed this hesitation as a promise of adherence in due course.[1] In May we find Melfort telling Hamilton that the success or failure of the King's plans depended on him, for many would delay decision until they saw what he was going to do, and expostulating with him on his contention that the Presbyterians' claim to relief was at least equal to that of the Catholics. At the beginning of June Hamilton was apparently concerned with the drafting of the second Act, for Melfort was troubled at what might happen to James's temper if there was delay over so small a matter as the wording of an Act of Parliament (nor, it may be added, is he very careful to preserve respect in his choice of words):

> Pray let us have no more debates (Melfort says), for this is the King's essay and any more jangling will give him the pet past all our power to cure.

On June 10 Melfort writes that the King is of opinion, and he himself agrees, that, "if there be not probability of its carrying", the Act should not be brought in. Hamilton no doubt heaved a sigh of relief at this conclusion of a period of uncertainty, and indeed he was given an eight months' respite from his uncomfortable seat on the fence.

But at the end of this period he had to decide whether or not he would sign an address to the King thanking him for the Declaration of

[1] Hamilton, either purposely or inadvertently, entirely deceived James, for Barrillon wrote of him at this time, "He professes now a great attachment to the person and interests of the King. He promises to employ all his credit in Parliament to give success to His Majesty's projects. It was believed that prominent people during his stay in England had persuaded him into different conduct. He has dissipated these suspicions and the King appears to be quite satisfied with him."

Indulgence, and he decided not to sign it. This refusal brought a strong reprimand from Melfort, who had apparently been entirely deceived by Hamilton's specious reasons against coming to a decision; he said that the refusal had "opened the mouths of all your enemies and given hopes to a party I am sure you are not of", and that it is tantamount to disputing the King's right to issue the Declaration. Hamilton had always contended that he had had the King's promise, when he came to London with Lockhart and Drummond, that he should not be called upon to announce this decision until he again came to London, but James denied that he had ever made such a promise, and in February 1688 he took the correspondence out of Melfort's hands and wrote demanding to know definitely and without further delay whether or no Hamilton

> can comply with what I desire and join with those of my loyal subjects who are for the repeal of those laws and test and for settling an entire liberty of conscience; (and he adds) If you cannot do this, tell noone. I expect your positive answer within two or three days.

Even then Hamilton would not commit himself definitely; he said he had been ill and unable to consult his friends and that he would like more time for consideration. Meanwhile he professed himself a firm adherent to the principle of religious toleration, "but how this is to be done with security to the Protestant religion, our laws and oaths is, in my humble opinion, what will deserve serious consideration, and is above what I can presently determine myself in".

After the issue of his second Scottish Declaration of Indulgence James's interest in Scotland declined. Perth, as Chancellor and First Commissioner of the Treasury, held the reins of power, and Melfort in London, now sole Secretary of State, was able to support his brother. In July 1686 Perth wrote to Bossuet saying that James had entrusted to him the interests of the Catholic religion in Scotland, but that his success had been slight, and eighteen months later he wrote a despondent letter to Cardinal Howard at Rome: they "had advanced little or nothing"; they had what Knox had left of the Abbey of Holyrood House for the order of St. Andrew, but there was no one to take possession; there was also a chapel at Aberdeen; some German missionaries had been brought over, but there had been very few conversions; not one man in a hundred in the army was a Catholic and very few officers. In the early spring of 1688 a prominent Catholic wrote thus of his return to Scotland after some years' absence,

> upon my arrival hither I found things as to the advancement of the Catholic faith far short of my expectations, for instead of finding

> good inclination of the people and many converts, to our grief we perceived that there were but few converts in this place, and a greater aversion in the people than there was five or six years ago when I left Scotland.

In fact, all that Perth was doing was to build up for himself day by day an immense unpopularity in a passively hostile country.

It was in Ireland, both during his reign and in his expedition to that country after his flight, that James revealed most clearly his characteristic defects as a ruler. Briefly it may be said that he failed at both times because he had made no study of the facts and had convinced himself that the only Irish grievance was on the score of religion, and that if the Irish Catholics were granted freedom of worship and their due share of public appointments they would be satisfied. He was unaware that two other major grievances, national and agrarian, focused in demands for the repeal of Poyning's Law and of the Act of Settlement, took precedence in the minds of most Irishmen over the religious grievance.[1] In common with all Englishmen of his time, he regarded Ireland as a conquered country, to be exploited for the benefit of England, and not at all on a par with Scotland; he regarded their grievances as unreasonable, and as far as possible ignored them. During his reign, however, he robbed himself of all chance of achieving a just view of the Irish situation by placing himself in Irish affairs unreservedly in the hands of Tyrconnel and Sunderland and by rejecting all information from other sources.

During the reign of Charles II the policy of the Government of Ireland had been determined in the main by James Butler, Duke of Ormonde. A period of nine years actually intervened between his two periods of office, but the three Lords Lieutenant during that period introduced few, if any, changes in general policy. Ormonde was one of the greatest men of his time; he cannot be classed as an enlightened statesman, since he regarded the existing political and economic constitution of Ireland as satisfactory and had no ideas beyond improving conditions within the existing framework by the preservation of peace and order; his loyalty also was so extreme as to prevent him from pressing his views strongly on the King. He was essentially a man of principle, a staunch Church and King man, and both from temperament and because of his long periods of residence in Ireland he took no part in

[1] As Clarendon wrote to Rochester in August 1686, "The contest here is not about religion but between English and Irish". He had written similarly to James in March and had reminded the King that he had agreed with him before he took up his Irish appointment.

political intrigue in England. Though he was a strong Protestant, he was of Catholic parentage on both sides, and his near relations were all, or nearly all, Catholics; he was therefore singularly fitted to conciliate the Catholics, though there was never a more rigid upholder of Protestant privileges; he was one of the very few who kept their heads during the agitation of the Popish Plot.[1]

The penal laws in force against the Catholics were considerably milder in Ireland than in England. Freedom of worship was permitted with the restrictions that priests were not allowed to appear in public places in their distinctive dress and that mass-houses could not be established within the walls of corporate towns; this latter prohibition was frequently relaxed by connivance. The legislation inspired by Oates in 1678 and 1679 left the secular priests untouched, and the only persons expelled from the country were the Jesuits and friars and other regulars, and such of the higher clergy as had received their appointments from Rome;[2] popish chapels were, however, suppressed not only in the principal cities and towns, but also in their suburbs, leaving to the Catholics in these places liberty to worship only in private houses. On the whole it may be said that except in the years 1678–81 the Catholics had absolute freedom of worship, unless they drew attention to themselves and challenged opposition by ostentatious ceremonies or by convocations of clergy.[3] This toleration is the more surprising because the Catholic Church in Ireland was almost avowedly disloyal. In 1670 there had been a movement among some of its members, known

[1] Colonel Edward Cooke, who was a member of Ormonde's household in the early part of his first Lord-lieutenancy, has left a glowing tribute to Ormonde's industry and regularity of life: ". . . my Lord Duke, a greater drudge than whom I believe breathes not. He always rises about five in the morning and keeps his closet till eight, despatching his devotions and private business; and then hath his public ministers till eleven; and then to prayers; and after till dinner gives free access to all people; and so for an hour after dinner; then to his closet; and if any of the three council days by three to council where he sits late; if not, then it may be if the weather serves, takes the air or keeps his closet till prayer; but is constant there; keeps great dinners but little suppers and after that sometimes twice a week or so plays ombre till ten; then to bed, and on Sundays now hath constantly two sermons in the Cathedral, and always at them; no swearing to be heard at Court, nor drinking seen, all things very regular and sober. I never was in love with a Court before."

[2] This regulation was of only temporary effect, for Ormonde wrote to Sunderland in January 1685 saying that there were as many Catholic as Protestant bishops and that "friars and other regulars do abound in all the parts of the kingdom".

[3] Thus in Galway in August 1683 a public display on the occasion of the habiting of two nuns gave rise to expostulation on the part of the authorities; the Catholic merchants of the town saw their mistake, and not only suppressed the nunnery and a priory, but closed four mass-houses in the town which had been tolerated, and begged Lord Longford "to interpose with the mayor not to disturb the secular priests and to allow them to worship in their own houses".

as the Remonstrants, to declare allegiance to the King of England in all secular matters; but they found themselves in a small minority and were crushed.[1]

But a modified freedom to exercise their religion was the only privilege of citizenship which the Irish Catholics enjoyed. They were entirely excluded from civil and military employment, and in February 1681 Ormonde challenged Lord Massarene, who had alleged that this rule was not strictly observed, "to find out any papists trusted in the civil or military part of the government". As regards the army, the rules laid down in December 1660 by Albemarle as Lord General were strictly observed: "Every officer and soldier to take the oaths of allegiance and supremacy, and no Papist officer or soldier to be at any time mustered in the Army". Allegations were made from time to time that these rules had been evaded, but Ormonde was able invariably to show that these allegations were baseless and were "a calumny cast on the army and government"; after the Popish Plot he instituted a system of rewards to soldiers who denounced as papists any of their officers or fellow-soldiers—apparently without result.

The Irish House of Commons was entirely Protestant, for though the Irish freeholders were not disfranchised, their numbers were small, and in the boroughs there were no Catholic freemen; many Catholic peers had been deprived of their seats in the House of Lords as a penalty for complicity in the rebellion of 1641. There were no Catholic judges or Commissioners under the Act of Settlement, and the justices of the peace were Protestants to a man, even though in many localities it was difficult to find properly qualified Protestants. But it was in the towns that the Catholics were made to feel their inferiority most keenly; they could not, except in rare cases, be members of the corporation, and they resided within the walls only on sufferance. Thus in 1661 a general permission was granted to "innocent" Catholics (*i.e.*, that small minority who had not taken part in the rebellion of 1641) to reside in cities and towns, "All others of the King's subjects may have leave to traffic and trade though they are forbidden to inhabit cities and walled towns". In 1670 Lord Berkeley of Stratton, who was then Lord Lieutenant, relaxed this order, and in February 1672 Charles wrote approving Berkeley's action. In the following November and January the King wrote further letters successively suspending the orders regulating the election of Common Councils and approving the appoint-

[1] In December 1686 Lord Clarendon stated that the Irish priests were so ignorant as to believe that Ireland was an appanage of the Pope and that the King of England "had no right further than the Pope gives him authority"; they also instructed Tyrconnel's Irish recruits "to take no oath but to be true to the Pope".

ment of nine Catholics to the Common Council of Dublin; meanwhile several Catholics had by some mysterious means got themselves appointed Justices of the Peace for that city. But the English House of Commons took alarm, and on March 25, 1673, they petitioned the King to withdraw the commission which had been appointed to inquire into the working of the Act of Settlement, to exclude Catholics from the army and from every public position, to expel from Ireland all Catholics in orders, including the secular priests, and to permit no Catholic to reside in a corporate town except under licence. This was at the time when Charles received his great rebuff over his Declaration of Indulgence, and in the lesser matter of the Irish corporations he also found it wiser to give way. Among the severities demanded at the time of the Popish Plot was the expulsion of all Catholics from corporations and garrison towns; but this measure was found to be impracticable, since many Catholics were valuable citizens and the Protestant merchants and others had need of their services; the expulsion was therefore restricted to "the useless and idle sort of them".

These grievances were local and in most cases merely personal. The national grievance—the subservience of Ireland to the English Parliament under Poyning's Law—was never absent from the minds of Irishmen, but no expression was given to it during Charles's reign; it was nursed in silence until a fitting opportunity should occur for demand for its redress. The agrarian grievance was kept more to the fore. The rebels of 1641 had suffered forfeiture of their estates, and these had been given to two classes of claimants: to the adventurers, the people who had advanced money (to Charles I and later to the Parliament) for the suppression of the rebellion on condition of being repaid in Irish land—and to the soldiers of Cromwell's Irish army who received land in satisfaction of arrears of pay. This land had been secured to both sections of the new proprietors by Charles's promise in the Declaration of Breda, and confirmed to them by the Act of Settlement in 1662; the Act of Explanation of 1665, which had become necessary when it was found that there was not sufficient land to satisfy all claims under the Act of Settlement, had indeed deprived the new proprietors of one-third of their estates, but had re-confirmed them in the possession of the remaining two-thirds. They were again confirmed in possession by a declaration by the King in 1673. But not only had the rebels been deprived, but the "innocent" Catholics had been compelled to give up the estates to which they were attached by family tradition in exchange for estates in Connaught; so that in 1665 the whole of the land in the three other provinces was out of the hands of the original Irish proprietors, in Munster and Leinster it was held in the main by Englishmen, and in Ulster by the descendants of the Scottish planters of James I's time. In these circumstances it was inevitable that the demand for the repeal of the Acts of Settlement and Explanation, from being a demand on the part of particular persons for the recovery of their estates, should become part of the national aspiration of Ireland for the Irish.

In the twenty years between 1665 and 1685 great changes took place among the possessors of land in Leinster and Munster. What happened in detail must be largely a matter of conjecture, but it is reasonable to suppose that most of the adventurers were speculators who never visited their estates and who took the first favourable opportunity of selling them, that many of the soldiers found life in Ireland uncongenial, sold their estates and returned to England, and that many Irish Catholics and English cavaliers had bought land. When the Act of Settlement was repealed by the Dublin Parliament of 1689 several Catholic judges were deprived of their estates; these judges were in a position to protest, but other purchasers, great and small, we must conclude to have been numerous, though they could not make their voices heard.

It seems probable that James was moved by his friend Richard Talbot to take an interest in Irish affairs some months before Charles died—probably in June 1684, when Talbot returned to England from Ireland after his return from exile. Talbot was a swaggering, impetuous man, very much the "stage" Irishman, who according to Grammont had been the companion of James's amours in the years immediately following the Restoration; he had no real ability and was quite incapable of applying himself to the details of business; his habit of lying was proverbial, and he had not the intelligence to abstain from unnecessary and unplausible lies; he had, however, two redeeming virtues: he was not personally corrupt (though he was ready to make use of the corruption of others, notably of Sunderland), and he had a very real passion for his country and his religion.[1] His first appearance in public life was as agent for certain Catholic peers and gentry to conduct their cases for reinstatement in possession of their lands under the Acts of Settlement and Explanation. In that capacity he appeared before the King and Council in February 1671, and he bettered the instructions of his clients by attempting to invalidate the Act of Settlement itself. From that time the main object of his life was the repeal of the Act of

[1] I omit as unimportant in a biography of James all reference to the division of the Catholic Irish into Old and New Irish. Talbot was descended from an Anglo-Norman family, and on occasion appeared as a strong partisan of the New Irish; he seems not to have been popular even with them. Conditions were such that no single leader would have been acceptable to the Irish Catholics as a whole.

Settlement. Talbot was three times imprisoned during Charles's reign, twice in the Tower for insults and worse against Ormonde, and once in Dublin Castle as a suspect of the Popish Plot. On all three occasions he was liberated by Ormonde's intercession. Ormonde appears to have liked him, but by no means to have taken him seriously;[1] in February 1683 Talbot wrote to Ormonde expressing his gratitude for past kindness, but this gratitude may have been only anticipation of favours to come, for he was asking Ormonde to use his influence to obtain permission for his return from exile. It is more than probable that he had been throughout working in secret against Ormonde.

In June 1684 Talbot came to England from Ireland, where he had been since his return from exile, and presented to the King a report on the administration of Ireland. Now, it is extremely improbable that Charles would have taken notice of a report which he had not asked for from a private person, unless it had been pressed upon him by someone of great influence, and James was at that time the only Catholic who could be so described. Ireland was prosperous and was giving no trouble—a great virtue in Charles's eyes; the direction of the royal policy was in the hands of the Church and King men, and he had no desire to court trouble by favouring Catholic claims. Nevertheless the report was accepted, it was decided to bring about an entire reformation of the civil and military administration of Ireland—that is to say, to make Catholics eligible for all public appointments—and to recall Ormonde, who indeed said himself that "if it be intended to place some papists in command in the army, I am really glad I shall not be commanded to do it".[2] There can be little doubt that James had never had a great affection for Ormonde; in his youth and early manhood in France and Flanders he had been aware of the older man's silent disapproval of his conduct on several occasions; later on Ormonde's uncompromising Protestantism had been an affront. There was never anything approaching an open quarrel—in fact, all the letters which passed between them—notably James's letter of condolence on the death of Ormonde's eldest son, and James's friend, the Earl of Ossory, and the letters which were exchanged in October and November 1684 on the subject of Ormonde's recall—are cordial in tone; but there is never a suggestion of mutual confidence. Ormonde's biographer, Carte, who spent years in studying Ormonde's papers, formed the opinion that

> King James II seemed always to stand in awe of him, and whatever esteem he could not help having of him, and whatever grateful

[1] Ailesbury's opinion of Tyrconnel was similar to Ormonde's.

[2] There was also, apart from the religious question, a scheme for remodelling the army and increasing its efficiency.

sense he entertained at some times of his services, yet he never really cared for him, purely on account of his being a zealous Protestant.

James's haughtiness and bullying manner were probably a mask for a secret sense of inadequacy, and Ormonde, who was very self-sufficient and sure of himself, induced in James a feeling of inferiority which he resented. In these circumstances it appears certain that James allied himself with Talbot to have Ormonde recalled. Charles was apt to get tired of his principal servants after a period of years, and James had many opportunities of hinting that Ormonde at seventy-four years of age had better be replaced.

Thus the revolution which took place in the administration of Ireland between 1685 and 1688 was initiated before Charles's death, though had Charles lived Rochester would have gone to Ireland as Lord Lieutenant and James and Talbot would have found in him an opponent less stubborn perhaps than Ormonde, but not so pliant as Rochester's brother Clarendon. But Rochester was reserved for a higher post on James's accession, and when Ormonde returned to England in April 1685 the government of Ireland was placed in the hands of Primate Boyle and the Earl of Granard as Lords Justices, and Granard was appointed Commander-in-Chief. Ormonde's official title had been "Lieutenant-General and General Governor of His Majesty's Kingdom of Ireland", but against his advice it had been decided in August 1684 to appoint a Commander-in-Chief independent of the Lord Lieutenant. Six weeks after his accession James made his first breach of the Test Act by giving Talbot an Irish regiment, and in May Talbot (now Earl of Tyrconnel) went to Ireland. Already there had been dismissals of officers in the Army, and Talbot, with scant regard to the authority of his superior officer, Lord Granard, laid the foundations of the wholesale conversion of the Protestant army into one predominantly Catholic. He singled out for removal officers in whom Ormonde had been personally interested, and Ormonde in retirement was very angry; he asked "under what qualification my Lord of Tyrconnel is, or is taken to be, that more should be done to him than to any other colonel in the Army", but he was told that "Tyrconnel is thought to have the King's authority to inspect and report on the army".

Tyrconnel took pains to justify to James his high-handed proceedings with the Army by insinuating that a great many of the officers and men had served under Cromwell and were still at heart disaffected. Against such an allegation James was in possession of the clearest evidence, and he should not have been deceived. Ormonde had been responsible for nearly all military appointments during the previous reign, he was very strongly prejudiced against the "fanatics" and no one could have been less inclined to tolerate subversive elements in the Army. Moreover there had been no less than three scrutinies of the Army List—in 1662, 1669 and in January 1685—for the purpose of eliminating officers of doubtful loyalty; and in the last James himself had taken part, and he had expressed himself satisfied except in the cases of two particular officers. Nevertheless Tyrconnel in August instituted a fresh inquiry, and all colonels were ordered to report (among other things) which of the officers under them had served under Cromwell. Apart from the fact that many of the officers were " '49 men", who had served the royal cause until in 1649 it had become hopeless, James should have secured in their employments men who had survived previous purges and had served his brother for twenty-five years. But this inquiry was pure bluff, for the wholesale dismissal of Protestant officers was conducted on no settled principle, and the officers lost their commissions at the whim of Tyrconnel or of the officers to whom he delegated his powers. One very mean circumstance of their dismissal was that in many cases the officers were not paid on the spot compensation for the commissions which they had previously purchased, or for their horses, but were forced to spend money on a journey to Dublin and to remain there for some time at their own expense while they were making good their claims.

With more plausibility, but with no greater basis in fact, Tyrconnel further convinced the King that the majority of the Protestants in Ireland were "fanatics" and enemies of the Government. James was well aware that during the exclusion agitation and at the time of his accession Ireland had remained perfectly quiet, but he had been led to believe that the rebellions of Argyll and Monmouth had had serious repercussions in Ireland, and his fixed opinion was that "many ill and disaffected persons were secured in their possessions" by the Act of Settlement. As a matter of fact this view was entirely erroneous: the soft airs of Ireland and their comparative isolation on their properties had wrought a great change in such of the adventurers and of Cromwell's soldiers as had remained in Ireland, and in their children. In the towns, particularly in Dublin and Cork, there were communities of dissenters, and the Ulster Presbyterians were a strong body; care had been exercised, as in the case of mass-houses, to prevent conventicles from existing except on sufference, and they were strictly watched after the Rye House Plot. But there was a general decline in opposition to the Church of England among the land-holders of Leinster and Munster; they took no concerted action, political or religious, and many of them came to church and received the Sacrament, though this conformity was in certain cases interested and with a view to qualifying for the commission of the peace. The numbers of the original settlers also was very much reduced: writing to the King in August 1686 Clarendon said:

> It is a great opinion, Sir, among some men (who may be better informed if they please) [*sc.* Tyrconnel], and they take the liberty to say that Your Majesty believes it, that the gross of the English in this kingdom are fanatics of Cromwell's brood, and the offspring of those who served in the rebellion against your sacred father; which I presume to say is a very great mistake,

and he goes on to say that there are not twenty families of adventurers left and no great number of soldiers, and that six parts of seven of the trade of the kingdom (apart from Ulster about which he is making inquiries) is carried on by Church of England men, and those not people who have recently taken to going to church.[1]

In August 1685 James's brother-in-law, the Earl of Clarendon, who was already Lord Privy Seal, was appointed Lord Lieutenant of Ireland. The Catholics were disappointed that James had not appointed a Catholic—not necessarily Tyrconnel—for they had hoped that a beginning of the domination of their faith in the three kingdoms would have been made at once in Ireland. Tyrconnel wrote a letter to James which is evidence either of deliberate disrespect or of inability to write a civil letter:

> My lord Sunderland's letter of the 20th bringing the news of Your Majesty's having named my lord Clarendon for the government of this country does so (disappoint)[2] your Catholic subjects here that they seem more struck with this change than any that hitherto has been in all the (tale)[2] of their miseries.

But James was still to a great extent in the cautious mood of the early months of his reign, and he was aware that the appointment of a Catholic would alarm and possibly exasperate the Parliament which he was to meet in November and from which he hoped great things for the Catholic religion. In appointing Clarendon he deviated from his customary line of conduct, he chose the one man who could serve his purpose and he behaved with a cynicism that was quite foreign to his

[1] It is alleged in a pamphlet of 1697 that many of Cromwell's soldiers, in default of women of their own kind, had married Irish women, and that their children had grown up without learning a word of English. It is difficult to believe that the writer is not exaggerating and founding his general statement on a few cases he has come across in his own locality.

[2] These two words are illegible in the MS.

nature; he did not tell Clarendon that he was merely to be a tool for the establishment of the domination of the Catholics in Ireland and that he was merely a stop-gap and would be removed as soon as was convenient, but this is the substance of his excuses to Barrillon:

> The King of England told me that he knew well that he could make Lord Clarendon obey him punctually and that one would see that in a short time he would put Ireland into a position not to fear the zealous Protestants.

Clarendon set out for Ireland with high hopes and undeterred by a letter from Doctor Fell (of the famous epigram) in which the Bishop wished him "good luck with his honour, which seems to me sufficiently hazardous". At the end of his term of office he claimed to have served the King "upon the English principle of the excellent Church of England", but the very instructions given him by James violated at every point what were then considered to be the principles of the Church of England, and in practice he had had to go very much farther from those principles.[1] There are many instances, particularly in the last hundred years, of English proconsuls complaining, and having reasons to complain, of lack of support from the home Government; but not one of them was so infamously treated as Lord Clarendon. In his case it was a matter not of lack of support, but of deliberate treachery and frustration and a persistent undermining of his authority. His viceroyalty is one of the best-documented episodes in English history, for he was almost too good a letter-writer, and his long letters to his brother, Lord Rochester, together with a few to Sunderland and the King, fill the greater part of two folio volumes.

Tyrconnel left Ireland as soon as he heard of Clarendon's appointment, and his presence in London and his possession of the King's ear, both direct and through Sunderland, enabled him to prevent Clarendon from exercising the authority due to his position. Time and again Clarendon had to complain that accusations had been made against him by persons living in Ireland, that the first he had heard about these accusations was that they had been accepted at Whitehall without question, and he had been reprimanded without opportunity of refuting the charges against him; sometimes even he had been reprimanded and had been unable to ascertain what his offence was supposed to be. His

[1] This was Ormonde's view: after Clarendon's dismissal he wrote to him, "The time of your government has been short, but it has produced alterations such as one would have thought a longer time could hardly have brought to pass. I heartily pray these changes may be for the King's service and that those who fear and those who wish the contrary may be deceived. . . . Your lordship has the approbation of many good and loyal men."

advice to the King was consistently good; in spite of the obstacles which were put in his way he succeeded in the difficult task of balancing the Irish budget, and he must be accounted an able officer, but nothing he could say carried weight with James: on one occasion James told him that he had been so short a time in Ireland that he could not possibly give "His Majesty so good an account as he had already received from persons of undoubted integrity and zeal in his service": a plain acknowledgement of Tyrconnel's commanding position and incidentally a claim that "integrity and zeal" were sufficient qualifications for high office. Clarendon noticed with regret that Ormonde, in spite of his long experience, was not consulted on Irish affairs.

In June 1686 Tyrconnel returned to Ireland with a commission as Lieutenant-General and Commander-in-Chief, and Clarendon's situation became even more unsatisfactory. It was to be expected that there would be an acceleration in the process of getting rid of the Protestants in the Army, and Clarendon had to conceal his chagrin at many irregularities which he was powerless to prevent; he had to see men deprived for no fault of commissions for which they had paid all the money they had, the dire effects on discipline when the new officers refused to obey their immediate superiors, to say nothing of the insubordination of the Army to the civil power instanced when soldiers boarded incoming ships and prevented the Customs officers from levying duties. But Tyrconnel went far beyond his province and invaded the civil administration, the appointment of sheriffs, the admission of Catholics to the freedom of boroughs and so on. Week by week Clarendon's letters to his brother are full of complaints on these heads; he summed them up in one letter to Sunderland written shortly after Tyrconnel's arrival:

> Certainly never any chief governor before me was directed to devolve all the power granted by his commission to another in command subordinate to him. There is nothing the King has directed to be done that I could not have performed as fully to His Majesty's satisfaction, even by the judgement of those whom my Lord Tyrconnel has employed, and whose advice and assistance I would have taken. The same work should have been done much more for His Majesty's service, and I will have the vanity to say not near that dissatisfaction given, which, I fear, is occasioned by the unhappiness of his lordship's temper; and I should not have been exposed to the descents of every man how little the King thought to trust me, and how ill an opinion he has of me.

There is no room to doubt that in the matter of Ireland James allowed himself to be hoodwinked by Tyrconnel and Sunderland. Except for a vague desire for the maintenance of the English interest and for the relief of the Irish Catholics—aspirations the mutual incompatibility of which could only be resolved by a great deal of hard thinking, and a settled policy—he took very little interest in the day-to-day affairs of Ireland and was a very easy dupe.[1] He accepted, for instance, Tyrconnel's statement that the Irish army was full of Cromwellians and disaffected officers, and that there could be no security against another rebellion unless they were removed and Catholics put in their places; if he had reflected he would have remembered the names of the lords-lieutenants of his brother's time, Ormonde's in particular, and have realised that they had appointed every officer then serving in the Irish army, and that it was at least unlikely that they would have given commissions to anyone except loyalists and churchmen. His credulity can only be accounted for by an apathy towards Ireland and a subconscious bias induced by his desire to have a Catholic army at his disposal; he was confirmed in his error when the cashiered officers crossed over to Holland and took service with William and eventually ranged themselves against him, partly because it was the only career open to them, partly also in disgust at the scurvy manner in which they have been treated—a further instance of James's failure to understand that no man's loyalty is proof against personal ill-treatment.

Tyrconnel was the head centre of the intrigues at Whitehall against Clarendon, and he had formed an alliance with Sunderland, based on self-interest and not at all on mutual esteem. The two men had been associated since the beginning of the reign in the Catholic Cabinet, Tyrconnel had been deep in Sunderland's intrigues against Rochester, and Sunderland had secured Tyrconnel's assistance by vague promises of helping him to the Lord-Lieutenancy; when Clarendon was appointed, Tyrconnel reproached Sunderland for his failure to fulfil his promises, and Sunderland assured him that his appointment was postponed only until the two Hydes had been ruined, as they would be by being separated. When, however, time went on and he found himself no nearer to the realisation of his ambition, Tyrconnel sent Sheridan to Sunderland to tell him that if he did not support his claims to the Lord-Lieutenancy he would reveal to the King the whole of their previous intrigues, and in particular would inform the Queen "that the true motive of removing Mrs. Sedley was to weaken Lord Rochester and gain herself to their party, and not the honour of religion". Sunderland refused to be blackmailed; he relied on James's invariable practice of refusing

[1] There can be little doubt, however, that if James had insisted on his own personal control of the Irish administration he would have made wholesale appointments of English Catholics to military and civil posts.

to listen to complaints against his trusted advisers. But he offered to get Tyrconnel made a Lieutenant-General in England, to secure for him an additional pension of £5000 a year, and "to make him as absolute in Ireland as Lauderdale had been in Scotland without the title"; eventually, when the penal laws had been abrogated, he might be made Lord-Lieutenant, but it would be very difficult on account of his known intentions, both to repeal the Act of Settlement, in which powerful persons in the three kingdoms were interested, and to hand over Ireland to France in the event of a Protestant succession; the King had also lately declared that he would not give the Lord-Lieutenancy to an Irishman.[1]

Though he could do little at the time to assist Tyrconnel in his main ambition, Sunderland was quite willing to serve his interests by weakening Clarendon's authority. Clarendon was quite certain that a number of his letters, whether addressed to the Secretary or to the King, were not seen by James himself, and that many of Sunderland's replies were written in the King's name, but without the King's knowledge or authority; and Tyrconnel was so indiscreet as to glory in the fact that the Lord Lieutenant had no effectual correspondence with the King. A stronger man than Clarendon would not have continued in such an invidious position, and a better man would not have so constantly violated his own principles by carrying out the illegal instructions which he received from the King and the Secretary. He clung to office until he was recalled, partly no doubt because he was very poor and needed the emoluments of office, but chiefly because his worship of royalty was proof against snubs and slights and because he regarded service to the King as the highest possible service. Many passages in his letters read like quotations from the penitential Psalms:

> I hope he knows that his breath may dispose of me and all I have; and whatever he determines will be submitted to with as much cheerfulness as is possible from an afflicted heart, which can never leave me while his displeasure lasts. . . .
>
> The wrath of the King is unsupportable and I am sure must crash me to nothing, who am next to nothing already, and must be altogether so without his support. . . .
>
> If I know my own heart I had rather not be in the world than remain under His Majesty's displeasure. . . .

[1] This anecdote is based on the account given by Thomas Sheridan. Sheridan is not a first-rate authority, for not only was he violently hostile to Tyrconnel a year or two later, but he did not put his notes into narrative form until 1702. However, the story is so consonant with what we know of the characters of Sunderland and Tyrconnel that it may be accepted as substantially true.

I do cast myself at Your Majesty's feet with all the submission the most afflicted heart is capable of, and do beg your pardon for whatever I have offended you in; and I will presume to say you never had and never can have a greater penitent among the many who have had the misfortune to offend you. . . . To die, sir, especially in your service, is no hard task.

But James had no intention of keeping Clarendon indefinitely in office; the success of his first essays in absolute government had led him to believe that he was now strong enough to appoint a Catholic to the government of Ireland. In August 1686 Sunderland saw in what direction the King's mind was working and that there was a chance that he could now be brought to appoint Tyrconnel to the Lord-Lieutenancy. He urged Tyrconnel to put in an appearance at Whitehall and to intrigue on his own behalf. Tyrconnel accordingly left Ireland on August 26 after a stay there of under three months, and on September 3 Barrillon told his master that Clarendon was to lose the Viceroyalty and that Tyrconnel was trying to get it, but that the King "has still some reluctance to give the appointment to an Irishman and fears that such a proceeding would excite unfavourable comment in England". No details are available of the long discussions which took place during the ensuing weeks. The names of the Marquis of Powis and of Lord Dover were suggested, but neither of these lords was a strong man, and James felt that "there was rough work to be done which no English lord could do"; there was also the consideration that Tyrconnel was such a turbulent person that he could not be controlled by a weak Lord Lieutenant, and in consequence, if he could not be appointed to the chief place himself, it would be necessary to take the command of the army from him, and probably even to keep him out of Ireland. Tyrconnel himself affected not to be unduly anxious for the promotion; he expressed himself unwilling, in view of the state of his health, to accept the appointment, and he proposed that he should serve as Lord Deputy under one of James's illegitimate sons, the Duke of Berwick or Henry Fitzjames, boys of seventeen and fifteen. Sunderland pursued his usual tactics of not coming forward in favour of any step until he was certain that the King would take it, and apart from Sunderland, Tyrconnel had very little support: even the Catholic lords on the English Privy Council were against him, and one of them, Lord Belasyse, said that he was capable of losing the King six kingdoms. The Queen was also said to exercise against him what little influence she had, there was no movement in his favour from the Catholics of Ireland, and the Protestants there were dismayed at the rumour of his appointment.

However, after nearly three months of indecision, in spite of all this opposition and of his own prejudice as a supporter of the English interest, James decided to appoint Tyrconnel, and the only concession he made to public opinion was to give him the title not of Lord Lieutenant, but of Lord Deputy.[1] At the same time he appointed Thomas Sheridan, a Protestant, Secretary to the Government, and Sheridan tells a story of these appointments which cannot easily be believed: he says that the King sent for him and said "that he knew Tyrconnel too well to trust him with the government without obliging him to consult with Mr. Fitton and him in everything relating to it, and that he was to have an account by Sunderland if they happened to differ and determine himself which of the opinions he would have followed". If this story is true, James cut himself off from all knowledge of what was going on in Ireland by making Sunderland the vehicle of information; he also failed to anticipate that Tyrconnel could ride rough-shod over any opposition and would prevent all direct communication by Sheridan with Whitehall by tampering with the mail-bags. In any case, to appoint a man to a post for which he is not fit, and to endeavour to control him by means of his subordinates, is not a device calculated to give strength and efficiency to a government.

Tyrconnel arrived in Dublin in January 1687 to take over the government. He was surprised and dismayed at the wholesale flight to England of Protestant merchants,[2] and he issued a proclamation calculated to reassure them. But his promises were no more believed than his master's were beginning to be; discretion was no part of Tyrconnel's nature, and he had made no secret of his intention to make Ireland a Catholic enclave in the King's dominions. There were many alive who remembered the massacres of 1641, and the traditions of that year were sufficiently fresh to give apprehension that Tyrconnel, if he did not himself initiate a proscription of the Protestants, would be powerless to prevent one.

All Tyrconnel's energies were now bent upon completing the work which the subservient Clarendon had begun, the domination of the boroughs by the Catholics. Under the Act of Settlement no Catholic could be a freeman, but James had from the first ignored this provision, and in April 1686 he had told Clarendon that the Act of Settlement

[1] Tyrconnel never achieved the higher title; in all his proclamations up to the landing of the King in Ireland, when his appointment lapsed, he described himself as Lord Deputy.

[2] This emigration had commenced in the summer of 1685, when the Protestants were disarmed and they saw that the army was passing into Catholic hands, and had continued throughout the year 1686. When Tyrconnel was appointed Lord Deputy it was accelerated.

should be honoured, but that there was no harm in putting in a few Catholics as freemen: he did not at that time go so far as to adopt the principle of equality between the two religions. In December his final instructions to Sheridan were "that no man was to be put out or into any employment, civil or military, on account of religion", and he added "that one of his chief injunctions to Tyrconnel was not to disoblige his Protestant subjects".

But Tyrconnel, safe from royal interference by the help of Sunderland, disobeyed his instructions and gave everywhere preference to the Catholics; in the boroughs he followed the English practice of forfeiting charters by *quo warranto* and granted fresh charters which permitted the admission of Catholics. His ultimate object was to induce the King to call a Parliament that would repeal the Act of Settlement. He had already remodelled the Army by getting rid of a very great number of Protestants—300 officers and 4000 non-commissioned officers and men, according to accepted estimates—and in a short time two-thirds of every corporation were Catholics; he reckoned that, when the land had been given back to its original owners, the Protestants would be reduced to insignificance. In November 1686, when Tyrconnel's appointment hung in the balance, his henchmen, Nagle, had published the famous Coventry Letter attacking the Act of Settlement. Tyrconnel about the same time had induced Sunderland to support the repeal by a bribe of either £5000 a year in Irish land or £50,000 in cash, to be paid when the Act was repealed; Sunderland had wisely chosen the cash, for he was doubtless aware that the uncertainty of the King's intentions with regard to the Settlement had reduced the price of land in Ireland from fifteen or sixteen years' purchase to eight. The two conspirators staged a farcical hearing before the King of a discussion about repeal, and Sunderland professed himself converted by Tyrconnel's arguments. But there can be little doubt that James remained firm against repeal. In 1686 he had told Clarendon and also Sir William Petty and the Chancellor, Sir Charles Porter, that he would not break the Settlement, and to that promise he adhered until he was forced to yield by the Dublin Parliament of 1689.

In the late summer of 1687 Tyrconnel saw the King at Chester, and was encouraged by him in his policy of bringing more Catholics into the administration and the corporations, but it does not appear that he was given hope that the Settlement would be upset. In October, indeed, Sunderland told Barrillon that James was preparing to repeal the Act of Settlement, but in this matter Sunderland was not a good witness, for the hope of £50,000 may have warped his judgement. In April 1688 Tyrconnel sent Nugent and Rice to England to explain to the King a scheme to hold an Irish Parliament and to get a supplementary Act passed to relieve the worst of the grievances under the Act of Settlement; James not only rejected the proposal as a subterfuge by which the Act would be virtually repealed and Ireland would be lost to the English Crown, but lent a favourable ear to those who hinted that it would be well to remove the Lord Deputy. What James failed to do was to make a general declaration of Irish policy, and, in particular, of his intentions with regard to the Settlement; Clarendon had never ceased to advise the King that Ireland could never be prosperous if steps were not taken to allay the prevailing apprehension among the landed proprietors that their lands would be taken from them. Possibly this advice never reached James; he certainly did not act upon it. From Nagle's Coventry Letter it appears that he had decided to issue such a proclamation; probably Sunderland and Tyrconnel found means to prevent him.[1]

[1] King (pp. 162–63) is additional evidence that during his reign James was firm against repeal; though King also says (p. 144) that the mission of Nugent and Rice was successful.

CHAPTER V

THE REVOLUTION

By the summer of 1688 all the elements of revolution were present, all that was lacking was a definite occasion for revolt. James had revealed the impossibility of the Stuart theory of government by using it in an attempt to bring back to Rome a nation fanatically and incurably hostile to the Roman faith; he had broken the law by establishing the Ecclesiastical Commission and he had strained the law by procuring a verdict favourable to the prerogative in the Hales *v.* Godden case; he had made the penal laws and Test Act inoperative; he had raised a host of private enemies by extensive dismissals of public servants in order to make room for Catholics and for Protestants who were willing to serve the Catholic cause. But even including the subversion of the rights of Magdalen College, there had been no single act of sufficient magnitude to rouse the nation to resistance. The effect of all these grievances was cumulative: the whole of the politically conscious part of the nation was in a state of profound discontent, but that discontent was spread over a variety of objects and it was without a recognised leader. James's Government was in appearance still strong and in no danger of attack from any particular quarter; there is no reason to believe that he himself had declined from the supreme confidence of the first months of his reign. Actually the Government was in a state of unstable equilibrium and was liable to destruction by the slightest shock: it was like a healthy octogenarian; its life might have been by good fortune prolonged indefinitely, but it was extremely vulnerable to accident. The two events which immediately preceded the Revolution—the prosecution of the Seven Bishops and the birth of the Prince of Wales—were in no sense its cause, but they were in a very real sense its occasion. Incidentally they led directly to the first overt act of rebellion, the invitation sent to William, Prince of Orange, and to his acceptance of the position of leader.

The Second Declaration of Indulgence, issued on April 27, 1688, repeated the words of the First Declaration, and concluded with an explanation of James's intentions in re-issuing it. This explanation was to the effect that an endeavour had been made to convince the public that his determination to secure the repeal of the penal laws and the Test Act was weakening and that he chose this means to counteract that endeavour; at the same time he excused the immense changes he had made among the holders of office up and down the country on the ground that no one ought to be employed in the public service "who will not contribute towards the peace and greatness of their country". In order to give the Declaration wider publicity than could be afforded by the *Gazette* (if for no other reason), he issued on May 4 an order in Council that the Declaration should be read twice in every church throughout the kingdom, on May 20 and 27 in London and on June 3 and 10 elsewhere.

There was nothing new in an order to the clergy to read important public pronouncements from their pulpits. In 1641 the House of Commons had caused their declaration to be read in churches. Charles II had employed the same means to make known his reasons for dissolving Parliament in 1681, and there had been a provision in the Exclusion Bills that James's ineligibility should be annually announced in the same manner. Nor does it appear that James and his Ministers, though the order was in all probability intended as an attack on the Church, expected less than complete acquiescence on the part of the clergy.[1] But this expectation is merely a supreme instance of the lack of contact between the Court and the nation. The clergy had no objection whatever to reading from the pulpit proclamations concerned with secular matters; but they held to the point of fanaticism the doctrine that any concession to the dissenters, particularly to the Catholic dissenters, was an injury to the Church; they had been convinced by James's conduct that what was aimed at went far beyond toleration and that his ultimate aim was to bring England to Rome and to reduce the Church of England to the position of a mere sect, and they resented vehemently a device which would place them under the implication of approving the Declaration of Indulgence and would make them accomplices in the destruction of their Church.

The Jacobite biographer of James thus speciously describes the situation:

> The Church of England clergy, nowithstanding their so much preached up doctrine of non-resistance and passive obedience,

[1] Ranke (IV, 345), however, says, apparently on the authority of the Imperial ambassador, "This order was, as it were, double-edged; indeed it was intended to be so. If the clergy complied they themselves recognised the legality of the step which was directed against them, and gave up their own cause; if they resisted they fell into contradiction with the doctrine of obedience and seemed likely to estrange the nonconformists by their conduct. . . . It was not certain beforehand whether the English Church would obey the commands. . . ." Ranke has stated the dilemma as it appeared to the clergy, but what is doubtful is that James and his advisers were aware that there was a dilemma. James's indignant astonishment when he saw the tenor of the bishops' petition appears conclusive evidence that he had no anticipation of their attitude, and Ranke himself says (IV, 353) that in the new situation set up by the neglect of the clergy to read the Declaration "even Sunderland and Petre were perplexed".

> began early to spread jealousies amongst the people, and, instead of suffering with patience, they complained before they felt any smart and thought imaginary dangers a good pretence to encourage a real sedition; they had preached prerogative and the sovereign power to the highest pitch while it was favourable to them, but when they apprehended the least danger from it, they cried out as soon as the shoe pinched, though it was of their own putting on.

Now there can be no doubt that the clergy of the Church of England had created a difficulty for themselves by their extravagant utterances on the royal prerogative since the Restoration; they had been entirely deceived by James's promises to uphold their Church, and had not realised that it was not possible for a Catholic monarch to keep those promises. So obsessed were they with the doctrine of passive obedience that their faith in James's pledges was only slightly shaken by a series of actions which to an unbiased mind would have proved them entirely hollow—the virtual abrogation of the penal laws, the appointment of Catholics to posts in central and local administration, the Ecclesiastical Commission, the First Declaration of Indulgence. What indignation they felt was as individual citizens and as peers, and they did not feel that any one grievance was of sufficient importance to justify a protest by the Church as a whole. The attacks on the Universities, in particular that on Magdalen College, were in a different category; the Universities were the nurseries of the Church, Fellowships were held exclusively by priests of the Church, and the future of the Church was bound up in the condition of the Universities. The bishops as a body could easily, without exceeding the bounds of their legitimate interests, have protested against the removal of Dr. Hough, and it is not to their credit that they kept silent.

But the edict for the reading of the Second Declaration of Indulgence they considered to be a direct attack on the Church as a whole. This edict took them entirely by surprise, a good many days were wasted before they got down to a discussion of what was best to do in these unforeseen circumstances, and though no doubt the tongues of the clergy were busy from the day of the issue of the Declaration, it was not until eight days later, May 12, that there was anything like formal discussion. On that day the Earl of Clarendon dined at Lambeth with Sancroft, the Archbishop of Canterbury, and there were also present the Bishops of London (Compton), Ely (Turner), Peterborough (White), Chester (Cartwright) and St. Davids (Watson); the two last-named were known to be in sympathy with the royal policy and out of touch with the general body of opinion of the Church of England, and it was not possible to commence discussion until they had left; by that time Tenison, Rector of St. Martin-in-the-Fields, a future Archbishop, had come in. It was then agreed to petition the King against the reading of the Declaration, but it was felt that their petition would have greater weight if it were signed by a larger number than three bishops. Accordingly letters were sent to seven other bishops of the province of Canterbury asking them to come to London to collaborate in such action as circumstances demanded; it is to be noted that no such invitations were sent to the Bishops of Rochester (Sprat), Hereford, Exeter (Lamplugh),[1] Coventry, Lichfield and Lincoln (Barlow), who were regarded at best as lukewarm supporters of the protest movement. Some of the bishops sent excuses, but the others acted so rapidly that by the morning of Friday May 18 the petition had been written out by the Archbishop (for he would trust no amanuensis with so secret a matter) and signed by himself and six other bishops: St. Asaph (Lloyd), Ely (Turner), Chichester (Lake), Bath and Wells (Ken), Peterborough (White) and Bristol (Trelawney).[2] Sancroft, as archbishop, signed first, but it is difficult to believe that he was more than nominally the leader: he was by nature retiring, and though he behaved on occasions with courage, it was with a passive courage, and he always refrained from justifying himself in public; it is more likely that the moving spirit was Henry Compton, Bishop of London, who was precluded from signing the petition by the fact that he had been suspended from episcopal functions by the Ecclesiastical Commission. Among prominent clergy who were present at the final discussions and approved of the petition were Tillotson, Dean of Canterbury, Stillingfleet, Dean of St. Paul's, Simon Patrick, Dean of Peterborough, Sherlock, Master of the Temple, and Tenison.

Sancroft was also under the King's displeasure and had been forbidden the Court. He did not therefore (to his small regret) accompany his brethren to Whitehall when they went to deliver their petition to James

[1] The attitude of Lamplugh was peculiar: when estimates were made of the likelihood of James getting the House of Lords to agree to repeal the Test Act, his name appears invariably with the opposition; he approved the draft of the Petition, but refused to sign the Petition itself and (according to Professor Browning) encouraged his clergy to read the Declaration. His behaviour when William entered Exeter has no bearing on this question: he might easily have approved the petition but refused to identify himself with the invasion.

[2] The bishops' petition is probably the shortest document of comparable importance. The gist of it (after proper expressions of loyalty) is contained in the words, "that declaration is founded upon such a dispensing power as hath been often declared illegal in Parliament, and particularly in the years 1662 and 1672 and in the beginning of Your Majesty's reign. . . . Your petitioners therefore most humbly and earnestly beseech Your Majesty that you will be most graciously pleased not to insist upon the distributing and reading Your Majesty's said declaration."

in person. The six bishops found Sunderland, offered him the petition and suggested that he should show it to the King so that he should not be taken by surprise. Sunderland refused to look at it, but went in to announce their arrival to the King, and they were at once admitted to audience. They were graciously received, for the secret of their meetings had been so well kept that James had no idea of the dismay and indignation which his Declaration had aroused among churchmen, and he expected that they had come merely to ask that the order for reading in churches should be sent not to them, but (as was more correct) to the Chancellors of their dioceses, and he was quite willing to accommodate them in so small a matter. When, however, he had glanced at the petition and realised its purport he completely lost his temper, and, as had happened at Oxford nine months earlier, he threw away all sense of royal dignity. "This is a great surprise to me," he said; "here are strange words. I did not expect this from you. This is a standard of rebellion."[1] The bishops on their side were no less surprised: they had been aware that their action in presenting their petition had been bold, but they had had no expectation whatever that they would incur so extreme a measure of the King's displeasure, and they were dismayed at being classed as rebels. (It may also be said that they had had no anticipation of the enormous results which their petition would have on the course of events; if they had had this anticipation it is unlikely that some of them would have concurred in the petition.[2]) Still on their knees, as they had been when they presented the petition, they protested their loyalty to the King, of which their conduct throughout his reign had given proof. James took no notice of what they said, but continued to rail at them: they had been guilty of rebellion, "the dispensing power was never questioned by men of the Church of England", "I will keep this paper, I will not part with it", "I will be obeyed in publishing any declaration", and in conclusion, borrowing the phraseology of the Puritans but conveying little meaning, "I tell you there are seven thousand men, and of the Church of England too, that have not bowed the knee to Baal".

A most important sequel to this audience was the printing of the bishops' petition the same evening and its wide distribution throughout London. The identity of the person who communicated to the Press this very secret document is one of the unsolved mysteries of history:

[1] Barrillon says that James "ajouta que l'écrit etait une trompette de rebellion (c'est une phrase Anglaise)".

[2] The *Life of James* (II, 155) says that the petition was deliberately kept back until two days before the Declaration should have been read, and then published with deliberate intent to inflame the people. But this view has no support in the facts.

the biographer of Bishop Ken suggests that Compton took this step; he certainly had the opportunity, and may have seen in the publication advantage to the popular cause. But Compton was not at all the man to betray his own party, and several other people, other than Compton and the Seven, saw and signed (or perhaps refused to sign) the petition in draft. The King also may not have kept it so private that it was not possible to make a copy. But whatever its source, the disclosure introduced an entirely new situation. In the King's closet the petition was not, as James said it was, "a standard of rebellion", but, dispersed in the streets, that is exactly what it became. For many months James had been exasperating his people, and everyone had been looking for the first open resistance to the royal will; the bishops (building better than they knew) had presented public opinion with an outlet for indignation and the clergy with popular support in their resistance to the royal decree. For without the publication, the text of the petition would have been a secret, there would no doubt have been a considerable body of rumour that the bishops had protested to the King, but the country was always full of rumours which had been proved baseless, and a great many of the clergy would have been quite as undecided in their attitude to the Declaration as the bishops had been when first it was promulgated.[1] In the event an overwhelming majority of the clergy both in London and in the provinces disobeyed the proclamation.[2] In some dioceses, notably in Durham, Chester, Rochester and St. Davids, the Declaration was circulated to the clergy, but according to Burnet only seven of them in London and not more than 200 elsewhere read it, and of these some read it once only.

The publication of the petition was also important as making it necessary for James to take notice of what he considered to be an affront: there could be no doubt that the disobedience of the clergy to his decree had been encouraged by the bishops' petition; he naturally felt that his authority had been challenged, and it was impossible for a man of his temperament to refuse to take up a challenge. He was determined that the bishops should be punished; a man less angry or more politic would have realised into what an *impasse* he had fallen by his misjudgement of the amount of strain which the loyalty of the Church of England could bear. For if he entered into conflict with the bishops he was bound in

[1] Macaulay, however, says that a letter was sent to every clergyman in the kingdom, in which the writer set forth the dilemma in which the clergy were, but urged them not to read the Declaration.

[2] One parson achieved fame by obeying the decree in the letter, but disobeying it in the spirit: he told his congregation that he was bound by law to read the Declaration, but that they were under no obligation to listen to it, and after a short pause it was read to an empty church.

the long run to be a loser: even if he were successful and punished them, the nation would look on them as martyrs in a national cause, and universal indignation would at the very least put an end to all the hopes which he had nourished, in spite of persistent discouragement, from the beginning of his reign of getting the principles of the Declaration of Indulgence accepted by the nation and legalised by Parliament.[1] It would have been better to have accepted defeat and humiliation at the outset either by ignoring the whole incident or by administering to the bishops a public reprimand and a pardon in view of their previous loyal conduct; but, as always happens, popular indignation in favour of the bishops had aroused equal indignation at Court against the bishops, and even the most moderate of James's counsellors could not advise so mild a solution, nor in fact could they have expected James to accept it. Several suggestions were made: one which was very nearly carried out was that the Declaration should be republished with an addition prescribing the penalty of suspension for all clergy who failed to obey it—a proceeding which would have meant depriving thirty-nine out of every forty parishes of their parsons and sixteen or seventeen of the twenty-four dioceses of their bishops; another suggestion was that the powers of the Ecclesiastical Commission should be used against the bishops, but if, as was still hoped, Parliament was to meet, the existing bishops (and Compton in spite of his suspension) could demand to be summoned to the House of Lords, and the Lords when they deliberated on their claims could not fail to pronounce the Ecclesiastical Commission an illegal body and its judgements null and void. Finally it was decided to cite the seven bishops before the King's Bench on a charge of seditious libel. There was no sound reason to believe that they had been guilty of this misdemeanour, but James relied on the judges he had put in, acting with a jury chosen by sheriffs of London whom he had selected, to return a verdict and to pass sentence according to his wishes. Various accounts have been given of the divisions among James's counsellors on this subject: Barrillon had the impression that Sunderland and Petre opposed the prosecution, but Sunderland was far too wary to oppose James openly on any subject on which he had made up his mind, and if Petre advised moderation before the decision was taken, he soon changed his opinion, and made no secret of his delight at the humiliation which the bishops were to undergo. James himself says that it was chiefly on the advice of Jeffreys that the decision was taken. But that again is unlikely, for Jeffreys, unscrupulous as he was,

[1] Possibly the best solution from James's point of view would have been a conviction followed immediately by a royal pardon. But there is no evidence that James would have been willing to pardon the bishops. (But see Adda June 29/July 9, quoted by Lingard, X, 308n., for a contrary opinion.)

had a respect for law, at any rate in courts which he could not himself dominate, and he must have realised the extreme weakness of the charge against the bishops; it appears also from his conversations with the Earl of Clarendon both before and after the trial that he was very much opposed to the prosecution; he was said also to be likely to lose his place because of his mismanagement of the trial. The real reason for the prosecution is the second reason which James himself gives, "his prepossession against the yielding temper which had proved so dangerout to his brother and so fatal to his father".

On May 28 Sancroft received a notification from Sunderland that he and the six other bishops were to appear before the Privy Council on June 8. The Council made two demands upon them: that they should acknowledge that the petition (which was shown to them) was in the handwriting of Sancroft and signed by all of them, and that they should enter into recognisances for their appearance before the King's Bench. They had been warned by their legal advisers to refuse both demands, but they yielded to the first after they had been subjected to a badgering by Jeffreys and James which almost amounted to "third degree", and in spite of their protest that they should not be forced into an acknowledgement which could be used against them at the trial. Against the second demand they pleaded their privilege as peers, and when this plea was over-ruled they remained obstinate in their refusal. The Council were very reluctant to commit them to the Tower,[1] for they were aware that a great crowd had assembled outside the palace and that it would be impossible to convey them through the streets without a large armed escort, but there was no alternative. They succeeded in frustrating the mob, and possibly an attempt at rescue, by sending the bishops to the Tower by water, but they could not prevent the people from crowding to the banks of the river and making the greatest anti-Government demonstration which London had seen since 1641.

The bishops appeared before the four judges of the King's Bench, Chief Justice Wright and Justices Allibone, Holloway and Powell, on June 15, the first day of term, after having been a week in the Tower. The proceedings were protracted by the objections raised by the bishops' counsel and spread over four hours; it is to be noted that there was already a breach in the unanimity of the Bench, for Justice Powell was far more ready than the other judges to admit the validity of the objections. In the end the bishops pleaded "Not Guilty" to the indictment, and were liberated after giving recognisances for their appearance for trial on June 29.

[1] There were twenty-one Privy Councillors present, and of these nineteen signed the order of committal. The Councillors who did not sign were both Catholics, the Earl of Moray and, very significantly, Father Petre.

The course of this trial does not concern us here: its importance lies in the grounds on which the bishops were acquitted, and for this reason it is fortunate that they were not acquitted or discharged on the technical pleas which were from time to time urged by their counsel—irregularity in the original order of commitment to the Tower, violation of the privileges of peerage, failure to prove fact or place of publication of the alleged seditious libel—for the Court was forced to pronounce judgement on one of the main points at issue between James and his political opponents: the legality of the Dispensing Power. The acquittal of the bishops involved by implication a judgement that James in issuing his two Declarations of Indulgence had acted illegally, and Chief Justice Wright himself, though he pronounced the petition a libel, was careful not to pronounce in favour of the dispensing power.

At the same time it must be admitted by the upholders of constitutional rights that the trial was not in a strict sense fair. James no doubt had the initial advantage of having judges who before the trial were entirely in his interests, and the method of choosing the jury was not disadvantageous to the Crown lawyers. But the cause of the bishops had in the eight weeks between the issue of the Declaration and the trial become a national cause, and both judges and jurymen could not fail to be aware of the intense odium they would incur if the bishops were convicted. This popular pressure (which had made itself felt in the courts at the time of Oates's Plot) was brought home to both judges and jury by the presence in court of a large number of prominent peers, who made no secret of their support of the bishops. As an eye-witness said, "At this great trial were between thirty and forty lords, which indeed frighted the judges and jury for they fancied that every one brought a halter in his pocket".

The London mob had watched all the proceedings of the prosecution with extreme and agitated interest. When the bishops on June 15 were brought by river to Westminster Hall from the Tower, the banks and the road from the river back to the Hall swarmed with people; when on the same day they were liberated on their own recognisances, a rumour went round that they had been acquitted, and the crowd so pressed upon them that the Bishop of St. Asaph was glad to take refuge in Lord Clarendon's coach and to be conveyed to his lodgings by side roads. When at last the verdict of "Not Guilty" was pronounced, Halifax in the court (to the indignation of the judges) led an enormous burst of cheering, which was taken up outside, and the good news spread across the country from village to village. At night there were illuminations and bonfires which James foolishly and in vain ordered the Lord Mayor to check. The national rejoicing could not have been greater at a great military or naval victory over a foreign enemy.[1]

James was at the military camp at Hounslow on the morning of the 30th. He heard the men outside cheering, and sent Feversham to inquire the cause; Feversham returned saying, "It is nothing, only the soldiers rejoicing at the acquittal of the bishops". "Nothing," said James; "you call that nothing", and he left the camp in violent agitation, and as he left he was heard to mutter over and over again, "Tant pis pour eux; tant pis pour eux".[2] For it was not the nature of a man afflicted with James's form of paranoia to accept defeat. He determined to proceed against the whole body of clergy who had followed the bishops in ignoring the Declaration. On July 12 the Ecclesiastical Commission sent out an order[3] to all Chancellors and archdeacons to make a return before August 16 of all those who had not read it; when, on August 16, it was found that the distances to be covered had made it impossible to make the return so early, the last date for submission was altered to December 6. The postponement to so distant a date seems to imply that the Commission was not so anxious as it had been at first to proceed with this wholesale prosecution; but at the same meeting they received a letter from the Bishop of Rochester who up to then had sat on the Commission (though a moderate member) and had himself read the Declaration in Westminster Abbey, as Dean;[4] in this letter he expressed himself unable to concur in the prosecution of the recalcitant clergy and resigned his seat on the Commission. The Commission was not formally dissolved until October 5, but apparently even Jeffreys lost heart when he found what little power the King and his instruments had over the Church, and he never again convened the Commission. In other ways James signified his reactions to the revolt of the clergy and to the trial of the bishops by distribution of rewards and punish-

[1] Stevens, an English Catholic, who later followed James to Ireland, considered that the first "hardened piece of insolence" in his neighbourhood (Welshpool) was the lighting of public bonfires in defiance of proclamation when the bishops were acquitted. Subsequently Lloyd of St. Asaph, one of the seven, made a triumphal progress through his diocese.

[2] Hoffmann, the Imperial Ambassador, interpreted this exclamation as meaning that if the bishops had been convicted James would have pardoned them, but that now they would feel the weight of his displeasure.

[3] The first words of this order in the *London Gazette* furnish a happy example of official meiosis: "Whereas we have received information that divers Vicars, Rectors and Curates have omitted or neglected to read the said Declaration . . ."

[4] Clarendon, however, wrote to the Princess of Orange, "The declaration . . . was read in only four churches in this great city and liberties. . . . One of the four places was Westminster Abbey, where the Bishop of Rochester is Dean; he ordered one of the petty canons to read it, but went out of town himself overnight; he's a poor-spirited man." But, as Plumptre says, "Lord Dartmouth's statement quoted in Stanley's *Memorials of Westminster* is . . . decisive. He was at Westminster at the time and heard Sprat read it."

ments. He made Timothy Hall, whose only qualification for the post was that he had read the Declaration, Bishop of Oxford, and he dismissed the two judges at the trial who had dissented from Wright and had been of opinion that the bishops' petition was not a libel.

The birth of the Prince of Wales took place at St. James's Palace a little after ten o'clock on the morning of Sunday, July 10. Rumours of the Queen's pregnancy had begun at the end of the previous October, but it was not until three weeks later that she herself was certain of it. In January, days of thanksgiving for the pregnancy were ordered by the Court, and three bishops were appointed to draw up appropriate forms of prayer. In the succeeding six months there were unfounded rumours that the Queen had had a miscarriage. The birth actually took place a month (or less) earlier than had been expected. The witnesses included Jeffreys, Sunderland, and a number of other Privy Councillors, the Queen-dowager, the Duchesses of Mazarin, de Bouillon and Portsmouth and other great ladies. There was nothing extraordinary in any of the physiological circumstances except that the Queen had had two miscarriages, in October 1683 and in April 1684, since the birth of a daughter to her in August 1682.[1]

But the political circumstances of the birth were unique. The main fact patent both to Catholics and Protestants was that the new Prince would take precedence in the succession to his half-sisters, Mary and Anne, and that it was likely that on James's death a Catholic would follow him on the throne. It is odd that both sides assumed that the baby would survive to manhood and not, as Mary Beatrice's five other children had done, die in infancy. Another chance was that James himself would die within a few years and that means would be found to bring up his son as a Protestant. Neither of these considerations influenced the minds of those whose hopes of the salvation of the country were founded on the expectation of the succession of William and Mary. It is difficult to believe that the doubts which were immediately cast on the genuineness of the birth arose spontaneously; the phenomenon of a fanatically held belief in what we now know to be utterly untrue in fact, is almost exactly a repetition of what had happened ten years earlier in connection with the so-called Popish Plot; but here was no Titus Oates to invent a tale which struck the public imagination at a moment when it was ready for such a tale; witnesses who believed or pretended to believe their own stories were no doubt produced, but

[1] Apart from these considerations, the doubts about the birth may have been due in part to the Queen's delicacy in talking about her condition, a delicacy which was not shared, or even understood, by Englishwomen of her time.

these witnesses did not originate the story that the Queen had never been pregnant (or, if pregnant, had had a miscarriage) and that a new-born baby had been found elsewhere at the right moment and produced as hers, and they so grossly contradicted one another in detail that it would have been impossible to compose a coherent narrative from their testimony. It is a saddening thought, but no less true, that, except for a small minority of the finest intellects, the hearts of men govern their heads, and their reasoning powers are subordinated to their prejudices; this is true of most individuals, and by mass-suggestion they infect their neighbours with their own disease, so that people in crowds are even more susceptible to it then are individuals. For several years no one in England, except a Jacobite here and there, publicly admitted a doubt that a fraud had been perpetrated. But no modern reader who studies the history of the royal exiles up to the time of Mary Beatrice's death in 1718, especially the pathetic account of her death, can doubt that James, and still more his Queen, were absolutely honest in declaring that James Francis Edward was her son.

In part, no doubt, James's hot-headed Jesuit followers were responsible for the incredulity with which the news of the birth was received: they had made such confident prophecies that the birth would take place, and that the child would be a boy, that they were suspected of taking measures to secure the fulfilment of their prophecy. In a letter which purported to have been sent from the Jesuits of Friburg to the Jesuits of Liége, James is said to have replied to a zealous Catholic who was apprehensive of the future, "God will be able to raise up an heir who is not a heretic and who will guarantee against this leprosy both us and our posterity"; the letter may have been a forgery, but the hope and faith which it attributes to James were everywhere expressed by the Jesuits. Nor did these men, or James himself, realise, in the delirious joy with which they welcomed the Prince, the reaction which the birth, quite apart from the doubts which were cast on its genuineness, would have on public opinion. For, not only had James's opponents been restrained from action by the hope that the conditions which they felt to be intolerable would be reversed by a Protestant successor, but the English Catholics as a body, between whom and Petre there was little contact or sympathy, had been restrained in their demands by the same expectation, for they were aware that a Protestant reaction would find them as defenceless as they had been in 1678. The prospect of a succession of Catholic kings gave a feeling of security to the Catholics in which the churchmen and Protestant dissenters found a danger to themselves. Three weeks after the birth the famous invitation to William to come to England with an armed force to vindicate the constitutional rights of the English people and his wife's right of succession was signed by Shrewsbury, Devonshire, Danby, Compton, Edward Russell and Henry Sidney.

There was an interval of twelve weeks between the acquittal of the bishops and the realisation by James that William's military and naval preparations were directed against himself; this period was marked by no diminution of James's hopes for the ultimate success of his plans and no slackening in his activities, but in fact the discontinuance of the sittings of the Ecclesiastical Commission was only one symptom of his steady loss of ground. Among his intimate advisors two parties were forming: Sunderland and Jeffreys were beginning to see that if James were to regain what he had lost by the prosecution of the bishops he would have to moderate his methods and to recover the support of a larger section of influential men; Petre and the Jesuits, on the other hand, shared their master's optimism and were for pushing home the victory which they thought was in their grasp. As early as December 1687 Skelton at Paris had been hinting that Sunderland was in correspondence with William and was encouraging him in his opposition to the repeal of the Test Act; but (as Barrillon says) Sunderland was consistently alienating himself from William by doing everything that he disliked, manipulating the constituencies to secure repeal by Parliament and backing up James in demanding the return of the British regiments. If Sunderland had any correspondence with William it was with the intention of keeping on good personal terms with the Protestant heir presumptive—a kind of insurance on James's life—and there is no more justification for the belief that he was in this instance playing a double game than there is at a later stage of his being in the secret of William's expedition.[1] But the suspicion engendered by Skelton, together with his opposition to their violent counsels, gave his Jesuit opponents a means of undermining him in the King's confidence, and his public avowal before the Council on June 24 of his conversion to the Catholic faith was a countermove. He himself said he had been a Catholic for two years, and in December 1687 Barrillon had told Louis that he was prepared to declare himself whenever James thought such a course advisable. Sunderland's declaration probably saved him from dis-

[1] There is, however, a letter of July 28 (which Dalrymple ascribes to Edward Russell) which says, "Since I came into England, Mr. Roberts [*i.e.*, Sunderland] is grown so warm that I can hardly prevail with him to stay for his being turned out. It is now resolved not to talk of the Test and Penal Laws nor indeed anything they would have him do. I believe he is so ill at Court that his reign there will hardly last a month. He has desired me to assure your Highness of his utmost service." It seems likely that Sunderland hoodwinked the writer of this letter.

missal, but it did James no good in the country: for the only remaining Protestants in high office were Jeffreys and Middleton, joint Secretary of State with Sunderland; Middleton had no great force of character, and Jeffreys had not been high in James's favour for a long time, and now the King attributed the acquittal of the bishops partly to his mismanagement. The admission at this time of three dissenters—Trevor, Titus and Vane—to the Privy Council was a gesture which still further alarmed the Church of England.

Among the signs of relaxation of the fear of the power of the King to bring retribution on anyone who opposed him was the action of the University of Oxford on receipt of the news of the death of their Chancellor, the Duke of Ormonde, on July 21, 1688. The graduates of the University, anticipating a mandate for the appointment of one of James's henchmen, met on Monday, July 23, and elected the late Duke's grandson, the second Duke, as Chancellor; only two hours later arrived a royal mandate to elect Jeffreys. The Vice-Chancellor wrote Jeffreys a letter excusing in very submissive terms the action of the University, but their rapid action can have had no other object than to defeat James's intentions. Nevertheless James had not even the slight pretext for interference which he had had in the case of Magdalen College, and he was compelled to swallow the rebuff.

Another symptom was the great disrespect with which the judges on circuit were treated by the local gentry. This disrespect was in part due to the contempt into which the Bench had fallen as exponents of the law; it was no longer felt that the judges even pretended to act impartially and according to law, for at all stages in the struggle between the royal prerogative and the people, judges had been dismissed who could not find law to justify the King's pretensions—Holloway and Powell, the two judges who had dissented from Wright's summing up against the bishops, had been dismissed as a matter of routine. But it was also due to the conduct of the judges themselves, acting on instructions originating with James. For in their charges at the opening of the Assizes, if the charge of Allibone at Croydon is a fair sample, they admittedly spoke for the King, made election speeches against the penal laws and Test Act and condemned the verdict in the bishops' trial.

But the most serious trouble was in the Army and Navy. Hounslow had been selected as a site for a camp of training and exercise for the Army on account of its proximity to London: partly no doubt because James wanted to be able to pay frequent visits himself, both from Whitehall and from Windsor, to supervise the organisation and drill and to gratify his own taste for military display; but he had a stronger motive, and that was to overawe the City of London, which, with memories of Shaftesbury in his mind, he regarded as the stronghold of Protestantism and Whiggery. But, as usual, he did not look all round before committing himself: if he had done so he would have realised that it was much more likely that London would keep the Army strong in its Protestant principles. James (according to Burnet) had connived at bad behaviour of the soldiers towards the civil population with a view to making the Army unpopular and therefore more devoted to himself, "but after all, though the soldiers were bad Englishmen and worse Christians, yet the Court found them too good Protestants to trust much to them". They had no objection to helping themselves to private property or to disturbing the peace of family life, but they openly showed their sympathy with the bishops when they mounted guard over them at the Tower, and did not forbear to cheer when they heard that the bishops were acquitted, though they well knew that the King was in the camp. It was probably this last incident which brought home to James that the implement of despotism which he had forged with such care was likely to break in his hands.

Again he took the most direct but least wise action: the camp at Hounslow was broken up early in August, and Irish Catholic troops were brought over to stiffen the loyalty of his Protestant Army. Now, the Irish, though Catholic, had no particular loyalty to the King of England; indeed, their chief feeling was one of resentment against the slavery in which they were held by him and by the Protestants who resided among them, and they owed no allegiance except to the Pope; in these circumstances it is said that Tyrconnel had to induce them to make the voyage to England by promises (which he had no intention of fulfilling) of grants of land. The Irish troops had small military value: they were imperfectly trained, and in their own country they had been under no sort of discipline when off duty. The English hated them as barbarians and foreigners, and their behaviour at Portsmouth, where a great many of them were quartered, was probably matched elsewhere; there the mayor was robbed when he was going the rounds of the sentries, and English soldiers prevented the Irish from robbing an alehouse at a cost of four or five deaths on the two sides. In any case, the numbers brought over from Ireland—three or four thousand[1]—were by no means sufficient for the purpose for which they were intended, but only served as an irritant to passions already roused by the prosecution of the bishops and the birth of the Prince.

This irritation came to a head at Portsmouth early in September. A

[1] Van Citters reported far higher numbers than these; he says that 18,000 was the number aimed at, that 2000 were to go to Portsmouth in addition to those already there, that 3000 had just (September 18) landed at Chester.

Colonel MacEllicot had arrived from Ireland with forty or fifty men above his proper quota; the Duke of Berwick, who was in command of the garrison, proposed that these men should be distributed among the English regiments; Colonel Beaumont, backed by five of his captains, represented to the Duke that it was not "consistent with our honours to have foreigners imposed upon us without being complained of that our companies were weak, or orders to recruit them": the captains were willing to recruit more men for their companies, as was their privilege and duty if the numbers were too small, but they were unwilling to affront their men by associating them with Irishmen, whom they despised.[1] When Berwick insisted on the men being taken, Beaumont and the captains offered to resign their commissions. When the incident was reported to James he sent a troop of horse to bring the recalcitrant officers to Windsor; there they were tried by court-martial and dismissed from the Army. James would have acted more wisely if he had treated the matter as trivial, as indeed it was at first, for Beaumont's original representation had been reasonable and respectful and in no sense defiant; by giving the case publicity James made it a test case for the Army, as the trial of the bishops had been a test case for the Church. The immediate effect of the court-martial was disastrous, for on September 18 it was said that at Portsmouth a great many officers had resigned their commissions, that a number of men had deserted and that James himself was going to Portsmouth to restore discipline.

In the Navy, before William actually landed in England, there had been less disturbance. But there was one incident which brought home to James the limitations of his power in a sphere in which he flattered himself he was supreme. The fleet of some twenty ships had been at sea since the beginning of the year, and James had recently appointed a Catholic, Sir Roger Strickland, to command it. Strickland dismissed his Anglican chaplain, took priests on board, and Catholic rites, possibly even the Mass, were celebrated on the flagship: the result was something like a mutiny, which Strickland failed to suppress. In the middle of July the condition of the Navy in the Thames estuary was so serious that James had to go down to see what he could do. He "flattered the seamen all he could, went from ship to ship and called the seamen his children, said he had nothing to say as to their religion, that he granted liberty of conscience to all, but expected that they should behave themselves like men of honour and courage when there was occasion for their service; but all the popish priests were brought on shore".

[1] James's biographer makes the unworthy and unsupported allegation: "Beaumont . . . being already engaged in the Prince of Orange's interest, was unwilling to have so many spies on him".

It is necessary now to consider the slow process by which James was convinced that his nephew and son-in-law was preparing for a descent upon England. It is a question that has little direct bearing on the history of the Revolution, for the extra weeks available for preparation could not have provided James with means to defeat William's invasion.[1] In the summer of 1688 James was on bad terms with the States-General: they had refused to send back to England the British troops in their employ and—a matter of scarcely less importance in James's eyes—to extradite Burnet; the Sweden–Denmark dispute, in which the English and Dutch navies were to have been employed on opposite sides, was in suspense at the Congress of Altona, but a half-hearted attitude of armed neutrality between the navies persisted. At the end of June, William made a gesture of personal friendship in sending Zuylenstein to England to congratulate James on the birth of his son, and at about the same time the Dutch ambassador had an audience with the King on the same subject. The ambassador took the opportunity to review the relations between his masters and the English Government; he said that James in general had a false impression that the States-General were hostile to him, and in particular that they harboured a design to attack the English coast, whereas they had a great respect for him, and as for the rumours of aggressive designs (which the minister hinted originated from Albeville) the fewness of the ships in commission was a sufficient refutation. The King had, Van Citters mildly suggested, been too prone to listen to French advice, and he even hinted that he had accepted financial help from Louis, and that Louis was no true friend of James, but sought only his own aggrandisement. James was in a gentle mood—the bishops had not yet been acquitted—and he did not take offence at the minister's frankness: he demurred at the description of Louis's motives, admitted that he had offered him assistance, but said that he did not think he would have to avail himself of it, and concluded with the harmless statement that he desired to live at peace with France, as with other States. A week later, before returning to Holland, Van Citters waited on James and obtained from him additional assurances that he had no treaty with France.

Albeville in Holland was persistent in his opinion that the Dutch fleet was being put in readiness for an attack on England. As early as the end of February he stated that it was intended to make a naval demonstration off the English coasts to encourage the opposition, and in the middle of July he reported that "the talk at The Hague is that

[1] An earlier enlightenment, however, might have persuaded James to accept the embassy of Bonrepaus in a more genial spirit and by consequence have altered Louis's military plans.

people of England and even the Army are on the point of revolution and it is openly said that if the Prince of Orange were to show himself in England the whole nation would declare for him". Unfortunately for James, he had appointed to a very important embassy a man in whom even he himself felt no confidence; there can be no doubt that the earliest conjectures of Albeville were without foundation, and that the activity of the Dutch Navy in the spring of 1688 was due in the first instance to an intention to assist Sweden in her quarrel with Denmark, and later, in connection with the same quarrel, to provide against a possible junction of the English and French fleets. But from July onwards Albeville's information was substantially correct; he continued to supply it, but it was consistently disregarded.

Meanwhile Louis had been receiving from Avaux, his minister at The Hague, a succession of despatches which left no doubt in the French King's mind of William's objective; he had the advantage over James of having an ambassador whom he could trust. Barrillon in England received Avaux's reports, both direct and from Paris, but nothing he could say convinced James that he was in imminent danger. In the middle of August, Louis determined to send an additional ambassador in the person of Bonrepaus, who had twice before been at James's Court, and had achieved a relation with the King almost amounting to intimacy. The mission of Bonrepaus was a complete failure: of his first interview he reported on August 25 that if James "believes that the Prince of Orange has any other design than to attack him, he is alone in Europe in that opinion". James was in a haughty and independent mood: he rejected all Louis's offers of military and naval assistance, though a naval treaty was actually drafted with blanks left for the numbers of ships, and to the Spanish ambassador, Ronquillo, he complained bitterly that Bonrepaus had been sent without the formality of a request that he would be willing to receive him. In the same mood when, at Louis's instigation, Skelton at Paris and Avaux at The Hague simultaneously and publicly declared that Louis would regard any attack on England as "a manifest breach of the peace and an open outbreak against my crown", James disavowed his envoy, recalled him and committed him to the Tower.

Ronquillo was very anxious to counteract the effect of French influence in the English Court, and in a two-hour audience with James he endeavoured to convince him that the States-General had no hostile intentions and that an alliance with Louis would make it impossible for Parliament to meet in a conciliatory spirit. On September 6 van Citters returned from Holland, and immediately had two audiences with the King. He was not in William's confidence, and he was therefore able with complete sincerity to express the indignation of his masters at the intimate relations subsisting between James and Louis and at his non-acceptance of their explanation of their military and naval preparations. According to the Imperial ambassador, he concluded his address to James:

> In such circumstances it is very painful for my superiors to see that Your Majesty has allowed himself to be deceived by France and to credit the insinuations that their intention is a descent upon England, so that Your Majesty has not only listened to the proposals of Bonrepaus but has even tolerated the publication of a declaration by Avaux, so grave, so scandalous and so prejudicial to the honour and glory of Your Majesty that it appears to place Your Majesty under the tutelage of France like another Cardinal Furstemberg, giving people cause to say that the King of England cannot defend himself against a petty republic.

James replied that the ambassador's reproaches were unmerited: that there were rumours abroad and that suitable precautions had been taken, but that he had respected all existing treaties, he had not accepted Bonrepaus's offers and that Avaux's declaration had been made without his knowledge. So convinced was James by the ambassador's protestations that he put aside the major issue of the threat to his safety and reverted to his permanent grievances against the States: their protection of Burnet and the pamphlets which he and others were publishing in Holland.

Meanwhile Albeville, seeing that no notice was taken of his warning by letter, crossed to England, and Skelton in Paris before his recall had got hold of a dismissed and disgruntled servant of William, called Budé de Verace, who had, or said he had, some authentic information to communicate. But Sunderland shared the blindness of his master and his Jesuit advisers, he got Albeville sent back with a reprimand for having left his post without leave and took so little notice of Budé de Verace's information that the informer decided against proceeding on his journey to England. On September 8 Louis and Barrillon wrote letters to one another:

> I am writing you today [said Louis] to tell you that I cannot tell by what wizardry the Court in which you are remains so fast asleep in the imminent danger which threatens it and so ill-informed about what is happening in England and elsewhere,

and Barrillon wrote:

> It is fashionable at Court to laugh at everyone who believes that

> the Prince of Orange intends to make a descent on England. Nevertheless I have omitted nothing in conversations with His Britannic Majesty and Lord Sunderland to cause them to reflect that the absolutely contrary opinion held by M. d'Avaux cannot be without foundation.

Two days later, however, James appears to have had some slight misgiving, for he told Barrillon that if, as appeared possible, William had designs on England, he would have no better success than Monmouth had had, for no one of quality would join him, and Barrillon's comment is that James is living in a fool's paradise: "Those who are nearest to him flatter him, and the least loyal pretend to be most zealous in his interests".

On September 15 Louis wrote to Barrillon saying that his army was besieging Philipsburg. Now, Philipsburg is in the heart of Germany, on the upper Rhine, and nearly 200 miles from the nearest Dutch frontier, so that the Dutch had no fear of attack by the French either through the Spanish Netherlands or by way of the lower Rhine. Louis had begun to believe about the middle of August that Avaux's warnings had foundation, and the ambassador's subsequent despatches had hardened his suspicions into conviction. His letter to Barrillon of September 15 was in the nature of an instruction to his ambassador on the line which he should take if James and his Ministers reproached his master for pursuing his own interests at such a time. But it cannot have been very helpful to Barrillon: in effect it merely says that Louis had no quarrel with the States-General on his own account, or with Spain, and that he proposes to observe his treaties with the one and the truce with the other; the implication is that he feels that James has rejected his offers and that he is not inclined to risk a further rebuff by repeating them James received the news with indifference.

It was on or about September 21 that James at last realised, from a despatch of Albeville's conveying information that could bear no other interpretation, what William's intentions really were; but he does not appear to have publicly acknowledged his conviction for several days, for on September 24 Lord Clarendon enters in his diary:

> I went to the King's levée and met His Majesty going to the Queen's side. He told me the Dutch were now coming to invade England in good earnest. I presumed to ask if he really believed it. To which the King replied with warmth, "Do I see you, my lord?" And then he said than an express arrived the last night with an account that 2000 men were already shipped off and 7000 more were marching to the sea-side.

Then James taunted Clarendon with his attachment to the bishops and to the Church of England with its boasted loyalty: "And now, my lord, I shall see what the Church of England men will do"; and Clarendon replied as much for himself as for his fellow-churchmen, "And your Majesty will see they will behave themselves like honest men, though they have been somewhat severely used of late".

James's reactions were those natural to a very obstinate man who suddenly finds that warnings which he has persistently scorned have been justified, that dangers which he thought chimerical are real and imminent and that the earth which had seemed so safe had crumbled beneath his feet: he completely lost his head, and took hasty and unconsidered steps to disarm his opponents at home and abroad. His first misguided step was to issue a proclamation saying that he had no aims inimical to the laws and religion of England and promising a Parliament in the following November, an action which, like so many which were to follow, was a measure of his fear rather than of his repentance, and which was entirely ineffective because his words, as ever, were belied by his deeds. He then did a far more foolish thing: he sent to Albeville on September 23 a memorial to be delivered by him to the States-General. With no reference to the projected expedition and with no suggestion of any other reason for choosing this time for making such an approach, he assured the States-General that he had no secret alliance with Louis, and offered, in the interests of the peace of Europe, to discuss with them measures for the preservation of the Peace of Nimeguen of 1678 and of the Truce of Ratisbon of 1684.

The States-General recognised this approach for what it was—a clumsy attempt to create a difference between them and the Prince of Orange. The memorial was delivered to the States at a meeting on September 25 by Albeville, whose manner of delivery "had no other effect than to confirm the impression that the King was frightened and to increase the confidence of his enemies". On October 4, William, in a secret session of the States-General, declared his intention to land in England with an armed force in order to secure the rights of the Protestant religion and to vindicate his wife's claim to the succession.[1] After that meeting a reply to Albeville's memorial was drafted: since James disavowed any alliance with France, the States-General had no hostile intentions against him or the English nation, but they desired to see peace re-established between James and his subjects with benefit to the Protestant religion, and in truth they had no other aim than the

[1] Avaux under date October 4/14 says that William did not allow the States-General to assemble, but approached the deputies separately, and mentioned, not his wife's rights, but only the religious question.

tranquillity of his kingdom; the offers of mediation between the States-General and France were tacitly rejected. The States-General by implication claimed a very doubtful right to intervene in the internal affairs of England and they provided an introduction to William's own declaration.

The effect of the memorial on the relations between James and Louis was even more disastrous, and it does not appear that Barrillon was informed of it before it was despatched. He wrote two letters to Louis on the same day, September 23; when he wrote the first he had evidently not seen the draft of the memorial, for he said that James had offered in certain circumstances to make war on France; later in the day, however, he had obtained more information, and he gave Louis the official version of the purpose of the memorial:

> The intention is to use it as a means of preventing or delaying the departure of the Prince of Orange and to commence a negotiation which will take time to conclude. D'Albeville has orders to discuss only methods of keeping the peace; a formal engagement has been avoided by this memorial. They hope here that Your Majesty will not take exception to their looking for a means of creating a division between the States-General and the Prince of Orange in the extremity to which the King is reduced, nor, when his very existence is at stake, to his having presented a memorial expressed in such terms that later on it will bear any interpretation that he likes to give it.

Sunderland pleaded (says Barrillon) that the memorial had little practical meaning, for the Prince of Orange might be in England in three or four days, and whether James was beaten or victorious the memorial would be forgotten. The minister also repudiated any suggestion that he himself was playing a double game and providing for his own safety: he said that "he could not save himself without saving the King his master, that the Prince of Orange would never pardon him for his attachment to the French court, for having declared himself a Catholic and for having taken the first step which led to the others in advising the recall of the British regiments". But it appeared to Louis that the explanations of James and Sunderland only covered an attempt to save themselves by an alliance with the Dutch against France, and that James had in effect proposed himself as a member of the League of Augsburg. Louis's feeling was not so much anger with James as pity for the depths of humiliation into which he had fallen; but if he had ever intended to declare war on the States-General, he was now precluded from doing so, because James was, or might presently become, their ally. When on October 7 he sent Barrillon 300,000 livres to be held in readiness for James's needs he explained his doubts more fully:

> I do not wish to examine my just causes of complaint when the King of England makes a request for my assistance. . . . But my interests would be seriously prejudiced if this money were employed to increase the army of the King of England so as to make it easier for him to make an agreement with the Prince of Orange to unite their forces against my crown (as is already rumoured) and if when this courier arrives the revolt has become general and the King's affairs are desperate you must say that I am collecting bills of exchange. . . . But if on the contrary the money is likely to be of real assistance to the King in maintaining himself, you may not only make over this money but you may even assure this Prince that I shall continue to give him effective pledges of my friendship; you will also discuss with his ministers the measures that should be taken to give him next spring naval forces superior to those of his enemy.

The proclamation of September 21 was the first indication that James saw the necessity of coming to some sort of accommodation with his subjects, but he could hardly hope that the vague promises contained in that proclamation would so far allay the popular discontents as to enable him to meet William's invasion at the head of a united nation. For his next moves he needed guidance and support, and characteristically he turned to the "loyal" Church of England. On September 24 Sunderland, by his order, wrote to nine bishops commanding them to wait on the King on the 28th. Six of these duly appeared—the other three being for different reasons unable to come—and James addressed them in general terms, saying that he was determined to support the Church of England; he did indeed announce that he had given orders for the restoration of Compton to the See of London, and he appears to have hinted that he might also give Magdalen College back to its Fellows, abolish the Ecclesiastical Commission, restore to the corporations their ancient charters and submit the question of the dispensing power to the decision of Parliament. These four points were in several quarters believed to have been definitely conceded, but subsequent events show that they were mentioned vaguely or not at all; James's policy at this time was to make promises so indefinite that they could be repudiated after the audience. The Bishop of Winchester said to those waiting outside, "Omnia bene", but the other bishops had small hopes of fundamental changes. Between the summoning of the bishops and their appearance before him there had been a stubborn conflict among the King's intimate advisers. Clarendon reports in his diary two interviews with Jeffreys;

on September 24 Jeffreys said that two days earlier James had determined to call a meeting of all peers, spiritual and temporal, who were in or near London, and to put everything back to the condition in which it had been at his accession, he had also ordered Jeffreys "to restore all the honest old aldermen of the City who had been turned out"; three days later the Lord Chancellor told Clarendon, "All was nought, some rogues had changed the King's mind, that he would yield in nothing to the bishops, that the Virgin Mary was to do all", and by implication the order to Jeffreys to restore the charter had been recalled.

This conflict in the royal counsels, between Sunderland and Jeffreys on the one hand and Petre and the Jesuits on the other, had been latent for some months; the certainty of William's invasion brought it to the surface. James's Jesuit advisers hardly made a claim to understand the political problem; they were not like their opponents, unscrupulous realists; in some ways they rose above them, in others they were their moral equals or inferiors: they undoubtedly worked (though with no wisdom) for the good of their Church, but they had a private motive which revealed itself obviously in the years of James's final exile. For the most important and fundamental of the concessions which James would have had to make for agreement with his people before his flight, or for restoration after his flight, was the dismissal from his counsels of themselves, and they could not contemplate so supreme an act of self-abnegation as to advise the King to make concessions that would inevitably lead to such a step. It is not necessary to assume that they acknowledged even to themselves or to each other their true motives: there is comprised in human nature an enormous power of self-deception, and no doubt they identified, as did their master, the cause of religion with their personal interests.

On September 30 James saw Sancroft alone (he had not been present at the previous meeting); Sancroft afterwards expressed himself satisfied with the King's general attitude, but he was apprehensive that the omission of mention of the clergy in the general pardon meant (as it probably actually did) that James had not given up hope of being revenged on them for their reception of the second Declaration of Indulgence. On October 3, James, having the previous day verbally promised the present and late Lord Mayor that he would restore the London charter, received a number of bishops. At that meeting Sancroft informed the King that the conversations he had previously had both with individual bishops and groups of them had been of too general a character to form a foundation for a settlement of grievances, and asked permission to "suggest to Your Majesty such advices as we think proper at this season and so leave them for your princely consideration". He then, with James's permission, read a statement under ten heads, humbly requesting the King: to put the local government of Lords-Lieutenant and Deputy-Lieutenants into the hands of legally qualified persons; to abolish the Ecclesiastical Commission; to employ only legally qualified persons in civil and ecclesiastical posts and in particular to restore Magdalen College to its rightful Fellows; to withdraw from Catholics licences to teach; to discontinue the use of the dispensing power until Parliament had decided for or against it; to deprive the four vicars apostolical of their offices; to fill the vacancies in archbishoprics and bishoprics both in England and Ireland; to restore the corporations; to call a Parliament in the near future; to revert himself to the faith in which he had been brought up.[1]

Up to this point James had been playing for time; the bishops' petition was on their part, or on the part of those who were advising them (Halifax probably among others), to commit the King to something more definite than hints of what he might do in certain circumstances and at no specified date. James was no doubt mortified and shocked at the advantage the bishops had taken of his gracious condescension in consulting them, but he took their petition and mumbled some words about not being offended at the freedom with which they had used him. The petition had some of the effect it had been intended to have, and several of the concessions demanded were made: the Ecclesiastical Commission was in any case moribund, and its abolition on October 5, by order in Council, was no great boon; on the 6th Jeffreys in person restored their charter to the City of London; on the 11th he replaced the Lords-Lieutenant, Deputy-Lieutenants and Justices of the Peace who had been dismissed for giving unsatisfactory answers to the three questions; on the 12th he gave the Bishop of Winchester a commission to reconstitute Magdalen College in accordance with the statutes;[2] and

[1] There are two versions of the bishops' petition; the first, in Sancroft's hand, seems likely to have been his own unaided first draft, for it is in the laboured, circumlocutary style which Macaulay condemned; the second covers the same ground, but is shorter and very much more to the point; its abruptness is thinly disguised by the forms of words customarily employed in addressing the sovereign. This is stated to be the petition delivered to James.

[2] There was a muddle about the restoration of Magdalen: the Bishop took his time about going to Oxford, and he did not arrive there until October 20; on the 21st he received an order by express to attend the meeting of notables before whom James was going to prove the genuineness of the Prince of Wales's birth. There was still time for the installation, but the Bishop appears to have thought that James intended to withdraw the concession and that the summons was only a pretext. He returned to London in spite of the efforts of the Protestant Fellows to detain him, and James was displeased with what he had done. He returned to Oxford and installed the Fellows on October 25. The delay caused a rumour that James had changed his mind because William's fleet had been scattered by the storm.

on the 17th he issued a proclamation restoring the corporations to the condition in which they had been in 1679, before Charles II had forfeited the charters by process of *quo warranto*. (The process of putting new men into corporations, and of substituting others for these new men when they proved unsatisfactory, had been steadily pursued by the Privy Council up to September 21 and had then suddenly ceased.) Of these five concessions, the one that James made with the greatest reluctance was that of Magdalen, and for the reason that it was the only one which directly betrayed the interests of the Catholic Church: he took, however, the advice of Leybourne, who awakened the royal conscience and convinced him that in this matter he had committed an obvious violation of the promises made at his accession. But James followed his father[1] in being obstinate about his friends and his religion, with the difference that his friends were Catholic advisers and his religion was Roman; still more did he cling to the dispensing power, though he could no longer hope to obtain a Parliament which would pronounce in its favour. This was the limit of James's public concession to popular demands, and he made no further gesture of putting everything as it had been at his accession. Though it was recognised that thanks were due to William rather than to James, the reversion to the traditional order in local government was generally welcomed, and there was even an expression of the old loyalty among the Deputy-Lieutenants in some counties. But this loyalty was tempered elsewhere by resentment at James's methods: they had been displaced for no fault, they were to be reinstated for no particular merit on their part and without any rénunciation of the principles for which they had lost their places; by a change of wind they might again find themselves dispossessed. Sir John Bramston recorded a conversation which he had with the Earl of Oxford, who had been restored as Lord-Lieutenant of Essex:

> He said he had refused at first but he had been advised to accept it, his circumstances considered. I told him he would find gentlemen not favoured to take commands; some would think one kick of the breech enough for a gentleman. He said we had all been ill-used, and he believed, this turn served, we shall be set aside again; but let us take our fortune together.

In Bedfordshire the deputy-lieutenants refused at first to be recalled to their appointments and only consented as a personal favour to Lord

[1] The similarity of character between James and his father is illustrated by a reference to the latter in a letter from Baillie to Henderson of May 9, 1646, "It has been his constant unhappiness to give nothing in time; all things have been given at last, but he has even lost the thanks and his gifts have been counted, constrained and extorted".

Ailesbury and under the condition that they should not be called on to serve under any other Lord-Lieutenant. And we may perhaps accept this as a fairly common attitude throughout the country.

In spite of his annoyance with them, James continued to consult with such bishops as were near at hand, and he induced them to compose special prayers against invasion—a proceeding inconsistent with his many statements that the Church of England was heretical. Those who wished him well but saw no hope for him without far more fundamental concessions disapproved of these meetings. Princess Anne at this time had several conversations with her uncle, Lord Clarendon; she was very much troubled at the ruin which she saw threatening her father, but she dared not say anything to him because he never discussed business with her; she saw no hope from the bishops and disapproved of the meetings: "The King will not hearken to them and they will only expose themselves". On October 22 James called a large meeting of Privy Councillors and notables to take evidence on the genuineness of the birth of the Prince of Wales and to counteract the Whig propaganda. The meeting had little practical effect, for James had called it with the mistaken notion that doubts about the birth were a cause and not a symptom of the discontents, but a significant incident occurred before people took their places: the Earls of Clarendon and Nottingham objected to sitting among the councillors because Petre was a councillor; James said that Petre would be seen no more at Council, though he had not gone to the length of formally dismissing him; the two lords rejoined that there were other unqualified persons on the Council, and, to James's annoyance, took their places apart from the Council, among the other persons invited.

But the chief event of October was the dismissal on the 26th of Sunderland from his posts of Lord President of the Council and Secretary of State. There were a number of rumours, particularly that he had been in treasonable correspondence with William and had sent him a very secret letter which Louis had written to James. James in council said he had dismissed him for private reasons best known to himself, and he was in no sense disgraced, for he remained a Privy Councillor, the day after his dismissal he was seen in company with the Queen, and Barrillon states that he was subsequently twice received in audience. If he had been caught in an act of treason it is unlikely that James would not have made that fact known, and it is quite certain that he would have spared no pains to humiliate the fallen Minister. There can be little doubt that the Jesuit faction in James's inner Cabinet had triumphed, and that the King had been swung back to his normal attitude of mind from the mood of conciliation in which he had in certain matters satisfied public demand. There is confirmation for this view in the unfounded rumour which was in circulation to the effect that there would be a clean sweep of moderate and Protestant counsellors, including Jeffreys and Godolphin. James was now entirely in the hands of Petre and the Catholic no-compromise party; in getting rid of Sunderland he had deprived himself of his last efficient Minister, for, if Sunderland followed his master rather than influenced him in his general policy, he at least had the ability to devise methods by which that policy could be carried out. It is probably from this time that we can date the rise of the Earl of Melfort in James's favour; Melfort had at first been a protégé of Sunderland. He had none of that Minister's capacity, but he was bold and active, and among the other Catholic advisers, with the Protestant advisers discredited, he had no difficulty in achieving pre-eminence.

During the second half of the month the first copies of William's declaration had been filtering into the country, and several copies were sent to the King. The declaration as a whole roused his indignation, especially the accusation contained in it that he was committing the worst betrayal of his sacred crown by putting forward a base-born heir. But what occupied his immediate attention was William's statement that he had been invited to England by a number of lords spiritual and temporal. In several meetings with bishops, individually and in groups, he was convinced that none of the bishops had been concerned in this invitation. Compton, who alone of the bishops had signed the letter of invitation and who indeed alone knew that such a letter had been sent, evaded James's question by saying that he was confident that the rest of the bishops would as readily answer in the negative as himself, a form of words which differs negligibly from a direct lie, but which will be condemned only by those who think that revolutions can be carried through without deception. James also sent for the Earls of Halifax, Burlington and Nottingham, and received from them assurances that they had not been concerned in the invitation to William. He was very much puzzled by this part of the manifesto, and had no idea who his enemies in England were.

Having satisfied himself that the bishops were not actively engaged against him, James now vainly attempted to enlist them actively on his side and to persuade them to subscribe their names to a public declaration expressing abhorrence of the invasion of the Prince of Orange. James had put such a proposal to Sancroft as early as October 16, but the Archbishop had been able to put him off by saying that the other bishops had returned to their dioceses and that he himself was not convinced of William's intentions. But with William's declaration in his hand James renewed to Compton on November 1 and to Sancroft and four other bishops on the following day his demand that the bishops should prepare and sign a paper denying their concurrence in the plans of the Prince of Orange and expressing their abhorrence of them. The bishops made no reply, and in the succeeding days their activity in consultation with each other was as great as it had been over the second Declaration of Indulgence. On November 6 the Archbishop was again summoned to the royal closet; he was accompanied by the bishops of London, Peterborough and Rochester. The two last had not been present at meetings with the King since the arrival of the Declaration, and they readily gave their word that they had had no hand in the invitation to William. Then ensued a battle of wits in which the King was soon put on the defensive, for the bishops were able to expose his entire lack of consistency in his treatment of the Church of England. James asked them for the "abhorrence" which he had previously demanded from them and which he understood they had promised to draft for his approval. They said they had made no promise and were not convinced of the genuineness of the Prince's declaration (which James, with singular fatuity, refused to let them read), and when James further pressed them they told him that the invasion was his own business and they as bishops had no concern with it; moreover, they had recently had a sharp lesson in the danger or interfering in matters of State and government.

> For (as Sancroft told the King) though we presented Your Majesty a petition of the most innocent nature and in the most humble manner imaginable, yet we were so violently prosecuted as it would have ended in our ruin if God's goodness had not preserved us; and I assure Your Majesty the whole accusation turned upon this one point—Your attorney and solicitor both affirmed that the honestest paper relating to matters of civil government might be a seditious libel when presented by persons who had nothing to do with such matters, as they said we had not but in time of parliament.

The Archbishop then referred to the scandal of the pronouncements by the judges on circuit on the trial and acquittal of the bishops, and, greatly daring, hinted that James himself had ordered the judges to make them on pain of dismissal.[1] James refused to be drawn into this dis-

[1] Sancroft at this point complained that one of the judges on circuit had accused him of writing bad English—an irrelevant and petty matter to bring in when great matters of state were under discussion. But it is very difficult to find in Sancroft's character clear evidence that he was fitted for the prominent position into which he was forced by circumstances.

cussion, saying that he hoped it had all been forgotten and that he was no lawyer and must do as his lawyers told him, and brought them back to the question of the abhorrence, and again asserted that they had promised to draw it up. But in this he was not supported by his only witness, Lord Preston (Sunderland's successor as Secretary of State), who had been present at the earlier meeting and agreed with the bishops that all they had promised was to discuss with their brethren the propriety of publishing an abhorrence. And they refused to yield to James or to recede from the position they had decided before the audience to take up—namely, that they four had no claim to represent the bishops and, further, that the whole bench of bishops had no *locus standi* in civil affairs except in association with the temporal peers. James was gravely disappointed: he admitted by implication that he expected nothing but hostility from the temporal peers, but he had hoped for unquestioning support from the bishops. He dismissed them saying, "This is the last time; I will urge you no farther; it you will not assist me as I desire I must stand upon my own legs, and trust to myself and my own arms". And he had no more meetings with the bishops.

Though James was not convinced until late in September that William contemplated an expedition againt him, he was aware of the extraordinary military and naval preparations of the Dutch, and he strengthened his own effective naval forces, both in the general interest of balance of power at sea, and in case he might be drawn into a war between Holland and France. There had been activity in the shipyards throughout the year with a view to co-operation with France if the Dutch intervened in the dispute between Sweden and Denmark, and in some quarters this activity, and the fact that James had contracted for the delivery of naval stores in December, pointed to a design on his part to make war on the Dutch in the following year. It was late in August before the extent of the Dutch preparations was brought home to James, and the uncertainty of the motive for those preparations caused him considerable trouble of mind. By this time he had plenty of grounds of complaint against William, he was well aware that the increasing body of malcontents in England looked to him as their leader and their ultimate hope, and he suspected him of a design to make a naval demonstration on the English coasts in order to influence the elections for Parliament which were to take place in October and November. But neither he nor the French Court were of opinion that the equipment of the Dutch fleet would be complete in time to take definite action against him or against France before the winter storms had shut down naval operations.

James was, however, shocked out of his customary complacency and serenity, and determined to leave nothing to chance. At an extraordinary Council held at Windsor on August 24 he announced his intention of calling a Parliament to meet on November 27, giving reasons "relating to the good and satisfaction of the nation", and he also took a number of steps to put the country in a state of defence. He had already stationed the fleet in the Downs; he now sent commissions to Chatham and Portsmouth to hasten on the fitting out of ten additional ships, he enlisted 6000 recruits for the Army and concentrated his troops at the ports and at places on the coast where a disembarkation was likely, and he stopped all leave to officers of the Army and Navy.[1] He was advised by the French Court to bring over a large contingent of Irish troops, for they thought that the mere knowledge that these troops were in England would deter William from making his attempt; but James was still listening to Sunderland's wiser councils, and decided that the presence of Irish troops would only irritate the English people and that he would use them only in the last resort if there was a long war.

At the end of September, when James was convinced that William intended to attack him and that the invasion was imminent, there was an acceleration in the naval and military preparations and Louis renewed his offer of military assistance. This offer James, regretfully and without finality, rejected. His dilemma was plain, for a small French contingent would unite the whole of England against it, and a large French army, if it succeeded in conquering the country, would threaten his own independence. Burnet says that Louis offered 12,000 or 15,000 men ("or as many more as he should desire") to hold Portsmouth and to keep open the communications of that place with France, and he continues:

> All the priests were for this, so were most of the popish lords. The Earl of Sunderland was the only man in credit that opposed it. He said the offer of an army of forty thousand men might be a real strength; but then it would depend upon the orders that came from France; they might perhaps master England, but they would become the King's masters at the same time, so that he must

[1] It is clear from Pepys's letter to Killigrew of September 3 that at this date James had no apprehension that the extraordinary activity in the Dutch shipyards was in preparation for an attack on England; he thought more likely that the attack would be on France and that in any case it was too late for a naval expedition. His own preparations were against any contingency and in making them he was very wise. Care must be taken to distinguish between war between the Dutch and English, which at this time he considered a remote possibility, and a personal and dynastic invasion by William of which he had no apprehension whatever.

> govern under such orders as they should give and thus he would become only a viceroy to the King of France; any army less than that would lose the King the affections of his people and drive the army to desertion, if not to mutiny.[1]

Louis relied for his information on Barrillon, who (as Burnet says) "knew the Court better than he knew the nation", and could not appreciate the reasons for the rejection of his offer. He also made another grave miscalculation: he under-estimated the estrangement of James from his people, and thought that the royalist party would be strong enough to support the King through a long civil war. He had abandoned any hope that James would be able to take the field as his ally; but the next best thing was to keep England neutral, and the longer the war the safer would Louis feel from attack in the rear;[2] moreover, the war, as he envisaged it, would keep a number of Dutch troops and William, his most dangerous enemy, locked up in England, and the French would probably be called in later and on their own terms. There was not the same objection to the co-operation with the English Navy of a French squadron; it could be based on French ports and could perform useful work even if it was considered advisable to keep it out of sight of the English coast and of the English fleet. But the greater part of the French fleet was in the Mediterranean, and Louis was able to offer immediately only sixteen ships to be kept for emergencies at Brest and forty to be got ready and in the Channel by the following spring.

On the eve of William's landing, the Imperial ambassador, Hoffmann (who seems to have made better use of his opportunities for observation than any other envoy), thus summed up James's chances of success:

> In appearance the King is far stronger than the Prince of Orange, for he has an army of 25,000, all old soldiers, well drilled and fully mobilised; and a fleet I will not say equal to the enemy's, but sufficiently strong and in good condition; while the Prince of Orange has a fatigued and sickly army and damaged cavalry;[3] one has to consider especially that the King has to wage only a defensive war and that all the strong places are in his hands.

[1] Military help from France would, in fact, have had the same effect, *mutatis mutandis*, as the evidence of the negotiations of the French Court with foreign Powers in 1791 had on the French Revolution: it would have united the whole country against the King.

[2] "France fears nothing so much as an accommodation", wrote the Imperial ambassador on November 23.

[3] Hoffmann is here, no doubt, referring to the effects of the storm of October 19 and 20.

> But it is doubtful if the King's soldiers are as faithful as those of the Prince, for nothing that the King has done hitherto to ingratiate himself with his subjects and to conquer their aversion has succeeded either with the nobles or with the people: the nobles, except a few loyalists, have persisted in their discontent and have remained on their estates, and the people, even more than the nobles, are welcoming the Prince of Orange and have no fear of him. The King has so completely lost credit that, if in present circumstances he made even more generous concessions than he has already made, he would only make the situation still more grave; it would have been another matter if he had made them when he had no invasion to fear.

In the French Court, on the other hand, there was a disposition to doubt the fighting qualities or fidelity of the English Navy, but no apprehension regarding the Army.

James himself had his moments of depression, but on the whole he was optimistic. On September 28 commenced in the Chapel Royal a forty-hour service of continuous prayer for divine assistance. The following day he issued a further proclamation stating that he had refused foreign help and was relying on the proved fidelity of his people to unite them against a common enemy. On October 8 Jeffreys issued instructions to the Middlesex justices to suppress all coffee-houses and to prevent the dissemination of news by news-letters; it was understood that even private letters should contain no news of public matters. At this time, too, there was a slight royalist revulsion; there were rumours that the Dutch had been so tactless as to speak of their coming "conquest" of England, and the national spirit had been roused; one observer said that the brisk apprentices of London were eager to come to blows with the invaders, the Earl of Newcastle was said to have enlisted in Yorkshire 2000 gentlemen on the King's behalf, and in other counties similar rallies were reported. The Jesuits advised a round-up of prominent men who might be suspected of collusion with William, and named Halifax, Danby, Shrewsbury and Nottingham—a curious example of the ignorance of these advisers of what was going on in England, for Shrewsbury was in Holland and Nottingham and Halifax had refused to lend their names to the conspiracy. Sunderland opposed this advice (and by his opposition possibly sealed his own fate) on the ground that "it would not be possible to seize on many at the same time, and the seizing a few would alarm all the rest, it would drive them to the Prince and furnish them with a pretence for it", and James agreed with him.

On October 19, William put to sea, but his fleet was scattered by a severe storm; the damage was not great, but the ships had to put back for repair, and there was a further twelve days' delay. James received the news of William's reverse at dinner; he assumed an attitude of devotion and said, "It is not to be wondered at, for the Host has been exposed these several days", a remark which provides obvious openings for the cynic.[1] About this time he appears to have had little doubt that the defeat of William would be as swift and easy as that of Monmouth had been. On October 1 he had removed the Catholic Strickland from the command of the fleet and had appointed in his place one of the few men who had stuck to him through all the vicissitudes of his brother's reign, the Protestant Lord Dartmouth. Lord Dartmouth had concentrated his ships at the Gunfleet, near the north shore of the Thames estuary, so as to be able to intercept William's fleet whether he sailed north for Yorkshire or south for the West of England; the English ships were not equal in numbers to the Dutch, and were under-manned, but they were probably superior in fighting value, for in a battle the Dutch would have been handicapped by having to protect the transports. To Dartmouth James wrote on October 23, "I grow stronger every day at land by the Scots and Irish coming near the town and the forwardness of some of the new raised regiments"; and on October 26, "With regard to all things if what is said of their [the Dutch] coming out with so small a quantity of victuals and water be true 'tis next to a madness". At the same time Barrillon and Bonrepaus were telling Louis, as Hoffmann had told the Emperor a month earlier, that the cashiered officers whom James had replaced in the Army were not to be relied on, and that the sailors were openly declaring that they would not fight against the Dutch.

On November 5, 1688, William landed at Torbay after a series of fortunate accidents which he took as confirmation of his belief in predestination; what James's views were on the workings of Providence in this instance are unrecorded. Four days later William entered Exeter, where he remained for twelve days. Lamplugh, the Bishop of Exeter, had fled to London as soon as he had heard of the landing; there is no reason to ascribe to him strong loyalist views, for, though he had refused to sign the bishops' petition, he had approved of it in draft, and his later conduct drew censure from loyalist quarters; a sufficient reason for his flight would have been a reluctance to be the first and possibly the only bishop to join the invader. James, however, put the best possible

[1] See Missons Travels in England, etc. (Eng. Trans. 1719), p. 243. It appears also in Dalrymple (Pt. I, Bk. VI, p. 192), and in Mazure (III, 61) who comments "But faith without works is not enough and the miracles of the Almighty do not concur with imprudence, feebleness, vows of vengeance or purely human ambition".

construction on his action, and rewarded it by translating him to the Archbishopric of York.

It was held by several people who were competent to judge, among them some of William's own generals, that if James had immediately marched to the West and attacked William in Exeter he would have forced him to re-embark. Certainly there was no subsequent time so favourable to James: William's troops were fatigued by the voyage and the cavalry were short of horses, the organisation of the Army for a campaign in a foreign country was incomplete and the accessions of English recruits were for the first fortnight negligible. It is true that the defeat of William would not be the end of his troubles, the King's victory would not have been popular and William would have carried with him back to Holland the wishes of almost the whole country for his speedy return. James would have been forced to deal with this rebellious sentiment, his only means would have been conciliation, there could be no conciliation without a Parliament, and the Parliament, in the conditions brought about by his recent concessions, would have been a free Parliament. There can be no question that if Parliament had met it would have made three immediate demands: the dismissal of the King's advisers, particularly of Petre and the other Catholics; the strict application of the penal laws and the Test Act; and a foreign policy hostile to France, if not an actual declaration of war against that country. This would have been, in James's eyes, to reduce him to the status of a "Duke of Venice", and he declared that rather than accept such conditions he would have abdicated. If he had not abdicated he would have been forced to rule as a constitutional monarch, and the Revolution would have come during and not at the end of his reign; for the constitutional questions which had been raised but not decided during his brother's reign had been brought into such prominence by his own actions that a decision on them could not have been delayed. James would have had to accept a Bill of Rights or something very like it.

Whether or no James's troops would have failed him in face of the enemy must be a matter of pure speculation. There would have been a certain amount of defection among the officers, but not nearly so great as there was later when William's propaganda had begun to do its work, and these defections would have to some extent disorganised the army. But in numbers he was overwhelmingly superior to William—the Imperial ambassador early in October estimated his army at 40,000 men—and the men as a whole, in spite of their Whiggish infection and in spite of their grievances against the Irish troops, would have followed bold and resolute leadership without too nicely considering what cause they were supporting; once engaged, they would have fought well: as a contemporary expressed it, "The truth is our countrymen love no cause nor man so well as fighting, even sometimes without any cause at all". Moreover, there is no evidence that the Army shared the reluctance of the Navy to fight against the Dutch. But neither James nor any of his loyal generals could provide the required leadership, nor, it may be said, had he at this time of his life the ruthlessness necessary to discourage desertion in face of the enemy. It appears also that in the Privy Council there was considerable opposition to the King's taking the field, it was felt that there was a danger that in his absence London would declare for William, and Petre conceived the notion that with James away William might elude the royal Army and appear in London with a small body of troops.

On the news of William's landing the English Army was ordered to rendezvous at Salisbury. James, after changing his mind several times, decided on November 16 to set out for Salisbury the following day. Five days before his arrival there on the 19th the first desertion to William on the part of an officer of distinguished family had taken place; Viscount Cornbury, eldest son of the Earl of Clarendon, and James's nephew by marriage, had attempted to take with him over to the enemy three regiments of cavalry. Most of the subaltern officers and troopers had found out his design in time and had returned to Salisbury, but Cornbury and some others remained with William, and they had set an example which many followed. James stayed only five days at Salisbury, during two of which he was incapacitated by a perpetual bleeding at the nose. There was a rumour that Kirke, who was commanding at Warminster, had concerted with Churchill to kidnap the King when he went to Warminster to inspect the troops there, and that the bleeding at the nose was an interposition of Providence to prevent him from falling into the trap. But James's nose had been bleeding the whole of November 20, and recommenced on the 21st, the day on which he had planned to go to Warminster. Moreover Churchill and Kirke would have been singularly ill-informed of William's wishes if they thought he would welcome the gift of his captive father-in-law.

On Thursday, November 22, a council of war was held, in which Feversham argued for a retreat from Salisbury and Churchill for making a stand;[1] James decided on a retreat, no doubt disheartened at what he saw of the condition of his army but not realising that to retreat in the circumstances must inevitably destroy what was left of the soldiers' morale. On Friday, November 23, there was a very serious loss to James:

[1] The Imperial Ambassador says that James was influenced in his decision by Lauzun, who proved himself a true Frenchman—"for they never fight except behind the walls of a fortress". James may also have been influenced by the rising in the North.

Lord Churchill left Salisbury in the night, accompanied by James's nephew, the Duke of Grafton, and joined William at Axminster. Contemporaries regarded Churchill's treason in a worse light than that of any other individual—as the Imperial ambassador put it, the King had raised him from the mud—and there is evidence, though the Earl of Marlborough (as he then was) was a very dim figure during the middle years of the succeeding reign, that he was exceedingly unpopular on this account, even among those who had been James's bitterest opponents. James himself regarded his defection as the blackest of crimes and put him at once at the head of the list of the enemies who were to feel his vengeance when he came to his own again. But there is no reason to suppose that Churchill's motives were entirely self-interested; we know very little of his political sentiments at this time, but we may be sure that his position at Court during James's reign, when his counsel was never sought and the King was falling more and more under the influence of his foolish and malicious Jesuit advisers, cannot have been very comfortable. He gave as the reason for leaving James his zeal for the Protestant religion, and the contemplation of James's Court may easily have increased the Protestant zeal of many men who were not pre-eminently Christian.[1]

James commenced his journey back to London on November 24, and the camp at Salisbury broke up. All accounts agree that the retreat from Salisbury was hurried and disorderly, a state of things for which there was no excuse, for William's outposts covering Axminster were still nearly sixty miles away. But there appears to have been in the royal army not even the most elementary intelligence service. Barrillon wrote a few days after the retreat commenced:

> Although I have been constantly with the King and have not let him out of my sight, and although since he left London I have passed the whole of the day and the greater part of the night with his confidential advisers, I have not yet been able to ascertain the condition of the Prince of Orange's army or what he is doing. I do not yet know that anyone has been sent to his camp and has returned to report. This will appear incredible to Your Majesty but it is nevertheless true; and Your Majesty will understand how difficult it is for the King of England to make plans when he has no knowledge of what his enemy is about. We were no better informed at Salisbury.

[1] It is possible that the occasion (but not the cause) of Churchill's flight was that he had heard that he was suspected of treason and was on the point of being arrested. Mr. Winston Churchill (*Marlborough*, I, 297–99) conjectures that he had failed to persuade his brother officers to join in compelling James to come to terms with William and to call a Parliament.

It would appear that the royal army had had no information about the enemy's movements except, in the first few days after the landing, from refugees whose fears had rendered them unreliable scouts. A corroboration of Barrillon's statement is given by George Clark, the judge advocate of the royal army, who found headquarters at Andover during the retreat; he says:

> The fright was so great that they were apt to believe an impossible report just then brought in that the Prince of Orange was come with 12,000 horse between Warminster and Salisbury. Upon hearing this the Lord Feversham the general never questioned the truth but cried out "Zounce, then Kirke be asleep". This I was an ear-witness of.

Of the general confusion in the royal counsels during James's journey to Salisbury and back Barrillon has a great deal to say. Plenty of advice was given to Ministers, but they were so dilatory that they "can hardly do anything promptly", the general officers are inexperienced and the King himself is irresolute—he issues orders and countermands them, he is very active, but he loses himself in a mass of detail which might be left to subalterns. In the ambassador's particular business—James's relations with France—there is the same hazy incompetence, and it is useless to try to formulate an agreement. All conferences finish with the appeal: "The King your master must save us or we are lost. It is to his interest to prevent the Prince of Orange from mastering England"; they all agree that the English and French fleets should unite, and they vaguely say that they will arrange the details; but they also agree that if the King were to make a treaty with Louis or should accept from him the services of a marshal of France he would be entirely ruined and would lose his small remnant of loyal servants—"In fact", Barrillon concludes, "Your Majesty must save him without any assistance on his part except his sincere and earnest prayers." Again George Clark confirms Barrillon's account:

> We [Clark and Dr. Radcliffe] went with the King to Andover and waited upon him at his quarters with the Prince of Denmark and the Duke of Ormonde. I can never forget the confusion the Court was in; the Lord Churchill had gone over to the Prince of Orange from Salisbury and the Duke of Grafton this morning; the King knew not whom to trust. . . . Everybody in this hurly-burly was thinking of himself and nobody minded the King who came up to Dr. Radcliffe and asked him what was good for the bleeding of his nose: it was the last time I ever saw him.

The words "nobody minded the King" are very significant: in a time of crisis he was temporarily, as he was later to become permanently, merely a pawn in the game. During the retreat from Salisbury he wrote to Tyrconnel in Ireland in very despondent terms.

James returned to London on November 26, and was mortified to find that Princess Anne had secretly left the capital the previous day under the escort of the Bishop of London. Her husband, Prince George, had left the royal camp at Andover during the retreat from Salisbury and had joined William; there can be little doubt that these defections were due to the influence of Churchill. The King had a long session with his Council a few hours after his arrival, and he summoned all the temporal and spiritual peers who were in London to attend a meeting the following day; nine bishops and thirty or forty temporal peers attended. The intention of the meeting was to discuss a petition which had been presented to the King ten days earlier when he was already making final preparations for his journey to Salisbury. This petition had been signed by nineteen peers, including six bishops, and was for a free Parliament and a settlement of the military situation by negotiation. Among the signatories there were no Catholics, and a large number of peers, including Halifax and Nottingham, refused to sign the petition because Rochester had signed it and because they regarded him as an accomplice in some of the illegal acts of the reign, notably the institution of the Ecclesiastical Commission. There were thus for the moment three parties among those who still hoped to keep James on the throne, the third party being the King's confidential advisers led by Petre and Melfort, mainly Catholic, but including the Protestant Secretaries of State, Middleton and Preston; these men were for no surrender, but they were already (according to one authority) contemplating taking James to France in their own custody.

James had already, before he received the petition, committed himself by a statement that anyone who proposed an accommodation with William was a traitor, and in spite of the defection of Cornbury he had been still hopeful that his presence with the Army at Salisbury would provide the necessary incentive for vigorous action. He had also (by his own unconfirmed account) called together a number of military officers who were in London, including Churchill and Grafton, and received from them an assurance that they would fight loyally in his Army. James was not easily accessible by petition, and this one was presented to him at a time when he was preoccupied with his journey, and it made him very angry: he adopted his customary attitude that everyone who questioned the justice or wisdom of anything that he had done was his enemy, and he reproached the bishops in that eleven days earlier they had refused to sign the abhorrence and to declare against William, but that now they were willing to declare against their King. When he had driven out the petitioners he detained Grafton for a particular reprimand.

> After the said Archbishop and his party had left His Majesty said to the Duke of Grafton that he was astonished and should never have expected him to have signed the petition, on which the other very resolutely answered that he conscientiously thought as a faithful subject to have thereby rendered an important service to his King and country, and further that, if His Majesty would employ him either on water or on land, he would openly give proofs of the utmost fidelity . . . and as this lay honestly in his mind he was by no means ashamed to warn His Majesty and he thought he should in no way stand suspected on account of it.

Another account says that James attacked Grafton, as he had attacked Admiral Herbert, for his personal lack of conscience, and that Grafton answered "that though he had little conscience yet he was of a party that had conscience"—a remark which had application to a very large number of public men of the time.

But James when he returned from Salisbury was in a different frame of mind: he had no longer any illusions about his freedom of action, he could no longer do what he wanted, he must either yield to the demands of all but a minute section of his subjects—demands which had overwhelming military force behind them—or fly the country. At the meeting he was mild and gracious, and there is no reason to suppose that at the moment he was not anxious to arrive at an accommodation or willing to retain his crown even at the expense of everything which had made that crown worth holding. There were a number of speeches—Rochester, Jeffreys, Halifax and others—all agreeing that the concessions demanded in the petition should be granted, but ominously hinting that it might even now be too late for James to save himself and keep the crown. The speech which called for most comment was that of Clarendon, who used "indecent and insolent words which were generally condemned", "behaved himself like a pedagogue to a pupil" and (according to James himself) "flew out into an indiscreet seditious railing, declaiming against popery, exaggerating fears and jealousies and blaming the King's conduct". Clarendon has been blamed for inconsistency, and this speech is coupled with the fact that the day after delivering it he travelled to William's camp. But there was no inconsistency, only incredible lack of judgement: to Clarendon, more than to any of his contemporaries, loyalty was a religion; he saw that James could only be saved if he got rid of his Catholic advisers and renounced all correspondence with Louis; and his speech, which indeed missed its mark, was a last desperate attempt to shake the King out of his complacency and so to save him. Moreover, in going to William, Clarendon did not consider that he was joining the King's enemies: he believed that William's manifesto, with its disavowal of any intention of supplanting James, still embodied the policy of William's adherents; he thought that by William's agency James could be induced or forced to reign according to law and custom, and would by that means be seated again firmly on the throne; but he was horrified to be unable to find among those who were with William anyone except the Earl of Abingdon who agreed with him, or who had any other view than that they were endeavouring to make James abdicate in favour of William or Mary.

The immediate effect of the meeting of November 27 was the issue of writs for a Parliament, to meet on January 15, and the despatch to William of a deputation consisting of Halifax, Nottingham and Godolphin. Of the other points in the petition James took no notice; like his father, there were certain particular concessions which he could in no circumstances be brought to make; the dismissal of his Catholic advisers was in this category. The following day James told Barrillon that a Parliament was the only means of saving him from absolute ruin and that the seven weeks which would elapse before it met could be employed in making himself safe, but he again asserted that he would do nothing contrary to Louis's interests. On the eve of James's flight Barrillon said that James had consented to the despatch of the deputation to William only to gain time to provide for the security of the Queen and the Prince of Wales. But it seems probable that he was impressed by the gravity of the demeanour of the wisest of the lords at the meeting of November 27, and had a transient hope that he might, by taking some of their advice, keep himself on the throne without sacrificing all that he had achieved for the Catholic religion.

But he had already lost all power of initiative: he turned in all directions for advice, and there was no lack of that commodity. The issue was now a simple one: should he remain and meet Parliament, and accept from them terms which would involve the abandonment of everything he had worked for in the last four years; or should he retire from the scene in the hope that his subjects would recall him and accept from him a settlement dictated by himself? If he had any clearness of mind he must have realised that if once he left the country, the causes of his expulsion would have to be removed before he could expect restoration. Melfort and the extreme Catholics urged him to go; they cited precedents from English history showing that some of James's predecessors had retired to exile and had returned to reign peaceably; they prophesied that William's reign would be short, that he would never be able to satisfy the ambitions of his adherents and that Louis would reinstate James. On the other side, Halifax and Godolphin, with the two Secretaries of State and the Catholic Lord Belasyse, who had never approved James's Catholic and autocratic policy, urged the King to satisfy his subjects in regard to law and religion and to trust Parliament to settle the affairs of the country, and they protested that once the people were by these means assured of security they would rally to him and there would be no danger of violence to his person. The one point on which all his advisers were in agreement was that he should not make armed resistance to William. The Duke of Hamilton urged him to take refuge in Scotland, where he could defend himself until reinforcements arrived from France, but warned him that if he went there he would have to leave his Catholic advisers behind. Tyrconnel wrote proposing that he should cross to Ireland, where he could be safe for an indefinite period if he could procure arms and ammunition. It would not have been difficult for him to get to Scotland if he could have assembled two or three thousand disciplined and loyal troops, but the journey to Ireland would have been very hazardous, with William's Navy in the Channel and his Army on the flank of the road to Chester.

With Barrillon James was constantly closeted, but he did not discuss with him the problem uppermost in his mind. Indeed, from the ambassador's letters and from those of Louis to him it appears that the French King hesitated to give James advice of any kind. Since the collapse of the royal Army and the news of disaffection in the Navy he had abandoned all hope of being able to render assistance by sending troops or ships. It had long been in his mind that James might be abandoned by his subjects and have to seek safety in flight: as early as August he had instructed Bonrepaus, when the ambassador-extraordinary was starting on his third and last visit to the English Court, "that he should endeavour to discover without indiscretion what plans the King of England has for the safety of his own person in case he finds himself abandoned". But since James had been roused to a sense of danger he had had hopes that James would succeed in defeating William, and there had been no mention of a necessity for flight. After the return from Salisbury there is constant allusion to this possibility, but Louis appears not to have thought of France as a possible asylum or to have given James any sort of invitation to come to him. In fact, on December 10, the day before James fled for the first time and, it can hardly be doubted, intended to go to France, Louis wrote to Barrillon offering an honourable asylum to the Queen and the Prince of Wales;

but apparently he had no knowledge of James's plans, for he told the ambassador that it would be dangerous to give James any advice whatever, and instructed him not to go with the King if he decided to go to Scotland or Ireland.

The Queen was the determining factor in making up James's mind; James was open to other influences, but she saw no one except the priests. She, poor woman, was utterly bewildered by the situation: except by giving general encouragement to James in his endeavours for what she thought to be the good of her religion, she had taken no interest in the problems of the reign. Clarendon relates a conversation with her on November 22, 1688, in which she repeated parrot fashion a few sentences about the King's intentions and was angry when Clarendon mildly put the constitutional position. It was an easy matter for Melfort, Petre and the rest to work on the fears of a woman who was in this condition of excitement and who was ignorant of the causes which had produced the existing situation. Of the motives of these people when they saw that there was a possibility of a compromise between James and William, Burnet says:

> But now strange counsels were suggested to the King and Queen. The priests and all the violent papists saw a treaty was now opened, they knew that they must be the sacrifice. The whole design of popery must be given up without any hope of being able in an age to think of bringing it on again. Severe laws would be made against them. And all those who intended to stick to the King and to preserve him would go into those laws with a particular zeal, so that they and their hopes must be now given up and sacrificed for ever. They infused all this into the Queen.

"They and their hopes"; in these words Burnet reveals the essential fairness and moderation of his mind; if he had been a mere party pamphleteer he could have justified to his own mind a statement that the advice these men gave the Queen was entirely self-interested, for in the reaction which would follow an agreement between the King and his subjects they must inevitably lose their posts and their power, possibly also their liberty, and even their lives. There is a letter written in this month of December from one Father Con to the Provincial of the Jesuits at Rome which from a point of view totally different from Burnet's conveys the same impression; he says:

> There is now an end of all the pleasing hopes of seeing our holy Religion make a progress in this country. The King and Queen are fled. . . . The great evil comes from ourselves, our own im-

> prudence, avarice and ambition. The good King has made use of fools, knaves and blockheads. . . . I am only sorry that I made one among so many madmen, who were incapable of directing and governing.

In short, the chief defect of James's Catholic advisers was, like his own, of the head rather than the heart; they had no wisdom to devise means of achieving their ends, and, in a minor degree, they allowed their personal ambition to be an obstacle to their ambition for their Church.[1] In any case, they thought it best for the monarchy, for the Church and for themselves that they should remain surrounding James's person, and if this contact could not be continued in England, then he and they should seek each other abroad.

As soon as James returned from Salisbury he made plans for transporting the infant Prince of Wales out of the country, and the only place of safety that occurred to his mind was France. He sent the child with an escort to Portsmouth and ordered Dartmouth, who commanded the English fleet there, to provide transport for him to some port in France. Dartmouth had a long record of faithful service to James, in particular he had stood by him in the period of his exile when his fortunes were at their lowest; he was not a man of outstanding ability or intelligence, but he was an ardent Protestant and, according to his lights, a good Christian; he was now one of the few Protestants of respectable position who remained true to the King without equivocation. He replied to James's command in a letter full of duty to his sovereign, but firmly refusing to have anything to do with the conveyance out of the country of the heir apparent; his refusal was on the ground that such an act would be high treason. Probably if he had been a free man Dartmouth would have taken the risk of accepting the commission, but the Duke of Berwick, who as Governor of Portsmouth had charge of the little Prince while arrangements for his embarkation were being made, says in his memoirs that Dartmouth's "true reason was that he had no more than the title of Admiral and that he was apprehensive, if the Prince were embarked, the fleet would deliver him to his enemies". This account is confirmed by George Byng (afterwards Lord Torrington), who left in his memoirs a long and circumstantial account

[1] The Imperial ambassador, writing on December 18, thus sums up the reasons for the collapse of James's system of government: "the great zeal His Majesty has for religion, his putting himself into the hands of unwise, ignorant and avaricious priests and inexperienced Catholics, together with his excessive affection for the Queen Consort, have undermined his courage and reduced him to his present position"; and he adds that his Catholic advisers were not intelligent enough to know that they had no capacity for politics and that their own insolence had been the undoing of the King.

of his own intrigues in the fleet in favour of William: he says that at the Gunfleet before William sailed disaffection was spreading among the captains, that during the pursuit of the Dutch fleet a number of them agreed to desert if they came up with the enemy, and that when they heard that a King's ship was to be used to convey the Prince of Wales to France they said openly that they would seize him as soon as he was put on board; "they were nigh succeeding, since all the baggage and necessaries for the child were then on board and he certainly upon the point of going off". James at the time was satisfied that Dartmouth was acting loyally and had been prevented from intercepting the Dutch fleet by circumstances beyond his control (though in his memoirs he expressed himself with less certainty), and he accepted these excuses without resentment. He was, however, annoyed with Dartmouth and his captains when, about the same time, they presented a memorial thanking him for his decision to call a free Parliament; if he had been wiser he would have kept his annoyance to himself, for the expression of it clearly implied that his decision to summon Parliament had been made under compulsion and not with a view to the public good.[1]

Meanwhile James had been making plans for the escape of the Queen, who by this time was thoroughly frightened and was eager to be off. Wanting, no doubt, to spare her a long period of sea-sickness, he first planned to send her by coach to Dover, and when, on December 8, the Prince was brought back from Portsmouth,[2] it was decided to send the Queen and the Prince together. But on Sunday, December 9, came news of disturbances at Dover, and at the last moment the plans had to be entirely changed. It is a striking proof of the state of pitiable weakness into which James's authority had sunk that everyone was agreed that secrecy must be observed and that no one proposed that the Queen should travel to the coast openly by day and with an escort of cavalry. No English nobleman was found sufficiently faithful and courageous to undertake the command of the little party, and the royal fugitives were put in charge of the Comte de Lauzun, who on this occasion accomplished the only efficient service of his life.

At two o'clock on the morning of Monday, December 10, in wind and rain, the Queen and her baby, two nurses, Lauzun and an Italian attendant of the name of Riva made their way by coach from Whitehall to the Horseferry and crossed, not without danger, to Lambeth in a boat

[1] There is a full and well-documented account of the revolt of the navy in Mr. Powley's *The English Navy and the Revolution of 1688*.

[2] James was seriously alarmed lest the Prince should have been intercepted between Portsmouth and London. As William was then at Hungerford, which is only 40 miles from Petersfield on the Portsmouth Road, James could not know how far to the South East William had extended his advance posts.

in which Riva had placed a gun and some provisions, as if for a shooting expedition. There they found that by some mistake the horses had not been put into the coach, and the Queen had to wait with no more shelter than the wall of a church. A harmless wayfarer took an interest in the proceedings, and was summarily dealt with by Riva: he collided with him as though by accident, and both men fell into the kennel; the stranger retired to the inn to clean himself, and Riva, with his sailor's disguise covered with mud, remained on watch. As the coach was passing through the southern suburbs of London they heard a remark from a bystander that the coach was full of papists and should be searched, but they were not molested, and reached the yacht which was awaiting them at Gravesend without incident. There was a considerable party on the yacht, including the Duke and Duchess of Powis and Lady Strickland, one account says as many as twenty-three persons. Lauzun stood over the captain for some time, to throw him into the sea if he proved treacherous, but the captain said he was glad to perform this service without reward; he begged, however, for the royal warrant (which he supposed they had), so that he could transmit it to his descendants. The only danger was from the two frigates which had been stationed in the Thames estuary to intercept the Prince; these they evaded, though they were at one time within hailing distance of one of them. Two of her attendants were sick over the Queen, and her later account of the voyage was, "It was a very sad voyage; I do not know how I survived it. I left the King not knowing what would become of him, and I feared to fall into the hands of our enemies". A courier had informed James of the Queen's successful embarkation.

James had promised his Queen before she left England that he would shortly join her in France. This promise resolved any lingering doubts he may have still harboured in his mind. Everybody expected that he would go. The Catholic camarilla and their Protestant associates had been seized with panic. Petre was the first to leave: he took the opportunity of slipping away while James was at Salisbury, travelling in the retinue of James's son-in-law, Lord Waldegrave, who had been appointed to the Paris Embassy in succession to Bevil Skelton, and taking with him, in violation of the principles of his order, "several great chests" containing the material acquisitions of his unofficial and official ministry; on December 3 Melfort left "with his family on a yacht"; all the Catholics, whether of the extreme or moderate party, were reported to be "in the most cruel anguish, and they will count themselves lucky if they escape a massacre". On the 7th Sunderland went to Holland; he was no longer in office, but he was held by the people to have had a greater share in the misgovernment of the reign than anyone except perhaps Petre; on the 8th Cartwright stole away; on the 9th Adda the nuncio left under the protection of the envoy of the Duke of Savoy; the Marquis of Powis had gone with the Queen; and it was said that Jeffreys would certainly not be left behind—unfortunately for him, he alone of the great Court figures of the last two years of the reign remained with his King to the end. James followed only twenty-four hours after Mary Beatrice, and he must have made his plans some days earlier; but on December 10 he concealed his intentions by making several appointments for the next day, and he asserted that "now that he has got the Queen and Prince away he will put himself at the head of his army and resist his enemies as long as he has breath"; he forgot that he was in formal negotiation with William and that he could not fight him unless and until that negotiation had broken down. Perhaps it was this inconsistency which made the public believe "that if he has expressed such a resolution it was merely to cover his own retreat and that he will hasten to follow the Queen". The same day he confided to the care of the Tuscan envoy the great boxes containing his memoirs, on which he placed a very high value, and which, after remarkable vicissitudes, reached him at Saint-Germain via Leghorn.

Before his first flight James had two communications from his commissioners at Hungerford. The first was dated December 8, and was received by Middleton the following day.[1] It gave an account of the reception by William of the commissioners and of various meetings and formalities; it also expressed the "conjectures" of the commissioners from conversations they had had with important persons in the Prince's camp. From these conversations they anticipated that the march of the invading army would not be delayed by negotiations and that two very unwelcome demands would be made on the King: that he should dismiss his Catholic advisers, and that, not only should he be forced to summon Parliament, but that restrictions should be placed on his power to interrupt its sittings. The first demand was of small practical importance, since most of the Catholic advisers had left the country, but it assumed in advance that Parliament would decide against the dispensing power; the second was a definite invasion of the royal prerogative. The second letter from the commissioners was sent by express, and arrived only a few hours before James left Whitehall; enclosed with it was a formal statement of William's terms. In this statement the dismissal of the Catholic Ministers was insisted on, but nothing was said directly about the King's power to prorogue or

[1] It is no doubt this letter to which the Imperial Ambassador referred when he wrote on December 9 that the Prince of Orange's terms had been received at Whitehall.

dissolve Parliament; by implication, however, this power was taken from him, for both he and William were to remain at a distance of thirty miles from London. The remainder of the provisions were framed with the objects of securing Parliament against interference while it was deliberating upon the settlement of the kingdom, and of preventing either of the antagonists from improving his military position.

It is unlikely that these communications had any effect whatever upon James's plans. It cannot be certain that he had determined on flight before he sent the commissioners, though Halifax believed that he had been used merely as a means to gain time, and was so angry that he ceased to labour for an accommodation, and went over whole-heartedly to the side of William. James may easily, in the state of mind he was in, have changed his mind between December 5 and 9. On December 9, however, when the first message from the commissioners arrived, he had already arranged for the departure of the Queen and the Prince of Wales, and had promised her that he would follow in twenty-four hours.

On December 10 James wrote the following letter to Feversham as Second-in-Command of the army:

> Things being come to that extremity that I have been forced to send away the Queen and my son the Prince of Wales that they might not fall into my enemy's hands, which they must have done had they stayed, I am obliged to do the same thing, and endeavour to secure myself the best I can, in hopes it will please God, out of His infinite mercy to this unhappy nation, to touch their hearts with true loyalty and honour. If I could have relied upon all my troops I might not have been put to this extremity I am in, and would at least have had one blow for it; but, though I know there are many loyal and brave men amongst you, yet you know you yourself, and several of the general officers told me, it was no ways advisable to venture myself at their head. There remains nothing more for me to do but to thank you and all those officers and soldiers who have stuck to me and been truly loyal; I hope you will still have the same fidelity to me and, though I do not expect you should expose yourselves by resisting a foreign army and poisoned nation, yet I hope your former principles are so rooted in you that you will keep yourselves free from associations and such pernicious things.

This letter deserves study, for it reflects the state of James's mind on the eve of his flight. It is certainly not the letter of a man in a panic, and it must go far to prove that at this date at any rate James was not actuated by personal fear; it preserves a sort of mournful dignity, but it admits that the nation is, for the time at least, hostile to him. It is chiefly interesting, however, for its two omissions. One of these should not have occurred in a letter to the man he was leaving in control of his troops—namely, clear instructions as to the disposal of the Army, and James's irresponsibility in this particular is of a piece with his later strictures on the action of the lords who took steps to preserve order in London after his flight. The second subject which is left untouched was not, however, directly Feversham's concern: an accommodation with his subjects and with William, which should have been preferable to flight or military defeat.

The last scenes at Whitehall on the evening of December 19 are vivaciously described by the Earl of Ailesbury. His description was written many years later, in his old age; it is likely that in the intervening period he frequently told the story and kept it fresh in his mind, but, on the other hand, it is probably not free from the embroidery that results from constant repetition. He was in attendance as Gentleman of the Bedchamber, and was the last person, except Middleton, to see the King before his flight. He says:

> The King . . . took me into his private closet with these words, "I know you love to be heard at leisure and 'twas for that reason I did not call for you into my ante-closet until all was over with the others"; and then went up the steps into his closet, and ordered me to shut the door and that he would hear me out. . . . I being well informed that the King was to go away after my separating from him, I fell on my knees with tears, humbly beseeching him not to think of going. He answered, "That is a coffee-house report, and why can you imagine it?" I replied, "For the love of God, sire, why will you hide it from me that knows that your horses are now actually at Lambeth and that you are to ride Bay Ailesbury,[1] that Sir Edward Hales is there to attend you, Mr. Ralph Sheldon your equerry, Labadie page of the back stairs and Dick Smith your groom?" This I found startled him and no doubt was the rise of what follows. After still persisting and refusing me his hand at parting, as I knew he would, but he said "No", but in a manner he begged the question, viz. "If I should go who can wonder after the treatment I have found? My daughter hath deserted me, my army also, and him that I raised from nothing the same, on whom I

[1] It had been James's practice for many years to name his horses after their previous owners. Bay Ailesbury no doubt had at one time belonged to the Earl himself.

heaped all favours; and if such betrays me, what can I expect from those I have done so little for?"

Ailesbury told him that he and some others were ready to get together a body of loyal horse and stand by him to the last drop of their blood. James asked to what purpose, and Ailesbury suggested he should go to Princess Anne at Nottingham, where there were many who had joined her only for fear of molestation if they remained in London, and who would join the King if he took the field. Alternatively he might march to York, where Danby and "his broomsticks and whistail militia and some raw bubbles he has drawn in will all run away"; he might secure Berwick and march into Scotland, where he would be sure of a welcome.

> To finish this melancholy conference, I humbly besought the King to stay at least until he had heard from his three Lords Commissioners . . . and again humbly beseeching him to give me his hand to kiss. He told me he would speak to me in the morning and so with tears I retired. In the guard room I met the Earl of Middleton and I asked him what news from the Commissioners; if I remember well his answer was, "Neither good nor bad". No doubt he made his report to the King but this I am not sure; he was not long with him, for the footman I left at the bottom of the stairs came to me in half-an-hour and told me that the King was gone.

James left Whitehall by coach about one o'clock[1] on December 11—less than twenty-four hours after the Queen had commenced her journey by the same route—and at the Horse-ferry found a boat waiting to take him across the river. He had brought the Great Seal with him, in order (as he says) to prevent a Parliament being called in his name and in his absence. When he was crossing the river he threw the seal overboard, probably because he thought it would be a cumbersome addition to his baggage. At Lambeth (which James erroneously calls Foxhall) there were horses waiting, and at about two in the morning he mounted and set out on his journey with Sir Edward Hales, a page of the back stairs, named Labadie, and a guide.[2] The guide was necessary

[1] So says Ailesbury. James put the departure an hour earlier, but he is less likely than Ailesbury to have known the exact time.

[2] There is a very curious conflict of authorities on this small point of the manner of conveyance of James from Lambeth to Elmley Ferry. Macaulay says he went by coach, but he misread his only authority, the *Life of James II*, which says that "horses were ready laid at Foxhall"; the other two independent circumstantial accounts (on which with the *Life* I have based my account of the journey) agree that the party rode, and Sir John Knatchbull says in his diary for December 11, "This day the King *rid* through Kent with Sir Edward Hales by way of Fainingham (Farningham?) and Alesford." Barrillon (De-

because they decided to lessen the risk of being intercepted by avoiding the main roads to Rochester and Maidstone and by using the country lanes—lanes which, after the weather in which the Queen had set out, would have been impassable by coach. After leaving the southern suburbs they went by Chislehurst and Farningham, and presumably along a road which still exists roughly parallel to the Maidstone road, and not a great deal longer. A couple of miles short of Maidstone they crossed the main road, found fresh horses waiting for them in charge of Ralph Sheldon at Aylesford Bridge, and took refreshment at the Woolpack Inn. It was about seven o'clock and still dark. From Aylesford, for some reason unknown, instead of taking the direct route to their destination they went east-south-east through Bearsted to Hollingbourne; there they took a right-angled turn to the left and passed through Bredgar and Tunstall; they crossed the Dover road near Sittingbourne to Little Marston on the Swale, where they arrived at about ten o'clock. The journey was roughly of fifty miles, and they had taken some eight hours over it—not bad going in the conditions, with only one change of horses, and a considerable feat for a man of fifty-five during an entirely sleepless night.

At Elmley Ferry, close to Little Marston, they found the customs hoy which it had been arranged was to take the party to France, and went on board. But here their plans miscarried, for the master of the hoy represented that he had neglected to ballast his ships sufficiently for the rough crossing that was to be expected; they therefore dropped down the Swale to Shellness, the most easterly point of the Isle of Sheppey, and there, by accident or design, they were left stranded by the ebb tide until eleven o'clock in the evening. No doubt all the travellers were glad of the opportunity for sleep.

Unfortunately there was a party out from Faversham to intercept fugitives to the Continent; Dr. Obadiah Walker had seen them, and had turned his coach back towards London, and when they were pursuing him they saw a man (probably Labadie) with two led horses coming out of a side turning leading to the river; they questioned this man, and got answers from him which they knew to be untrue, and accordingly made him go with them to Sittingbourne; there they heard that Sir Edward

cember 19–24, Instr. Données, XXV, 417) is correct in this part of the narrative, though he goes astray elsewhere. On the other hand, a newsletter (H. M. C. Rep. XII, vii, 228), the Imperial Ambassador (Campana II, 417, 433), Burnet (I, 795) Reresby and Evelyn said that he travelled to Elmley Ferry by water. The account that reached William's camp at Abingdon at three o'clock the same day was that James had gone in disguise in a hackney coach "towards the Port of London", and had there taken a boat; four days later at Windsor it was reported that he had left Whitehall in the hoy in which he intended to cross to France (Japikse, I, ii, 638).

Hales with two or three companions had been seen earlier in the day crossing the road towards the ferry, and, putting two and two together, they concluded that Sir Edward Hales was trying to escape by water. Sir Edward was thoroughly hated throughout Kent, and it was unfortunate that James had chosen him as a companion, for if the cavalcade had consisted of persons unknown it is unlikely that trouble would have been taken to pursue them.

Edwards, who had questioned the man with the led horses, returned hurriedly to Faversham and manned three boats with about forty men and went down to the Swale to look for Hales and his companions. It seems likely that they spent many hours on the search, for it was not until the hoy was actually afloat that they found her. James was disguised, and they took him for a Jesuit; if he had told Ames, who led the party, who he was, instead of offering him a bribe of fifty guineas, he would possibly have been left unmolested. Hales showed a pistol, but James dissuaded him from using it; it would, indeed, have been a very foolish thing to do, for they were outnumbered ten to one, and if they had killed one of the attackers they would all have been put to death. The King was subjected to very gross indignities: they rifled his pockets, and even partially undressed him to see if he had valuables concealed under his clothes; they took from him £200 in gold, his watch and his gold-hilted sword, and they treated him "with such harsh expressions as old rogue, ugly, lean-jawed, hatchet-faced Jesuit, popish dog, etc." They continued in this unpleasant company all night, and in the morning the hoy was taken across the Swale to the mouth of the Faversham creek and there they were transferred to Sir Thomas Jones's coach, which had been captured the previous day with the judge in it. It was remarked that at the shore Sheldon was carried, and Hales, too, because he was lame, but that James, who was in riding boots, was made to walk through the ooze. They went by coach to Faversham, where they were conducted to the Arms of England: there he was recognised, and he was treated with more respect, but a party of sailors under Ames kept him a close prisoner and refused all his demands that he should be allowed to proceed on his journey; their motives were fear lest William might punish them for letting him go, and hope of reward for preventing his flight.

Napleton, who had first recognised James, went forthwith to Canterbury with a letter from the King to Lord Winchelsea, the Lord Lieutenant of the county, who had assembled there a volunteer troop of horse as a protection against the disbanded Irish. Sir John Knatchbull's account of the discussion on this letter reflects the uncertainty of the country gentlemen regarding William's plans and intentions, and their conviction that the safest way to avoid the Prince's displeasure was to do nothing:

> I plainly saw that my lord and most of the gentlemen were disposed to let the King go if he desired, and indeed so was I, for I knew it was the Prince's desire; but then I considered he was in the hands of seamen, and I thought it very probable they would value themselves much upon so great a prize, and, thinking they had done great service, might take such a proposal from the gentry very ill, and to what degree their passions might rise I did not know; . . . though the Prince might have been pleased with the event, I had little reason to expect any thanks for it; nay, according to the methods of state it might have proved the ruin of me and my family; therefore, though on the Prince's behalf I was contented he should go, I was not willing to be accounted the sole author of his escape; so I took leave. . . .

Winchelsea himself, though he had been moved to tears by the King's letter, was in very grave doubts about the course he should take; it was only after two hours of discussion that he and a small party of gentlemen set out for Faversham, and it was not until late in the evening of December 12 that he arrived there. He disavowed to the sailors any intention of delivering their captive out of their hands, but he persuaded them to consent to his removal from the inn to a private house, where the sailors mounted guard; but James himself was given rooms of his own, and two of the local inhabitants volunteered to wait on him; his privacy was not, however, respected, and he had to endure the affront of a reading of William's manifesto under his windows.

On Friday, December 15, certain Lords, who in James's absence, in the interests of public security, had constituted themselves an unofficial Council of Regency, received a letter from James, and in consequence the Earls of Feversham, Ailesbury, Middleton and Yarmouth were sent with three coaches and 120 guards to bring him back. Ailesbury has left a very spirited account of their journey: he describes the panic on the roads at the reports of the Irish troops being out of hand, and says that they were only just in time to reassure the people of Rochester and to prevent the bridge there from being blown up; and he continues,

> The Earl of Winchelsea . . . conducted me to the house. I passed the hall through all those seamen and entered into the parlour. The King was sitting in a great chair his hat on and his beard being much grown, and resembled the picture of his royal

> father at the pretended High Court of Justice. He rose up to meet me, I bent my knee not being able to kneel by reason of my jack-boots. He took me to the window with an air of displeasure, indeed quite contrary to what I expected, and said, "You were all kings when I left London". I could not dissemble but spoke my mind in these terms, "Sir, I expected another sort of welcome after the great dangers I ran last night by repairing to you". "I know," said the King, "you meant well as to your particular." I replied, "It is certainly so, and give me leave to tell Your Majesty that your going away without leaving a Commission of Regency, but for our care and vigilance the City of London might have been in ashes; but the Lord Mayor and city respecting us, all was kept in a calm."

James's immediate grievances were the lack of a clean shirt and the insolence of the deputy-lieutenants of the county who had superseded the sailors and constituted themselves the King's gaolers. Shortly afterwards the coaches arrived, and James showed his good spirits by telling Ailesbury that he had now a shirt to lend him instead of trying to borrow one.

James now determined to return to London, or rather was determined by the four lords, for he had lost all power of initiative and had no plans for the future. He graciously forgave those who had treated him with such indignity, and refused to receive back the money they had stolen from him. On Saturday, December 15, they went to Rochester, where James slept at Sir Richard Head's house; on Sunday he rode as far as Dartford, and then took coach. He had intended to return to Whitehall by the Horse-ferry, but several gentlemen persuaded him that a welcome was prepared for him in the City, and he crossed London Bridge. Though some accounts try to belittle the welcome London gave to the returning King in the dusk of that December evening, and to confine the shouting to a few boys, there is overwhelming preponderance of evidence that the acclamations were loud and enthusiastic:

> After dinner [at Dartford] the King went in his body-coach and I attended [says Ailesbury]. . . . Vast numbers of persons out of the city and suburbs came out on horseback and the road filled with spectators on foot with faces of joy. Blackheath was covered with gentlemen and citizens on horseback, and two eminent merchants came to the coach-side for to beg of me to beseech the King to pass through the City. . . . From St. George's Southwark to Whitehall, a long march, there was scarce room for the coaches to pass through and the balconies and windows were thronged, with loud acclamations beyond whatever was heard of. . . .

This spontaneous outburst of popular approval at the King's return is very extraordinary, and it confirms impressions, already formed in the later years of Charles's reign, of lack of steadiness of sentiment on the part of the London mob. James himself adduced it as evidence that he had not lost his personal popularity and that "the anger was not at his person but at his religion". The general opinion was that it was inspired by personal pity for a King suddenly plunged from magnificence to helplessness under the indignities heaped on him at Faversham. This sentiment had no doubt a place in the minds of the cheering crowds,[1] but the feeling uppermost in their minds was one of relief at an unexpected return to security in their persons and property;[2] for the citizens of London had since the King's departure been through a terrible time of panic (in common with other parts of the country) at the news that the disbanded Irish troops were marching to sack the City, and though the committee of lords had to a great extent restored confidence, they had acted without authority, and were regarded as temporary and provisional.

Once re-installed at Whitehall, James behaved as if he had never left his capital or as if his absence had been in the nature of an excursion for pleasure. The experiences he had undergone had finally reduced his mind to the condition in which it was to remain for the thirteen years he had yet to live. The second Lord Dartmouth relates that:

> the night King James returned to Whitehall, where I stood by him during his supper, and he told me all that had happened to him at Faversham with as much unconcernedness as if they had been the adventures of some other person, and directed a great deal of his discourse to me, though I was but a boy.

He reassumed, as if by habit, his regal state, and he was, temporarily, elated at the splendid reception he had had in the City. He missed no opportunity of expressing displeasure at the means that had been taken to preserve order during his absence.

One of his first acts was to make good his claim to be still King of England by calling a council. It can hardly have been a regular meeting of the Privy Council, though its proceedings were duly minuted, but in the absence of any code of procedure for Privy Council meetings it is impossible to be certain: at such notice and in the circumstances a summons cannot have been delivered to more than a few of the persons entitled to attend, and in fact only eight councillors were present, all

[1] In common with the previous reactions in his favour in October 1679, February 1680 and April 1681, the basis in sentiment was that James had sinned, but had been, perhaps excessively, punished.

[2] I am indebted for this view to Sir Charles Firth, *Commentary on Macaulay*.

Protestants: the Duke of Hamilton, the Earls of Craven, Berkeley and Middleton, Lords Preston and Godolphin, the Master of the Rolls and Colonel Silius Titus. There were only two items of business: His Majesty was pleased to direct Lords-Lieutenants and other local officers to suppress riotous and tumultuous meetings; and, being informed that "during his absence from London" an embargo had been laid on various ports, is pleased to direct Mr. Samuel Pepys to remove the embargo. He also proposed to send a warrant to release from imprisonment various Catholics who had been seized—the Earls of Salisbury and Peterborough, Sir Edward Hales and others—but the Council persuaded him that such an action would involve conflicts which were better avoided.[1]

On one section of James's followers—his fanatical Catholic adherents—the acclamations of the City had an extraordinary effect. Their leaders had decamped or were in custody, and they themselves had for five days been in hiding for fear that the panic of the mob would find expression in a general massacre of papists. They now emerged from their holes and trooped to Whitehall, believing (as is barely credible) that the King's return to London was a genuine triumph and that he was again firmly seated on the throne with themselves as his chief advisers. It was said that at Court that evening there were five Catholics for every Protestant. If James had really thought at the time that his unpopularity was solely on account of his religion (and, it may be added, if he had been capable of definite resolution), he would at least have made some gesture of getting rid of his exclusively Catholic counsellors. At midnight he heard Mass—a privilege, as we are told, "which the canons allow only to a King".

Meanwhile William had heard at Abingdon of James's flight; he had at once changed his plans, and instead of going to Oxford, he had proceeded towards London on the direct route; on December 12 he went to Wallingford, on the 13th to Henley and on the 14th to Windsor. When the news of the stoppage at Faversham arrived, with the detail that the sailors had said that they would not release James without an order from the Prince, William sent Zuylestein with an order for his release and a message to him suggesting that for the present he should reside at Rochester. When Zuylestein reached Rochester, however, he found that James had just passed through the town on his way to London, and he followed the King back to Whitehall, where he had a prolonged audience before returning to William to report. Zuylestein

[1] The holding of this Council is sufficient proof that James's withdrawal on December 11 was not an act of abdication. It is interesting in this connection to note that no Treasury business was transacted between December 11 and 23 inclusive, except on December 17 and 18, when James was in London.

pointed out to James that William could not be in London except with sufficient troops to protect his person, and James replied, "He may bring as many as he will; I will have myself even only those which he may think necessary, or rather, not being sure of my own troops, I would as lief have none at all"; and he at once gave orders that St. James's Palace should be prepared for William and that quarters should be provided for the Dutch troops.

After the crowded business of the Sunday evening, Monday was a quiet and undisturbed day. James had a long talk with Barrillon (as he had had on his arrival); he spoke of the chaotic condition of the country, where no stranger could travel without being questioned[1] and an important town like Dover was governed by the mob; he had no longer any hopes founded on the acclamation of the previous day, he had no doubt that William would seize the throne, but he spoke in a detached manner of a preliminary difficulty the Prince would have in summoning Parliament without the Great Seal, which, as he said, was lost; he renewed his protestations that he would never take action against Louis. The ambassador received a strong impression that the King was still resolved on flight. During the day James wrote to Louis commending his wife and child to his care and saying that he would have been making the same requests for himself had he not been stopped.

William did not welcome James's proposal that the two of them should be in London at the same time and (presumably) that Parliament should meet and settle the affairs of the kingdom while they were there. James's reply to the Hungerford terms had been flight. William had been delighted at the simplification of the problem of settlement which this virtual abdication had brought about, and he was correspondingly annoyed at the officiousness of the Faversham fishermen in interrupting it. Whether, as many believe, he had determined before he left Holland to supplant his father-in-law on the throne of England and his manifesto had been a cloak for more drastic action, or he had come to England in good faith to secure his wife's succession and to adjust the differences between the King and his Protestant subjects, there can be little doubt that from the time of James's first flight he abandoned any scruples he may have had against usurpation and pressed on almost without disguise to his own immediate accession. At Hungerford he had been content that he and James should be on an equal footing—both at some distance from London while Parliament mediated between them; at Windsor there were divided counsels, but none of William's advisors appear to have been in favour of repeating the terms offered from Hungerford;

[1] This account of the condition of the country is confirmed by the incidents described in his journal on a journey from Chester to London by John Stevens.

some apparently (though it is not necessary to accept allegations that either Clarendon or Churchill were among them) were for imprisoning James either at Breda or in the Tower. William decided that he himself would be in London, while James remained some distance away. What followed was certainly a breach of the good behaviour which William had observed and had imposed on his troops since his landing, and, if James had had the power or disposition to take advantage of it, might have caused him considerable embarrassment through the universal condemnation of his conduct to the fallen King and the consequent revulsion of feeling. Thus the Imperial ambassador wrote that William's treatment of James was unduly harsh, that it was urged in William's favour that James had shown no intention of abandoning his papist and pro-French policy, and that it was hopeless to bring him to an accommodation by gentle methods, but that nevertheless a reaction in James's favour had appeared even among those who approved of reform, and Burnet wrote to Admiral Herbert, "Compassion has begun to work, especially since the Prince sent him word to leave Whitehall".

In the first place William had the Earl of Feversham arrested, whom James had sent to him to invite him to St. James's; the pretext was said to be that he was a general of the opposing forces and had come into the lines without a safe conduct;[1] but, as was pointed out at the time, exactly the same consideration applied to Zuylestein, and he had been allowed to come to James and to return freely; it was said—and probably truly—that William took this unjustifiable course to express his irritation at the disbandment of the royal troops; in any case it was a gross piece of discourtesy to James. Then a deputation consisting of Halifax, Shrewsbury and Delamere was sent to James by William, and arrived at midnight between December 17 and 18, demanding, "for the quiet of the city and the safety of his person", his removal within ten hours to the Duchess of Lauderdale's house at Ham. James was in a heavy sleep when Middleton came to announce the arrival of the three lords, but he received them courteously and discussed the proposal dispassionately: he did not at all object to leaving London and at such short notice, but he did not relish the idea of living at a damp house like Ham in the winter; he therefore proposed to go to Rochester instead, and entered into some detail about the tide, and concluded that it would serve next morning for the journey in his barges to Rochester. The lords had no commission from William to give James a choice of residences, but a reference back to William, who had now moved nearer London to the

[1] But Bentinck, who was with William at Windsor, does not mention this pretext, but says that Feversham's offence was having disbanded the troops when he had assured the Prince that he would give them no orders.

Duke of Somerset's seat, Zion House, secured the necessary permission, and it was agreed that James should leave for Rochester at ten o'clock on the following morning.

The departure for Rochester was almost funereal in its atmosphere; there was no exultation in the faces of the many spectators—indeed, many were moved to tears. The King was conducted to his barge by the three lords who had brought William's peremptory message, and in his memoirs he contrasts Halifax's brusqueness with Shrewsbury's courtesy, a distinction that may have been due merely to their different reactions to a situation which was equally painful to both to them. It is a curious coincidence that two of the instruments of his ejection from his capital (the hot-headed and ineffectual Delamere being the third) should have been the only two men in the country who possessed the qualities of statesmanship, who had the ability to choose the best means to achieve a distant end, and who were able, not invariably but from time to time, to make personal sacrifices for the public good. If James had been willing to submit himself to the advice of Halifax and Shrewsbury, or of either of them, his reign would not have ended in this tragedy. But it is an idle speculation, for James's mind was incapable of compromise or of estimating all the effects of a course of action; he proceeded by impulse, and was convinced that whatever he considered desirable must be done at once, without regard to ultimate effects.

The royal barge accommodated James and his personal attendants, Ailesbury, Dumbarton, Arran and others; it was followed by other barges and boats containing Dutch guards, and a troop of horse was sent by road to Rochester; and James appeared in the sight of the world as a prisoner, though he was not under restraint. The night of December 18–19 was spent at Gravesend, and the following day James journeyed to Rochester and installed himself at Sir Richard Head's house—a significant choice, for the grounds at the back of the house reached to the river bank. No one doubted that his intention in choosing Rochester for his residence was to take the earliest opportunity to follow the Queen to France; it was also obvious to everyone that William wanted him to go, and local evidence of this desire was furnished by the absence of guards at the rear of the house. James himself said that the only matter on which he and William were in agreement was that he should leave the country. He was now among the best friends still left to him—Protestants and moderate Catholics—and they were nearly unanimous in their entreaties that he should stay. They saw that as long as he remained in England he could claim to be king *de facto* and could demand the right to be heard in any proposals for settlement, and that the high Tories who had disapproved of his policy would nevertheless, as their declaration of December 11 had shown, refuse to countenance his deposition; but that if once he left the realm he might retain the academic rights of a king *de jure*, but would virtually have abdicated. Clarendon in London made a last desperate effort to settle James's mind by sending to him one Belson, a moderate Roman Catholic, with the message that "his enemies wished that he would be gone and his friends feared it". On the evening of December 22 James received Belson, but told him he had letters to write and would see him in the morning.

It was said that the second flight was determined by a letter which James received from Queen Mary, but it seems clear that he had made up his mind before he left London, and that he affected to listen to argument merely to gain time to make his arrangements for flight. The day after his arrival at Rochester he wrote to William Chiffinch, his own and his brother's "confidential man", telling him to collect all portable articles of value at Whitehall and to give them to James Graham, the Keeper of the Privy Purse, presumably for despatch to France, and also to Sir William Turner and Sir Benjamin Bathurst to secure his holdings in public companies. His last words to Ailesbury were:

> If I do not retire I shall certainly be sent to the Tower, and no king ever went out of that place but to his grave. It is a cruel thing for a subject to be driven out of his native country, much more for a king to be driven out of his three kingdoms. . . . I declare to you that I retire for the security of my person, and I shall always be ready to return when my subjects' eyes may be opened. All you keep together and live in unity for my good. And my Roman Catholic officers etc. I have directed them to retire and live quietly. . . . Can you advise me to stay?

He also left a letter addressed to Middleton giving his reasons for his withdrawal: after reciting his grievances against William since his first flight, the arrest of Feversham, the midnight deputation at Whitehall and the propaganda designed "to make me appear as black as Hell to my own people as well as to all the world besides", he says that he would never be free in England to make good against the forces hostile to him, and that he is withdrawing to no great distance, "but so as to be within call when the nation's eyes shall be opened so as to see how they have been abused and imposed upon by the specious pretences of religion and property". We may conclude without undue conjecture that personal fear was at least a small element in the motives underlying the second flight: he had before him the example of his father's death, his mind had crystallised before the Restoration and he did not see that what had been possible forty years earlier was no longer possible, nor did he reckon that the mere fact of relationship would inhibit William from doing personal injury to his uncle and father-in-law.

James was well aware that his departure would not be impeded; he could easily have gone by day, and he could probably have made use of one of his own ships of war; but some latent dramatic sense induced him to observe all the operations of hazard and secrecy. He undressed and went to bed in his usual manner, rose and dressed again shortly after midnight (this was the morning of December 23), and with his son, the Duke of Berwick, and some of the minor officers of his household and servants, he got into the pinnace of the *Henrietta* yacht and was rowed down the Medway. It blew so hard from the east that the going was slow and the tide had turned against them before they reached the northern mouth of the Swale, and it was nearly six o'clock before they reached Queenborough, where the *Henrietta* was moored; they failed to find her, however, until daylight, as she had had to shift her moorings on account of the gale, but they were able to take shelter on the *Eagle* fire-ship, whose captain and crew were said to be "honest and loyal". At daybreak they transferred to the *Henrietta*, but the wind was dead ahead, and they crossed to the Essex shore and lay there all day; in the evening the gale slackened, and they dropped down on the tide as far as Red Sand, where they anchored for the night. The next day the weather had cleared and they had a fairly comfortable passage, though they failed to make Calais, and had to put in at Ambleteuse. There they found French men-of-war which had been stationed to look out for them, and James actually concluded his voyage in a French frigate. They had had small arms on board sufficient to repel any casual attack, but the ship was small and the accommodation so meagre that James and Berwick entirely filled the small cabin; provisioning was bad, and the only frying-pan had a hole in it which had to be stopped "with a pitched rag, and to tie an old furred can about with a cord to make it hold the drink they put in it". But James made light of these hardships, and ate and drank as heartily as he had ever done in his life. It is not surprising, however, that he was glad of a sleep as soon as he got ashore.

CHAPTER VI

THE FINAL EXILE

From Christmas Day, 1688, the date of his landing at Ambleteuse, until his death on September 16, 1701, the life of James II has very little psychological interest. He was present, and by courtesy in a position of importance, on a number of occasions, but he did not by any exercise of will-power influence events: he was merely a puppet in the hands of the men who had possession of his person and of the little that remained of his mind. Certain habits, indeed, persisted with him, notably his obstinacy in refusing to part with advisers to whom he had grown accustomed, in spite of incompetence obvious to everyone except himself.

The symptoms of James's degeneration of mind were similar to those of extreme senility, and are very rare in a man so young and so physically fit, for he still hunted whenever he could. Briefly these symptoms may be described as a complete apathy towards his misfortunes and in respect of the plans for his restoration, perfect contentment with his present surroundings, a lack of sense that he had sunk from a crown to a pension, and a distressing proneness to fits of garrulity in which he would relate dispassionately, as if he were speaking not of himself but of a third person, the incidents of his past life. Descriptions of his public conduct abound in the letters of those who saw him in France; the most favourable, perhaps the only favourable, account is that given by Rizzini, who had been Modenese envoy at St. James's.

> The dethroned King [he says] enjoys perfect tranquillity in the haven of security provided for him in this country by the brotherly love of its ever glorious and victorious monarch; and he finds his condition less unhappy as an exile and a fugitive than reigning, even peacefully, over perfidious and ungrateful subjects. Unfavourable comment is passed on his indifference to his misfortunes; but those who know him best are aware that his outward imperturbability gives no indication of the deep wounds he has inwardly received.

This imperturbability had been a recognised feature of James's character before his flight, but it can hardly be counted a virtue: it was, indeed, in accordance with his obstinate, stupid, sluggish and withal sanguine nature; it was not evident in those periods of his stay in Scotland in which his prospects had appeared to be hopeless—his letters to Legge are anything but complacent—but once he was on the throne he *knew* that he would achieve his ends in spite of temporary setbacks.

Other observers contrast the attitude of Mary Beatrice, proud, resentful and anxious to do anything to regain what they had lost in England, with that of James, happy and contented in the negative way of a very old man, and gradually losing all rancour against those who had taken his crown from him and, as he thought, betrayed him. Thus Madame de Sévigné says in one place:

> Everything she says is fitting and sensible; her husband is not like her in this, he has plenty of courage but a mean mind. He speaks of everything that has happened in England with an insensibility which makes him look a fool. He is sociable and enjoys all the pleasures of Versailles.

And in another:

> The Queen of England, it is very evident, would reign if God willed, in the great kingdom of England where the court is magnificent, rather than be at Saint-Germain where she is overwhelmed with the magnificent favour of our King. The King of England appears to be content, and that is why he is here.

In a later letter she says that this judgement on James has become a current saying at Versailles: "When one listens to him one realises why he is here".

Madame de La Fayette writes of him as hunting "like a man of twenty who has no other care than to amuse himself". She is also one among many Catholics who believed in moderation even in religion, and who regretted that he sank more and more into what his brother Charles had called his "sottise", and allowed himself to be dominated by his priests: "He had not been long in France before he was known for what he was, a man infatuated with religion and abandoned in an extraordinary manner to the Jesuits". The accounts of Madame[1] are of a somewhat later date, and are concerned with James as he was after his return from Ireland; she was very fond of James, but with the sort of affection women feel for men who have relapsed into something like the simplicity and helplessness of childhood. She writes in October 1690, "Now that I have come to know more of this good king I like him better. He is the best fellow in the world for he sometimes sighs fit to break one's heart." And again in June 1692, "Our dear King James is good and honest but the most incompetent man I have ever seen in my life. A child of seven

[1] Elizabeth Charlotte of the Palatinate, who had married the Duke of Orleans after the death of James's sister Henrietta.

would not make such silly mistakes as he does. . . . His piety makes him very stupid." She also reports a conversation she heard between James and Mary; Mary said: "Money! he never had any; I never knew him to have a half-penny". James replied that he had had plenty and had spent it on ships and guns, and Mary closed the conversation by saying, with a malice which we may hope was rare with her, that all the good he had got out of that was that these armaments had been used against him.

But Madame's most interesting contribution to an understanding of James's character in these last years is a revelation of the continuance of the twenty-year-old conflict between his spiritual aspirations and his carnal desires:

> If the prophecy of the previous King of England comes true the worthy King will not even make a good saint. Lady Portsmouth (Charles's mistress), who was here a few days ago, told me indeed, that the late King used to say, "You will see that when my brother there becomes King he will lose his kingdoms through his religious zeal and his soul through his unsightly wantons, because he has not even the niceness to like them beautiful!" The prophecy seems to be coming true already, for his kingdoms are lost to him and one hears that at Dublin he had two frightful scarecrows (laiderons) with whom he was always carrying on. The more one sees of this King the more favourably one feels towards the Prince of Orange, and the more excuses one finds for him;

and a few weeks later:

> I am sure [the Queen] would be glad if her husband never saw any ladies more beautiful than I am! Then her mind would be at rest and not troubled with jealousy, and dear King James would not have his ears boxed. His lackey says he had two mistresses at Dublin, but here his conduct is irreproachable. I know not whether it is from fear of his wife or merely from desire to follow present fashions here and to play the saint, he certainly attends sermons regularly.

This is, however, the last we hear of James's easily besetting sin (or "predominant sin", as he called it in his Papers of Devotion); he was now fifty-seven years of age, and could claim with many an old *roué* that he had abandoned his vices, when in fact his vices had abandoned him.

To support the testimony of these three ladies, Rizzini, weakening somewhat from his former defence of James, writes:

> He lives always surrounded by friars and talks of his misfortunes with indifference, as if he did not feel them or had never been a king; in this way he has entirely lost the respect of the French and those who knew him in Flanders as Duke of York [forty years previously] say that he was quite another man then, so great is the change they find in His Majesty, who, however, is as affable and courteous to everyone as could be desired.

And in the summer of 1693 a man who had just returned to England from Saint-Germain said that King James "minds little but hunting, and loves not to talk of England".

It would be easy to produce further evidence of James's degeneration of mind, but perhaps too much has already been said; it is necessary, however, to counteract a tendency to regard James's life as all of a piece and to consider him after the Revolution as a fully responsible person.[1] It may be added that all the evidence tends to the same conclusion, and that it is fully confirmed by a number of independent witnesses who were with James in Ireland.

It is not difficult to imagine that a king in this pathetic condition gave very little trouble to the men who had his ear. Mary for her part had neither the knowledge nor the independence of mind to supply her husband's deficiencies; she indulged in a marked degree the vice of queens of governing through favourites and not through men of ability. If James had been capable of detached thought he would have realised that he could not get back to England except by placating Protestant opinion, and if during his first days at Saint-Germain he had happened to have Protestants about him he might (conceivably but improbably) have been induced to give his name to their proposals and they might have kept Catholics from getting near him. But by natural inclination his first Cabinet was Catholic, and by the very act of consulting them he was lost; for they were at once able to prevent him from consulting with anyone who was not in their interests, or even from receiving letters which had not passed their censorship. It was not long before it was said that "My Lord Melfort had ruined the King and would suffer nothing to come to him but what came from his party". It must be remembered also that James was living at the court of Louis XIV at a time when that monarch had become such a bigot that he could barely tolerate the presence of English Protestants in his kingdom; indeed, a few years later he advised James to dismiss all his Protestant servants—

[1] Macaulay, for example, quoting many of the same authorities as I have done, speaks of the contempt with which James was regarded by the French courtiers, but criticises his subsequent conduct as if he were still in possession of all his faculties, and might be blamed for what was done in his name but to a great extent without his knowledge.

and such advice was in the circumstances tantamount to a command. Of Petre very little is heard after the flight: during the first weeks in Paris James found occasion to say that he had never given any but good advice, but subsequently he was not mentioned either by James or Mary, except in terms of abuse:[1] It is significant that before James went to Ireland Petre had ceased to be Clerk of the Closet; it is said, however, that he was at Saint-Germain, incognito, towards the end of 1693. Adda was also "coldly received" by James as not having been sufficiently zealous in the royal policy, and Louis was so angry with him that he would not allow him to remain in France. Queen Mary Beatrice, however, thought more highly of Adda than did James; she sent him to Rome with a very cordial introduction to her uncle, the Cardinal d'Este. He (or possibly someone of the same name) was subsequently made a Cardinal.

King Louis received the fugitives with every mark of respect and with munificent hospitality. He treated them as if they were actual sovereigns in full possession of their kingdoms, he insisted that his own near relations should give them the precedence due to their rank and he repressed a tendency among his courtiers to make James an object of ridicule. James and Mary accepted his kindness as the simple expression of a generous disposition, and to a great extent they were justified in so accepting it. But Louis had an additional motive in his conduct towards his cousin and towards the Queen who had owed to him her splendid marriage: he saw in them a means of strengthening himself against his great enemy, William of Orange. He was singularly ill-informed about political sentiment in England, he was convinced that the Jacobites were a large and powerful party there, and that by their means he could create difficulties for William at home that would handicap him in the Continental war. He was no doubt confirmed in that error by the reports of spies, who made much of the inevitable reaction after the Revolution, when those who had nursed extravagant hopes had been disappointed. From the moment Mary landed at Calais, Louis was determined to keep her in France and to prevent her from carrying out her early intentions of returning to England; Siegnelay wrote to Lauzun telling him that if she had not left Boulogne he was to see that she made no further delay there; and when there was a danger that James, after his detention at Faversham, would want her to return to England, Louvois issued instructions that she should be told that her escort had orders to conduct her to Vincennes and could not disobey those orders.

[1] The Grews (*The English Court in Exile*, p. 83, note) say that it appears from a letter of Rizzini in the Archives of Este at Modena that the Queen had used her influence to get Petre dismissed.

When Mary lay down in her lodging at Calais she said she had not felt so easy and safe for three months; but she had been in no personal danger, and her words are merely a measure of the fears which had been excited in her mind by her priests. Her first intention was to wait at Calais for James, but after two days she consented to go as far as Boulogne. On the road she met a company of dragoons which had been sent to meet her, and from that time her arrangements were made for her. On December 19 she heard at Boulogne that James was a prisoner, and she wanted to return to England, but the following day she journeyed to Montreuil, where she was met by a distinguished body of officers of Louis's household, and she was reassured by the news of James's return to Whitehall. At Beaumont on the 26th she heard that James had landed at Ambleteuse, and (as reported by a lady who was with her), "Without thinking of the loss of three kingdoms, she said immediately, 'Oh, God! I am the happiest woman in the world'."

Madame de Sévigné wrote to her daughter that the sheet of paper she was writing on would soon be full if she began to tell of the generosity of Louis to James and Mary, and three days later she gave a description of the meeting of the French King with Queen Mary:

> He met the Queen with his whole household and a hundred carriages-and-six. When he saw the coach of the Prince of Wales he got down from his own coach . . . and embraced him tenderly; then he hastened to the Queen who had left her coach, he kissed her and talked to her for a short time; then he took her in his coach, placed her on his right hand and presented to her Monseigneur and Monsieur, who were also in the coach. He conducted her to Saint-Germain, where she found herself waited on as a Queen.

Admirable stage-management! Well might Madame de Sévigné say, "His beautiful spirit takes pleasure in playing this great part". James travelled in less splendour but more rapidly by post-chaise, and arrived the following day; he went to Versailles to pay his respects to Louis, but found that the King was waiting for him at Saint-Germain. Madame de Sévigné continues her narrative:

> The King met him at the end of the Salle des Gardes; the King of England bent low as if to embrace his knees; the King stopped him and embraced him three or four times very cordially. They conversed in low tones for a quarter of an hour, the King presented the King of England to Monseigneur, Monsieur and Cardinal Bonzi and then led him to the chamber of the Queen, who had great difficulty in restraining her tears. After they had

talked for some time the King brought them to the Prince of Wales and stayed with them some minutes and then left saying, "This is your house; when I come here you will do the honours for me as I will for you at Versailles".

In spite, however, of Louis's distinguished hospitality, the first impression made by James on the French courtiers was very unfavourable. Madame de La Fayette relates that in one of his first interviews with Louis, in company with several French gentlemen, James gave an account of his recent experiences and that this account was so incoherent and that he stammered so badly[1] that excuses had to be made for him on the erroneous ground of his lack of knowledge of French.

By his flight to France and his dependence on Louis, James had done what he had throughout his reign avoided doing: he had definitely taken the French side in the European conflict, and he could no longer claim to be a neutral and to demand assistance from Louis's enemies. He wrote to both the Emperor and the Pope, urging that to help him to regain his throne was to benefit the Catholic religion; but neither sovereign was willing to embark on a crusade whose success would only have added to the strength of Louis. As the Papal nuncio in Paris told Queen Mary Beatrice in May 1689, neither the Pope nor the Catholic princes could assist the British King; they were obliged to look to their own preservation against the preponderance of France.

Six weeks were spent in the ordinary trivialities of Court life, in hunting at Saint-Germain and in various other royal forests, in religious exercises and in visiting convents and other holy places. James would rather have remained where he was, but Louis decided that he had better earn his keep, and that he could not do it better than by making a diversion in William's rear by raising his standard in Ireland: as the Abbé Melani wrote at the time, James was "tranquil and insensible; he would rather stay in France occupied with devotional exercises and hunting, but he is driven to Ireland not only by Tyrconnel but by the French". Shortly after arriving at Saint-Germain, James had written to Tyrconnel a letter which in the circumstances must be regarded as irresponsible: he says that he hopes Tyrconnel will be able to maintain himself in Ireland "till summer at least", that Louis will send at present no more help than seven or eight thousand muskets, but may do more when he hears how Tyrconnel is situated, and that Tyrconnel must make haste and send a report. In reply (or more probably crossing

[1] There are several references to James's stammering after but not (I think) before his flight; the defect may have been due to the shock of disillusionment which occurred at Salisbury. On the other hand, I have seen it stated that his father stammered, and he may have been subject to a hereditary defect.

James's letter) Tyrconnel wrote what must have stung even James's sluggish spirit, "Sir, I beg of you to consider whether you can with honour continue where you are when you possess a kingdom of your own plentiful of all things for human life"; he said that money was their chief need, and that with the 200,000 livres they expected from the French King they would do very well; that he has 35,000 or 36,000 men enlisted, but they are without arms, equipment and means of subsistence; that they are at present living on pillage, "which in six months' time will destroy both nation and army"; and that the Catholic population everywhere preponderates except in Dublin and Ulster, where the numbers of Catholics and Protestants are about equal.

From the French point of view it was urged that James would have no difficulty in getting together a large army, and his presence in Ireland would inspire it;[1] that the Protestants would flock to him for fear of being robbed; that he could easily pass to Scotland, where he would be welcomed by the episcopalian party; that the English Jacobites would find him more accessible in Ireland than in France and would hasten to join him; and that he would be of great assistance to France in compelling William to fight on two fronts. These views reveal the usual French ignorance of conditions in the three kingdoms and ignore many of the difficulties of James's enterprise, but in the main they furnish the plan most likely to succeed in a not very hopeful enterprise. For, unless Louis had been prepared to make Ireland a major theatre of the war and to provide money, troops and generals in far greater quantities than he ever consented to supply, the resources of England must eventually have prevailed.

James left Saint-Germain for Brest on February 15, 1689. Louis's dramatic instinct did not fail him at parting; when James told him that he had given him all the equipment for his army that he could desire but that he had forgotten to give him arms for his own person, he gave James his own cuirass and arms, to that he might appear in the field as a king should appear; and his last words to him were, "I am deeply grieved at parting with you, but I hope never to see you again; but if you do return you may be assured that you will find me as you leave me". On the eve of his departure James wrote to his wife's uncle, the Cardinal d'Este, a long and optimistic letter saying, among other things, that Tyrconnel had a Catholic army of 20,000 men, that Ireland was a land

[1] Vauban wrote to Louvois on February 15, "I have an idea that when a man plays his last stake he ought to play it himself or to be on the spot. The King of England seems to be in this condition. His last stake is Ireland; it appears to me that he ought to go there, where with the help which the King may give him he can get on his legs again and be supported by those of his subjects who remain loyal to him."

full of food and forage, that the people there were ready to spill the last drop of their blood in his defence and that it was only a short step from Ireland to Scotland, where (save the mark!) there were many Catholics both among the gentry and the common people. Before starting he fasted for twenty-four hours.

At Brest he found a squadron of ten ships loaded with all that was necessary for his own equipment and that of his army—saddle-horses, coaches, linen, furniture, dinner services for ceremonial and for camp use, arms for 20,000 men, guns and ammunition; Louis also allowed him 200,000 livres a month for the pay of the troops, in addition to nearly two million livres for his personal use. No French troops were sent with James, but there were over a hundred French officers of various grades, including six generals[1] and a number of specialists, such as engineers and gunners. There is no evidence that James had been actively employed in organising this expedition; on the contrary, he was continuously occupied with other matters. But the most important of James's companions was Avaux, who had been appointed French ambassador at James's Court. Avaux had been for some years previous to Louis's declaration of war against the States-General ambassador at The Hague, and had been able to supply Louis with accurate information about William's intrigues with the English malcontents, his military and naval preparations and the object of those preparations. Barrillon had been ambassador in England for eleven years, but he had known little of that country except the Court, he had not sufficiently corrected Louis's own prepossessions and had been taken by surprise by the Revolution. He appears to have taken his supersession by Avaux in a philosophic spirit, and general opinion in France commended Louis's choice. We are indebted to the despatches of Avaux for the fullest and most accurate account we have of the expedition to Ireland until his recall in March 1690. These despatches reveal him as a man of great ability, integrity and devotion to his master's service. He was in a strong position, for Louis was providing the greater part of the money and material of the expedition, and he could claim a considerable voice in James's counsels. He stood out among James's advisers as the only man who had any real conception of the problems which had to be faced and the only man who wanted to get things, not merely talked about, but done. He formed at once the lowest opinion of James's capacity—at Brest, for example, before the expedition started, he found that James was chattering to everyone about his plans and that no

[1] An indication that Louis regarded Ireland as a "side-show", and not a main theatre of war, is furnished by the fact that he sent there at first no general of the highest reputation except Rosen.

secrecy could be observed; and he failed on the whole to gain the King's confidence. The conflict between the King and the ambassador was partly due to James's resentment at being persistently reminded of his failures in organisation, partly also to a fundamental difference in policy. Avaux agreed with Tyrconnel that the loyalty of the Irish Protestants was not to be relied on, and that James's best chance of success was to treat them as potential enemies and to rally the native Irish to his cause by making large concessions to their national aspirations; James was obsessed with the belief that the majority of the people of England and Scotland were still at heart faithful to his cause and were longing for his return, and he dared not alienate his supporters on the other side of the Irish Channel by adopting the policy of Avaux and Tyrconnel.

In these views James was strongly supported by John Drummond, Earl of Melfort, who until the end of August 1689 was in effect his sole adviser and entirely dominated his mind. Melfort, as a pupil of Sunderland, gave James only such advice as accorded with his prepossessions—Avaux was infuriated by this sychophantic procedure; he was greedy of power and aimed at concentrating all authority in his own hands, and he jealously guarded his position by insinuations against his rivals in James's confidence. But he was neither so able nor so unscrupulous as Sunderland, and he was universally unpopular. Avaux admitted that he was plausible and conveyed an impression of ability on first acquaintance, but he soon found him out as the most incompetent Minister that ever held high office, and Avaux's judgement is unanimously supported by men of all shades of Jacobite opinion. Louis for a long time tried to convince his ambassador that he had under-rated Melfort, but he came round to his opinion, and even James admitted to Avaux that Melfort was incompetent, but argued that there was no one to replace him. Melfort was as great but not nearly so convincing a liar as Sunderland, but he was not, like Sunderland, open to bribes. Nor was he, like Sunderland, totally devoid of convictions and principles: he was as strong as James himself in contempt for the Irish and in belief that the best chance of a restoration lay in a direct attack on England or Scotland.

The exclusive character of Melfort's connection with James left Tyrconnel out in the cold, and he did not trouble to conceal his chagrin. As long as James was in the country his post as Deputy-Lieutenant was in abeyance, but he was still Commander-in-Chief of the Army and he was a third member with Melfort and Avaux of the King's inner Council. Avaux naturally had a high opinion of Tyrconnel's pro-French principles, but said he was very lazy; for several months he withdrew to his country house on the pretext of illness, which may have been the effect of disappointment at his relegation to comparative obscurity.

The Irish situation when James landed at Kinsdale presented such difficulties as to defeat the wisest and most resolute of rulers. James was neither wise nor resolute: he cannot be blamed for failing to solve the Irish problem, but he did not even see it clearly, far less did he make comprehensive plans to solve it or a steady effort to carry out such plans. As Louis's Minister Louvois subsequently told Lord Dover:

> I am sensible of the difficulties in a country destroyed by war, and where the method of arms and sieges being new, few had any experience in their employment. But I am convinced that no industry was used to obviate these difficulties.

Fundamentally the problem was racial and to be solved only by a compromise—a means never popular in Ireland. Among the Irish themselves there was still, in spite of centuries of intermarriage, a deep division between the Old Irish and the Norman-Irish whose forefathers had come to Ireland mainly in the twelfth and thirteenth centuries, and who had been followed by middle-class English who had populated Dublin and other east coast towns. Two independent contemporary estimates make the proportion of Old to New Irish ten to one, but the New Irish were in wealth and culture superior to the Old, and claimed an ascendency over them. The effect of the Reformation on the Irish population was very slight indeed, and it may be broadly stated that among the Old and New Irish there were no Protestants.[1] Plantations by Elizabeth and the great Plantation of Ulster by James I had given Protestants large possessions of land, and considerable tracts had been made over to Cromwell's soldiers in lieu of arrears of pay, and to the "Adventurers", and there had been an influx of English merchants and others to the towns. But there were very few Protestants whose families had been for more than three generations in Ireland; the Protestants regarded themselves and were regarded by their neighbours as English, and were not identified with the soil of Ireland, and they shared with their mother country a great contempt for the Catholic Irish and a conviction that Ireland was a conquered country and possessed no rights against the conqueror.

Great as were the jealousies between the Old and New Irish, they were as nothing compared with the hatred of both for the English. Their grievances (as has been already stated) can be summed up under three

[1] The outstanding exception among the Norman-Irish was the Duke of Ormonde.

heads, in order of importance, Agrarian, national, and religious: they demanded a repeal of the Acts of Settlement and Explanation of 1667 by which the actual holders of landed property were confirmed in their possession; a repeal also of Poyning's Law of 1494 under which the Irish Parliament could take no action which was not endorsed by the English Parliament; they did not, indeed, question James's right to be King of Ireland, but, as far as can be judged, they would have been content with a status similar to that of Scotland, which would have given them complete independence of England in matters of legislation, justice, industry and commerce. In the third place, they were strongly attached to their religion (though possibly not so fanatically as the Irish of the nineteenth century), and required not only complete toleration of it, but a suppression of Protestant worship. Of disinterested loyal sentiment for the House of Stuart they had hardly a trace: James I had planted Ulster, the rebellion of 1641 had been against the rule of Charles I, Charles II had confirmed Cromwell's confiscations, James II had as Duke of York accepted an enormous grant of Irish land and had throughout his brother's reign steadily supported the "English Interest". At the same time they had high hopes that, now that they had got him among them, they could make use of the English King for their own ends: he had already during his reign done much for the benefit of their religion, and they trusted him to satisfy their land-hunger and their national aspirations. Avaux saw the situation clearly when he had been only a fortnight in Ireland and witnessed the enthusiasm at James's first entry to Dublin.

> The Catholics [he wrote] . . . hope that the arrival of the King and the conjuncture of affairs will release them from servitude to the English. . . . The people and nobility of Ireland look on this as an opportunity to recover their liberty.

But their hopes of James were entirely without foundation; his only point of contact with them was in religion. His sentiments were entirely English, he concurred with the low opinion of the Irish which was universal in England, he had no intention of making them independent and he accepted the economic theories of the time and believed that Ireland could not be prosperous except at the expense of England. He was opposed to the repeal of the Act of Settlement both on the statesmanlike ground that the repeal would create as many injustices as it would remove, and because it would prejudice vested interests in England and Scotland. Even in religion James was not prepared to give entire satisfaction to the Irish—less satisfaction, in fact, than Tyrconnel had given before his arrival. Here the situation was extremely delicate.

In his letter to James of January 29, 1689, Tyrconnel had told James that "amongst the Protestants generally tainted with the ill principles of England there are not in the whole kingdom one hundred that may be relied on to serve Your Majesty". Tyrconnel was a separationist and had no reason for wishing to placate James's subjects in England and Scotland; but his estimate of the loyalty of the Irish Protestants was probably correct. They had no reason whatever for being loyal to James: he had for the past two years delivered them to their worst enemy and had placed no check upon his endeavours to render them of no account in a country where they had enjoyed ascendancy; and they had every reason to distrust his intentions. The invasion of William and the completion of the Revolution in England had made their condition even more deplorable than it had previously been: by successive proclamations on February 25 and March 1 and 7 Tyrconnel had deprived them of their arms and their horses, and those of them who had not the means of fleeing the country were left defenceless against the depredations of the rapparees.

One particular incident must have had a very disturbing effect on the Protestants. Their natural leader, Lord Mountjoy, the officer commanding the King's artillery, had been active in calming the excitement which William's expedition to England had aroused among the Protestants of Ulster and in inducing them to be loyal to James. Tyrconnel, with what an Irish Catholic called "wise and seasonable dissimulation", played Claudius to Mountjoy's Hamlet and sent him on a diplomatic mission to Paris in company with Stephen Rice, whose instructions were to deliver him to James as a traitor. James wanted to give Mountjoy permission to leave France, but Louis shut him up in the Bastille, and he remained there until he was exchanged for Richard Hamilton some eighteen months later.[1] There can be little doubt that Tyrconnel honestly suspected Mountjoy, but there were other ways of rendering him harmless which were less open to objection. This act of treachery confirmed the Irish Protestants in their distrust of Tyrconnel and drove many waverers among them into active opposition; these betook themselves to the strongholds of Londonderry and Enniskillen, which, however, were not yet in open rebellion, but had refused to admit Catholic troops. The remainder of the Ulster Protestants waited in passive apprehension for their deliverance by William.

[1] It is only fair to Tyrconnel to say that Avaux was later convinced (he may, of course, have obtained all his information from Tyrconnel) that Mountjoy had already made preparations to go over to William, and that he was so able that he would have held part at least of Ireland against James; moreover, Dr. King, the apologist of the Irish Protestants, stated that Mountjoy was "the likeliest man to lead" them.

When James landed in March there was a large Protestant population in Ulster and there were Protestant communities in Dublin, Cork, Brandon and Galway; elsewhere they had been driven off the land, and two hundred and fifty of them were in Galway jail. The instructions given by Louis to Avaux, his ambassador, and to Maumont, the Chief of the French military mission, are mutually contradictory: Avaux is to

> make every endeavour to reconcile the Protestants with the Catholics so that the Protestants may be convinced that the Catholics have no violent designs against them and that the King their master will treat them with the same gentleness and goodness without distinction of religion;

while Maumont is told to encourage Tyrconnel to pillage the Protestants and to employ their goods for the upkeep of the Army. But Louis had modified his instructions to Avaux by a marginal note saying that the just rights of the Catholics must not be disregarded and that the kindness to the Protestants should continue only until James is restored to his kingdoms; and in the first letter which Avaux received from his master in Ireland this modification was confirmed. Louis was a very simple man if he believed that the Protestants could be deceived by so obvious an artifice. Avaux from the first disregarded his formal instructions; he saw clearly that every Protestant, with but few exceptions, was at heart a Williamite, that he kept quiet only from fear, and that as soon as an expedition landed from England all the Protestants would flock to join it. He was also afraid that the Protestants in certain places—Galway, for instance—might suddenly rise in the night, massacre the Catholics and seize and defend the town. He strongly urged James to take severe measures with the Protestants and to render them harmless,[1] but he found the King very irresolute and soft. One of the ambassador's first complaints to Louis is that James has pardoned some Protestants whom the French general Pusignan has seized, and he says that there is fear among all James's followers that he will continue to pardon to the end.

But James's point of view in the matter of the Protestants did not coincide with that of Louis and his ambassador. They regarded the war in Ireland merely as part of the general European war, and to them

[1] The allegation of Macaulay and Klopp that Avaux recommended a general massacre of the Protestants in case any of them joined Schomberg on his landing seems to be denied by implication in Avaux's next letter. The passage on which the allegation is founded contains the phrase "*faire main basse sur les Protestants*", and Jusserand maintains that in the usage of the seventeenth century "*faire main basse*" was not equivalent to the English "to exterminate" or presumably to the German "vernichten".

the Irish Protestants were open or concealed enemies and a legitimate sacrifice to military exigencies. But to James it was essentially a civil war and the Protestants were his subjects, who, he hoped, would return to their allegiance and who must not be exasperated; (it may be remarked, however, in passing that he had not been so tender with rebellious subjects four years earlier). When Avaux asked him what he had decided about the measures he had proposed against the Protestants, James replied angrily that he had no desire to cut his subjects' throats; Avaux disavowed any intention of inhumanity, but again urged that the Protestants were a menace which must be suitably dealt with. But James was incapable of deciding on a settled policy. A month after he landed he issued a proclamation offering a full pardon to all Protestants who would return to their allegiance, he fixed a date before which those who had fled might return to Ireland and promised to give back their land to all loyal Protestants. He also issued "protections" to all who undertook to live quietly under his government, and these protections not only made them safe from the depradations of the royal troops, but in certain cases enabled them to protect themselves against the rapparees. The result was that in certain localities, notably the neighbourhood of Belfast, there was a security and prosperity not easily to be found in any other part of Ireland. There is a remarkable anonymous diary still extant giving the experiences of a man who landed with Schomberg in August 1689; under date August 23 he states that he returned to Belfast from Carrickfergus,

> and find that a Protestant may already safely . . . march through the whole province of Ulster . . . not a Papist anywhere to be found, except about 2000 who are fled to the Red Glin about twenty miles northward of this place. To our great surprise and no less joy we found the whole country full of corn and all manner of provision, whose plenty you may guess at by the following Table of Rates set up at the market cross at this place [Belfast],

and he proceeds to give a long list of prices: wheat, 13*s.* a barrel; oatmeal, 1*s.* a peck; butter, 2*d.* a pound; cheese, 1*d.* a pound; hay, 8*d.*; hens, 4*d.*; eggs, eight a penny; white bread, 15 oz. for a penny, and so forth, and says that one of the vendors told him that these prices were "enough in all conscience, and almost double what they got before our landing".

The Protestants, on their side, accepted the protection with a cynicism which does them little honour, but after the treatment they had received from Tyrconnel they had small faith in James's promises;

they regarded them as dictated by immediate military necessities, and made the best use they could of their precarious immunity. On the other hand, James's indulgence to them alienated the Catholics, whom from all points of view it was most important to placate. According to them he was incapable of learning from experience that his lenity only provided the Protestants with opportunities to betray him; he was infatuated with this rotten principle—"provoke not your Protestant subjects"; and the non-juror Leslie writes of the Catholic attitude to this question:

> Some of them moving him for leave to cut off the Protestants, which he returned with indignation and amazement saying "What, gentlemen? Are you for another Forty-one?" which so galled them that they ever after looked on him with a jealous eye and thought him though a Roman Catholic too much of an Englishman to carry on their business. And I am told that the generality of the Irish papists do at this day [*i.e.*, in 1692] lay all their misfortunes upon King James because he would not follow their measures and was so inclinable to favour the Protestants.

Five months after his landing, Avaux reported to Louis that James had entirely lost the affection of the Irish people, who at his arrival had been ready to do anything for him.

The Irish Catholics touched the centre of James's problem when they said he was "too much of an Englishman to carry on their business", for there is no evidence whatever that he tried to identify himself with his Irish subjects. There was no idea in his mind of making Ireland prosperous and strong, and of ruling there as an independent monarch until such time as an opportunity should occur to regain his kingdoms in Great Britain. He was obsessed with the notion that England and Scotland were groaning under William's tyranny and that vast numbers of the population there were longing for his return and would rise to support his restoration as soon as he appeared among them. This obsession had no basis in evidence: one of the main defects in his organisation was that he had no efficient spies in England; this deficiency had existed at the time of his landing, for as late as March 15, 1689, Tyrconnel was unaware of the very important fact that the Duke of Hamilton had declared for William, though that news was three months old. William obtained all the information he could require from the Protestants who passed freely from Ireland, but the few letters which Jacobites sent from England, anxious as the writers were to present affairs in the most favourable light, contained accounts of the frustrated hopes of those who had expected an "age of gold" to follow the Revolution and of minor grievances which they exaggerated, but no word of a widespread desire to welcome James's return. Avaux once put the direct question to James and asked him on what information he founded his belief that the English were still loyal to him at heart. James merely replied "that he had no news from England but that the greater part of the troops had been deceived, that he was popular with the common people and that his friends would flock to him as soon as he appeared in England".

James's anxiety to cross the Irish Channel led to a perpetual conflict between the King and Melfort on the one hand and Avaux, Tyrconnel and the whole of the Irish nation on the other. Neither Avaux nor Tyrconnel was whole-heartedly in James's interest. Avaux regarded James primarily as a means of weakening William, Tyrconnel wanted Ireland separated from England as long as England was under a Protestant king, but both were, for their different reasons, anxious to restore James to the English throne. Avaux's declaration in a letter to Louis that "if it had been a Frenchman who is Viceroy of Ireland he could not have been more zealous in Your Majesty's interest" merely meant that for the time Tyrconnel's views were identical with his own and that Tyrconnel realised that only with French assistance could Ireland be saved from falling under the rule of William. Tyrconnel cared little about England, the ultimate aim of Avaux and his master concurred with that of James—namely, his restoration to the crowns of England and Scotland. But there was serious difference on the question of strategy: James was for an immediate descent on Scotland or Wales; Louis was of opinion that the descent should be deferred until a base had been created by the consolidation of James's position in Ireland. In Louis's instructions to Maumont the General was told that he could assure James that if he could hold on in Ireland until the following winter he would be furnished with sufficient French troops not only to defend himself, but to carry the war into Scotland or England. At the end of May 1689 Avaux sent Louis a vague but very optimistic report from a Jacobite spy in England, whom he calls M. Pen,[1] and asked the French King whether or no the time had arrived for an invasion of England; he suggested that if an immediate descent was practicable Louis could save himself expense at a later date by assisting it with arms and men three weeks later the ambassador is still inclined to favour the plan. In a

[1] Both Avaux's orginal despatch at the French Foreign Office and the copy in Avaux's letter-book at the Public Record Office give the name as Pen; but Baschet's transcript gives it as Parrquez, obviously a French version of Parker (Colonel James Parker was certainly in England in the Jacobite interest at that time), but where Baschet obtained this version is a mystery. The style of the report is as different from William Penn's as it could possibly be.

letter which crossed these two from Avaux, Louis said that he was not impressed by the reports from Scotland, and ordered Avaux to advise James to defer asking for assistance for an expedition overseas until he had put his affairs in Ireland in good shape and had reorganised his finances. Throughout the correspondence there are many direct allusions to James's projects for the invasion of England, and there is never a hint that Louis, Louvois or Avaux disapproved of these projects in principle; but except for momentary hesitations, they were convinced that definite plans for invasion should be postponed until James had achieved a sound military and financial position in Ireland.[1] Louvois is very contemptuous of James's judgement; writing on June 3, 1689, he puts the consistent policy of Louis in concise form:

> What is necessary (he says) is that he should forget that he has ever been King of England and Scotland and think only of what will benefit Ireland and will provide him with means to maintain himself there; if God gives him grace to return to England he must behave as a King of England should, and he must not play into the hands of the Prince of Orange by making it easy for him to conquer Ireland.

Again in the same letter Louvois asks Avaux how he can think that Louis can send troops to Ireland when England and Holland control the sea and how James can believe that the French fleet could possibly cruise off the north of Ireland to cover an expedition to Scotland, and he continues:

> Such propositions are very disconcerting for there can be no hope that the affairs of the King of England can recover when he is seen to be capable of putting forward such impracticable propositions; the project of crossing to Scotland without assurances of help on landing and of occupying Anglesey is of the same nature, and, if the King of England will not remain in Ireland and establish himself there and wait until the English are tired of the tyranny of the Prince of Orange, and send for him, he will deliver himself and Ireland into the hands of the Prince of Orange. . . . If the King of England does not take steps to settle Ireland and make it safe for himself before crossing to England he is lost.

[1] Klopp says that Louis thought he could make the best use of James by keeping him in Ireland; this statement is not supported by Avaux's correspondence, nor does it appear reasonable; for James restored to the English throne would obviously be of more use to Louis than James in Ireland. In this connection see "Reasons why King James should go to Ireland" in the Archives of the French Ministry of Marine and ascribed to Vauban.

But James and Melfort were deaf to all argument. James was appalled at the disorder he found in Ireland, and his imagination boggled at a task of reconstruction which he had not the authority, moral energy or driving power to accomplish. To a man in his lethargic condition of mind what was immediate and pressing was very troublesome, and he could not bring himself to concentrate on his present difficulties.[1] But beyond them and beyond the Irish Channel he saw himself in an entirely different set of circumstances: he would be among the people he had known and loved, they would rally to him and, when by their help he had driven out his unnatural son-in-law, he would return to conquer Ireland. In May he drew up the scheme which was in the mind of Louvois when he wrote the diatribe just quoted: by the help of Chateaurenaud's fleet (which had just landed troops and stores in Bantry Bay and driven off an inferior detachment of the English fleet) he was to land with 10,000 men at Troon in Ayrshire, ten miles from Glasgow (the distance is actually 30 miles); from there it is only two days' march to Stirling, "where there is a very weak castle in which are stored all the arms of the country"; from Stirling to Edinburgh is only three short days' march, and once in Edinburgh he would be master of Scotland; William would be obliged to send his troops against him at Edinburgh and to provide Louis with an opportunity to land a French army on the east coast of England and to cut communications between William's troops and London. If this plan was not considered feasible, James and his troops could equally well land in Anglesey, whence with the eight or ten thousand troops which Louis would provide they could either march straight on London, or wheel to the left into the most fertile part of England, according to the amount of support afforded by James's subjects. A man who could put his name to such schemes was wanting not only in military judgement, but in elementary common sense; it is not worth while to criticise in detail a plan in which there is confusion of mind between the conceptions of an invasion and of a triumphal procession, but it may be pointed out that the first scheme presupposes the existence not only of one but of two French fleets—in the Irish Channel and in the North Sea—capable of holding the English fleet, and assumes that an army which had failed to take Londonderry would carry Stirling by assault and proceed to a victorious march on Edinburgh.

James continued to harbour the hope that Louis would change his mind even after Ulster was lost to him by Schomberg's invasion, and in November he sent Lord Thomas Howard to Versailles to arrange with Louis plans for the invasion of England. It was in vain that it had been

[1] Avaux said of him, "He tries to hide from himself everything which might give him trouble; he does not like one to talk to him about such things and is content to live from day to day".

pointed out to him that, of the two invasions which had been made in his own reign, Monmouth's had failed because he had had in advance no assurance of support from influential people, while that of William had succeeded because he had had such an assurance. Louis's final word was that James should not think of crossing to Great Britain until he had organised a considerable body of his supporters there and until these supporters had seized a port at which invading troops could land. At the same time he reminded James that before entering upon the reconquest of his kingdoms it would be well to determine the principles on which he would re-establish his government.

If there was disagreement in James's counsels about the treatment of the Protestants and about the strategy of the struggle against William, there was no room for doubt that the first necessity was an efficient army. But even here there was a difference, if only in degree. For if we are to believe Avaux (and there is no reason why we should not), he himself was during the first months one among very few persons in Ireland who realised the gravity of James's situation and the entire inadequacy of his military preparations. Very few of the Irish were aware that they were in any danger whatever; they thought that the long battle against England was already won, and that they might take possession of the lands of their ancestors without fear of disturbance. This attitude of mind may be excused in men of the extremely low education of the home-bred Catholic Irish, but in James and Tyrconnel, who had fought in and observed, not only the contending armies in the English Civil War, but the French and Spanish forces, it is unaccountable. The letters of Tyrconnel to James at the end of January 1689 and to Hamilton and Perth six weeks later show that he had no appreciation of the difficulties that lay ahead: to James he wrote that he was in desperate straits for money to pay his newly raised army of 40,000 and to prevent them from destroying themselves and the country by pillage; and to Hamilton and Perth that now that James had arrived with money and arms he had 50,000 horse, foot and dragoons "well armed and disciplined", and committed himself to the phrase "the good posture of His Majesty's affairs". James had written from Saint-Germain the long and optimistic letter, already mentioned, to the Queen's uncle, the Cardinal d'Este, describing his plans for Ireland: and on March 29, when he had had plenty of opportunity to inform himself of his actual situation in Ireland, he wrote from Dublin to Lord Dundee in Scotland saying that he was not only in a position to defend Ireland, but proposed to send Dundee 5000 men if he wanted them. Melfort wrote in similarly confident terms to his brother Perth and to Balcarres.

It appears therefore that James, his Secretary for War Melfort and his commander-in-chief Tyrconnel were of opinion that an army had only to be loyal, well-armed and well-clothed to be invincible; they were unaware that of equal importance to an army are training and discipline and an efficient auxiliary service to supply it with food and equipment; and of these necessities there was almost complete deficiency. The Irish army in 1685 had consisted of about 8000 men under Protestant officers. These officers had been gradually replaced by Catholics, and this process had been completed in November 1688 by the dismissal of the remaining Protestants. At the same time four or five thousand men—more than half of the regular army—were sent over to England to fight for King James. After the Revolution the greater part of this Irish contingent was shipped off to Hamburg and compelled to join the Emperor's army and to fight against the Turks. Some of the Irish officers, among them the redoubtable Sarsfield, found their way back to Ireland, but if any private soldiers accompanied these officers it was as individuals and not as organised troops.[1]

The position in Ireland when William landed at Torbay was therefore that Tyrconnel had at his disposal less than four thousand trained troops, under officers who, except for the very few who had seen service in France, had had at most four years' experience. He proceeded to raise a new army by giving captain's rank to anyone who could get a nominal roll of a hundred followers and would undertake to feed, clothe and house them until the Government could afford to give them regular pay. Some of these new captains were members of the old Irish aristocracy, but the majority were, according to Avaux, tailors, butchers and shoemakers; with few exceptions they were miserably poor and unable to pay the men who were supposed to fill their companies, so that they either lived at home and pursued their ordinary avocations or, more frequently, lived at free quarter on the neighbourhood and by pillaging farther afield. The officers were drawn from the same class as the men, and they were so ignorant of soldiering as to be unaware of their own deficiencies and to resent any attempt to teach them their duties. Captain John Stevens, an English Catholic who served through the Irish war, gives a very vivid picture of the condition of a company:

> They will follow none but their own leaders, many of them as rude, as ignorant and as far from understanding any of the rules of

[1] Melfort wrote to James from Paris in October 1689 saying that four or five hundred of these troops had found their way from Hamburg to Lille and had been given passes to France by the Duke of Lorraine; Louis was sending them to Ireland at his own expense, and they probably arrived with Lauzun in March 1690.

> discipline as themselves. This was the utter ruin of the army, none fitter to raise men than he that had been ever bred in the mountains. When raised there was no respect from soldier to officer, they were all fellow mountaineers. The commissioned officer could not punish his sergeant or corporal because he was his cousin or foster-brother, and they durst not correct the soldier lest he should fly in their face and run away.

When James arrived in Ireland there had been no real effort to form these local levies into regiments and to establish camps of exercise. The very numbers were exceedingly vague. In a sense the army comprised the entire Catholic manhood of the country, for the priests compelled every man to arm himself with "a skean and a half-pike", and in another sense the actual numbers were far less than those on paper, for the new captains were under no compulsion to produce the men whose names appeared on the muster roll, and "false musters", that bane of all armies in which the men's pay is handed over to the officers in a lump sum, were prevalent. So loose was the organisation that as late as the end of May 1689 the arrival for orders in Dublin of two majors from different regiments was the first intimation to Melfort that these regiments existed.

The men themselves were of splendid physique, they had lived hard and were accustomed to privation, and they had great fighting spirit, which could have been turned to advantage by discipline and by skilful and spirited leadership. But at the moment they were worthless: Rosen thus described them in May 1689:

> Nearly all are without arms and quite naked; the greater part of the officers are miserable fellows without courage or honour, a single cannon-shot passing at the elevation of a clock-tower throws a whole battalion to the ground, and the only way to get them to their feet is to send horses over their bellies.

During the first few months Avaux was constantly repeating that if William were to send to Ireland a force of only 10,000 men they would find no army to oppose them. In season and out of season he urged James to organise his army and to administer Ireland in such a way as to support the army; he drew up two elaborate memorials in which he exposed the most obvious deficiencies and suggested immediate remedies. James could hardly bear to hear the memorials read, he was dimly aware that everything was wrong, but exact statement of fact appeared to him exaggeration, and Melfort was able to insinuate that Avaux's remonstrances lacked deference. A proclamation had been issued by

Tyrconnel in February against looting by the army, and at the end of July James issued a further proclamation prescribing the death penalty for desertion, but these proclamations had no effect; James was an entirely different person from the James who had a few months earlier taken a personal interest in the execution of a deserter, had rejected the judge's recommendation for mercy and had insisted that though he had been convicted at Reading he should be hanged at Plymouth, where his regiment was; there is no record that during his fifteen months in Ireland he took disciplinary action against a single soldier. In June, for instance, a colonel was ordered to occupy Beltarbet; he disregarded the order and went unpunished. Very little also was done in training the new officers in their duties or in drilling the men and teaching them the care and use of their arms. Boisseleau, indeed, one of the French major-generals, had a camp near Cork, and by unremitting labour and patience achieved some little success, but no other similar effort was made.

But there was an obstacle in a prejudice which was deep-rooted in all the Irish, and from which James himself was not entirely free—a jealousy of the French officers. In James it showed itself chiefly in his obstinacy in keeping the incompetent Richard Hamilton in command of the army which was besieging Derry and by his anxiety that the French should not have the credit of taking that city. The professional competence of the French officers showed up the incompetence of their Irish colleagues and was resented by them, while the Irish non-commissioned officers and men were so intensely nationalist that they deserted in large numbers to avoid serving under French or Catholic English officers. When Lauzun in May 1690 proposed to complete with Irish recruits the French regiments which had accompanied him from France, he found it necessary to include Irish officers also in these regiments to prevent wholesale desertions. The French officers strongly resented the ungrateful attitude of people for whom they were fighting, and hated the Irish so much that after a very few months they regarded an appointment in Ireland as little short of a disgrace. James did not affront Irish sentiment by unduly favouring the French, but the Irish were even more jealous of the English, and Tyrconnel remonstrated with the King in a private audience for giving the best civil and military posts to Englishmen. For an English Catholic was as much hated by the Irish Catholics as were the Irish Protestants. A striking example of this last general statement is that of John Stevens, a Catholic collector of excise from Montgomeryshire; his devotion to the Stuart cause was so great that he took a journey of over 1200 miles—via Chester, London, Paris, Brest and Bantry—in order to join James's army, and yet when he arrived in Dublin was kept waiting two months, at a time when there was a great shortage of officers, before he could obtain a commission. He says that the English and French officers were so unacceptable to the men that they had to be carried on the regimental books as supernumeraries (or "reformadoes" as they were called), and he reveals his own slight influence over his men in his account of the Battle of the Boyne:

> Looking about I wondered what madness possessed our men to run so violently, nobody pursuing them. What few men I saw I called to, *no commands being of force*, begging them to stand together and repair to their colours.

As late as October 1689 Avaux wrote:

> There is neither order nor discipline in the army, soldiers draw their swords against their officers; officers of the advanced guard when we were a league and a half from Schomberg were found every night asleep on the straw and their horses unsaddled and unbridled; plenty of complaints have been made to the King but he merely says it is very bad.

When James landed from France he had the money to pay the army and to remove all excuse for free quarter and pillage, but, in a spirit of pure parsimony, he kept the money in his hands; nor was there a concerted effort to form the companies into regiments and to give every officer and man a definite status; the army remained for months an amorphous body of indefinite numbers, and as long as there was uncertainty whether a particular man was a soldier or not there could be no progress in discipline. The arms which James brought with him also remained for a long time undistributed to the troops, and Avaux reported as late as September 10 that munitions which were absolutely necessary for the army which was facing Schomberg were lying in store at Athlone, Limerick and Cork, and that there were 8000 pike-heads at Dublin which had not been fitted with shafts. Moreover, the constant desertions and the negligence of the officers and their ignorance of their duties resulted in a very serious depletion of the stock of muskets; the deserters took their muskets with them, whether they deserted in a body or as individuals, and formed themselves into bands of rapparees; the soldiers who remained with their regiments were entirely unused to firearms, and they were not taught to handle their muskets or punished for damaging them. Among the troops which were besieging Derry in May not one man in ten had a serviceable musket, and two months later an official return showed in the same force 2770 muskets out of repair and 1105 missing. The armourers who were engaged in repairing them were all Protestants (and therefore in Avaux's opinion unreliable) and inadequate in number.

Supply services were practically non-existent. The roads were so bad that transport by sea, with all the risks of capture and storms, and in spite of the immensely greater distances, was often preferred to transport by land. There was a deficiency of waggons which was never made up. When James landed at Kinsale there were not even ten horses to take him and his companions to Dublin, and there were only three waggons in the country. In the result he had to leave all the munitions behind with a great number of the French officers, and to travel to Dublin with only his personal retinue and their baggage. A year later, when Lauzun landed with his French reinforcements, he encountered the same difficulty. At the end of July 1689, when the abandonment of the siege of Derry appeared imminent, there was urgent necessity for carts to evacuate 3000 sick and wounded from Strabane. Melfort in council stated that sixty carts were ready and more were being put together; four days later he had to confess that the sixty carts had vanished.

> I asked him (says Avaux) how they had vanished and he replied that they had vanished because they could not be found; then the King turned to me and said, "You see, Monsieur, that we are doing everything that is possible".

There was the same difficulty with regard to gun-carriages, but, as Pusignan complained, the supply of artillery ammunition was so inadequate that it was hardly worth while to take the guns into action. Pusignan also demanded that permanent posts should be established between Derry and Dublin so that regular communication could be kept up between James and his forces in the field; Avaux supported the appeal and urged that the Dublin–Kinsale road was also important, but nothing was done.

In the important matter of raising money James achieved no success whatever. The administration of Tyrconnel had left Ireland in complete anarchy. All the local revenue officers had been Protestants and had either been dismissed or had fled. The Catholic Irish who took their places were without experience. Moreover, the recruitment for the army and the fears of pillage caused an almost complete cessation of agriculture and internal trade, so that in the autumn of 1689 there was something like a famine. The customs revenue depended entirely on the trade with England, and that trade had practically ceased. Avaux strenuously endeavoured to make a beginning of a trade with France by exchanging Irish linen for French wines. But when first the question was broached, James thought he would have peaceably recovered the throne of England in two months, and he would do nothing to annoy the English merchants who had had a monopoly of Irish trade; he and Melfort put every obstacle in the way of the conclusion of a commercial treaty; in particular they declared that no readjustment of duties would be valid without the consent of Parliament, and then prevented Parliament from legislating in the matter. Another means of raising money of which Avaux did not fail to remind James was the estates of men who were in rebellion against him. James's reply to this suggestion was that no confiscation could be made until the proprietors had been proved traitors in a court of law—a unique instance in James of an exaggerated respect for law; but perhaps it was merely an additional excuse for doing nothing. On the whole he may be said to have drawn no appreciable revenue from the country and to have existed precariously on what Louis gave him. In July he embarked on the ruinous expedient of coining brass token money. This money obeyed the same economic rules as paper money would have done and kept its value only as long as it was exchangeable at par with silver. Neither the Protestants nor the French would accept it and it was useless for external trade. It did not seriously depreciate, however, until the Battle of the Boyne made certain that it would never be redeemed. The worst of the financial situation was that in this constant want of money there was no control of expenditure, and very little of the money spent was employed on the objects for which it was intended: James's biographer (who got the figures from James) states that pay was drawn for 50,000 troops, but that there were never more than 18,000[1] actually under arms—the system of giving the soldiers' pay to the officers had resulted in a widespread use of "false musters".

The chief events of James's sojourn in Ireland may be rapidly summarised. The situation when he arrived in Dublin was that the whole country was in submission to him except Derry and Enniskillen, together with a few towns near them, which were speedily taken. The position at Derry was confused, negotiations were on foot for surrender, but it is unlikely in any case that the party in the town which was in favour of surrender would have prevailed. James was convinced that no subject of his could defy him to his face, and determined to travel immediately to Derry and to make a personal demand to the citizens.

[1] Lauzun gives the same figures, but his was probably not an independent estimate. Also the difference between these figures is undoubtedly exaggerated. The Irish army was in May 1689 reduced to 35,000; there were 22,000 at Ardee in the autumn of 1689 and a few thousand Irish less at the Boyne. Just estimates would be between 25,000 and 35,000, the latter figure allowing for garrisons and other contingents elsewhere.

He had a terrible journey through desolate country, and once returned on his tracks on a false alarm that a hostile force was approaching. When he reached the neighbourhood of Derry he violated a convention under which his troops had undertaken, pending negotiations, not to advance within four miles of the city, and he and his escort were fired on from the walls. After two days' fruitless parleying he had to swallow the rebuff and to return to Dublin.

Before leaving Dublin, James had yielded to pressure by the Irish Catholics and had summoned a Parliament. This was his worst single mistake, and it is curious that James, who throughout his life had hated Parliaments and striven to prevent their meeting, should in the end consent to call a Parliament at a time when he had every reason, personal and public, to refuse. It could not be a legal Parliament, for under Poyning's Law the Irish Parliament could not be summoned except with the consent of the English Parliament; moreover, James must have seen enough even during the few weeks he had been in the country to realise that in the excited state of national feeling the Parliament would do all it could to establish the independence of Ireland from England, and that it would by its action exasperate the English against him and make his restoration to the English throne impossible. This last reason it would have been impolitic to bring forward, but he had an even sounder argument against the meeting of Parliament, and one which should have been urged on the Irish people unremittingly: they should have been told the truth about the precarious state of their present independence and urged to employ all their endeavours to defeating the national foe; for while the leading men were deliberating in Dublin, who was to organise the country for war? What Ireland wanted in the state of anarchy in which it was, was a strong central government, and James had neither the resolution to initiate and control, nor the reliable civil and military officers to conduct such a government.

The members knew what they wanted, and they passed a number of Acts in a great hurry and with considerable impatience of opposition. They gratified James by recognising him as King, by voting liberal supplies (which, as he says, was a sum "more agreeable to the King's necessities and their own good will than to the present abilities of the people") and (somewhat grudgingly) they passed an Act instituting Liberty of Conscience. But almost every other Act was in direct conflict with James's wishes. In his opening speech he promised to consent to the amendment of the Act of Settlement "so far as may be consistent with reason, justice and the public good of my people", but Parliament demanded a return of all lands to the proprietors who had held them in 1641 or to their heirs, except in so far as these proprietors or their heirs had by sale or otherwise voluntarily alienated them. No consideration was shown to the original adventurers and soldiers, but in cases in which the present holders had acquired land by purchase they were to be compensated from lands forfeited by William's adherents.[1] James saw in this measure a tremendous blow to vested interests in England and Scotland: he did not dare to oppose it directly, but he delayed for a time giving his consent on the ground that certain prominent Catholics who had purchased lands would be dispossessed, and he went so far as to threaten to prorogue the Parliament if these men were not left in possession; the answer was that in that case the Irish would refuse to fight for him, or presumably for their own security.

The Parliament also forced on James an Act of Attainder so violent and comprehensive as to be ridiculous. Procedure by attainder is open to strong objection on the ground that legislative bodies are not courts of law, that they have no experience in hearing evidence and that they are apt to be swayed by party passion. In the past this procedure had been very sparingly used, and it was discontinued after the conviction of Sir John Fenwick in 1695. The Irish Attainder Bill contained upwards of 2000 names, no definite charge was preferred against any of the condemned persons, and there was no pretence of a trial. The persons condemned were roughly of four classes: those actually in arms against James, absentee proprietors, Protestants who had fled the country, and personal enemies of members of Parliament. There was some ground for condemning those in the first category, but no proscription has ever included the whole body of rebels; against the other three classes no case could have been made out. Finally the Bill invaded the King's prerogative and took away his right to pardon the attainted persons.

Various accounts are given of James's resentment at being forced by Parliament to do what he had determined not to do. It was said that the Duke of Powis told the Earl of Granard that "the King durst not let them know that he had a mind to have them stopped", and that, when Granard was going to the House to record his protest against the repeal of the Act of Settlement, James said "that he was fallen into the hands of a people who rammed that and many other things down his throat". Another story is that James was so moved by the opposition to his expressed will that his nose bled and that he summed up his experience of Parliaments in the aphorism, "All Commons are alike". To a Scottish gentleman who came to ask for assistance for his country

[1] Lecky (*Ireland in the Eighteenth Century*, Cabinet Edn., I, 120–23) shows that Macaulay was grossly unjust in alleging that these purchasers were expropriated without compensation, but Avaux writing to Louvois on April 26 seems to think that this concession is temporary and that it would be withdrawn at the end of the war.

James said, "What can I do; You see I am left alone. I have none to do anything for me". Writing many years later, the Earl of Ailesbury, a life-long Jacobite, confessed that "King James, to speak naturally as affairs stood between him and his (Irish) parliaments was a cipher rather than a king".

The Parliament constituted a crisis in James's affairs. There were no ultimate effects, for all its proceedings were nullified at the Boyne a year later. But the immediate effects were disastrous, for the fundamental cleavage between James and his Irish subjects was made manifest: though he had given way to their demands, he had given way with such ill grace that there could be no doubt that he was yielding to compulsion, they had no longer an illusion that he had any intention of restoring them to what they considered their just rights and he entirely lost his popularity with them. To James himself it was a profound shock to discover that he could exercise no personal ascendency over his Parliament and that the Irish were unconcerned about his restoration to the Crown of England. From this time onward he ceased to take any interest in Ireland or to think of being happy and prosperous there; there were signs that he was contemplating flight early in August, five months after his arrival, but he did not want to retire, as he had done from England, without first striking a blow.

In August three events occurred which, paradoxically enough, created a temporary improvement in James's fortunes. On the 13th Derry was relieved by William's forces, and it was at last possible to withdraw the besieging troops, to concentrate the army near Dublin and to make some attempt to organise it. The following day Schomberg landed in Carrickfergus Bay and blew away for ever the ignorant sense of security in which the Irish had been living. Immediately Parliament had repealed the Act of Settlement the Irish officers had dispersed themselves all over the country to take possession of their hereditary lands and had left the army still further disorganised. Now at last it was brought home to them that the lands were not theirs until they had fought for them, and a new spirit of enthusiasm appeared in the army. The third event was the departure of Melfort on August 25. For some time hatred against him had been growing, and after the prorogation of Parliament an extensively signed memorial was submitted to James by gentlemen and military officers complaining of his mismanagement of the army; this was a product of the new feeling of danger and of eagerness for efficiency, but no doubt Melfort's well-known anti-Irish prejudices supplied an additional motive. Melfort bowed before the storm and asked to be relieved of the Secretaryship for War. Eleven days later James consented to let him leave Ireland; he gave him a commission to report to Louis on the situation in Ireland. At the end he was so afraid of assassination that he left Dublin secretly and at night.[1]

Avaux's despatches of the early part of September contain his only expressions of satisfaction since his arrival in Ireland. After the first consternation and the despair at seeing nothing ready for resistance to Schomberg's advance, there was a feverish display of activity: disbanded troops were re-enlisted, with great trouble transport was found to fetch a new French consignment of arms, and these arms were distributed. Melfort's successor as War Minister was Tyrconnel's friend Nagle, and in spite of his French prejudice against civilian war ministers, Avaux had to admit his competence.[2] On September 10 he wrote to Colbert de Croissy:

> A fortnight ago we hardly hoped to put things into so good a condition, but, since Lord Melfort left, Lord Tyrconnel and all the Irish have worked so hard that we have been put in a state of defence,

and a week later he wrote to Louvois,

> Things have improved a good deal in the past week, reinforcements have come in and there are now sufficient arms.

But Avaux realised the essential weakness of the army and that the eagerness it showed to attack the enemy was not enough. With few exceptions, the field officers were unreliable, and the subalterns worse, and it was doubtful whether they would lead their men with courage; the men still broke their muskets, and only those who had been at Derry had ever fired a shot.

Schomberg was, as Avaux had anticipated, joined by all the Protestants of Ulster, as well as by the relieved garrisons of Derry and Enniskillen. In opposition to the advice of Avaux and Rosen that he should destroy Dublin and retreat behind the Shannon, James determined to advance against the enemy. On August 26 he established his headquarters at Drogheda, thirty miles north of Dublin, and Tyrconnel in Dublin worked hard fitting out regiments and sending them to James as soon as they were ready. On September 12 Tyrconnel joined the army and James held a review and expressed his satisfaction,

[1] There was a fourth event in the same month from which James and Louis expected great profit: the death of Pope Innocent XI. The new Pope, Alexander VIII, was less hostile to France, but he lived for only one year, and his successor, Innocent XII (the Pope of *The Ring and the Book*), pretended sympathy for James, but did nothing for him.

[2] Clarendon had had a high opinion of Nagle.

especially with the cavalry. Schomberg's headquarters were now at Dundalk, and on September 14 James moved his headquarters forward to Ardee, where he lodged in the Castle; 500 enemy cavalry evacuated Ardee on his approach. After a day there James went forward with his cavalry to Allardstown, and immediately sent back for the infantry to join him. Allardstown was a hamlet on the south bank of the River Fane, and the best accommodation James could find was a miserable thatched hut. The river was fordable, but beyond the river, and continuing to Schomberg's lines four miles away, was a morass, extending to the sea on the east and several miles to the west, and crossed only by a few narrow causeways. The river was bridged in two places and the troops were established along the river between them in tents and bivouacs. On September 21 James drew out his whole army in order of battle in full view of Schomberg's outposts, but Schomberg did not stir from his trenches, nor did any attempts by James to bring on a general engagement by sending out skirmishing and foraging parties have any effect.

On October 6 James burnt his camp and fell back on Ardee, where there was better and more healthy accommodation. By this time rain had begun to fall in torrents and both the opposing armies suffered severely from sickness. James had the advantage that his men were accustomed to the conditions, but his camp was very badly supplied with food, and the huts were so constructed that they had the choice of being deluged with rain or choked with smoke from their fires; Schomberg was well supplied by ships in the Bay of Dundalk and his tents were good; he had to camp, however, on lower and less healthy ground, his troops were very raw and, particularly in the English section of his polyglot army, he complained bitterly of the inefficiency of the officers—they would neither train their men nor look after their health; he was also greatly troubled by conspiracies in the French Huguenot regiments. He was probably justified in not attacking James, but had he been fully aware of the condition of the Irish army he might have done so. Avaux estimated the loss from sickness in each camp as about the same—between 7000 and 8000 men. James's personal activity was immense; he was constantly in the saddle, and Avaux was worn out by following him about. He said the King was as active as a man of twenty.

James was tremendously pleased at the issue of this campaign, and in a sense he had scored a victory, for he had certainly frustrated Schomberg's hope of spending Christmas in Dublin. Towards the end of September James wrote to his son-in-law, the Earl of Waldegrave:

> On the 6th of September we came . . . within three [Irish] miles of Dundalk where Schomberg lies encamped. Since which

> time we have often offered him occasions of battle. We have omitted nothing that might provoke him to it by excursions of parties to his out-grounds, by foraging near his camp and consuming with fire what we could not transport; yet he continues within his trenches without accepting a battle or even a fair skirmish although his parties have been often much superior in number to ours.

James's followers were also very pleased with themselves, and Avaux feared, with reason, that the mood of enthusiasm and warlike ardour would quickly pass and that things would fall back into their former condition of muddle and disorder. No sooner had the army got itself into winter quarters than the officers left it and flocked to Dublin. The picture which Stevens paints of the Irish army, and in particular of Dublin in that winter of 1689–90, the final appearance of the Jacobites and their Irish allies in independence on the territory of a Stuart King, is one of complete irresponsibility: there was no realisation of the desperate struggle which the following summer was to bring. The Protestant Jacobites laughed at the boasts of the Catholics that they would drive Schomberg back into Derry and Enniskillen.

> This too great confidence of the good posture of our affairs produced in all men such a security as proved without doubt very prejudicial to our interest in the end. Everyone laying aside the care of the public wholly devoted himself either to his private affairs or to his pleasure and ease.

For a long time no efforts were made in recruiting fresh troops and in training and discipline. In Colonel Thomas Butler's regiment, for example, there were 600 men on the muster roll, but only 200 could be brought on parade.

> Notwithstanding His Majesty's repeated orders for all officers to repair to their commands the city swarmed with them, the greatest part of them not blushing to give the King daily testimonies of their disobedience by presuming to appear in his presence. But what is worse, if worse can be than disobeying and cheating our sovereign, the money ill gotten was as ill spent in all manner of debauchery, luxury and riot.

And Stevens enlarges on this theme and remorsefully admits that he himself gambled, drank and drabbed with the rest, nor apparently did James's Court set an example of conduct conformable to James's pretensions to sanctity. He himself worked hard—that is to say, he was hours daily in the saddle—but the sort of details in which he interested himself had no bearing on the success of his plans. From the time of the return to Dublin, Avaux had made an effort to bring home to James the necessity for repairing the defects in the army which the late campaign had laid bare, but it was impossible to stiffen his will; with a very bad grace he admitted that there was something in Avaux's strictures, but he had long been past any steady endeavour to put things right. In the course of the winter, however, a small council was unofficially formed, consisting of Avaux, Nagle and Tyrconnel, and a little was done to fill up the ranks and to clothe the troops; but by this time the officers and men had hardened into their mischievous habits and very little progress could be made.

The campaign of 1690 opened under the worst auspices. There was great shortage of provisions because of the neglect of agriculture; the Irish troops were hardly more numerous or better trained than they had been the previous year, and McCarthy, their best general, had been sent to France in command of the 6000 Irish recruits who were to form the nucleus of the Irish Brigade in the French army. True, a body of 6000 trained French troops had been sent in exchange, but this splendid addition to James's army was largely neutralised by the appointment to its command of the Comte de Lauzun.

Lauzun had earned the gratitude of James, and still more of Mary Beatrice, by his conduct in organising the flight of the Queen and Prince of Wales in December 1688. This action has also restored him in the favour of Louis, but Louvois hated him, and it is difficult to find anyone who had a good word to say for him. He had served as a soldier in his youth, but his middle years had been spent in prison and he had had no experience in high command. It was said by those competent to judge that he had forgotten all the military science he had ever known. He had tried to accompany James from France as Louis's representative, but he had annoyed Louis by requiring to be made a Duke; since Avaux's appointment he had been intriguing in Paris against him and had insinuated to the Queen that Avaux had sent to Versailles damaging and libellous reports against King James and had in Dublin treated the King very haughtily and disrespectfully. Mary Beatrice knew that there were many stories derogatory to James current in Paris—hardly had there been time for the news of James's landing at Kinsale to reach Paris when the current opinion there was that in Ireland he was an obstacle to the success of his own plans—and she believed Lauzun when he told her that Avaux was the author of these stories. She also believed him when he told her that he himself was a great general.

But Paris in the autumn of 1689 held more intriguers than Lauzun.

Lord Dover arrived there from Ireland in August and at once commenced to declaim against Tyrconnel; Melfort appeared in the following month, not at all humiliated by the obloquy under which he had left Dublin, and held the same language. Neither of these men gained personal credit in the eyes of the people of Paris, but it was inevitable that their activities should in some degree assist Lauzun in injuring Avaux, whose close ally Tyrconnel was. Louis knew all about Lauzun, and it is almost incredible that he should have consented to so bad an appointment; it seems likely that Mary Beatrice obtained it through Madame de Maintenon and that it is one more example of the degree to which Louis in his later years yielded to that lady's influence.

James himself was not sorry for the change. In his active days he had always been impatient at advice which ran contrary to his own fixed ideas; now his fixed idea was that he did not want to be bothered to make definite plans or to take definite decisions, and Avaux's clear brain and remorseless advice had been a constant reproach. Avaux had commenced his mission by treating James with all the deference due to a king, but he had been advised by the English Jacobites that he would not penetrate James's mind unless he spoke to him plainly; he had therefore changed his tactics, and Louis, after some hesitation, had approved of his new attitude. But Melfort saw his opportunity, and James was made to believe that Avaux was haughty and insolent; the result was that for several months Avaux found his counsels entirely disregarded. Even before Melfort left, James saw his error—a performance for which it would be difficult to find a parallel in his whole life; he actually expressed regret for what he had written to the Queen about Avaux and he showed for a time a tendency to rely on Avaux's advice. But the change was short-lived. In November 1689 Avaux wrote to Louis, "However respectfully I do it, the King of England does not like me to show him the disorder that there is in his affairs". The final parting of James and the French ambassador supplies a touch of comic relief to the almost unbroken tragedy of James's later history. He sent him off from Dublin in a hurry without giving him the customary letter in answer to Louis's letter of recall, but expressed the warmest sentiments of esteem; he excused himself on grounds of poverty from giving him the honorarium usual in such cases, but promised that when he was restored to the English Crown he would make him a present larger than any he had ever given an ambassador. Avaux wrote ruefully to Colbert de Croissy:

> You will see by the letter which I had the honour to write to the King that I was not born to get presents; the present which the

States-General had in mind to give me I lost by accident, and now the King of England refers me to London for the magnificent gift he will make me there.

Lauzun in Ireland was in the double capacity of Louis' ambassador and commandant of the French troops. A casual glance at the Irish troops convinced him that even with the moral and material support of the French regiments, it would not be possible to make a stand against William in the country between Dublin and Dundalk. His first despatches from Ireland contained very much the same complaints as had been common in Avaux's. On May 10 he wrote to Louvois:

> We cannot take the field yet as it is a late season and the grass has not grown for the horses; the treasury has failed to store hay, straw and oats and the treasury has all the power. If the King gives orders the treasury first delay and then fail to carry them out. I kill myself representing the reason and necessity we have for forming an army immediately so that we can defend ourselves or perish with honour but only the King and Lord Tyrconnel listen to me; the others regard me as importunate or inspired by French interests.

Four weeks later he wrote that there was not enough food to support the army for more than a month, that Lord Dover had been so careless in storing what had come over with the French troops that half of it had perished, that strenuous efforts were being made to collect wheat, but that there were no waggons, so that it had to be transferred by pack-horses and on men's backs.

His plan of campaign, in which he copied the ideas of Avaux and Rosen in the previous September, was that the army should retreat behind the Shannon, laying waste the country as they went and burning Dublin. James and Tyrconnel disapproved of this plan, and James could not bear the idea of the sacrifice of his Irish capital city. The army was advanced to Dundalk and took up a position which Schomberg regarded as almost impregnable. William's headlong march, however, disconcerted them—they had no doubt expected a repetition of Schomberg's Fabian tactics of the previous autumn. They had a fear that William would execute a flank march to Dublin and cut them off from their base—a fear which appears to have been groundless, because in order to reach Dublin by any road except through Drogheda, William would have had to make a very wide detour by way of Armagh. Be that as it may, a decision was made to fall back upon a strong, though less strong, position on the Boyne.

The many accounts of the Battle of the Boyne present the confusion common to all descriptions of battles by those who took part in them.

Several facts, however, emerge with something like certainty. The confusion in James's counsels reflected itself in the conduct of the battle, for it was not decided whether to make a decisive stand or to fight a rear-guard action to enable the main body of the army to fall back in good order: when half the small train of artillery—that is to say, six guns—were already on their way to Dublin and no great trouble had been taken to dig trenches to protect the fords, an attempt by the whole army was made to dispute the passage of the river. Two other fatal mistakes were made: it was anticipated that William would send a detachment up the river to cross by Slane Bridge, three miles away, to outflank the Irish left wing, but James decided (and it appears that he was personally responsible for the decision) to send only 800 dragoons to meet this danger; moreover, the position against which the strongest attack was expected, and against which it actually took place—at Oldbridge, on James's left wing—was in the first instance entrusted to the French troops; had they remained there they would have had against them the Dutch Blue Guards and there would have been a stiff engagement; but the Irish insisted on holding the "post of honour", and the Blue Guards went through them with slight loss. The crisis of the battle was when James realised that the flank movement by Slane bridge was not a mere diversion, but an attack in force—one authority says that William had sent no fewer than 12,000 infantry and 5000 cavalry and dragoons by that route. James hastily withdrew troops from his front to meet this force and to prevent it from cutting the line of retreat to Dublin by Duleek, and in this they succeeded. But meanwhile the weakened front was outnumbered and overwhelmed by the enemy and there was a general and disorderly retreat. The French regiments alone kept their formation, and by skilful and courageous rear-guard action prevented William's troops from following up their victory. It is customary to praise the Irish cavalry at the expense of the Irish infantry, but the longest contemporary account by a man who was in the thick of the battle—that by Story, a chaplain in William's army, who wrote a long account of the campaign—mentions quite a number of occasions when the infantry stood for a time against superior numbers. On the other hand, the Irish cavalry, if they did well at the commencement of the engagement, were responsible for the final rout; for when they were repulsed by the Blue Guards they turned and galloped through their own infantry and scattered them without hope of re-formation.[1]

[1] William watched the engagement between his guards and the cavalry and said that the guards had accomplished an unprecedented feat—unsupported infantry defeating cavalry. It is with some diffidence that I connect Story's account of this encounter with Stevens's description of the dispersal of his own men by the retreating Irish cavalry.

> For the horse in general (says Stevens) taking their flight towards the left broke the whole line of the foot, riding over all our battalions. The Lord Grand Prior's wherein I served was then in Duleek Lane enclosed with high banks marching ten in rank. The horse came on so unexpected and with such speed, some firing their pistols, that we had no time to receive or shun them, but all supposing them to be the enemy (as indeed they were no better to us) took to their heels, no officer being able to stop them even after they were broken and the horse past, though at the time no enemy near us . . . some throwing away their arms and even their coats and shoes to run the lighter.

And looking at the hills in the rear, he saw them covered with fleeing men of all regiments.

Of James's own conduct during the battle there is a slight confusion of evidence. His son Berwick says that he marched towards Slane with the reinforcements which he drew from the centre, but if that is true it was the only occasion when he came among his troops, and he certainly did not, as thirty years before at the Battle of the Dunes, "go where the fight was hottest"; what was generally believed is that he watched the battle from the hill of Dunore, about a mile from the river, and made no attempt to direct it. When the battle appeared to be irretrievably lost, Lauzun advised James to leave the field, and James rode hard for Dublin. The story goes that he was met there by Lady Tyrconnel (Sarah Churchill's sister), that he told her that the Irish had run away, and that she replied, "But Your Majesty has run still faster". Next morning early he sent for the Lord Mayor and made a speech in which he cast the blame of his defeat upon the cowardice of the Irish troops. His last command as King on his own soil did him more credit: that Dublin should not be destroyed to prevent it from falling into William's hands. Then he took horse and rode hard for Waterford; from Waterford he proceeded by water to Kinsale, where he found a French frigate which landed him at Brest. He need not have hurried out of Ireland: William had no more desire to burden himself with a royal prisoner than he had had eighteen months earlier, and he was relieved to hear that James had escaped uninjured; he had had a piteous letter from his wife begging him to do her father no harm, and he was glad to be able to tell her that James was safe.

Avaux's prophecy that James would bolt to France at the first check, but that he would not wish to go without striking a blow, was fulfilled in both particulars. Louis received him graciously and without reproaches, but it is clear from his letters to Avaux that he had no longer any hope that James had the capacity to contribute to his own restoration. In August of the previous year he had written that it was evident from Avaux's despatches that James could not put himself into a condition to resist Schomberg, and that he (Louis) found it difficult to believe that James could take the pusillanimous resolution of abandoning Ireland and of losing all hope of regaining his throne.

James had also lost among the French gentry the last remnants of reputation which had survived after their contact with him in the few months before he went to Ireland. The adverse reports from Avaux had been kept secret, but returning French officers and letters from Ireland had given an indelible impression of James's conduct and abilities. In April 1690 Louvois had written to Louis, "All I can say to Your Majesty in advance is that, unless God works a miracle to the advantage of the King of England, I fear that the Prince of Orange will accomplish the conquest of Ireland with far greater ease than he imagines"; in the following month de Bussy Rabutin wrote to Madame de Sévigné, "Things are going well enough in Ireland; it is only King James who spoils everything and shows by his daily conduct that he deserves his misfortunes"; Marshal Luxembourg's opinion given to Louvois was, "Those who love the King of England should be glad to see him in safety, but those who love his glory will deplore the figure he has made of himself"; and Madame de Sévigné wrote, "We are utterly astonished at Paris and Versailles at the return of the poor King of England. Our King continues his generosities on a heroic scale. There is as yet no definite news of what has happened in Ireland." What gave additional point to these strictures was the atmosphere of victory in which the French had lived for a generation: the defeat of Louis's ally was a disgrace which reflected upon Louis and the French nation.

James's behaviour on his return to France still further increased the contempt with which he was regarded there. He had created an unfavourable impression during the weeks of his sojourn after his flight, and he confirmed that impression by his readiness to chatter about his misfortunes and by his entire lack of shame. Foucault, the intendant of Lower Normandy, who accompanied James on part of his journey from Brest to Paris, wrote that James gave him so confused an account of the Battle of the Boyne that it was impossible to understand it, and continued, "The King of England seems as insensible of the bad condition of his affairs as if they did not concern him; he laughs when he talks about his experiences". The Comte de Bouridel, who also saw him shortly after his landing, concluded from his conversation that he knew nothing about the Battle of the Boyne except that he had been defeated; and another witness says that he did not know whether French troops had taken part in the battle or not. The Duchess of Orleans also wrote of his muddled notions about the Battle of the Boyne and contrasted his gaiety with his wife's gravity.

From the time of his return from Ireland, James was always a distinguished figure at the French Court, but he ceased to be of any value to Louis except such value as a child might have had who had a claim to the English crown. The Jacobite cause remained, and there were many who were willing to fight for it; but no one, least of all Louis, expected any assistance to that cause from its nominal head. During the passage from Kinsale to Brest, James's essentially sanguine nature had enabled him to forget the past and to form plans, or rather fantasies, for the future. In the intervals of his confused account to Foucault of the Battle of the Boyne, James had talked about the manners and customs of the English, their politics and the number of families who were attached to him; he said that the English people were entirely on his side, but that they were prevented from showing their loyalty to him by the remorseless tyranny of William and his foreign troops, and Foucault's comment is, "This poor prince thinks his subjects still love him". James had already forgotten Ireland, lost to him (he was convinced) by Irish cowardice, and there is no evidence that he ever again took more than a passing interest in that country. His new scheme was a direct invasion of England by himself in command of French troops, and this scheme he urged upon Louis with great enthusiasm, but, we may be sure, with no precision of detail. He was very importunate, but he was unable to shake Louis's resolution to make no attempt upon England until there was tangible proof of support within that country, such as the seizure of a port at which troops could be landed. In the end Louis feigned illness in order to avoid James's persistency and refused to see him. James was just clever enough to see through this subterfuge and he was deeply wounded. In the spring of 1691 he had to endure a second rebuff from Louis: the French King was about to set out for the siege of Mons, and James was very anxious to accompany him, but he was warned beforehand that a request for permission would be refused, and he decided in intense mortification (as he told his friend the Abbé Rancé) not to make it. Thenceforward James enjoyed the hospitality of Louis on many occasions, but it was understood that the two kings met purely on a social footing and there was to be no direct discussion between them on public affairs; the French Minister, however, kept touch with the Ministers of the exiled Court.

After his return from Ireland the restoration by any other means than the conquest of England by French troops was out of the question. Twice did Louis make preparation for a descent upon England, and on both occasions James travelled to the shores of the English Channel so as to be in readiness to land with the French forces; the first attempt, in 1692, was foiled by the defeat of the French fleet in the Battle of La Hogue, and the second, in 1696, by the failure of the Jacobite insurrection which was to have been the prelude to the French invasion. During the period between these events James paid little heed to the projects of his supporters; he was absorbed in his day-to-day occupations and was increasingly preoccupied with religion. In the summer of 1693 a gentleman who had just returned from Saint-Germain reported that "King James minds little but hunting, and loves not to talk of England"; and in February 1694 James wrote:

> There has never been less prospect of my restoration than there is at present, for the King [of France] is unable to transport me to England at a time when my friends are urgently demanding my presence there, my enemies fear it, and the King himself is I am sure even more eager for it than I am.

The Duke of Berwick records in his memoirs that in the early months of 1696 it was with great difficulty that his father was induced to intermit his devotions and to take an interest in the projected invasion of England.

The various proclamations of the people of England which emanated from Saint-Germain in the early years of the exile have little bearing on the biography of James. They were, indeed, issued in his name, but they were drafted by his Catholic advisers, and for that reason they did not offer the one concession which might have appealed to the English people—a promise to observe the Test Act in letter and in spirit. Such a promise would have entailed an act of disinterested loyalty far beyond the capacity of human politicians, for it would have been tantamount to an undertaking on their part to retire into obscurity. In the utterances of these men, of Queen Mary and of James himself there is no hint of any appreciation of the causes which led to the Revolution or of admission that James had been guilty of illegal acts or of errors of policy. What they now demanded was that he should be reinstated in his three kingdoms, and in the position he had held in the summer of 1688; the only concession they proposed was that, in addition to those who resisted his reinstatement, only a few of those who had taken part in the Revolution should be put to death; James's one undoubted contribution to the text of the proclamations was the inclusion in this proscription of the fishermen of Faversham who had interrupted his first flight and had treated him disrespectfully.

But by no means all the Jacobites supported the official policy of Saint-Germain. The Protestants [1] were well aware that James had no chance whatever of returning to his kingdoms unless he was prepared to give guarantees that he would not unduly favour the Catholic religion—unless, that is to say, he acknowledged by implication the chief mistake of his reign. These men were known as the Compounders, while those who were against all concession to Protestant susceptibilities were called Non-Compounders; and the Non-Compounders were in control, for they alone had access to James's ear and could control his actions, and Queen Mary was wholeheartedly on their side. Melfort, equally hated by the other members of the Court and by the French Ministers, but still in the confidence of James and Mary, and employed as Secretary of State for brief periods, was the most uncompromising and unscrupulous of the Non-Compounders. Two of his remarks may be quoted as typical of his general attitude: in a memorial on the affairs of Scotland sent to Queen Mary in April 1690 he said:

> He who gains time gains life, and therefore the King should show [the Scottish Presbyterians] all the confidence in the world, write most affectionately to them, seem to grant more than he intends to perform . . .

and he described James's conciliatory declaration of April 1693 as merely a means for his return to England: "It will be far easier to argue the business of the Catholics at Whitehall than at Saint-Germain". It is evident that he had adopted the Stuart maxim of state that the only value of concessions is to achieve a position in which these concessions can be safely withdrawn.

It would ill become one brought up in the Protestant tradition to pretend to a final judgement on the claims made for him by the Catholic friends of James of the halo of sainthood; we can only say that these things are a mystery. In middle life Burnet relates that he remonstrated with James at the irregularity of his life and its incompatibility with his religious aspirations, and that James replied hotly, "If a man is religious need he become a saint?" And for many years—indeed, until the age at which women cease to be attractive—he lapsed from time to time into

[1] It does not appear that the moderate Catholics—except for a localised faction in Lancashire—were active on either James's or William's side. They had foreseen the disaster to themselves which resulted from James's religious policy, and they can hardly have been eager for his restoration. They were also under constant suspicion from their neighbours.

carnal sin, nor does it appear that until he came to the throne he made any great effort to overcome his passions. Moreover, while it is true that during the lethargy of his last years James made no effort to regain his kingdoms, the hope that he would eventually regain them was never absent from his mind, so that he cannot be said to have entirely renounced the world. As late as 1697, during the discussions preceding the Peace of Ryswick, it was proposed that James should abdicate his pretensions to the throne of England and that the Prince of Wales should be adopted as the successor of William, and James scornfully rejected the proposal. It was, in any case, only the useless fag-end of his life that he in any real sense devoted to God, and to merit the title of saint he should have given himself heart and soul to the religious life, abandoning all thoughts of his earthly kingdoms and cutting himself off from the adulation of his courtiers and from the honours done to him at Versailles and Fontainebleau. Nevertheless, there can be no doubt that before he died James acquired a very considerable reputation as a saint; after his death Queen Mary habitually referred to him in correspondence as "our holy King".

The atmosphere of the Court at Saint-Germain must have been terribly gloomy. In contrast with the Court of Charles in exile some forty years earlier, it had a permanent abode and a constant and indulgent patron; also, although James and Mary were unable to support as many exiled Jacobites as they would have wished, and though times of financial stress occurred when the French Government failed to pay James's pension regularly, he was never reduced to the state of abject penury which was Charles's chronic condition. But in spite of its uncertain domicile and absence of money, the Court of Charles was a young Court: the King demanded distraction, and courtiers who sought his favour found it to their advantage to be cheerful and witty; there was plenty of laughter in the intervals between depressions. But it is nowhere recorded that anyone laughed at Saint-Germain. It was a court of middle-aged and elderly people: the titular Duke of Powis (who stood highest in rank) was seventy-one at the time of the Revolution, Melfort and Middleton were both about fifty, and Caryll sixty-four; only Sir Edward Herbert at forty was comparatively young.

Furthermore the Court was dominated by the austerities of the King's religion. Anthony Hamilton, the author of Grammont's Memoirs, has left a melancholy picture of life at Saint-Germain. Accommodation in the Chateau was so fully occupied by priests and Jesuits that most of the exiles had to find lodgings elsewhere; everyone was so poor that there was not enough to eat and the general standard of behaviour was low; there were plenty of women of sense and beauty but so few men that it was barely possible to compose a household for the Prince of Wales. He adds:

> Our occupations appear to be serious and our exercises entirely Christian, for there is no mercy here for those who do not spend half the day at their prayers or at any rate make a show of doing so. Misfortunes suffered in common, which usually create a bond between the sufferers, seem to have spread discord and bitterness among us; the friendship we openly profess is often feeble; the hatred and envy which we conceal is always sincere; and while we make in public vows to our unity, we tear them in pieces by our behaviour to each other individually. Innocent flirtation is frowned upon; love-making there is and, though it is carefully concealed, it suddenly bursts forth in some surprising adventure.[1]

He proceeds to relate a recent experience of his own, when wandering in the grounds he had to take cover from an importunate widow "whose husband had died of apoplexy in the service of the King", and who, from morning till night, dressed in mourning, haunted the galleries of the Castle and the garden paths in order to demand a pension.

In addition, the Jacobites at Saint-Germain reverted to the absurdities of the exiled Royalists, and indulged in intrigues against one another for sinecures and precariously paid posts.

But these were personal and superficial enmities, and were of no account in comparison with the antagonisms which separated the Jacobites in England. There, in addition to the cleavage between Compounders and Non-Compounders, there was deep mutual distrust and entire lack of agreement about the means to achieve their end. They were scattered about the country in small groups, and the more prominent among them were closely watched by the authorities; discussion between groups was thus made very difficult, and it was not possible to bring them together to concert an armed rising in James's interest. It is significant that the Earl of Ailesbury, the wealthiest and (save Clarendon) the most distinguished in rank of the Jacobites, and of whose whole-hearted attachment to the Stuart cause there could no doubt, refused to enter into any of the little conspiracies which occupied the minds of men whose abilities he despised and who would be as likely as not to betray him, though he held himself in readiness to risk his life in a well-planned insurrection which gave hopes of success. This disunion was recognised at Saint-Germain as a serious handicap to the cause; in October 1689 Melfort wrote to James in Ireland:

[1] The reference is, no doubt, among others to a scandal in which James's own daughter, the widowed Countess of Waldegrave, was involved.

> There are several gangs which trust not one another, and all these must be managed separately according to their tempers and desires, and what is possible to be done must be to keep them in heart.

The object of keeping the Protestant Jacobites in heart could not, however, be achieved merely by Melfort's specious half-promises. They had proved their unalterable devotion to their Church before the Revolution when, in spite of the material advantages which conversion to Rome would have brought them, and in spite of their loyalty to a Catholic King, they had refused to transfer their religious allegiance. As long as there was no full and clear-cut pronouncement on the religious question they remained in a conflict of loyalties: in restoring their King would they not be betraying their Church? And no such pronouncement was forthcoming; not only that, but they were enabled to contemplate in miniature at Saint-Germain what would happen at Whitehall in the event of the success of their plans. Two of the small band of Catholic peers, of respectable character but moderate talents, whom James had employed in high offices of state—Lord Belasyse and Lord Arundel of Wardour—had not accompanied him to France,[1] and there was still greater difficulty than formerly in finding Catholics of sufficient ability and dignity to perform almost formal duties about the Court. It became necessary, therefore, in certain cases to employ Protestants—Middleton, for example, as Secretary of State (sometimes alone, sometimes uneasily yoked with Melfort) and Sir Edward Herbert as Lord Chancellor. But no pretence was made of giving the Protestants a position of equality with the Catholics; Middleton as Chief Executive Officer could not be excluded from the Council, but Herbert was persistently excluded. A petition to James from the Compounders embodied the request,

> that your Majesty would be pleased to admit of the Chancellor of England into your Councils

and the reply was:

> The King will be on all occasions ready to express the just value and esteem he has for his Lord Chancellor.

This exclusion of Herbert was an extraordinary breach with tradition, for the association of the Chancellorship with a seat on the King's Council was as old as the Council itself.

In other ways the Protestants were made to feel that they were

[1] Lord Belasyse died in 1689 and Lord Arundel of Wardour in 1694.

tolerated rather than welcomed at Saint-Germain. A contemporary thus sums up their disabilities in respect of religious exercises:

> The Protestant Jacobites were refused a chapel at Saint-Germain; Dr. Granville whom they proposed as Chaplain was so insulted that he had to leave Saint-Germain; Dr. Gordon, a Scottish Bishop, was reduced to abjuring his religion for bread, and King James sent a message to Scotland asking his friends there not to employ divines as messengers.

No doubt James was to a great extent not his own master in this matter. Since the *volte face* which had culminated in the Revocation of the Edict of Nantes, Louis had regarded France as holy ground and the celebration of any but Roman rites on French soil as a desecration, and James was persistently pressed to dismiss his Protestant servants.

But not many of the Catholics were as unscrupulous as Melfort; he continued to be universally hated,[1] and at Saint-Germain he had no support except from the King and Queen. Even the French Ministers after a time entirely ceased to trust him. In May 1690 James and Mary yielded very reluctantly to the demands of his enemies at Saint-Germain and dismissed him, he retired to Bourbon and was consoled by patent for a Dukedom, which, however, was not to take effect until James returned to England. Melfort's disgrace was short, for he was reinstated as Secretary of State in the autumn of 1691, but he was finally dismissed in May 1694. After James's death Queen Mary in 1704 recalled him to her counsels, saying that James had discovered shortly before his death that the accusations against him were untrue. It was clearly impossible to convince James and Mary that anyone to whom they had given their confidence was unworthy of it, unless he overtly took a side against them.

Of the lack of loyalty and of deference to James's wishes in the Court of Saint-Germain a very striking instance is given in the memoirs of the Earl of Ailesbury. In the spring of 1693 Ailesbury decided to make a secret visit to Saint-Germain; in order that he should not fall under suspicion of active Jacobitism, he stipulated that not more than two or three persons in James's Court should know of his visit, and it was given out at Saint-Germain that a distinguished visitor was arriving and that his identity should not be known. Nevertheless the courtiers openly plotted to discover who it was, they blocked the staircase so

[1] E.g., Dangeau writes, " Il y avait à Saint-Germain une cabale fort opposée à lui [Melfort]".

that he would have to descend from the curtained chair in which he was being conveyed to the royal presence, and when that plan did not succeed they seized on the little Prince of Wales, then a child of five, when he came from being presented to Ailesbury, and by questioning him found out who it was. The result was disastrous to Ailesbury, for the news of his visit was conveyed to William, and three years later he was exiled for life, though this visit has been his single overt act against the Government.

The Court was riddled with spies, for neither James nor Mary had any knowledge of men or could distinguish an honest adherent from a traitor: any specious person who paid lip service to the Jacobite cause was accepted and taken into confidence; Madame de Caylus, an intimate friend of Madame de Maintenon, alleges in her memoirs that Lady Strickland made use of her confidential relations at Court to pick the Queen's pockets for confidential documents and to send copies of them to England. By these spies William's government was kept fully informed of activities at Saint-Germain and of plans for James's restoration. James was also at the mercy of old servants who went over to the enemy. Of these the most notorious was William Fuller, who had been for some years in Melfort's service; in the spring of 1690 he was entrusted with important despatches to the Jacobites in England, and he not only handed over those despatches to William, but betrayed into his hands Crone, a fellow-spy, who had accompanied him to England. Spies in England, indeed, furnished James's Ministers with long reports, but these reports were of no practical value: they unanimously represented the people of England as anxious for James's return, and were thus in harmony with James's own obsession; but not one of the spies was able to point out any considerable group of people who would at a given signal commence an insurrection.

When, by the Peace of Ryswick in 1697, Louis recognised William as King of England, James's last hopes of restoration were removed; in fact, his own last half-hearted attempt to gain recognition of his rights was his claim to be represented at the Peace Conference. Up to that time hopes had been steadily fading, but as long as the war lasted there was a remote chance that the tide of victory would turn in Louis's favour. When the news arrived that peace had actually been signed James and Mary were Louis's guests at Fontainebleau. Saint-Simon says that they recognised the necessity of the peace, and that there could be no peace without a settlement in William's favour of their particular problem; they were grateful, on the other hand, for Louis' firmness in not consenting to remove them from Saint-Germain to Avignon or some other locality remote from England. Louis remained their friend, and may well have been the only friend they had in France, or indeed anywhere. As early as September 1691 there had been a rumour that they were to leave France because of their unpopularity there and were to take up their residence in Rome; it was said that the Cardinals were strongly opposed to the project, for they found they would have to maintain the exiled Court and, in addition, they had had recent experience of the troubles which another ex-monarch, Queen Christina of Sweden, had brought to the city. In 1694 there was wide-spread famine and misery, and in the bread riots that ensued it was a common cry that James was the cause of the war and of the calamities which had fallen upon France. James himself on one occasion met a mob which killed some of his guards, and at Saint-Germain itself there was rioting and clamour against him. At Court, however, he continued to be received with the same honours as at first, Louis's disavowal of intention to help him by arms to regain his throne did not imply that he did not remain King *de jure*, and he suffered no decline in social status. When Bentinck (since April 1689 Earl of Portland) came to Paris on his splendid embassy in 1698 he was shocked to find that men who had been implicated in the Assassination Plot of 1696 were countenanced and that no particular care was taken to prevent a meeting between him and James himself.

The first serious illness which James is reported to have suffered in his whole life occurred in the spring of 1695, and his Queen was proportionately alarmed. His last recorded appearance on the hunting-field was in the summer of 1699, when he was nearly sixty-six. In the autumn of 1699 he had another illness, but a year later Mary Beatrice wrote that both she and the King were extremely well; Matthew Prior had written in 1698, in language which does not savour of Christian charity—"You never saw such a strange figure as the old bully is, lean, worn and rivelled", and we can conclude that James had aged very much since he left England. His seizure in the spring of 1701 appears to have been sudden; he recovered sufficiently for a journey to Bourbon (at Louis' expense) to drink the waters, but on August 24 he had a stroke when he was hearing Mass, and he died three weeks later. On his death-bed he charged his son, the Prince of Wales, then aged thirteen, to die rather than to change his religion, and so long as he could speak he poured forth words of edification to all his visitors. Immediately before he died there was a dramatic incident in his bed-chamber, when King Louis declared that he would recognise his son as King of England. It was said that he took this step because of the importunity of the boy's mother, and that his whole Council, except the Dauphin, was against the declaration; and he explained that he meant only to recognise James III as *de jure* king, as he had recognised his father for the past four years, and that he had no intention of helping him to conquer his dominions. But to the English his words were a breach of the Peace of Ryswick, and while they might not have been eager to follow William into the War of the Spanish Succession for an abstraction such as the Balance of Power, they were prepared to resist what they thought to be Louis's determination to force a Catholic King upon them.[1]

[1] Anyone interested in the " Posthumous Vicissitudes of James II " will find the subject exhaustively treated in an article under that title by J. G. Alger in the *Nineteenth Century and After*, Vol. XXV, p. 104.

REFERENCES

ABBREVIATIONS

Adda.	Transcripts in the British Museum.
Ailesbury.	*Memoirs of Thomas, Earl of Ailesbury*, Roxburgh Club, 2 vols., 1890.
Arlington.	*Letters of Arlington*, 2 vols., 1701.
Avaux Holland.	*Négociations de M. le Comte d'Avaux en Hollande . . .* 6 vols., Paris, 1673.
Avaux Ireland.	*Négociations de M. le Comte d'Avaux en Irlande*, 1689–90, Intr. by J. Hogan, Dublin, 1934.
Barlow.	Edward Barlow, *Journal of His Life at Sea*, 1914.
Baschet.	Transcripts of despatches of French ambassadors, at the Public Record Office.
Berwick.	*Memoirs of the First Duke of Berwick*, 2 vols., 1779.
Bloxam.	J. R. Bloxam, *Magdalen College and James II*, Oxford, 1886.
Bramston.	*Autobiography of Sir John Bramston*, ed. T. W. Bramston (Camden Society), 1845.
Buckingham.	John Sheffield, Duke of Buckinghamshire—*Works*, 2 vols., 1753.
Bulstrode.	Sir Richard Bulstrode, *Memoirs and Reflections upon the Reign and Government of Charles I and Charles II*, 1721.
Burnet.	Gilbert Burnet, *History of My Own Times* (references to the text are from the folio edition, to the notes from the Oxford Edition of 1852).
Cal. Clar. S.P.	Calendar of Clarendon State Papers.
Cal. S.P.	Calendar of State Papers, Domestic.
Cal. S.P. Ven.	Calendar of State Papers, Venetian.
Cal. T.B.	Calendar of Treasury Books.
Campana.	Campana di Cavelli, *Les Derniers Stuarts à Saint-Germain en Laye*, 2 vols., 1871.
Carnock.	*Journal of the Hon. John Erskine of Carnock*, Scottish Historical Society, 1893.
Carte, Ormonde.	T. Carte, *History of the Life of James, Duke of Ormonde*, 6 vols., 1851.
Cartwright.	*Diary of Thomas Cartwright* (Camden Society), 1843.
Cary, Memorials.	Henry Cary, *Memorials of the Great Civil War*, 1646–52, 1842.
Caylus.	*Souvenirs de Madame de Caylus*, Paris, 1881.
Charlotte Elizabeth.	*Letters of Charlotte Elizabeth, Duchess of Orleans* (various editions).
Chesterfield.	Letters of Philip, 2nd Earl of Chesterfield, 1834.
Christie.	W. D. Christie, *Life of Anthony Ashley Cooper, Earl of Shaftesbury*, 2 vols., 1871.
Chron. Notes.	Sir John Lauder of Fountainhall, Bart., *Chronological Notes of Scottish Affairs*, 1680–1701, Edinburgh, 1822.
Clar. Corresp.	*Correspondence of Henry Hyde, Earl of Clarendon, and Laurence, Earl of Rochester, with Clarendon's Diary, etc.*, ed. S. W. Singer, 2 vols., 1828.
Clar. Hist.	Edward Hyde, Earl of Clarendon, *History of the Rebellion and Civil Wars in England.*
Clar. Life.	*Life of Edward, Earl of Clarendon . . . written by himself*, 3 vols., 1827.
Clark, Ruth.	Ruth Clark, *Sir William Trumbull in Paris*, 1685–6, 1938.

Clarke Papers. *Clarke Papers*, ed. C. H. Firth (Camden Society and R.H.S.), 4 vols., 1891–1901.

Dalrymple. Sir John Dalrymple, *Memoirs of Great Britain and Ireland*, 3 vols., 1790.

Dangeau. *Journal de Philippe, Marquis de Dangeau, 1684–1720*, 19 vols., 1854–60.

D'Orleans. Père d'Orleans, *Histoire des Revolutions d'Angleterre*, 4 vols., 1724.

D'Oyley. George d'Oyley, *Life of William Sancroft*, 2 vols., 1821.

Du Boscq. Du Boscq de Beaumont et de Bernos, *La Cour des Stuarts à Saint-Germain en Laye*, Paris, 1912.

Dutch Despatches. Transcripts in the British Museum.

E.H.R. *English Historical Review*.

Ellis Corresp. *The Ellis Correspondence, 1686–88*, 2 vols., 1829.

Essex. *Essex Papers* (Camden Society), 2 vols., 1890.

Evelyn. *The Diary of John Evelyn* (references under dates).

Evelyn Corresp. *Memoirs of John Evelyn, with Letters*, ed. E. H. Bray, 5 vols., 1827.

Familiar Letters. *Some Familiar Letters from Charles II and James Duke of York . . . to the Countess of Litchfield*, ed. Viscount Dillon in *Archæologia*, Vol. LVIII.

Fox, App. Charles James Fox, *A History of the Early Part of the Reign of James II*, with Appendix, London, 1808.

Foxcroft. H. C. Foxcroft, *Life and Letters of Halifax*.

Grey. Anchitel Grey, *Debates in the House of Commons, 1667–94*, 10 vols., 1769.

Haile. Martin Haile, *Queen Mary of Modena*.

Halkett. *Autobiography of Anne, Lady Halkett*, ed. J. G. Nichols (Camden Society), 1875.

Halstead. Robert Halstead, *Succinct Genealogies of . . . the Houses of Alno*, etc., London, 1685.

Hatton. Hatton Papers (Camden Society), 2 vols.

Hay. M. V. Hay, *The Enigma of James II*.

Hist. Memoirs. *Some Historical Memoirs . . . of James, Duke of York and Albany*, London, 1683.

Hist. Notices. Sir John Lauder of Fountainhall, Bart., *Historical Notices of Scottish Affairs*, Bannatyne Club, 2 vols., Edinburgh, 1848.

Hist. Observes. *Historical Observer . . . 1680 to 1686*, by Sir John Lauder of Fountainhall, Edinburgh, 1840.

H.M.C. Historical Manuscripts Commission.

Hoskins. S. E. Hoskins, *Charles II in the Channel Islands*, 2 vols., 1854.

Inst. Données. *Recueil des Instructions données aux Ambassadeurs . . .*, Tom. XXV, ed. J. J. Jusserand, Paris, 1929.

Jacobite Narrative. *A Jacobite Narrative of the War in Ireland*, ed. John T. Gilbert, Dublin, 1892.

Japikse. *Correspondentie van Willem III en Portland*, ed. Japikse, 3 vols., 1932–37.

Joly. A. Joly, *Un Converti de Bossuet, James Drummond, Duc de Perth*, Lille, 1934.

Jusserand.	J. J. Jusserand, *A French Ambassador at the Court of Charles II*, 1892.
King.	*The State of the Protestants in Ireland under the Late King James's Government*, London, 1691.
Klopp.	O. Klopp, *Fall der Hauses Stuart*, 14 vols., 1875–88.
La Fayette.	*Mémories de Mme. de La Fayette*, 1890.
Lake.	*Diary of Dr. Edward Lake*, Camden Miscellany, Vol. I.
Lauderdale.	*The Lauderdale Papers*, ed. Osmond Airy (Camden Society), 1885.
Law, *Memorials*.	Robert Law, *Memorials of Memorable Things . . . in Britain*, 1638–84, ed. C. K. Sharpe, Edinburgh, 1819.
Leslie.	[Charles Leslie], *An Answer to a Book intituled The State of the Protestants in Ireland under the late King James's Government*, 1692.
Life.	*Life of James II*, published from the original MSS. in Carlton House by J. S. Clarke, 2 vols., 1816.
Lonsdale.	John, Viscount Lonsdale, *Memoir of the Reign of James II*, York, 1808.
Ludlow.	*Memoirs of Edward Ludlow*, ed. C. H. Firth, 2 vols., Oxford, 1894.
Luttrell.	Narcissus Luttrell, *Brief Relation of State Affairs 1678–1714*, 6 vols., 1857.
Mac. Exc.	Macariae Excidium.
Macky.	*Memoirs of the Secret Services of John Macky*, London, 1733.
Macpherson.	James Macpherson, *Original Papers*, 2 vols., 1775.
Mazure.	F. A. J. Mazure, *Histoire de la Révolution de 1688 en Angleterre*, 3 vols., 1825.
Mignet.	*Négociations relation à la Succession d'Espagne . . .*, 4 vols., Paris, 1835–42.
Misc. Aul.	*Miscellanea Aulica . . . State Treaties, etc.*, collected by T. Brown, London, 1702.
Motteville.	*Mémoires de Mme. de Motteville*, 4 vols., Paris, 1886.
Nicholas.	*Nicholas Papers* (Camden Society), 4 vols., Vols. I–III, ed. G. F. Warner, 1886. Vol. IV, ed. Sir Charles Firth.
North, Lives.	Roger North, *Lives of the Norths*, 3 vols., 1826.
Ormonde, *Letters*.	*A Collection of Original Letters . . . 1641 to 1660, found among the Duke of Ormonde's Papers*, ed. T. Carte, 2 vols., 1739.
Parl. Hist.	*Parliamentary History of England* [Cobbett].
P. C. Reg.	*Privy Council Register* (at the Public Record Office).
P.C. Reg. Scot.	*Register of the Privy Council of Scotland*, 3rd Series.
Plumptre.	E. H. Plumptre, *Life of Thomas Ken*, 2nd ed., 2 vols., 1860.
Prinsterer.	Groen van Prinsterer, *Archives de la Maison d'Orange Nassau*.
Ranke.	Leopold von Ranke, *History of England Principally in Seventeenth Century*, 6 vols., 1875.

Rawdon. *The Rawdon Papers*, 1819.
Reresby. *Memoirs of Sir John Reresby*, ed. A. Browning, 1936.
Rousset. C. F. M. Rousset, *Histoire de Louvois*, 4 vols., 1862–3.

Sacharissa. Julia Cartwright, *Sacharissa*, 1893.
Sandwich. *Journal of the Earl of Sandwich*, Navy Records Society, 1929.
Savile. *Savile Correspondence*, ed. W. B. Cooper (Camden Society), 1858.
Sévigné. Mme. de Sévigné, *Lettres*.
Sidney, A. *Letters of Algernon Sidney to Henry Savile*, London, 1742.
Sidney, H. Henry Sidney, *Diary of the Times of Charles II*, ed. R. W. Blencowe, 2 vols., 1843.
Sourches. L. F. du Bouchet, *Marquis de Sourches, Memoires*, 1836.
S.P. Dom. State Papers, Domestic (at the Public Record Office).
Sprat. [Thomas Sprat, Bp. of Rochester] *A True Account . . . of the Horrid Conspiracy Against the Late King . . .*, London, 1685.
S.T. Charles II. *State Tracts . . . privately printed in the Reign of Charles II*, London, 1689.
Steele. *Tudor and Stuart Proclamations*, ed. Steele (in Bibliotheca Lindesiana, Vol. V).
Stevens. *The Journal of John Stevens, 1689–91*, ed. R. H. Murray, 1912.
Stuart Papers, Roxburgh. *Stuart Papers*, Roxburgh Club, London, 1879.

Temple. *The Works of Sir William Temple*, 3 vols., 1770.
Thoresby. Ralph Thoresby, *Diary* (1677–1724), 2 vols., 1830.
Thurloe. *State Papers of John Thurloe*, 7 vols., 1742.

Ven. Trans. Translations of Despatches of the Venetian Ambassadors (at the Public Record Office).

Walker. George Walker, *The Siege of Londonderry*, ed. P. Dwyer, 1893.
Welwood. James Welwood, *Memoirs of . . . the last Hundred Years preceding the Revolution of 1688*, London, 1736.
Williamson. Sir Joseph Williamson, *Letters*, ed. W. B. Christie (Camden Society), 2 vols., 1874.
Wodrow. Robert Wodrow, *History of the Sufferings of the Church of Scotland from the Restoration to the Revolution*, ed. Rev. Robert Burns, 4 vols., 1837.
Wood. *Life and Times of Antony Wood*, ed. A. Clark, Oxford, 1891–1900.

REFERENCES

PAGE

10 **l. 17,** Baschet 13.10.65; also quoted Jusserand, pp. 171–72. **l. 33,** Cal. S.P., 31.10.33. **l. 37,** *ibid.*, 24.4.33. **l. 41,** *ibid.*, 11.12.35, 5.2.38/9.

11 **l. 3,** *ibid.*, 26.11.36. **l. 4,** *ibid.*, 7.4.38. **l. 8,** H.M.C. Hastings, p. 118. **l. 11,** Life, I, 1. **l. 17,** *ibid.*, I, 2; H.M.C. Buccleuch, I, 294; Clar., Life, I, 129; H.M.C. Rep. V, App., p. 141. **l. 33,** Life, I, 2; Clar., Hist., V, 88–91; H.M.C. Rep. V, App., p. 147.

12 **l. 7,** Life, I, 16; H.M.C. Dartmouth, p. 40. **l. 13,** Clar., Hist., IX, 35. **l. 32,** *Camden Miscellany*, I, 26. **l. 35,** Clar., Hist., XIV, 74 and note. **l. 38,** Clar. MSS., 14.11.48 (quoted Hoskins, II, 249); Cal. S.P., 1663–64, p. 526. **l. 40,** Carte MSS., 130, f. 182; Shorthouse, *John Inglesant*, Ch. IX, gives an interesting reconstruction of Oxford during the siege.

13 **l. 1,** Cal. S.P., March 1664; 1667, p. 439. **l. 4,** Nicholas, I, 76. **l. 15,** *A Short View of the Life and Actions of . . . James, Duke of York*, 1660. **l. 23,** Cal. S.P., 31.1.63/4. **l. 25,** H.M.C. Bath, II, 97.

14 **l. 10,** Life, I, 548. **l. 30,** *ibid.*, p. 29. **l. 38,** Clar. MSS., 26, f. 79.

15 **l. 1,** Charles I to Henrietta Maria, Oxford 4.1.45/6; Newcastle, 26.9.46 (quoted Headlam, *Oxford*). **l. 5,** Life, I, 30. **l. 20,** Clar. MSS., 29, f. 165. **l. 31,** *ibid.*, 30, f. 261. **l. 33,** Clar. S.P., I, 329.

16 **l. 1,** Life, I, 30. **l. 3,** Clar., Hist., X, 103, 115, 116; Life, I, 31. **l. 19,** Cromwell to Fairfax, 21.12.46 (Carlyle); Life, I, 30, 31; H.M.C. Rep. VII, App., p. 455. **l. 20,** Cal. S.P., Ven., 1647–52, p. 47. **l. 39,** Clar. MSS., 30, f. 301.

17 **l. 1,** Life, I, 32–3. **l. 7,** Cal. S.P., 1648–49, p. 19; L.J., 22.4.48. **l. 10,** Whitlocke, *Memorials*, 22.4.48.

18 **l. 41,** Life, I, 34–39; Clar. S.P., App., p. xlvii; Clar., Hist., XI, 20; H.M.C. Rep. III, App., p. 283; Halkett, pp. 21–22; Cal. S.P., Ven., 1647–52, p. 58; Motteville, II, 51–52.

19 **l. 24,** Prinsterer, V, 437, 462; Life, I, 734.

20 **l. 3,** Life, I, 43, 45.

21 **l. 25,** Clar., Life, III, 468; Ormonde, I, 189. **l. 29,** Clar. S.P., II, 416. **l. 36,** Clar., Hist., XI, 35–36.

22 **l. 6,** Cary, *Memorials*, II, 60. **l. 20,** Life, I, 46. **l. 36,** Mademoiselle, *Mémoires*.

23 **l. 3,** Clar., Hist., XII, 59; Nicholas, I, 150, 156. **l. 17,** Ormonde, II, 263. **l. 20,** *ibid.*, I, 238. **l. 22,** *ibid.*, II, 306–7. **l. 40,** Hoskins, I, 351–427.

24 **l. 18,** Life, I, 47. **l. 31,** Hoskins, II, 314. **l. 36,** *ibid.*, p. 318. **l. 39,** Ormonde, I, 316 *et seq.* **l. 42,** Carte, Ormonde, III, 480–82.

25 **l. 2,** Ormonde, I, 326. **l. 10,** Life, I, 48; Clar. MSS., Journal of Mr. Trethewy. **l. 15,** Nicholas, I, 190. **l. 25,** Clar. S.P., II, 520. **l. 33,** *ibid.*, p. 529.

26 **l. 1,** Christie, II, 313. **l. 5,** Ormonde, I, 338, 342. **l. 12,** Clar. MSS., 39, f. 122. **l. 25,** H.M.C. Rep. VI., App., p. 695. **l. 30,** *ibid.*, II, App., p. 173. **l. 40,** *A Brief Relation*, quoted *Charles II in Scotland* (Scottish Historical Society), p. 40.

27 **l. 11,** *ibid.*, pp. 24–25. **l. 25,** Life, I, 679; cf. Welwood, p. 129. **l. 36,** Clar. MSS., 39, f. 121. **l. 39,** Nicholas, I, 191, 194.

28 **l. 8,** Hoskins, II, 324. **l. 21,** Clar., Hist., XII, 36. **l. 29,** Nicholas, II, 344; cf. Burnet, I, 95. **l. 38,** *loc. cit.*

29 **l. 2,** H.M.C. Ormonde, I, 168. **l. 7,** Nicholas, I, 229. **l. 10,** Carte MSS., 22.7.81, quoted Burghclere, *Life of Ormonde*. **l. 12,** H.M.C. Ormonde, I, 178. **l. 14,** Clar., Hist., XIII, 121. **l. 18,** H.M.C. Ormonde, I, 178, 181. **l. 29,** Clar. MSS., 64, f. 84. **l. 35,** Clar.,

PAGE

Life, II, 223–24; Nicholas, I, 90, and *passim*; cf. Burnet, I, 98. **l. 37,** Nicholas, I, 116, 128, 149. **l. 39,** Reresby, p. 29. **l. 41,** Clar., Hist., XIII, 129; Nicholas, I, 97, 160.

30 **l. 9,** Life, I, 273. **l. 11,** Nicholas, I, 156. **l. 19,** Clar., Hist., XIII, 36. **l. 28,** Clar., Life, I, 284. **l. 31,** Nicholas, I, 97. **l. 35,** Burnet, I, 267; Clar., Hist., X, 130, XIII, 122; Nicholas, II, 343.

31 **l. 3,** Life, I, 43; Clar., Hist., XI, 33, XIII, 36. **l. 6,** Whitlocke, *Memorials*, 19.12.49. **l. 9,** Ormonde, II, 232–34; Clar. MSS., 51, f. 108. **l. 13,** Clar., Hist., XI, 150 n. **l. 16,** *loc. cit.*; Ormonde, I, 199. **l. 19,** Clar. MSS., quoted Hoskins, II, 249. **l. 25,** Clar., Life, I, 285; Ormonde, I. 222. **l. 26,** Clar., Hist., XIII, 38. **l. 32,** Nicholas, I, 202. **Note,** H.M.C. Ormonde, VI, 460, VII, 348.

32 **l. 5,** Life, I, 84; Cheruel, *Minorité de Louis XIV*; H.M.C. Bath, II, 97; Clar., Hist., XII, 38; Clar., Life, I, 288. **l. 13,** Life, I, 48. **l. 18,** H.M.C. Bath, *loc. cit.*; Nicholas, I, 196. **l. 21,** *loc. cit.*; Ormonde, I, 441. **l. 25,** Nicholas, I, 97; Clar., Life, I, 285; Clar., Hist., XIII, 36. **l. 27,** Ormonde, I, 404. **l. 34,** Clar., Hist., XIII, 38. **l. 37,** *loc. cit.*; Nicholas, I, 198, 202.

33 **l. 5,** Nicholas, I, 242–46; Ormonde, I, 439, 449, II, 3, 9; *Hibernia Anglicana*, II, 59–61; H.M.C. Ormonde, I, 182; H.M.C. Portland, I, 595. **l. 7,** Cal. S.P., 1650, p. 414; *Misc. Aulica*, p. 154. **l. 11,** *loc. cit.* **l. 13,** Nicholas, I, 207; cf. H.M.C. Bath, II, 97. **l. 16,** Nicholas, I, 204. **l. 17,** Clar. MSS., 41, f. 93. **l. 27,** Nicholas, I, 208–9. **l. 37,** H.M.C. Portland, I, 595; Nicholas, I, 209–10; H.M.C. Heathcote, p. 5; Cal. S.P., 1650, p. 182. **l. 39,** Nicholas, I, 213.

34 **l. 3,** *ibid.*, p. 214; Cal. S.P., 1650, p. 482. **l. 7,** Life, I, 50. **l. 9,** Carte MSS., 29, f. 197; Nicholas, I, 218. **l. 11,** Life, *loc. cit.* **l. 13,** Nicholas, I, 228, 230; Ormonde, I, 423. **l. 18,** *ibid.*, II, 4. **l. 24,** Life, I, 51; Ormonde, I, 18; Nicholas, I, 248; Clar., Life, I, 283; Clar., Hist., XIII, 46; Carte MSS., 29, f. 522. **l. 26,** Nicholas, I, 247. **l. 30,** *Parl. Hist.*, IV, 1196, 1238. **l. 40,** Clar. MSS., 49, f. 193.

35 **l. 6,** Nicholas, I, 299. **l. 9,** *ibid.*, pp. 284, 300, 304. **l. 13,** *ibid.*, pp. 264–65; Ormonde, II, 37, 41; Carte MSS., 29, f. 619. **l. 32,** Ormonde, I, 441.

36 **l. 1,** Carte MSS., 29, f. 522. **l. 5,** Ormonde, I, 422, 428; Carte MSS., 29, f. 215. **l. 9,** Nicholas, I, 247. **l. 11,** H.M.C. Ormonde, I, 208. **l. 33,** *ibid.*, p. 281. **l. 40,** Carte MSS., 213, f. 38.

37 **l. 1,** H.M.C. Ormonde, I, 263 n. **l. 5,** Whitlocke, *Memorials*, 1.10.50; Cal. S.P., 1650, p. 355. **l. 6,** H.M.C. Ormonde, I, 216. **l. 11,** Life, I, 51–52. **l. 17,** *Evelyn Corresp.*, I, 352. **l. 22,** Clar., Hist., XIII, 149. **l. 28,** *ibid.*, p. 151; Cal. S.P., Ven., 1647–52, p. 207.

38 **l. 3,** H.M.C. Ormonde, I, 176, 181; Ormonde, II, 40. **l. 7,** *A Bloudy Fight in France*, London, 1651/52. **l. 12,** Life, I, 54; Clar., Hist., XIII, 128. **l. 18,** *A Bloudy Fight in France*.

39 **l. 25,** Life, I, 54–264. **l. 27,** *ibid.*, p. 72.

40 **l. 3,** Thurloe, I, 319. **l. 29,** Life, I, 187. **l. 34,** *ibid.*, p. 106; Clar., Hist., XV, 136. **l. 35,** Life, I, 106, 185. **l. 38,** Burnet, I, 168. **l. 40,** H.M.C. Bath, II, 103.

41 **l. 2,** *ibid.*, I, 106. **l. 3,** Clar. S.P., III, 67. **l. 5,** *Evelyn Corresp.*, IV, 294. **l. 7,** Thurloe, I, 590. **l. 12,** Clar. MSS., 49, f. 31. **l. 17,** Nicholas, II, 97. **l. 21,** Clar. MSS., 49, f. 89. **l. 25,** *ibid.*, 55, f. 54. **l. 27,** Nicholas, II, 34. See also for James's reputation for courage: *Hist. Observes*, p. 148; Sévigné, 14.11.88, 16.3.89; *Memoires du Comte de Bussy*, Paris, 1882, I, 425.

42 **l. 9,** *Hist. Memoirs*, p. 19; cf. *Hist. Observes*, p. 148. **l. 14,** Life, I, 284. **l. 27,** *ibid.*, p. 274. **l. 34,** *ibid.*, p. 275. **l. 39,** Nicholas, II, 230, 297.

43 **l. 3,** Clar., Hist., XIV, 95; Thurloe, II, 418. **l. 10,** cf. Burnet, I, 99. **l. 18,** Clar. MSS., 48, f. 316. **l. 24,** Life, I, 274; Nicholas, II, 123, 135, 156, 166–67, 173, 297, 343, III, 4. **l. 27,** Life, I, 280; H.M.C.

PAGE

Bath, II, 105; *Misc. Aulica*, p. 109. **l. 29,** H.M.C. Ormonde, I, 313; H.M.C. Bath, II, 99, 105; Ormonde, II, 78. **l. 32,** Nicholas, II, 166–67. **l. 35,** *ibid.*, p. 297.

44 **l. 4,** Life, I, 279. **l. 24,** Clar. MSS., 48, f. 316. **l. 38,** *ibid.*, *loc. cit.* **l. 40,** Clar. S.P., III, 153.

45 **l. 4,** *ibid.*, pp. 153, 155. **l. 9,** Nicholas, II, 112. **l. 21,** *Evelyn Corresp.*, IV, 203. **l. 24,** Nicholas, II, 132. **l. 28,** *ibid.*, p. 135; Clar. MSS., 49, ff. 167, 193.

46 **l. 18,** Thurloe, I, 666. l. 23, Nicholas, III, 264–65. **l. 36,** Sévigné, 16.3.89.

47 **l. 2,** Clar. MSS., 51, f. 76. **l. 6,** Carte MSS., 213, f. 40; Cal. S.P., Ven., 1655–56, pp. 207, 212. **l. 14,** *ibid.*, p. 195; Carte Letters, II, 75. **l. 18,** Life, I, 265; Nicholas, III, 281; Clar. S.P., III, 287. **l. 24,** Life, I, 266; Nicholas, II, 184–85. **l. 28,** H.M.C. Ormonde, I, 316. **l. 31,** Cal. Clar. S.P., III, 69–118. **l. 39,** Clar. MSS., 51, f. 98. **l. 42,** Thurloe, I, 666.

48 **l. 5,** Life, I, 269. **l. 12,** *ibid.*, I, 270. **l. 20,** Thurloe, I, 690. **l. 27,** Clar. MSS., 51, f. 291. **l. 29,** Thurloe, I, 667. **l. 36,** *loc. cit.* **l. 41,** Clar. MSS., 51, f. 91.

49 **l. 3,** *ibid.*, f. 108. **l. 7,** Thurloe, V, 120, cf. Clar. MSS., 51, f. 244. **l. 12,** Thurloe, V, 293, 320. **l. 22,** *ibid.*, p. 511. **l. 25,** Life, I, 276. **l. 36,** *ibid.*, p. 277.

50 **l. 3,** Thurloe, V, 432. **Note,** Clar. Hist., X, 13.

51 **l. 14,** Thurloe, V, 736. **l. 26,** Life, I, 290. **l. 27,** Carte MSS., 30, f. 418.

52 **l. 14,** Clar. S.P., III, 317–18. **l. 16,** *ibid.*, pp. 318–21.

53 **l. 27,** Nicholas, IV, 4. **l. 29,** Clar. S.P., III, 360. **l. 37,** Clar. MSS., 55, ff. 299, 333. **l. 38,** *ibid.*, f. 162.

54 **l. 3,** Clar., Life, III, 64. **l. 19,** Clar. S.P., III, 407. **l. 40,** Life, I, 306–8, 321.

55 **l. 13,** *ibid.*, p. 351 *et seq.*; Ludlow, II, 4; Clar. Hist., XV, 37; Clarke Papers, III, 153–59. **l. 18,** Nicholas, IV, 46. **l. 20,** *ibid.*, p. 58. **l. 25,** *ibid.*, p. 40. **l. 26,** Pepys, 4.6.64; cf. Motteville, IV, 112. **l. 32,** *Hist. Memoirs.* **l. 39,** Life, I, 360–61; Clar. Hist., XV, 37.

56 **l. 2,** Life, I, 367; Nicholas, IV, 66. **l. 22,** Clar. MSS., 60, f. 509. **l. 31,** Clar. MSS., 60, ff. 518, 520, 563; 61, ff. 131, 341. **l. 34,** *ibid.*, 60, f. 402; cf. Carte MSS., 213, f. 357.

57 **l. 5,** Clar. MSS., 60, f. 403. **l. 9,** *ibid.*, 63, ff. 1, 122. **l. 13,** *ibid.*, 61, f. 341; Cal. Clar. S.P., III, 86. **l. 25,** Life, I, 371. **l. 31,** Clar. MSS., 63, f. 123. **l. 32,** Ormonde, II, 192.

58 **l. 6,** Life, *loc. cit.* **l. 7,** Carte, Ormonde, *Letters*, II, 186. **l. 16,** *ibid.*, pp. 192, 193. **l. 18,** *ibid.*, p. 195. **l. 20,** H.M.C. Bath, II, 139. **l. 29,** Ormonde, II, 259, 268; Clar. S.P., III, 598, 604. **l. 35,** H.M.C. Heathcote, p. 14. **l. 42,** Life, I, 381; H.M.C. Bath, II, 152; Cal. S.P. Ven., 1659–60, p. 129.

59 **l. 7,** Clar., Hist., XVI, 168. **l. 17,** Barlow, I, 43. **l. 21,** Ludlow, II, 71; Cal. S.P., 4.2.60/61. **l. 26,** Pepys, 16.5.60. **l. 30,** *ibid.*, 22.5.60.

60 **l. 7,** Cal. S.P., Ven., 1661–64, p. 87. **l. 35,** Grammont; Pepys, 3.11.62, 19.1.62/3; H.M.C. Heathcote, p. 55.

61 **l. 41,** Savile, 6.11.77. **l. 7,** Ailesbury, I, 132. **l. 10,** Burnet, I, 169. **l. 12,** *Instr. Données*, XXV, 217. **l. 19,** Pepys, 23.6.67. **l. 22,** H.M.C. Rutland, II, 44. **l. 25,** *Familiar Letters.* **l. 32,** Pepys, 23.9.67; Marvell, 14.11.67. **l. 34,** Harl. MSS., 6584, f. 27. **l. 39,** Baschet, 5.4.85; cf. H.M.C. Frankland-Russell-Astley, p. 60. **Note,** Ailesbury, I, 105.

62 **l. 8,** *N. & Q.*, 3rd Series, V, 392. **l. 11,** H.M.C. Dartmouth, p. 40. **l. 15,** Burnet, I, 689. **l. 24,** Pepys, 15.9.62, 3.11.62, 17.11.62, 1.6.63, 13.10.66, 28.11.66. **l. 26,** H.M.C. Bucc. & Q., II, 19, 33, 37, 130, 133, 163, 164; cf. Baschet, 12.4.85.

63 **l. 7,** H.M.C. Rep. VIII, App., Part I, p. 281. **l. 9,** *ibid.*, p. 279. **l. 11,** H.M.C. Dartmouth, p. 37. **l. 15,** *loc. cit.*, *ibid.*, p. 74. **l. 17,** *The*

PAGE

Old Charlton Hunt, by the Earl of March, 1810. **l. 19,** Cal. S.P., 1673–75, p. 490. **l. 27,** They were kept up after James's Accession, see Cal. T.B., VIII, i, 83. **l. 31,** Reresby, p. 45. **l. 35,** *Victoria County History, Bucks*, II, 228. **l. 38,** Bramston, pp. 226–27 ; Reresby, p. 423.

64 l. 4, Burnet, I, 168. **l. 21,** Harl. MSS., 6584, f. 27. **l. 25,** Life, I, 387. **l. 31,** *loc. cit.* ; *Memorials of the Civil War*, ed. by R. Bell, II, 272.

65 **l. 2,** Pepys, 23.2.60/61. **l. 13,** Life, *loc. cit.* ; Cal. S.P., Ven., 1659–60, pp. 210, 212. **l. 22,** Clar., Life, I, 371–92. **l. 25,** Pepys, 7.10.60. **l. 30,** Burnet, I, 168, 353 ; Cal. S.P., Ven., 1659–62, p. 228. **l. 35,** H.M.C. Rep. IX, App., p. 445 ; Carey, *Memorials*, II, 272.

66 **l. 2,** P. C. Reg. 18.2.60/61. **l. 25,** Ailesbury, I, 246. **l. 30,** Pepys, 27.1.66/67. **l. 36,** Christie, II, 104. **l. 39,** Clar., Life, II, 457.

67 **l. 6,** *loc. cit.* ; Life, I, 453. **l. 11,** Pepys, 14.5.67. **l. 18,** Dartmouth's note to Burnet, I, 170. **l. 24,** Clar. MSS., 49, f. 70 ; Clar., Life, I, 302–7 ; Nicholas, III, 4. **l. 31,** Lans. MSS., 1236, f. 126.

68 **l. 1,** Pepys, 1.1.60/61 ; Clar., Life, I, 393–96 ; Cal. S.P., Ven., 1659–60, p. 237 ; Motteville, IV, 226–29 ; *Mémoires de Mademoiselle.* **l. 61,** Burnet, I, 298 ; Clar., Life, III, 65 ; Pepys, 13.4.62. **l. 10,** Grammont. **l. 14,** Baschet, 7.4.64. l. 15, Reresby, p. 55. **l. 17,** Pepys, 20.4.61., **l. 18,** *ibid.*, 4.3.68/69. **l. 21,** Burnet, I, 170 ; Harl. MSS., 6584, f. 27. **l. 26,** Burnet, I, 309 ; Courtin to Lionne, 7.4.64, 16.1.68/69, 4.3.68/69. **l. 28,** Pepys, 16.1.68/69, 4.3.68/9 ; Baschet, 2.10.64. **Note 1,** the reference is Clar., Life, I, 396. This was found when this book was in the press.

69 **l. 3,** Life, I, 388. **l. 9,** Pepys, 3.11.62, 15.5.63, 30.7.67. **l. 10,** Jonson, *Epicene*, IV, 2. **l. 20,** Burnet, I, 227 ; Reresby, p. 55 ; Pepys, 16.11.65, 9.1.65/66. **l. 26,** *ibid.*, 24.6.67. **Note 1,** Reresby, p. 338. **Note 2,** Burnet, I, 170 ; Baschet, 13.12.65 ; Oldmixon, *History of England* ; cf. H.M.C. Portland, III, 489 ; Cal. T.B., I, 308–9, 603, 605 ; II, 97 ; III, 1352 ; Rawlinson MSS., A 243, f. K ; Russell and Prendergast, *Report on the Carte MSS.*, pp. 174–80.

70 **l. 11,** Pepys, 27.1.67/68. **l. 16,** H.M.C. Rep. VIII, App., Part I, p. 280 (2 places). **l. 27,** Clar., Life, I, 382. **l. 30,** Life, I, 392. **l. 36,** Clar., Life, I, 405.

71 l. 2, Rawdon, p. 143. **l. 5,** L.J., *passim.* **l. 16,** P.C. Reg., *passim.*

72 **l. 22,** See Granville Penn, *Life of Sir William Penn.* **l. 35,** cf. Clar., Life, II, 326. **l. 36,** Pepys, 20.11.68.

73 **l. 33,** *ibid.*, 9.8.67. **l. 35,** Macaulay, *History of England*, 1855 ed., I, 447.

74 **l. 3,** *Instr. Données*, XXV, 323–24. **l. 8,** Baschet, 18.2.86. **l. 22,** *ibid.*, 25.8/4.9.87. **l. 27,** Pepys, 3.5.60.

75 **l. 1,** Burnet, I, 170. **l. 11,** Baschet, 6.11.64. **l. 24,** Dalrymple, Part II, Bk. IV, 168–77. **l. 34,** Pepys, 1.9.61, 20.11.61, 27.6.62, 2.7.62, 2.6.63. **l. 36,** Pepys, 2.6.63. **l. 39,** Add. MSS. 11,602, f. 128 (I am indebted to Mr. Ogg for this reference); Baschet, 3.6.72. **l. 40,** Pepys, 27.6.62, 2.7.62, 2.6.63, 24.6.63, *Tanjier Papers*, pp. 106, 122–24 and *passim.*

76 **l. 2,** Baschet, 18.2.86. **l. 16,** Clar., Life, II, 226, 327 ; Pepys, 1.4.64 ; Baschet, 5.5.64, 18.9.64. **l. 17,** Mignet, III, 97. **l. 18,** Mignet, 19.8.69. **l. 40,** *Instr. Données*, XXV, 109.

77 **l. 7,** Pepys, 6.9.64 ; cf. Life, I, 401–2 ; Macpherson, I, 28. **l. 11,** Clar., Life, II, 303, 353 ; Baschet, 6.11.64. **l. 20,** Life, I, 403 ; Macpherson, I, 28 ; Pepys, 3.12.64 ; H.M.C. Hastings, II, 146–47 ; Sandwich under given date, Arlington to Hollis, 28.11.64 (*Letters*, II, 61). **l. 27,** Barlow, I, 49–50. **l. 36,** Arlington to Hollis, 30.3.65. **l. 39,** Sandwich, 23.3.64/65. **Note,** Tedder, *The Navy of the Restoration*, quoting S.P. Dom. Charles II, CV, f. 125.

78 **l. 8,** Clar., Life, II, 354, 385 ; Pepys, 3.10.64. **l. 14,** Granville Penn, *Memorials of Sir William Penn.*

PAGE

79 **l. 7,** Marvel, 18.4.68, 25.4.68, 13.11.69; Barlow, I, 106. **l. 14,** Colenbrander, p. 211; Sir Thomas Allies, quoted by Tedder, *The Navy of the Restoration*, p. 125 n. **l. 22,** Burnet, I, 219; Pepys, 21.10.67. **l. 35,** Add. MSS., 27962 S, f. 441; Marvel, 18.4.68, 25.4.68, 13.11.69; C.J., IX, 106.

80 **l. 7,** Pepys, 8.6.65; Colenbrander, p. 189. **l. 16,** Clar., Life, II, 395; Pepys, 17.10.62, 15.5.63. **l. 19,** Pepys, 3.12.64. **l. 21,** Burnet, I 99. **l. 23,** Clar., Life, II, 385. **l. 29,** Pepys, 30.8.68. **l. 40,** James's own account of the battle is in Life, I, 405 *et seq.*

81 **l. 29,** Cal. S.P., Ven., 1664–66, p. 146. **l. 33,** Burnet, I, 525. **l. 34,** *ibid.*, I, 634.

82 **l. 10,** C.J., 25/6.10.65; *Parl. Hist.*, IV, 327, 331; Pepys, 4.7.65, 15.10.65, 28.10.65; Sandwich, 2.7.65; *Misc. Aulica*, p. 364. **l. 18,** Colenbrander, p. 218. **l. 28,** Airy, note to Burnet, I, 447, quoting Marvel, *Last Instructions*, pp. 317–24. **l. 31,** Life, I, 487. **l. 34,** Pepys, 3.10.60. **l. 38,** Life, I, 399. **l. 40,** Cal. S.P., 2.9.63. **l. 41,** Douglas Mackay, *The Honourable Company*, 1937.

83 **l. 7,** Baschet, 6.11.64. **l. 11,** *Ven. Trans.*, 21.12.74. **ll. 15, 17,** Barrillon deals with these matters in several places, but Baschet is not available at the moment. **l. 28,** Pepys, 11.9.60, 18.9.60; Barlow, I, 46; Cal. S.P., 1660–61, pp. 267, 268, 277, 325 (2 places); Cal. S.P., Ven., 1659–60, p. 201. **l. 29,** Burnet, I, 170–71. **l. 37,** Cal. S.P., Ven., 1659–60, p. 213; Burnet, I, 171. **l. 41,** Cal. S.P., *loc. cit.*

84 **l. 6,** Life, I, 394; **l. 9,** Arlington, II, 82. **l. 16,** Clar., Life, II, 384. **l. 20,** H.M.C. Hastings, II, 46. **l. 24,** Life, I, 421; Arlington, 29.6.65. **l. 31,** Arlington, I, 17. **l. 33,** Hatton, I, 47. **l. 36,** Clar., Life, II, 454–7. **l. 41,** Reresby, p. 55.

85 **l. 4,** *loc. cit.* **l. 10,** Grammont. **l. 25,** Wood, *Ath. Oxon*, art. " Sir Chas. Sedley "; Bramston, p. 270 (2 places). **l. 28,** H.M.C. Portland, II, 145.

86 **l. 5,** Wood, III, 58–73. **l. 17,** Cal. S.P., 1670, p. 213. **l. 20,** Pepys, 18.2.61. **l. 21,** Burnet, I, 232; Evelyn, 6.9.66; H.M.C. Hastings, II, 370. **l. 25,** Life, I, 446; Macpherson, I, 51.

87 **l. 14,** Cal. S.P., 1675–6, p. 475. **l. 20,** Life, I, 393; Macpherson, I, 39; Clar., Life, II, 382, 405; Rawdon, p. 143. **l. 27,** Clar., Life, II, 258–60. **l. 30,** Burnet, I, 196, 197; Pepys, 2.9.67. **l. 32,** *Parl. Hist.*, IV, 276; Jusserand, p. 214. **l. 35,** Pepys, 24.6.67.

88 **l. 13,** Life, I, 429; Clar., Life, III, 282. **l. 16,** *ibid.*, p. 332; Burnet, I, 256; cf. Bramston, p.256 n. **l. 19,** Life, I, 431; Burnet, I, 255; Clar., Life, I, 431. **l. 21,** *ibid.*, III, 292; Ormonde, II, 57. **l. 26,** Pepys, 29.8.67; Reresby, pp. 139–40. **l. 27,** Life, I, 431. **l. 33,** Pepys, 30.8.67, 2.9.67. **l. 40,** Pepys, *passim*; H.M.C. Rep. VIII, App., Pt. i, p. 280; Clar., Life, III, 293; Coventry to Savile, 3.9.67, quoted Foxcroft, I, 54.

89 **l. 1,** Baschet, 24.12.68; Burnet, I, 100. **l. 4,** *ibid.*, 7.6.68. **l. 14,** Cominges to Louis, 7.4.60 (Jusserand). **l. 20,** Clar., Life, III, 62–63. **l. 25,** Pepys, 17.11.65; Marvel, II, 297. **l. 27,** H.M.C. Buccleuch, I, 441.

90 **l. 3,** Pepys, 30.10.68, 5.11.68. **l. 11,** Life, I, 433; Macpherson, I, 44; Burnet, I, 469; Pepys, 12.11.68. **l. 21,** Life, I, 439. **l. 32,** Pepys, 12.11.68. **l. 38,** Life, I, 441–42; Macpherson, I, 130 and note.

91 **l. 1,** Christie, II, App., p. xxxvi. **l. 3,** Baschet, 9.2.72/3. **l. 6,** Macpherson, I, 73; Burnet, I, 379; Buckingham. **l. 9,** Macpherson, *loc. cit.* **l. 13,** Pepys, 30.10.68. **l. 17,** H.M.C. Buccleuch, I, 441. **l. 28,** Haile, p. 72. **l. 29,** Life, I, 750. **l. 32,** Essex, I, 140; *Camden Misc.*, XI, 35.

92 **l. 15,** Reresby, p. 120. **l. 24,** Mignet, III, 10; Baschet, 21.5.68. **l. 28,** Baschet, *loc. cit.* **l. 30,** Cal. S.P., 1675–76, p. 19. **l. 34,** Christie, II, 201–2. **l. 37,** Prinsterer, V, 357. **Note,** H.M.C. Bucc. & Q., I, 181.

PAGE

93 **l. 1,** Japikse, II, ii, 568. **l. 4,** Mignet, IV, 257. **l. 7,** Prinsterer, V, 360. **l. 9,** H. Sidney, I, 259. **l. 36,** Steele, pp. 408–51. **l. 37,** *e.g.*, Baschet, 18.2.74/5.

94 **l. 8,** Baschet, 13.8.74. **l. 10,** cf. King, p. 58. **l. 12,** Dalrymple, I, i, App., p. 77. **l. 14,** Life, I, 482, 484; Christie, II, App., p. xxvii. **l. 17,** Lake, 30.12.77. **l. 29,** Baschet, 15.4.76, 4.6.76, 8.6.76, 11.8.76, 5.11.76, 21.6.77 and elsewhere.

95 **l. 4,** Ven. Trans., 14.12.74. **l. 23,** Life, I, 540; H.M.C. Portland, I, 534; Cal. S.P., 1650, pp. 271–414; Cary, *Memorials*, II, 229–32. **l. 28,** H.M.C. Bath, II, 97; Cary, *loc. cit.* **l. 34,** Life, 209–10. **Note,** I have made great but fruitless endeavours to re-discover this reference and I am unable to assess its authority.

96 **l. 10,** Pepys, 14.10.60. **l. 16,** Thurloe, I, 619. **l. 32,** Clar. S.P., III, 458. **l. 37,** Cal. S.P., Ven., 1659–60, p. 129; *Appeal from the County to the City* (Parl. Hist., IV, App., p. C). **l. 28,** Pepys, 18.2.60/61.

97 **l. 2,** Marvell, II, 127. **l. 31,** cf. Bulstrode, p. 417. **l. 35,** C. J., *passim*; Life, I, 391. **l. 37,** Marvell to Ackham, 7.2.71.

98 **l. 5,** Life, I, 483. **l. 7,** *Instr. Données*, XXV, 109; Baschet, 10.7.73. **l. 8,** Evelyn, 30.3.73; Wood, II, 244 n. **l. 9,** Haile, p. 69. **l. 20,** Life, I, 440; Macpherson, I, 130 n. **Note 2,** Lord John Russell, *Life of William, Lord Russell*, pp. 37, 38; Belloc, *James II*.

99 **l. 24,** Dalrymple, I, 123. **l. 27,** Life, I, 443. **l. 32,** Life, I, 554, 614; cf. Hartmann, *Madame*, p. 254.

100 **l. 1,** *op. cit.*, p. 57.

101 **l. 7,** *Instr. Données*, XXV, 120. **l. 31,** Life, I, 450. **l. 37,** Life, I, 449; Macpherson, I, 54.

102 **l. 1,** Dalrymple, I, 80; Hartmann, *Madame*, p. 241. **l. 7,** *op. cit.*, p. 299. **l. 19,** Dalrymple, I, 122. **l. 24,** Life, I, 451. **l. 28,** Cal. S.P., 1670, p. 333. **l. 29,** Cal. S.P., Ven., 1669–70, p. 244. **Note 1,** Life, I, 448; Hartmann, *Madame*, p. 308; Cal. S.P., Ven., 1669–70, p. 202. **Note 2,** *Stuart Papers* (Roxburgh Club), p. 393.

103 **l. 8,** Life, I, 450. **l. 18,** Baschet, 10.6.72. **l. 21,** Life, I, 463; Macpherson, I, 61; *Ven. Trans.*, 10.6.72, 24.6.72, 1.7.72; Baschet, 14.6.72. **l. 34,** Life, I, 466. **Note,** *Ven. Trans.*, 18.3.71/72, 28.3.72, 10.4.72.

104 **l. 3,** Life, I, 466. **l. 7,** Burnet, I, 323; Ludlow, II, 431. **l. 12,** Williamson, I, 39. **l. 15,** Marvel, II, 318. **l. 18,** Life, I, 477. **l. 28,** Baschet, 7.2.72/73. **Note,** *Ven. Trans.*, 24.6.72, 1.7.72.

105 **l. 9,** *Parl. Hist.*, IV, 515–70. **l. 23,** *Ven. Trans.*, 17.3.72/73; Christie, II, App., p. xxxi. **l. 26,** Reresby, p. 356; Bramston, p. 180. **l. 33,** P.C. Reg., 13.6.73, 18.6.73; Burnet, I, 352; Baschet, 26.6.73. **l. 36,** Williamson, I, 55, 68, 176. **l. 39,** *ibid.*, p. 68.

106 **l. 1,** Life, I, 484. **l. 5,** Burnet, I, 352; Essex, I, 258, 259.

107 **l. 4,** Arlington, II, 324; H.M.C. Ormonde, III, 447. **l. 24,** H.M.C. Rep. VII, App., p. 489. **l. 28,** Burnet, I, 309; *Ven. Trans.*, 10.4.71. **l. 30,** Life, I, 452–53; Macpherson, I, 56–57. **l. 32,** Reresby, p. 416; Harl. Misc., V, 44. **l. 35,** Cal. S.P., 1673–75, p. 131.

108 **l. 5,** Life, I, 539. **l. 9,** Campana, II, 130. **l. 10,** Steele, p. 449. **l. 19,** Life, I, 453; Clar., Life, I, 457. **l. 33,** Burnet, I, 352. **l. 36,** H.M.C. Rep. VIII, App., Pt. i, p. 498. **l. 38,** *ibid.*, VI, App., p. 369. **Note,** Burnet, I, 227.

109 **l. 15,** *Instr. Données*, XXV, 120. **l. 22,** Baschet, 31.7.73. **l. 34,** *ibid.*, 17.7.72. **l. 38,** *ibid.*, 24.4.73, 31.7.73. **l. 39,** *ibid.*, 17.4.73, 10.7.73.

110 **l. 5,** Cal. S.P., 1673, p. 29; Baschet, 20.2.72/73; *Ven. Trans.*, 27.10.72, 4.11.72; Hartmann, *Clifford of the Cabal*, pp. 236–38. **l. 8,** Cal. S.P., 1672, pp. 29, 137, 628, 631; Baschet, 20.2.73, 24.4.73; *Misc. Aulica*, pp. 65–107; Halstead, pp. 680–82. **l. 11,** *ibid.*, pp. 684–87. **l. 20,** Life, I, 485. **l. 29,** Baschet, 10.8.73; *Ven. Trans.*, 22.9.73, 6.10.73, 13.10.73. **l. 32,** *ibid.*, 25.8.73. **l. 36,** *ibid.*, 6.10.73, 13.10.73, 3.5.75.

PAGE

111 **l. 3,** Cal. S.P., 12.11.73. **l. 16,** Essex, I, 142. **l. 21,** *Clar. Corresp.*, II, 261. **l. 30,** Baschet, 17.7.73. **l. 34,** *Parl. Hist.*, IV, 585; Williamson, I, 144. **l. 40,** C.J., 20.10.73; Williamson, II, 51, 70.

112 **l. 1,** C.J., 30.10.73; *Parl. Hist.*, IV, 591; Life, I, 485; Essex, I, 130; H.M.C. Portland, III, 341; *Ven. Trans.*, 10.11.73. **l. 3,** C.J., 31.10.73; *Parl. Hist.*, IV, 603; Cal. S.P., 1673–75, p. 73. **l. 7,** Essex, I, 130. **l. 9,** Life, I, 503. **l. 11,** Haile, p. 52; Luttrell, I, 213. **l. 33,** Halstead, p. 428. **l. 37,** Williamson, II, 86; Essex, I, 145. **Note 1,** *Stuart Papers* (Roxburgh), p. 376

113 **l. 14,** Reresby, p. 121. **l. 18,** Baschet, 21.7.87. **l. 20,** Caylus, p. 166. **l. 29,** *Stuart Papers* (Roxburgh), p. 373. **l. 33,** *ibid.*, p. 369; *Ven. Trans.*, 15.12.73. **l. 37,** Essex, I, 145; *Ven. Trans.*, 15.12.73, 22.12.73. **l. 40,** Macpherson, I, 103. **l. 41,** *Stuart Papers* (Roxburgh), p. 437.

114 **l. 5,** Cal. S.P., 1678, pp. 421, 444, 460, 466; Luttrell, I, 1; Haile, p. 64; H.M.C. Ormonde, IV, 217; H.M.C. Rep. IV, App., p. 406. **l. 9,** Williamson, II, 87; Essex, I, 145. **l. 12,** Williamson, II, 103. **l. 16,** H.M.C. Rep. VII, App., p. 491. **l. 19,** Life, I, 385; Macpherson, I, 70, 71; *Ven. Trans.*, 27.10.73. **l. 23,** Essex, I, 159. **l. 24,** Life, I, 733. **l. 29,** Haile, p. 54. **l. 31,** *Instr. Données*, XXV, 181 n.; Baschet, 15.4.76. **l. 36,** H.M.C. Rutland, II, 34. **Note,** Luttrell, I, 1; *An Appeal from the Country to the City.*

115 **l. 13,** Pepys, 27.10.66. **l. 17,** *ibid.*, 7.11.66. **l. 21,** Wood, II, 93. **l. 26,** Pepys, 21.5.68. **l. 32,** Life, I, 602.

116 **l. 14,** Steele, p. 449. **l. 21,** Baschet, 19.3.73/74. **l. 24,** Temple, II, 506.

117 **l. 9,** quoted by Hartmann, *Clifford of the Cabal*, p. 284. **l. 19,** Williamson, I, 24. **l. 25,** Baschet, 21.1.73/74. **l. 36,** Christie, II, App., p. xxxvii. **l. 39,** Williamson, II, 67, 71.

118 **l. 1,** Haile, p. 60. **l. 9,** Grey, VII, 238; *Parl. Hist.*, IV, 1131. **l. 23,** Baschet, 10.7.73.

119 **l. 5,** Life, I, 487. **l. 11,** Baschet, 17.4.73, 10.7.73. **l. 13,** *ibid.*, 17.4.73, 10.7.73. **l. 17,** *ibid.*, 17.11.73. **l. 28,** *ibid.*, 10.7.73. **l. 36,** Burnet, I, 345. **Note,** Bolingbroke, *Works*, 8 vols., 1809, III, 118 n.

120 **l. 1,** Burnet, I, 366. **l. 4,** Baschet, 3.10.77, 1.11.77, and elsewhere. **l. 11,** *Clar. Corresp.*, I, 46. **l. 12,** Life, I, 487. **l. 27,** Christie, II, 127. **l. 35,** Dalrymple, II, App., p. 90.

121 **l. 12,** Martyn, *Life of Shaftesbury*, quoted Christie, II, 118. **l. 25,** *Ven. Trans.*, 2.2.73/74. **l. 31,** *Instr. Données*, XXV, 117; *Ven. Trans.*, 22.12.73. **l. 34,** *ibid.*, 15.12.73. **l. 35,** Ogg, probably quoting *Ven. Trans.* **l. 36,** Colbert to Louis, 9.11.73. **l. 42,** *Ven. Trans.*, 8.3.74/75.

122 **l. 6,** Essex, I, 258; Baschet, 13.8.74, 27.1.74/75. **l. 25,** Mignet, IV, 257. **l. 26,** *Parl. Hist.*, IV, 1167; Life, I, 602. **l. 40,** *Ven. Trans.*, 15.2.74/75, cf. Life, I, 499, 500.

123 **l. 16,** Baschet, 8.4.75. **l. 23,** Burnet, I, 386. **l. 37,** Baschet, 12.11.76; Mignet, IV, 434. **Note,** Burnet, I, 393.

124 **l. 2,** Baschet, 8.4.75. **l. 10,** *ibid.*, 30.11.76, 3.12.76, 10.12.76. **l. 12,** *ibid.*, 21.1.76/77, 8.3.76/77, 3.6.77. **l. 17,** *ibid.*, 25.10.77. **l. 29,** *ibid.*, 15.4.76. **l. 37,** *ibid.*, 3.12.76. **l. 39,** Reresby, pp. 120, 121. **l. 41,** H.M.C. Rep., V, App., p. 318.

125 **l. 11,** Christie, II, 283 (to whom I am indebted for the comparison of the two documents). **l. 19,** Life, I, 513; Macpherson, I, 88. **l. 33,** Baschet, 3.12.76; Haile, p. 69. **l. 34,** H.M.C. Rep. VII, App. p. 467.

126 **l. 2,** Wood, II, 343; Mignet, IV, 405. **l. 6,** Baschet, 3.12.76; Mignet, *loc. cit.* **l. 11,** Baschet, *loc. cit.*, 31.12.76. **l. 14,** *ibid.*, 3.12.76, 3.6.77. **l. 18,** *ibid.*, 12.10.76. **l. 21,** *ibid.*, 22.6.76. **l. 38,** *ibid.*, 8.6.76.

127 **l. 4,** Baschet, 8.6.76. **l. 7,** *ibid.*, 2.11.76, 3.6.77. **l. 12,** *ibid.*, 3.6.77, 12.7.77, 2.9.77, 6.9.77.

128 **l. 5,** Reresby, p. 82. **l. 7,** Essex, I, 130; Baschet, 27.11.73. **l. 9,** H.M.C. Kenyon, p. 99. **l. 15,** Baschet, 23.4.76. **l. 28,** Dalrymple, I, 158.

PAGE

129 **l. 23,** Baschet, 23.4.74. **l. 28,** H.M.C. Hastings, II, 160, 5.11.72: 'many of the Council were against her marrying with the King of France's son'. **l. 35,** Mignet, IV, 323; Dalrymple, I, 158

130 **l. 6,** Burnet, I, 377; Carte Ormonde, IV, 495; Baschet, 19.11.74. **l. 10,** Life, I, 502; Carte Ormonde, *loc. cit.*; Temple, II, 294; Baschet, 23.4.70. **l. 11,** Prinsterer, V, 246, 259; *Ven. Trans.*, 18.1.74/75. **l. 22,** Courntenay, *Memoirs of Temple*, I, 431. **l. 39,** Temple, II, 324–27.

131 **l. 2,** *ibid.*, p. 420. **l. 11,** Elizabeth Charlotte, I, 162. **l. 14,** H.M.C. Rutland, II, 32. **l. 17,** Prinsterer, V, 348; H.M.C. Ormonde, IV, 376. **l. 27,** Baschet, Sept. 23, 27, 30, Oct. 4, 1677. **l. 28,** *ibid.*, 19.10.77. **l. 29,** *ibid.*, Oct. 21, 25, 28, 1677. **l. 34,** *ibid.*, 25.10.77. **l. 38,** *ibid.*, 28.10.77. **l. 40,** *ibid.*, Oct. 28, 30, 1677.

132 **l. 27,** Temple, II, 420; cf. Life, I, 508. **l. 30,** Lake, 21.10.77. **l. 36,** *loc. cit.*; Hatton, I, 151, 153. **l. 38,** *Instr. Données*, XXV, 254; Japikse, II, ii, 208. **l. 42,** Lake, 4.11.77.

133 **l. 2,** *ibid.*, 16.11.77. **l. 13,** H.M.C. Rutland, II, 42. **l. 29,** Baschet, 1.11.77. **l. 34,** *loc. cit.* **l. 39,** *ibid.*, 4.11.77.

134 **l. 4,** Temple, *loc. cit.* **l. 6,** Burnet, I, 410. **l. 11,** H.M.C. Rep. XIV, App., Pt. ix, p. 387. **l. 15,** Hatton, I, 151, 153. **l. 16,** Cal. S.P., 1677–78, pp. 422, 427, 452, 454. **l. 20,** Temple, *loc. cit.* **l. 22,** Cal. S.P., 1677–78, pp. 438, 449. **l. 25,** Christie, II, 281. **l. 27,** Cal. S.P., 1677–78, p. 547. **l. 30,** Mignet, IV, 545. **l. 40,** *ibid.*, p. 514.

135 **l. 11,** *ibid.*, p. 545. **l. 14,** *ibid.*, p. 514. **l. 23,** *ibid.*, p. 517. **l. 27,** *ibid.*, p. 516. **l. 32,** *Instr. Données*, XXV, 255. **l. 35,** *loc. cit.* **l. 40,** *Parl. Hist.*, IV, 897.

136 **l. 2,** *ibid.*, IV, 907. **l. 8,** Mignet, IV, 533. **l. 12,** *ibid.*, p. 541. **l. 20,** *loc. cit.*

137 **l. 7,** Prinsterer, V, 354. **l. 11,** Mignet, IV, 520. **l. 13,** Haile, p. 69. **l. 15,** Burnet, I, 407–8; *Instr. Données*, XXV, 258.

138 **l. 2,** Dalrymple, I, 194. l. 22, *Parl. Hist.*, IV, 896–977; C.J., Jan. 15 to March 8, 1677/78. **l. 31,** Dalrymple, I, 199–209.

139 **l. 11,** Reresby, p. 131. **l. 17,** *Instr. Données*, XXV, 259. **l. 21,** *Parl. Hist.*, IV, 975. **l. 42,** Prinsterer, V, 358–59.

140 **l. 3,** Mignet, IV, 545; Christie, II, 281. **l. 6,** Mignet, IV, 583. **l. 10,** *ibid.*, pp. 587–88. l. 20, Dalrymple, I, 209. **l. 21,** *Instr. Données*, XXV, 260. **l. 30,** Dalrymple, I, 221.

141 **l. 11,** Cal. S.P., 1678, p. 182. l. 23, Christie, II, App., p. cxviii. **l. 27,** Temple, II, 412. **l. 32,** Mignet, IV, 600. **l. 34,** *ibid.*, p. 601.

142 **l. 9,** Dalrymple, I, 319. **l. 11,** *ibid.*, p. 321. **l. 16,** *ibid.*, p. 363. **l. 26,** Savile, p. 92. **l. 36,** Evelyn, 13.6.73. **l. 32,** H.M.C. Rep. VII, App., p. 343. **l. 39,** H.M.C. Rutland, II, 44, 50.

143 **l. 4,** Sacharissa, p. 273. **l. 7,** Prinsterer, V, 423. **l. 15,** cf. Dartmouth's note to Burnet, I, 683. **l. 19,** Pepys, 26.10.77. **l. 21,** *ibid.*, 1.7.63, 16.11.67.

144 **l. 36,** Dalrymple, I, 246.

145 **l. 5,** Burnet, I, 425; H.M.C. Ormonde, IV, 380. **l. 12,** Ailesbury, I, 27; North, *Examen*, p. 136. **l. 16,** *Parl. Hist.*, IV, App., pp. lxxx–lxxxi. **l. 19,** *ibid.*, pp. lxxix–xciv. **l. 24,** Baschet, 21.1.76/77. **l. 40,** Life, I, 534.

146 l. 6, H.M.C. Ormonde, IV, 460; Steele, p. 449. **l. 10,** H.M.C. Foljambe, pp. 123–25. **l. 23,** H.M.C. Ormonde, IV, 463. **l. 27,** *loc. cit.* **l. 28,** Baschet, 24.11.78.

147 **l. 14,** *Parl. Hist.*, IV, App., p. xciii. **l. 21,** H.M.C. Ormonde, IV, 465. **l. 27,** *ibid.*, p. 507. **l. 32,** *loc. cit.*

148 **l. 6,** Pollock, *The Popish Plot*, pp. 149–66. **l. 31,** Burnet, II, 163; *Brief History*, III, 187. **l. 41,** Reresby, p. 365.

149 **l. 19,** *ibid.*, p. 178. **l. 26,** H.M.C. Ormonde, IV, 227; cf. Baschet,

PAGE

14.11.78. **l. 28,** *Parl. Hist.*, IV, 1026. **l. 32,** Macpherson, I, 91. **Note 2,** Baschet, *loc. cit.*

150 **l. 13,** Reresby, p. 156; *Parl. Hist.*, IV, 1030. **l. 15,** *Parl. Hist.*, *loc. cit.* **l. 18,** *ibid.*, 1031. **l. 33,** Reresby, p. 157. **Note,** Life, I, 550.

151 **l. 1,** *Parl. Hist.*, IV, 1035; H.M.C. Ormonde, IV, 467. **l. 4,** *Parl. Hist.*, IV, 1024. **l. 10,** Baschet, 24.11.78. **l. 38,** Dalrymple, I, 252. **Note,** Baschet, 1.12.78.

152 **l. 35,** Burnet, I, 248, and Dartmouth's note to I, 157. **l. 37,** H.M.C. Ormonde, IV, 106; cf. North, Lives (1826), " King Charles would not suffer his mimics to fool with the persons of his ministers that he had a value for ".

153 **l. 2,** *Parl. Hist.*, IV, 1035. **l. 7,** Baschet, 17.11.78, 24.11.78. **l. 28,** H.M.C. Foljambe, p. 126. **l. 31,** *Parl. Hist.*, IV, 1074, 178. **l. 36,** *ibid.*, 1115, 1129.

154 **l. 4,** Campana, I, 271, 277, 279. **l. 11,** H.M.C. Rep., XIV, App., Pt. ix, p. 414; cf. H.M.C. Portland, III, 165. **l. 24,** Reresby, p. 331.

155 **l. 13,** Burnet, I, 364–65; Temple, II, 288. **l. 29,** Burnet, I, 452; Reresby, pp. 171, 239; Dalrymple, I, 292–93; Lindsey MSS., 399, 407, 409. **l. 33,** H.M.C. Ormonde, IV, 340. **l. 36,** Burnet, *loc. cit.*; Luttrell, I, 10; Reresby, p. 175; *Stuart Papers* (Roxburgh), p. 372.

156 **l. 2,** H.M.C. Hastings, II, 388. **l. 11,** Clar. S.P., III, 458. **l. 14,** Life, I, 537–40; Hatton, I, 177; Dalrymple, I, 293; H.M.C. Ormonde, IV, 340; *Clar. Corresp.*, II, 467–71. **l. 18,** H.M.C. Dartmouth, p. 30. **l. 23,** *ibid.*, pp. 30–37; Dalrymple, I, 296–309. **l. 24,** *Clar. Corresp.*, I, 43–46.

157 **l. 3,** Dalrymple, I, 352. **l. 11,** *Parl. Hist.*, IV, 1092–1111; H.M.C. Ormonde, IV, 346. **l. 14,** *Parl. Hist.*, IV, 1122. **l. 18,** H.M.C. Foljambe, p. 129. **l. 22,** H.M.C. Dartmouth, pp. 32, 36. **l. 23,** Baschet, 1.5.79. **l. 27,** Ailesbury, I, 36. **l. 31,** *Parl. Hist.*, IV, 1125. **l. 40,** Grey, VII, 150–51.

158 **l. 17,** *Parl. Hist.*, IV, 1128; Grey, VII, 158–59. **l. 24,** *Parl. Hist.*, IV, 1133; Grey, VII, 243. **l. 33,** *ibid.*, VI, 148. **l. 36,** *Parl. Hist.*, IV, 1182, 1190; S.P. Charles II, p. 177.

159 **l. 1,** *Parl. Hist.*, IV, 1131; Grey, VII, 236. **l. 9,** *Parl. Hist.*, IV, 1136; Grey, VII, 285 n. **l. 16,** *Parl. Hist.* and Grey, *loc. cit.* **l. 19,** *Parl. Hist.*, IV, 1149; Grey, VII, 345. **l. 24,** *Clar. Corresp.*, I, 44; Dalrymple, I, 300, 301. **l. 28,** *Parl. Hist.*, IV, 1135.

160 **l. 28,** Life, I, 551–52. (This letter is clearly genuine in substance, for it is mentioned in James's letter to Legge of May 18/28, and is also similar in content to that letter.)

161 **l. 10,** H.M.C. Dartmouth, pp. 34–35. **l. 16,** Dalrymple, I, 302. **l. 22,** *e.g.*, H.M.C. Foljambe, pp. 129–32. **l. 30,** H.M.C. Rep. XIV, App., Pt. ix, p. 405. **l. 34,** Rochester, *The Farewell.*

162 **l. 4,** Dryden, *Absalom and Achitophel.* **l. 7,** Clar., Life, II, 252–56. **l. 11,** Pepys, 22.2.63/64. **l. 12,** *ibid.*, 16.12.66. **l. 14,** *ibid.*, 10.10.62, 4.5.63, 14.5.63, 15.5.63, 11.9.67. **l. 16,** *ibid.*, 4.5.63. **l. 30,** Baschet, 4.5.63, 14.5.63, 15.5.63, 11.9.67. **l. 16,** *ibid.*, 4.5.63, 22.2.63/64. **l. 19,** Macpherson, I, 44. **l. 22,** Buckingham, p. 19. **l. 30,** Baschet, 18.3.69; Mignet, III, 79, 80. **l. 35,** *Instr. Données*, XXV, 97. **l. 42,** Williamson, I, 119.

163 **l. 9,** Williamson, II, 72. **l. 16,** Macpherson, I, 73; H.M.C. Dartmouth, p. 35. **l. 19,** Life, I, 446; Macpherson, I, 52. **l. 28,** *ibid.*, p. 52, 74. **l. 29,** Buckingham, p. 19. **l. 32,** Essex, I, 261. **Note,** Evelyn, 18.8.73; Life, I, 481.

164 **l. 3,** Buckingham, II, 37. **l. 5,** Cal. S.P., 1673–75, p. 490. **l. 7,** Reresby, pp. 136, 176. **l. 12,** Cal. S.P., 1678, p. 358. **l. 16,** Baschet, 24.11.78. **l. 18,** Reresby, p. 176. **l. 23,** H.M.C. Ormonde, IV, 341; H.M.C. Dartmouth, p. 36; Hatton, I, 177. **l. 27,** Life, I, 559. **l. 32,** *loc. cit.*

PAGE

l. **35**, Burnet, I, 472–73; Macpherson, I, 93; *Parl. Hist.*, IV, 1206, Dalrymple, I, i, App., p. 127. **Note**, Sprat, p. 149.

165 l. **5**, H.M.C. Dartmouth, pp. 30, 31, 33; Cal. S.P., 1679–80, pp. 123, 186. l. **11**, H.M.C. Dartmouth, p. 37; Cal. S.P., 1679–80, p. 231. l. **15**, H.M.C. Rep. VII, App., p. 532. l. **22**, H.M.C. Ormonde, IV, 542. l. **28**, H.M.C. Dartmouth, pp. 31, 32; H.M.C. Ormonde, *loc. cit.* l. **35**, Add. MSS., 32095, f. 196 (I am indebted for this reference to Pollock, *Popish Plot*). l. **37**, *Parl. Hist.*, IV, 1132; Reresby, p. 156. l. **41**, H.M.C. Ormonde, IV, 542.

166 l. **2**, Life, I, 555; H.M.C. Dartmouth, pp. 31, 33; H.M.C. Rep. VII, App., p. 472. l. **6**, H. Sidney, I, 122. l. **14**, Life, 564; Macpherson, I, 93; Temple, II, 517–18.

167 l. **19**, Carte MSS., 232, f. 51, quoted Winston Churchill, *Marlborough, His Life and Times*, I, 56, cf. an inexact account in H.M.C. Rep., XIII, App., vii, p. 21; Cal. S.P., 1679–80, p. 234. l. **26**, Life, I, 565; H. Sidney, I, 101. l. **32**, Dalrymple, I, 327. l. **36**, *Parl. Hist.*, IV, 1154. l. **41**, Cal. S.P., 1679–80, p. 240; Dalrymple, I, 328; H.M.C. Ormonde, IV, 536.

168 l. **3**, Cal. S.P., 18.9.79. l. **9**, Reresby, p. 185; Luttrell, I, 21; H.M.C. Ormonde, *loc. cit.* l. **14**, Savile, p. 123. l. **18**, Life, I, 563–64; Prinsterer, V, 457; Dalrymple, I, 331. l. **22**, Luttrell, I, 21; Cal. S.P., 1679–80, p. 251. l. **27**, H.M.C. Dartmouth, p. 137; H.M.C. Foljambe, p. 139. l. **32**, *loc. cit.* l. **35**, Life, I, 573.

169 l. **1**, Luttrell, I, 179, 241, 312, 323; H.M.C. Rutland, II, 53; Add. MSS. 6308, f. 39. l. **27**, Luttrell, I, 24; Hatton, I, 47–49; Wood, II; Reresby, p. 261; H.M.C. Ormonde, IV, 551; H.M.C. Rep. VII, App., p. 476; "A True Account of the Invitation and Entertainment of the Duke of York. . . ."

170 l. **8**, Campana, I, 302.

171 l. **1**, *Parl. Hist.*, IV, 1154. l. **13**, Life, I, 574. l. **21**, *loc. cit.* l. **27**, Cal. S.P., 1679–80, p. 271. l. **30**, *ibid.*, p. 272. l. **33**, A. Sidney, pp. 155–56.

172 l. **19**, H.M.C. Ormonde, V, 231, 234–35; Luttrell, I, 25–27; H.M.C. Foljambe, p. 140; Reresby, pp. 190, 191 and note. l. **26**, Cal. S.P., 1679–80, p. 278; Life, I, 575; H. Sidney, I, 191; Bulstrode, pp. 308–9. l. **31**, Reresby, pp. 191–92. l. **38**, H.M.C. Rep. VII, App., p. 495.

173 l. **1**, H.M.C. Dartmouth, p. 42; *Clar. Corresp.*, I, 82. l. **6**, Hay, pp. 26–29. l. **14**, Lauderdale, III, 184. l. **21**, Hay, *loc. cit.* l. **41**, *loc. cit.*

174 l. **2**, Law, *Memorials*, p. 205; Luttrell, I, 138. l. **6**, Cal. S.P., 6.10.79; l. **8**, *ibid.*, 1673–75, p. 250. l. **12**, *Decisions of the Lords of Session*, I, 67; Cal. S.P., 30.11.79; Wodrow, III, 175; Lauderdale, III, 181–86. l. **14**, Life, I, 575–78, 580; Burnet, I, 510–11; Hay, p. 29. l. **28**, H.M.C. Dartmouth, p. 41. l. **31**, Life, II, 634; Dalrymple, I, 363; *Familiar Letters*, 6.6.81, 20.8.81.

175 l. **2**, Reg. P.C. Scot., VI, 293. l. **12**, Macpherson, I, 202. l. **19**, Cal. S.P., 1679–80, p. 399; Hay, pp. 32–33. l. **21**, H.M.C. Rep. VI, App., p. 725. l. **28**, Wodrow, III, 233. The Privy Council of Scotland had in 1674 more than forty members apart from those not resident in Scotland (Cal. S.P., 18.5.74), and there can hardly have been many less in 1680. Even allowing for absences from illness, etc., 28 seems a small number. l. **36**, H.M.C. Ormonde, IV, 480. l. **39**, Prinsterer, V, 435.

176 l. **3**, Cal. S.P., 1679–80, p. 399. l. **4**, Luttrell, I, 37, 38; H. Sidney, I, 301. l. **7**, Cal. S.P., 1679–80, p. 414. l. **9**, *ibid.*, p. 475. l. **20**, H. Sidney, II, 55; North, Lives (1826), II, 57. **Note 2**, Cal. S.P., 1694–95, pp. 118, 217.

177 l. **28**, Prinsterer, V, 415. l. **32**, H. Sidney, II, 173. l. **34**, Reresby, p. 193. **Note**, Haile, p. 72.

PAGE

178 **l. 3,** Burnet, I, 479; Reresby, *loc. cit.*; Prinsterer, V, 397, 400, 401, etc.; Baschet, 19.4.80, 6.6.80. **l. 6,** Prinsterer, V, 401. **l. 12,** H. Sidney, I, 259, 292. **l. 20,** Baschet, 15.4.80. **l. 25,** *ibid.*, 22.4.80. **l. 39,** Prinsterer, V, 393.

179 **l. 3,** H.M.C. Dartmouth, p. 38. **l. 9,** Cal. S.P., 1679–80, p. 240; Life, I, 578; Luttrell, I, 27; Prinsterer, V, 460. **l. 12,** Luttrell, I, 53, 56; Life, I, 579. **l. 17,** *ibid.*, I, 589–90; H.M.C. Finch, II, 76–77; Baschet, 6.5.80, 9.5.80, 13.5.80. **l. 23,** *ibid.*, 9.5.80. **l. 26,** Life, I, 590. **l. 41,** *ibid.*, p. 590–91; Luttrell, I, 49; *Parl. Hist.*, IV, 1274.

180 **l. 5,** Baschet, July 8–11.1680. **l. 9,** H. Sidney, I, 376, 187; Cal. S.P., 1679–80, p. 21. **l. 15,** Burnet, I, 487; Sacharissa, p. 258. **l. 16,** H.M.C. Dartmouth, p. 53; Prinsterer, V, 176. **l. 20,** Baschet, 3.8.80, 9.9.80. **l. 26,** *ibid.*, 11.6.80. **l. 37,** *ibid.*, 19.8.80. **Note,** H.M.C. Rutland, II, 46, Ruvigny to Louis, 20.1.76, quoted by Forneron, *Louise de Keroualle*; Baschet, 8.11.85.

181 **l. 8,** Baschet, July 15, Aug. 3–19.1680. **l. 12,** H. Sidney, II, 82; Prinsterer, V, 422. **l. 15,** Sacharissa, p. 278. **l. 21,** Baschet, 19.7.80. **l. 27,** Luttrell, I, 53, 56; Baschet, 22.8.80. **l. 30,** Prinsterer, V, 422. **l. 37,** Life, I, 593–95; H. Sidney, II, 104; Prinsterer, V, 423; Hatton, I, 238; Baschet, 18.10.80. **l. 41,** Prinsterer, V, 426.

182 **l. 5,** Life, I, 596; Prinsterer, V, 22, etc. **l. 13,** Dalrymple, I, 344. **l. 16,** Baschet, 31.10.80. **l. 20,** Reg. P.C. Scot., VI, 565; Wodrow, III, 238. **l. 26,** Life, I, 593; Dalrymple, I, 345.

183 **l. 3,** *Chron. Notes*, p. 3. **l. 12,** *Hist. Observes*, p. 5. **l. 19,** Reg. P.C. Scot., VI, 568; Lauderdale, III, 210, 211; Baschet, 10.10.80; *Decisions of the Lords of Session*, I, 114.

185 **l. 12,** Wodrow, III, 274. **l. 17,** H.M.C. Hamilton, pp. 148–49. **l. 31,** *Chron. Notes*, p. 11; Hay, p. 51. **l. 41,** Whytford to Innes, 2.12.80, quoted Hay, p. 53.

186 **l. 2,** Burnet, I, 510–12. **l. 6,** Reresby, p. 239. **l. 17,** Burnet, I, 583. **l. 36,** Macaulay, *History of England* (1855), I, 271.

187 **l. 2,** *ibid.*, p. 498. **l. 6,** Wodrow, III, V, sect. 11. **l. 9,** Macaulay, *op. cit.*, p. 558. **l. 17,** H.M.C. Rep., XV, App., Pt. VIII, p. 205. **l. 29,** Law, *Memorials*, p. 202.

188 **l. 2,** Lauderdale, III, 223–25. **l. 5,** H.M.C. Dartmouth, p. 63. **l. 6,** Luttrell, I, 113. **l. 7,** H.M.C. Dartmouth, p. 66. **l. 14,** *Hist. Notices*, I, 301. **l. 16,** *ibid.*, p. 310.

190 **l. 2,** Wodrow, III, 299; Burnet, I, 513; Hay, p. 21. **l. 11,** Dartmouth's note to Burnet, II, 44. **l. 30,** Wodrow, III, 300. **Note 1,** *Diary of T. Burton*, II, 279, quoted by Sir C. Firth, *E.H.R.*, LII, 642. **Note 2,** Foxcroft, I, 119–20.

191 **l. 6,** Wodrow, III, 314. **l. 9,** *ibid.*, p. 315; *Hist. Notices*, p. 335. **l. 15,** *Decisions of the Lords of Session*, I, 166; *Hist. Observes*, pp. 51, 184, 342, 434, 533; Suppl. to Burnet, pp. 5–7, 83, 84. **l. 25,** Life, I, 706; Wodrow, III, 291. **l. 41,** *ibid.*, p. 318.

192 **l. 3,** Life, I, 710–11; Burnet, I, 521; *Hist. Observes*, p. 55. **l. 10,** Wodrow, III, 319. **l. 13,** Life, I, 709; Prinsterer, V, 538. **l. 19,** Wodrow, III, 359. **l. 27,** H.M.C. Dartmouth, p. 41 (letter misdated). **l. 37,** Law, *Memorials*, p. 210; Prinsterer, V, 538.

193 **l. 12,** Life, I, 710. **l. 26,** Baschet, 31.10.80; cf. Wodrow, III, 236–37. **l. 30,** Dalrymple, I, 351; Baschet, *loc. cit.* **l. 36,** Dalrymple, I, 364. **Note,** H.M.C. Kenyon, p. 125.

194 **l. 3,** Christie, II, 383 n. **l. 10,** *ibid.*, App., p. cv; *North Examen*, p. 89. **l. 17,** Dalrymple, I, 321. **l. 20,** *ibid.*, p. 319. **l. 24,** *ibid.*, p. 363. **l. 31,** *ibid.*, p. 356. **l. 37,** *Instr. Données*, XXV, 267.

195 **l. 2,** *loc. cit.* l. 4, Louis to Barrillon, 24.1.81, quoted by Ogg. **l. 7,** Dalrymple, I, 364. **l. 22,** *Familiar Letters*, 6.6.81. l. 28, *ibid.*, 20.8.81. **l. 29,** *ibid.*, 18.7.81; Luttrell, I, 112; H.M.C. Dartmouth,

PAGE

p. 65. l. **31,** *Familiar Letters*, 26.11.81. l. **34,** Prinsterer, V, 276. l. **36,** *ibid.*, p. 538; *Familiar Letters,* Dec. 1681, 11.1.81/82. l. **39,** *ibid.*, 18.10.81, 19.2.81/82.

196 l. **1,** Prinsterer, V, 287. l. **9,** *ibid.*, p. 497. l. **11,** *Familiar Letters,* 31.1.81/82; Hay quotes *Archæologia Scotica* for a further reference to James's golf. l. **12,** H.M.C. Bucc. & Q., II, 137. l. **14,** *Familiar Letters,* 11.1.81/82. l. **17,** Life, I, 670; Prinsterer, V, 483; Baschet, 13.3.81; H.M.C. Hamilton, p. 198. l. **25,** Campana, I, 353.

197 l. **4,** H.M.C. Dartmouth, pp. 43–64; a great many of these letters are misdated. l. **7,** Life, I, 659, 679. l. **15,** *ibid.*, p. 616; *Parl. Hist.*, IV, 1161; Grey, VII, 358 *et seq.* l. **22,** Life, I, 601 *et seq.*; C.J., 26.10.80; *Parl. Hist.*, IV, 1162, 1175; Grey, VII, 358, 413. l. **34,** *ibid.*, p. 396. **Note,** *ibid.*, p. 399.

198 l. **2,** *ibid.*, p. 405. l. **3,** *Parl. Hist.*, IV, 1192. l. **9,** *ibid.*, 1186; Grey, VII, 409–10, gives the speech similar in substance, but in different words.

199 l. **3,** *Parl. Hist.*, IV, 1195–96. l. **10,** *ibid.*, 1206; Grey, VII, 448–49. l. **20,** *ibid.*, p. 401–2; cf. *Parl. Hist.*, IV, 1181. l. **23,** C.J.; Grey, VII, 477; *Parl. Hist.*, IV, 1215. l. **25,** Reresby, p. 203. l. **39,** quoted Foxcroft, I, 241.

200 l. **19,** Reresby, *loc. cit.*; Burnet, I, 482; H.M.C. Finch, II, 96. l. **26,** L.J., 16.11.80. l. **32,** Grey, VIII, 21–23, 41–51; *Parl. Hist.*, IV, 1221; H.M.C. Finch, II, 96, 97. l. **33,** Grey, VIII, 38–40, 73–97, 233. l. **36,** *ibid.*, VII, 460–71, VIII, 61–71. l. **38,** *ibid.*, VIII, 52–60; *Parl. Hist.*, IV, 1216. l. **40,** *ibid.*, 1293–94.

201 l. **4,** Reresby, p. 209. l. **7,** *Parl. Hist.*, 1231–32. l. **9,** *ibid.*, 1279 et seq.; H.M.C. Finch, 100–1. l. **20,** *Parl. Hist.*, IV, 1291 and note. l. **41,** H.M.C. Dartmouth, pp. 53–54.

202 l. **7,** Life, I, 718. l. **19,** Burnet, I, 398. l. 21, H.M.C. Dartmouth, p. 36. l. **27,** *ibid.*, pp. 44, 46, 47, 60, 62; Temple, II, 527; Reresby, p. 239; H.M.C. Ormonde, VI, 274. l. **30,** H.M.C. Dartmouth, pp. 62, 65, 66. l. **37,** *ibid.*, pp. 40, 41.

203 l. **8,** H.M.C. Dartmouth, p. 58; *Clar. Corresp.*, I, 48. l. **12,** H.M.C. Dartmouth, p. 49. l. **19,** Life, I, 613, 629 *et seq.*, 635, 642, 645, 655, 659, etc. l. **21,** H.M.C. Dartmouth, pp. 40, 44, 45 (2 places), 54, 57, 58, 59, 60 (2 places). l. **26,** *ibid.*, p. 42. l. **38,** *ibid.*, p. 45.

204 l. **9,** Burnet, I, 498; Reresby, p. 220; Lindsey, MSS., p. 428. l. **20,** Christie, II, App., p. cxvi; H.M.C. Rep. XII, App. IX, pp. 83, 84. l. **24,** *Parl. Hist.*, IV, 1339. l. **36,** H.M.C. Dartmouth, p. 57, see also following letter.

205 l. **9,** Life, I, 678. l. **16,** Macpherson, I, 117–18. l. **22,** Dalrymple, I, 364. l. **33,** *ibid.*, p. 367. l. **39,** H.M.C. Dartmouth, p. 31.

206 l. **6,** H.M.C. Dartmouth, p. 65. l. **21,** Sitwell, *The First Whig.* l. 22, Life, I, 693.

207 l. **1,** Prinsterer, I, 490, 492; H. Sidney, II, 123. l. **2,** *ibid.*, p. 177. l. **5,** Life, I, 690 *et seq.* l. **8,** Campana, I, 378. l. **23,** Prinsterer, V, 484. l. **37,** *ibid.*, pp. 493–94.

208 l. **1,** *ibid.*, p. 494. l. **7,** H. Sidney, II, 143. l. **9,** *ibid.*, p. 93. l. **12,** *ibid.*, II, 120. l. **15,** *ibid.*, p. 126. l. 18, *ibid.*, II, 138. l. **24,** Prinsterer, V, 589; see also as a general reference Temple's long letter to William of 23.12.80, commencing Prinsterer, *loc. cit.* l. **27,** Life, I, 626–27. l. **34,** H.M.C. Dartmouth, p. 47 (both letters are antedated by a year).

209 l. **19,** H.M.C. Dartmouth, p. 36. l. **28,** *ibid.*, p. 40. l. **34,** Life, I, 632, cf. H.M.C. Dartmouth, p. 55. **Note 1,** Clar. S.P., II, 284. **Note 2,** Grey, VII, 162.

210 l. **3,** Life, I, 699. l. **7,** *loc. cit.*; Campana, I, 361; Wood, II, 440. l. **18,** Life, I, 701. l. **20,** Reresby, p. 258. l. **29,** H.M.C. Dartmouth, p. 67. l. **32,** Life, I, 678. l. **34,** Dalrymple, I, i, App., p. 177.

PAGE

211 l. **7,** Reresby, p. 239. l. **10,** *ibid.*, p. 244. l. **16,** *Hist. Notices*, p. 327.

212 l. **30,** Life, I, 724–29; H.M.C. Rep. III, App., p. 289; H.M.C. Ormonde, pp. 229, 271.

213 l. **8,** Luttrell, I, 171; cf. Life, I, 727; H.M.C. Rutland, II, 66; H.M.C. Rep. VII, App., p. 533. l. **10,** Reresby, p. 259. l. **12,** H.M.C. Ormonde, VI, 357. l. **24,** H.M.C. Rutland, II, 69. l. **27,** *Hist. Notices*, I, 354.

214 l. **15,** Prinsterer, V, 550. l. **19,** Life, I, 731; Macpherson, I, 730. l. **22,** Churchill, *Marlborough*, I, 730.

215 l. **4,** Dalrymple, I, i, 128; cf. *Stuart Papers* (Roxburgh), I, 371; *Clar. Corresp.*, I, 70 *et seq.* l. **22,** Life, *loc. cit.* l. **25,** *Chron. Notes*, pp. 10, 24; *Hist. Observes*, p. 69. l. **28,** Life, I, 732–33; H.M.C. Rutland, II, 74; H.M.C. Buccleuch, I, 337. l. **30,** Luttrell, I, 189. l. **33,** *ibid.*, pp. 214–30; H.M.C. Rep. XV, App., Pt. viii, pp. 84, 85, etc. l. **37,** *ibid.*, p. 171; Life, I, 735; Prinsterer, V, 559.

216 l. **2,** *loc. cit.* l. **3,** Luttrell, I, 221. l. **4,** *ibid.*, p. 247; Reresby, p. 288. l. **11,** Hatton, II, 17; Life, I, 734. l. **26,** H.M.C. Rep. VII, App., p. 480. l. **34,** Life, I, 738; Luttrell, I, 241, 307, 310; Prinsterer, V, 586; Cal. T.B., 10.8.87; Bulstrode, p. 321.

217 l. **1,** H.M.C. Ormonde, VI, 444; H.M.C. Rep. VII, App., p. 533. l. **6,** H.M.C. Ormonde, VI, 452. l. **10,** Luttrell, I, 216, 219, 222, 230, 240. l. **19,** *ibid.*, p. 263; Cal. S.P., 1683, July to Dec., pp. 130, 211, 213, 249, 258, 383; H.M.C. Bucc. & Q., II, 193. l. **28,** H.M.C. Rep. XV, App., Pt. viii, p. 194. l. **32,** *ibid.*, VII, App., p. 263. **Note,** Christie, II, 271.

218 l. **5,** H.M.C. Rep. XV, App., Pt. viii, pp. 200, 201. l. **6,** Prinsterer, V, 579. l. **13,** Luttrell, I, 150, 293. l. **15,** H.M.C. Dartmouth, p. 39. l. **19,** Luttrell, I, 263. l. **27,** *ibid.*, p. 292; Life, I, 742; Reresby, p. 319; Dalrymple, I, i, App., p. 114; H.M.C. Rep. XI, App., Pt. viii, p. 199; H.M.C. Bucc. & Q., II, 168. l. **30,** P.C. Reg., 25.11.83. l. **33,** Luttrell, I, 293. **Note,** Bulstrode, p. 356.

219 l. **1,** P.C. Reg., 12.12.83; H.M.C. Rep. XV, App., Pt. viii, pp. 99–221; Sprat, pp. 151–57; Bulstrode, pp. 352–57; Dalrymple, I, i, 115–16; Welwood, pp. 110–20. l. **4,** H.M.C. Rep. XI, App., Pt. vi, p. 197. l. **7,** *ibid.*, p. 318; H.M.C. Rep., XV, App., Pt. viii, p. 205; H.M.C. Hamilton, p. 197. l. **9,** Dalrymple, I, i, App., p. 118; Prinsterer, V, 587. l. **30,** Burnet, I, 499–501. l. **34,** Luttrell, I, 259; Wood, III, 45–54. **Note,** Welwood, App., XIV; *E.H.R.*, XX, 730–35.

220 l. **2,** H.M.C. Kenyon, pp. 163 *et seq.* l. **9,** Wood, III, 72. l. **22,** *Hist. Notices*, I, 354. l. **27,** H.M.C. Bucc. & Q., II, 110. l. **30,** Macky, p. 243.

221 l. **10,** H.M.C. Bucc. & Q., II, 119–63. l. **15,** *ibid.*, p. 129. l. **23,** *ibid.*, pp. 130, 131, 138, 144. l. **24,** *ibid.*, pp. 137, 160. l. **28,** *ibid.*, p. 163. l. **31,** *loc. cit.*

222 l. **1,** H.M.C. Laing, I, 426. l. **11,** H.M.C. Rep. XV, App., Pt. viii, pp. 168–215. l. **14,** Burnet, I, 582–3. l. **27,** *loc. cit.* l. **30,** Reresby, p. 329; cf. Welwood, pp. 119, 129. l. **32,** Bulstrode, p. 346. l. **36,** Life, I, 745; Evelyn, 12.5.84; Reresby, pp. 338–39; Luttrell, I, 308; Prinsterer, V, 586. **Note,** *Hist. Notices*, II, 745.

223 l. **6,** Off. Etr. Angleterre, 152, f. 292, quoted Ogg, p. 654. l. **10,** Life, I, 727. l. **22,** *ibid.*, p. 746. l. **27,** *ibid.*, p. 736. l. **41,** *loc. cit.*; Fox, App., p. viii; *Spalding Club Miscellany*, Vol. III; *Stuart Papers* (Roxburgh), p. 372; H.M.C. Stuart Rep., VI, App., p. 2; H.M.C. Bucc. & Q., II, 37, 38, 199, 203, 204, 206–10.

224 l. **3,** Luttrell, I, 272. l. **7,** Life, I, 745; Dalrymple, I, Pt. i, App., p. 129. l. **10,** Burnet, I, 562. l. **15,** H.M.C. Rep. XV, App., viii, p. 189.

228 l. **26,** Fox, App., pp. xi to xv. l. **30,** Evelyn, 6.2.84/85. l. **32,** Luttrell,

PAGE

I, 420. **l. 36,** *Stuart Papers* (Roxburgh), pp. 254–61, 287–88. **l. 37,** Life, I, 746–49.

229 **l. 21,** Christie, II, 313. **l. 43,** I am indebted to Mr. Alan Fremantle for this parallel.

234 **Note 2,** *Stuart Papers* (Roxburgh), II, 393; Reresby, p. 423; Campana, II, 124; *Ellis Corresp.*, I, 82, 271, 293.

235 **l. 10,** *Instr. Données*, XXV, 309. **l. 13,** *ibid.*, p. 313. **l. 18,** Baschet, 7.2.86. **l. 25,** Bloxam, p. 99. **l. 32,** North Lives, II, 153.

236 **l. 7,** *Instr. Données*, XXV, 312–13. **l. 21,** Ailesbury, I, 126. **l. 38,** *Instr. Données*, XXV, 340. **l. 40,** *loc. cit.*

237 **l. 4,** Campana, II, 28; *Hist. Observes*, p. 152; Soudres, I, 199. **l. 8,** *Instr. Données*, XXV, 306. **l. 12,** Add MSS. 28,569, f. 54. **l. 15,** *Instr. Données*, XXV, 312. **l. 19,** Campana, II, 27, 112; Dalrymple, Pt. I, Bk. II, App., p. 55, and Bks. III and IV, p. 103; H.M.C. Rep. XII, Pt. V, App., p. 109. **l. 28,** Dalrymple, Pt. I, Bk. II, App., p. 28. **l. 34,** *Instr. Données*, XXV, 307–8; Campana, II, 19; H.M.C. Ormonde, VII, 323; *Hist. Observes*, p. 152. **l. 36,** Campana, II, 89; H.M.C. Rutland, II, 99. **l. 38,** Baschet, 5.4.85; *Hist. Observes*, *loc. cit.*

238 **l. 2,** Cal. T.B., 84, 102, 470 and *passim*; Life, II, 7–8; Haile, p.122. **l. 35,** La Fayette, p. 209. **Note 2,** *Le Siècle de Louis XIV*, Ch. XV.

240 **l. 21,** Steele, p. 457; S. P. James II, 6.2.84/85. **Note,** quoted Ranke, IV, 215.

241 **l. 2,** H.M.C. Rep. XII, App. VII, p. 197. **l. 5,** S.P., *loc. cit.*; Evelyn, 6.2.84/85; Life, II, 2–5. **l. 13,** Steele, p. 457; Burnet, I, 620. **l. 20,** Campana, II, 6. **l. 22,** Fox, App., p. xvi. **l. 23,** Evelyn, 10.2.84/85. **l. 28,** S.P. James II, 13.2.84/85. **l. 34,** H.M.C. Rep. XIV, Pt. VIII, App., p. 111. **l. 37,** H.M.C. Rep. XI, Pt. vii, p. 199. **l. 39,** H.M.C. Ormonde, VII, 325. **l. 42,** S.P. James II, f. 27.

242 **l. 7,** Wood, II, 127–30. **l. 13,** Welwood, p. 154. **l. 19,** Calamy, *Account of his own Life*. **l. 24,** Fox, App., p. xvi. **l. 31,** *ibid.*, p. xxxii. **l. 32,** H.M.C. Ormonde, VII, 317. **l. 36,** Campana, II, 16. **l. 40,** Baschet, 22.2.84/85; Fox, App., p. xxxv.

243 **l. 3,** *Clar. Corresp.*, I, 109, 110; H.M.C. Ormonde, VII, 325–26. **l. 9** S.P., James II, 7.2.84/85. **l. 11,** *ibid.*, various dates; for precautions at Carlisle see H.M.C. Rep. XII, App. vii, p. 196. **l. 14,** Fox, App., p. xvi; Reresby, pp. 349–52; North, Lives, II, 108–9. **l. 18,** Fox, App., p. lxxviii. **l. 22,** *Parl. Hist.*, IV, 1208. **l. 25,** Grey, VII, *Parl. Hist.*, IV. **l. 35,** *Life of Seth Ward.*

244 **l. 2,** Oldmixon, II, 694. **l. 5,** Evelyn, 14.2.84/85. **l. 6,** Life, II, 6; Add. MSS., 28569, f. 54. **l. 13,** Luttrell, I, 330. **l. 16,** S.P. James II. **l. 31,** *London Gazette*, Feb. 12–16; Campana, II, 11; Fox, App., p. xxxiv; Evelyn, *loc. cit.*; Baschet, 22.2.84/85; H.M.C. Ormonde, VII, 322–23. **Note,** Bramston, p. 200.

245 **l. 4,** Bramston, *loc. cit.* **l. 9,** North, Lives, II, 110. **l. 10,** Steele, p. 458. **l. 14,** Ailesbury, I, 125–26. **l. 23,** North, Lives, *loc. cit.* **l. 27,** Bramston, pp. 200, 201. **l. 21,** Steele, p. 458. **l. 34,** Luttrell, I, 328; Evelyn, 19.2.84/85. **l. 41,** Haile, p. 69; Williamson, II, 106; H.M.C. Rep. VII, App., p. 467.

246 **l. 3,** Life, I, 483; Evelyn, 30.3.73. **l. 4,** H.M.C. Bath, II, 98; Thurloe, I, 619, etc. **l. 10,** Campana, II, 17. **l. 12,** Reresby, p. 356. **l. 16,** Life, II, 79; Evelyn, 15.2.84/85, 19.2.84/85, 5.3.84/85. **l. 20.** Baschet, 20.9.85; Campana, II, 37–38. **l. 23,** Evelyn, 18.10.85, **l. 26,** *L.C.C. Survey of London*, XIII, 102–8; Wood, III, 201. **l. 30,** *L.C.C. Survey*, *loc. cit.* **l. 32,** Cal. T.B., VIII, 1326. **l. 37,** Fox. App., p. liv. **l. 38,** Baschet, 22.2.84/85. **Note 2,** " Leader," 16.1.46,

247 **l. 10,** Fox, App., p. xxxiii. **l. 16,** Evelyn, 15.2.84/85, 5.3.84/85. **l. 24,** Fox, App., pp. xxxvii–xxxviii, xliv. **l. 29,** *Instr. Données*, XXV, 319–20. **l. 41,** Fox, App., pp. lxvi–lxvii.

PAGE

248 **l. 1,** *Ellis Corresp.*, I, 91. **l. 13,** Fox, App., p. xvi. **l. 22,** Reresby, p. 360. **l. 36,** Campana, II, 19; Fox, App., p. xxxiv; Baschet, 8.3.85; Add. MSS., 34508, f. 83. **Note,** H.M.C. Ormonde, VII, 323.

249 **l. 9,** Fox, App., p. xvii. **l. 13,** Ailesbury, I, 98–99; Burnet, I, 258, 484; II, 117. **l. 18,** Ailesbury, I, 104; Barrillon, quoted Ranke, IV, 281. **l. 22,** Fox, App., p. xxxiv; Baschet, 23.4.85. **l. 25,** Fox, App., p. cxliii. **l. 32,** H.M.C. Dartmouth, p. 58; Prinsterer, V, 440. **l. 40,** Baschet, 19.2.85.

250 **l. 2,** Fox, App., p. xvii. **l. 8,** *ibid.*, p. l. **l. 10,** Baschet, 26.3.85. **l. 12,** Fox, App., p. cix. **l. 18,** *ibid.*, p. xxv. **l. 21,** *ibid.*, pp. cxliii *et seq.*, cxlviii; Campana, II, 113. **l. 26,** H.M.C. Stuart, VI, 5; Barrillon 25.2.85, quoted Lingard. **l. 30,** Burnet, I, 621 and Dartmouth's note; Campana, II, 143; Fox, App., pp. xxxiv, l. **l. 35,** *ibid.*, pp. xvi, xxix, xxxiv. **l. 37,** *ibid.*, p. xxxviii; P.C. Reg., 18.2.84/85.

251 **l. 7,** Reresby, p. 360. **l .20,** Burnet, I, 621. **l. 28,** Fox, App., p. xxxviii.

252 **l. 15,** *ibid.*, pp. xlvii–xlviii.

253 **l. 6,** Fox, App., p. xvii. **l. 13,** Baschet, 19.2.85. **l. 24,** *loc. cit.* **l. 30,** Fox, App., p. xxvii. **l. 32,** *ibid.*, p. xli. **l. 38,** Luttrell, I, 341.

254 **l. 5,** S.P. James II. **l. 17,** H.M.C. Rutland, II, 86.

255 **l. 3,** The above and following paragraphs are based on documents in S.P. James II, in the Public Record Office; some details are taken from authorities quoted in Porrit, *Unreformed House of Commons*, II, 396; see also Baschet, 2.4.85; Ailesbury, I, 99–101. **l. 9,** H.M.C. Frankland-Russell-Astley, pp. 59–60. **l. 10,** *loc. cit.*; Bramston, p. 172. **l. 33,** *Letters of Eminent Literary Men*, ed. Sir Henry Ellis (Camden Society), p. 190. **Note 1,** H.M.C. Bucc. & Q., II, 215.

256 **l. 4,** Burnet, I, 626; Coke, 19.5.85, quoted Somerville, *Political Transactions*. **l. 9,** Baschet, 29.3.85, 9.4.85, 5.4.85, 23.4.85. **l. 14,** *ibid.*, 5.4.85. **l. 23,** Fox, App., pp. xxxix, xl. **l. 27,** *loc. cit.* **l. 32,** Baschet, 9.4.85. **Note,** Fox, App., p. lxiii.

257 **l. 2,** Reresby, p. 362. **l. 4,** O. F. Morshead in *The Listener* of May 12, 1937. **l. 10,** Life, II, 10; Campana, II, 63. **l. 14,** Burnet, I, 628. **l. 18,** Campana, II, 62. **l. 21,** H. Sidney, Introduction. **l. 26,** Burnet, *loc. cit.* **l. 31,** Baschet, 2.4.85. **l. 33,** Adda, 1.2.86. **l. 35,** D'Orleans, IV, 289. **Note,** Cal. T.B., VIII, 70.

258 **l. 2,** Reresby, p. 367. **l. 10,** *ibid.*, p. 360; Campana, II, 39. **l. 39,** *Instr. Données*, XXV, 311–12; Baschet, 15.3.85, 19.3.85, 9.4.85, 19.4.85, 23.4.85. **l. 16,** Cal. T.B., VIII, 176. **l. 33,** Fox, App., p. xxxiii.

259 **l. 1,** *ibid.*, pp. xliv–xlv. **l. 8,** *Instr. Données*, XXV, 312. **l. 35,** Coventry to Halifax, 29.5.77, quoted Foxcroft, I, 129 n.

260 **l. 12,** Fox, App., p. lx. **l. 27,** Baschet, 19.4.85. **l. 28,** *ibid.*, 30.4.85. **l. 31,** *ibid.*, 11.10.85, 18.10.85.

261 **l. 9,** *ibid.*, 26.3.85; Louis to Barrillon, 4.4.85 (quoted Lingard), Bonrepaus to Seignelay, 18.3.86 (quoted Mazure); Documents quoted by Mazure, II, 188, 192, 251–55. **l. 17,** Avaux Holland, IV, 346–47 and *passim*. **l. 20,** Bulstrode, pp. 377, 384, 425–26.

262 **l. 6,** Avaux, Holland, IV, 334; Baschet, 19.3.85. **l. 12,** *ibid.*, 22.2.85. **l. 21,** Fox, App., p. xli. **l. 23,** *ibid.*, p. lv. **l. 28,** *ibid.*, pp. xxxv, xxxvi. **Note,** Avaux Holland, IV, 283.

263 **l. 1,** Fox, App., p. xl. **l. 16,** *ibid.*, p. xliii. **l. 24,** H.M.C. Bucc. & Q., II, 46. **l. 30,** H.M.C. Ormonde, VII, 334. **l. 33,** *ibid.*, p. 335.

264 **l. 6,** Avaux, Holland, IV, 328. **l. 10,** *ibid.*, p. 272; Fox, App., p. xlii. **l. 21,** Baschet, 5.4.85. **l. 25,** Fox, App., p. cviii.

265 **l. 7,** Dalrymple, I, i, 75; Pt. I, Bk. II, App., p. 13; Supp. to Burnet, p. 161; Bourepaus to Seignelay, 14.2.87. **l. 10,** Dalrymple, Part I, Bk. II, pp. 18, 19. **l. 23,** Dalrymple, *loc. cit.* **Note 1,** Avaux, Holland, IV, 338; Prinsterer, V, 502, 506, 508, 525.

PAGE

267 l. **17,** Fox, App., p. xlv. l. **19,** Baschet, 23.4.85. l. **26,** Barrillon, 12.3.85, quoted Ranke, IV, 229 n.; Baschet, 15.3.85, 19.3.85. l. **28,** *ibid.*, 9.4.85.

268 l. **5,** *ibid.*, 19.4.85. l. **10,** Fox, App., p. lxix. l. **12,** Baschet, 23.4.85. l. **24,** *Instr. Données*, XXV, 311–12. l. **32,** Bramston, p. 196.

269 l. **13,** C.J., 22.5.85.

270 l. **2,** Evelyn, 22.5.85. l. **5,** Bramston, p. 199. l. **8,** C.J., 22.5.85. **Note,** North, Lives, II, 119 n.

271 l. **15,** Evelyn, 22.5.85; Fox, App., pp. xc, xciii; Coke, quoted Oldmixon, II, 698; Burnet, I, 639. l. **24,** Lonsdale, pp. 5–7. l. **35,** Fox, App., p. xc.

272 l. **5,** Reresby, pp. 368–69; *Parl. Hist.*, IV, 1357. l. **25,** Fox, App., p. xcvi. l. **32,** C.J., 26.5.85; Reresby, p. 369. l. **39,** L.J., 30.5.85.

273 l. **1,** Fox, App., p. xcix. l. **12,** *ibid.*, pp. xcvi–xcvii. l. **29,** *loc. cit.* l. **34,** C.J., 30.5.85. **Note,** *Memoirs de Louis XIV*, ed. Dreyes, II, 7.

274 l. **6,** Life, I, 51–55; cf. W. A. Shaw, *Introduction to Cal. T.B.*, VIII, pp. xii, xiii. l. **11,** L.J. and C.J., June 13–19, 26; Dutch Despatch, 26.6.85; Reresby, p. 374. l. **35,** Burnet, I, 639 and notes; Fox, App., p. xci.

275 l. **13,** Avaux Holland, IV, 265. l. **21,** *ibid.*, p. 280. l. **29,** *ibid.*, p. 284. **Note,** Bulstrode, pp. 377, 384, 425–26.

276 l. **16,** Avaux Holland, V, 16–20. l. **31,** Fox, App., pp. lxxxi *et seq.*

277 l. **1,** Japikse, I, i, 20–29. l. **7,** Dalrymple, Pt. I, Bk. II, App., pp. 22–23. l. **10,** *ibid.*, pp. 23, 24. l. **19,** *ibid.*, p. 26. l. **24,** Life, II, 32. l. **30,** Japikse, *loc. cit.* **Note 2,** Avaux Holland, V, 38–39.

278 l. **4,** H.M.C. Bucc. & Q., p. 41. l. **10,** S.P. James II. l. **13,** H.M.C. Rep. III, App., p. 97. l. **19,** *loc. cit.* l. **32,** cf. Churchill to Clarendon, 4.7.85; *Clar. Corresp.*, I, 141.

279 l. **9,** Life, II, 35. l. **27,** Bramston, pp. 187–88; cf. Burnet, I, 644 and Dartmouth's note. **Note,** Reresby, p. 384.

280 l. **3,** Dalrymple, Pt. I, Bk. II, App., p. 25. l. **8,** Macpherson, I, 144–46; Life, II, 26; cf. Campana, II, 70. l. **19,** Bramston, p. 207. l. **23,** Wood, III, 164. l. **25,** Evelyn, 6.9.85, 31.10.85. l. **30,** *Parl. Hist.*, IV, 1374; Lans. MSS., 253; Harl. MSS., 7187; but see Lady Russell's letter of 15.1.85/86. **Note,** Baschet, 13.9.85.

281 l. **4,** Hatton, II, 60; cf. Lonsdale, pp. 12–13. l. **7,** Ailesbury, I, 121–22; Life, II, 43–44. l. **12,** North, Lives, II, 125. l. **17,** S.P. James II, 22.9.85. l. **22,** Evelyn, Sept. 15–17, 1685; Baschet, 24.9.85. l. **27,** Dalrymple, Pt. I, Bk. II, App., p. 52. l. **32,** *loc. cit.*

282 l. **11,** Macpherson, I, 144–45; Life, II, 43. l. **25,** D'Orleans, preface; cf. Ailesbury, I, 121–22. l. **32,** S.P. James II. l. **39,** Bramston, p. 207.

285 l. **7,** Fox, App., p. civ. l. **23,** *ibid.*, p. cvi. l. **26,** *ibid.*, p. cxvii. **Note,** Bramston, pp. 205–6; Reresby, p. 390.

286 l. **5,** Fox, App., p. xx. l. **11,** Burnet, I, 652. l. **35,** Chesterfield, pp. 296–97; cf. Reresby, p. 393; Campana, II, 84; Harl. MSS., 6584, f. 127 (*a*). l. **41,** Fox, App., p. cxliv; P.C. Reg., 4.12.85.

287 l. **5,** Baschet, 26.3.85. l. **7,** Fox, App., p. cvii. l. **9,** *ibid.*, p. cix. l. **14,** Burnet, I, 684. l. **42,** Fox, App., pp. cxliii *et seq.*

288 l. **3,** H.M.C. Stuart, VI, 3. l. **18,** Avaux Holland, V, 152. l. **28,** *Instr. Données*, XXV, 314 n.; Fox, App., pp. cxvii *et seq.*, cxix, cxxi. l. **30,** Baschet, 3.9.85. l. **32,** *Instr. Données*, XXV, 314 n.; Baschet, 10.9.85, 24.9.85. l. **38,** Fox, App., p. cxxv.

289 l. **3,** *Instr. Données*, XXV, 322. l. **14,** *Clar. Corresp.*, I, 163; Diest, 27.10.85 (quoted Ranke, IV, 249). l. **29,** Fox, App., p. cxxix. l. **33,** Baschet, 8.11.85. l. **37,** Fox, App., p. cxxvi.

290 l. **10,** *ibid.*, p. cxxxii.

291 l. **8,** C.J., 9.11.85. l. **22,** *Parl. Hist.*, IV, 1372.

292 l. **16,** *The Times*, 5.5.1938. **Note,** cf. Reresby, p. 561.

293 l. **6,** C.J., Nov. 14, 16, 1685. l. **17,** *ibid.*, Nov. 16. l. **37,** *ibid.*, Nov. 18.

PAGE

294 l. **9**, *Parl. Hist.*, IV, 1385. l. **17**, C.J., Nov. 18; Reresby, p. 398; H.M.C. Rutland, II, pp. 85–87; Bramston, p. 216. l. **22**, Bramston, p. 214. l. **33**, Lans. MSS., 253; Harl. MSS., 7187; l. **42**, Reresby, p. 398.

295 l. **4**, *loc. cit.* l. **11**, Bramston, pp. 216–17. l. **30**, *loc. cit.* l. **36**, Ranke, IV, 277, and authorities there cited. l. **40**, Burnet, I, 65; H.M.C. Rep. VI, App., p. 463.

296 l. **2**, Evans, *Life of Frampton*, p. 197; Macaulay, *History of England*, (1855), III, 402–3 and authorities cited. l. **4**, Reresby, p. 398. l. **7**, Ranke, *loc. cit.*; Baschet, 10.12.85. l. **10**, Luttrell, I, 364. l. **12**, Bramston, p. 216. l. **18**, Baschet, 3.12.85. l. **21**, Fox, App., p. cxv. l. **26**, Baschet, *loc. cit.* l. **34**, Dalrymple, Pt. I, Bks. III & IV, App., p. 105.

297 l. **2**, Fox, App., p. cxlvii. l. **7**, Baschet, 3.12.85. l. **11**, *ibid.*, 13.12.85. l. **22**, Baschet, 24.12.85, 27.12.85. l. **24**, *ibid.*, 3.1.86. l. **30**, Reresby, p. 409; Campana, II, 75, 88–89. l. **31**, Evelyn, 19.1.85/86. l. **33**, *loc. cit.*; *Instr. Données*, XXV, 308 n.

298 l. **2**, Campana, II, 90; cf. *Instr. Données*, *loc. cit.* l. **21**, Burnet, I, 682–83. l. **36**, H.M.C. Rutland, II, 103. **Note**, Burnet, I, 683.

299 l. **20**, H.M.C. Stuart, VI, 7. l. **32**, Reresby, p. 410. l. **33**, Add. MSS., 28569, f. 58. **Note**, H.M.C. Montagu of Beaulieu, p. 192.

300 l. **16**, *ibid.*, f. 91. l. **18**, *loc. cit.*; H.M.C. Rutland, II, 105; Campana, II, 98; *Clar. Corresp.*, I, 288. l. **23**, *ibid.*, p. 577. l. **25**, H.M.C. Rep. XII, *loc. cit.*; Add. MSS., 28569, f. 91. l. **28**, *Ellis Corresp.*, I, 92. l. **30**, Burnet, I, 683; *Clar. Corresp.*, I, 544; Campana, II, 117, 118; Luttrell, I, 386. l. **32**, Campana, *loc. cit.* l. **37**, Baschet, 4.6.87. **Note**, *Clar. Corresp.*, I, 304.

301 l. **16**, Baschet, 21.7.87. l. **20**, Campana, II, 74. l. **23**, Evelyn, 13.7.86; Haile, p. 233; Caylus, p. 166. l. **27**, Baschet, 22.10.85; Campana, II, 157–58. l. **31**, *ibid.*, 151, 152; Burnet, *Letter from Rome*. **Note**, Campana, II, 158.

302 l. **1**, H.M.C. Rutland, II, 103. H.M.C. Rep. XII, Pt. VII, p. 225. l. **17**, *Instr. Données*, XXV, 384. l. **23**, Burnet, I, 356.

303 **Note**, Campana, II, 84, 108, 153, 154, 168, 199; Fox, App., pp. xxii, li, cxxxi; *Instr. Données*, XXV, 313; Mazure, II, 130–31.

304 l. **16**, Cal. S.P. 1689–90, p. 16; Add. MSS., 28053, f. 384. l. **18**, Dartmouth's note to Burnet, I, 756. l. **23**, Campana, II, 143. l. **32**, Baschet, 4.6.87. l. **37**, Burnet, I, 672. **Note 1**, Bonrepaus, 28.3.86, quoted Lingard.

305 l. **2**, *Ellis Corresp.*, I, 68, 155, 196. l. **5**, Campana, II, 113; Supp. to Burnet, pp. 259, 271; Ailesbury, I, 128. l. **7**, Campana, II, 482. l. **10**, Life, II, 76. l. **12**, Lingard, X, 123, and his authorities. l. **15**, Campana, II, 125. l. **18**, H.M.C. Stuart, VI, 11. l. **21**, Mazure, II, 390. l. **24**, *ibid.*, pp. 242–43. l. **32**, *Ellis Corresp.*, I, 68, 155; Rouquillo, 17.3.87. l. **36**, Baschet, 3.3.87. **Note**, Cal. T.B., VIII, Pt. I, Intr.

306 l. **4**, Ailesbury, I, 104. l. **10**, Cal. T.B., VIII, 176. l. **12**, *ibid.*, p. 204. l. **13**, *ibid.*, pp. 454–56. l. **16**, *ibid.*, pp. 610–11 ; Add. MSS., 34508, f. 103. l. **17**, Cal. T.B., VIII, 1020–22. l. **27**, *ibid.*, p. 1245. l. **36**, *ibid.*, p. 1246.

307 l. **2**, Cal. T.B., VIII, 1262. l. **7**, *ibid.*, p. 1321; for Burnet's view of James's change of attitude to the Protestant Dissenters *see* Harl. MSS., 6584, ff. 222 (*b*) and 223 (*a*). l. **13**, *ibid.*, p. 1393. l. **31**, Macpherson, I, 51.

308 l. **3**, Sewell, *History of the Quakers* (1811), p. 436. l. **8**, Hatton, I, 138. l. **27**, Sir Henry Ellis, *Original Letters*, 1st series, III, 339. l. **33**, Barrillon, 12.3.85, quoted Ranke, IV, 227 n. **Note 2**, Fox, App., p. xix.

309 l. **5**, H.M.C. Bucc. & Q., p. 215. l. **25**, Carte MSS., XL, ff. 212 *et seq.*,

PAGE

quoted Firth, *Commentary on Macaulay*. **l. 32,** Clarkson, *Life of Penn*, Ch. XXI, quoting letter of Gerard Croese ; Baschet, 6.10.86 ; Supp. to Burnet, pp. 218–19 ; cf. Reresby, p. 538. **l. 39,** Cal. T.B., VIII, 629–34, 932 ; Luttrell, I, 378 ; Add. MSS., 34508, f. 110.

310 **l. 3,** Cal. T.B., VIII, 991. **l. 9,** King, p. 16 ; Eachard, *History of the Revolution*, p. 70. **l. 34,** Cartwright, 20.4.87.

311 **l. 5,** Blair's Archives, quoted M. V. Hay, *Winston Churchill and James II*, p. 51. **l. 12,** Add. MSS., 34502, f. 61. **l. 25,** Baschet, 1.10.85. **l. 27,** *ibid.*, under dates in text. **l. 38,** *ibid.*, 29.10.85.

312 **l. 6,** *Instr. Données*, p. 337. **l. 17,** *ibid.*, p. 319. **l. 26,** Baschet, 22.10.85. **l. 38,** *ibid.*, 1.10.85.

313 **l. 6,** Ranke, IV, 267. **l. 10,** Baschet, *loc. cit.* **l. 12,** *Instr. Données*, XXV, 317 n. **l. 96,** Evelyn, 5.5.86 ; Baschet, 13.5.86. **l. 31,** *ibid.*, 19.11.85. **l. 35,** Lady Russell, Jan. 15, 22, 85/86. **Note 1,** Luttrell, I, 140. **Note 2,** Plumptre, *Life of Ken* (1890), II, 97 *et seq.*

314 **l. 12,** Baschet, 25.2.86. **l. 24,** *ibid.*, 4.3.86 ; cf. Camden Misc., XI, 88. **l. 26,** *Instr. Données*, XXV, 326 *et seq.* **l. 31,** Baschet, 28.3.86. **l. 33,** Steele, p. 462 ; *London Gazette*, 15.4.87 ; there was apparently no announcement in the current gazette ; Luttrell, I, 374. **l. 35,** *Chron. Notes*, p. 67. **Note 2,** *Ellis Corresp.*, I, 46 ; Dutch Despatches, 5.3.86.

315 **l. 7,** Lady Russell, 14.4.86 ; Barrillon, 19.4.86, quoted Macaulay. **l. 16,** Baschet, 19.4.86. **l. 21,** *London Gazette*, *loc. cit.* ; P.C. Reg., March 5, 11, 17, 18, 86/7, April 15, 87 ; Luttrell, I, 434. **l. 26,** Burnet, I, 501. **l. 36,** Campana, II, 25.

316 **l. 2,** Ranke, IV, 293–94 (no authority given). **l. 9,** Baschet, 4.3.86. **l. 18,** *Life of Sharp*, by his son ; Thoresby, *Diary and Correspondence*, *passim* ; H. Prideaux, *Letters* (Camden Society), p. 148. **l. 21,** Burnet, I, 674. **l. 34,** Bramston, pp. 232–34. **l. 41,** P.C. Reg., 17.7.86.

317 **l. 2,** *Ellis Corresp.*, I, 144 *et seq.* ; *Instr. Données*, XXV, 320. **l. 13,** Barrillon, 22.7.86, quoted Mazure, II, 130 ; c.f. Lonsdale, p. 22. **l. 17,** Adda 2.8:86. **Note 2,** *Clar. Corresp.*, App

318 **l. 17,** Burnet, I, 675. **l. 21,** Steele, p. 464 ; Bramston, p. 265 ; *Ellis Corresp.*, I, 172–73. **l. 32,** Burnet, I, 676.

319 **l. 4,** Burnet, I, 677. **l. 17,** *State Trials*, XII, 257–64. **l. 28,** Reresby, p. 422 ; Eachard, *History of England*, III, 797. **Note,** Ranke, IV, 301 n. ; Burnet, *loc. cit.*

321 **l. 20,** Dartmouth's note to Burnet, I, 755. **l. 30,** Porrit, *The Unreformed House of Commons*, II, 396. **Note 2,** Steele, p. 468.

322 **l. 19,** quoted Ranke, IV, 309*a*. **l. 35,** Bramston, pp. 268–70.

323 **l. 22,** *ibid.*, p. 234 ; P.C. Reg., 17.7.86, 8.10.86. **l. 24,** *ibid.*, 11.3.86/87. **l. 37,** H.M.C. Rutland, II, 109. **l. 40,** P.C. Reg., 7.1.86/87 ; Japikse, II, i, 7.

324 **l. 3,** Evelyn, 3.1.86/87 ; Bulstrode, p. 386. **Note,** *Letter-book of Sir G. Etheridge*, ed. Rosenfeld, pp. 139–40 ; Lauzun to Louvois, 26.6.89, quoted Ranke, VI, 109–13 ; Macpherson, I, 324.

325 **l. 5,** Burnet, I, 705–6. **l. 29,** Campana, I, 302. **l. 36,** Burnet, *Letter from Rome*.

326 **l. 2,** Baschet, 4.10.85. **l. 3,** *ibid.*, 29.10.85 ; Campana, II, 82 ; Life, II, 75. **l. 11,** Burnet, I, 704 ; Baschet, *loc. cit.* **l. 15,** Barrillon, quoted Mazure, II, 76–77 ; Adda, quoted Ranke, IV, 375 n. **l. 21,** Campana, II, 132, 147 (2 places) ; Baschet, 7.7.87. **l. 27,** Campana, II, 120. **l. 30,** Welwood, p. 185. **l. 34,** Burnet, I, 704 ; Campana, II, 127–28.

327 **l. 2,** Campana, II, 81, 82, 93–95, 98 ; Baschet, 22.11.85. Fox, App., p. cxxxii ; Dutch Despatches, 23.11.85, 27.11.85. **l. 7,** Welwood, p. 184. **l. 10,** Baschet, 10.7.87. **l. 16,** Barrillon, 12.5.87, quoted Macaulay ; Cartwright, 1.5.87 (p. 52). **l. 18,** Wood, III, 222. **l. 25,** *loc. cit.* **Note,** Campana, II, 93–95.

PAGE

328 l. **6,** Lonsdale, pp. 23–24; cf. Burnet, I, 716; and Bramston, pp. 280–81. l. **13,** Baschet, 14.7.87 (2 letters), 21.7.87. l. **28,** P.C. Reg., 22.10.86, and list inserted after minutes for 17.12.86. l. **30,** Bramston, p. 251; for Lancashire and Durham at this and later dates, H.M.C. Le Fleming, pp. 202, 203, 210; Luttrell, I, 388, 391–92, 398. l. **33,** Aielsbury, I, 162–67.

329 l. **16,** Cal. T.B., VIII, 1816; Dalrymple, Pt. I, Bk. V, App., p. 101. l. **30,** Luttrell, I, 433; Reresby, p. 478; H.M.C. Le Fleming, pp. 203, 205–8. l. **35,** Reresby, p. 478. **Note,** Luttrell, I, 412–13; *Ellis Corresp.*, pp. 338, 339.

330 l. **1,** Ailesbury, I, 162–67; Burnet, I, 719, and Dartmouth's note. l. **7,** Luttrell, I, 422; Baschet, 17.10.87.

331 l. **5,** H.M.C. Le Fleming, p. 208. l. **7,** *ibid.*, p. 209. l. **16,** Campana, II, 160. l. **26,** *ibid.*, p. 186. l. **29,** Reresby, pp. 496–97; H.M.C. Rep. V, App., p. 197. l. **35,** Luttrell, I, 420–21. **Note 2,** Ailesbury, I, 165.

332 l. **1,** Luttrell, I, 420–21. l. **9,** e.g., P.C. Reg., 12.6.85, 20.1.86/87; H.M.C. Rep. XI, App. VI (Reading Corpn.), p. 199. l. **11,** Reresby, pp. 365–68; H.M.C. Rep. XI, App. VII, p. 201; Cartwright, 30.10.87. l. **34,** Life, II, 71; H.M.C. Rep. V, App., p. 187. l. **35,** Luttrell, I, 384. l. **38,** Life, II, 140.

333 l. **5,** This is Ranke's opinion, see IV, 333–34 and authorities quoted; Burnet (I, 717) takes a different view. l. **26,** Plumptre, *Life of Ken* (1890), I, 280–81. l. **30,** *Ellis Corresp.*, I, 336–37; Luttrell, I, 411–12. **Note,** Cal. T.B., VIII, 28, 100 and *passim*; Luttrell, I, 378; Bramston, p. 231; Reresby, p. 426 n.; Evelyn, 5.11.86; Wood, III, 233.

334 l. **3,** Cartwright, 28.8.87. l. **4,** *ibid.*, 30.10.87. l. **17,** Burnet, I, 717. **Note,** Baschet, 22.10.87.

335 l. **20,** Burnet, I, 697–98. **Note 2,** Thoresby, *passim*; Life of Dr. Radcliffe published by Curll.

336 l. **7,** Bloxam, pp. 2–4. l. **14,** *ibid.*, pp. 12–13. l. **10,** *ibid.*, p. 14. l. **32,** *ibid.*, pp. 50–51.

337 l. **3,** Bloxam, pp. 16–19. l. **9,** *ibid.*, p. 22.

338 l. **11,** Wood, III, 217. l. **39,** Bloxam, pp. 65–67, 72; cf. Wood, III, 217; Cartwright, 22.6.87; Ailesbury, I, 167–68.

339 l. **12,** Bloxam, pp. 77–78. l. **17,** Cartwright, 6.6.87. l. **38,** Tanner MSS. in *State Trials*, XII; cf. Wood, III, 223.

340 l. **7,** cf. Cartwright, p. 63 n. l. **10,** Cartwright, 18.10.87. l. **21,** Bloxam, p. 82. l. **23,** *ibid.*, p. 83. l. **29,** Wood, III, 226 *et seq.* l. **34,** Ailesbury, I, 131.

341 l. **15,** Bloxam, pp. 85–86. l. **22,** *ibid.*, p. 87. l. **26,** H.M.C. Leybourne-Popham, pp. 265–66; cf. Burnet, I, 700. l. **33,** Wood, III, 233. l. **36,** *loc. cit.*

342 l. **1,** Bloxam, p. 91. l. **7,** *ibid.*, p. 92. l. **10,** *ibid.*, p. 94. l. **28,** *ibid.*, p. 153. l. **34,** *ibid.*, p. 169. **Note 1,** Wood, *loc. cit.* **Note 3,** *State Trials*, XII, 355.

343 l. **4,** Bloxam, pp. 185–214. l. **11,** *ibid.*, pp. 219, 221. l. **24,** *ibid.*, p. 240. l. **28,** *ibid.*, p. 4. **Note,** *ibid.*, p. 106.

344 l. **15,** Ailesbury, I, 167–69; *European Magazine*, XXVII, 22. l. **38,** Avaux Holland, V, 130. **Note,** Dalrymple, Pt. I, Bk. II, App., pp. 50–52.

345 l. **14,** Baschet, 13.12.85. l. **29,** Quoted Mazure, II, 164–65. **Note,** Rousset, IV, 104–5; Ranke, IV, 384.

346 l. **13,** Japikse, II, i, 720. l. **29,** Quoted Ruth Clark, pp. 31–32. l. **36,** *ibid.*, pp. 52–53. l. **40,** *ibid.*, p. 69.

347 l. **2,** Ruth Clark, p. 38, quoting R.O., Vol. 148, ff. 136, 7. l. **6,** reference lost; see also for the Orange Question, Dalrymple, Pt. I, Bk. II, App., pp. 46 *et seq.* l. **12,** R.O. France, 148, f. 118, quoted Ruth

PAGE

Clark, p. 20. **l. 23,** *ibid.*, p. 75 n. **l. 25,** *ibid.*, p. 70. **l. 33,** *ibid.*, pp. 81–82, 84.

348 **l. 1,** Burnet, I, 707–8. **l. 4,** *Instr. Données*, XXV, 315; Avaux Holland, V, 317–18. **l. 9,** *loc. cit.* **l. 11,** Burnet, I, 734; Avaux Holland, *loc. cit.* **l. 12,** *Instr. Données*, XXV, 315 n. **l. 18,** Mazure, II, 185, quoting Avaux. **l. 23,** Burnet, I, 733; Harl. MSS., 6584, f. 242 (*a*). **l. 33,** Dalrymple, Pt. I, Bk. II, App., pp. 54–56.

349 **l. 2,** Mazure, II, 409. **l. 7,** Mazure, *loc. cit.*, quoting Avaux. **l. 31,** Japikse, 23.7.86.

350 **l. 12,** Dalrymple, Pt. I, Bk. II, p. 29; Mazure, II, 409. **l. 19,** *ibid.*, pp. 30, 31. **l. 24,** *ibid.*, pp. 31–32; cf. Baschet, 13.9.86.

351 **l. 3,** *ibid.*, 8.12.87; Dangeau, 11.1.88; Mazure, II, 409–13; Campana, II, 168, 171. **l. 4,** Dangeau, 2.1.88. **l. 9,** Dalrymple, Pt. I, Bk. II, App., p. 141. **l. 10,** Avaux Holland, VI, 130. **l. 15,** Baschet, 13.10.87. **l. 23,** Dalrymple, Pt. I, Bk. II, App., p. 141.

352 **l. 27,** Burnet, I, 693–94; Harl. MSS., 6584, f. 226 (*a*); cf. Avaux Holland, VI, 21–24. **l. 35,** Burnet, I, 709.

353 **l. 5,** Bonrepaus, 21.6.87, quoted Macaulay, *History of England* (1855), II, 234 n. **l. 9,** Lady Russell, 9.2.86/87. **l. 22,** Burnet, I, 708; among others whom Dykvelt approached was Clarendon, *see* H.M.C. Buccleuch, II, i, 31. **l. 33,** Campana, II, 30; Mazure, II, 192, 252. **Note 2,** Burnet, I, 762.

354 **l. 6,** Dalrymple, Pt. I, Bk. V, App., pp. 116–21. **l. 37,** Letters of Bonrepaus and Barrillon of June 1687, quoted Mazure, II, 251–55.

355 **l. 14,** *loc. cit.* **l. 31,** Burnet, I, 731–32. **Note,** *ibid.*, p. 731.

356 **l. 3,** For English text of Fagel's letter *see Somers Tracts*, IX, 183–88. **l. 7,** Campana, II, 166–67. **l. 16,** *ibid.*, II, 184. **l. 21,** Mignet, 19.8.69. **l. 35,** Campana, II, 169–70. **Note,** *ibid.*, p. 167.

357 **l. 23,** Burnet, II, 689. **l. 34,** Campana, II, 169.

358 **l. 7,** Burnet, I, 708. **l. 11,** Campana, II, 131. **l. 19,** *ibid.*, p. 169. **l. 24,** Burnet, I, 726. **l. 28,** Add. MSS., 25859, ff. 64, 65; Clarke and Foxcroft, *Life of Burnet*, pp. 232–37 and authorities cited. **l. 33,** Lady Russell, 5.10.87. **Note,** Campana, II, 157.

359 **l. 7,** *ibid.*, p. 171. **l. 15,** quoted Mazure, II, 160. **l. 19,** Mazure, II, 390.

360 **l. 5,** Evelyn, 10.3.87. Dalrymple, Pt. I, Bk. V, App., pp. 57, 69, 84; **l. 29,** *ibid.*, p. 95. **Note,** Ailesbury, I, 153.

361 **l. 15,** Dalrymple, Pt. I, Bk. V, App., pp. 96–97. **l. 23,** *ibid.*, p. 118. **l. 25,** *ibid.*, pp. 59, 90.

362 **l. 12,** *ibid.*, p. 78. **l. 18,** *ibid.*, pp. 57, 83. **l. 24,** *ibid.*, p. 57–58. **l. 29,** *ibid.*, p. 84.

363 **l. 4,** Dalrymple, Pt. I, Bk. V, App., p. 117. **l. 12,** *ibid.*, p. 80. **l. 38,** Barrillon, quoted Mazure, II, 399–400.

364 **l. 15,** *Instr. Données*, XXV, 313; Mazure, II, 130–31. **l. 19,** Campana, II, 84. **l. 31,** *ibid.*, p. 108. **l. 40,** Baschet, 21.7.87.

365 **l. 7,** *ibid.*, 9.10.87. **l. 30,** *ibid.*, 6.10.87. **l. 40,** *ibid.*, 9.10.87.

366 **l. 33,** H.M.C. Bucc. & Q., II, 142. **Note 2,** Baschet, 27.10.87.

367 **l. 3,** Avaux Ireland, pp. 85, 247. **l. 6,** H.M.C. Bucc. & Q., II, 103 *et seq.* **l. 7,** Lans. MSS., 1163 A. **l. 14,** H.M.C. Bucc. & Q., II, 85. **l. 18,** Avaux Ireland, p. 347. **l. 23,** H.M.C. Bucc. & Q., II, 33. **l. 27,** *ibid.*, pp. 40, 47, 55, 70, 73, 76, 82. **l. 29,** *ibid.*, p. 216. **Note,** Avaux Ireland, pp. 173, 182; cf. Rosen to Louvois, 20.5.89, quoted Rousset, IV, 198.

368 **l. 8,** Lauderdale, II, 142. **l. 13,** Life, II, 10–13; Joly, p. 120; Mazure, I, 407. **l. 23,** H.M.C. Bucc. & Q., II, 90 *et seq.* **l. 26,** *Hist. Notices*, II, 676; cf. H.M.C. Bucc. & Q., II, 106. **l. 29,** *ibid.*, p. 62. **l. 34,** *ibid.*, pp. 103–4. **l. 36,** *ibid.*, p. 90. **Note,** *ibid.*, pp. 301, 310, 327.

369 **l. 3,** H.M.C. Bucc. & Q., II, 100, 101. **l. 5,** *Hist. Notices*, II, 654; Wodrow, III, 347. **l. 11,** H.M.C. Bucc. & Q., II, 52. **l. 19,** *Hist.*

PAGE

Notices, *loc. cit.* **Note 1,** *Hist. Observes*, pp. 236–37. **Note 2,** H.M.C. Bucc. & Q., II, 107. **Note 3,** *Commentary on Macaulay*, ed. Godfrey Davies.

370 **l. 12,** H.M.C. Rep. X, Pt. I, App., p. 137. **l. 23,** Sibbald, *Memoirs of My Life*, ed. F. P. Hett, 1932, pp. 86–87. **l. 26,** Johnson, *Life of Dryden*. **l. 32,** Macky, p. 241. **l. 37,** Joly, pp. 154–55.

371 **l. 2,** *Correspondence de Bossuet*, III, 328. **l. 8,** Baschet, 4.10.85. **l. 15,** Burnet, I, 653. **l. 17,** H.M.C. Hamilton, p. 169. **l. 21,** Burnet, *loc. cit.* **l. 26,** H.M.C. Hamilton, pp. 169–72. **l. 37,** *ibid.*, p. 171.

372 **l.** 6, H.M.C. Bucc. & Q., p. 97. **l. 15,** Trials of Mowbray and Keith in *State Trials*; Burnet, I, 678; *Hist. Notices*, II, 700, 704; *Hist. Observes*, pp. 243–44; H.M.C. Bucc. & Q., II, 97; Wodrow, IV, 397. **l. 21,** H.M.C. Bucc. & Q., II, 153. **l. 23,** Joly, p. 167. **l. 36,** H.M.C. Bucc. & Q., *loc. cit.*; cf. *Hist. Notices*, II, 712; *Ellis Corresp.*, I, 50–51.

373 **l. 8,** Bramston, p. 246; *Hist. Notices*, p. 750; Wodrow, IV, 389–90. **l. 11,** *Ellis Corresp.*, I, 96; Dutch Despatch, 23.4.86. **l. 27,** Barrillon, 29.4.86, quoted Macaulay, *History of England* (1855), II, 119 n. **Note 1,** *e.g.* by Sir Charles Firth, *loc. cit.*

374 **l. 10,** Bramston, p. 230; cf. Luttrell, I, 376. **l. 15,** *Hist. Notices*, II, 715; Life, II, 64–69; Wodrow, IV, 362. **l. 18,** Carnock, p. 191. **l. 21,** *Instr. Données*, XXV, 319. **l. 24,** Carnock, p. 195.

375 **l. 3,** H.M.C. Le Fleming, p. 200; Wodrow, IV, 366. **l. 7,** Life, *loc. cit.*; Wodrow, IV, 387; Barrillon, 13.6.86, quoted Ranke, IV, 304 n. **l. 10,** Carnock, p. 199. **l. 16,** *ibid.*, p. 213; *Hist. Notices*, II, 750, 1117. **l. 19,** Burnet, I, 713. **l. 24,** Wodrow, IV, 471 n. **l. 26,** Barrillon, quoted Ranke, IV, 305 n. **l. 30,** *Hist. Notices*, II, 725, 727, 752, 806. **l. 42,** H.M.C. Hamilton, p. 197; Wodrow, III, 301.

376 **l. 3,** H.M.C. Hamilton, pp. 168, 170. **l. 5,** *ibid.*, pp. 164, 169, 171.
l. 6, *ibid.*, p. 172. **l. 21,** *ibid.*, p. 173. **l. 29,** *loc. cit.* **l. 32,** *loc. cit.* **Note,** Baschet, 29.4.86.

377 **l. 6,** H.M.C. Hamilton, p. 174. **l. 16,** *ibid.*, pp. 174–75; cf. Dalrymple, Pt. I, Bk. V, App., p. 99. **l. 19,** *ibid.*, pp. 100–1; H.M.C. Hamilton, p. 175. **l. 30,** *Correspondence de Bossuet*, III, 297. **l. 36,** H.M.C. Stuart, I, 30–31.

378 **l. 4,** Nicholson to Leslie, 8.2.88, quoted Hay, *Enigma of James II*, p. 85. **l. 19,** *Clar. Corresp.*, I, 339, 460, II, 38. **Note,** *Clar. Corresp.*, I, 298, 559.

379 **l. 3,** Carte, *Ormonde*, IV, 672. **l. 6,** *ibid.*, p. 138. **l. 11,** *ibid.*, pp. 553–54; Essex, I, 137–38. **l. 16,** Carte, *Ormonde*, IV, 550. **Note 1,** H.M.C. Rep. XV, App., Pt. VIII, p. 165. **Note 2,** Carte, *Ormonde*, IV, 311–13, cf. p. 559. **Note 3,** H.M.C. Ormonde, VII, 115–16, 119.

380 **l. 3,** Carte, *Ormonde*, IV, 431, 435–38; Essex, I, 150–51. **l. 9,** Carte, *Ormonde*, IV, 158. **l. 13,** *ibid.*, IV, 673, V, 42, 150, 158, 159; Cal. S.P. Ireland, 1660–62, p. 122. **l. 16,** Carte, *Ormonde*, V, 158. **l. 18,** *loc. cit.* **l. 23,** *ibid.*, V, 109. **l. 26,** *ibid.*, p. 42; H.M.C. Ormonde, VI, 478, VII, 68. **l. 29,** Carte, *Ormonde*, V, 109, 111, 120; Essex, I, 135–36. **l. 34,** Cal. S.P. Ireland, 1660–62, p. 397. **l. 35,** Carte, *Ormonde*, IV, 439. **Note,** *Clar. Corresp.*, II, 124.

381 **l. 9,** Grey, II, 159–61; C.J., 25.3.73; Carte, *Ormonde*, IV, 477; Essex, I, 92 *et seq.* **l. 12,** Carte, *Ormonde*, *loc. cit.*; Essex, I, 111–13. **l. 17,** Carte, *Ormonde*, IV, 564. For a fuller account of the state of Ireland before 1685 see O'Brien, *Economic History of Ireland in the Seventeenth Century*. **l. 37,** Carte, *Ormonde*, IV, 378.

382 **l. 14,** *Clar. Corresp.*, I, 536. **l. 18,** Avaux Ireland, pp. 191–92, 215–16. **l. 22,** H.M.C. Ormonde, VII, 239. **l. 26,** Avaux Ireland, pp. 138, 182, 292–93. **l. 31,** *Clar. Corresp.*, I, 221, 507, 509, 541, etc.; H.M.C.

PAGE

Ormonde, VII, 430, 432, 433, 434, 477; Berwick, p. 95. **l. 36,** Cal. S.P. Ireland, 1669–70; Carte, *Ormonde*, V, 105–8.

383 **l. 4,** *ibid.*, IV, 73, 451; H.M.C. Ormonde, VI, 533. **l. 5,** Carte, *Ormonde*, V, 60. **l. 8,** H.M.C. Ormonde, VI, 533–34. **l. 14,** *ibid.*, VII, 239. **l. 23,** Carte, *Ormonde*, IV, 669. **l. 27,** *ibid.*, p. 673. **l. 34,** H.M.C. Rep. VII, App., p. 741. **l. 36,** Carte, *Ormonde*, V, 166–67. **Note 1,** Ailesbury, I, 147. **Note 2,** H.M.C. Ormonde, VII, 57, 75, 94, 177, 189, 233, 235, etc.

384 **l. 21,** H.M.C. Ormonde, VII, 325. **l. 23,** P.C. Reg., 6.2.84/85. **l. 24,** *Clar. Corresp.*, I, 111. **l. 27,** H.M.C. Ormonde, VII, 300; Reresby, p. 360; Fox, App., p. lxxxiii. **l. 30,** H.M.C. Ormonde, VII, 356, 360, 363. **l. 35,** *ibid.*, p. 372. **l. 36,** *ibid.*, p. 380. **l. 39,** H.M.C. Stuart, VI, 5.

385 **l. 3,** H.M.C. Ormonde, VII, 76, 78, 104, 124, 152, etc. **l. 8,** Carte, *Ormonde*, IV, 118, 358; H.M.C. Ormonde, VII, 310, 314. **l. 12,** *ibid.*, p. 310. **l. 23,** *Clar. Corresp.*, I, 499–503 and elsewhere. **l. 32.** *ibid.*, p. 339. **l. 39,** H.M.C. Ormonde, VII, 65, 78, 81, 88, 89, 90, 96.

386 **l. 3,** H.M.C. Ormonde, VII, 68–69, 78, 91. **l. 15,** *Clar. Corresp.*, I, 536–37. **l. 28,** Add. MSS., 32095, f. 224. **Note 1,** *True Way to Render Ireland Happy and Secure*, quoted Prendergast, *The Cromwellian Settlement of Ireland*, p. 130.

387 **l. 8,** Baschet, 13.9.85. **l. 12,** Hatton, II, 61. **l. 14,** *Clar. Corresp.*, II, 128. **l. 36,** *ibid.*, p. 23–24. **Note,** H.M.C. Ormonde, VII, 487.

388 **l. 3,** *ibid.*, p. 417–18, 483–84. **l. 7,** *ibid.*, I, 294; cf. *ibid.*, pp. 342–43. **l. 11,** *Clar. Corresp.*, II, 8; H.M.C. Ormonde, VII, 451. **l. 16,** *ibid.*, pp. 398, 416, 418, 425, 444. **l. 22,** *Clar. Corresp.*, II, 4, etc. **l. 25,** *ibid.*, I, 440–42, 449–50, 455, etc. **l. 39,** *ibid.*, p. 466.

389 **l. 8,** H.M.C. Stuart, VI, 5. **l. 17,** Life, II, 60; H.M.C. Stuart, VI, 21. **l. 32,** *ibid.*, p. 5.

390 **l. 11,** *ibid.*, p. 7. **l. 19,** *Clar. Corresp.*, II, 10, 26. **l. 32,** *ibid.*, p. 43. **l. 35,** *ibid.*, p. 39. **l. 37,** *ibid.*, p. 16.

391 **l. 6,** *Clar. Corresp.*, II, 43. **l. 14,** H.M.C. Stuart, VI, 6. **l. 15,** H.M.C. Ormonde, VII, 442; H.M.C. Stuart, VI. **l. 19,** Baschet, 13.9.86. **l. 24,** H.M.C. Stuart, VI, 14. **l. 33,** *ibid.*, p. 7; *Clar. Corresp.*, II, 38. **l. 38,** Life, II, 61; *Clar. Corresp.*, II, 55, 68; Mazure, II, 112. **l. 41,** *Clar. Corresp.*, II, 138, 152; Life, *loc. cit.*

392 **l. 5,** *Clar. Corresp.*, II, 134 n.; Grey, VIII, 152. **l. 6,** King's Pamphlets, No. 100*h* 7*a* quoted by Saxe Bannister, intr. to Sheridan, *Some Revelations in Irish History*. **l. 12,** H.M.C. Stuart, VI, 14. **l. 17,** *ibid.*, p. 35–36. **l. 23,** *Clar. Corresp.*, II, 138, 152; King, p. 86. **l. 24,** *ibid.*, p. 144; Wodrow, IV, 398 n. **Note 1,** *e.g.* London Mercury, Jan. 10–Feb. 6, 1688/89. There is a valuable collection of Irish proclamations in the British Museum. **Note 2,** Proclamation of the Lords Justices, etc., 24.7.88; H.M.C. Ormonde, VII, 353, 395, 417; *Clar. Corresp.*, I, 296, 415, 497–98; H.M.C. Stuart, VI, 21.

393 **l. 2,** *Clar. Corresp.*, I, 339. **l. 7,** H.M.C. Stuart, VI, 16. **l. 10,** H.M.C. Ormonde, VII, 469. **l. 16,** Fortescue, *History of the British Army*, IV, ch. 1. **l. 27,** H.M.C. Le Fleming, p. 200. **l. 30,** Adda, 15.11.86, quoted Lingard, X, 240 n. **l. 33,** *Clar. Corresp.*, I, 346, 351; Petty to Southwell, 30.9.86, quoted Fitzmaurice, *Life of Sir William Petty*, p. 281. **l. 40,** Dalrymple, Bk. V, App., p. 137.

396 **l. 1,** H.M.C. Ormonde, VII, 448. **l. 6,** P.C. Reg., 4.5.88. **l. 9,** Clar., Hist., IV, 3. **l. 13,** Burnet, I, 736; Life, I, 601; D'Oyley, I, 252. **Note,** Campana, II, 206.

397 **l. 7,** Life, II, 70.

398 **l. 8,** *Clar. Corresp.*, II, 171. **l. 12,** H.M.C. Le Fleming, p. 210; H.M.C. Buccleuch, II, i, 32. **Note 2,** There is a copy of the petition in *Somers Tracts*, Vol. IX.

PAGE

399 **l. 10,** Burnet, I, 739. **l. 33,** Tanner MSS., quoted *State Trials*, pp. 453–57; *Clar. Corresp.*, II, App.; Campana, II, 197.

400 **l. 1,** Plumptre, *Life of Ken*, I, 309. **l. 24,** Life, II, 167–68; Luttrell, I, 440. **l. 26,** *loc. cit.*; Burnet, I, 740; Campana, II, 197. **l. 31,** *ibid.*, p. 235. **Note 1,** Macaulay, *History of England* (1855), II, 354. **Note 2,** Burnet, *loc. cit.*; H.M.C. Charlemont, II, 347.

401 **l. 19,** Burnet, I, 738; Campana, II, 205; H.M.C. Le Fleming, p. 210. **l. 21,** Mazure, II, 446–47. **l. 33,** *ibid.*, p. 448. **l. 37,** Life, II, 158; Macpherson, I, 151.

402 **l. 5,** *Clar. Corresp.*, II, 177, 179, 180, 185. **l. 9,** Macpherson, *loc. cit.* **l. 12,** *Clar. Corresp.*, II, 173. **l. 30,** Campana, II, 210; Evelyn, 8.6.88; *Clar. Corresp.*, App. **l. 37,** *Clar. Corresp.*, II, 177. **Note,** P.C. Reg., 8.6.88.

403 **l. 29,** Add. MSS., 34514. (Macaulay has misquoted this document, making it appear that the writer had said that Wright was the only person "frighted"); cf. H.M.C. Portland, III, 412–13; Campana, II, 234. **l. 37,** *Clar. Corresp.*, II, 177. **l. 41,** Mazure, II, 472, quoting Barrillon.

404 **l. 2,** Campana, II, 234–35. **l. 9,** Mazure, II, 472; Campana, II, 234–35; cf. Burnet, I, 744. **l. 14,** *London Gazette*, 12.7.88. **l. 24,** Bramston, p. 312; *Ellis Corresp.*. II, 137; Evelyn, 23.8.88. **Note 1,** Stevens, pp. 4–5. **Note 2,** Campana, II, 236. **Note 4,** H.M.C. Buccleuch, II, i, 31; Plumptre, I, 310 n.

405 **l. 2,** Burnet, I, 740; Luttrell, I, 440. **l. 4,** *Ellis Corresp.*, II, 26; Campana, II, 239. **l. 8,** many references in Barrillon's letters cited Mazure, II, 365–69. **l. 11,** *ibid.*, p. 165. **l. 16,** Campana, II, 215, 220–21, 222. **l. 19,** Luttrell, 284, 307; H.M.C. Rep. VII, App., p. 481; H.M.C. Rutland, II, 81. **l. 35,** Campana, II, 223.

406 **l. 15,** H.M.C. Stuart, VI, 419. **l. 27,** Mazure, II, 219.

407 **l. 22,** Barrillon, quoted Mazure, II, 374; cf. *Instr. Données*, XXV, 396. **l. 28,** Barrillon, quoted Mazure, III, 164. **l. 32,** Campana, II, 233; Luttrell, I, 446. **l. 35,** *Instr. Données*, XXV, 396; Mazure, II, 374; he had had leanings to Rome as early as 1671, see Dalrymple, I, 123. **Note,** Dalrymple, Pt. I, Bk. V, App., p. 119.

408 **l. 21,** *Ellis Corresp.*, II, 180; *Clar. Corresp.*, App., pp. 490–91. **l. 30,** Luttrell, I, 449; Campana, II, 239; *Ellis Corresp.*, II, 26; Evelyn, 2.7.88. **l. 35,** *State Trials*, XII, 503–4; *Ellis Corresp.*, II, 137–38.

409 **l. 5,** This passage was suggested to me by Sir Charles Firth's, *Commentary on Macaulay*, p. 157. **l. 10,** Burnet, I, 746; cf. *ibid.*, p. 755. **l. 29,** Barrillon, 23.9.88, quoted Mazure, III, 74. **l. 34,** H.M.C. Le Fleming, pp. 213–14, 218.

410 **l. 7,** Bramston, pp. 314–15; cf. Reresby, pp. 509, 510; *Ellis Corresp.*, II, 167–68, 184; Dutch Despatches, 17.9.88, 28.9.88; Burnet, I, 767. **l. 15,** H.M.C. Leybourne-Popham, p. 266. **l. 23,** *Ellis Corresp.*, II, 192, 196. **l. 39,** Reresby, p. 503; cf. Burnet, I, 755; Caveat against the Whigs. **Note,** Life, II, 168–69.

411 **l. 32,** Campana, II, 232–33. **l. 34,** *ibid.*, pp. 237–38. **l. 38,** *Instr. Données*, XXV, 397.

412 **l. 3,** *ibid.*, 403. **l. 12,** *loc. cit.*; Mazure, III, 69. **l. 25,** *Instr. Données*, XXV, 409. **l. 28,** *ibid.*, p. 410. **l. 35,** *ibid.*, pp. 403–4; Luttrell, I, 462; Sourches, II, 231. l. 40, Mazure, III, 170. **l. 42,** *loc. cit.*

413 **l. 15,** Campana, II, 257–58. **l. 23,** *ibid.*, pp. 258–59; cf. Reresby, p. 509. **l. 32,** D'Orleans, IV, 320–21; Life, II, 176; Berwick, I, 22–23. **l. 37,** *Inst. Données*, XXV, 404.

414 **l. 4,** *loc. cit.* **l. 11,** Barrillon, 20.9.88, quoted Mazure, III, 73. **l. 19,** Avaux Holland, VI, 217–54. **l. 28,** Campana, II, 266. **l. 31,** *ibid.*, p. 263; Rousset, IV, 105 n.; Haile, pp. 197–98. **l. 41,** *Clar. Corresp.*, II, 189.

415 **l. 6,** *loc. cit.* **l. 15,** Steele, p. 469; Campana, II, 263–64, 270–71. **l. 25,**

PAGE

ibid., p. 271; Mazure, III, 106; Dutch Despatches, 22.9.88, etc., quoted Ranke, 420–21. l. **28**, Mazure, III, 104–5. l. **31**, *ibid.*, p. 109. **Note**, Avaux Holland, VI, 283–84.

416 l. **2**, Mazure, III, 115–16; cf. Campana, II, 298. l. **24**, Barrillon, 3.10.88, quoted Mazure, III, 104–5. l. **34**, *loc. cit.*

417 l. **16**, quoted Mazure, III, 135–36. l. **25**, Tanner MSS., quoted *State Trials*, XII, 489. l. **35**, H.M.C. Portland, III, 418; *Ellis Corresp.*, II, 226–27; Bonnet and Dutch Secretary, quoted Ranke, IV, 423–24. l. **39**, *Clar. Corresp.*, II, 191; cf. Campana, II, 279–80.

418 l. **5**, *Clar. Corresp.*, p. 190. l. **8**, *ibid.*, p. 191. l. **35**, *ibid.*, p. 192; Tanner MSS., quoted *State Trials*.

419 l. **12**, Bramston, p. 322–24; *Ellis Corresp.*, II, 230–31; Tanner MSS., quoted *State Trials*, XII, 489–92; cf. Foxcroft, *Supplement to Burnet*, p. 529. l. **24**, P.C. Reg., 5.10.88. l. **25**, Bramston, p. 320; Campana, Campana, II, 285. l. **28**, H.M.C. Rep. V, App., p. 385. **Note 2**, Bloxam, pp. 257–59.

420 l. **3**, Steele, p. 470; P.C. Reg., 17.10.88. l. **6**, *ibid.*, *passim.* l. **12**, Adda, 22.10.88. l. **35**, Bramston, p. 326; cf. Ailesbury, I, 181–82. **Note**, Baillie's Letters.

421 l. 6, *Clar. Corresp.*, II, 193. l. **15**, *ibid.*, pp. 194. l. **26**, *ibid.*, pp. 195–96. l. **31**, Dartmouth's note to Burnet, I, 783. l. **35**, *Ellis Corresp.*, II, 237–38. l. **36**, Barrillon, quoted in *Continuation to Mackintosh's History*. l. **42**, Burnet, I, 783; Bramston, p. 327; Campana, II, 313; *Ellis Corresp.*, II, 264.

422 l. **3**, *ibid.*, p. 268. l. **13**, Campana, II, 312; *Clar. Corresp.*, II, 197; Mazure, III, 148. l. **26**, *Clar. Corresp.*, II, 199, 494, 502–3.

423 l. **4**, *ibid.*, p. 494.

424 l. **18**, *ibid.*, pp. 497–501; cf. Life, II, 210; Dutch Despatches, 16.11.88. l. **26**, Campana, II, 190. l. **29**, *ibid.*, p. 251. l. **37**, Baschet, 13.5.88, 20.5.88; cf. *Instr. Données*, XXV, 397. l. **41**, Campana, II, 254–55; cf. *Ellis Corresp.*, II, 131.

425 l. **5**, Reresby, p. 506. l. **11**, Pepys to Strickland, 16.8.88; Pepys to Killigrew, 3.9.88, quoted *E.H.R.*, VIII, 273, 274; Barrillon, 13.9.88, quoted, Mazure, III, 73; H.M.C. Rep. V, App., p. 198; Campana, II, 251. l. **17**, Barrillon, 23.9.88, quoted Mazure, III, 73. **Note**, Admiralty Letters, XIV, p. 236, quoted J. R. Tanner, *E.H.R.*, VIII, 274.

426 l. **4**, Burnet, I, 767–68. l. **6**, Burnet, I, 768. l. **10**, *loc. cit.* l. **24**, Campana, II, 300; Mazure, III, 68. **Note 2**, Campana, II, 335.

427 l. **12**, *ibid.*, 306–7. l. **15**, *ibid.*, pp. 303–4, 320–21. l. **18**, *ibid.*, p. 280. l. **21**, *ibid.*, pp. 281, 289. l. **24**, *Ellis Corresp.*, II, 243. l. **29**, *ibid.*, pp. 232, 233. l. **30**, *ibid.*, p. 241. l. **40**, Burnet, I, 783; cf. Barrillon, 23.9.88, quoted Mazure, III, 74; Ailesbury, I, 184.

428 l. **20**, Campana, II, 300. l. **22**, *ibid.*, p. 303. l. **26**, *Instr. Données*, XXV, 404, 410, 412; Campana, II, 265. l. **30**, Japikse, I, ii, 626. l. **35**, Campana, II, 332.

429 l. **6**, Buckingham, *Account of the Revolution*; Campana, II, 445–46. l. **27**, cf. *ibid.*, p. 335. l. **39**, *ibid.*, p. 287. l. **42**, cf. Ailesbury, I, 213; Onslow's note to Burnet, I, 791.

430 l. **2**, Buckingham, *loc. cit.* l. **12**, Campana, II, 279; Mazure, III, 183. l. **15**, Campana, II, 323; *Ellis Corresp.*, II, 301. l. **31**, Life, II, 222–23; D'Orleans, IV, 339; Campana, II, 336–37, 349; Ailesbury, I, 188–89; cf. Firth, *Commentary on Macaulay*, p. 297. l. **36**, Life, *loc. cit.*; Ranke, IV, 448 (giving no authorities); Barrillon, 1.12.88, quoted Macaulay. **Note**, Campana, II, 343, 356.

431 l. **2**, Japikse, I, i, 61; Burnet, I, 765; H.M.C. Leybourne-Popham, p. 267; Reresby, p. 534. l. **5**, Campana, II, 345. l. **23**, Japikse, I, ii, 629; Luttrell, I, 480. l. **38**, quoted Mazure, III, 214.

432 l. **12**, H.M.C. Leybourne-Popham, p. 267. l. **30**, Mazure, *loc. cit.* l. **40**, H.M.C. Leybourne-Popham, *loc. cit.*

PAGE

433 **l. 4,** *Jacobite Narrative*, p. 36. **l. 7,** Conduct of the Duchess of Marlborough; *Ellis Corresp.*, II, 338–39; Burnet, I, 792; Dalrymple, Bk. VI, App., p. 250; Dutch Despatches, 6.12.88. **l. 10,** Ailesbury, I. 190; Life, II, 226; Prince George's letter in *1st Collection of Papers.* **l. 23,** Bramston, pp. 334–35; Campana, II, 331–34; *Clar. Corresp.*, II, 205. **l. 29,** Buckingham. **l. 32,** Campana, II, 322–23; Mazure, III, 185. **l. 38,** Life, II, 219; but see Campana, *loc. cit.*, and *Clar. Corresp.*, II, 205.

434 **l. 14,** Dutch Despatches, 30.11.88; cf. Campana, *loc. cit.* **l. 18,** Burnet, I, 791. **l. 33,** *ibid.*, p. 794. **l. 34,** Ailesbury, I, 193. **l. 37,** Life, I, 239; cf. *Clar. Corresp.*, II, 209; Dutch Despatches, 7.12.88, 10.12.88; H.M.C. Dartmouth (Rep. II), p. 11.

435 **l. 13,** *Clar. Corresp.*, II, 215–16, 218. **l. 17,** Campana, II, 355. **l. 24,** Barrillon, 9.12.88, quoted Ranke, IV, 458 n. **l. 33,** Mazure, III, 214.

436 **l. 10,** Barrillon, 13.12.88, quoted Mazure, III, 221–22. **l. 17,** Barrillon, 15.12.88, quoted Mazure, III, 224–25. **l. 23,** Campana, II, 361; Mazure, *loc. cit.* **l. 34,** *Instr. Données*, XXV, 408.

437 **l. 4,** quoted Mazure, III, 238; *Instr. Données*, XXV, 416. **l. 6,** Campana, II, 432. **l. 13,** *Clar. Corresp.*, II, 206. **l. 27,** Burnet, I, 795.

438 **l. 4,** quoted in App. to 1765 ed. of *State Letters of Henry, Earl of Clarendon.* **l. 12,** Buckingham. **l. 18,** Dalrymple, Pt. I, Bk. VI, App., p. 243. **l. 27,** *ibid.*, pp. 245–48. **l. 34,** Berwick, I, 31. **Note,** Exact reference lost, but cf. Campana, II, 424.

439 **l. 9,** Memoirs relating to Lord Torrington (Camden Society), pp. 33–34. **l. 11,** James to Dartmouth, 9.11.88. **l. 12,** Life, II, 207. **l. 15,** H.M.C. Rep. V, App., p. 198. **l. 25,** H.M.C. Dartmouth, p. 228; Campana, II, 382, 393.

440 **l. 26,** Life, II, 246–47; Campana, II, 381–95; *Stuart Papers* (Roxburgh), pp. 372, 373; Dangeau, 23.12.88. **l. 37,** Life, II, 221–22; Campana, II, 341, 350 (letter wrongly dated), 360, 366; Luttrell, I, 480, 481, 482; H.M.C. Rep. XII, App., VII, p. 220.

441 **l. 1,** Campana, II, 373. **l. 4,** *loc. cit.* **l. 11,** *loc. cit.* **l. 16,** *loc. cit.* **l. 19,** *ibid.*, pp. 377, 431. **l. 31,** Rawlinson A. 139, B, p. 278, quoted Foxcroft, II, 24–26. **l. 37,** H.M.C. Finch, II, 194. **Note,** Campana, II, 374.

442 **l. 37,** Life, II, 249–50; Campana, II, 376–77.

444 **l. 22,** Ailesbury, I, 194 *et seq.* **l. 28,** H.M.C. Stuart, I, 77. **l. 30,** Burnet, II, 17.

448 **l. 18,** Ailesbury, I, 202; Campana, II, 433–36; Add. MSS., 32095, ff. 303–7, 308 *et seq.*; Add. MSS., 33923, ff. 429–81 (two of these three MSS. are transcribed in *N. & Q.*, 3rd Series, V & VI). **l. 23,** *Ellis Corresp.*, II, 363. **l. 41,** Ailesbury, I, 214; cf. *Ellis Corresp.*, II, 362–63; Buckingham, *Account of the Revolution*; D'Orleans, IV, 348; Wood, III, 288; *Instr. Données*, XXV, 418; Berwick, I, 34.

449 **l. 6,** Bramston, p. 340; cf. Wood, III, 289. **l. 8,** Burnet, I, 799. **l. 27,** Dartmouth's note to Burnet, II, 47. **l. 13,** Thoresby, *Review of the Year 1688.* **l. 31,** Buckingham, *Account of the Revolution.*

450 **l. 8,** P.C. Reg., 16.12.88. **l. 12,** Bramston, p. 340. **l. 22,** *loc. cit.*; Burnet, I, 799; Wood, III, 289; Desertion, p. 93; *Evelyn Corresp.*, III, 287; Buckingham. **l. 27,** Bramston, p. 340. **Note,** Cal. T.B., VIII, 2140–41.

451 **l. 5,** *Clar. Corresp.*, II, 226 n. **l. 21,** Campana, II, 431. **l. 29,** Foxcroft, *Supplement to Burnet*, p. 536. **Note,** Stevens, pp. 7–12.

452 **l. 3,** Harl. MSS. 6584, f. 280 (*b*); Conduct of the Duchess of Marlborough; The Dear Bargain. **l. 10,** Burnet, I, 802; *Clar. Corresp.*, II, 231, 238. **l. 15,** Campana, II, 442–43; H.M.C. Le Fleming, p. 228. **l. 17,** Foxcroft, *Supplement to Burnet*, p. 535. **l. 26,** Campana, II, 487; *Evelyn Corresp.*, III, 287; Life, II, 273. **l. 30,** Burnet, I, 801; *Clar. Corresp.*, II, 230; Japikse, I, ii, 632–33. **Note,** *ibid.*, pp. 25–26.

PAGE

453 **l. 3,** Japikse, I, ii, 26; H.M.C. Rep. II, App., p. 14. **l. 6,** Evelyn, 18.12.88; *Evelyn Corresp., loc. cit.*; H.M.C. Le Fleming, p. 228; Barrillon, quoted Mazure, III, 270; *Clar. Corresp.*, II, 238. **l. 8,** Life, II, 266–67. **l. 27,** Wood, III, 290; H.M.C. Rep. X, App., Pt. IV, p. 329. **l. 37,** Campana, II, 401.

454 **l. 3,** I am indebted for this conjecture to Keith Feiling, *History of the Tory Party*, p. 340. **l. 8,** *Clar. Corresp.*, II, 232, 234. **l. 10,** Burnet, I, 804. **l. 18,** H.M.C. Rep. X, *loc. cit.* **l. 27,** Ailesbury, I, 224. **l. 37,** Life, II, 274.

455 **l. 8,** Berwick, I, 37. **l. 33,** Life, II, 275–78; Berwick, *loc. cit.*; Campana, II, 456.

456 **l. 30,** Campana, II, 477.

457 **l. 13,** Sévigné, 14.1.89. **l. 19,** *ibid.*, 2.2.89; cf. Caylus, p. 166. **l. 22,** La Fayette, p. 210. **l. 27,** *ibid.*, p. 211. **l. 30,** *ibid.*, p. 230. **l. 36,** Elizabeth Charlotte, 20.10.90.

458 **l. 2,** *ibid.*, 16.1.92. **l. 8,** *ibid.*, 20.8.90. **l. 24,** *loc. cit.* **l. 33,** *ibid.*, 6.9.90.

459 **l. 7,** Campana, II, 504. **l. 10,** H.M.C. Portland, III, 529. **l. 34,** *Clar. Corresp.*, II, 290. **l. 39,** Maloney to Tyrrel, Feb. 26/March 8, 1689/90, quoted King, p. 371.

460 **l. 4,** Campana, II, 482. **l. 6,** King, p. 371. **l. 7,** *Renandot Papers*, quoted Haile, p. 201. **l. 10,** Campana, II, 476; Haile, p. 241. **l. 12,** *ibid.*, p. 296. **l. 14,** Sourches, 13.2.90. **l. 34,** Campana, II, 439. **l. 36,** *ibid.*, p. 450. **l. 39,** *ibid.*, p. 395; cf. Campana, II, 439.

461 **l. 2,** Campana, II, 395. **l. 15,** *ibid.*, p. 399, 10.1.89. **l. 18,** Sévigné, 7.1.89. **l. 27,** *ibid.*, 10.1.89.

462 **l. 4,** *loc. cit.* **l. 11,** *Mémoires de la Cour de France*, LXV, 60. **l. 15,** Avviso, 21.2.89, quoted Haile, p. 215 n.; Campana, II, 424, and elsewhere. **l. 19,** *ibid.*, 483–84, 488–90, 495–501. **l. 22,** Haile, p. 251; cf. Dangeau, 10.5.89. **l. 25,** Campana, II, 525–26. **l. 32,** *ibid.*, p. 528. **l. 38,** Life, II, 319–20.

463 **l. 11,** Campana, II, 509–11. **l. 19,** *ibid.*, pp. 524–25. **l. 34,** Sévigné, 28.2.89, 2.3.89; Campana, II, 525; La Fayette, p. 228. **Note,** Rousset, IV, 187.

464 **l. 4,** Campana, II, 509–11. **l. 5,** *ibid.*, p. 525. **l. 11,** Sourches, II, 43–44; H.M.C. Buccleuch, II, i, 36–37; Dangeau, 2.4.89. **l. 28,** Sourches, pp. 43–44. **l. 37,** Avaux Ireland, pp. 23, 36. **Note,** La Fayette, pp. 225–26, 250–51; cf. Sourches, p. 345.

465 **l. 1,** Avaux to Louis from Brest, quoted Macaulay (III, 170) from French archives, transcribed by Baschet (date missing). **l. 17,** Avaux Ireland, pp. 85, 247 and elsewhere. **l. 20,** *ibid.*, p. 181. **l. 23,** *ibid.*, p. 293. **l. 26,** *ibid.*, pp. 166–67, 239, 408–9, 416. **l. 29,** *ibid.*, p. 218. **l. 42,** *ibid.*, pp. 138, 182; cf. Berwick, I, 95.

466 **l. 2,** *ibid.*, p. 182. **l. 12,** Letter of Waldegrave, quoted Macpherson, I 316–17 (Nairne DN1, f. 44). **l. 22,** H.M.C. Stuart, VI, 6. **l. 42,** Avaux Ireland, pp. 138, 182; cf. Berwick, I, 95.

467 **l. 13,** Leslie, p. 124. **l. 29,** Avaux Ireland, p. 50.

468 **l. 4,** Add. MSS. 28053, f. 387. **l. 17,** There is a valuable collection of Irish proclamations in the British Museum. **l. 19,** For Clarendon's opinion of Mountjoy see *Clar. Corresp.*, I, 241, 251. **l. 23,** *Jacobite Narrative*, p. 43. **l. 27,** Avaux Ireland, p. 89; Add. MSS., 28053, ff. 386–88. **Note,** *ibid.*, p. 93; King, VIII, 14.

469 **l. 4,** Avaux Ireland, pp. 262–63, 372, 378–79. **l. 11,** *ibid.*, p. 2. **l. 17,** *ibid.*, p. 10. **l. 18,** *ibid.*, pp. 31–32. **l. 24,** *ibid.*, pp. 189–90. **l. 26,** *ibid.*, pp. 372, 374, 389. **l. 28,** *ibid.*, pp. 189–90, 372. **l. 32,** *ibid.*, p. 88. **Note,** *ibid.*, p. 372; *Instr. Données*, XXV, 444–45 (the phrase in question is not in Avaux's copy of his letter, but according to Jusserand and Macaulay it is in his letter in the French archives).

470 **l. 10,** Avaux Ireland, pp. 378–79.

PAGE

471 l. **18,** Leslie, p. 125, App., 23–25. l. **21,** Avaux Ireland, pp. 392–93; cf. Pointis to Seignelay, 30.8.89, quoted Rousset, IV, 211. l. **37,** H.M.C. Buccleuch, II, i, 36. A Journal of what has passed in the North of Ireland since the Landing of the Duke of Schomberg, 1689.

472 l. **8,** Avaux Ireland, p. 112. l. **18,** *ibid.*, p. 148. l. **31,** *ibid.*, p. 11. l. **36,** *ibid.*, pp. 188–89. l. **37,** *ibid.*, pp. 221–22.

473 l. **5,** *ibid.*, pp. 244–45. l. **10,** *loc. cit.* and *ibid.*, pp. 61, 162, 400, 404–5, 412, 552–54, 649. l. **19,** *ibid.*, p. 277. l. **35,** *ibid.*, pp. 284–87. **Note,** Klopp, V, 9; Campana, II, 524–25.

474 l. **27,** Avaux Ireland, pp. 150–52. l. **40,** *ibid.*, pp. 573–74. **Note,** *ibid.*, pp. 298–99.

475 l. **4,** *ibid.*, pp. 552–54. l. **10,** *ibid.*, p. 649. l. **21,** Stevens, p. 61. l. **34,** H.M.C. Buccleuch, II, i, 36–37. l. **42,** H.M.C. Hamilton, p. 178.

476 l. **14,** Cal. S.P., 1689–90, pp. 26, 44. Luttrell, I, 525. l. **27,** Avaux Ireland, p. 78. **Note,** Macpherson, I, 330, quoting Nairne, D.N.I., f. 74.

477 l. **7,** Stevens, pp. 63–64. l. **20,** Avaux Ireland, p. 210. l. **30,** Rousset, IV, 198. l. **35,** Avaux Ireland, p. 136 and elsewhere. l. **36,** *ibid.*, pp. 253–54, 342, 359–70. l. **40,** *ibid.*, pp. 218, 289.

478 l. **8,** Bramston, pp. 272–73. l. **11,** Avaux Ireland, p. 220. l. **16,** *ibid.*, p. 119. l. **22,** *ibid.*, pp. 280, 288, 298. l. **28,** Rousset, IV, 209; Stevens, p. 68; Letter from Dublin, 12.6.89, p. 17; *An Exact Account, of the Most Considerable Transactions that hath occurred in Ireland since the late King James's Arrival There*, 1689; Great News from Ireland, 1689. l. **30,** Lauzun to Louvois. l. **33,** Sourches, 13.5.90, 17.1.91, 28.1.91. l. **37,** Avaux Ireland, p. 390. l. **42,** Stevens, pp. 7 *et seq.*

479 l. **2,** *ibid.*, pp. 54–59. l. **11,** *ibid.*, p. 122. l. **18,** Avaux Ireland, pp. 498–99. l. **21,** *ibid.*, p. 92. l. **31,** *ibid.*, p. 470. l. **33,** *ibid.*, p. 357. l. **38,** *ibid.*, p. 57. l. **39,** *ibid.*, p. 156.

480 l. **1,** *ibid.*, pp. 335–36. l. **3,** *ibid.*, pp. 79, 357. l. **7,** *ibid.*, pp. 52, 161–62. l. **12,** *ibid.*, pp. 23, 29, 52, 54. l. **14,** *ibid.*, p. 699; Sourches, 20.5.90. l. **22,** Avaux Ireland, p. 354. l. **25,** *ibid.*, pp. 81–82. l. **28,** *loc. cit.* l. **30,** *ibid.*, p. 110.

481. l. **7,** *ibid.*, pp. 55–56, 75, 80, 90–91, 108, 223–24, 226, 237, 254–55, 277, 308, 340–41. l. **11,** *ibid.*, pp. 216, 263, 268–69. l. **19,** *ibid.*, pp. 294, 502, 642. l. **26,** Life, II, 390.

482 l. **6,** Walker. l. **7,** *Jacobite Narrative*, p. 63. l. **9,** Proclamation of 25.3.89. l. **13,** Leslie, p. 124. l. **25,** Stevens, p. 70. l. **35,** Life, II, 356. l. **37,** Avaux Ireland, p. 89. l. **40,** Leslie, p. 101.

483 l. **9,** Avaux Ireland, pp. 191–92, 215–16; cf. Life, II, 354–58. l. **27,** King, p. 37. l. **34,** Leslie, p. 100. l. **37,** King, p. 37.

484 l. **2,** Leslie, p. 124. l. 5, Ailesbury, I, 251. l. 14, Rousset, IV, 211. l. **21,** Avaux Ireland, pp. 379, 390. l. **31,** *A True Account of the Present State of Ireland*, 1689; *An Exact Account of the Most Considerable Transactions* . . ., 1689. l. **38,** *ibid.*, p. 429. l. **42,** *ibid.*, p. 433.

485 l. **3,** *ibid.*, pp. 434; H.M.C. Stuart, I, 46. l. **12,** Avaux Ireland, pp. 445, 501. l. **17,** *ibid.*, p. 466. l. **20,** *ibid.*, p. 475. l. **26,** *ibid.*, pp. 460–61, 464–65, 468, 470. l. **29,** Life, II, 372–73. l. **32,** Avaux Ireland, p. 599. **Note 1,** Haile, p. 315. **Note 2,** *Clar. Corresp.*, I, 273, 411, 417, 422.

486 l. **1,** Avaux Ireland, p. 601. l. **31,** *ibid.*, pp. 473, 475–76, 478, 540, 546, 589, 609. l. **33,** *ibid.*, p. 532. l. **35,** *ibid.*, p. 516.

487 l. **7,** Macpherson, I, 314–15, quoting Nairne D.N.I., f. 42. l. **11,** Avaux Ireland, p. 497. l. **24,** Stevens, p. 97. l. **35,** *loc. cit.* l. **39,** *ibid.*, pp. 91–92; cf. *Jacobite Narrative*, pp. 89–90; Mac. Exc., p. 41.

488 l. **2,** Life, II, 390. l. 7, Avaux Ireland, p. 548. l. **9,** *ibid.*, p. 651. l. **12,** *ibid.*, pp. 630, 651. l. **29,** *ibid.*, p. 521; Berwick, pp. 75–76; Nairne D.N.I., f. 44, quoted Macpherson, I, 317. l. **31,** La Fayette, p.

PAGE

225; Nairne, *loc. cit.* **l. 35,** Avaux Ireland, pp. 250–51, 312, 317, 318, 428, 521, 566. **l. 39,** Sourches, pp. 74–75. **l. 41,** Life, II, 388.

489 **l. 2,** Sourches, p. 134. **l. 4,** *ibid.*, p. 159; Avaux Ireland, p. 441. **l. 11,** La Fayette, p. 254; cf. Macpherson, I, 317. **l. 19,** Avaux Ireland, p. 104. **l. 21,** *ibid.*, p. 484. **l. 27,** *ibid.*, p. 319. **l. 30,** *ibid.*, p. 548.

490 **l. 3,** *ibid.*, p. 675. **l. 19,** Lauzun to Louvois, 20.5.90, quoted Ranke, VI, 108. **l. 25,** Ranke, VI, 109–13; Sourches, 10.2.40. **l. 29,** Lauzun to Seignelay, 26.7.90, quoted Ranke, VI, 117. **l. 38,** Lauzun to Louvois, 1.7.90, quoted Ranke, VI, 113.

491 **l. 15,** *True and Perfect Journal of the Affairs in Ireland since His Majesty's arrival in that Kingdom*, 1690. **l. 25,** *op. cit.* **l. 27,** Life, II, 396. **l. 33,** *e.g.*, H.M.C. Finch, p. 328. **l. 36,** Story, *Impartial History of the Wars of Ireland.*

492 **l. 13,** Stevens, pp. 122–23. **l. 16,** Berwick, I, 63. **l. 21,** *True and Perfect Journal. . .* **l. 25,** H.M.C. Finch, pp. 344, 352; the source of this anecdote is apparently unknown, see *D.N.B.*, art. "Richard Talbot". **l. 27,** Leslie, App. 21. **l. 30,** *loc. cit.* **l. 32,** Macpherson, I, 229–30. **l. 37,** Dalrymple, V, 96.

493 **l. 1,** Avaux Ireland, p. 493. **l. 9,** *ibid.*, pp. 487–88. **l. 19,** Louvois to Louis, April 1690; Sévigné, 31.5.90. **l. 25,** quoted Du Boscq, p. 89. **l. 22,** Sévigné, *circ.* 1.8.90. **l. 42,** quoted Du Boscq, pp. 87–89.

494 **l. 2,** MS. letter in Archives of French War Office quoted du Boscq, p. 87. **l. 6,** Elizabeth Charlotte, 30.7.90, 20.8.90. **l. 21,** Du Boscq, *loc. cit.* **l. 33,** Life, II, 411–12; Macpherson, I, 233. **l. 38,** James to Rancé, 26.3.91 (Philobiblion Society, XIV); Berwick, I, 83.

495 **l. 13,** H.M.C. Rutland, III, 529. **l. 19,** James to Rancé, 19.2.94.

496 **l. 12,** Haile, p. 305; Macpherson, I, 497. **l. 22,** Lans. MSS., 1163 A, f. 75. **l. 25,** quoted Mazure, App. **l. 35,** Burnet, I, 356.

497 **l. 18,** King's MSS., 140; Haile, pp. 351, 368, 370. **l. 23,** *ibid.*, pp. 234–35, 292, 326–27.

498 **l. 18,** Anthony Hamilton, *Zeneyde*, Introductory Letter. **l. 37,** Ailesbury, *passim.* **Note,** Dangeau, 10.1.95.

499 **l. 3,** Macpherson, I, 329. **l. 33,** *ibid.*, I, 493; Macky, pp. xxx, *et seq.*

500 **l. 8,** Macky, pp. 29 *et seq.* **l. 19,** Haile, p. 306. **l. 23,** *ibid.*, p. 313.

501 **l. 8,** Ailesbury, I, 322–31. **l. 16,** Caylus; cf. Haile, p. 292; *Souvenirs*, Paris, 1881, p. 167. **l. 23,** *Life of William Fuller*, passim.

502 **l. 5,** Cal. S.P., 6.9.91; Wood, III, 441. **l. 13,** Cal. S.P., 15.5.94. **l. 24,** Haile, p. 314. **l. 25,** Mary Beatrice to Caryll, 21.9.99, quoted E. and M. S. Grew, p. 405. **l. 26,** Haile, pp. 339–40. **l. 27,** *ibid.*, pp. 340, 345. **l. 30,** Prior to Halifax, quoted Haile, p. 334. **l. 34,** Stuart, Roxburgh, II, 263 *et seq.*, 323 *et seq.*; Sourches, 2.9.1701. **l. 39,** *ibid.*, 13.9.1701; Joly, pp. 333–34.

INDEX